MW00989491

In this volume Dr Reymond offers a substantial and clear defence of the traditional Christian assertion that the Bible represents Jesus as the Divine Messiah. In an age when this claim is debated by many and dismissed by some, the first part of this volume re-examines many of the messianic texts of the Old Testament. The second part looks at how the New Testament authors regarded Jesus and drew on the Old Testament material to show that Jesus was indeed the long-expected Messiah and was himself Divine. This is an inspiring and challenging work from a strong evangelical scholar. It is a worthy summary of the Biblical evidence that Jesus is the Divine Messiah and offers an excellent resource for all evangelicals seeking to defend this vital biblical teaching.

Revd Dr Paul D Gardner
Chairman of the Church of England Evangelical Council
and Vicar of Hartford, Cheshire

Robert L. Reymond is a major evangelical theologian. The systematic theologians whose theological works are not only the most reliable but also the most deeply satisfying are those who are equally at home in biblical studies. One thinks, for instance, of superb exegetes like John Calvin and Charles Hodge, whose commentaries are as valuable as their theological works. Christian Focus are to be congratulated for their recent publication of two impressive volumes by Professor Reymond in the realm of biblical studies, his books on Paul and on John, and now for publishing this robust presentation of the evidence for the divine messiahship of Jesus. The range of scholarship is extensive, and there is no exegetical or theological nettle that he hesitates to grasp here. He never fudges an issue and the reader is left in no doubt as to what his own view is on any of the issues he handles. His opening chapter, in which he deals with present denials of the deity of Jesus, is of special value, and I would make it required reading for every theological student.

Geoffrey Grogan
former Principal, Glasgow Bible College

Since the birth of classical Liberal Theology in the middle of the 19th century, there has been a gradual weakening of the Church's willingness to claim that Jesus Christ is the only way to God. Many theologians have lost their nerve in the face of a multicultural and postmodern society and have ceased to insist on the uniqueness of Christ. Indeed, some supposedly Christian theologians have even denied the incarnation and asserted that Jesus Christ was a mere human being. Over against all of that, Robert Reymond has powerfully reaffirmed the biblical view that Jesus Christ is God incarnate. With his usual thoroughness and with that characteristic blend of exegesis and systematic theology, Professor Reymond has provided us with a superb summary of the biblical case, which will be a valuable help in defending the faith.

Andrew T. B. McGowan
Principal, Highland Theological College

'Dr. Reymond has given us a magnificent study of the biblical teaching about Jesus Christ. He has patiently sifted through a mass of evidence and has demonstrated the strength of the case for seeing Jesus as indeed the divine Messiah. Dr Reymond has an impressive acquaintance with the literature on the subject, and he has not shirked the difficult issues. He has rendered a service to the whole church in dealing so thoroughly with the evidence and giving his up-to-date assessment of its significance.

Leon Morris
Formerly Principal of Ridley College, Melbourne, Australia

This volume displays a truly impressive breadth of scholarship, and is a consistently conservative summary of the biblical evidence as well as the critical arguments at every conceivable point of importance in the contemporary christological debate. The book is thorough, competent, and orthodox; it brings together in one volume much helpful material for the convenience of both teacher and student.

Robert Strimple
Westminster Theological Seminary in California

Dr. Reymond has produced a massive analysis of the biblical witness to the deity of Jesus, the Messiah. He takes great care to analyse various critical views of recent vintage and to show how they fail to give us a consistent picture of Christ. Probably not since H.P. Liddon's The Divinity of our Lord (1867) has such a massive defence of the deity of Jesus appeared in print. Dr. Reymond worthily functions in the train of G. Vos, B.B. Warfield, and J.G. Machen.

Roger Nicole
Reformed Theological Seminary, Orlando

Jesus, Divine Messiah

Robert L. Reymond

Mentor

All rights reserved. No part of this publication may be reproduced, stored in a retrieval system, or transmitted, in any form, by any means, electronic, mechanical, photocopying, recording or otherwise without the prior permission of the publisher or a license permitting restricted copying. In the U.K. such licenses are issued by the Copyright Licensing Agency, 90 Tottenham Court Road, London W1P 9HE.

©Robert L. Reymond

ISBN 185792 802 4

Published in 2003
in the
Mentor imprint
by
Christian Focus Publications, Geanies House,
Fearn, Tain, Ross-shire, IV20 1TW, Scotland

www.christianfocus.com

Edited by Malcolm Maclean
Cover design by Alister MacInnes

Printed and bound by
WS Bookwell, Finland

Contents

PREFACE

In 1990 Presbyterian and Reformed Publishing Company published the results of my sabbatical research at Tyndale House, Cambridge under the title, *Jesus, Divine Messiah: The New Testament Witness.* Shortly thereafter, Christian Focus Publication published its counterpart, *Jesus, Divine Messiah: The Old Testament Witness.* Even though both books served as resources in many seminary classrooms and pastors' studies, over time both titles went out of print. For the words of appreciation I received over the years concerning them I am still very grateful and humbled by them. I assure those readers that I appreciated their words very much.

Some five years or more have passed since these books went out of print, yet I and the publishers have continued to receive requests for them. Therefore, the editors of Christian Focus Publications requested that I grant them permission to republish both books in one volume to meet the continuing demand for them. Because I believe that there is wisdom in having both books within one cover, I happily acceded to this request and want to express my appreciation, first, to P & R for returning all publishing rights of its book to me and, second, to CFP for its confidence that the earlier books still have lives to live. The volume you the reader now hold in your hands is the result of this republishing effort.

I want to say three things about this combined edition of these earlier books. First, their republication gave me the opportunity to reread every sentence and every footnote and to rewrite both books where I felt it would be an improvement to do so. Second, I have also added new material to both. Third, I have transliterated into English every Hebrew and Greek word I employ (something I did not do in either of the earlier books) to make this edition more accessible and readable to people who do not know the biblical languages.

Having been forced by this task of revision to rethink the conclusions of both earlier works, I will simply say that I am as assured now as I was over ten years ago that what I concluded then is still correct. In this edition I have reaffirmed and hopefully have even strengthened the argument that the Bible uniformly teaches that Jesus of Nazareth was no mere man. True man (*vere homo*) Jesus was, indeed, but he was and is more than simply a man. He was and is also God the Son, the second person of the Holy Trinity, who through the virginal conception in the womb of Mary became man in order to fulfill his Father's investiture in him of the messianic task to accomplish a "so great salvation" not only of personal but also of cosmic proportions. It is my hope that this new edition will strengthen the faith of Christians and will persuade my skeptical readers to consider seriously Christ's and the Bible's claims concerning him.

Robert L. Reymond
Fort Lauderdale
May 2002

CHAPTER ONE

INTRODUCTION: PRESENT DENIALS OF THE DEITY OF JESUS

"What's the problem?"

The Christian church, it would seem, has always been embroiled in controversy, not always of its own making, true enough, but in controversy nonetheless. And it has often been the case that the controversy has been "within the family," as views at variance with sound doctrine were developed and espoused. For example, in the Nicene and Post-Nicene Periods of the church, running roughly from A.D. 300-600, the Greek church, centered mainly in the Catechetical Schools of Alexandria and Antioch, was engaged in heated dispute regarding the Trinitarian/Christological controversies dealing respectively with (1) the related issues of the deity of Christ (and the Holy Spirit) and the implications of that teaching for the doctrine of the triune nature of God and (2) the manner in which the divine and human natures are to be related to each other and to the one person of Christ. The Latin or Western church, on the other hand, found itself in the fifth century involved in the soteriological controversy[1] precipitated by the great conflict (A.D. 411-431) between Pelagius and Augustine. In sum, this controversy centered in the question of whether it is God who saves man or whether a man can and must save himself. The church, of course, determined rightly at that time (at the Sixteenth Council of Carthage in A.D. 418 and the Council at Ephesus in A.D. 431) that Christianity was to remain "a religion of rescue" and not rot down into "a religion of self-help."[2]

---

[1]Philip Schaff, in his monumental *History of the Christian Church* (Revised fifth edition; Grand Rapids: Eerdmans, 1960), *Nicene and Post-Nicene Christianity, A.D. 311-600*, III, 783, speaks of these as "Anthropological Controversies," in that they raise the question of the degree to which men are involved in their own salvation.

[2]See Schaff, *History*, III, 785-815, and Benjamin B. Warfield, *The Plan of Salvation* (Grand Rapids: Eerdmans, 1955), for more detail.

Now while the soteriological controversy has again and again engaged the church's interest and energies (for instance, in the Gottschalk controversy in the ninth century, in the doctrinal struggles of the Reformation Period in the sixteenth century, in the Calvinist/Arminian debates within the Reformed church in the seventeenth century, and in our own day in the church's opposition to secular humanism's contention that men must save themselves from whatever ills that beset them), it is a striking fact that once the doctrines pertaining to the two-natured person of Christ and the Trinity had been hammered out and settled in the intense struggle at Nicaea in A.D. 325 and the debates leading up to and culminating at Chalcedon in A.D. 451 (except for the monophysite and monothelite controversies mainly in the Eastern church in the succeeding two centuries which at heart entailed relapses into contradictions that Chalcedon had already substantially overcome), they saw virtually no challenge but rather only refinement (see, for example, the *enhypostasis* of Leontius of Byzantium [or Leontius of Jerusalem] and Calvin's later insistence upon the autotheotic character of the Son) until the so-called European Enlightenment (*Die Aufklärung*) of the eighteenth century which encouraged a rationalistic criticism of the Bible and opposition to all supernatural religion. The formulations of Nicaea and of Chalcedon, in other words, became the touchstone of Christological orthodoxy for catholic Christendom for the next fifteen hundred years, even through the turbulent divisions of the church into Eastern church and Western church in A.D. 1054, and then in Western Christendom into Roman Catholic Church and Protestant Church in the sixteenth century. Indeed, to this very day, if not in men's minds at least still in the church's creeds and confessions, both the doctrine and the language of the Nicene Creed and the Definition of Chalcedon may be found.[3]

But for the last two centuries, beginning with Schleiermacher's *The Christian Faith* (see sections 95-96) and continuing into our day

---

[3]See Augsburg Confession (A.D. 1530), Article III; First Helvetic Confession (A.D. 1536), Article XI; Second Helvetic Confession (A.D. 1566), Article XI; Heidelberg Catechism (A.D. 1563), Question 35; Belgic Confession (A.D. 1561), Articles X, XVIII, and XIX; First Scotch Confession (A.D. 1560), Article VI; Thirty-Nine Articles of the Church of England (A.D. 1563, 1571), Article II; and Westminster Confession of Faith (A.D. 1647), Article VIII, ii.

particularly, the conciliar formulations of Nicaea and Chalcedon that espouse a two-natured Christ have fallen upon hard times. Today, one can find evidence virtually everywhere—on every continent, in both Protestant and Roman Catholic circles—that the theologically "in thing" is to contend for a Jesus who was only a man by nature and for a Bible which is virtually silent regarding the classical incarnational Christology of a two-natured Christ—true God and true man in the one person of Jesus Christ.[4] As we shall see, it is very much in vogue to believe that the better case can be made for understanding Jesus as only a man—a very unusual man, of course, with a special mission from God—with the biblical ascriptions of divine qualities to him to be explained in other than in ontological terms.[5] Illustrations of this trend abound virtually without end, but four will suffice to make my point.

In his lecture on "The Christological Confession of the World Council of Churches" that Jesus Christ is "God and Saviour" (the confession of the WCC meeting in 1948), Rudolf Bultmann, the German New Testament form-critical scholar, responded to the question whether this confession accords with the New Testament thus: "I don't know." It all depends, he said, on what is meant by the word "God." "Is Christ's nature intended to be designated in the designation of him as 'God'—his metaphysical nature or his

---

[4]Throughout this book I may refer, for the sake of variation in style, to this doctrine of Christ's two natures in a variety of ways: for example, classical incarnational Christology, biblical incarnationalism, and so on; but I will always have the doctrine of Christ's two natures in mind.

[5]I recognize that there are those who, while they fully accept the *biblical* doctrine of incarnational Christology, believe that the *classical* formulations of Nicaea and Chalcedon, the latter particularly, in one way or another distort the biblical portrayal of Christ. A. N. S. Lane, Lecturer in Historical Theology at London Bible College, may be cited as a representative of this group. He faults the Chalcedon statement for asserting the impassibility of the eternal Son, thereby leading to a "dualistic Christ," a Christ who can suffer and a Christ who cannot suffer, which is "foreign to the New Testament portrait of Christ." Lane also believes that the Chalcedonian Christ is docetic, that is to say, he is in some sense something other than true man (a further result of the "unabashedly dualist" tendency in the Chalcedonian definition of Christ), this docetism, Lane contends, evidencing itself in the Definition's "practical denial" of human limitations in Christ. See his "Christology Beyond Chalcedon" in *Christ the Lord* (Leicester: Inter-Varsity, 1982), 257-81.

significance? Does the pronouncement have soteriological or cosmological character or both?"[6] "Neither in the Synoptic Gospels nor in the Pauline Epistles," he declared, "is Jesus called God."[7] Any significance that one might attach to his concession with regard to the one "certain passage" in John 20:28 (Thomas' confession) is immediately blunted by his remark that everywhere else Jesus is always spoken of as subordinate to God.[8] Bultmann's conclusion is that "the formula 'Christ is God' is false in every sense in which God is understood as an entity which can be objectified.... It is correct, if 'God' is understood here as the event of God's acting."[9] We will have many occasions to refer to Bultmann's views later, but we have seen enough to conclude that it is clear that, for Bultmann, Jesus in himself (*in se*) was only a man. Now a second illustration.

In 1977 a symposium of seven British theologians published *The Myth of God Incarnate* in which they called upon the church to recognize "that Jesus was...'a man approved by God' for a special role within the divine purpose, and that the later conception of him as God incarnate, the Second Person of the Holy Trinity living a human life, is a mythological or poetic way of expressing his significance for us."[10] John Hick summarized how he thinks it happened that Jesus, though only a man, came to be regarded also as God:

> ...it was natural and intelligible both that Jesus, through whom men had found a decisive encounter with God and a new and better life, should come to be hailed as son of God, and that later this poetry should have hardened into prose and escalated from a metaphorical son of God to a metaphysical God the Son....[11]

Maurice Wiles, another contributor, categorically declared:

---

[6]Rudolf Bultmann, *Essays Philosophical and Theological*, translated by James C. G. Greig (New York: Macmillan, 1955), 275.

[7]Bultmann, *Essays Philosophical and Theological*, 275.

[8]Bultmann, *Essays Philosophical and Theological*, 276.

[9]Bultmann, *Essays Philosophical and Theological*, 287.

[10]John Hick (ed.), *The Myth of God Incarnate* (Philadelphia: Westminster, 1977), ix.

[11]Hick, *The Myth of God Incarnate*, 176.

> 'Incarnation, in its full and proper sense, is not something directly presented in scripture.'[12]

My third example is taken from an American Roman Catholic scholar. In his review of I. Howard Marshall's commentary on the Johannine letters in the NICNT series, Raymond E. Brown on two accounts criticized Marshall's suggestion that the Johannine letters can be profitably read as an introduction to the theology of the New Testament as a whole since they stress (states Marshall) a "real Christianity" which is "based on the incarnation and sacrificial death of the Son of God": first, because Marshall implies "a continuity in NT thought" which Brown believes never existed, and second, because, while "Incarnation is truly characteristic of Johannine Christology," it is "quite uncharacteristic of about 90% of the rest of the NT."[13] Brown's remarks simply mean, if he is right, that by far the major portion of the New Testament does not espouse an incarnational Christology but reflects rather "other forms of NT theology."

My final example is taken from James D. G. Dunn's book, *Christology in the Making*, sub-titled, *A New Testament Inquiry into the Origins of the Doctrine of the Incarnation*. Dunn asserts:

> ...if we are to submit our speculations to the text and build our theology only with the bricks provided by careful exegesis we cannot say with any confidence that Jesus knew himself to be divine, the pre-existent Son of God.[14]

Of the three Synoptic passages (Mark 12:6, Mark 13:32, and Matthew 11:27 with its parallel in Luke 10:22), according to Dunn, which might offer some basis for classical incarnational Christology, the contrast between "servants" and the "Son" in the first passage

> provides no sure foundation since the contrast can be fully explained as part of the dramatic climax of the parable. As for the other two, it

---

[12]Maurice Wiles, "Christianity Without Incarnation?" in *The Myth of God Incarnate*, 3.

[13]Raymond E. Brown, *The Catholic Biblical Quarterly*, vol. 42, no. 3 (July 1980): 413.

[14]James D. G. Dunn, *Christology in the Making* (London: SCM, 1980), 32.

[15]Dunn, *Christology in the Making*, 28.

> is precisely in Jesus' reference to himself as "the Son" that most scholars detect evidence of earliest Christians adding to or shaping an original saying of less christological weight.[15]

Dunn, in fact, can find an explicit statement of incarnation in *only one passage* in the New Testament—the so-called "Logos Poem" of John 1![16] But even this "poem," states Dunn, reflects not Jesus' own self-understanding but the theology of subsequent Christian reflection.[17]

Dunn believes that incarnational Christology began to emerge in Christian thought when Paul pressed into service both pre-Christian Jewish Wisdom language to express what for him was the "cosmic significance of the Christ-event" and "mystery" language to express the conviction that Christ was the eschatological fulfillment of God's purpose from the beginning. But the idea never occurred to Paul, according to Dunn, to think of Christ "as a heavenly being who had pre-existed with God from the beginning."[18] It was when these language forms (found particularly in Colossians and Ephesians) were later read apart from their original contexts that pre-existence and a role in creation began to be ascribed to Christ. Here, Dunn declares, "we see the most immediate antecedent to the doctrine of the incarnation, the womb from which incarnational christology emerged...."[19] Then when a second-generation Christianity in the last decades of the first century extended the "Son of God" language "backward"—from resurrection, to death and resurrection, then to the beginning of Jesus' ministry, then to his conception and birth, and finally to a timeless eternity—the Christian mind was ready for the

---

[16]Dunn, *Christology in the Making*, 241.

[17]Dunn, *Christology in the Making*, 30. Dunn believes, because the style of the Fourth Gospel is "so consistent" and "so consistently different" from the Synoptic Gospels, "that it can hardly be other than a Johannine literary product...elaborated in the language and theology of subsequent Christian reflection" (30). Again, because of the "complete lack of real parallel in the earlier tradition: no other Gospel speaks of Jesus coming down from heaven and the like," Dunn writes: "...it would be verging on the irresponsible to use the Johannine testimony on Jesus' divine sonship in our attempt to uncover the self-consciousness of Jesus himself" (31).

[18]Dunn, *Christology in the Making*, 255.

[19]Dunn, *Christology in the Making*, 256.

full-blown Logos Christology of John's Prologue in which degrees or stages of his Sonship are left behind and a divine Sonship of unchanging timelessness is reached.[20]

Dunn's book claims to demonstrate the development of the Christ-idea from "Christ-event" in which *God acted for men* in Jesus to "incarnation" in which Christ as pre-existent Son of God became flesh and *acted for God among men*. Of course, if all this is so, then the formulations of Nicaea and of Chalcedon have, at best, enshrined only one Christological model of the New Testament—the latest to develop—and their value as descriptions of the person of Christ is reduced virtually to zero since they now can command only that degree of appreciation which one is willing to yield to the last among several other New Testament Christological models.

Clearly, if these four examples are representative expressions of what is being said generally today across the spectrum of enlightened New Testament scholarship, classical incarnational Christology as defined by Nicaea and by Chalcedon in terms of a two-natured Christ is no longer held in the high esteem which it once enjoyed. In short, both Nicaea and Chalcedon are in trouble.

"What's behind it all?"

Even though a significant portion of modern New Testament scholarship has apparently determined that it is necessary to urge major modifications in the church's understanding of Christology, the Christian can hardly be blamed if he expresses some hesitancy about a theological shift that discards the central feature (one person/two natures) of a doctrinal formulation which virtually all of Christendom for fifteen centuries has adjudged to be the doctrinal reflection of the teaching of Holy Scripture itself. I think that all will agree that this is no light matter. Furthermore, the resultant radical revision which an outright rejection of incarnational Christology would require not only in Christology (which would become a variant of anthropology if Bultmann is to be believed) but also—because of the interrelatedness of the doctrines of the Christian system one with the other—throughout the entirety of Christian dogmatics (for example, Trinitarianism would give way to Unitarianism; salvation would become a variant of

[20] Dunn, *Christology in the Making*, 256.

philosophical existentialism or socio-religious humanism), I would submit, is no small matter either. In fact, unless there are uncommonly sound and necessary reasons approaching the level of unimpeachability for such a shift, the average Christian is justified if he should conclude that such a revisionary departure from the established Faith of the centuries is grossly irresponsible. Are there such reasons, and if there are, what are they? What precisely is behind this present furor in Christology?

In this chapter I will present seven modern objections raised against the classical doctrine of a two-natured Christ. Although there may be others, I believe that they will be found, upon analysis, only to be variations of one or more of these seven. I will also offer some general responses to them along the way, not as my final word on them since I will, of necessity, interact with them either directly or indirectly, either explicitly or implicitly, throughout the book. But my responses may persuade the reader, whether evangelical or not, that it is not a waste of time or energy to continue with me as I consider again the biblical material concerning a Christ who is very God and very man.

"It is a Christology 'from above.'"

The first objection against classical Christology is the charge that it begins "from above" rather than "from below." What this means is that the classical formulation begins from God, more specifically, from the triune God and from a Christ whose deity is already a given, who is already God the Son, who as the pre-existent Son of God, as the eternal Logos, became man, rather than with the human Jesus, the Jesus of history. As a result, it is urged, such questions thrust themselves to the fore: How is it that God can also be a man? What does it mean that the Son of God became a man? What does it mean to say that Jesus is a man in such a construction? Indeed, *is* Jesus truly a man under such conditions? And finally, is any Christology "from above," which always entails a Christ of faith, really the earthly historical Jesus? A Christology "from above," it is maintained, always threatens the genuinely human existence of Jesus. Maurice Wiles, whom I quoted earlier, puts the matter thus:

> ...throughout the long history of attempts to present a reasoned account of Christ as both fully human and fully divine, the church

> has never succeeded in offering a consistent or convincing picture. Most commonly it has been the humanity of Christ that has suffered; the picture presented has been of a figure who cannot by our standards of judgment...be regarded as recognizably human.[21]

Raymond E. Brown even speaks of "the perils created by [the] brilliant insights" of John's Gospel and says:

> ...the Gospel Prologue opens up the possibility of neglecting the human career of Jesus: if one stresses the incarnation as the unique moment of contact with God, what difference does it make what the Word did once the Word had become flesh?[22]

Gerald O'Collins, another Roman Catholic scholar, characterizes this concern in this fashion:

> The figure in the manger may cry like any baby. He may grow up seemingly just another boy playing on the streets of Nazareth. He may preach in the style of a wandering rabbi. The Roman forces of occupation can put him to death by that hideous combination of empalement and display which they call crucifixion. But all the same we know he is really God and this injects an element of make-believe into the whole life-story from Bethlehem on. He looks like a man, speaks like a man, suffers and dies like a man. But underneath he is divine, and this makes his genuine humanity suspect.... [A]long lines suggested by Christmas pantomimes, Daisy looks something like a cow and moos better than most cows. But all through the act we know she is no real cow at all. Right from the manger does Jesus simply play at the role of being a man?[23]

There are several things that need to be said in response to this objection. First, I think evangelicals must heed its implicit warning and admit that it is altogether possible in their theologizing so to concentrate both their own and the church's attention on the deity of Christ that his humanness suffers eclipse in the church's witness and proclamation. The church must say "Enough!" to Docetism wherever

---

[21]Wiles, *The Myth of God Incarnate*, 4.

[22]Brown, *The Catholic Biblical Quarterly*, 42.3, 414.

[23]Gerald O'Collins, *What Are They Saying About Jesus?* (New York: Paulist, 1977), 2.

it appears, and recognize anew the marvelous attraction in the *human* face of our sympathizing heavenly High Priest (see *Belgic Confession*, Chapter 26).

It is also true that the evangelical witness may have been unduly hasty at times in "beating the world over the head" with biblical "proof texts" for the deity of Christ. Evangelicals must reclaim lost high ground here by recognizing that there is something tremendously compelling and powerfully winsome about the *man* Jesus Christ,[24] his ethical teaching, his conflicts with temptation, his attitude toward the pain and felt alienation of other human beings, and his sensitive views on life in this world in general as set forth in the Gospel narratives. This is doubtless one reason that such men as Mahatma Gandhi found him so fascinating. The church surely can use Jesus' humanity to real apologetic advantage to define what true humanness is in a day when men feel "dehumanized" in so many ways. Indeed, it should not be overlooked that in the days of our Lord's earthly ministry men first encountered him and perceived him as a man (Phil 2:8; Heb 2:14-17). So there is certainly something that can be said for a biblically-oriented Christology "from below" as long as it does not lose sight of everything else that the New Testament says about him.

But beyond this, we must question the character of any Christology "from below" which claims to be the key for unlocking the real meaning of Jesus for us. We must ask, what are its underlying presuppositions? What philosophical, sociological, psychological, and psychoanalytic theories control it in its effort to isolate out of the whole biblical picture of Jesus the "truly human" elements of Jesus in order to build a Christology that is a scientific Christology "from below" which will also address the real needs of men? After all, in the modern world, whose thought-forms are so thoroughly shaped by the human social sciences, can one afford to neglect Freud, Jung, Erikson, or Schweitzer in his attempt to erect a Christology "from below"? Do any of the diverse portraits of the Christ "from below" proposed to date which substitute another picture of Jesus for the one advanced by classical Christology deserve our intellectual allegiance? Are we to follow Bultmann's "demythologized" Jesus to "authentic existence"? Or

---

[24]We must be careful here to recall, if classical Christology is correct, that we never have to do just with the man Christ Jesus at any point in his career.

J.A.T. Robinson's Jesus as God's "representative to man"? Or Tillich's Jesus as the "Bearer of the New Being"? Or Pannenberg's Jesus as "the man for the future"? Or Küng's Jesus as the "Advocate and Deputy of God"? What about Rahner's Jesus as the "unique, supreme case of the total actualization of human destiny"? Or Schoonenberg's Jesus as "the embodiment of God's presence?" Or Schillebeeckx's Jesus as "the revelation of the eschatological face of all humanity"? Or Goulder's Jesus as "the man of universal destiny"? Or Lampe's Jesus as the "supreme exemplar of perfect and unbroken response to the Father"? Which? And are we to pinpoint the uniqueness of his humanity in his "being for other," his "being for God," his "sinlessness," or what?

Whatever one's answer here, every humanist Christology "from below," while it may stress the genuine humanness of Jesus,[25] must still face this problem: does it say enough to justify the church calling him, in its worship and in its confessions, "true God and true man"? Every Christology "from below" presupposes that there is some kind of continuity, which can be displayed by the theologizing process, between the human and the divine in Jesus which makes it possible to ascend in thought from reflecting in some fashion upon Jesus' humanity to a "divinity" which requires the ascription of "Godness" to Jesus. The results thus far, however, have been dismally disappointing[26] since none of these representations of Jesus' "divinity," whether represented in terms of "being open to God" or "being for God" or "being open for others" or being even "sinless," pushes us that far. Even his being the *supreme* revelation of God to man does not require that we believe, when we reflect upon Jesus, that we are considering God himself. For as O'Collins rightly observes: "The agent of divine revelation cannot automatically be assumed to be identical with God."[27] Not even a real historical resurrection from the dead, derived simply from the evidence of the empty tomb and subsequent post-crucifixion

---

[25]I personally do not think it will safeguard his true humanness inasmuch as it must "mythologize" the human Jesus by some existential vision if he is to be unique and final for men into some kind of "superman" in order to accredit to him the universal human esteem which it deems he deserves.

[26]See Colin E. Gunton, *Yesterday & Today: A Study of Continuities in Christology* (Grand Rapids: Eerdmans, 1983), chaps. 2 and 3.

[27]Gunton, *Yesterday & Today*, chaps. 2 and 3.

appearances, in and of itself necessarily requires that one ascribe ontological deity to him as some evangelicals mistakenly maintain. Pinchas Lapide, for example, declares that Jesus was really raised from the dead but he remains an orthodox Jewish theologian! He understands Jesus' resurrection simply as part of God's providential purpose to spread the knowledge of the God of Israel throughout the world.[28] Herein resides the fundamental problem that every Christology "from below" must honestly face: Does its construction compel us to move beyond Jesus' humanness to Thomas' great confession in John 20:28? Or does it offer to the church and to men a Jesus whose "deity" in the final analysis is only his total dedication to God or to be viewed as his special mission from God or as the fullness of Spirit within him? The church must seriously inquire whether such Christologies "from below" do not rule out at the outset, by their very methodologies, one alternative, namely, the ascription of deity to him in the classical sense, inasmuch as one cannot by induction (Paul would say "by [human] wisdom"—1 Cor 1:21) ascend from the finite to the infinite, Thomas Aquinas' famous (but logically flawed) theistic arguments notwithstanding.

The church must clearly understand what is at stake when asked to grant legitimacy to these modern efforts to explain Jesus "from below." If he is only a man in these Christologies and their advocates urge on grounds they have discovered that we should "worship" him, that act of devotion constitutes *idolatry* and stands under the Bible's anathema. But if he is not only a man but also God in the classical sense and we either refuse to acknowledge him as such or fail to recognize him as such, that refusal or that failure constitutes either apostasy or unbelief respectively. The Scripture informs us that only divine judgment awaits such recalcitrance (John 8:24).

While they may argue that classical Christology has insurmountable, inherent tensions and difficulties within it, "Christologists from below" should be willing to face the fact that their Christologies also have their own set of tensions and problems. They would do well to heed and to work within the constraints of the following feature which Gunton observes in the New Testament's depiction of Jesus:

---

[28]See Pinchas Lapide, *The Resurrection of Jesus* (London: SPCK, 1984).

> ...amidst all the diversity of [the New Testament's] Christology one thing remains constant, and that is the refusal to abstract the historical events from their overall theological meaning. The historical man Jesus is never construed apart from his meaning as the presence of the eternal God in time. The New Testament...will not allow us to choose between time and eternity, immanence and transcendence, in our talk about Jesus. The two are always given together.[29]

The reader will have to decide as he continues this study which set of problems he prefers—those of classical Christology (which are not, as charged, insurmountable) or those of the new Christologists.

"It is an ontological Christology."

A second objection to classical Christology is framed in the charge that its depiction of Jesus is exegetically insensitive to the intention of Scripture, that is to say, that it depicts Christ in *ontological* terms rather than along New Testament *functional* lines. What this simply means is that the Definition of Chalcedon is charged with being concerned to set forth who Christ is *in himself* (*in se*) rather than to represent him, as does the New Testament, in terms of what he is *for us* (*pro nobis*). Such is the conclusion today of many biblical scholars, notably Oscar Cullmann, who writes in his *The Christology of the New Testament:* "When it is asked in the New Testament 'Who is Christ?', the question never means exclusively, or even primarily, 'What is his nature?', but first of all, 'What is his function?'"[30]

The Nicene and Post-Nicene church, it would seem, child that it was of its own time and influenced by the Aristotelianism of the Antiochene Catechetical School and (mainly) the Platonism of the Alexandrian Catechetical School, in its conciliar descriptions of Christ against heretics was imbued with a philosophical metaphysic which unwittingly but nonetheless inexorably compelled it to conceptualize the person of Christ in terms of "natures." As a result, it viewed him in so-called ontological categories rather than in the rich functional language of the "theologies" of the New Testament. Even though Cullmann concedes that the Fathers were narrowly restricted to a

---

[29]Gunton, *Yesterday & Today*, 207.

[30]Oscar Cullmann, *The Christology of the New Testament*, translated by Shirley C. Guthrie and Charles A. M. Hall (London: SCM, ET 1959), 3-4.

concentration upon the person of Christ because of the "necessity of combating the heretics," he still contends that their emphases were misplaced, with the ensuing discussion of "natures" being "ultimately a Greek, not a Jewish or biblical problem."[31] Their emphases, as a result, injected an unrelievable tension into the church's creedal portrayal of Christ which either has threatened to rend asunder the unity of his person or has placed his essential manhood in jeopardy. The resultant Christ of the Definition of Chalcedon is neither descriptive of the Christ of the Gospels nor relevant in a modern world where men no longer think in ontological categories but rather in functional categories. In short, for men today, it is argued, classical Christology is unreal and unintelligible because of its ontological conceptualization of Jesus.

It is difficult not to grow a bit impatient with twentieth-century theologians who think they would have reacted differently or done better than the fifth-century Fathers in combating the heresies that faced them, particularly when they fail to make clear how they would have responded differently to the specific views which were then circulating with regard to the person of Christ. The issues before the Councils of Nicaea and Chalcedon, as Cullmann acknowledges, were not primarily, "What is Christ's function? What has he done for us?" but "Was the Logos created or uncreated, and if the latter, how is the divine Logos to be related to Jesus' manness so that justice is done to both Christ's deity and his humanity." A. N. S. Lane, pointing out that Chalcedon was not disinterested in the soteriological (functional) question at all, as is evident from the words, "for us men and for our salvation," which appear in the Definition, also rightly observes that Chalcedon simply did not set out to present an all-embracing, totally comprehensive Christology:

> Its essential task was to protect Christology against heresy in four particular forms, and to expound the essential points which those heresies undermined. With such a limited, albeit important, aim there [was] no need to represent the full range of New Testament teaching about Christ.[32]

---

[31]Cullmann, *The Christology of the New Testament*, 17.

[32]A. N. S. Lane, "Christology Beyond Chalcedon" in *Christ the Lord*, 264.

Furthermore, for Cullmann to contend that such ontological considerations were "Greek" and foreign to Hebraic thought is simply not so. The Jews of Christ's day had a good grasp of their God's ontological distinctiveness from all that he had created. It was precisely this conviction of the Creator-creature distinction that underlay their horror that a man standing in their midst would claim that God was his Father in such a unique and essential sense that he made himself equal with God (John 5:17-18; see also John 8:58-59; 10:33; 19:7). This was for them clearly a blasphemous claim. And, I suggest, the reason that it was for them blasphemous was that Jesus was claiming *ontological* continuity between himself as God's Son and the Creator God as his Father.

I would also insist that it is really rather superficial to suggest that men can forever concentrate on what Jesus did for them and never address the ontological question of who he is. Indeed, I would urge that it is as psychologically impossible for modern men as it was for the men of New Testament times to be satisfied with an interest only in Jesus' functional significance and never raise the question of or address the ontological issue which his functional significance forces upon them.

Let us not forget that while it is true that often it was what those first men saw him do that drew them to him, they were also quick to begin to speculate as to who he might be. We are informed that, upon beholding his miracle of the stilling of the storm, both his disciples and the men in the other boats were driven by the absolutely staggering character of the miracle to ask themselves, not "What has he done here? And what does it all mean for us?," but: "Who is this, that even the wind and sea obey him!" (Mark 4:41) Even more pointed, if that is possible, is Matthew's report of their question on the same occasion: "*What kind of person* [Ποταπός, *Potapos*] is this that even the wind and the sea obey him?" (8:27).

The force of their question can only be fully appreciated when one recalls that for them as Jews there could only be one proper response to this question (Pss 93:3-4; 104:7-8; 107:23-32), though admittedly to apply this conclusion to Jesus was to prove unsettling in coming days to their view of the monadic nature of God. And to respond to the question at all intelligently, I say with no fear of refutation, would have required them to enter deeply—let us speak frankly—into what we have to call "ontological considerations."

Even more significant for our present point is the fact that Jesus himself was not content to allow men to bask only in the brilliance of his teachings and the wonder of his deeds and to concern themselves solely with the functional significance of his mission. At the appropriate moment in the process of educating his disciples, it was Jesus who raised the ontological question: "Who do people say I am?" And after hearing their report concerning what others had been saying about him, he drew his disciples still more deeply into the ontological issue with his question: "But what about you? Who do you say I am?" (Matt 16:13-15). Now if it was only a functional response which he was hoping to receive we can only conclude that he was disappointed since Peter responded with both a functional and an ontological answer: "You are the Christ [functional], the Son of the living God [ontological]" (Matt 16:16). We can be assured that the second part of Peter's response was ontological in its intent because Jesus declared that Peter, by saying this, gave evidence that he was the blessed beneficiary of the Father's revelatory activity (Matt 16:17; see 11:25), a pronouncement hardly necessary if Peter were only confessing Jesus to be the Messiah since this was a perception which many other people were entertaining about him as well (see John 7:31). It is also noteworthy that it was not until he was satisfied that his disciples understood *who* he was (the ontological question) that he began to indoctrinate them regarding his saving mission by the way of the cross (Matt 16:21-23).

Germane also to this same point is the fact that Jesus forced the religious authorities of his day to face the "metaphysical" issue which later had to be addressed by the Council of Nicaea in A.D. 325 when he asked them: "What do you think about the Messiah? [note: he is already talking about the Messiah, admittedly a functional title] *Whose Son is he?*" (Matt 22:41-42). And when the response of these religious leaders seemed to limit the Messiah's origin only to his human ancestry ("The son of David") and therefore of only human origination, Jesus asked them:

> How is it then that David, speaking by the Spirit, calls him "Lord"? For he says, "The Lord [κύριος, *kurios*; Heb: יהוה, *Yahweh*] said to my Lord [κυρίῳ, *kuriō*; Heb: אֲדֹנִי, *'ădōnî*]: 'Sit at my right hand until I put your enemies under your feet.'" If then David called him "Lord," *how can he be his Son?* (Matt 22:43-45)

How indeed! If ever a question was designed to compel a consideration of "natures," this is it! For not only is the Messiah David's lineal descendant but, according to Psalm 110, he is also David's Lord and the "Son of God" in a sense that entitles him to sit on God's throne and to exercise universal and everlasting dominion (see the Psalm in its entirety and Heb 1:5-13). It was in order to sort out and to provide an answer to just this quandary, which Jesus himself forced the Pharisees to face that day, that the church of the fourth and fifth centuries, confronted by what it was to determine by its deliberations were heresies and doctrinal aberrations concerning him, was forced to gather together periodically in ecumenical councils.

So whatever one may say about the concerns and interests of the New Testament witness to Jesus, the one thing he should not say is that the New Testament does not raise "ontological" questions concerning Christ's person. Reginald H. Fuller and others have also argued as much,[33] G. C. Berkouwer even calling into question the academic integrity of a theology which would dismiss the ontological aspects of New Testament Christology:

> ...certainly theology is in bad form when, in discussing [Christ's utterances pointing to the mystery of his origin], it reaches for such depreciatory words as 'speculation' and 'ontology.' For in order to eclipse *this* origin, *this* miraculous being, *this* gracious reality, it has to set aside the whole gospel.[34]

Walter Kasper, in fact, dismisses the choice between functional and ontological Christologies as "illusory and a position into which

---

[33]Reginald H. Fuller, *The Foundations of New Testament Christology* (London: Lutterworth, 1965), 247-250; see also his *Who Is This Christ?*, co-authored with Pheme Perkins (Philadelphia: Fortress, 1983), 9-10, and Gerald Bray, "Can We Dispense With Chalcedon?" in *Themelios*, 3, 2 (Jan 1978): 2-9.

[34]G. C. Berkhouwer, *The Person of Christ*, translated by John Vriend (Grand Rapids: Eerdmans, 1954), 165.

theology must not allow itself to be maneuvered."[35] And the New Testament is willing to go even beyond these somewhat mild statements in support of the recognition of the legitimacy of the ontological questions concerning the person of Christ in the Gospels. So far does the New Testament seem to press the importance of the ontological issue that it is willing to report that Jesus grounded a man's eternal destiny in a right view of who he is: "If you do not believe that I am, you will die in your sins" (John 8:24). It bears saying again, in light of Jesus' solemn warning here, that whatever else one may say about the concerns of the New Testament witness to Christ, he should not say that its interests are purely functional and never ontological. Neither should he say, I hope to show, that the church was in error when it depicted Christ as "perfect in deity and perfect in manhood, truly God and truly man,...of the same essence with the Father according to deity and of the same essence with us according to manhood."

My emphasis on ontological considerations in this section is not intended in any sense to suggest that it is only with ontological considerations that one should concern himself when considering who Christ is. This would be tantamount to reducing soteriology to a narrowly conceived ontological Christology. But it is intended to erect a hedge against the other extreme which, by means of a functional Christology, virtually reduces Christology to soteriology. A balance must be struck and always maintained between an ontological and a functional Christology.

"It is an incarnation-centered Christology."

A third objection to classical Christology—closely related to the preceding objection but one which I am treating separately because of the somewhat different manner in which its concern is represented—is that it makes the event and effect of the Incarnation rather than the cross and resurrection of Christ the central doctrine about him. Both Wolfhart Pannenberg and Walter Kasper oppose a classical Christology for this reason. Kasper writes:

---

[35]Walter Kasper, *Jesus the Christ*, translated by V. Green (London: Burns & Oates, 1976), 24.

> If the divine-human person Jesus is constituted through the Incarnation once and for all, the history and activity of Jesus, and above all the cross and the Resurrection, no longer have any constitutive meaning whatsoever. Then the death of Jesus would be only the completion of the Incarnation. The Resurrection would be no more than the confirmation of his divine nature. That would mean a diminution of the whole biblical testimony. According to Scripture, Christology has its centre in the cross and the Resurrection.[36]

Now there is no question that a Christology which makes the event of the Incarnation the virtual "be-all and end-all" of the New Testament's statements about Jesus must be faulted for its insensitivity to the equally strong emphasis which it places on the significance of his death and resurrection. It is not an accident that the four Evangelists devote a major portion of their respective Gospels to the *last week* of Jesus' life. Clearly, they intend for Christ's cross work and his resurrection to be kept at the center of any Christology which would lay claim to a sensitive reading of their story. For one to concentrate primarily if not exclusively on the event of the Incarnation is clearly unbiblical. But who, in fact, does this? The Nicene and Post-Nicene Fathers may have done so to a degree. Medieval theology did do so to a certain degree. But certainly since the Reformation few evangelical Protestant scholars could be faulted for doing so. Evangelical Protestantism has made the cross and resurrection central to its theological interests and to church proclamation. But it also recognizes, as did the early Fathers, that for the New Testament writers it is because Christ is who he is that his death and resurrection have the transcendent value that they have in behalf of men's salvation. For this reason evangelical Protestants have been solicitous to hold tenaciously to the ontological deity of Jesus.

The one Protestant theologian who can be faulted for making the Incarnation *the* reconciling event is the Swiss theologian Karl Barth. And it is against Barth's Christology, most directly, that Pannenberg and others have erected their Christologies "from below" as antidotes. In Barth's view the Incarnation is the really crucial event in man's reconciliation to God:

---

[36]Kasper, *Jesus the Christ*, 37.

> ...the being of Jesus Christ, the unity of the living God and this living man, takes place in the event of the concrete existence of this man. It is a being, but a being in history. The gracious God is in this history, so is reconciled man, so both are in their unity. And what takes place in this history, and therefore in the being of Jesus Christ as such, is atonement. Jesus Christ is not what He is—very God, very man, very God-man—in order as such to mean and do and accomplish something else which is atonement. But His being as God and man and God-man consists in the completed act of the reconciliation of man with God.[37]

Clearly, for Barth the Incarnation as such is the reconciling act! Jesus' death on the cross is little more than revelatory of the depth of the humiliation resulting from God turning himself into his opposite, namely, man. And the resurrection is essentially revelatory of the height of man's exaltation that takes place in the being of Jesus Christ.

This construction of the significance of the Incarnation, however, does not do justice to the biblical doctrine of reconciliation which sees the reconciliation of God to the world as being effected by the cross work of Christ. Again and again during his earthly ministry, Jesus himself declared: "My hour has not yet come." Then, standing in the shadow of the cross, he exclaimed: "The hour has come...and what shall I say? 'Father, save me from this hour?' No, it was for this very reason I came to this hour" (John 12:23-27). The New Testament nowhere speaks of our being reconciled by the event of the Incarnation *per se*, but rather insists that our reconciliation to God is through the death of God's Son (Rom 5:10; Col 1:22). It affirms that Christ effected peace between God and men through the blood of his cross (Col 1:20; Eph 2:16). Barth is unable to square the emphasis of these passages with his Christological construction. As a result, all of his claims to the contrary notwithstanding, he does not stand in the mainstream of Reformation thought when by his Christological reconstruction he interprets the person of Christ in terms of his work and his work in terms of his person. The Reformed faith, with Paul, has uniformly and consistently proclaimed the centrality of the cross (1 Cor 1:17, 18, 23; 2:2) in its soteriological thinking and preaching. Of course, the Reformed faith has also recognized that the value of the cross as

---

[37]Karl Barth, *Church Dogmatics*, IV/1, 126ff.

God's saving instrument resides in the fact that at the cross it was the *Lord of glory* who was crucified (1 Cor 2:8), who thereby rendered up to God, because of his intrinsic personal worth, a propitiatory sacrifice of infinite value to satisfy the offended holiness and divine justice of God over against man's sin. So it is important to the New Testament—indeed, critically so—that one never lose sight of who it is who did the cross work, namely, the Lord of glory. While Barth's Christology is guilty of diminishing the glory of the cross, placing the event of the Incarnation as such at the center of his theology, it has never been characteristic of evangelical Christianity or, for that matter, of classical Christology to do so. Consequently, this objection is not really against classical Christology as much as it is against Barth's modern Christological reconstruction.

"It is a Hellenized Christology."

A fourth charge which warrants some discussion is the accusation that the Christ of Nicaea and of Chalcedon is "the philosopher's Christ." The Christ of the early Fathers, it is said, is so thoroughly Hellenized by both the language and metaphysical garb of Greek philosophy that he bears little if any resemblance to the Christ of Scripture, the very human Jesus of Nazareth. The point is sometimes facetiously put in the form of a question: Can one really imagine Jesus responding to a seeker's inquiry concerning who he was with the words: "I am truly God and truly man, consubstantial with the Father according to my deity and consubstantial with you according to my manness, having two natures which are not confused, which do not change, which are not divided, but which are not separated either, the difference of my natures being be no means removed by their union in me but the properties of each nature being preserved and coalescing in my one person and one subsistence, not parted or divided into two persons but still one and the same Son and only-begotten God, Word, the Lord Jesus Christ"?

What is one to say in rejoinder? Resisting the impulse to say: "Yes, had he lived in the fifth century, given the circumstances of the fifth-century situation, I can imagine that he might have responded precisely in this fashion," let me be the first to admit that the Fathers did employ terminology derived from the Greek philosophical tradition, such as the Greek words, οὐσια, ***ousia***, ὁμοούσια, ***homoousia***, φύσις, ***phusis***, and ὑπόστασις, ***hupostasis*** ("essence," "same essence," "nature," and "subsistence") and the Latin words, *substantia*, *consubstantia*, *natura*, and *persona* ("substance," "same substance," "nature," and "person") in their efforts to define as precisely as they knew how just who Jesus Christ is. I readily admit that these words had as their background the thought-form of Greek philosophy. But are they to be faulted for this? Is this really the pertinent issue?

Consider the following facts. The Greek autograph of the Definition of Chalcedon (there was also a Latin translation), although philosophical in appearance, can be translated almost in its entirety by any second-year Greek student with a standard Greek New Testament lexicon as an aid. It is not difficult Greek syntax. And as I said, with only a few exceptions every word can be located in a standard lexicon for the Κοινή (*Koinē*, "common") Greek of the New Testament. What is truly striking about the Definition, when one takes into account how difficult the Fathers could have made it, is its brevity, its simple phrasing, and its common Greek vocabulary. As for its Hellenistic cast, can we of all people—we who live at a time when as never before there is the steady, strident call for "contextualizing" the biblical message—fault them for speaking to their age and culture in such fashion? "Hellenize" the New Testament portrayal of Christ they certainly did; compromise or distort the New Testament portrayal—that needs yet to be demonstrated. Reginald Fuller writes in this regard:

> If the church was to preserve and to proclaim the gospel in the Graeco-Roman world, it had to answer [the ontological questions, how can the Son share the same being as the Father and yet be distinguishable, how can Jesus be God and man at the same time, etc.] in terms of an ontology which was intelligible to that world. Its answer to these questions was the doctrine of the Trinity and the Incarnation....
>
> We must recognize the validity of this achievement of the church of the first five centuries within the terms in which it operated. It is sheer biblicism to maintain that the church should merely repeat "what the Bible says"—about Christology as about anything else. The church has to proclaim the gospel into the contemporary situation. And that is precisely what the Nicene Creed and the Chalcedon formula were trying to do. [As Montefiore says], "The

> Definition of Chalcedon was the only way in which the fifth-century fathers, in their day, and with their conceptual apparatus, could have faithfully creedalized the New Testament witness to Christ."[38]

I agree. The question then that should be asked is not, Did they "Hellenize" Christ, that is, describe the Christ of the New Testament with philosophical language? Of course, they did. But I would hasten to say that *any historical fact of transcendent significance such as the event of the Incarnation must inevitably require the language of metaphysics if men are to explain it theologically.* Serious theological discussion of Jesus Christ—and this is true for every Christology "from below" and every "functional Christology" as well—will of necessity invoke the aid of philosophical language and concepts inasmuch as issues concerning the final and ultimate meaning of reality are being addressed. As a case in point, Pannenberg's *Jesus—God and Man* is a sustained attempt to write a Christology "from below," but when Pannenberg teaches that "Jesus' essence is established retroactively...from his resurrection...in its being,"[39] he has entered deeply into metaphysics by the claim that Jesus' resurrection has ontic retroactive significance for the essence of Jesus. Pannenberg would be the first, in fact, to acknowledge as much. So the question of "Hellenization" is not really to the point.

The much more critical question is: In their attempt to describe precisely who Jesus Christ is for their own time did they deviate from the intention of the New Testament data in any way? Is the New Testament portrayal of Christ's person in some way falsified? These questions are, of course, what the remainder of this book seeks to address. But I think it can be said even at this juncture that whatever one may finally think of their end product, their resultant Christology is anything but "Greek" in theological content. As Lane says, it was "profoundly un-Greek" in content, "challenging Greek culture at a fundamental point."[40] This challenge may be seen first in their "un-Hellenistic" willingness to accept something (the Incarnation) as true that they could not first entirely comprehend. This submitting of their

---

[38]Fuller, *The Foundations of New Testament Christology*, 249-50.

[39]Wolfhart Pannenberg, *Jesus—God and Man*, translated by Lewis L. Wilkins and Duane A. Priebe (London: SCM, 1968), 136.

[40]Lane, "Christology Beyond Chalcedon" in *Christ the Lord*, 263, 264.

minds to an authority external to themselves is to be traced to their conviction that they, possessing the New Testament as they did, possessed the very revelation of God, the only proper response to which is human submission. It is this attitude of submission that explains their employment of γνωριζομένον (*gnōrizomenon*, "being made known") in the middle of their Christological definition, this word indicating that "the Chalcedonian Fathers were accepting, and giving conciliar authority to, what had had its distinct place in the Church's Christological thought from earliest days."[41] The "un-Greek" character of their Definition is discernible also in their perception of the nature of the Incarnation itself as the uniting of God and man in one person so that of Christ it is both appropriate and necessary to say that he is "very God and very man." It is not that in the Greek philosophical strain of the period there were no mediators between God and man; to the contrary, there were mediators galore, usually represented as "emanations" of God between God and man. But all such mediators, on the one hand, were created, and thus subordinate to the "One," the utterly transcendent God. The world, on the other hand, with which the lowest mediator came in contact was viewed as intrinsically evil. It was because of this latter condition concerning the nature of matter that levels of mediators had been posited between the world of men and the transcendent God in the first place. Consequently, a mediator who was in himself both the uncreated God and a sinless man as well was totally unlike anything in the Greek (and Gnostic) scheme of things.

All of this means that we must, in fairness to these Fathers, conclude that, while their words had for their background the history and language of Greek metaphysics, this factor was not the decisive, controlling influence on their thinking. Rather, as they themselves would have certainly insisted, it was simple fidelity to the New Testament witness concerning Jesus that was their primary concern.

"It is a pre-scientific Christology."

A fifth objection to classical Christology is that it is "pre-scientific" in its understanding of the relationship that obtains between the "other world" and the "this world" order of things. It presupposed the

---

[41]R. V. Sellers, *The Council of Chalcedon* (London: SPCK, 1953), 217.

literalness of both the "unseen" and the "seen" worlds, and along with the culture of its time accepted the literal penetration of the former into the latter in the form which biblical supernaturalism assumes. The Incarnation, in terms of "the Word became flesh" motif, was literally comprehended. This perception of the Incarnation is said to be part and parcel of the widespread inclination of virtually that entire age toward grand wholesale legitimacy of the occurrence of miracles. But that, it is now said, was before man "came of age" through the Enlightenment and the ensuing modern scientific revolution. Now, according to Bultmann and his followers, for example, modern man knows better. Today, the world, as the totality of the spatio-temporal phenomena and the only legitimate object of human knowledge, may be approached both externally in an objectifying way that is appropriate to the physical sciences and internally in a manner appropriate to the social sciences. But regardless of one's approach, the world must be understood as a closed system of cause and effect. Every this-world effect has a this-world cause. God can no longer be introduced as the *Deus ex machina* device to explain this-world phenomena or events. Bultmann avers: "...modern man acknowledges as reality only such phenomena or events as are comprehensible within the framework of the rational order of the universe...."[42] He also states: "Modern men take it for granted that the course of nature and of history like their own inner life and their practical life, is nowhere interrupted by the intervention of supernatural powers."[43] Again he declares: "...modern science does not believe that the course of nature can be interrupted or, so to speak, perforated by supernatural powers."[44] The classical doctrine of the Incarnation, for Bultmann, is consequently the result of the later conciliar failure to recognize in the New Testament the presence of the influence of Jewish Apocalyptic and Gnostic mythology. The New Testament, according to Bultmann,

> proclaims in the language of mythology that the last time has now come. 'In the fulness of time' God sent forth his Son, a pre-existent

---

[42]Rudolf Bultmann, *Jesus Christ and Mythology* (New York: Charles Scribner's Sons, 1958), 37.

[43]Bultmann, *Jesus Christ and Mythology*, 16.

[44]Bultmann, *Jesus Christ and Mythology*, 15.

> divine Being, who appears on earth as a man.... All this is the language of mythology, and the origin of the various themes can be easily traced to the contemporary mythology of Jewish Apocalyptic and in the redemption myths of Gnosticism.[45]

"What a primitive mythology it is," he continues, "that a divine Being should become incarnate, and atone for the sins of man through his own blood!"[46] Bultmann's conclusion is that "man's knowledge and mastery of the world have advanced to such an extent through science and technology that it is no longer possible for anyone seriously to hold to the New Testament view of the world."[47] Where it is so held, as in the case of classical Christology and the beliefs of evangelical Christianity in general, it is simply indicative, as far as Bultmann is concerned, of the regrettable fact that some, "ostrich-like," are still living as "pre-scientific" men.

Does this conclusion necessarily follow? Is it true that modern science has necessarily relegated all present-day belief in the supernatural and the miraculous to the category of "baggage from the pre-scientific age of man"? There is no question that this opinion is widely held today. But if there is a *modern* myth (and I recognize that I am using the word in a different sense from that of Bultmann), this is it. I must ask, over against Bultmann *et al.*, is it so that modern science compels both the necessity of "demythologizing" classical Christology and its reinterpretation along Heideggerian existentialist lines? Is the mindset of modern man really such that he is incapable of believing anything that is not scientifically demonstrable. What I find truly amazing is just how many *unscientific* things (more than Lewis Carroll's "seven before breakfast") modern man is able to believe today, such as the modern "scientific" view that this present physical universe with all of its interrelatedness, interdependency, complexity, and awe-inspiring beauty is the result of impersonal forces evolving through aeons of times by chance mutations, catastrophic interruptions of nature, and so on, or that man is the result solely of these same impersonal forces latent in nature plus time plus chance,

---

[45]Bultmann, "New Testament and Mythology" in *Kerygma and Myth*, edited by Hans Bartsch (New York: Harper, 1961), 2, 3.

[46]Bultmann, "New Testament and Mythology," 7.

[47]Bultmann, "New Testament and Mythology," 4.

or that man is essentially good and morally perfectible through education and social manipulation, or that universal morals need not be grounded in ethico-religious absolutes.

In fact, Bultmann's view of the implications of modern science for the historical understanding of the cardinal doctrines of the Christian faith is not scientifically established at all but is rather the reflection of an *a priori* secular or positivistic "scientism" which many scientists reject today. He ascribes an infallibility, a finality, and powers to modern science which in fact it simply does not, cannot, and never will have. No scientific fact, in and of itself, can prove that this universe is a closed system of cause and effect. Nor can the scientific enterprise by the accepted canons of the scientific method demonstrate that the supernatural has never before and will never in the future intrude itself into this world or that the miraculous has never occurred before and will never occur in the future. The most astute philosophers of science among us would never claim that science can so demonstrate nor would they try so to demonstrate. They recognize that to believe that modern science has demonstrated that the miraculous (in the New Testament sense) cannot occur is blind dogmatism. This explains why literally thousands of scientists today, at work in every field of the pure sciences, are quite comfortable both as men of science and men of faith, standing without apology in the historic tradition of the church's teaching and submitting to the full, sweeping supernaturalism of the Scriptures. I refer, for example, to the membership of the American Scientific Affiliation and the Creation Research Society. These scientists are quite adamant in their opposition to any suggestion that this world is a closed system of cause and effect. Still further, they recognize that even from the standpoint of logic such a position as Bultmann espouses, since it involves a universal negation, is incapable of empirical proof.

Bultmann's "modern man," the man who has "come of age," who can no longer tolerate the "mythical" idea of a real incarnation, had his counterpart, in fact, in the days of the New Testament. Doubtless for other reasons but just as certainly, there were men who could not believe some one aspect or other of the Christian proclamation. Thomas, for example, declared that he would not believe in Jesus' resurrection until he saw the nail marks (John 20:25). Second-century

Gnostics were unable to reconcile Christianity's insistence that "the Word became flesh and dwelt among us" with their philosophical view regarding the nature of matter as evil. So they refused to believe in the Incarnation. Unbelief in the supernatural is not a phenomenon new to the church in this age—the result of modern man's newly learned sophistication—and unknown to the Apostles. Unbelief is simply *man's* problem, and it has ever been the case that some have mocked at the supernaturalism of the Bible, others have said, "We want to hear you again on this subject," but some have always believed (Acts 17:32-34).

The upshot of all this is that while it will always be opposed as unscientific or pre-scientific by a positivistic scientism which is not real science at all, New Testament Incarnationalism has nothing to fear from true science.

"It is a triumphalist Christology."

The next objection has to do with the implications in classical incarnational Christology for the truth character of the other religions of the world and for the world's political states as well.

If, as classical Christologists contend, God in a unique and final way became incarnate in Jesus of Nazareth and in no other, then it follows, according to this objection, that Christianity may lay claim not only to the exclusive possession of religious truth but also to monarchical transcendence over the other world religions. This precludes any ultimate peaceful commerce within the "brotherhood" of world religions. Furthermore, this "triumphalist" vision—traceable, it is alleged, to the doctrine of the Incarnation—has controlled Christian theology all too long and inevitably has led to Western Christendom's absolutist and authoritarian claims in the political arena as well, with Jesus Christ himself being made the theological basis of the Christian Empire and of political and ecclesiastical power in the present age. This world—the ever-shrinking "global village" that it is and faced as it is with all kinds of political and economic forces working at cross-purposes with one another—can ill afford, it is urged, the unbecoming triumphalist exclusivism implicit in the church's incarnational Christology.

None to my knowledge has voiced this concern more fervently of late than some of the contributors to *The Myth of God Incarnate*. Maurice Wiles, for example, writes:

> ...where the categorical and absolute character of the religious demand, as it impinges on the Christian, is tied to the historical person of Jesus in a strict metaphysical way (as in traditional incarnation doctrine), that does involve a pre-judgment of the potential significance of other religious faiths..., of a kind that is very hard to justify from our standpoint within one particular stream of religious and cultural development.[48]

Wiles goes on to call for the abandonment, not of Christian religious demand as such, but of its linkage "in its absoluteness" to the figure of Jesus set forth in traditional incarnational Christology.[49] John Hick, editor of *The Myth of God Incarnate*, also writes:

> ...understood literally the Son of God, God the Son, God-incarnate language implies that God can be adequately known and responded to *only* through Jesus; and the whole religious life of mankind, beyond the stream of Judaic-Christian faith is thus by implication excluded as lying outside the sphere of salvation. This implication did little positive harm so long as Christendom was a largely autonomous civilization with only relatively marginal interaction with the rest of mankind. But with the clash between the Christian and Muslim worlds, and then on an ever broadening front with European colonization throughout the earth, the literal understanding of the mythological language of Christian discipleship has had a divisive effect upon the relations between that minority of human beings who live within the borders of the Christian tradition and that majority who live outside it and within other streams of religious life.
>
> ...If Jesus was literally God incarnate, and if it is by his death alone that men can be saved, and by their response to him alone that they can appropriate that salvation, then the only doorway to eternal life is Christian faith. It would follow from this that the large majority of the human race so far has not been saved.... Is not such an idea excessively parochial presenting God in effect as the tribal deity of the predominantly Christian West? . . .

---

[48]Maurice Wiles, *Incarnation and Myth: the Debate Continued* (Grand Rapids: Eerdmans, 1979), 10-11.

[49]Wiles, *Incarnation and Myth: the Debate Continued*, 11.

> It seems clear that we are being called today to attain a global religious vision which is aware of the unity of all mankind before God...we must affirm God's equal love for all men and not only for Christians.... If, selecting from our Christian language, we call God-acting-towards-man the Logos, then we must say that *all* salvation, within all religions, is the work of the Logos.... But what we cannot say is that all who are saved are saved by Jesus of Nazareth. The life of Jesus was one point at which the Logos—that is, God-in-relation-to-man—has acted.... From now onwards...we have to present Jesus...in a way compatible with our new recognition of the validity of the other great world faiths as being also, at their best, ways of salvation. We must therefore not insist upon Jesus being always portrayed within the interpretative framework built around him by centuries of Western thought.[50]

Don Cupitt, yet another contributor to *The Myth of God Incarnate*, traces the roots of early and medieval concepts of the Christian Empire with all of its absolutism and authoritarianism in the political and ecclesiastical spheres, by an unmitigated inevitability, to the dogma of the Incarnation which makes Christ "the manifest Absolute in history."[51] If the church is to reestablish Jesus' moral (and eschatological) lordship in the world as a guide for the world's improvement, maintains Cupitt, it must abandon the dogma which is at the root of Jesus' temporal lordship, namely, the doctrine of the Incarnation.[52]

In response to Wiles' and Hick's calls for the church to abandon its "exclusivist" doctrine of incarnational Christology in favor of a religious pluralism which sees the Logos "savingly" at work in all of the world's great religions, we must say that there is no question, as John Stott writes, that every Christian should normally support *legal* tolerance toward other religions. That is to say, Christians should actively support laws which adequately protect the rights of the individual to profess, practice, and propagate his religious views, with due allowance being made at the same time, of course, for the protection of the rest of the citizenry from the excesses of religious fanaticism which would inflict physical harm upon others. Furthermore,

---

[50]Hick, *The Myth of God Incarnate*, 179, 180, 181, 182.

[51]Don Cupitt, *The Myth of God Incarnate*, 140-41.

[52]Cupitt, *The Myth of God Incarnate*, 140-41.

every Christian should cultivate in himself and encourage in others *social* tolerance toward other religions. In other words, the Christian should respect the religious views which others hold and should seek to understand them and to encourage the same in others with respect to his own faith. But when it comes to *intellectual* tolerance, that is to say, the cultivation of "a mind so broad that it can tolerate every opinion, without ever detecting anything in it to reject"—this "is not a virtue; it is the vice of the feeble-minded."[53] Of course, neither Wiles nor Hick can be charged with such feeble-mindedness, for they have reference to the "other great world faiths" such as Islam and Judaism when they speak of the Logos as being at work in other faiths. They would not and do not attribute to the work of the Logos the superstitious and demonic elements which loom large, for example, in so many of today's third-world primitive cultures. Stott himself recognizes that such intellectual tolerance is rare, the more popular expression of it being the demand for a religious syncretism in which the *best* of the differing religious beliefs are harmonized into a single system.[54] It is this "inter-faith dialogue" of religious pluralism for which Wiles and Hick are calling, to which incarnational Christology is said to be a major stumbling block. The *Myth* contributors sincerely believe that such a religious syncretism as they envision will aid in bringing about the universal brotherhood of men which the world so badly needs.

But this entire argument ignores the question of truth. *If* Jesus is in fact God incarnate (and this book will examine the biblical testimony reputedly said to favor the doctrine), Christians cannot accept this rationale for an intellectual religious pluralism. And if Jesus is in fact God incarnate, and if the church would be governed by truth, as presumably it should be, it must continue to insist that Jesus is *unique*, finally and transcendentally so. Historically, this uniqueness resides in his birth, his obedient, perfectly sinless life and sacrificial death, his resurrection, ascension, and present session at the Father's right hand, and his eschatological return as the Judge and Savior of men. Theologically, it resides in the Incarnation and its implicates, the Atonement, and the several (including the cosmically final) aspects

---

[53]John Stott, *The Authentic Christ* (Basingstoke: Marshalls Paperbacks, 1985), 70.

[54]Stott, *The Authentic Christ*, 70.

of his exaltation. *If* Jesus Christ is in fact God incarnate, Jesus must continue to be proclaimed as the *only saving way* to the Father, as he said (John 14:6), his the *only saving name* among men, as Peter said (Acts 4:12), and his the *only saving mediation* between God and man, as Paul said (1 Tim 2:5). Furthermore, the church must declare that the goal which the religious pluralist so devoutly seeks—a universal religious brotherhood binding all men everywhere joyously together in one world of common humanity—is, on his grounds, unobtainable, not only because such pluralism does not transform the human heart, but also because *only the genuinely and transcendentally unique has such universal significance that it deserves to be universally proclaimed and universally received.* Without the transcendent finality that is displayed, for example, in the biblical witness to Jesus—directing and energizing the innate and explicit religious demands of the community of men—there can be no universal significance or power in such an appeal. And any religious commerce, if it is achieved, will finally have to be imposed upon men against their will (see Rev 13:11-17).

As for Cupitt's contention, if Brian Hebblethwaite's assessment that such an opinion reflects "sheer perversity in moral judgment"[55] should seem too strong, it is certainly true that his related insight—that what has ever given Christianity its characteristic moral and religious power is its "conviction that its Lord has humbled himself and taken the form of a servant"[56]—is right on target! The un-Christlike political triumphalism of the organized church in the West during certain periods of its existence can be traced to any number of other forces and influences, not the least of which is man's *hubris* ("pride"). But to charge it to the church's doctrine of the Incarnation is a glaring piece of theological "reaching" for the sake of making a point in harmony with a highly individualistic and questionable religious vision.

To abandon biblical incarnationalism in favor of a religious pluralism, *if* Christ is indeed God incarnate, is tantamount to the gravest breach of the First Commandment and would be to involve oneself in

---

[55]Brian Hebblethwaite, "The Moral and Religious Value of the Incarnation" in *Incarnation and Myth: The Debate Continued*, 89.

[56]Hebblethwaite, "The Moral and Religious Value of the Incarnation," 89.

unspeakable infidelity to the Lord of Glory who wears a diadem which out-rivals all the diadems of all the world's religious and political leaders. In a word, to do so would mean that the church had simply ceased to be *Christian*! The Christian church can afford to follow the modern call for religious pluralism only at the greatest of costs both to itself and to the world to which it has been sent. Moreover, to follow this call would be to set the church on a course which can only lead ultimately to disappointment and judgment in the end.

"It is a 'pre-critical' Christology."

The last and probably the most significant objection raised against classical incarnational Christology—because it is at the base of and directly or indirectly accounts for all the other modern objections—is the contention that the Nicene and Chalcedonian formulations were drawn up prior to the rise of the methods of critical analysis of the Gospels and Epistles which dominate the field of New Testament research today.

In the late eighteenth and throughout the nineteenth and twentieth centuries a negative biblical criticism, assuming the evolutionary development of religious thought, began to dominate the thinking of the great centers of learning, particularly in Europe and England. This attitude surfaced in the field of Old Testament under the academic aegis of such notable scholars as Graf, Keunen, Wellhausen, Cornill, Driver, and Briggs and rapidly spread to the field of New Testament within which such names as Strauss, Wrede, Weiss, Schmiedel, and Bousset coming readily to mind. Then with the rise to dominance of "form criticism" (*Formgeschichte*) in Gospel studies in the early twentieth century through the influence of K. L. Schmidt, Martin Dibelius and Rudolf Bultmann, and then "redaction criticism" (*Redactionsgeschichte*) through the influence of Willi Marxsen, G. Bornkamm, and Hans Conzelmann, any remaining significant knowledge of the historical Jesus of the Gospel records was pushed so far back into the dark recesses of first-century church tradition that today it is generally argued by the more skeptical practitioners of the methods that reliable knowledge of Jesus is quite illusory. And while there is a noticeable reaction today among the so-called "new questers of the historical Jesus" away from the agnostic stance captured in Bultmann's famous judgment, "I do indeed think that we can know almost nothing concerning the life and personality of Jesus,"[57] Maurice Wiles still felt it academically legitimate to say in his 1973 Hulsean Lectures at Cambridge: "...it is essential that the doctrinal theologian recognizes that the kind of information about Jesus that theology has so often looked to New Testament scholars to provide is not available."[58] And John Bowden concludes his article entitled "Jesus" in *A New Dictionary of Christian Theology* with these words:

> There is a good deal that we probably do know about Jesus; the trouble is that we cannot always be sure precisely what it is. Because of the very nature of historical research, discussions about Jesus always contain countless approximations, and one of the most confident recent studies (A. E. Harvey, *Jesus and the Constraints of History*, 1982) concedes that "it can still be argued that we can have no reliable historical knowledge about Jesus with regard to anything that really matters" (p. 6). This being so, it is remarkable that attempts to restate the significance of Jesus without the doctrine of Incarnation can be based on what amounts to an interpretation of the character of Jesus which is actually based on very little historical evidence. However christology may be worked out, there is no escaping our considerable ignorance about actual facts.[59]

Why, it may legitimately be asked, is there such skepticism regarding the acquisition of significant factual information about the Jesus of history? Why does one so often hear it said today that the only Jesus that is now recoverable by New Testament research is the non-historical "created" Jesus of the early church's κήρυγμα, *kerugma*. To understand all of this, it will be necessary to give a brief overview of the methods which have dominated twentieth-century New Testament Gospel research.

---

[57]Rudolf Bultmann, *Jesus and the Word*, translated by Louise Pettibone Smith and Erminie Huntress Lanters (New York: Charles Scribner & Sons, 1934), 8.

[58]Maurice Wiles, *The Remaking of Christian Doctrine* (London: SCM, 1974), 48.

[59]John Bowden, "Jesus" in *A New Dictionary of Christian Theology*, edited by Alan Richardson and John Bowden (London: SCM, 1983), 312.

Source Criticism of the Synoptic Gospels

Virtually from the time that the Gospels were originally composed, for all their similarities (particularly between the Synoptic ["look alike"] Gospels—Matthew, Mark, and Luke[60]), their dissimilarities have attracted the special attention of New Testament students. For example, the sequence of events occasionally varies from Gospel to Gospel. Where Matthew, for instance, gives the sequence of Jesus' temptations one way (4:3-10), Luke reverses the order of the second and third temptations (4:3-12). Then there are the frequent variations from Gospel to Gospel in the way Jesus' sayings and parables are reported. For example, where Matthew reports that Jesus concludes his lesson on prayer with the words: "...how much more will your Father in

---

[60]Biblical scholarship throughout the Christian era has recognized that the Fourth Gospel is "different" in some respects from the other three. For example, (1) the Synoptic Gospels are concerned largely with Jesus' ministry in Galilee whereas John's Gospel concentrates primarily on an early Judaean/ Samaritan ministry (about which the Synoptics say nothing) and after that on Jesus' ministry centering around three more trips to Jerusalem; (2) in the Synoptics only one Passover—our Lord's last one—is mentioned whereas in John there are at least three Passovers, possibly four; (3) John's Gospel records the details of only 7 miracles, 5 of which are unique to his Gospel, and makes no mention of Jesus' miraculous birth, his transfiguration, many of the Synoptic miracles and no exorcisms of demons at all; (4) John's Gospel does not mention Jesus' baptism, his Passion Week cleansing of the temple, his Olivet Discourse, his institution of the Lord's Supper, or his agony in Gethsemane; (5) while the Synoptists highlight the Jewish trial of Jesus, John scarcely mentions Jesus' trial by the Sanhedrin but gives considerable attention to the Roman trial, particularly to Pilate's interview of Jesus; (6) not only do Jesus' discourses in John's Gospel concentrate chiefly on his person rather than on the ethics of his kingdom as in the Synoptics but also the literary genre of his teaching is different: whereas in the Synoptics the most distinctive literary form is the parable and many short vivid sayings, in John's Gospel Jesus' narrative parables have been largely replaced by long and, for the most part, private or semi-private discourses; (7) prominent Synoptic themes are lacking in John, for example, John's Gospel has nothing to say about repentance and Jesus' teaching on the kingdom of God has almost disappeared (but see 3:3, 5; 18:36), its place being taken by his teaching on eternal life, while prominent Johannine themes are missing in the Synoptics, for example, Jesus' "I am" sayings and the lengthy "bread of life," "light of the world," "good Shepherd," "vine and branches," and upper room discourses; (8) the structure of the eschatological thought of John's Gospel

heaven give *good gifts* to those who ask him!" ((7:11), Luke reports his words this way: "...how much more will your Father in heaven give the *Holy Spirit* to those who ask him!" (11:13). Then the words of others are variously reported: where Matthew, for example, reports Peter's confession in the words: "You are the Christ, the Son of the living God" (16:16), Mark reports his confession more simply as "You are the Christ" (8:29). What is the explanation for these differences?

No doubt there is merit to the suggestion that many of the variations can be explained by the fact that Jesus repeated his sermons and parables on more than one occasion and in different contexts. The Evangelists could then be reporting sermons and parables similar in substance but different in detail, given the fact that they were given on different occasions.[61] But this suggestion will not explain every variation, for example, the variation in the sequence of Jesus' temptations, or in the form of the question which Jesus put to his disciples at Caesarea Philippi: where Matthew reports Jesus asking, "Who do people say the *Son of Man* is?" (16:13), Mark records his question this way: "Who do people say that *I* am?" (8:27). Here is clearly the same occasion and the same question. Why does Matthew use the title "Son of Man" while Mark employs the first person personal pronoun? Could it be that underlying our present canonical Gospels at a more primitive level of Gospel tradition were earlier literary sources

---

is somewhat different: whereas the Synoptics emphasize the two consecutive temporal ages of Jewish apocalyptic—this age and that which is to come (but see 11:24), which is not completely absent from John's Gospel—the Fourth Gospel emphasizes the dualism between the above and the below, heaven and earth, the sphere where God the Father is and this world; (9) Jesus' vocabulary in John's Gospel is different, that is to say, many common words in the Synoptics are missing in John whereas many common words in John are missing in the Synoptics; (10) finally, there are what seem to be at least suface contradictions between some Synoptic details and some Johannine details. For discussions of these differences see my *John: Beloved Disciple* (Ross-shire, Scotland: Mentor, 2001), 21-7, and G. R. Beasley-Murray, "Synoptics and John" in *Dictionary of Jesus and the Gospel*, edited by Joel B. Green, Scot McKnight, and I. Howard Marshall (Downers Grove, Illinois: InterVarsity, 1992), 792-94.

[61]See Everett F. Harrison, "*Gemeindetheologie:* The Bane of Gospel Criticism" in *Jesus of Nazareth: Saviour and Lord*, edited by Carl F. H. Henry (London: Tyndale, 1966), 162.

upon which the Synoptic Evangelists relied in which such variations occurred? If so, why did these more primitive literary sources vary? Could it be, if these "aboriginal Gospels" could be isolated one from the other through minute analysis, that the scholarly world could gain not only answers to these questions but also a portrait of the Jesus of this primitive Gospel tradition that is more historically accurate than (perhaps even different from) that given in the canonical Gospels?

To find the answers to these questions, during the first two decades of the twentieth century such scholars as E. D. Burton and B. H. Streeter engaged in a method known as "source criticism" which sought to discover the supposed literary sources which underlay the first three Gospels. Two basic proposals were put forth: the "two-document theory" (Mark, or *Ur-Markus*, a written tradition thought to be so close to the canonical Gospel of Mark that for all intents and purposes we actually possess it in Mark's Gospel, and "Q," standing for the German noun *Quelle* meaning "source," referring to the non-Markan material used by Matthew and Luke) and the "four-document theory" (Mark [or *Ur-Markus*], Q, M [the special material found only in Matthew], and L (the special material found only in Luke]) gained the widest general acceptance.

Granting for the sake of argument their existence, did these "sources," now "isolated," present a Christ different in kind from the canonical Gospels? Benjamin B. Warfield, in his study of Jesus' titles in the New Testament, for the sake of argument demonstrated that the so-called "primitive Mark," even if its contents are confined only to the matter common to all three synoptic Gospels, still portrays a Christ in whom deity is "ineffaceably imbedded."[62] All the more so is this true if one adds the fragments peculiar to Mark and M,[63] or Mark and L.[64] The same conclusion holds true, he demonstrated, for Q.[65] A. T. Robertson demonstrated the same thing in 1924 in his *The Christ of the Logia*.[66] In addition, Warfield pointed out, if we grant for the sake of argument that the canonical Gospels are "second

---

[62]Benjamin B. Warfield, *The Lord of Glory* (Reprint; Grand Rapids: Baker, 1974), 149.

[63]Warfield, *The Lord of Glory*, 152-53.

[64]Warfield, *The Lord of Glory*, 153.

[65]Warfield, *The Lord of Glory*, 153-55.

[66]A. T. Robertson, *The Christ of the Logia* (New York: G. H. Doran, 1924).

generation" documents and that behind them lay these still more primitive documents, "we have simply pushed back [from the seventh decade of the first century] ten, fifteen, or twenty years our literary testimony to the deity of Christ: and how can we suppose that the determinative expression of the Church's faith in A.D. 50 or A.D. 40 differed radically from the Church's faith in A.D. 30—the year in which Jesus died?"[67]

Historical Criticism

In the face of these undeniable conclusions, those biblical scholars—and there were many—who were predisposed philosophically and theologically against the doctrine of a two-natured Christ continued to place confidence in another critical approach to the Gospels known as "historical criticism," in which the critic attempted by the most searching critical analysis to get back to the Jesus "that really was" behind the Jesus of the Evangelists who, it was assumed, had read their own ideas about him into his teachings and who had attributed much to Jesus which he never said. Scholars such as W. Bousset, P. Schmiedel, O. Pfleiderer, and S. Matthews worked with the assumption that the Evangelists, because they were men of faith, that is, because they revered Jesus and wrote out of a commitment to him, were incapable of writing objectively about him. As a result, they have given to us not a portrait of Jesus as he really was but as they, in their devotion as spokesmen of the believing community, envisioned him to be. Warfield states their working thesis in these words:

> Faith [became] the foe of fact: and in the enthusiasm of their devotion to Jesus it was inevitable that His followers should clothe Him in their thought of Him with attributes which He did not possess and never dreamed of claiming: and it was equally inevitable that they should imagine that He must have claimed them and have ended by representing Him as claiming them.[68]

The results of their labors proved to be quite meager. After "the utmost sharpness of inquisition," Schmiedel, for example, concluded that there were only nine "absolutely credible passages" in the Gospels

---

[67]Warfield, *The Lord of Glory*, 147-48.

[68]Warfield, *The Lord of Glory*, 157-58.

which could serve as "the foundation pillars for a truly scientific life of Jesus,"[69] these nine incidentally proving to Schmiedel that the real Jesus was only a man like other men. All else that the Evangelists report had been so retouched from the standpoint of faith, maintained Schmiedel, that it should be discarded insofar as aiding in the discovery of the Jesus that really was. Pfleiderer even concluded that the real Jesus was irretrievably hidden under the devotional layers with which faith had enveloped him.[70]

This eviscerated picture of Jesus, however, was simply incapable of explaining the supernatural Christianity which sprang from him. Moreover, the assumption with which the historical critics worked—that faith is the foe of fact, the enemy of real historical reporting—is defective beyond redemption. That the Evangelists wrote as men of faith is, of course, not to be doubted. Two of them admit as much. Luke acknowledges that his Gospel stood in the train of other Christians' efforts before his (does he include Mark and Matthew among them?) to "set in order a narrative of those things which have been fulfilled among us...that [his reader] may know the certainty of the things you have been taught" (1:1-4). And John forthrightly declares that he wrote with the aim of bringing his readers to faith in Jesus as the Christ, the Son of God (John 19:35; 20:31). Sympathetic they undoubtedly were to Christ and his cause—beyond any question. But "are we to lay it down as the primary canon of criticism that no sympathetic report of a master's teaching is trustworthy; that only inimical reporters are credible reporters"[71] —in spite of the fact that Luke and John expressly state respectively that their concern was to testify "carefully" (ἀκριβῶς, *akribōs*, Luke 1:3) and truthfully (ἀληθινή, *alēthinē*, ἀληθής, *alēthēs*, John 19:35; 21:24). Surely, Warfield was right when he declared:

---

[69]Paul W. Schmiedel, "Gospels" in *Encyclopaedia Biblica* (1901). The nine passages are Matthew 12:31ff., 27:46 (and its Markan parallel); Mark 3:21; 10:17ff., and 13:32; to which he added Matthew 11:5 (and its Lukan parallel); Mark 6:5ff., 8:12, and 8:14-21. See Warfield's response in his "Concerning Schmiedel's Pillar-Passages" in *Christology and Criticism* (New York: Oxford, 1929), 181-255.

[70]Otto Pfleiderer, *The Early Christian Conception of Jesus*, cited by Warfield, *The Lord of Glory*, 162.

[71]Warfield, *The Lord of Glory*, 159.

> ...the procedure we are here invited to adopt is a prescription for historical investigation which must always issue in reversing the portraiture of the historical characters to the records of whose lives it is applied. The result of its universal application would be...the writing of all history backwards...every historical character [being] the exact opposite to what each was thought to be by all who knew and esteemed him.[72]

Warfield may be guilty in the eyes of some of simply resorting to the *argumentum reductio ad absurdum* here, but the fact that the historical critic's canon is so vulnerable to the argument is an indication of its weakness. Nor should it be denied that the historical critic's canon that would suggest that only *uninterpreted* facts about Jesus—divested of any and all personal views about him, theological or otherwise—are grist for the historian's mill is asking for facts, as James Denney cautioned, that stand out of relation to everything in the universe, which have no connection with any part of our experience, a blank unintelligibility, a mere irrelevance in the mind of men.[73] C. H. Dodd also has pointed out that events "can take their true place in an historical record only as they are interpreted,"[74] while Leon Morris urges that the historian who would simply content himself with a "factual" account of what takes places is to fail as a historian.[75] Even A. E. Harvey, who is no friend of the teaching of a two-natured Christ, acknowledges that

> it is a mistake to contrast the admittedly heavily interpreted gospel record with an imaginary ideal of objective, completely uninterpreted "history." Such history is never in fact written. Bare objective facts exist only, if at all, in archives and account books. History is what makes sense out of the raw material by a complex process of selection, arrangement, and interpretation.[76]

---

[72]Warfield, *The Lord of Glory*, 161.

[73]James Denney, *Studies in Theology* (London: Hodder and Stoughton, 1895), 106; see also A. M. Hunter, *Interpreting the New Testament 1900-1950* (London: SCM, 1951), 46-7.

[74]C. H. Dodd, *History and the Gospel* (London: Nisbet, 1938), 104.

[75]Leon Morris, "The Fourth Gospel and History" in *Jesus of Nazareth: Saviour and Lord*, 124.

For these reasons then—first, its inability to explain the existence of the supernatural Christianity which sprang from Jesus on the basis of the minimal amount of "trustworthy" material which it recovered about him from its labors, and second, the defective canon which governed it—the historical-critical movement was and must be adjudged a failure.

Form Criticism

For the last seventy years or so a third method of New Testament research has increasingly dominated the field. I refer to form criticism. Though there had been predecessors of these form critics such as Herder, Overbeck, Wendland, and Nordern, it was Martin Dibelius and Rudolf Bultmann who pioneered the form-critical method. The method, technically known as the *Formgeschichtliche* ("form-historical") method, signalizes the effort to penetrate behind the written Gospels and even behind the presumed more primitive literary sources underlying them (*Ur-Markus*, Q, M, L) to the even more primitive *oral* stage of the Gospel tradition and to classify and to examine the various "forms" or types of material present in that oral tradition. These "oral forms," it was presumed, provided material for the aboriginal literary sources of the Gospels, but it was also urged that the oral forms were so thoroughly shaped by the racial and socio-cultural character and needs of the several early Christian communities in which they originated that they preclude any real historical basis for the events which are recorded in the Gospels. The error of the historical-critical method, according to these form critics, was the assumption that there was real historical data, however scant, still to be obtained about Jesus in the Gospels which could provide a portrait of a Jesus who could still be a moral guide to the Enlightenment if only the layers of theological encrustation encasing him could be removed by the historical-critical method itself. What these earlier practitioners of the art had failed to realize, the first form critics maintained, is that the Gospel material had already been so thoroughly reshaped ("mythologized," to employ Bultmann's term) at the level of

---

[76]A. E. Harvey, "Christology and the Evidence of the New Testament" in *God Incarnate: Story and Belief*, edited by A. E. Harvey (London: SPCK, 1981), 46.

oral tradition as the post Easter church[77] sought to meet its evangelistic and apologetic needs that there is virtually nothing remaining of the historical Jesus in the Gospels beyond his mere "thatness." Bultmann declares, in fact, in the opening paragraph of his *Theology of the New Testament* that the post-Easter church "frequently introduced into its account of Jesus' message, motifs of its own proclamation."[78] The church was also clearly influenced, according to Bultmann's analysis of the *Sitze im Leben* ("settings in life") of the isolated forms of tradition (which have been "form-critically" categorized into prophetic sayings, wisdom sayings, legal sayings, parables, "I" sayings, and narrative units of paradigm, conflict stories, miracle stories, Passion stories, and so on), by Jewish Apocalyptic and Gnostic mythology.

Developments in the method have, of course, occurred. For example, Reginald H. Fuller, both refining and reacting to the views originating with W. Bousset (*Kyrios Christos*) and developed by R. Bultmann (*Theology of the New Testament*) and F. Hahn (*The Titles of Jesus in Christology*), has subjected the Christological statements of the New Testament to a critical analysis in accordance with the particular *Sitze im Leben* which they occupy in their assigned first-century milieu.[79] As a result of his labors Fuller argues that Jesus himself understood his earthly mission entirely in functional terms, seeing his task to be the announcement of the future coming of the Son of Man. After his death the earliest Aramaic-speaking Christians of Palestine thought of Jesus in a functional/prophetic manner but they also identified him with the eschatological Son of Man which identification, Fuller contends, Jesus himself had never made. (The teachings of Peter in Acts and James are often thought to reflect this Christological stage.) As the gospel spread to the Jews of the Diaspora,

---

[77]The reader should bear in mind that when the anti-incarnational form critic uses the phrase "post-Easter church," he does not intend to suggest that he believes that Jesus actually rose from the dead. Rather, he refers to the church which grew out of the "dawning" upon Jesus' disciples after his death that he still "lived" among them in a spiritual or "existential" sense in order to transform them.

[78]Rudolf Bultmann, *Theology of the New Testament*, translated by Kendrick Grobel (London: SCM, 1971), 3.

[79]Reginald H. Fuller, *The Foundations of New Testament Christology* (New York: Charles Scribner's Sons, 1965).

these Hellenistic (Greek-speaking, "Grecianized") Jewish Christians combined with these functional categories certain ontological categories as well, heightening the representation of Jesus' person during his earthly ministry and adding the thought of his present reign as exalted "Lord." (Paul and the Author of Hebrews (who may well be Paul) would reflect this stage of development.) Finally, in the church's mission to Hellenistic Gentiles, still more ontological categories were added, resulting in the pre-existent, incarnational, "divine man" Christology reflected by the Johannine corpus.[80]

Of course, such a Christological construction, if true, would mean the end to anything truly transcendentally significant in classical incarnational Christology since it both precludes any real, knowable, historical basis for the events which are recorded in the canonical Gospels and contends rather that there never was *one* recognized Christology in the first century but rather that there was a variety of Christologies—a "Synoptic" Christology, a "Pauline" Christology, a "Johannine" Christology, and so on, that in substantive detail differed from each other. Without realizing it, the church simply creedalized that Christological form which had taken shape during the church's Hellenistic Gentile mission. But W. D. Davies' *Paul and Rabbinic Judaism* and Martin Hengel's *Judaism and Hellenism* have both demonstrated that the alleged distinctions that Fuller draws between Palestinian and Hellenistic Judaism cannot be asserted in that no part of Judaism had escaped the influence of Hellenization already by 150 B.C. I. Howard Marshall has argued similarly that no significant differences can be drawn between a Jewish and a Gentile Christianity[81] because of (1) the short span of time (some twenty years) that transpired between the death of Jesus and the writing of the earliest Pauline letters in which a fully developed Christology is already present, and (2) the improbability that a special Jerusalem theology developed independently of a special theology in Antioch (which latter

---

[80]James D. G. Dunn's *Christology in the Making* reflects a similar vision of the development of New Testament Christology from a non-incarnational to an incarnational kind.

[81]I. Howard Marshall, "Palestinian and Hellenistic Christianity: Some Critical Comments" in *New Testament Studies* 19 (1972-1973), 271-287; see also his *The Origins of New Testament Christology*, 32-4.

church was deeply involved in the Gentile mission) because of the many contacts that existed between these two Christian centers. He concludes that the three-stage scheme of development is "an inexact means of plotting Christological thought" because the boundaries between the three areas of thought were simply "too fluid."[82]

Redaction Criticism

Other form-critical scholars, beginning with Willi Marxsen, have now added a fourth critical method known as redaction criticism which asserts that allowances have to be made in the final appearance which the Gospels assumed not only for the mythologized oral strata behind the literary Gospels but also for the theological and literary preferences of the Gospel writers themselves who in their selecting and arranging of the material for their respective Gospels did not hesitate, as they "redacted" or edited their material, to *create* a new story in order to meet the needs of their respective communities of belief.

A careful exegetical study of the early sermons of Peter in Acts and the sixty odd occurrences of εὐαγγέλιον (*euangelion*, usually translated "gospel"; literally "good news") in Paul's writings will disclose that the *apostolic* gospel was simply (1) the proclamation (κήρυγμα, *kērugma*) of the *historical* facts of the death, resurrection, and exaltation of Jesus, (2) together with the apostolic explication of the significance of these events for God and for man, (3) followed by the summons to repent and the invitation to receive forgiveness through faith in Christ's work.[83] While the church has historically been satisfied that what it possesses in the four canonical Gospels is simply the literary "fleshing out" of the essential facts of the life and ministry of that one who is central to the apostolic proclamation—this "fleshing out" itself described by Mark as "the gospel of Jesus Christ" (1:1), recent redaction criticism has given rise to the effort by scholars to discern which *genre* a given Gospel writer was patterning his account after as he "created" it: was it (1) the history format genre form comprised of ancient memoirs and biography segments, (2) the Semitic model genre form, such as apocalypse, the legend of Achikar, Exodus,

---

[82]Marshall, *The Origins of New Testament Christology*, 40.

[83]See Robert H. Mounce, "Gospel" in *Evangelical Dictionary of Theology*, 472-74.

the book of Jonah, a Passover Haggadah, Midrashim, and the Mishnah, (3) the kerygma/history genre form, (4) the Greco/Roman biography genre form, (5) the aretalogy genre form in which the miraculous deeds of a "god" or "hero" are narrated, (6) the Christian novel genre form, (7) the dramatic history genre form, (8) the Greek tragicomic genre form, (9) a combination of these, or (10) the cult of Christ/kerygma genre—the latter unique among genre forms? Whatever genre a given scholar finally endorsed, there is general agreement among scholars that "it is not the construing of what Jesus did and said that determined the genre, but the genre that determined how what he did and said was construed" (Via).

Critique of These Critical Methods

It should now be evident to anyone who has followed this brief overview of the history of twentieth-century New Testament research why Wiles and Bowden, whom we quoted earlier, express such skepticism about ever knowing anything about the historical Jesus that is really significant. And it should not be surprising that scholars, faced with the specter of total skepticism in the field of New Testament studies, have reacted—some more mildly, some more vigorously—against the conclusions of the form-critical/redaction-critical methods which have shifted the object of faith away from the Jesus of the canonical Gospels to the "demythologized" Christ of the church's proclamation. Though still committed to the form-critical method itself, they have begun to search for ways to isolate out of the Gospel tradition at least some, if not all, of the authentic sayings of Jesus (assuming there might be some) in order to lay hold upon something of the historical Jesus in the interest of justifying the church's continuing interest in him.

J. Jeremias, for example, argued for years that the presence of certain patterns in the reported speeches and sayings of Jesus can only be explained on the ground that we have in them, if not the *ipsissima verba Jesu* ("very words of Jesus") very likely the *ipsissima vox Jesu* ("very voice of Jesus"). He advanced such characteristic patterns of speech in Jesus' recorded teaching as his use of *Abba* (*Abba*, Greek transliteration of the Aramaic אַבָּא, '*abbā*', "Father") without a suffix as an address to God in prayer, his use of ἀμήν (*amēn*, "in truth") to introduce and to authenticate his own words, his frequent use of antithetic parallelism, his parables, and his employment of circumlocutions (for example, the passive verbs in the Matthean Beatitudes) to avoid the use of the divine name.[84] Jeremias concluded as a result of his detailed study that

> ...the linguistic and stylistic evidence...shows so much faithfulness and such respect towards the tradition of the sayings of Jesus that we are justified in drawing up the following principle of method: In the synoptic tradition it is the inauthenticity and not the authenticity of the sayings of Jesus that must be demonstrated.[85]

C. H. Dodd echoed Jeremias' conclusion, saying that after full allowance has been made for all the possible limiting factors—changes in oral transmission, the effects of translating Jesus' Aramaic into Greek, and the "redactional" intent of the Evangelists—

> it remains that the first three gospels offer a body of sayings on the whole so consistent, so coherent, and withal so distinctive in manner, style, [and] content, that no reasonable critic should doubt, whatever reservations he may have about individual sayings, that we find reflected here the thought of a single, unique teacher—[even Jesus Christ].[86]

But such optimistic conclusions have not gone unchallenged by a good many form critics, such as V. Hasler, K. Berger, and H. Conzelmann. And Norman Perrin declares, contrary to Jeremias' conclusion:

> ...clearly, we have to ask ourselves the question as to whether [Jesus' sayings] should now be attributed to the early Church or to the historical Jesus, and *the nature of the synoptic tradition is such that the burden of proof will be upon the claim to authenticity*.[87]

---

[84]Joachim Jeremias, *New Testament Theology, I: The Proclamation of Jesus*, translated by J. Bowden (London: SCM, 1971), 8-37.

[85]Jeremias, *New Testament Theology*, I:37.

[86]C. H. Dodd, *The Founder of Christianity* (New York: Macmillan, 1970), 21-2.

[87]Norman Perrin, *Rediscovering the Teaching of Jesus* (London: SCM, 1967), 39, emphasis original.

Faced with the need then to authenticate a historical Jesus which will stir even minimal interests of faith in him, in their "new quest of the historical Jesus" form-critical scholars such as E. Käsemann, H. Conzelmann, N. Perrin, and R. Fuller among others have resorted to three criteria for isolating authentic sayings of Jesus and thus for establishing a genuinely historical base sufficiently broad for the grounding of faith in him. These are the criteria of dissimilarity, coherence, and frequency of attestation. The *criterion of dissimilarity* is applied as follows: if a saying of Jesus has no obvious source in Jewish tradition (apocalyptic and Rabbinic tradition) or in the traditions of the early church (their faith, their practice, their life situations), then it is likely that the saying originated with Jesus.[88] By this criterion a pool of authentic teaching is isolated. Then the *criterion of coherence* is applied to increase the number of sayings. This is done by noting other sayings which, although they do not fit into the previous category, nonetheless cohere with those that do. Finally, *the criterion of frequency* of occurrence in the so-called independent strands of Synoptic tradition (Ur-Markus, Q, M, L) comes into play. It assumes that a saying found in two or three sources is more likely to be authentic than a saying found in only one source unless the latter meets the criterion of dissimilarity.

As with Jeremias' proposals, needless to say, these criteria have not gone unchallenged and, quite frankly, properly so. With regard to the criterion of dissimilarity, since Jesus was a Jew, "to excise from his teaching all that agreed with previous Jewish tradition is certainly to remove some genuine material."[89] Moreover, it assumes that there was no continuity between Jesus and the post-Easter church that emerged from his teaching; Morna Hooker,[90] for example, points out that this criterion eliminates from the teaching of Jesus those areas in

---

[88]See Ernst Käsemann, "The Problem of the Historical Jesus" in *Essays on New Testament Themes*, translated by W. J. Montague (London: SCM, 1964), 15-47, for his programmatic argument for the validity of the criterion of dissimilarity.

[89]P. H. Davids, "Tradition Criticism" in *Dictionary of Jesus and the Gospels*, 830.

[90]M. D. Hooker, "On Using the Wrong Tool" in *Theology*, Vol. LXXV, No. 629 (Nov 1972): 570-81; see also her article, "Christology and Methodology" in *New Testament Studies* 17 (1970-1971): 480-87. R. T. France, "The

which he would have been in agreement with both Judaism and the church. Which is just to say that if the church is, in fact, the outcome of his ministry it is utterly improbable that no continuity would obtain between his teaching and the post-Easter faith of the church. But on the basis of the criterion of dissimilarity, if Jesus, for example, actually claimed to be the Messiah, this teaching would have to be disallowed because the church makes it on his behalf. Hooker notes:

> ...this particular criterion...*may* perhaps be able to give us a collection of sayings concerning whose authority we may be reasonably confident, but those sayings will not represent the kernel of Jesus' teaching, or be his most characteristic thought. Indeed, they would seem to offer us those sayings which the church treated as peripheral.[91]

Hooker also notes that the criterion of dissimilarity is faulty because it assumes that our knowledge of pre-Christian and first-century Judaism and early Christianity is sufficient to serve as a control of what is unique in Jesus' teaching. But the discovery of the Qumran community and its library (not to mention materials found since Hooker wrote) illustrates that New Testament scholars still have much to learn about New Testament times. "It could be," she writes, "that if we knew the whole truth about Judaism and the early Church, our small quantity of 'distinctive' teaching [on the basis of this criterion] would wither away altogether."[92]

The criterion of coherence is also suspect because sayings that may seem incoherent to us in our twenty-first-century milieu may have been quite coherent in first-century Palestine—and vice versa. And all the more is it difficult to assess coherency if Jesus intended some of his sayings to contain an element of paradox.

Hooker also faults the form-critical scholar for applying these

---

Authenticity of the Sayings of Jesus" in *History, Criticism, and Faith*, edited by Colin Brown (Downers Grove, Illinois: InterVarsity, 1976), 101-43, also provides a very helpful treatment of the issue. For I. Howard Marshall's critical analysis of the criterion of dissimilarity, see his *The Origins of New Testament Christology*, 54-8.

[91] Hooker, "On Using the Wrong Tool," 575.

[92] Hooker, "On Using the Wrong Tool," 575.

criteria with a degree of subjectivity. To illustrate, she points out that the term "Kingdom of God" is often used by both Jesus and the early church while, with rare exceptions (once in Acts and twice in the Revelation), the "Son of Man" title is used exclusively by Jesus. On the principle of dissimilarity one would think that form critics should conclude that Jesus never spoke of the Kingdom of God but spoke often about the Son of Man. But what have the form critics concluded? They all regard the Kingdom of God as the very core of Jesus' teaching but have reduced the authentic references in Jesus' teachings to the Son of Man to (at most) a mere handful—those dealing with the future coming of the Son of Man! She concludes by stating the obvious: "...in the end, the answers which the New Testament scholar gives are not the result of applying objective tests and using precision tools; they are very largely the result of his own presuppositions and prejudices."[93]

This much is plain from Hooker's penetrating analysis of the "tools" of form criticism: the specter of skepticism about the historical Jesus from which these criteria were supposed to deliver the form-critical scholar still hovers over all his labors, and the prospect is still frighteningly real that, on form-critical grounds alone, nothing for sure can ever be said about the historical Jesus.

But if I grant for the sake of argument that on form-critical grounds some things can be said about Jesus for certain, does even the reduced amount of new material with which the form critic will allow himself to work portray a Jesus *different in kind* from the Jesus of the canonical Gospels? If the Jesus of history is in fact the two-nature God incarnate, as classical Christology has insisted, it should come as no surprise to learn that, even in the highly circumscribed "authenticated" material of the form critic, this divine Christ still seems to preside. Royce Gruenler has attempted to meet the form critic on his own ground in this regard. Choosing Norman Perrin's book, *Rediscovering the Teaching of Jesus*,[94] because it is "still the best compendium of 'authentic' sayings of Jesus arrived at by the most

---

[93]Hooker, "On Using the Wrong Tool," 581.

[94]For Perrin (as also for R. Fuller) the criterion of dissimilarity is not simply one way of proving some traditions are authentic; it is the *only* criterion of authenticity. All traditions not established by it he rejects.

radical application of the criterion of dissimilarity,"[95] Gruenler examines Perrin's pool of authentic sayings, using as the criterion of his analysis the later Wittgenstein's theory of the intentionality of language. He shows that even on the basis of Perrin's highly circumscribed pool of authentic sayings the Jesus portrayed by them believed himself to have the divine prerogative to forgive sins, that he stood in such a relationship to God that the Kingdom (authority) of God was present in his person, that he stood in the very place of God himself, and that through him men can be received back into fellowship with God. Here, Gruenler concludes, is an implicit, if not explicit, high Christology indeed![96]

Is there nothing that can be said positively about the form-critical method and the redaction-critical method as tools for doing New Testament research? Regarding the former, as long as the New Testament scholar seeks to determine the "form" (genre) of a given pericope—for example, whether it is narrative, poetry, parable, hymn, or passion account—for the benefit such knowledge will yield as he does exegesis, since he must apply different canons of interpretation when interpreting predictive prophecy from those he will apply when interpreting historical narrative, and yet again still other hermeneutical rules when interpreting poetry from those he applies when interpreting a parable, no harm is done so long as the *meaning* of the passage is still finally derived from grammatical/historical and biblical/theological hermeneutics.

Regarding redaction criticism, the church virtually from the beginning has recognized and happily acknowledged that the four Evangelists carefully selected and arranged their material (derived from whatever sources—other Gospels, eye-witnesses, etc.) in order to highlight their respective portrayals of Jesus. This recognition is what lies behind the oft-drawn generalization that Matthew portrays Jesus as the Messianic King, that Mark portrays him as the Lord's active Servant, that Luke portrays him as the Man concerned for others, and that John portrays him as God's Son. This is not only harmless redaction criticism, it is actually quite helpful inasmuch as the composite picture they give of Jesus is richer than any single

---

[95]Royce Gordon Gruenler, *New Approaches to Jesus and the Gospels* (Grand Rapids: Baker, 1982), 34.

[96]Gruenler, *New Approaches to Jesus and the Gospels*, chapters 2 and 3, *passim.*

Gospel portrayal could have achieved.

But when the New Testament scholar further assumes that the Gospels or Epistles have undergone a warping away from the actual history of the event or the actual teaching of Jesus which they purport to depict as the result of an earlier process of theologizing on the part of the early church or the Evangelists so that they no longer portray Jesus as he really was and hence are no longer historically reliable, or when he asserts that the Gospels simply reflect genres necessitating that they be read as mere secular literature of some kind, I would submit that he is being governed more by dogmatic prejudice than by what the facts of the case will allow. What actual biblical evidence we have would take us in precisely the opposite direction!

For example, there are indications in the New Testament that the Apostles were jealous to preserve the teachings of Jesus intact by maintaining the distinction between what Jesus had said and what they themselves were saying to the church. Twice in 1 Corinthians 7, Paul employs a turn of phrase which distinguishes Jesus' earlier teaching on marriage and divorce from his later teaching (see 7:10: "To the married I give this command, not I, but the Lord"; 7:12: "To the rest I say this, I, not the Lord"). And though the Gospels were being written either after with respect to some portions of the New Testament or contemporaneously with other New Testament material, a clear line of demarcation is maintained throughout between what Jesus in his public ministry had employed as his most common self-designation prior to his death ("Son of Man") and what came to be for the church the most common designation for him in light of his resurrection and ascension ("Lord"). "Son of Man" as a post-resurrection title of Jesus is found only in Acts 7:56 and Revelation 1:13 and 14:14. If the church had no commitment regarding the preservation of Jesus' precise words, as the form critic implies, it is most unlikely that the Son of Man title would be found almost exclusively in the Gospels. Finally, if the church, as the form critic alleges, freely molded the original sayings of Jesus and actually created others to meet its emerging evangelistic and apologetic needs, one can only conclude that it missed some golden opportunities for doing so, indeed, that it went about this activity in a woefully inadequate if not inept fashion.

One would think, if the church were accustomed to doing so, that "Jesus' teaching" on the issue of Gentile circumcision would have been brought into the debate at the Jerusalem council in Acts 15 or on other issues in scores of places in the New Testament material where vital "life and death" matters were being debated. But in the most unnecessary places, as far as the vitals of the Faith are concerned, they are introduced. Paul, for example, quotes Jesus in a charge to fellow believers: "It is more blessed to give than to receive" (Acts 20:35), a saying which admittedly does not appear as such in any Gospel although certainly the spirit of it is evident in other sayings which are recorded (Matt 10:8; John 13:34). For another example of this "non-vital" application of a saying of Jesus to a situation in the life of the church, the reader is invited to compare 1 Timothy 5:18 with Luke 10:7 where Paul is treating the subject of materially providing for the faithful elder. The only fair conclusion that one can draw from the facts that are actually present in the New Testament text is that there is no warrant for the form-critical conclusion that at the oral level of early church tradition which underlies our canonical Gospels the life and teaching of Jesus were so completely reconstructed that we have very little real historical information about him. David Wells' observation on this whole issue is quite relevant:

> Why is it that only now, two thousand years after the event, we are at last beginning to understand what Christianity is all about? But, of course, by the word *we* what is in view is only an elite coterie of scholars. There are masses of Christians, all over the world, who have no ability to pick their way through the layers of literary tradition in Scripture.... Are we to suppose that the real interpretation of Jesus is alone accessible only to a tiny minority in the church—its learned scholars—and that the remainder of Christian believers is excluded from such knowledge? To suppose such a thing is to subject the meaning of Scripture to a far more restrictive "tradition" than anything proposed by Rome in the sixteenth century and to invest our new magisterium—the coterie of learned scholars—with an authority more stifling and far-reaching than the Roman Catholic magisterium ever exercised.[97]

---

[97]David F. Wells, *The Person of Christ* (Westchester, Illinois: Crossway, 1984), 35-6.

And we must not lose sight of the fact that even this tiny minority of scholars in the church cannot agree on what is authentic in the New Testament portrayal of Jesus.

Convinced as I am that Wells' trenchant observation is right on the mark and that the biblical, particularly the New Testament, material records reliable history and sober truth, I will proceed to look to the Bible for its doctrine of Christ. Of course, it needs to be borne in mind that, when examining the teachings of Jesus with regard to his self-witness, because the precise wording of a saying can vary from Gospel to Gospel and because what Jesus is reported as saying in Greek he may have said originally in Aramaic, we must be aware that we are probably not working for the most part with the *ipsissima verba Jesu* ("very words of Jesus"). But for the reasons already given, I am proceeding on the assumption that we still possess at every point, accurately and substantively as the essential equivalency of the *ipsissima verba Jesu*, the *ipsissima vox Jesu* ("very voice of Jesus"), with the words employed by the Gospel writers representing truthfully and reliably the content of Jesus' sayings.

* * * * *

We have completed our survey of modern objections raised against the classical doctrine of a two-natured Christ. As we have seen, the reasons for such vary today within academia. A strictly human Jesus who is the "man for others" or the "man for God" or any number of other perceptions of him is much preferred. These reasons run the gamut from the sincere missiological concern for a Christian witness before the world that avoids all claim to an "achieved transcendence" for itself over the other world religions to the skeptical claim that it is simply impossible to obtain any information that is really significant and at the same time historically reliable about Jesus. I have attempted to offer rebuttals to these objections along the way.

Although those who have advanced these objections are for the most part scholars of great breadth of learning and recognized literary achievement, I am convinced that the biblical portrayal of Jesus is still sound and offers the basis for an intellectually satisfying faith. When one takes into account the alternative—the utter confusion which abounds in modern Christological research in both the exegetical and dogmatic fields—the proof is abundant that something has gone dreadfully awry. That is all the more reason for the reader to continue in this present study with me. I will suggest at the end of our study together that I believe something far more vital than an intellectually satisfying faith is at stake.

We will begin our journey then by considering several highly significant Old Testament passages that establish the direction, if not also the parameters, of the biblical trajectory pertaining to the question: "What should one think about Jesus Christ?" We will then turn to the pages of the New Testament and assess the picture that we find there of Jesus of Nazareth.

PART ONE

The Old Testament Witness

The Hebrew word from which we derive the title 'Messiah' is מָשִׁיחַ (*māshîach*) which literally means 'anointed one'. It is twice transliterated Μεσσίας (***Messias***) in the Greek New Testament (John 1:41; 4:25). In both instances it is accompanied with its Greek equivalent, Χριστός (*Christos*), which also means 'anointed one'. In the Old Testament, Israel's *prophets* (1 Kgs 19:16; Isa. 61:1; see Ps. 105:15), *priests* (Ex. 28:41; 29:7; 30:30-33; Lev. 4:3; 6:22; 8:12, 30) and (most relevant for our present purpose) *kings* (Jud. 9:8; 1 Sam. 10:1; 16:13; 24:10; 26:11; 2 Sam. 2:4; 19:21; 1 Kgs. 1:34; 2 Kgs. 9:6-13; Ps. 89:20) were installed in their respective offices to perform their respective functions through an 'anointing' ritual. If fact, because of King Cyrus's typical significance in his role as Israel's 'deliverer' from Babylonian exile, Isaiah, son of Amoz, even speaks prophetically of this Persian ruler as Yahweh's 'anointed one' (45:1).[1] As a result,

---

[1]Cyrus' 'messiahship' has proven problematic for Old Testament students because, while it is true that Yahweh called him his 'anointed one' (45:1), he declared twice of Cyrus in Isaiah 45:4-5: 'though you do not acknowledge me.' Indeed, on the Cyrus Cylinder Cyrus gives to Bel and Nebo the glory for his peaceful conquest of Babylon. J. A. Motyer, however, points out that Cyrus 'messiahship' is in fact 'specially helpful in defining the term'. He writes:

> There are here five features which, in the light of the rest of Scripture, are clearly definitive of certain main lines of OT Messianism. Cyrus is a man of God's choice (Is. 41:25), appointed to accomplish a redemptive purpose toward God's people (45:11-13), and a judgment on his foes (47). He is given dominion over the nations (45:1-3); and in all his activities the real agent is Yahweh himself (45:1-7).... There could be no better summary of the OT view of the 'anointed' person; furthermore it is quite clear that these five points are pre-eminently true of the Lord Jesus Christ, who saw himself as the fulfilment of the OT Messianic expectations ('Messiah. I In the Old Testament,' *The Illustrated Bible Dictionary* [Wheaton: Tyndale House, 1980]), 2, 987)

the title 'Messiah,' that is, '[God's] anointed one,' gradually came to be a popular designation of Israel's future Davidic Deliverer who would usher in the promised universal reign of God over men (see Ps. 2:2; Dan. 9:25-26; Psalm 17 of the Pseudepigraphal Psalms of Solomon; and the New Testament Gospels).[2]

Anthony Hoekema summarizes the Old Testament messianic vision and hope by calling attention to seven specific revelational concepts in which that perception and hope were embodied. There were, he writes:

1. The expectation of the coming Redeemer, revealed first as the 'seed of the woman' (Gen. 3:15), then the 'seed of Abraham' (Gen. 22:18), then a descendant of the tribe of Judah (Gen. 49:10) and specifically a son of David (2 Sam. 7:12-13), who would in some not completely clear (to them) but unique and final way fill the offices of prophet (Deut. 18:15), priest (Ps. 110:4), king (Zech. 9:9), suffering servant of God (Isa. 42:1-4; 49:5-7; 52:13-53:12), and son of man (Dan. 7:13-14).
2. The anticipation of the kingdom of God when God's rule would be fully experienced, not just by Israel, but by the whole world (Dan. 2:44-45);
3. The making of a new covenant with Israel by which instrument God would forgive His people of their sins and idolatry (Jer. 31:31-34);
4. The restoration of Israel from her captivity by hostile nations (Isa. 11:11; Jer. 23:3; Ezek. 36:24-28);
5. The outpouring of the Spirit upon all flesh (Joel 2:28-32);
6. The approach of the Day of the Lord which would mean judgment upon the unbelieving nations and deliverance for the people of God (Obad, 15-16; Joel 1:15; 2:1-17; Isa. 13; Amos 5:18-20; Zeph. 1:7, 14-16; Mal. 4:5)[3]; and

---

[2] Daniel 9:25-26, declaring that 'Messiah will be cut off and will have nothing,' intimates that the future Messiah's ministry would contain a tragic as well as a regal dimension.

[3] In connection with the coming Day of the Lord the Old Testament prophets also envisioned the resurrection of both the righteous and the unrighteous (Job 19:25-27; Ps. 73:24-25; Is. 26:19; Dan. 12:2; see Matt. 22:29:32;

7. The creation of a new heaven and a new earth (Isa. 11:6-69; 32:15; 35:7; 65:17; 66:22).[4]

This study will attempt to show that Jesus of Nazareth believed himself to be the unique and final embodiment of that messianic vision and hope. By his method of Old Testament interpretation Jesus established for his church the prerogative both to exegete the Scriptures of the Old Testament in such a way that it finds him there and to draw from those Scriptures by theological deduction its messianic understanding of his person and work. For example, in addition to those specific occasions when Jesus applied the Old Testament to himself (see, for example, his use of Ps. 110:1 in Matt. 22:41-45; Isa. 61:1-2 in Luke 4:17-21; Isa. 53:12 in Luke 22:37; probably Deut. 18:15-19 in John 5:43-47, and the 'man-like figure' of Dan. 7:13 as his favourite self-designation), Luke informs us that after his resurrection, the risen Christ said to his perplexed disciples on the road to Emmaus: 'How foolish you are, and how slow of heart to believe all that the prophets have spoken! Did not the Christ [the Messiah] have to suffer these things and then enter his glory?' Then Luke declares: 'And beginning with Moses and all the prophets, he *explained* to them what was said in all the Scriptures *concerning himself*' (24:25-27). That Luke intended by his phrase, 'all the Scriptures,' specifically the Scriptures of the Old Testament is clear from the words of Jesus which he cites a few verses later: 'Everything must be fulfilled that has been written about me [περὶ ἐμοῦ, *peri emou*] in the Law of Moses and the Prophets and the Psalms' (Luke 24:44).[5] 'Then,' Luke

---

Heb. 11:10, 13-16, 19) and a judgment to follow (Ps. 50:4-6; Eccles. 12:14; Mal. 3:2-5).

[4]Anthony Hoekema, *The Bible and the Future* (Reprint; Grand Rapids: Eerdmans, 1979), 3-12. It should be noted in passing that during the Inter-Testamental Period a variety of messianic views sprang up that would have diverged from this Old Testament vision in significant ways.

[5]Jesus' description of the Old Testament here as 'the Law of Moses and the Prophets and the Psalms' probably reflects the tripartite division of the Old Testament canon (תּוֹרָה, נְבִיאִים, כְּתוּבִים) that clearly already existed in some form in the second century B.C. See Edward J. Young, *An Introduction to the Old Testament* (Grand Rapids: Eerdmans, 1960), 32, and Gleason L. Archer, Jr., *A Survey of Old Testament Introduction* (Chicago: Moody, 1964), 63.

recounts, 'he opened [his disciples'] minds so they could understand *the Scriptures*. He told them, "*This is what is written*: The Christ [the Messiah] will suffer and rise from the dead on the third day, and repentance and forgiveness of sins will be preached in his name to all nations, beginning at Jerusalem"' (Luke 24:45-47). From this Lukan material one learns, according to Jesus, that the Old Testament prophets taught that in his own person, (a) the Messiah would suffer, (b) the Messiah would be glorified, (c) his suffering would precede his glorification, and (d) salvation should be preached in his name throughout the entire world.

In light of such explicit declarations as these, the church from the beginning to the present has believed itself to be justified in seeing both adumbrations and explicit descriptions of Jesus of Nazareth and what befell him in the Old Testament scripture. In his *According to the Scriptures*, C. H. Dodd, the Cambridge scholar, writes:

> At the earliest period of Church history to which we can gain access, we find in being the rudiments of an original, coherent and flexible method of biblical exegesis which was already beginning to yield results.
>
> ... Very diverse scriptures are brought together so that they interpret one another in hitherto unsuspected ways. To have brought together, for example, the Son of Man who is the people of the saints of the Most High, the Man of God's right hand, who is also the vine of Israel, the Son of Man who after humiliation is crowned with glory and honor, and the victorious priest-king at the right hand of God, is an achievement of interpretative imagination which results in the creation of an entirely new figure. It involves an original, and far-reaching resolution of the tension between the individual and the collective aspects of several of these figures, which in turn makes it possible to bring into a single focus the 'plot' of the Servant poems..., of the psalms of the righteous sufferer, and of the prophecies of the fall and recovery (death and resurrection) of the people of God, and finally offers a fresh understanding of the mysterious imagery of apocalyptic eschatology.
>
> This is a piece of genuinely creative thinking. Who was responsible for it? The early Church, we are accustomed to say ... but creative thinking is rarely done by committees, useful as they may be for systematizing the fresh ideas of individual thinkers, and for stimulating them to further thought. It is individual minds that originate. Whose was the originating mind here?
>
> Among Christian thinkers of the first age known to us there are three

> of genuinely creative power: Paul, the author to the Hebrews, and the Fourth Evangelist. We are precluded from proposing any one of them for the honor of having originated the process, since even Paul, greatly as he contributed to its development, demonstrably did not originate it ... the New Testament itself avers that it was Jesus Christ Himself who first directed the minds of His followers to certain parts of the scriptures as those in which they might find illumination upon the meaning of His mission and destiny.... I can see no reasonable ground for rejecting the statements of the gospels that (for example) He pointed to Psalm cx as a better guide to the truth about His mission and destiny than the popular beliefs about the Son of David, or that He made that connection of the 'Lord' at God's right hand with the Son of Man in Daniel which proved so momentous for Christian thought, or that he associated with the Son of Man language which had been used of the Servant of the Lord, and employed it to hint at the meaning, and the issue, of His own approaching death. To account for the beginning of this most original and fruitful process of rethinking the Old Testament we found need to postulate a creative mind. The Gospels offer us one.[6]

Surely Dodd, in his main point here, is right. Beyond all dispute the Gospels depict Jesus of Nazareth as drawing from the Old Testament fascinating messianic deductions and applying them to his own person and mission. It is he then who established for his church the prerogative of interpreting the Old Testament the way it has, that is, that it is a covenantal and prophetic witness to Jesus Christ and his mission. If we today would follow Jesus in his hermeneutical method, we must make the exegesis of the Old Testament, no less than the New, the basis of our Christology. And if we would also follow him in his

---

[6]C. H. Dodd, *According to the Scriptures* (London: James Nisbet, 1952), 108-10. I would issue two caveats here, however. First, while we obviously appreciate Dodd's granting to Jesus alone the creative genius to bring these several Old Testament themes together to enhance our understanding of his person and work, it is extremely important to insist that, in doing so, Jesus did not bring a meaning to the Old Testament that was not intended by the Old Testament itself. See I. Howard Marshall, *The Origins of New Testament Christology* (Downers Grove: Inter-Varsity, 1976), 76-8, and Gerald Bray, *Creeds, Councils and Christ* (Reprint: Ross-shire, Scotland: Mentor, 1997), 49. Second, I take exception to Dodd's suggestion that the Danielic 'man-like figure' is a collective entity only. I will explain my divergence here from Dodd when I discuss Daniel 7:13.

exegetical understanding of the Old Testament, we must by our exegesis of the Old Testament, no less than the New, likewise finally see *him* – Jesus of Nazareth – there.

This then is my hermeneutical rationale for treating the following vignettes of the Old Testament Messiah the way I do. The reader will have to judge whether I have interpreted them fairly and accurately. Because of the special interest I have throughtout this book in the *nature* of the Messiah's person and work, I am going to treat – to use Warfield's delightful expression[7] – only the 'high lights shining out brightly on the surface of a pervasive implication' that lend themselves to this particular concern of Old Testament messianism. I will restrict myself to a consideration of Genesis 3:15; 16:7-13 *et al.*, Psalms 2:7; 45:6-7; 102:25-27; 110:1; Isaiah 7:14-16; 9:6-7; 52:15-53:12; Micah 5:2; Daniel 7:13; Zechariah 12:10; and Malachi 3:1. From these contexts I hope to provide answers to the following questions:

1. How does the Old Testament represent the Messiah's role?
2. Is Jesus Christ in some sense the God (Yahweh) of the Old Testament and, if so, in what sense?

---

[7]Benjamin B. Warfield, 'The Divine Messiah in the Old Testament,' *Biblical and Theological Studies* (Philadelphia: Presbyterian and Reformed, 1952), 123. In this same vein, Warfield quite properly writes earlier:

> The complete synthesis of the various representations [of the whole body of Messianic hopes] waits, of course, for the fulfilment of them all in one Person. But it becomes clear at least that the hope of the coming of the world-savior, which includes in it the more specifically defined 'Messianic' hope, is but another aspect of the hope of the coming of Jehovah to judge the world and to introduce the eternal kingdom of peace. One of the results of this is that the testimony of the Old Testament to 'the transcendent Messiah' becomes pervasive. We no longer look for it in a text here and there which we are tempted to explain away as unexpected, perhaps intolerable, exaggerations, but rather see it involved in the entire drift of the eschatological expectations of the Old Testament, and view the special texts in which it finds particularly poignant expression as only the natural high lights thrown up on the surface of the general picture. (100)

CHAPTER TWO

THE OLD TESTAMENT WITNESS TO THE MESSIAH

THE "SEED OF THE WOMAN"

Biblical messianism begins early in the Old Testament and highlights the fact that it would include a tragic dimension within it. Immediately after Adam's transgression of the "covenant of works" which had been sovereignly imposed upon him by his Creator (Gen 3:1-7; see Hos 6:7), God came to the garden of Eden and in the hearing of Adam said to the serpent, the instrument of Satan, and by extension to Satan himself: "I will put enmity between you and the woman, and between your offspring and hers; he will crush your head, and you will strike his heel" (Gen 3:15; see Rom 16:20). Long have Christian theologians recognized in these words both the inauguration of the "covenant of grace" and God's first gracious promise to men of salvation from sin. Not without good reason then has this divine promise been designated the "first gospel proclamation" (*protevangelium*). The promise is given in "seed-form," true enough, but God clearly stated that someone out of the human race itself ("the woman's offspring"), although fatally "wounded" himself in the conflict, would destroy the serpent (Satan). Geerhardus Vos has quite correctly observed that "it is unhistorical to carry back into the O.T. mind our developed doctrinal consciousness of these matters,"[1] but it is possible to address the issue of the Old Testament saints' understanding of redemption so one-sidedly from the "biblical-theological" perspective that one permits the hermeneutic of that discipline to overpower the "analogy of faith" principle of systematic theology, and as a result neither the teaching of the Old Testament itself nor what the New Testament writers expressly report or imply that the Old Testament meant and that the Old Testament saints knew about the suffering Messiah and his resurrection from the dead is given its rightful due.

---

[1]Geerhardus Vos, *Biblical Theology* (Grand Rapids: Eerdmans, 1948), 64.

In my opinion Vos himself commits this error when he construes "the seed of the woman" in Genesis 3:15 in a collective rather than a personal sense: "As to the word 'seed' there is no reason to depart from the collective sense in either case. The seed of the serpent *must* be collective, and this determines the sense of the seed of the woman."[2] But it does not necessarily follow, because the seed of the serpent is collective, that the seed of thc woman must also be collective. I would submit that it was precisely of Christ that God spoke, just as Paul

---

[2] Vos, *Biblical Theology*, 54. Interestingly, after Vos urges that it is the collective sense that must be placed on the "seed of the woman," he writes:

> ...indirectly, the possibility is *hinted at* that in striking this fatal blow the seed of the woman will be concentrated in one person, for it should be noticed that it is not the seed of the serpent but the serpent itself whose head will be bruised. In the former half of the curse the two seeds are contrasted; here the woman's seed and the serpent. This suggests that as at the climax of the struggle the serpent's seed will be represented by the serpent, in the same manner [that is, at the climax of the struggle] the woman's seed *may find representation* in a single person. (54-5, emphasis supplied)

But having said this, Vos then reverts back and declares:

> ...we are not warranted, however, in seeking an exclusively personal reference to the Messiah here, as though He alone were meant by "the woman's seed." O. T. Revelation approaches the concept of a personal Messiah very gradually. (55)

Meredith G. Kline, "Genesis," *The New Bible Commentary: Revised* (London: Inter-Varsity, 1970), 85, seems to concur with Vos's basic position:

> *Between your seed and her seed.* Beyond the woman, the whole family of the true humanity, becoming her spiritual seed by faith, will stand in continuing conflict with those descendants of fallen Adam who obdurately manifest spiritual sonship to the devil...*He shall bruise your head, and you shall bruise his heel.* The 'you' still contending in the remote future points past the mere serpent to Satan. This focusing on an individual from one side in connection with the eventual encounter suggests that the *he* too is not the woman's seed collectively but their individual champion.

insisted that it was precisely of Christ that God later spoke in his reference to Abraham's "seed" in Genesis 13:15 and 17:8 (Gal 3:16). Furthermore, it is inexplicable why Vos makes nothing of the "death wound" which "the woman's seed" would experience in his conflict with the *Serpent*, *not* the Serpent's seed, stating only that the *protevangelium* promised that "*somehow* out of the human race a fatal blow will come which shall crush the head of the serpent."[3] I would not say "somehow" here. I would contend, on the basis of the clear allusion to his death in the *protevangelium*, that from the very beginning of redemptive history the saints' everlasting hope rested in the triumphant "conflict work" carried out by a specific individual, namely, the *mortally wounded* "seed of the woman." Thus begins the history of Old Testament (and biblical) messianism.

Accordingly, "the Lamb of God who takes away the sin of the world" (John 1:29) is here in Genesis 3:15 covenantally prophesied; in Genesis 22:8, 13 he is symbolized; in Leviticus 16:15-16 he is typified; in Isaiah 7:14, 9:6, 53:1 he is "deified"; in Isaiah 53:3-6 he is "personified"; in John 1:29 he is identified; in all four Gospels he is crucified; and in John's Revelation—"as the object of the worship offered by the hosts of heaven and earth (chaps 4-5); as the unveiler of the destinies of the ages (chaps 5-6); as the one enthroned before whom and to whom the redeemed render the praise of their salvation (7:9-12); as the controller of the book of life (13:8); as the Lord of the hosts on mount Zion (14:1); as the victor over the hosts of Antichrist (17:14); as the spouse of the glorified church (19:7); as the temple and light of the new Jerusalem (21:22-23); and as the sharer in the throne of God (22:1)"[4]—the Lamb is glorified!

But if the "he" may be (Vos) or is to be (Kline) construed, not collectively, but as an individual, why is "the woman's seed" not an individual as well, since "the woman's seed" is the antecedent of the "he"? Are we to believe, *contra* Westminster Confession of Faith I/ix, that "seed" here has or may have a dual meaning?

[3]Vos, *Biblical Theology*, 54.

[4]I have paraphrased Isbon T. Beckwith, *The Apocalypse of John* (Reprint: Grand Rapids: Baker, 1967), 315, here.

THE "ANGEL OF THE LORD"

Our next subject for study in our selected Old Testament references to the Messiah is the Angel (or Messenger) of the Lord (מַלְאַךְ יהוה, *mal'ak Yahweh*), that mysterious Old Testament figure whom Geerhardus Vos terms "the most important and characteristic [usually, but not always, ephemerally human] form of revelation in the patriarchal period."[5] A careful analysis of the relevant passages[6] will disclose that God *differentiates* himself from this Angel by the very title itself as well as by the fact that he refers to him in the third person and may even address him in the second person in 2 Samuel 24:16, and yet the Angel in his speeches, while also often distinguishing himself from God, lays claim to divine attributes and prerogatives, indeed, to *identity with God*. In the following verses, for example, the Lord clearly distinguishes himself from the Angel:

1. In Genesis 24:7 Abraham says to his servant: "The Lord, the God of heaven...will send his Angel before you." The servant later reports Abraham's words as follows: "[Abraham] replied, 'The Lord...will send his Angel with you'" (24:40).

2. In Exodus 23:20-23 the Lord declares: "See, I am sending an Angel ahead of you to guard you along the way...My Angel will go ahead of you and bring you into the land." Later still, in Exodus 32:34 the Lord declares again: "My Angel will go before you."

On the other hand, the Angel quite clearly represents himself as deity. For example,

1. In Genesis 16:7-13 the Angel of the Lord appears to Hagar and commands her: "Go back to your mistress and submit to her."

---

[5]Vos, *Biblical Theology*, 85.

[6]Genesis 16:7-13; 21:17-18; 22:11-18; 24:7, 40; 28:10-18 (see 31:11-13); 32:24-30 (see 48:15-16; Hos 12:3-4); Exodus 3:2-6; 13:21 (see14:19); 23:20-23 (see 33:14-15); 32:34; Numbers 22:21-35; Judges 2:1-5; 6:11-24; 13:3-22; 2 Samuel 24:16; 1 Kings 19:7; 2 Kings 19:35; Isaiah 63:9; Zechariah 1:10-11; 12:8; and Malachi 3:1 all contain references in some way to the Angel of the Lord.

Then he says: "I will so multiply your descendants that they will be too numerous to count," and he proceeds to issue a prophetic oracle. The narrative then adds the statement: "[Hagar] named Yahweh who had spoken to her, 'You are a God who sees me.'"

2. In Genesis 22:11-18 the Angel of the Lord calls to Abraham from heaven and commands: "Do not lay your hand upon the lad, and do nothing to him, because now I know that you fear God, since you have not withheld your only son *from me*."

3. Genesis 28:10-18 declares that Yahweh spoke to Jacob in a dream at Bethel in the following words: "I am Yahweh, the God of your father Abraham and the God of Isaac." Upon waking from his dream, Jacob is so moved by the experience that he names the place Bethel ("the house of God"), saying: "Surely Yahweh is in this place." But later, according to Genesis 31:11-13, the Angel of the Lord appeared to him and said: "I am the God of Bethel."

4. In Genesis 32:24-30 Jacob wrestles with a "man" (אִישׁ, *'îsh*) who blesses him and says: "Your name will no longer be Jacob, but Israel, because you have struggled with God...and have overcome." Jacob then names the place Peniel ("the face of God"), saying, "I have seen God face to face." Hosea 12:3-4 declares that Jacob had "wrestled with God, yes, he wrestled with [the] Angel and prevailed."

5. In Genesis 48:15-16, through the employment of a striking parallelism in his invocation, Jacob implies the Angel's equality with God:

   The God before whom my fathers Abraham and Isaac walked,
   the God who has been my Shepherd all my life to this day,
   the Angel who has redeemed me from all evil—
   may he [note the singular "he"] bless the lads.

   About the three titles that Jacob employs here for God, Gerhard von Rad writes:

   The little hymn reaches the climax of its attempt to identify Jahweh in descriptive terms in the third title. Any idea that the "angel" means a being subordinate to Jahweh is of course ruled out. This מַלְאָךְ [*mal'āk*] too is Jahweh—but in contradistinction to the Jahweh of general providence, he is the Jahweh of the specific saving action (גֹּאֵל [*gō'ēl*]).[7]

6. In Exodus 3:2-6 the Angel of the Lord appeared to Moses in a blazing fire from the midst of a bush, and identified himself to Moses as "the God of your father, the God of Abraham, the God of Isaac, and the God of Jacob."

7. In Exodus 23:21 Yahweh declares to Israel: "Pay attention to [My Angel] and listen to what he says; do not rebel against him; he will not forgive your rebellion, since My *Name* is in him." About this intriguing statement Vos writes:

> The entire tenor of this passage forbids our thinking that an ordinary angel is spoken of...We learn from the statement that the Angel's function was the comprehensive one of leading the people to Canaan. We further learn that in respect of sinning against him he is identical with God...Nothing short of identification [with Yahweh] can be meant by [the fact that Yahweh's name is in him], for it is stated as the ground why sin committed against the Name-bearing Angel will not be pardoned by him.[8]

10. Where Yahweh promises in Exodus 23:20-23 and 32:34, as we have already noted, that his Angel would go with Israel, he declares in Exodus 33:14 that "my [own] presence" (פָּנַי, *pānay*) would go with them. That the Angel and Yahweh's "presence" are one and the same figure seems clear from the later reference to "the Angel of his presence" in Isa 63:9.

11. Also instructive is the Angel of the Lord's response to Manoah's request for his name in Judges 13:18: "It is פֶּלְאִי [*peli' (y)*]," that is, "a Wonder," or "beyond human comprehension"), he replied, "performing [then] the wonderful thing" מַפְלִא לַעֲשׂוֹת, *maphli'*

---

[7]Gerhard von Rad, *Old Testament Theology* [New York: Harper & Row, 1962], I, 287.

[8]Vos, *Biblical Theology*, 122-23.

la'ᵃsôth, 13:19) of ascending in the flame of Manoah's sacrifice (13:20). Manoah then concluded: "We have seen God [אֱלֹהִים, *ᵉlōhîm*]" (13:22).

This biblical/theological phenomenon of an apparently personal distinction within Yahweh one may also find in Psalms 2:7, 45:6-7, 110:1, *et al.* Many liberal theologians explain this phenomenon as the reflection of a late trend within Israelite religion of softening the concept of theophany toward angelophany, but they can offer no explanation why this process does not occur consistently and uniformly. For alongside the several appearances of the Angel are continuing manifestations of Yahweh himself. Von Rad suggests that Israelite storytellers inserted the Angel of the Lord into earlier traditions in place of an original Canaanite *numen* or deity, but he provides no evidence that this really happened.[9] Vos quite rightly affirms that the only way to do justice to both features of this "differentiation-identity pattern"[10]—is to

---

[9]Gerhard von Rad, *Old Testament Theology*, I, 286.

[10]Other places (which we do not intend to address in this work) where this "differentiation-identity pattern" appears to be present are, first, those passages in which the Messiah as the divine speaker refers to the Lord and/or the Spirit as having sent him, as in

> Isaiah 48:16: "From the first announcement I [Yahweh is the speaker here] have not spoken in secret; at the time it happens I am there. And now the *sovereign Lord has sent me*, and his *Spirit.*"
>
> Isaiah 61:1: "The *Spirit* of the sovereign *Lord* is on *me*, because the *Lord* has anointed *me* to preach good tidings to the poor" [see Luke 4:16-18])."
>
> Zechariah 2:10-11 (MT, 2:14-15): "'Shout and be glad, O Daughter of Zion. For *I am coming, and I will live among you*,' declares the Lord. 'Many nations will be joined with the Lord in that day and will become my people. *I will live among you* and you will know that the *Lord Almighty has sent me* to you.'"

and second, those passages in which the prophet speaks of the Lord, the Angel of his presence, and his Holy Spirit as virtually distinct Persons, as in

> Isaiah 63:9-10: "In all their distress *he* too was distressed, and the *Angel of his presence* saved them. In his love and mercy he redeemed them; he lifted them up and carried them all the days of old. Yet they rebelled and grieved *his Holy Spirit.* So he turned and became their enemy and he himself fought against them."

> assume that back of the twofold representation there lies a real manifoldness in the inner life of the Deity. If the Angel sent were himself partaker of the Godhead, then he could refer to God as his sender, and at the same time speak as God, and in both cases there would be reality back of it. Without this much of what we call the Trinity the transaction could not but have been unreal and illusory.[11]

He notes further, with trenchant insight, that the Angel's declarations of identity with God (which he terms God's "sacramental" intent) underscored God's desire to be present with his people in order to support them in their frailty and limitations; but without the Angel's differentiation from God (which he terms God's "spiritual" intent), the real spiritual nature of the Deity would have been threatened. Hence, the Angel speaks of God in the third person. From his analysis Vos concludes:

> In the incarnation of our Lord we have the supreme expression of this fundamental arrangement.... The whole incarnation, with all that pertains to it, is one great sacrament of redemption. And yet even here special care is taken to impress believers with the absolute spirituality of Him Who has thus made Himself of our nature. The principle at stake has found classical expression in John 1:18: "No man has seen God at any time; God only begotten, who is in the bosom of the Father, He has declared Him."[12]

The biblical data suggests accordingly that the Angel, as a *divine person*, was uncreated. On the other hand, the varied forms of appearance which he assumed in these Old Testament texts, for example, the "man" of Genesis 32:24, Judges 13:6-11, and Zechariah 1:10-11, the "blazing fire" of Exodus 3:2, and the "pillar of cloud" and the "pillar of fire" of Exodus 13:21 (see 14:19), were doubtless created. Writes Vos:

> The only difference in this respect between [the incarnate Christ] and the Angel is that under the O. T. the created form was ephemeral, whereas through the incarnation it has become eternal.[13]

---

[11]Vos, *Biblical Theology*, 86-7.
[12]Vos, *Biblical Theology*, 88.
[13]Vos, *Biblical Theology*, 89.

Here then, in the revelational form of the Old Testament figure of the Angel of the Lord, we find the first visible expression of that "sacramental-spiritual" character of God's redemptive program which was to find its ultimate tangible expression in that supernatural act which John captures in his great Christological affirmations, ὁ λόγος ἦν πρὸς τὸν θεόν, καὶ θεὸς ἦν ὁ λόγος, *ho logos ēn pros ton theon, kai theos ēn ho logos*, "the Word was *with* God [the Word here is distinguished from God by the preposition "with"], and the Word *was* God [the Word here is identified as himself God]" (John 1:1) and ὁ λόγος σὰρξ ἐγένετο, *ho logos sarx egeneto*, "the Word became flesh" (John 1: 14). It would find its ultimate doctrinal resolution in the church's trinitarian construction of God and the redemption which the triune God effected in Christ and the Holy Spirit.

THE PSALMISTS' MESSIAH

The glorified Christ declared to his disciples that certain things had been written (γεγραμμένα, *gegrammena*) in the Psalms about him (Luke 24:44). The New Testament writers took him seriously, relating no less than forty-eight statements from sixteen different Psalms either directly or indirectly to him.[14] Evangelical scholars accordingly have followed their example, customarily distinguishing between the suffering messianic Psalms and the royal messianic Psalms—the former portraying the Messiah in some sense in his humiliation, the latter portraying him in some sense in his exaltation. We will look at four—Psalms 2, 45, 102, and 110.

The Enthroned Son (Psalm 2)

The second Psalm, a Psalm of David (Acts 4:25),[15] speaks of the ultimate victory of the Messiah's kingdom over the kingdoms of the

---

[14]This count is based upon the "Index of Quotations" in *The Greek New Testament*, edited by Aland, Black, Martini, Metzger, and Wikgren (Third edition; New York: United Bible Societies, 1975), 898-99.

[15]Mitchell Dahood, *Psalms I, 1-50* (AB), (Garden City, New York: Doubleday, 1966), 7, dates the Psalm on linguistic grounds to the tenth century B.C. which would tend to support a Davidic authorship although it does not prove the same.

world. Though modern Old Testament scholarship, for the most part, prefers to regard it as a Psalm composed for the coronation of an unspecified human king in Israel,[16] I agree with such older commentators as E. W. Hengstenberg, J. A. Alexander, and H. P. Liddon that it is directly messianic and therefore exclusively prophetic of David's greater Son, the Lord Jesus Christ.[17] My reasons for this view, briefly, are as follows: First, David, in addition to serving in the kingly office, was also a prophet and therefore *capable* of writing predictive prophecy pertaining directly and exclusively to the Messiah. Psalm 16 is a case in point concerning which psalm Peter in Acts 2:25-31 tells us it was written by David who, "being a prophet" and "seeing beforehand," spoke therein (Ps 2:8-11) not of his own resurrection but of the resurrection of the Messiah. Second, the special application which the New Testament makes of its content to conditions pertaining to Jesus Christ and the Christian dispensation points directly to this conclusion (see Ps 2:1-2 with Acts 4:25-26; Ps 2:7 with Acts 13:33; Heb 1:5; 5:5; Ps 2:9 with Rev 2:27; 12:5; 19:15). The Psalm divides itself neatly into four strophes of three verses each:

<u>Strophe 1:</u> Verses 1-3 speak prophetically of the united, hostile voice of man as the *voice of revolt* (or rebellion) arrayed against the Lord and against his Messiah (מָשִׁיחַ, *māshîach*, lit, "anointed one").

---

[16]See Millar Burrows, *An Outline of Biblical Theology* (Philadelphia: Westminster, 1946), 99; Helmer Ringgren, *The Messiah in the Old Testament* (London: SCM, 1956), 11-13. But see J. Barton Payne, *The Theology of the Older Testament* (Grand Rapids: Zondervan, 1962), 22-24, for a conservative answer to the modern critical interpretation. The fact that it was composed by David is itself a strong argument against the critical view.

[17]See also George Eldon Ladd, *A Theology of the New Testament* (Grand Rapids: Eerdmans, 1974), 136, who writes of מָשִׁיחַ, *māshîach*, in Psalm 2:2 that it is "the most outstanding messianic use of the word in the Old Testament" because "the coming king is both God's son and the anointed one who will rule in behalf of God and over all the earth." I recognize the plausibility of the argument put forth by Derek Kidner, *Psalms 1-72* (London: Inter-Varsity, 1973), 18-20, that the Psalm applied initially to Solomon and to the subsequent kings of the Davidic dynasty but I disagree with him. So does R. Laird Harris, "Psalms" in *The Biblical Expositor*, edited by Carl F. H. Henry (Philadelphia: A. J. Holman, 1960), 438-39.

"Against" (עַל, *'al*) occurs twice in the Hebrew text of verse 2, thus distinguishing the Lord in some sense from his Messiah. Acts 4:25-26 records the fulfillment of this predicted hostility in the opposition which Herod, Pilate, the Gentiles, and the leaders of Israel mounted against Jesus.

Strophe 2: Verses 4-6 confront us with the voice of the Lord as the *voice of rebuke* (or retribution). He declares that all such hostilities against him and his Messiah will come to nought, for he will yet enthrone his King upon his holy hill of Zion.

Strophe 3: Verses 7-9 record the voice of the Lord's Messiah as the *voice of rule*, who announces that as God's "Son" he will assume universal dominion after his resurrection (see Acts 13:33), requesting of his Father and receiving and exercising "rod of iron" rule (that is, judgment prerogatives) over the nations of the world.

Strophe 4: Verses 10-12 feature the voice of the Holy Spirit speaking through David as the *voice of reprimand*, warning the kings and judges of the earth and calling them to repentance toward God and faith in the Son ("Kiss [the] Son"[18]), lest the wrath of the Son who reigns over them be kindled against them.

This then is the dramatic movement of the Psalm, which finds its fulfillment both in the crucifixion and resurrection of Christ and, following upon these events, in the present missionary outreach of the church and the judgment, both currently and eschatologically, against those nations which spurn him.

Our present interest in the Psalm, however, arises from the fact that it is this Psalm which provides the two titles—"Messiah" (or

---

[18]This is the literal translation of the phrase in the original but because David uses the Aramaic בַּר, *bar*, for "Son" in verse 12 rather than the Hebrew בֵּן, *bēn*, of verse 7, the phrase has suffered considerably at the hands of conjectural emendationists. But there is no need to emend the text. While we will probably never know for certain the reason for the Aramaic בַּר, *bar*, it has often been suggested that David employed it here to avoid the assonance of בֵּן פֶּן, *ben pen* in 2:12 ("Son, lest"). See בַּר, *bar*, #277 in Harris, Archer, and Waltke, *Theological Wordbook of the Old Testament* (Chicago: Moody, 1980) I, 126-27.

"Christ") and "Son [of God]"—which became current in New Testament times as titles of Jesus, and about which titles the high priest inquired specifically of Jesus as to whether he thought they applied to him (Matt 26:63). The former ("Messiah") is directly applied to the promised World-Ruler in only one other passage in the Old Testament (Daniel 9:25-26, twice); the latter ("Son") is directly applied to him in only two other passages in the Old Testament (1 Chr 17:13; Isa 9:6).[19] The reference to the former in verse 2 puts beyond all reasonable controversy the direct and clear application of this Psalm to the Messiah. And, I submit further, when the Psalm refers to the Messiah by the latter designation of "Son" in verse 7, or perhaps more pointedly, when it ascribes sonship to God to him, it is ascribing, according to the Author of Hebrews, such *superangelic* dignity to him that the supreme titles of "God" (θεός, *theos*, 1:8) and "Lord" (κύριος, *kurios*, meaning יהוה, *Yahweh*, occurring as it does in the Old Testament quotation], 1:10)—with all the dignity, attributes, and functions which these titles connote— may also rightly be ascribed to him, *not, however, as new names additional to "Son," but rather as explications of the content of that one "more superior name [than "angel"]" of "Son"*! To be God's *Son* in the sense in which God intended it in Psalm 2:7, in short, is just to be divine too.

If the Author of Hebrews is allowed to serve as a legitimate

---

[19]I would suggest that the quotation in Hebrews 1:5b is from 1 Chronicles 17:13 and not from 2 Samuel 7:14 where the expression is also found. Of course, the two expressions are related, but the expression in 1 Chronicles 17:13, having been purged of the earlier negative threat ("When he does wrong, I will punish him with the rod of men, with flogging inflicted by men.") which does indeed apply to Solomon and the subsequent kings of the Davidic dynasty but which disqualifies the Samuel statement from being a direct reference to the righteous Messiah is the Chronicler's elevated rendering of the earlier declaration in the Davidic Covenant of 2 Samuel 7:14. This means, I would suggest, that the divine promise in 2 Samuel 7 (as also in Psalm 89; see especially vss 19-32) pertained directly to the promulgation of the Davidic dynasty and only by indirect extension to the Messiah as the culminating point of that dynasty while the promise in 1 Chronicles 17 moves beyond the mere promise of perpetual dynastic blessing to the promise of a direct and personal fulfillment of that promise in the Messiah himself. I might add that Hosea 11:1 also *indirectly* refers to Jesus as God's Son (see Matt 2:15).

commentator on the title "Son [of God]" in Psalm 2:7 (and only the non-evangelical critical scholar will deny the admissibility of his insights), then we may conclude that Psalm 2:7 clearly speaks of a *divine* Messiah. Here also is suggested that personal manifoldness in the being of God which we observed earlier in connection with the Angel of the Lord, for the Lord (Yahweh) addresses Another as his Son, this "Son" designation not only distinguishing between them but also ascribing deity to his Son.

The Divine King/Bridegroom (Psalm 45)

Psalm 45, a Korahite Psalm from the mid-tenth century B.C., under the imagery of a royal wedding, portrays the divine-human (see 45:2, 6) Messiah in the role of a royal Bridegroom in all his grace and might and in all his splendor and majesty (45:2-9), then addresses his bride, the "true Israel" of both dispensations, admonishing her respecting her duties to her royal Consort (45:10-15), and closes with a benediction upon the Groom (45:16-17). This bridegroom-bride metaphor describing the relation of the Messiah to his people is a familiar one to every student of Scripture (see Song, Isa 62:5; Hos 1-3; Jer 2:2; Matt 9:15; 22:2-14; Mark 2:19-20; Luke 5:34-35; John 3:29-30; 2 Cor 11:2; Eph 5:25-32; Rev 19:7-9; 21:2, 9; 22:17).

While the ancient synagogue and virtually all the older Christian commentators viewed the Psalm as a royal messianic Psalm along lines suggested above, modern Old Testament critical scholarship has tended to regard it simply as a wedding song (*epithalamium*) composed most probably for an unspecified royal marriage. Some modern scholars admit that, though the subject is a purely human king of Israel, he (honorifically) "is...called God."[20] This acknowledgement at least recognizes the vocatival force of אֱלֹהִים, *'ᵉlōhîm*, ("God") in verse 6. More customarily, critical Old Testament scholarship has urged alternative translations which in effect rid the verse of its vocative "O God" such as "Your divine throne," "Your throne is of God," "Your throne is [or, will be] God's throne," and "Your throne is like God's throne." Even among those acknowledging the vocatival force of אֱלֹהִים, *'ᵉlōhîm*, there have been sponsors of translations

[20]Ringgren, *The Messiah in the Old Testament*, 18.

commending something other than "God" for אֱלֹהִים, *'ᵉlōhîm*, such as "Ruler," "majesty," and "god" (in the sense of "noble one"). Some scholars, in what Murray Harris calls an "ill-advised counsel of despair,"[21] have even proposed emending אֱלֹהִים, *'ᵉlōhîm*, to יִהְיֶה (*yihyeh*, "will be") or omitting it altogether as a later gloss. Dahood has proposed revocalizing the noun "throne" to make a verb "has enthroned" ("God has enthroned you"), acknowledging, however, that "the only evidence for this is its manifest good sense, its concordance with the Ugaritic-Hebrew proclivity for coining such verbs...and, negatively, the unsatisfactory nature of the numberless solutions which have been proffered on behalf of this *crux interpretum*."[22]

Warfield reviewed the expedients resorted to in the literature prior to and during his own day to avoid the conclusion that Psalm 45 both ascribes superhuman nature and powers to the Messiah and addresses him in the course of its description of him as "God," and concluded that they were all just that—mere expedients.[23] Two significant studies in our own day by Leslie C. Allen and Murray Harris[24] have defended the vocatival force of אֱלֹהִים, *'ᵉlōhîm*, in 45:6. And, of course, over against all modern scholarship which would argue otherwise, the Author of Hebrews, guided by the Holy Spirit, understood אֱלֹהִים, *'ᵉlōhîm*, vocatively, and in the course of his exposition in Hebrews 1 employed it to contribute to his explication, as we have already suggested, of the content of that one "more superior name [than "angel"]" of "Son."[25]

---

[21]Murray J. Harris, "The Translation of *Elohim* in Psalm 45:7-8" in *Tyndale Bulletin* 35 (1984): 70.

[22]Dahood, *Psalms I, 1-50*, 273.

[23]Benjamin B. Warfield, "The Divine Messiah in the Old Testament" in *Biblical and Theological Studies* (Philadelphia: Presbyterian and Reformed, 1952), 88-95.

[24]Leslie C. Allen, "Psalm 45:7-8 (6-7) in Old and New Testament Settings," in *Christ the Lord* (Leicester: Inter-Varsity, 1982), 220-42; Murray J. Harris, "The Translation of *Elohim* in Psalm 45:7-8" in *Tyndale Bulletin* 35: 65-89; see also Kidner, *Psalms 1-72*, 21, 172; and R. Laird Harris, "Psalms" in *The Biblical Expositor*, 437-38.

[25]See Murray J. Harris's definitive article, "The Translation and Significance of Ο ΘΕΟΣ in Hebrews 1:8-9" in *Tyndale Bulletin* 36 (1985): 129-62.

Thus in God's address to the King, "Thy throne, O God, is forever and ever," we have another biblical datum supporting the personal manifoldness in the being of God, for here we have God as אֱלֹהִים, *'elōhîm*, addressing the royal Bridegroom (his Son, according to the Author of Hebrews) as אֱלֹהִים, *'elōhîm*.

The Eternal Lord (Psalm 102)

Psalm 102, an anonymous (but perhaps Davidic) Psalm, according to its superscription, is the "prayer of an afflicted man" in which he "pours out his lament before Yahweh" ("Yahweh," God's personal name, is employed through verse 22).

The content of the Psalm reflects the Psalmist's keen awareness of the contrast between his own and Israel's frailty (102:4-9, 13-17) and transient existence (102:3, 10-11) on the one hand and the eternality of Yahweh who "sits enthroned forever" (102:12, 25-27) and who "remains the same forever" on the other. As a consequence, he cries out to this אֵל ('ēl, "God") (102:24)—in whom resides his only hope of aid and restoration—in behalf of both himself and Israel for respite from their mutual humiliation and their otherwise certain end. In his petition for help in Psalm 102:25-27 (MT, 102:26-28), he confesses:

> In the beginning you laid the foundations of the earth,
> and the heavens are the work of your hands.
> They will perish, but you remain;
> they will all wear out like a garment.
> Like clothing you will change them
> and they will be discarded.
> But you remain the same,
> and your years will never end.[26]

The Author of Hebrews applies this passage to Jesus in 1:10-12 as further explication of the content of the Son's "more superior name

[26]Derek Kidner (*Psalms 73-150* [London: Inter-Varsity, 1975], 362-63) writes: "The Greek, reading the Hebrew consonants with different vowels,...makes the whole passage, including the tremendous words of verses 25-28, the words of God to the psalmist, whom God addresses as the Lord and Creator.... On this understanding, the whole Psalm is messianic."

[than "angel"]." His use of this particular Psalm calls for two comments.

First, his use of this passage in order to explicate Jesus' designation as God's "Son" illustrates what Warfield refers to as the pervasive testimony of the Old Testament to the transcendent Messiah. We have to acknowledge that, apart from the use to which it is put in Hebrews 1, we probably would not have been quickly drawn to this Psalm and to this particular passage in order to find a direct allusion to the divine Messiah. But the Author of Hebrews having done so, we not only can see immediately his rationale for doing so, but also are instructed by his method regarding the correct way to read and to interpret the Old Testament. What he ascribes to Christ by applying these verses in Psalm 102 to Jesus accords perfectly with what Paul (Col 1:16-17) and John (John 1:3, 10-11) teach elsewhere; and here he simply affirms what he himself had earlier affirmed in Hebrews 1:2: "...through whom [the Son] he made the universe." The Christian is thus reminded that the Old Testament Creator is the Son of God who acted as the Father's agent in creation. He may, therefore, in keeping with the Author's insight, view the one described throughout the Old Testament as the Creator and Sustainer of all things as also the one who was to come as the Messiah.

We can only guess how many other such references there are to the divine Messiah in the Old Testament corpus. Doubtless there are many, but may we suggest one other fruitful line for Christian reflection; and here we permit William Binnie to instruct us:

> ...no one who heartily believes in the inspiration of the Psalter will be at a loss to discern in it more testimonies to the proper Divinity of the Hope of Israel than could well have been discovered before His incarnation and death lighted up so many dark places of the ancient Scriptures. It will be sufficient for our purpose to indicate a single example. The coming of Jehovah to establish a reign of righteousness in all the earth is exultingly announced in several lofty Psalms [see 96:13; 98:9]. It may be doubted, indeed, whether the ancient Jews were able to link these to the person of the Messiah; but we are enabled to do it, and have good ground to know that it was of Him that the Spirit spoke in them from the first. The announcement is thus made in the Ninety-sixth Psalm:

> 11. "Let the heavens rejoice and let the earth be glad;
> Let the sea roar, and the fulness thereof;
> 12. Let the field be joyful, and all that is therein:
> then shall all the trees of the wood shout for joy
> 13. Before Jehovah: for He cometh,
> for He cometh to judge the earth:
> He shall judge the world with righteousness,
> and the peoples with His faithfulness."
>
> We know whose advent this is. No Christian can doubt that the proper response to the announcement is that furnished by the Book of Revelation, Amen. Even so, come Lord Jesus.[27]

Numerous similar parallels between other of the prophesied activities of Yahweh in the Old Testament and the person and work of Christ in the New could be drawn. Space limitations permit us here only to underscore the fact itself.

Second, in keeping with his appreciation of the fact that this Old Testament passage was applicable to Jesus as the Son of God, the Author of Hebrews deliberately follows the LXX and inserts κύριε, ***kurie***, the vocative of κύριος (***kurios***, "Lord"), into the Old Testament quotation from 102:25 even though there is no corresponding vocative at this place in the Hebrew text and even though in the Hebrew Psalm it is אֵל ('*ēl*, "God") who is addressed from verse 24 to the end. Κύριος, ***kurios***, is the LXX's choice for regularly translating God's Old Testament name of Yahweh (יהוה). Given this fact, plus the twin truths that the Author of Hebrews inserts κύριε, ***kurie***, into this Old Testament quotation which speaks of the unchanging eternality of Yahweh, and that he speaks of Christ in these terms in 13:8, it is evident that he intended to identify the Yahweh of the Old Testament as directly as is humanly possible with the "Son," of Hebrews 1 who, of course, is Jesus Christ.

This being so, we are now in a position to respond to an objection that has been raised against θεός, ***theos***, in Hebrews 1:8 being construed as a vocative. It has been suggested by E. C. Wickham

---

[27]William Binnie, *The Psalms: Their History, Teachings and Use*, 200ff., cited by Warfield, "The Divine Messiah in the Old Testament" in *Biblical and Theological Studies*, 86.

and others that if θεός, *theos*, were vocatival, verse 8 would of necessity have to be the climax of the Author's argument. But since the Author goes on in verse 10 to describe the Son as κύριε, *kurie*, this further development, it is suggested, would be anticlimactic if the Son is indeed addressed as θεός, *theos*, in verse 8. This further development, in sum, it is argued, has the effect of weakening rather than strengthening the case for θεός, *theos*, as a vocative ascription of deity to the Son.[28]

In response, I would counter that this argument fails to apprehend the significance of the two words θεός, *theos*, and κύριος, *kurios*, respectively with regard to their basic and essential connotations. Θεός, *theos*, while it is a term of the most exalted significance, refers to God simply in terms of his divine essence, for example, in terms of his attributes of omnipotence, omniscience, omnipresence, and omnicompetence. But it is κύριος, *kurios*, coming to us out of the Old Testament quotation here, that is God's *personal name*. And in the covenantal sense it is the more sacred of the two![29] So actually, the argument of the Author of Hebrews *does not* reach its climax in 1:8 with its reference to the Son as θεός, *theos*, but rather, having affirmed of the Son along the way the great truth that he is θεός, *theos*, it reaches its climax in 1:10-12 by its reference to the Son as κύριος (*kurios* or *Yahweh*)—not only the Creator and the Eternal One but also Yahweh the covenant God who is "the same yesterday and today and forever" (Heb 13:8). By his application of this title—κύριος, *kurios*—to the Son as the highest form of explication of the content of that "more superior name [than "angel"]," the Author of Hebrews can say nothing higher: not only is the Son in some sense the אֱלֹהִים, *'ᵉlōhîm*, the God of the Old Testament but he is also in some sense יהוה, *Yahweh*, the *covenant* God of the Old Testament—himself *identical with* Yahweh but in some sense *distinguishable from* Yahweh (a further datum which must be taken into account in any Christian construction of the nature of God).

---

[28]E. C. Wickham, *The Epistle to the Hebrews* (London: Methuen, 1910), 8.

[29]See Raymond E. Brown's comment in *Jesus, God and Man* (Milwaukee: Bruce, 1967), 29: "If Jesus could be given this title [κύριος, *kurios*], why could he not be called θεός, *theos*, which the Septuagint often used to translate אֱלֹהִים, *'ᵉlōhîm*? The two Hebrew terms had become relatively interchangeable, and indeed YHWH was the more sacred term."

The Lordly Priest/King (Psalm 110)

No Psalm is alluded to more in the New Testament as having explicit and emphatic application to our Lord's person and work than Psalm 110 (see Matt 22:44; 26:64; Mark 12:36; 14:62; Luke 20:42-43; 22:69; Acts 2:34-35; 5:31; 7:55-56; Rom 8:34; 1 Cor 15:25; Eph 1:20; Col 3:1; Heb 1:3, 13; 5:6, 10; 7:17, 21; 8:1; 10:12-13; 12:2; 1 Pet 3:22; Rev 3:21). And yet probably no Psalm is more consistently declared by modern Old Testament critical scholarship to be an enthronement oracle composed either for David's or for one of his successor's coronation and spoken to him by an anonymous cultic official.[30] Kidner's biting comment is both a sufficient and appropriate reply to this view: "Our Lord and the apostles, it is understood, were denied this insight."[31]

It is not our present purpose to treat the New Testament's use of verse 4 pertaining to our Lord's high-priestly ministry other than to say that its repeated use by the Apostles confirms our view that Psalm 110 is directly messianic and therefore prophetic (Alexander, Delitzsch, Kissane, Kidner, and R. L. Harris also assert its directly messianic character). Again and again the "priest forever after the order of Melchizedek," who after offering himself up once for all as a sacrifice to satisfy divine justice sat down on the right hand of God (Heb 10:12), is identified with Jesus Christ. The Author of Hebrews even declares that verse 4 was expressly *spoken* (by David through the Spirit; see Matt 22:44) *to* the coming Messiah, Jesus Christ (7:21; see 7:22).

Reflection upon *all* that David affirmed elsewhere of the Messiah, his descendant according to the flesh, can leave little doubt that his "greater Son" here in Psalm 110—as his "Lord" (אֲדֹנִי *'adhōnî*—would be divine. He affirmed, as we have already argued in our consideration of Psalm 2, that the Messiah (see "his Anointed One"

---

[30]See Leslie C. Allen, *Psalms 101-150* (Waco, Texas: Word, 1983), 83-6, for an excellent summary of critical views regarding the authorship, date, and occasion of Psalm 110. It is indeed sad, when David's authorship is so clearly affirmed by the Lord Jesus in all the Synoptic Gospels (Matt 22:43; Mark 12:36; Luke 20:42) and when our Lord's argument hangs so directly on Davidic authorship, to see Allen, an evangelical, opting for a "court poet" as the author (86).

[31]Kidner, *Psalms 73-150*, 392, fn. 1.

in Psalm 2:2), as *God's* "Son," possessed such transcendent dignity that the Author of Hebrews later believed that he was not distorting the sense of David's title of "Son" when he ascribed such superangelic dignity to him in that role that the supreme titles of "God" (θεός, *theos*) and "Lord" (κύριος, *kurios*) might also be quite properly ascribed to him as further explications of that exalted title of "Son" (see Heb 1:5, 13). Apparently, when David spoke of the Messiah as God's "Son," his perception of the Messiah was a much more exalted one than the Bible student might presume upon first consideration. In fact, in keeping with his transcendent view of the Messiah here in Psalm 110:1, he ascribes such "lordship" to the Messiah that his superiority over David, as Jesus later would suggest in Matthew 22:45, cannot comport with merely human lordship but transcends such human lordship just to the degree that divine lordship transcends human lordship.

If the interpretation suggested here should be regarded as granting too advanced a view of the Messiah to a man who lived a millennium before Christ, perhaps it might help to be reminded that David, being a prophet, also knew that the Messiah would die (see also in this connection, Ps 22:16), for he expressly declared that God would raise the Messiah from the dead (Ps 16:8-11; see Acts 2:25-31). And he knew still further that God would exalt this risen Messiah to his own right hand (see the verse presently under discussion and Acts 2:32-35). This one's exaltation apparently was understood by David as entailing not merely occupancy of the place of highest honor in the heavens but also *such participation in the dignity and power of God* that (1) he himself ascribes to that Messiah all the prerogatives of lordship over his life (see "The Lord said to *my* Lord [אֲדֹנִי, *ᵓᵃdhōnî*]") that one normally reserves for God alone, (2) Jesus can later employ David's statement concerning the exaltation of David's Lord to Yahweh's right hand in connection with his own claims to *divine* Sonship when he describes his apocalyptic glory (Matt 26:64 and Synoptic parallels), (3) Peter can later affirm that such transcendent glory could only mean that God himself was confirming by it that David's "Lord" is "both Lord and Christ," the title "Lord" here entailing overtones of deity in light of Peter's reference to "God" in Acts 2:17 (see 2:33) and "Lord" in 2:20, 21 where the Old Testament counterpart in Joel 2:31, 32 is Yahweh (Acts 2:36) and (4) as we have already noted, the Author of Hebrews can see in it, as his final explication of the content of that all-surpassing name of "Son," the Son's essential superiority to angels (1:13). The most exalted angels, like Gabriel, are those who are privileged to "stand in the presence of God" (Luke 1:19), but none of them has ever been invited to *sit* before him, much less to sit in the place of *unique* honor beside him at his right hand. We may deduce from all this that David's "Lord" at Yahweh's right hand was himself divine.

I have considered only four Psalms—2, 45, 102, and 110. A biblical/theological study of these as well as certain other Psalms, such as Psalms 16, 24, 72, 96, and 98, will lead the unprejudiced scholar, I submit, to adduce that these Psalms do foretell the coming of a divine Messiah. That same objectivity will also conclude that Jesus was, both as he himself claimed (Mark 14:62; John 4:26; 17:3) and as Peter and Martha confessed (Matt 16:16-17; John 11:27), that very Messiah who was to come.

ISAIAH'S IMMANUEL CHILD

Gleason L. Archer, Jr., opines that "Isaiah sets forth the doctrine of Christ in such full detail that he has rightly been described as 'the evangelical prophet.' Deeper Christological insights are to be found in his work than anywhere else in the Old Testament."[32] Surely he is right, with the exception, perhaps, of some of David's messianic Psalms such as Psalms 2, 16, 22, 40, 69, 110. Isaiah's prophecy of the עַלְמָה, *'almâ*, who would conceive and bear a son who would be Immanuel (7:14-16) is a classic case in point.

The Historical Setting of the Prophecy

Its historical setting is well known. During the reign of King Ahaz of Judah, probably around 734 B.C., Rezin, king of Syria, and Pekah, king of Israel, formed an alliance against Ahaz of Judah to dethrone him and to install in his place the son of Tabeel as a puppet king who would do their bidding and bring Judah into their coalition against

[32]Gleason L. Archer, Jr., *A Survey of Old Testament Introduction* (Chicago: Moody, 1964), 314.

Assyria.[33] News of their alliance produced great anxiety throughout the southern kingdom of Judah, so God sent Isaiah to Ahaz to assure him that the plot against him would come to nought. But as a warning to Ahaz not to rely on an alliance of his own with Assyria (see 7:9), God informed him that within sixty-five years the northern kingdom, in spite of its Syrian alliance, would be "broken." We may note here that, historically, the alliance was "broken" in three stages: Assyria overran Damascus and despoiled the northern kingdom in 732 B.C. (2 Kgs 15:29), then Samaria fell to the Assyrians in 722 B.C., and finally, with the Assyrians' deportation of the Israelite population and the colonization of the land with non-Israelites (see 2 Kgs 17:24ff. and Ezra 4:2, 10), by 669 B.C. (sixty-five years from 734 B.C.), when Ashurbanipal began to reign over Assyria, Ephraim's destruction became complete.[34]

To give a pointed lesson to the faithless Ahaz that he should put his confidence in God and not in Assyria, and also to encourage him to do so, God graciously invited Ahaz to ask him for a "sign" (אוֹת, *ʾôth*) as a confirmation or attestation of his power to save Judah. Ahaz was informed, in so many words, that he was not to feel the slightest restriction in what he could request, for he was granted unfettered latitude of request "whether in the deepest depth or in the highest heights." Any request within the bounds of this antonymic venue, which is just to say any righteous request at all, was permissible.

Since it has often been suggested that the word "sign" in 7:14 does not mean that the thing it signified should be understood as necessarily entailing something out of the ordinary, I think it important to stress here that at least in Isaiah 7:11 it is quite apparent that it was precisely the "extraordinary" or the "miraculous" that God had in mind when he extended to Ahaz his invitation. And had Ahaz requested of him a miracle, God was prepared to perform one. This is evident from the proximate purpose which the sign was to serve (a proof that God was

---

[33]See Edward J. Young, "The Immanuel Prophecy" in *Studies in Isaiah* (London: Tyndale, 1954), 145-48, for a reconstruction of the historical background to the prophecy in which reconstruction he harmonizes the details of 2 Kings 15:37; 16:1-9; 2 Chr 28:5-21; and Isaiah 7:1-9.

[34]This is essentially the view of Gleason L. Archer, Jr., as well. See his "Isaiah" in *The Wycliffe Bible Commentary*, edited by C. F. Pfeiffer and E. F. Harrison (Chicago: Moody, 1962), 617.

able to deliver and to keep his people) and from the unrestricted latitude in the invitation which was extended to Ahaz. It is not too much to say that upon this occasion God was "thinking miracle" and was ready to perform one as a sign to Ahaz of the certainty of his promise. So while it does not prove that the sign spoken of in verses 14-16 must be construed as entailing the miraculous, the fact that the referent of the word "sign" in verse 11 clearly is of that order lends strong credence to the presumption that, when God declared in verse 14 that he himself would give a "sign" since Ahaz had refused to ask for one, the words that then followed upon his declaration that he would give a "sign" also entailed the miraculous.

Ahaz, because he had doubtless already determined to rely upon a coalition with Assyria (see 2 Kgs 16:5-9), feigned great piety and refused God's gracious invitation, hypocritically declaring that to ask for a sign was to test God (an appeal to Deut 6:16). At this, God declared that he himself would give a sign—not only to Ahaz, but to the whole House of David, implying by this latter statement that the sign carried implications for the entire nation and for its future. God's sign is then stated in these words (7:14-16):

> Behold, the עַלְמָה, *'almâ* [that is, the specific one before the prophet's mind in his vision], is [or, will be] with child and will give birth to a son and will call[35] his name Immanuel. Curds and honey he will eat when he knows enough to reject the wrong and choose the right. For before the child knows enough to reject the wrong and choose the right, the land which you dread will be forsaken of her two kings.

---

[35] I regard the verb וְקָרָאת, *w^eqārāth*, of the MT as a *third* feminine singular ("and *she* will call") (supported by the καλέσει, *kalesei*, in א) in spite of the fact that it has the appearance of a *second* feminine singular (supported by the καλέσεις, *kaleseis*, in A and B). Some scholars (see Walter C. Kaiser, Jr., *Toward an Old Testament Theology* (Grand Rapids: Zondervan, 1978), 208, stress that the verb should be construed as a second feminine singular ("and *you* [the עַלְמָה, *'almâ*, will call"), and that it indicates that the עַלְמָה, *'almâ*, was standing before the prophet as he spoke. But *Gesenius' Hebrew Grammar* (Corrected second English edition; Oxford: Clarendon, 1910) explains this particular form as a "rarer form" of the *third* feminine singular in ל"א, *l-a*, verbs (see 120, par. 44 f, 206, par. 74 g). Besides, Matthew's citation of Isaiah 7:14 reads καλέσουσιν, *kalesousin* ("and *they*

The Meaning and Referent of the עַלְמָה, *'almâ*

What does עַלְמָה, *'almâ* mean here, and to whom does it refer? These questions have invoked many responses. Two such studies of this word were conducted by Robert Dick Wilson and Edward J. Young respectively, in which the nine occurrences of the word in the Old Testament (five times in the plural—Song of Solomon 1:3; 6:8; Pss 46, superscription; 68:25 (MT, 68:26); 1 Chr 15:20; four times in the singular—Gen 24:43; Ex 2:8; Prov 30:19; Isa 7:14) were investigated (1) contextually, (2) against their historical background, and (3) in the versions, including in the case of Young's study a consideration of the Ras Shamra material from ancient Ugarit. Both came to the same conclusion: *never is the word employed to describe a married woman.* Their conclusions are worthy of quotation. Robert Dick Wilson wrote:

> ...two conclusions from the evidence seem clear; first, that *'alma*, so far as known, never meant "young married woman"; and secondly since the presumption in common law and usage was and is, that every *'alma* is virgin and virtuous, until she is proven not to be, we have a right to assume that Rebecca and the *'alma* of Is. vii. 14 and all other *'almas* were virgin, until and unless it shall be proven that they were not.[36]

E. J. Young's conclusion is similar:

> We are far from asserting that this word is the precise equivalent of the English "virgin." It rather seems to be closer to words such as "damsel" or "maiden", words which most naturally suggest an unmarried girl. In fact the Hebrew word *'almâ* would seem to be a shade stronger than the English words "maiden" and "damsel", since there is no evidence that it was ever used of a married woman. Consequently, one is tempted to wish that those who repeat the old

---

will call"), the third common *plural* form, suggesting, to say the least, that in the final analysis precisely who it was who would actually do the "naming" apparently is of no great moment. The verb form simply cannot support the exegetical freight that these scholars want it to carry.

[36]Robert Dick Wilson, "The Meaning of 'Alma (A.V. "Virgin") in Isaiah VII. 14" in *Princeton Theological Review* XXIV (1926), 316.

> assertion that it may be used of a woman, whether married or not, would produce some evidence for their statement.
>
> In the light of this fact that the word is never used of a married woman, and in the light of the Ras Shamra texts, where it is found as a practical synonym of *bethûlâh*, ["virgin"], both words there referring to an unmarried goddess, we believe that the translators of the Septuagint brought out the true force of the passage when they rendered the word by *hē parthenos* ["virgin"].[37]

In my opinion, Matthew, guided by the Holy Spirit, had already placed the validity of their shared conclusion beyond all doubt when he declared (1) that the Lord meant "virgin" when he said what he did to Ahaz, and (2) that Jesus' miraculous conception and birth were the fulfillment of Isaiah's prophecy:

> All this took place to fulfill what the Lord had said through the prophet: "The virgin will conceive and give birth to a son, and they will call him Immanuel"—which means, "God with us." (Matt 1:22-23)

If Matthew is following the LXX here, as many scholars urge, an interesting feature of the LXX translation is that it reflects the *pre-Christian Jewish interpretation* of Isaiah 7:14. It is simply not the case, as some modern Jewish scholars have maintained, that the original reading of the LXX was ἡ νεᾶνις (*hē neanis*, "the young woman") rather than ἡ παρθένος (*hē parthenos*, "the virgin") and that early Christians tampered with the text by substituting the latter for the former. The truth of the matter is that Aquila, a second-century convert to Judaism, did an independent Greek translation of the Hebrew Bible and deliberately substituted the former for the latter to avoid the Christian interpretation. But the original LXX translator, doing his work one to two centuries before the birth of Christ and knowing nothing of the fact itself, translated עַלְמָה, *'almâ*, by παρθένος, *parthenos*, because he was attempting to deliver a competent translation. Cyrus H. Gordon, one of the most knowledgeable Jewish scholars in Mediterranean studies in this generation, acknowledged as much:

---

[37]Young, "The Immanuel Prophecy" in *Studies in Isaiah*, 183-84; see also J. Gresham Machen, *The Virgin Birth of Jesus Christ* (New York, Harper and Brothers, 1930), 288.

> The commonly held view that "virgin" is Christian, whereas "young woman" is Jewish is not quite true. The fact is that the Septuagint, which is the Jewish translation made in pre-Christian Alexandria, takes '*almah* to mean "virgin" here. Accordingly, the New Testament follows Jewish interpretation in Isaiah 7:14...The aim of this note is...to call attention to a source that has not been brought into the discussion. From Ugarit of around 1400 B.C. comes a text celebrating the marriage of the male and female lunar deities [Nikkal and Yarih]. It is there predicted that the goddess will bear a son....The terminology is remarkably close to that of Isaiah 7:14. However, the Ugaritic statement that the bride will bear a son is fortunately given in parallelistic form; in 77.7 she is called by the exact etymological counterpart of Hebrew '*almah* "young woman"; in 77.5 she is called by the exact etymological counterpart of Hebrew *bethulah* "virgin." Therefore, the New Testament rendering of '*almah* as "virgin" for Isaiah 7:14 rests on the older Jewish interpretation, which in turn is now borne out for *precisely this annunciation formula* by a text that is not only pre-Isaianic but is pre-Mosaic in the form that we now have it on a clay tablet.[38]

Two caveats are necessary here, however. Even though Gordon's remarks support the view that Isaiah 7:14 was regarded by Jewish scholars before the birth of Christ as referring to a *virgin* birth, the reader must be cautioned not to follow Gordon in his implied suggestion that the New Testament *via Isaiah* is simply reflecting an ancient pagan annunciation formula used to announce the birth of gods and kings. It may well have been such originally, but in Isaiah, as Young trenchantly notes,

> this formula is lifted from its ancient pagan context and made to introduce the announcement of the birth of one who is truly God and King. No longer must this phrase serve the useless purpose of heralding the birth of beings who had never existed and never would exist. Now, for the first time in its history, it becomes a true "divine-royal *euangelion* formula."[39]

---

[38]Cyrus H. Gordon, "'Almah' in Isaiah 7:14" in *The Journal of Bible and Religion* XXI, 2 (April 1953): 106.

[39]Edward J. Young, "The Immanuel Prophecy" in *Studies in Isaiah*, 160; see Luke 1:31 for the *final* occurrence of the formula in Gabriel's "birth annunciation."

Second, Gordon's last comment implies a post-fifteenth century date for Moses, when in actuality Moses was contemporaneous with the Ugaritic corpus from ancient Ras Shamra.

Now there can be no doubt that Matthew, even granting that he followed the LXX (but only because of the propriety of its translation), intended by παρθένος, *parthenos*, the meaning of "virgin" (*virgo intacta*). This is clear from his statements on both sides of his citation of the Immanuel prophecy, specifically, his statements "before they came together" (1:18), "what is conceived in her is from the Holy Spirit" (1:20), and "[Joseph] had no union with her until she gave birth to a son" (1:25). We conclude, then, at this point in our discussion that God's "sign" to the House of David entailed the announcement that a virgin would both conceive and *while still a virgin* bring forth a son—definitely a miracle and answering thereby the demands of the implied meaning in the word "sign" which was God's characterization of the future event. This interpretation necessarily eliminates as referents of the עַלְמָה, *'almâ*, both Ahaz's wife, whom Vriezen and Kaiser suggest,[40] and Isaiah's own wife (see 7:3, 8:3-4 for the evidence that Isaiah was married), as Archer has urged.

The virginal conception, however, does not exhaust the miraculous features of the sign, for it is apparent, if the mother was to conceive virginally, that the Child, having no biological father, while certainly

[40]Th. C. Vriezen, *An Outline of Old Testament Theology* (Newton, Mass.: Charles T. Branford, 1958), 360, fn. 1; Walter C. Kaiser, Jr., *Toward an Old Testament Theology*, 209-10; see also Kaiser's article, "The Promise of Isaiah 7:14 and the Single-Meaning Hermeneutic" in *Evangelical Bulletin* 6 (1988): 55-70. In his treatment of the passage Kaiser urges specifically that the עַלְמָה, *'almâ*, was Abi (a variant form of Abijah), daughter of Zechariah and wife of Ahaz (2 Kgs 18:2), and that the Immanuel child was Hezekiah. But this cannot be, since, as Kaiser himself recognizes (but discounts because of dating problems surrounding the latter's reign), "on present chronologies [Hezekiah] must have been nine [*sic*] years old at that time (about 734 B.C.)" (209). Actually, in my opinion, Hezekiah may have been around nineteen years old in 734 B.C., coming to the throne as he apparently did in 728/27 B.C. at the age of twenty-five (see 2 Kgs 18:1-2, 9, 10). The reference to his "fourteenth year" in 2 Kings 18:13 may refer to the fourteenth year of the special fifteen year dispensation of *additional* life which God granted him (see 2 Kgs 20:1-11). This would be 701 B.C., which Old Testament scholars assert was the year in which Sennacherib invaded Judah.

human would himself necessarily be *unique*. Young aptly comments: "The emphasis which has been placed upon the mother of the child leads one to the conclusion that the child himself is unusual."[41] Of course, the direction in which the text itself prompts one to look for help in apprehending the nature of his uniqueness is toward the name he was to be given—Immanuel. What does this name tell us about his character?

The Hebrew proper name עִמָּנוּ אֵל, *'immānû ēl* (Gr.' Εμμανουήλ, *Emmanuēl*), meaning "With us [is] God," occurs only three times in the Bible (7:14; 8:8; Matt 1:23). It is employed as a proper name in all three verses, and, I would urge, as the name of the same person. (The occurrence of עִמָּנוּ אֵל, *'immānû ēl* , in Isaiah 8:10, following as it does the Hebrew particle כִּי [*kî*, "for"], should be taken as a statement and not as a proper name; that is to say, the clause should be rendered "for God is [shall be] with us" rather than "for—[I am] Immanuel!" Therefore, I will not lay any weight upon it in the present discussion except to say that it is an obvious play on the proper name in 8:8 and gives the reason why Assyria's impending devastation of Judah would not prove to be ultimately fatal for Immanuel's land—"for God [in the person of עִמָּנוּ אֵל, *'immānû ēl*] is with us.") Now it does not do justice to the child's uniqueness among men *as virginally conceived* to argue as some do[42] that the name Immanuel was intended merely to symbolize the fact that God was present with the nation in her coming deliverance and nothing more. The name by itself, I grant, *might* symbolize nothing more than that, but a *virginally-conceived* child who would bear the name "Immanuel"—one could be excused were he to conclude—might well *be* in fact what his name suggests. I say this for the following reasons:

First, in Scripture the name which was given to one (or which one bore) quite often was *descriptive or declarative of what one was* (see, for example, Gen 17:5, 15-16; 27:36; Ex 3:13-14; 6:2-3; 1 Sam 25:25; 2 Sam 12:25; Matt 1:21). Just as in Isaiah 4:3 where those who are "called holy" are not simply *nominally* so but *are in fact* holy (see also Hos 1:10, Isa 1:26; Luke 1:31, 35), so also in Isaiah 7:14, to

---

[41]Young, "The Immanuel Prophecy" in *Studies in Isaiah*, 194.

[42]See, for example, Raymond E. Brown, *The Birth of the Messiah* (New York: Macmillan, 1977), 148; see also 150, fn. 52.

call the child "Immanuel" can and, I would submit, did intend to designate what he would in fact be.

Second, the other occurrence of the name in Isaiah suggests that the Child of the Immanuel prophecy was divine. From 8:8 we learn that Immanuel was the *Owner* of the land of Israel, and that he would protect the people of God (see 8:10), clearly implying that the Child would possess divine prerogatives and attributes.

Third, the fact that Matthew "by-passed" the name "Jesus" (but see the angel's explanation of "Jesus" which is reminiscent of Ps 130:8) which was equally "un-Greek" and translated "Immanuel" (the third occurrence of the name) into Greek (1:23) surely suggests, against the background of the angel's earlier statement that "what is conceived in her is from the Holy Spirit" (1:20), that he intended to teach that in the person of the virginally conceived offspring of Mary God himself had come to dwell with his people ἐν σάρκι (*en sarki*, "in flesh") (see Jesus' later promises to *be with his people* in Matt 18:20 and 28:20).

Fourth, the further descriptions of this Child in Isaiah 9:6—"wonderful Counselor, mighty God, everlasting Father, Prince of peace" (not to mention the numerous New Testament applications to Jesus of other descriptions of the Child found in Isaiah 7-12, the so-called "Volume of Immanuel"[43])—indicate that the Child of the Immanuel prophecy was to be, as virginally conceived, the divine Son of God.

[43]For example, (1) the "Lord of hosts" of 8:13 is the "Lord Christ," according to 1 Peter 3:14-15; (2) this same "Lord of hosts" of 8:14 who is "a stone that causes men to stumble and a rock that makes them fall" is the Christ whom the Jews rejected, according to Romans 9:33; (3) and yet he is to be distinguished from the Lord in some sense for, according to the Author of Hebrews, it is the Christ who says in 8:17: "I will put my trust in him" (Heb 2:13), and who speaks of having received children from the Lord in 8:18 (see "everlasting Father" in 9:6) (Heb 2:13); (4) the geographic locale specified in 9:1-2 is applied to the locale of Jesus' ministry in Matthew 4:13-16; (5) the nature of the Child's reign described in 9:7 is the background to Gabriel's statement in Luke 1:32-33; (6) the statement that only a remnant in Israel rely upon the Lord and return to the mighty God in 10:20-23 (see "mighty God" in 9:6), Paul in Romans 9:27-28 applies to the then-current wide-scale rejection of Jesus Christ; and (7) the Root of Jesse to whom the natives will rally in 11:10 is the Christ, according to Paul in Romans 15:12. Clearly, the Child of the "Volume of Immanuel" is Deity incarnate and yet is in some sense to be

Only such an understanding of the name as we have suggested here, in my opinion, explains the uniqueness of the Child who was to be conceived in the womb of the virgin mother without the benefit of a human biological father. The biblical evidence, in sum, is quite overwhelming in support of this virginally conceived Child being God in the flesh and thus the rightful bearer of the descriptive name "Immanuel"—"With us [is] God!"

Of course, it should be clearly understood that, while the virginal conception is declared by Scripture to be the *means* whereby the Son of God became man and thus entered into the world, nothing that I have said or have intended to say should be construed to suggest that the virginal conception *per se* was the *cause* or source of the deity of Immanuel. Geerhardus Vos has aptly sounded a cautionary note here when he writes:

> ...there is truth in the close connection established between the virgin birth of our Lord and His Deity. It is, however, a mistake to suspend the Deity on the virgin birth as its ultimate source or reason. The impossibility of this appears when we observe that the virgin birth has reference to the human nature of our Lord, and cannot, therefore, without confusion of the two natures, be regarded as the cause of Deity. Being an event in time, the virgin birth cannot be productive of something eternal. To suspend the Deity of Christ on his virgin birth would lead to a lowering of the idea of Deity itself. Yet, the feeling is quite correct that those who deny the supernatural birth are also prone to deny the true Deity of our Lord and His eternal existence with God before the world was. The combination of affirming the true Deity of Christ while denying the fact of His virgin birth is not a normally sane position, but a mere theological oddity.[44]

---

distinguished from Deity. Only the postulation of the correlative doctrines of the Incarnation and the Trinity can resolve this otherwise clear contradiction. More examples could be given: As a further explication of the content of that one "more superior name [than "angel"]" of "Son," the Author of Hebrews declares that when this Child was born, God commanded that all the angels should worship him (Heb 1:6; see Deut 32:43 LXX), and that as God's Son he is himself the "God" of Psalm 45:6-7 and the "Lord" of Psalm 102:25-27. Surely he is Deity.

[44]Geerhardus Vos, *The Self-Disclosure of Jesus* (Reprint; Phillipsburg, New Jersey: Presbyterian and Reformed, 1978), 191, fn. 15.

The Problem of Relevance

The major exegetical objection raised against this interpretation of Isaiah 7:14 is that the prophecy would have had no relevance for Ahaz's day. A "sign" that was not to be fulfilled for seven and a half centuries, it is often urged, could hardly have been of any value to the House of David in the eighth century B.C. This objection is found in both non-evangelical and evangelical studies of the passage. Of course, in the case of the latter, a valiant effort is made so to interpret the passage that it portends a birth in Isaiah's own day *and* the birth of Christ later. For example, William Sanford LaSor has argued that the Hebrew word עַלְמָה, *'almâ*, must be interpreted broadly enough so that, in addition to its ultimate application to the *virgin mother* of Jesus Christ, it may refer penultimately to an earlier *young woman* in Isaiah's day who would conceive and bear a son *by natural means* whose son would bear the name Immanuel and who would thus become a sign of hope to Ahaz of a deliverance which God was to bring to pass within a dozen years.[45]

Gleason Archer also understands the Immanuel prophecy in 7:14 as having a dual fulfillment, the first and typical fulfillment being in Maher-Shalal-Hash-Baz (8:1-4), son of Isaiah, with the second and antitypical fulfillment being, of course, in Jesus, son of Mary.[46] But in order to justify this interpretation, Archer must postulate, first, that Shear-Jashub (7:3) was Isaiah's son by a previous wife who had died leaving Isaiah a widower, and second, that he was engaged to be married to a prophetess who was at the time of the prophecy and her marriage to Isaiah a virgin but who, of course, would not have been a virgin at the time of her conception and delivery. But both of these features in his interpretation—Isaiah's widowerhood and his engagement to be married again to the prophetess—are pure assumptions since the Scriptures say nothing about *two* wives. They are simply assumptions which Archer must necessarily make if he is to hold the dual-fulfillment view.

A careful reading of both Isaiah 7:14 and Matthew 1:22-25 will disclose, however, that the עַלְמָה, *'almâ*, was to be a virgin not only at

[45]William Sanford LaSor, "Isaiah 7:14—'Young Woman' or 'Virgin'?" (Pasadena: privately published, 1952), 8-9.

[46]Archer, "Isaiah," *The Wycliffe Bible Commentary*, 618.

the time of her marriage but also *at the time of her conception and her delivery*. Consider the following: the παρθένος, *parthenos*, whom Matthew expressly affirms was a "virgin" (and whom Archer happily acknowledges was a virgin at the time of the prophecy), both Isaiah and Matthew also represent as the *same* subject who both *conceived* and *delivered*: "the *virgin* shall *conceive* and [the virgin shall] *bring forth* a son." There is no hint that the virginal status of the παρθένος, *parthenos*, changed between the description of her as such and the two verbs ("conceive" and "bring forth") that follow. An analogy would be John 1:14 where we are informed that "the Word *became* flesh and *dwelt* among us." The Word, evangelicals would argue, without changing into something else and ceasing to be all that he is as the Word *became* flesh. And the same Word is the subject of the next verb—"dwelt"—as well. Similarly, the παρθένος, *parthenos*, without ceasing to be a παρθένος, *parthenos*, both conceived and delivered. This is the reason—what other reason can account for it?—that Matthew underscored the truth that Joseph had no sexual relations with Mary until *after* she had given birth to Jesus (1:25). He clearly intimates that Mary's virginity throughout the duration of her pregnancy was necessary as a fulfillment feature of the Isaiah 7:14 statement which he had cited. In my opinion, this fact necessarily eliminates a dual fulfillment for Isaiah 7:14 and requires that the Immanuel prophecy be applied exclusively to Christ. The reader will have to judge whether a woman who would be a virgin at her marriage but a virgin neither at conception nor at delivery (that is, the prophetess) could have possibly served as a type of the future antitypical woman who prior to her marriage would still be a virgin both at conception and at delivery (that is, Mary), and whether Isaiah 7:14 can be so read that it allows both of these quite dissimilar situations to fall within the parameters of the linguistic tolerances of the verse. In my opinion, this resort to "double fulfillment" or "double meaning," as J. Barton Payne urges, fails to take seriously the fact that "the *'alma* of Isa 7:14 either was a virgin or was not and cannot simultaneously predict these two opposing meanings."[47] As I have

[47]J. Barton Payne, *Enyclopedia of Biblical Prophecy* (New York: Harper and Row, 1973), 292, fn. 61; see J. A. Alexander, *Isaiah Translated and Explained* (Philadelphia: Presbyterian Board of Publication, 1851), I, 106-07.

said, it flies in the face of Matthew's assertion that the Immanuel prophecy describes the עַלְמָה, *'almâ*, as a virgin *not only at the moment of conception but also throughout her pregnancy up to and including her time of delivery.*

The Solution to the Problem of Relevance

What is the solution, then, to the problem of relevance for its contemporaries of a "sign" prophecy which was not to be fulfilled for seven and a half centuries? At least four solutions have been proposed in response to this objection:

1. Joseph Addison Alexander in his great critical commentary on Isaiah argued that the assurance that Christ was to be born in Judah, of its royal family, might be a *sign* to Ahaz that the kingdom should not perish in his day; and so far was the remoteness of the sign in this case from making it absurd or inappropriate that the further off it was, the stronger the promise of continuance of Judah which it guaranteed.[48] The problem with this response is that it seems to make the relevance of the prophecy turn on an awareness on the part of the original recipients that its fulfillment was to be in the *distant* future.

2. J. Barton Payne, with keener insight, argued that the relevance of the prophecy for the eighth century B.C. was dependent neither upon the immediacy of its fulfillment nor upon Ahaz's awareness of its distant future fulfillment. A prophecy, he writes,

> may serve as a valid force in motivating conduct [and instilling consolation], irrespective of the interval preceding its historical fulfillment, provided only that the contemporary audience *does not know* when this fulfillment is to take place. Even as the Lord's second coming should motivate our faithful conduct, no matter how distant it may be..., so Isa 7:14, on His miraculous first coming, was equally valid for motivating Ahaz, 730 years before Jesus' birth.[49]

---

[48]J. A. Alexander, *The Earlier Prophecies of Isaiah* (New York: Wiley and Putnam, 1846), I, 119; Charles Lee Feinberg, "The Virgin Birth in the Old Testament and Isaiah 7:14)" in *Bibliotheca Sacra* 119 (1962): 258, also seems to support this proposal.

[49]Payne, *Enyclopedia of Biblical Prophecy*, 292, emphasis supplied.

That is to say, according to Payne, precisely because Ahaz *did not know* when the prophecy would be fulfilled, "the time lapse need not diminish the contemporary relevance of Isaiah's warning" even though Immanuel was not to appear for more than seven centuries.[50] Payne's interesting solution is the antithesis to that proposed by Alexander inasmuch as Alexander's view looks to the recipients' *awareness* of the prophecy's distant fulfillment as the ground of its relevance whereas Payne's view roots the relevance of the prophecy in the recipients' *lack of awareness* of the time of its fulfillment. Payne's view resolves the difficulty implicit in Alexander's proposal. But his view also appears to cut off from 7:14 the following two verses, verses which as a part of the sign statement seem to provide the very measure of time (in relative terms) between that moment and Judah's subsequent deliverance from the threat from the north which Payne seems to suggest is absent from the passage.

3. As did John Calvin, Robert I. Vasholz attempts to show the relevance of the prophecy by arguing that, while 7:14-15 predicts the virgin birth of Christ, 7:16 does not refer to him.[51] He thinks it "regrettable" that English translations invariably suggest by their translation of הַנַּעַר (*hanna'ar*, "the boy") that 7:16 speaks of the same child that is in 7:14-15. He translates 7:16: "Before a boy knows enough to reject the wrong and choose the right, the land of the two kings you dread will be laid waste." He recognizes that the Hebrew employs the article with the word "boy," but he cites *Gesenius' Hebrew Grammar*, 126 q-r to the effect that the Hebrew article may denote an indefinite person or thing which is present to the mind of the narrator as the ground for his translation.

I acknowledge the validity of the syntactical rule he cites but question its applicability in this instance since in verse 14 specific reference is made to the virgin's "son" (בֵּן, *bēn*) and in verse 15 *that* son is the antecedent referent of the third masculine singular form of the verb יֹאכֵל (*yō'kēl*, "he will eat") and the third masculine singular suffix attached to the infinitive construct לְדַעְתּוֹ, *l^edha'tô*, "when he knows"). It is not likely, against this background, that הַנַּעַר *hanna'ar*,

---

[50]Payne, *Enyclopedia of Biblical Prophecy*, 291.

[51]Robert I. Vasholz, "Isaiah and Ahaz: A Brief History of Crisis in Isaiah 7 and 8" in *Presbyterion: Covenant Seminary Review* XIII/2 (Fall 1987): 82-3.

in the very next verse (7:16) would then refer to just any boy in general and not to the boy just mentioned. It is also striking, to say the least, that when precisely the same terms (הַנַּעַר, *hanna'ar*...בֵּן, *bēn*) occur again only a few verses later (8:3-4), Vasholz himself translates: "Before the boy [the "son" referred to in the preceding verse] knows."

4. Therefore, I believe that the solution proposed by J. Gresham Machen, E. J. Young, and R. Laird Harris is the best to date, all three arguing that the "sign" is not to be restricted to the virgin's miraculous conception and to the unique character of her Son (7:14) but must include the words of 7:15-16 as well, and who, accordingly, make *the period of the early years of the miraculous child's life the measure of the time of Judah's dread.*[52]

In these two verses we are informed that the child would "eat curds and honey when he knows enough to reject the wrong and choose the right." What does this mean? According to Isaiah 7:21-22, "curds and honey" would be the common fare of the remnant who remained in the land after the king of Assyria had assaulted the nation and deported much of its populace. Because of the diminished number of people in the land, there would be an abundance of milk, with the result that they "will have curds to eat. All who remain in the land will eat curds and honey." In other words, this aspect of God's sign to the House of David warned of a coming period of humiliation which, in light of verse 17, would envelop not only Israel but Judah as well *for a time*. The statement that the marvelous Immanuel Child would eat curds and honey symbolically meant then for Judah that the Immanuel child would identify himself with the remnant people from whom he would eventually come. But that the nation's then-present distress was to be a relatively short period of humiliation is evident from the fact that God declared that "before the child knows enough to reject the wrong and choose the right, the land of the two kings you dread will be laid waste." This time frame may be understood in either of two ways. It may mean that in the time it would take for the child to come to years of *moral* discretion, that is, within a period of a couple of years or so, the threat from the northern alliance would have been removed. If this is the intent of the "time phrase," God was saying that the time of dread for Judah would come to an end

---

[52]They do differ on details.

with the Assyrian invasion in 732 B.C. at which time Damascus fell and the northern kingdom was so despoiled (see 2 Kgs 15:29) that for all intents and purposes it was only a "rump" state during Hosea's reign. It could also be taken to mean that in the time it would take for the child to reach the age of *legal* accountability, that is, within a thirteen year period (twelve years plus the original gestation period of the Child), the time of dread would come to an end. If this is the intent of the "time phrase," then God was referring to the period of time (if we commence the period from 734 B.C.) from 734 B.C. to 721 B.C. during which period of time both Damascus (in 732 B.C.) and Samaria (in 722 B.C.) were overthrown.

To sum up, then, it is not the time between the giving of the sign and its fulfillment that should be made the basis of relevance for Ahaz's day; rather, it is the time between the birth of the miraculous child and his coming to the age of discernment that makes the prophecy relevant to Ahaz's day.

Taking now the entire sign together, it is as if Isaiah had said, to employ Machen's paraphrase,

> I see a wonderful [virginally-conceived] child...whose birth shall bring salvation to his people; and before such a period of time shall elapse as would lie between the conception of the child in his mother's womb and his coming to years of discretion [or legal accountability], the land of Israel and of Syria shall be forsaken.[53]

This paraphrase, endorsed in principle by both Young[54] and Harris,[55] takes all of the features of the sign into account and demonstrates how the sign, specifically because of the "time" indicator attached to it, although not to be fulfilled for hundreds of years, nevertheless could have had—and did in fact have—relevance for Isaiah's contemporaries in that it provided them a measurable, relatively short time frame within which Judah's period of humiliation would come to an end.

---

[53]J. Gresham Machen, *The Virgin Birth of Christ* (New York: Harper and Brothers, 1930), 293.

[54]Young, "The Immanuel Prophecy" in *Studies in Isaiah*, 190, 195-96.

[55]See R. Laird Harris's comment on Isaiah 7:14 in Buswell, *A Systematic Theology of the Christian Religion* (Grand Rapids: Zondervan, 1963), II, 548.

As a parallel short-term prophetic sign that Judah's period of humiliation would be relatively short, God had Isaiah write on a large scroll the name, Maher-Shalal-Hash-Baz, which name—meaning as it does "Quick to the plunder; swift to the spoil"—suggested an imminent assault from the Assyrians. He then had this act witnessed by two reliable witnesses. Then Isaiah "went to the prophetess [doubtless his wife, and most likely at God's command], and she conceived and gave birth to a son." God then commanded that the child should be named Maher-Shalal-Hash-Baz, and declared that before the boy would know how to say "my father" or "my mother," Assyria would plunder Judah's two northern enemies (8:1-4). This prophecy was surely fulfilled within the space of a year or so with Tiglath-pileser III's capture of Damascus and the spoliation of Samaria in 732 B.C. And its fulfillment, in accordance with its stated short-term time feature, both confirmed and illustrated the similar time feature attached to the previous long-term Immanuel prophecy—enhancing thereby the latter's relevance to Isaiah's contemporaries.[56]

In my opinion, the interpretation of Isaiah 7:14-16 shared by Machen, Young, and Harris is to be preferred above all the others. I believe that they have demonstrated that the prophecy *exclusively* predicted Mary's virginal conception and the supernatural birth of Jesus Christ, and that in doing so it provided at the same time the time measure for the length of duration of Judah's eighth-century B.C. trouble as well. I would suggest also that Jesus' uniqueness as the

---

[56]A variation on this explanation of the Isaiah 8 prophecy is that of Motyer in "Context and Content in the Interpretation of Isaiah 7:14" in *Tyndale Bulletin* 21 (1970): 118-25, who, with the "Machen-Young-Harris proposal," understands the Immanuel prophecy to have single and direct fulfillment only in Christ but who also argues that Isaiah knew from the start that Judah and Jerusalem would ultimately fall, necessarily projecting the birth of Immanuel as the nation's ultimate hope into the undated future. Immanuel, in other words, was to inherit a "disestablished" Davidic dynasty. Therefore, Isaiah "introduced the second child into the sequence of prophecies (8:1-4), allowing Maher-Shalal-Hash-Baz *to take over from Immanuel* the task of providing a time-schedule for the immediately coming events" (124; emphasis supplied). But this proposal, it seems to me, "disestablishes" the minority years of Immanuel from being the time indicator of a short period of devastation for Judah, the very thing which God himself declared that it was to be.

uniquely-conceived son of Mary came to expression precisely in terms of his being God incarnate, "the Word become flesh," as the name "Immanuel" suggests.

ISAIAH'S CHILD OF THE FOUR EXALTED TITLES

When onc considers the prophetic utterances in Isaiah 9:6-7 there can be no doubt that Isaiah of Jerusalem intended that we should recognize that we stand on messianic ground, as virtually all Old Testament scholars, even the most critical ones, will acknowledge. In his great article on Isaiah 9:6, John D. Davis could list such scholars of his day as Briggs, Cheyne, Driver, G. A. Smith, Kirkpatrick, Skinner, Davidson, Dillmann, Kuenan, Guthe, Giesebrecht, Duhm, Cornill, Hackmann, Volz, Marti, Smend, and Nowack who admitted as much.[57] The list could certainly be extended today to include Davis himself, Alexander, Hengstenberg, Delitzsch, Mowinckel, Lindblom, Ringgren, Zimmerli, E. J. Young, J. Barton Payne, R. Laird Harris, Bruce K. Waltke, and Gleason L. Archer, Jr. In spite of the fact that some scholars, such as Gerhard von Rad, espouse the view that Isaiah—using "high court language" on the order of that found in Egypt—speaks here of Hezekiah's ascension to Judah's throne,[58] nothing has been uncovered by modern Old Testament research that has convinced any evangelical scholar that he must abandon the traditional Christian interpretation which applies this prophecy to the Lord's Messiah.

The Setting of the Prophecy

The setting for this messianic prophecy is readily apparent from the context. Spiritual darkness blankets the land of Immanuel. Because God's chosen nation has resorted to sources other than the voice of God's prophets for spiritual guidance (8:19-20), the people "roam through the land" in distress and gloom. But it will not always be so, declares the prophet Isaiah. It will come to pass that the spiritual darkness will be overcome. Suddenly, "the people walking in darkness

---

[57]See Davis's article, "The Child Whose Name is Wonderful" in *Biblical and Theological Studies* (New York: Charles Scribners, 1912), 93-108.

[58]Gerhard von Rad, *Old Testament Theology* (New York: Harper & Row, 1965), II, 172.

will see a great light; on those living in the land of the shadow of death a light will shine" (9:2; MT, 9:1). And where precisely does this "great light" shine? In the regions of Zebulun and Naphtali (upper and lower Galilee), declares Isaiah (9:1; MT, 8:23), around the Sea of Galilee and the Jordan River, in the "district of the nations" (or "Galilee of the Gentiles") in which a large mixed population of Jews and Gentiles lived—a specific prediction, according to Matthew 4:13-16, of the Galilean portion of Jesus' ministry[59] (see also John's references to Jesus as "the Light" in the universal sense in John 1:4, 7-9; 8:12; 9:5). The effect of this sudden appearance of "the great light" is two-fold (9:3; MT, 9:2): first, it enlarges the now-illumined nation (through the bringing in of the Gentiles) and, second, it replaces the people's previous gloom with joy (note that לֹא, *lō*', "not," should be read לוֹ, *lô*, "to him"; see Isa 54:1; Luke 2:10; John 15:11; 16: 20-24; 17:13; Rom 14:17; Gal 5:22). Isaiah then gives three grounds in verses 4-7 (see the introductory כִּי [*ki*, "because"] at the beginning of 9:4, 5, and 6; MT, 9:3, 4, 5) for this new-found joy of the people:

---

[59]O. Palmer Robertson in his *Understanding the Land of the Bible* (Phillipsburg, N.J.: Presbyterian and Reformed, 1966), 13, observes about this geographical location:

> When the Christ actually came, the biblical perspective on the "land" experienced a radical revision.... By inaugurating his public ministry in Galilee of the Gentiles along the major international trade route, Jesus was making a statement. This land would serve as a springboard to all nations. The kingdom of God [the central theme of Jesus' teaching] encompassed a realm that extended well beyond the borders of ancient Israel. As Paul so pointedly indicates, Abraham's promise of a new covenant perspective meant that he would be heir of the cosmos (Rom. 4:13).
>
> The radical implications of Jesus' pointing his ministry toward the whole world rather than confining himself to the land of Canaan need to be appreciated fully. By setting this perspective on his ministry, Jesus cleared the way for the old covenant "type" to be replaced by the new covenant "antitype." The imagery of a return to a "land" flowing with milk and honey was refocused on a rejuvenation that would embrace the whole of God's created order. It was not just Canaan that would benefit in the establishment of the kingdom of the Messiah. The whole cosmos would rejoice in the renewal brought about by this newness of life.

first, their deliverance from the bondage which had enslaved them;

second, the destruction of all hostility (symbolized by the instruments of war) against them;

and third and climactically, the birth of the Davidic King who will reign over them and through whom the previously-mentioned deliverance and destruction were to be accomplished.

There can be no doubt that Isaiah intended this climactic third ground for rejoicing to be prophetic of the birth and ministry of the Messiah, which prophecy the New Testament declares in turn saw its fulfillment in the birth and ministry of Jesus Christ.

Grammatical Issues in Isaiah 9:6

The Number of Titles: Five, Four, or One?

It is grammatically possible to construe the two nouns, פֶּלֶא, *pele'* ("wonder[ful]") and יוֹעֵץ, *yô'ēts*, "counselor"), separately as two names, thus bringing the number of the Messiah's names here to five rather than four. The *telisha*, the least powerful of all the disjunctive accents, on פֶּלֶא, *pele'*, might appear slightly to favor keeping the two nouns separate as distinct titles. But there are two decisive arguments in favor of overriding the Massoretic accenting and taking the two nouns together as forming one title: first, the fact that the other three are compound titles, אֵל גִּבּוֹר, *'ēl gibbôr*, obviously a single title ("mighty God") as evidenced by its usage as a single designation for God in Isaiah 10:21 (see also Deut 10:17; Ps 24:8; Jer 32:18; and Neh 9:32), and the other two names being construct-absolute relationships ("Father of eternity," "Prince of peace"); and second, Isaiah's description of the Lord of Hosts as being "wonderful in counsel" in Isaiah 28:29 where the same two roots are united to denote *one* characteristic in God.

As for the interpretation that makes the name "Prince of peace" *alone* the Child's name, with "wonderful Counselor, mighty God, eternal Father," being construed as the compound subject of the verb וַיִּקְרָא, *wayyikrā'*, that is, "...his name will be called by the wonderful Counsellor, the mighty God, the eternal Father, Prince of peace," the following needs to be said by way of rejoinder:

first, this rendering unnnecessarily construes the active verb וַיִּקְרָא,

wayyikrā', as a passive verb; it also forces upon the compound subject a singular verb;

second, in no other instance in the Hebrew Bible is the word "name" separated by the subject of the sentence from the name itself;

third, one does not expect to find attributes of God being named here but such as would be characteristics of the child.[60]

As for the suggestion of some that all of the titles are to be read as the sentence, "The mighty God, the eternal Father, the Prince of peace is counseling [יוֹעֵץ, *yô'ēts*] a wonderful thing," which translation takes all of these titles away from the Messiah and makes the Messiah's name to be descriptive of the nature of the God for whom he is to rule, Davis, after noting that it has "caused merriment among solemn commentators"—with Dillman calling it an "un-paralleled monstrosity" and Delitzsch speaking of it as a "sesquipedalian name"— notes the following objections to it:

first, if the intention of the name is to emphasize the divine wisdom, it is just a fact that the epithets of God that are here given do not contribute to that object;

second, while it is true that "Counselor" is a participle (in the classical interpretation, the participle as a verbal adjective is construed nominally), nevertheless, since a verb is needed in such a sentence, it is strange that a participle is employed rather than a perfect or imperfect verb form;

third, the title, "Prince of peace," belongs to the child and not to God according to the unmistakable context."[61]

The Prophetic Perfects

That the two verbs in the perfect tense in 9:6a (יֻלַּד, *yulladh*; נִתַּן, *nittan*; MT, 9:5a) are to be understood as prophetic perfects,[62] that is, as verbs which describe the birth (and thus the reign) of this child as yet future but also certain to Isaiah, is evident from the entire context

[60]Davis, "The Child Whose Name is Wonderful" in *Biblical and Theological Studies*, 96.

[61]Davis, "The Child Whose Name is Wonderful" in *Biblical and Theological Studies*, 97.

[62]See O.T. Allis, *The Unity of Isaiah* (Philadelphia: Presbyterian and Reformed, 1950), 29-33, for his discussion of the prophetic perfect.

and also from the fact that no Davidic king prior to or during Isaiah's time, *including* Hezekiah, ever governed as Isaiah predicted that this king would do. This king, in fact, Isaiah prophesies, would realize in himself the consummation of the Davidic dynasty and reign forever:

> Of the increase of his government and peace there will be no end. He will reign on David's throne and over his kingdom, establishing and upholding it with justice and righteousness from that time on and forever. (9:7)

These words are the prophetic soil from which later were to spring the words of the angel Gabriel who spoke to Mary of her future Child:

> He will be great and will be called the Son of the Most High. The Lord God will give him the throne of his father David, and he will reign over the house of Jacob forever; his kingdom will never end. (Luke 1:32-33)

Surely Alexander's words, spoken almost a century and a half ago, are as true today as they were when he wrote them:

> Upon the whole, it may be said with truth that there is no alleged prophecy of Christ, for which it seems so difficult with any plausibility to find another subject; and until that is done, we may repose upon the old evangelical interpretation as undoubtedly the true one.[63]

I will approach this passage, and Isaiah 9:6 in particular, then, standing on the well-founded assumption that it is directly and prophetically descriptive of the Messiah (who also fulfilled the earlier Immanuel prophecy of Isaiah 7:14), and proceed to a discussion of the significance of his names. The following is my translation of Isaiah 9:6:

> For a [male] child will be born to us,
>   A son will be given to us.
> And one will call his name:
>   wonderful counselor, mighty God,
>   everlasting father, prince of peace.

---

[63]J. A. Alexander, *The Earlier Prophecies of Isaiah* (New York: Wiley and Putnam, 1846), 167.

The Four Titles

As a prophetic description of the Messiah, the opening couplet of this climactic ground of rejoicing (9:6, MT, 9:5) is remarkable. The similarity between Isaiah's "a child *will be born to us*,...and the *government* will be" and the angel's "a Savior *has been born to you* ...in the *city of David*" (Luke 2:11) are, from a biblical-theological perspective, hardly accidental or incidental—the one predicts and the other announces the fulfillment. The same can be said for Isaiah's "a son shall be given to us" (which means, when the passive voice is rendered actively, "God shall give a son to us") compared to the New Testament phrase, "God gave his Son" (John 3:16; Rom 8:32; see John 4:10; 6:32). Neither can the similarity be accidental between this couplet together with the phrase following it, namely, "and one *will call his name*..." (which means, "and his name *will be called*..."), and Gabriel's later announcement: "You will become pregnant and give birth to a son, and you will call his name Jesus. He will be great and *will be called* the Son of the Most High...the Power of the Most High will overshadow you; that is why [διὸ καὶ, *dio kai*] the one to be born *shall be called* holy. [After all, he is] the Son of God" (Luke 1:31-32, 35). According to Isaiah, this ruling child would be called by four exalted names; and according to the angel Gabriel, this ruling child would be called "Son of the Most High," and "Holy." I am drawing attention to this parallel in "name-calling" now, before we consider the names themselves in Isaiah 9:6, to make the point that, though the phrase "to call a name" is an idiom that can in fact mean "to name" in the sense of attaching an identifying proper noun to someone as in the case of "Jesus" (Matt 1:21; Luke 1:31, but even here it describes Jesus in his functional role as Savior), it may also intend that the "name" one is given descriptively designates what one in fact is ontologically (see Isa 1:26; Hos 1:10), as in the cases of "Immanuel" in Matthew 1:23 and (clearly from the context) "Son of the Most High" and "holy" in Luke 1:32, 35. It is in this latter sense, as with "Immanuel" in Matthew 1:23 and "Son of the Most High" in Luke 1:32, that the four Isaianic names, I would submit, are to be construed: not as names which the Child/Son would only bear nominally (no child before or since Jesus was or has been so named), but as names which *descriptively designate him as to his nature*, that is, names which designate his characterizing attributes. Just as Mary's Son as "Savior" was named "Jesus" but was in fact "God with us," "Son of the Most High," and "holy," so here, I would suggest, we now learn that he is also in fact what these four marvelous names indicate. To discover what these names intend with respect to his character we will consider each name in turn.

"Wonderful Counselor"

The translation, "wonderful counselor," is arrived at either (1) by construing "wonder" (פֶּלֶא, *pele'*) as standing in epexegetical construct to "counselor" (יוֹעֵץ, *yô'ēts*), that is, "a wonder of a counselor," which means "wonderful counselor"), after the analogy of כְּסִיל אָדָם (*k*ᵉ*sîl 'ādām*, "a fool of a man," that is, "a foolish man") in Proverbs 15:20,[64] or (2) by construing "wonder" independently as an absolute noun in apposition to "counselor" ("a wonder [who is] a counselor," that is, "a counseling wonder"), after the analogy of נַעֲרָה בְתוּלָה (*na'ᵃrâh bh*ᵉ*thûlâh*, "a damsel [that is] a virgin," that is, "a virgin damsel") in Deuteronomy 22:23.[65] The meaning is virtually the same in either case: "As a counselor, he is a wonder," which is just to say that the child/son is a "wonderful counselor."

As for its meaning, we must not ascribe to the word "wonder" its modern debased denotation which permits it to be attached to the most mundane of things ("I had a wonderful time in the country," "You have a wonderful schedule," etc.). The significant feature about this first title is that the word for "wonder" (פֶּלֶא, *pele'*) and the niphal participial form from the same root (the root meaning of both being "separation," and hence remoteness, inaccessibility, and impossibility) is always employed only in relationship to God (the occurrence in Lam 1:9 is not really an exception when one recalls that it was God who effected the "wonder" of Jerusalem's destruction before both Israel and the surrounding nations) to denote his wondrous miracles in behalf of the salvation of his people and his horrible judgments

---

[64] Gesenius-Kautzsch-Cowley, *Gesenius' Hebrew Grammar* (Second English edition; Oxford: Clarendon, 1910), 416, par. 128 l.

[65] Gesenius-Kautzsch-Cowley, *Gesenius' Hebrew Grammar*, 423, par. 131b.

against his enemies (Ex 3:20; 15:11; 34:10; Josh 3:5; Neh 9:17; 1 Chr 16:12; Pss 40:5 (MT, v 6); 77:11 (MT, v 12), 14 (MT, v 15); 78:12; 136:4; 139:14; Isa 25:1). Particularly instructive for our present purpose is its occurrence in Judges 13:18 when in response to Manoah's request for his name, the Angel of the Lord replied: "It is פֶּלִאי [*peli'(y)*]" (that is, "wonderful," or "beyond human comprehension"), following his announcement by doing the "wonderful thing" (מַפְלִא, *maphli'*, vs.19) of ascending in the flame of Manoah's sacrifice (13:20). Then when we read in Isaiah 28:29 that the Lord of Hosts is "wonderful in counsel and magnificent in wisdom," literally, that the Lord of Hosts "caused [his] counsel to be wonderful and [his] wisdom to be magnificent," we must conclude that when the child/son of Isaiah 9:6 is named "wonderful counselor," this title is ascribing an attribute characteristic only of the Lord of Hosts himself to the one so named, indicating thereby his divine wisdom and by extension his deity. In the execution of his prerogatives as Davidic ruler, the child/son will govern with the wisdom which is nothing short of just the wisdom of God himself for he is himself divine.

"Mighty God"

The Messiah's second name אֵל גִּבּוֹר,[66] *'ēl gibbôr*, is arrived at by construing גִּבּוֹר (*gibbôr*, "mighty") adjectively with אֵל, *'ēl* ("God") after the analogy of שַׁדַּי, *shadday*, in the joint name of אֵל שַׁדַּי, *'ēl shadday* ("Almighty God") in Genesis 17:1. All of the efforts through such translations as "a God-like hero" (Kautzsch) or "a mighty hero" (Gesenius) to reduce the title in meaning to something less than deity, as Delitzsch says, "founder, without needing any further refutation," on the recurring instances of this title as a designation of God himself in Deuteronomy 10:17, Psalm 24:8, Jeremiah 32:18, Nehemiah 9:32, and especially Isaiah 10:21 where it is used beyond all question of God himself.[67] There can be no doubt that its meaning is "mighty God."

---

[66]See Benjamin B. Warfield, "The Divine Messiah in the Old Testament" in *Biblical And Theological Studies* (Philadelphia: Presbyterian and Reformed, 1952), 104-16, for his trenchant analysis of the critical handling of this name by the leading Old Testament scholars of his day.

[67]Franz Delitzsch, *Biblical Commentary on the Prophecies of Isaiah*,

But are we to understand this title as a description of the nature of the Messiah? In response to this question, it is important to note that in Psalm 45:6 (MT, 45:7) the Messiah is addressed as "God" (אֱלֹהִים, *'elôhîm*) in the fullest sense of the word (see Heb 1:8). We may also take note of the additional fact that earlier in the same Psalm (vs 3; MT, vs 4), the Messiah is addressed as "mighty One" (גִּבּוֹר, *gibbôr*). Thus we see that there is a willingness on the part of the Old Testament witness elsewhere to address the Messiah by both terms in the same context. Isaiah is hardly setting a precedent then when he utilizes a title for God in which the two terms have been brought together as an epithet of the divine Messiah. And if, as the Author of Hebrews affirms (1:8), the intention of Psalm 45 is to ascribe nothing less than unabridged deity to the Messiah, then there is nothing (except dogmatic prejudice) which prohibits the conclusion that Isaiah intended to do the same thing here. Since this is what Isaiah 7:14 intends as well by its description of the Messiah as Immanuel ("God [is] with us"), I would submit that the second title in Isaiah 9:6 intends to predicate of the child/son just deity itself and specifically the divine might of the Deity. And in this context this means that the Messiah, as he governs with divine wisdom (see "wonderful Counselor"), exercises the attribute of divine might as well. His first two names then describe what the Messiah is in himself, with the former describing his wisdom to counsel (govern) and the latter his power to execute it.

"Everlasting Father"

Because of the construct-absolute relationship between the two nouns in the third name אֲבִי־עַד, *'abhî 'adh* and because the noun עַד, *'adh*, means here "perpetuity" as it does in the genitive connection in Isaiah 45:17 (see 57:15), there can be no doubt that the phrase is to be translated "everlasting father," after the analogy of הַר קָדְשִׁי, *har qodhshî* (lit, "the hill of my holiness," that is, "my holy hill") in Psalm 2:6.[68] The efforts by some scholars, through such translations as "father of booty," to rid the title of the implication of unendingness shatters on

---

translated by James Martin (Third German edition; Grand Rapids: Eerdmans, 1877), I, 252.

[68] *Gesenius' Hebrew Grammar*, 440, par. 135 n; see also 417, par. 128.

the phrases surrounding it in the context: "Of the increase of his government and peace there will be no end" and "He will reign...from that time on and forever" (9:7; MT, 9:6). At the very least, this title suggests that the Messiah in some sense is possessed of no mere mortality. And this perception is strengthened by the fact that the passage itself teaches that he, as the realization in himself of the culmination of the Davidic line with no succession of rulers after him, will reign over his kingdom as long as the latter endures, which is just to say, forever.

The Christian mind must be careful not to confuse the "son" here with God the Father because the "son" is designated here as a "father." The prophet had already made it clear that the Messiah is God's "son" ("a son shall be given"). What then does the word "father" as a characterization of the Messiah mean here? This name, as with the other two, must be restricted to its contextual universe as a description in some sense of the "given Son," which is just to say that the title affirms that as the Messiah rules with divine wisdom and power from David's throne, his rule—notwithstanding his might—will be *paternal in character*. he will view his subjects as his *children* and will, as a result, wield his scepter for their benefit. Citing Gesenius, Delitzsch, Dillmann, Cheyne, Skinner and Marti, Davis writes:

> It is exegetically needful...to give to the word עַד [*'ad*] in the messianic title its customary sense of endurance, continuance, and render the title "father of endurance" and understand the designation to denote *a continual father, one who enduringly acts as a father to his people.*[69]

This paternal "father to child" relationship is precisely that which the Author of Hebrews declares governed the Son in his willingness (as their messianic king and priest after the order of Melchizedek) to share in the humanity of his "children" (Heb 2:13-14). And it is precisely this caring paternity which we see the incarnate Son exercising already toward the paralytic in Mark 2:5 and Matthew 9:2 when he addressed him as "child" (τέκνον, *teknon*) and toward the sick woman in Mark 5:34 whom he addressed as his "daughter" (θυγάτηρ, *thugatēr*). In this third name, then, we see yet another

---

[69]Davis, 'The Child Whose Name is Wonderful' in *Biblical and Theological Studies*, 105 (emphasis supplied).

divine quality—the quality of mercy—ascribed to the Messiah as he enduringly acts as a father toward his people.

"Prince of Peace"

The fourth name שַׂר־שָׁלוֹם (*sar shālôm*, "prince of peace"), like the third a construct-absolute construction in the Hebrew, adds nothing to the Messiah's character insofar as his deity is concerned. It does, however, provide insight into his kingly office, suggesting that the Messiah by his reign will institute, promote, and maintain peace (see Isa 2:4; 9:6; 11:6-9; Mic 4:3-4; 5:4-5a; Hos 2:18). And to the degree that this particular work of the Messiah is divine work alone, just to that same degree his own divine character is reflected in the specialized work which he does. All the more is this evident when it is recalled, first, that Messiah's "peace work" necessarily involves the cessation of all earthly warfare and the destruction of the cause of all this warfare—human sin (Jam 4:1-2), and second, that he extends this work *universally* (see the phrases, "Of the increase of his government and peace there will be no end [geographically]"), and, "from now on and forever [to the farthest reaches of the future]").

Such "peace work" in turn certainly means that God and man must be reconciled. But can anyone doubt that only the Messiah in the person of Jesus Christ, through whom alone, according to Scripture, men may find peace with God (Rom 5:1), who himself

> *is our peace*, who made both [Jews and Gentiles] one and destroyed the enmity, the regulations, in order that he might create in himself one new man out of the two, *thus making peace*, and [in order] that he might *reconcile both in one body to God* through the cross, slaying the enmity [of God] by it. And having come he preached the good news of peace to you who were far off and of peace to those who were near (Eph 2:14-17)—

can anyone doubt, I say, that Scripture would have us believe that Jesus Christ alone is Isaiah's "prince of peace" and that he alone completely fulfills the role implied in this fourth great name. And surely in doing so, he floods the name with all the divine glory and power of his own essential being!

We have seen that Isaiah confronts us with the divine "Child of the Four Exalted Titles"—"wonderful counselor, mighty God, everlasting father, prince of peace." As a summary of this great messianic passage, I cannot improve upon Delitzsch's insight—surely he is right—when he declares:

> ...the words [of Isaiah 9:6] in their strict meaning point to the Messiah, whom men may for a time, with pardonable error, have hoped to find in Hezekiah, but whom, with unpardonable error, men refused to acknowledge, even when He actually appeared in Jesus. The name Jesus is the combination of all the Old Testament titles used to designate the Coming One according to his nature and his works. The names contained in ch. vii. 14 and ix. 6 are not thereby suppressed; but they have continued, from the time of Mary downwards, in the mouth of all believers. There is not one of these names under which worship and homage have not been paid to Him. But we never find them crowded together anywhere else, as we do here in Isaiah; and in this respect also our prophet proves himself the greatest of the Old Testament evangelists.[70]

THE SUFFERING SERVANT IN ISAIAH'S "FOURTH SERVANT SONG"

It is striking that in the two passages in the Old Testament where Israel's future Deliverer actually receives three times the title of "Messiah," there is the strong intimation that his ministry will entail not only a regal but also a tragic dimension as well. In Psalm 2:2, read in the light of verse 7 which speaks of his resurrection from the dead (see Acts 13:33), the Lord's "Anointed One" is confronted with united hostility from Jew and Gentile which apparently eventuates in his death. And in Daniel 9:25-26, we are informed that "Messiah will be cut off and will have nothing [or, "...off but not for himself"]." This tragic dimension in Messiah's work is both poignantly and powerfully displayed in Isaiah's "Fourth Servant Song," foretelling that the Messiah would suffer unto death for sinners. We may outline this Song as follows:

---

[70]Delitzsch, *Biblical Commentary on the Prophecies of Isaiah*, 251.

Introduction: The enigma of the Lord's servant (Isa 52:13-15)

1. His infancy and youth (Isa 53:1-2)
2. His maturity (Isa 53:3)
3. His sufferings (Isa 53:4-6)
4. His trial and death (Isa 53:7-8)
5. His burial (Isa 53:9)
6. His resurrection and vindication (Isa 53:10)
7. The fruit of his labors (Isa 53:11-12)

Conclusion: Alternative responses to the Lord's servant (Isa 52:15b and 53:1)

The Literary Setting of this Song

In Isaiah 41-53 are found what most scholars, following Bernhard Duhm's 1892 commentary on Isaiah,[71] designate as the four "Servant Songs." The first is found in Isaiah 42:1-4, the second in 49:1-6, the third in 50:4-9, and the fourth in 52:13-53:12. The principle underlying this specific selection of Songs is that all four portray a single distinctive figure. Because the limits of these songs are not always clear, some scholars have added verses 5-7 to the first, verse 7 to the second, and verses 10 and 11 to the third, and some, O. T. Allis,[72] for instance, even regard Isaiah 61:1-3 as a fifth Song.

It is true, because the nation of Israel is addressed in the second song (49:3) as "my [God's] servant," that some scholars read a *corporate* notion into the "servant" in *all* these songs. As we will see, this cannot be made to work exegetically. Other scholars, while acknowledging that the "servant" refers to an *individual*, suggest that that individual is either some unknown contemporary of Isaiah or the so-called "Deutero-Isaiah" or a known individual such as Cyrus, Jeremiah, Zerubbabel, or Isaiah himself. This view, we will see shortly, cannot be made to work exegetically either. The most satisfying view, I maintain, is the *three-dimensional* view put forward by Franz Delitzsch[73] using the figure of a pyramid, in which

---

[71]Bernhard Duhm, *Das Buch Jesaia* (Fifth edition; Göttingen, 1892).

[72]O. T. Allis, *The Unity of Isaiah* (Philadelphia: Presbyterian and Reformed, 1950), 82.

(1) Israel, as the base of the pyramid, in some contexts is God's servant who is charged with the twofold responsibility of bearing witness to the true God before the heathen nations and serving as the custodian of his revealed and inscripturated Word (Isa 41:8-9, 42:18-19, 44:1, 44:21, 45:4, 48:20, 49:3 [within the second song]);

(2) in one context (43:10), as the central section of the pyramid, the elect remnant in Israel ("Israel not only of the flesh but also of the spirit") is God's servant charged with the responsibility of bearing witness to God's character before their unspiritual countrymen; and

(3) in the four contexts mentioned above, as the apex of the pyramid, the Messiah himself is God's servant.

If we are right about this three-dimensional division of the Servant material in Isaiah, then interestingly, in the first of the songs about him, the Messiah is set forth as one who has the task of establishing justice in the earth and who will complete that mission successfully. In the second are intimations that he will be confronted with opposition in the execution of his mission of restoring Israel to God's favor (see "I have labored to no purpose; I have spent my strength in vain and for nothing," 49:4). In the third the Messiah himself speaks about the personal suffering which he will face but he gives no reasons for his suffering (see "I offered my back to those who beat me...I did not hide my face from mocking and from spitting," 50:6). Accordingly, it is reserved for the fourth, climactic Servant Song to inform us why the Servant must suffer: he must bear the sin of many! This then is the literary setting of the Song.

The Corporate Interpretation of this Song

As we have noted, many scholars would want us to believe that the servant of Yahweh in this Song is to be viewed corporately as the nation of Israel. Can this view be sustained? A careful reading of the Song by the unbiased student will show

---

[73]Franz Delitzsch, *Biblical Commentary on the Prophecies of Isaiah* (reproduction of the 1877 translation by James Martin; Grand Rapids: Eerdmans, n. d.), II, 174.

1. that the servant is
   a. portrayed as divine ("the arm of the Lord," 53:1[74]);
   b. portrayed in detailed features as a human personality (52:14; 53:2-3);
   c. an innocent, indeed, sinless sufferer (53:4, 5, 8d, 9c-d, 12d);
   d. a voluntary sufferer (53:7a);
   e. an obedient, humble, and silent sufferer (53:7); and

2. that his suffering
   a. springs from his love for sinners, including his executioners who act in ignorance (53:4c-d, 7, 12);
   b. is ordained by God in love and fulfills the divine intentional will and purpose (53:10);
   c. deals with sin in all its aspects (see the word "sin," that is, specific acts of missing the mark, 53:12; "transgressions," that is, willful acts of rebellion, 53:5; "iniquities," that is, moral evil, 53:5);
   d. is vicarious, that is, substitutionary (53:4a-b, 5a-b, 6c, 8-9d, 10b, 11d, 12e);
   e. is redemptive and spiritual in nature (53:5c-d, 11d);
   f. ends in his death (53:8a, c-d, 10a, 12c) which leads to his being buried with the rich (53:9-10), which condition gives way to his resurrection (53:10b-d, 11);
   g. leads the straying people for whom he died to confession and repentance (53:4-6); and finally,
   h. as his redemptive work, in implementing a divine plan in which suffering, humiliation, and death are central, inaugurates a fruitful and victorious life for endless ages (53:10c-d, 11a-b, 12a-b).[75]

Can these characteristics of the servant's suffering designate the nation of Israel, viewed either historically, spiritually, or ideally? I am compelled to answer in the negative for the following reasons:

---

[74]See J. Alec Motyer, *The Prophecy of Isaiah: An Introduction and Commentary* (Downers Grove, Ill.: InterVarsity, 1993), 427, for the exegetical argument.

[75]I have adapted these points from Frederick Alfred Aston, *The Challenge of the Ages* (Scarsdale: New York: Research Press, 1968), 8.

1. Scripture knows no parallel case where, without any hint of allegory, a passage maintains a personification of Israel throughout the entire section with no indication of its meaning.

2. The words in Isaiah 53:8, "...for the transgression of my people [פֶּשַׁע עַמִּי, *peshaʿ ʿammî*] he was stricken," makes the application of the passage to Israel as the servant untenable since the prophet's "people" are clearly Israel, but if the servant is Israel how can Israel be slain for Israel?

3. Israel as a nation has never been an innocent sufferer. In Isaiah 1:4 the prophet speaks of Israel as a "sinful nation, a people loaded with guilt, a brood of evildoers, children given to corruption," and in the nearer context of 42:23-25 he states that Israel's affliction is God's judgment upon the nation for its sins.

4. Israel as a nation has never been a voluntary sufferer. Never did the nation voluntarily go into exile; each exile was the result of a humiliating national defeat.

5. Israel as a nation has never been an obedient, humble, and silent sufferer. No sooner was the nation delivered from Egypt than it rebelled and complained against the privations of the wilderness. Even such great biblical personalities as Job, Moses, David, Elijah, and Jeremiah complained bitterly about their lot at times.

6. Israel as a nation never endured suffering out of love for others. Since the nation's suffering was neither innocent nor voluntary nor silent, it cannot be said that its suffering was motivated by love for others.

7. Israel as a nation never suffered because God out of love for the nation divinely ordained that it would *innocently* suffer. Israel's suffering is always portrayed as the consequence of her transgressions (Deut 28:62-68; Isa 40:2b; 42:23-25).

8. Israel as a nation never suffered vicariously for other nations. Yet throughout this passage the idea of vicarious suffering providing atonement for others occupies the most prominent place, being expressed no less than 23 times in 9 of the 15 verses.

9. Israel's suffering as a nation *per se* has not brought redemption to the world. Nowhere does Scripture teach that Israel will be redeemed by its own suffering, far less that it can or will redeem other nations or that *its* suffering will redeem the nations of mankind from the power of sin. Since Israel's suffering as a nation has been neither innocent nor voluntary nor silent, it can have no intrinsic moral value and no redemptive power.

10. Israel's suffering as a nation has not ended in its demise, either historically or ideally, while every ancient nation that existed in the Old Testament contemporaneously with Israel has long since passed into oblivion.

11. Israel's suffering as a nation has not brought about its experiencing moral or spiritual resurrection, either historically or ideally. Since there was no national death there cannot be and there has been no national resurrection. And spiritually speaking, the nation remains by and large in unbelief to this day.

12. Israel's suffering as a nation has not produced a moral transformation of the nations or caused them to come to Israel's God with the penitence and confession of guilt which occupies the prominent place that it does in this passage.

13. Israel's suffering as a nation has never resulted in the nation's glorification. No restoration of Israel from exile lifted the nation from extreme humiliation to sublime exaltation.

14. If Israel's suffering as a nation has in the past and will in the future bring great redemptive blessing to the other nations of the world, one must wonder why the synagogue readings from the prophets always omit this "Fourth Servant Song" while the portions immediately preceding and following it are read? If the leaders of world Jewry really believe that this chapter depicts the nation of Israel by its suffering atoning for the nations, why do they not read it in public? What could be more comforting in a memorial service for Jews who perished in the gas chambers of Treblinka and Auschwitz or who struggled to survive in the Warsaw ghetto than the divine promise, "My [suffering] servant justifies many and bears their guilt" (53:11)? To the thousands who mourn relatives killed in

> the Nazi fury what could be more consoling than the assurance that their loved ones' deaths were not in vain but were in fact the climactic aspect of God's grand plan for the redemption of the nations?[76]
>
> As the situation stands now, however, unless it changes, I believe that someday world Jewry will rise up and condemn its rabbinic leadership for refusing to acquaint the Jewish people with Isaiah's marvelous predictive prophecy of their Messiah who would lay down his life for sin and rise again for the justification of his own.

In sum, I must conclude that the corporate view does not fit and cannot be made to fit the terms of the Song exegetically. One could even conclude with some justification that the corporate view is put forward primarily to avoid the prophet's obvious design—that the passage depicts, and is intended to depict, an individual.

The Individualistic Interpretation of the Song

Among the voices who contend that the Song speaks of an individual—a fact not generally known—is that of the Ancient Synagogue that taught that the prophet is speaking here of an individual of transcendent influence who ranks morally and spiritually above any and every other character of the Old Testament, and therefore it applied the passage to the Messiah.[77] In fact, according to R. T. France, "the evidence... suggests that in Palestinian Judaism of the time of Christ and afterward a messianic exegesis of the Servant was so firmly established that even the demands of the anti-Christian polemic could not unseat it."[78] Later, such rabbis as Rabbi Naphtali Ben Asher Altschuler and Rabbi Mosheh Alsheh in the late sixteenth/early seventeen centuries also applied this Song specifically to the Messiah.

---

[76]I have adapted these points from Aston, *The Challenge of the Ages*, 8-14.

[77]See Aston, *The Challenge of the Ages*, 14-17, who cites the *Targum Yonathan ben Uzziel*, the *Midrash Cohen*, the *Midrash Rabbah* of Rabbi Mosheh Haddarsham, and the Musaph service of the Day of Atonement to this effect.

[78]R. T. France, "Servant of the Lord" in *The Zondervan Pictorial Encyclopedia of the Bible*, edited by Merrill C. Tenney (Grand Rapids: Zondervan, 1975), 5.361.

The Referent of this Song

There are scholars, however, who argue that the individual is simply a martyr, perhaps Isaiah himself or perhaps Jeremiah. But an insuperable burden rests upon these scholars to make the case that the martyrdom of Isaiah, "Deutero-Isaiah,"[79] Jeremiah, or some other Israelite saint[80] meets the demands of a fair reading of the Song. After all, they were all sinners who would need redemption themselves. Indeed, Isaiah himself declares: "All we [this "all" would necessarily include Isaiah, Jeremiah, and any other Old Testament saint] like sheep have gone astray; we have turned every one to his own way" (53:6). Moreover, to assert that the martyrdom of even the most pious forgiven saint would or ever could bring about the redemption of the world is entirely foreign to the entire Old Testament where one will search in vain for a eulogy of even the greatest of Israel's heroes save one, that is, the Messiah.

Who then is the Servant, if not some Old Testament saint? Find such a person as this Song describes and one finds the Servant/ Messiah. All the difficulties which the other views entail disappear when the passage is applied to Jesus of Nazareth, for he (and, we may say parenthetically, he alone[81]) meets all the demands of the details of this magnificent prophetic Song. This assertion is clearly substantiated by the following New Testament data:

---

[79]The mere fact that the verb tenses of the Fourth Song are perfects means nothing. The "prophetic perfect" is a recognized use of the perfect aspect of the verb. Moreover, just as the Cyrus prophecy in 44:24-28 places Cyrus in the distant future from the perspective of the writer, so also the Fourth Song places the suffering Servant in the distant future. See O. T. Allis, *The Unity of Isaiah*, chapters 5-7.

[80]According to O. T. Allis, in his *The Unity of Isaiah*, 90, in his own time some fifteen different individuals who had figured more of less prominently in Old Testament history had been suggested as the servant intended by the Fourth Song.

[81]One must decide whether Jesus alone bore the sins of his people or whether someone other than he could do and in fact did this. For myself, only Jesus could and did die for my sins.

1. Jesus was both a historical person, born in lowliness (Matt 2:1; Luke 2:1-2) and divine (Rom 9:5; Titus 2:13; Heb 1:8; 2 Pet 1:1; John 1:1, 18; 20:28; 1 John 5:20).
2. He was an innocent person (John 8:46).
3. He was despised and rejected by men and was unjustly executed as a felon (Luke 23:13-15).
4. He was a voluntary sufferer (John 10:17-18; Gal 2:20).
5. He was an obedient, humble, and silent sufferer (Matt 27:12, 14; Phil 2:8; 1 Pet 2:23).
6. He suffered out of love for others (Luke 23:34).
7. He suffered in order to fulfill the divine plan and will (Eph 3:11).
8. He suffered vicariously for his people (1 Pet 2:24).
9. He suffered in order to provide a redemptive intervention in the course of history leading to the justification of the evildoer from his sin (1 Cor 1:30; 1 Pet 1:18-19).
10. He suffered to the point of death (Matt 27:50).
11. His death gave way to the resurrection (1 Cor 15:4).
12. He ascended, after his resurrection from the dead, to heaven and is now highly exalted, sitting on the right hand of God (Phil 2:9-11).[82]

All of these features of Jesus' life comport beautifully with the demanding details of the fourth Servant Song. Can anyone validly write any other name under the Song's amazing portrait than the name of Jesus of Nazareth? Beyond all controversy, the New Testament regards him as the Song's referent.

New Testament Teaching about the Song's Referent

John the Baptist, by his use of the descriptive phrase with reference to Jesus, "the Lamb of God who takes away the sin of the world" (John 1:29, 36), seems to have been drawing from Isaiah's Fourth Servant Song when he said this. Morna D. Hooker may believe that there is "no convincing evidence to suggest that Isaiah 53 played any

---

[82] I have adapted these points from Aston, *The Challenge of the Ages*, 18.

significant role in Jesus' own understanding of his ministry,"[83] but Jesus self-consciously applied the role of the sacrificial Servant of Isaiah 53 to himself and taught others to believe that he was the Servant spoken of there. For example, he expressly applied the vicarious death of Isaiah's suffering Servant to himself in Luke 22:37: "This Scripture [referring to Isaiah 53:12]," he declared, "must be fulfilled *in me*. Yes, what is written about me is reaching its fulfillment." After his resurrection the risen Christ said to his perplexed disciples on the road to Emmaus: "How foolish you are, and how slow of heart to believe all that the prophets have spoken! Did not the Messiah have to suffer these things [I just suffered] and then enter his glory?" Luke then declares: "And beginning with Moses and all the Prophets [which surely would have included this Song], [Jesus] *explained* to them what was said in all the Scriptures *concerning himself*" (24:25-27). That Luke intended by his phrase, "all the Scriptures," specifically the Scriptures of the Old Testament is clear from the words of Jesus which he cites a few verses later: "Everything must be fulfilled that has been written *about me* in the Law of Moses and the Prophets and the Psalms" (Luke 24:44).[84] "Then," Luke recounts, "he opened [his disciples'] minds so they could understand *the Scriptures*. He told them, '*This is what is written*: The Messiah will suffer and rise from the dead on the third day, and repentance and forgiveness of sins will be preached in his name to all nations, beginning at Jerusalem'" (Luke 24:45-47).

Students of the four Gospels have detected other references to Isaiah 53 even in single words and phrases in the sayings of Jesus, for example, his use of the word "rejected" in Mark 9:12 (see Isa 53:3), and his expression "taken away" in Mark 2:20 (see Isa 53:8).

---

[83]Morna D. Hooker, "Did the Use of Isaiah 53 to Interpret His Mission Begin with Jesus" in *Jesus and the Suffering Servant: Isaiah 53 and Christian Origins*, edited by William H. Bellinger, Jr., and William R. Farmer (Harrisburg, PA: Trinity Press International, 1998), 88.

[84]Jesus' description of the Old Testament here as "the Law of Moses and the Prophets and the Psalms" probably reflects the tripartite division of the Old Testament canon that clearly already existed in some form in the second century B.C. See Edward J. Young, *An Introduction to the Old Testament* (Grand Rapids: Eerdmans, 1960), 32, and Gleason L. Archer, Jr., *A Survey of Old Testament Introduction* (Chicago: Moody, 1964), 63.

Furthermore, Isaiah 53:7 seems to be reflected in Jesus' deliberate silence before his judges (see Mark 14:61; 15:5; Luke 23:9; John 19:9), Isaiah 53:12 in his intercession for his executioners (see Luke 23:34), and Isaiah 53:10 in his "laying down his life" for others (see John 10:11, 15, 17). Martin Hengel, in fact, has argued that Isaiah 53 as a whole provides the basis for both Jesus' famous "ransom sayings" (Matt 20:28; Mark 10:45) and his "supper sayings" (Matt 26:26-28; Mark 14:22-24).[85] R. T. France does not appear to be amiss then when he states that all the Evangelists "accepted [the figure of the Servant of Yahweh] as an appropriate and illuminating model for Jesus mission of vicarious suffering and death for the sins of his people."[86]

Jesus' disciples clearly grasped from his teaching the connection which he specifically drew between Isaiah 53 as prophecy and himself as its fulfillment, for we find the following things recorded in the New Testament about this Song:

1. Philip, when asked by the Ethiopian eunuch about whom Isaiah spoke in 53:7-8, "beginning with this scripture, told him about Jesus" (Acts 8:30-35);
2. Paul refers to Isaiah 53:12 in Philippians 2:7;[87]
3. Peter alludes to Isaiah 53:5, 6, 9, and 11 in 1 Peter 2:22-25; 3:18;
4. Matthew refers to Isaiah 53:4 to Jesus in Matthew 8:17;
5. the Author of Hebrews (whom I have argued elsewhere[88] was

[85]Martin Hengel, *The Atonement: The Origin of the Doctrine in the New Testament*, translated by John Bowden (London: SCM, 1981), 33-75.

[86]R. T. France, "Servant of Yahweh" in *Dictionary of Jesus and the Gospels*, edited by Joel B. Green, Scot McKnight, and I. Howard Marshall (Downers Grove, Illinois: InterVarsity, 1992), 746a.

[87]See my treatment of Philippians 2:7 in *A New Systematic Theology of the Christian Faith* (Nashville, Tenn.: Thomas Nelson, 1998), 263, where I have argued that the Pauline phrase "himself he emptied" is the dynamic equivalent to Isaiah's expression in 53:12, "He poured himself out unto death." The so-called kenosis phrase in this pericope has for its background then our Lord's high-priestly ministry and refers to the Messiah's sacrifice of his life for sinners and not a "self-emptying" on his part of some of his divine attributes alleged by some to have occurred in the act of the Incarnation.

[88]See my *Paul: Missionary Theologian* (Fearn, Ross-shire, Scotland: Christian Focus, 2000), 257-79.

Paul) alludes to Isaiah 53:4-6 when he declares that "Christ was once offered to bear the sins of many"; and

6. John uses Isaiah 53:1 in John 12:38.

In light of both the predictive character of Isaiah's Fourth Servant Song and these explicit usages of Isaiah 53 by Jesus and the New Testament writers, the church from the beginning to the present has believed itself to be justified in seeing both adumbrations and explicit descriptions of the cross work of Jesus Christ throughout Isaiah 53. Therefore, we must not hesitate to call the world's attention to this passage and teach it about Jesus from it.

MICAH'S DIVINE/HUMAN RULER

As with Isaiah 9:6-7 the setting of this prediction in Micah 5:2 is one which envisions the people of God in dire straits. The city of Jerusalem is under siege, but more significant, the Davidic dynasty is at a low ebb. Israel's "judge" (שֹׁפֵט, *shōphēt*) has been "struck on the cheek with a rod" (5:1; MT, 4:14). Micah then delivered the prophecy presently under discussion:

> But you, Bethlehem Ephrathah, [though you are] small among the thousands of Judah,
> From you for me will go forth [the one] to be ruler in Israel, whose goings forth [have been] from of old, [even] from everlasting.

The prophetic utterance itself provides ample warrant for viewing the oracle as a messianic prediction: (1) Bethlehem, being David's birthplace, was a "royal" city; (2) the prediction speaks of him who was to come forth from Bethlehem as being "ruler in Israel"; and (3) as Israel's ruler he would "shepherd" Yahweh's flock in the strength of the Lord and be "great to the ends of the earth" (5:4). This is also clearly the New Testament's understanding. For when Herod inquired of the chief priests and teachers of the Law "where the Messiah was to be born," Matthew reports that they answered, "In Bethlehem of Judea," and that they then cited Micah 5:2 (and 2 Sam 5:2, doubtless due to the suggestion in Mic 5:4) as the basis of their response (Matt 2:3-6).[89] It would be asking a whole lot of the reader to believe that

Matthew, who cites the Old Testament himself a great deal, was merely recording their response with no concurrence on his part in their answer, particularly when we learn from John 7:42 that it was common belief in Israel that the Messiah would come "from David's family and from Bethlehem." Such official (and common) opinion could have come only from Micah 5:2 since it is the only passage that teaches so. Consequently, it is a fair deduction that by his inclusion of the religious leaders' Old Testament citation in his Gospel Matthew was agreeing with both their response and the Old Testament basis for it. I will proceed, therefore, on the assumption that Micah 5:2 is directly messianic and a prediction concerning the Messiah.

There is little significant difference of opinion respecting the meaning of the first two lines: Micah is simply prophesying that the Messiah would be born in Bethlehem. Beyond all doubt, then, being *born* in Bethlehem, the Messiah was to be a man like other men. The true humanity of the Messiah is a clear implicate of this verse but that is not the issue before us now.

The point of dispute turns rather on the intention of the third line—between those who see and those who do not see in it an intimation of the Messiah's pre-existence prior to his birth in Bethlehem. Those who do not see it[90] insist, first, that the noun translated above by "whose goings forth" (מוֹצָאֹתָיו, *môṣāʼōtha*[*y*]*w*) really means "whose origin," and second, that the time phrases, "from of old" (מִקֶּדֶם, *miqqeḏem*) and "from days of eternity" (מִימֵי עוֹלָם, *mîmê ʻôlām*),

---

[89]See D. A. Carson, *Matthew* in *The Expositor's Bible Commentary* (Grand Rapids: Zondervan, 1984), 87-8, for the resolution of the merely formal and not real contradictions between the Hebrew of Micah 5:2 and Matthew's citation of Micah 5:2 which, strictly speaking, follows neither the Massoretic text nor the LXX.

[90]For example, J. M. P. Smith, *A Critical and Exegetical Commentary on Micah, Zephaniah, Nahum, Habbakuk, Obadiah, and Joel* (ICC) (Edinburgh, T. & T. Clark, 1912), 104; John Naish, *The Books of Micah and Habbakuk* (London: National Adult School Union, 1934), 22; Leslie C. Allen, *The Books of Joel, Obadiah, Jonah, and Micah* (Grand Rapids: Eerdmans, 1976), 343-44; Hans Walter Wolff, *Micah the Prophet*, translated by R. D. Gehrke (Reprint; Philadelphia: Fortress, 1981), 93; James D. G. Dunn, *Christology in the Making* (London: SCM, 1980), 70-1, 293, fn. 24; Ralph L. Smith, *Micah-Malachi*, Vol. 32 in *Word Biblical Commentary* (Waco, Texas: Word, 1984), 43-4.

actually refer, as the latter phrase does in Amos 9:11, most probably to the days of David. On this construction, a paraphrase of the third line would read: "whose origin [or roots] goes back to the time of David."

This interpretation, in my opinion, however, is suspect on two accounts, one biblical/theological, the other exegetical. First, this view implies that the messianic idea in Israel (and thus the hope of a messianic King) originated in and grew out of the failed monarchy in Israel. That is to say, as the elect remnant saw less and less reason to pin their hopes on the kings of Israel and Judah, more and more did they begin to long for a King in whom there would be only virtues and no vices and who would be able to do (and would do) for them what the kings before him were unable (or unwilling) to do: to provide for them and to protect and to care for them. But as Edmond Jacob rightly says:

> ...the messianic hope...has...roots which go further back than the institution of Kingship, though the latter gave it its dominant orientation. Since the return of the golden age formed part of the most ancient religious patrimony of Israel it is quite natural to suppose that it also included the hope of the return of man as he existed in the beginning.[91]

The point I am making here is that it is arbitrary, simply on the basis of the reference to Bethlehem, David's city, to insist that Micah's intention was to trace the Messiah's origin back to David and no farther as if that origin sufficiently marked out the point of beginning of Israel's messianic hope. Although the Davidic covenant of 2 Samuel 7 is indeed significant for Israel's messianic vision, the idea of kingship in Israel went back at least to Abraham (Gen 17:6) and was anticipated in Genesis 49:10 and in the Deuteronomic covenant renewal treaty (17:14-20) of the Mosaic age. Ezekiel alludes to Genesis 49:10 in Ezekiel 21:27, evidencing his awareness of the antiquity of the idea of the monarchy and messianism. Certainly the New Testament is also aware of the idea's antiquity (see Matt 1:1-2; Luke 3:23-37; Rom 9:5; Gal 3:16; Heb 7:14). Consequently, as I said, it is arbitrary to suggest

---

[91]Edmond Jacob, *Theology of the Old Testament* (New York: Harpers, 1958), 327.

that the intention of the third line is simply to trace the Messiah's origin back to the time of David and the Davidic covenant and no farther. I am aware that I have offered nothing to this point that proves that another idea is present in the passage. But I have shown that the Messiah's "origin," assuming for the moment that this is the meaning of the noun, can be and often is traced in Scripture back before the time of David. Consequently, there are no grounds for insisting that the verse's intention is simply the tracing of Messiah's origin back to David. In fact—and this feature should not be overlooked—David is not expressly mentioned by name anywhere in the passage.

The issue, of course, must be determined finally exegetically, and this is the second questionable feature about this proposal. The meaning of the clause, all admit, turns ultimately upon the meaning of both the noun מוֹצָאֹתָיו, *môṣā'ōthā(y)w*, and the time phrases following it. The noun is a *hapax*, that is, it occurs only this one time in the Old Testament (the euphemistic Qere reading for מוֹצָאֹתָיו, *môṣā'ōthā(y)w*, has a quite different meaning, namely "latrine," and is meaningless in the context. It is the feminine plural form of מוֹצָא (*môṣā'*), the masculine singular noun, and it is interesting that the feminine *plural* of this noun occurs only here in the Old Testament. The noun in the singular, derived as it is from יָצָא, *yāṣā'*, ("to go forth"), can denote, first, *a concrete entity*, such as an exit (Ezek 42:11), an export (of horses) or (by interpretation) an import (1 Kgs 10:28), or an utterance (Deut 8:3); second, *a place of going forth*, such as a spring of water (2 Kgs 2:21) or a point of departure ("stage"—NIV) (Num 33:2), including within this idea the meaning of "east," as the place of the sun's "going forth" (Ps 75:6 [MT, v 7]), and a "mine," as the place from which silver is drawn (Job 28:1). And it can mean, third, simply the *act itself of going forth* (Hos 6:3). Reflection will show, I think, that a concrete entity of any kind does not fit the context of Micah 5:2. Nor does the idea of a place of departure (the closest idea to "origin") suit the time predicates that follow the plural noun, particularly when one factors in the plurality of the noun ("whose *places* of going forth...are from of old"). This leaves as the most plausible meaning the act itself of going forth, which meaning also most admirably suits the meaning which the *same* root has in the *immediately preceding line*, which we translated "will go forth." To feel the force of what I have just said, perhaps it will help to put the two lines together thus:

> From you [that is, from Bethlehem as his *place* of birth, thereby underscoring his humanity] for me *will go forth* [יֵצֵא, *yēṣē'*] [the one] to be ruler in Israel,
>
> Whose [note that the subject is the ruler in Israel] *goings forth* [מוֹצָאֹתָיו, *môṣā'ōthā(y)w*, from the same root as the verb in the preceding line] [have been] from of old, even from days of eternity [which underscores his deity].

The plural form of the noun hardly allows the RSV's "origin" (the NIV's "origins," though still a somewhat strange turn of phrase in the context does at least take cognizance of the plural form of the noun), whereas the adjacency of the noun to the same root in the preceding line where its meaning is unquestionably "will go forth," powerfully argues for this same meaning for the noun in the third line. And it is not without significance that the LXX construed it this way, translating the noun מוֹצָאֹתָיו, *môṣā'ōthā(y)w* ("goings forth") by ἔξοδοι (*exodoi*, "goings out"), the plural of ἔξοδος (*exodos*, "going out").

As for the time phrases, it is true that מִקֶּדֶם, *miqqeḏem*, "from of old") intends nothing more than "from former times" in isolated contexts, but מִקֶּדֶם, *miqqeḏem*, can also mean "eternity" as in Deuteronomy 33:27 where God is described as the "God of eternity" (אֱלֹהֵי קֶדֶם *'ᵉlōhê qeḏem*) And while מִימֵי עוֹלָם, *mîmê 'ôlām*, "from days of old," may refer to nothing more than to hoary antiquity as in Micah 7:14 where the words refer to the Mosaic (or Patriarchal) Age, עוֹלָם, *'ôlām*, occurs in Proverbs 8:22-23 with מִקֶּדֶם, *miqqeḏem*, to denote the eternity preceding the beginning of the creation of the world! Occurring, then, as these time phrases do with the unusual noun meaning "[*acts* of] going forth," it seems more plausible to think that it is this last sense that is intended. And again, for what it is worth, this is the way the LXX seems to have understood the phrases, for they are rendered in the Greek, ἀπ' ἀρχής (*ap' archēs*, "from the beginning", see 1 John 1:1) and ἐκ ἡμέρον αἰῶνος (*ek hēmeron aiōnos*, "out of days of eternity").

There is no legitimate warrant, then, for interpreting the third line simply as a reference to Messiah's ancient Davidic pedigree. To the contrary, if we give the plural noun its full force, pointing as it does to prior *repeated acts* of going forth on the part of the ruler who was to be born in Bethlehem, we have every reason to include within the time frame allowed by the phrases themselves the idea even of eternity past, and to affirm that the third line refers to the "goings forth" of the Messiah (in the person of the pre-existent Son or Logos) in eternity past to create the world (see John 1:1-3; Col 1:16-17; Heb 1:2), to his numerous subsequent "goings forth" as the "Angel of the Lord" from Patriarchal to Davidic times,[92] and to his constant "goings forth" providentially to sustain and to uphold all things by the word of his power (Col 1:17; Heb 1:3).

If it should be objected that this interpretation (which has an eighth-century B.C. prophet teaching the eternal pre-existence of the Messiah) grants too high and too advanced a Christology for the man and his time, I would simply point out, first, that this Christological perception goes not one iota beyond the conceptions which we have already seen were advanced by David and Isaiah. Keil, of this same opinion, rightly remarks:

> ...this thought [of the Messiah's pre-existence and divine nature] was not strange to the prophetic mind in Micah's time, but is expressed without ambiguity by Isaiah, when he gives the Messiah the name of "the Mighty God."[93]

I would also insist—if the Old Testament prophets were in fact inspired by the Spirit of God as they themselves affirm (see Deut 18:15-20 and the prophetic phrase, "Thus the Lord says") and as the New Testament affirms of them (2 Tim 3:16; 1 Pet 1:10-11; 2 Pet 1:20-21)—that it would have been no more difficult for an inspired prophet to speak of the Messiah's pre-existence and eternality than for him to predict by name the precise place of his birth seven hundred and fifty years prior to the event.[94] If he could do the latter, what obstacle, in principle, stands in his way of doing the former? No such

---

[92]See our discussion of the Angel of the Lord above.

[93]Carl Friedrich Keil, *The Twelve Minor Prophets* in *Biblical Commentary on the Old Testament*, translated by James Martin (Grand Rapids: Eerdmans, 1949), I, 481.

[94]An unnamed prophet also spoke of Josiah by name three hundred years before his time (1 Kgs 13:2), and Isaiah spoke of Cyrus by name two hundred years before his time (Isa 44:28; 45:1).

obstacle exists. Therefore, for these reasons, I would urge that Micah intended to refer to the Messiah's pre-existence prior to his birth in Bethlehem and thus by implication he taught the deity of the Messiah. And I may add, this is the historic interpretation of the Christian church and the position of most evangelicals today.

I will conclude our study of this messianic vignette by citing the opinions of two Old Testament theologians. E. J. Young affirms:

> In vs. 2 the future birth of the messianic king is declared. His humanity is set forth, in that he is to come forth out of Bethlehem, and his true deity, in that the places of his going forth...[are] from of yore...from days of eternity.[95]

And J. Barton Payne writes:

> Micah's revelation...describes the Bethlehem-born Messiah as One "whose goings forth are from of old, from everlasting" (5:2), a quality which constitutes further witness to his eternal deity.[96]

DANIEL'S "MAN-LIKE FIGURE"

During the Babylonian exile, Daniel the prophet, whose historicity is vouched for by both Ezekiel (14:14, 20; 28:3), himself an exilic prophet, and Jesus the Prophet *par excellence* (Matt 24:15), had a "vision at night" (Dan 7), in which he saw "four great beasts" rising out of the churning sea (7:3), these four beasts corresponding to the four great ancient empires of Daniel 2 (Neo-Babylonia, Medo-Persia, Greece, and Rome) (see 7:17). Just as he saw a fifth kingdom appear in the former chapter ("the Kingdom of God") which crushed the previous four kingdoms, then filling the earth (2:35) and enduring forever (2:44),

---

[95]Edward J. Young, *An Introduction to the Old Testament* (Grand Rapids: Eerdmans, 1949), 26. Note should be taken that apparently Young believes that the idea of "place" is in the noun מוֹצָאֹתָיו, *môṣāʼōthā(y)w*. While he does not state his reason, it may be due to the מ, *m*, prefix on the noun which admittedly can specify "place" on the analogy of מַמְלָכָה, *mamlākâ* ("kingdom"). See *Gesenius' Hebrew Grammar*, 236-37, par. 85 e-m, particularly g. See also Young, *The Study of Old Testament Theology Today* (London: James Clarke, 1958), 98.

[96]J. Barton Payne, *The Theology of the Older Testament* (Grand Rapids: Zondervan, 1962), 263.

so also in this latter vision in chapter 7, after the fourth beast had appeared on the world scene, as Daniel looked, "thrones were set in place and the Ancient of Days took his seat" (7:9). Then unfolds a court scene (7:10), in which the "terrifying, frightening, and very powerful fourth beast" (7:7) and its boastful "little horn" (7:8, 11, 20) who had been persecuting the people of God (7:25) are judged, slain, and destroyed (7:11, 26). At this point Daniel tells us:

> In my vision at night I looked, and there before me was one like a son of man [Aram, בַּר אֱנָשׁ, *bar ᵉnāsh*], coming with the clouds of heaven. He approached the Ancient of Days and was led into his presence. He was given authority, glory, and sovereign power; all peoples, nations, and men of every language worshiped him. His dominion is an everlasting dominion that will not pass away, and his kingdom is one that will never be destroyed. (7:13-14)

Just as the people of Jesus' day, perplexed by his use of this title, inquired of him, "Who is this Son of man?" (John 12:34), so also we would ask the same question of Daniel here.

Daniel, of course, was not the first Old Testament writer to employ the "son of man" phrase. The term בֶּן־אָדָם, (*ben 'ādhām*, lit., "a son of man") occurs in Numbers 23:19; Job 16:21; 25:6; 35:8; Psalms 8:4 (Heb, 8:5); 146:3; Isaiah 51:12; 56:2; Jeremiah 49:18, 33; 50:40; 51:43; and Daniel 10:16 where it simply means "[a] man" ("men" in Dan 10:16), each occurrence standing as it does in parallel to אִישׁ, *'îsh*, אֱנוֹשׁ, *ᵉnôsh*, or אָדָם, *'ādhām* (with the exception of the occurrence in Job 16:21 where it is parallel with גֶּבֶר, *gebher*, and the occurrences in Psalm 146:3 and Daniel 10:16 where the phrase stands alone). It also occurs in Psalm 80:17 (Heb, 80:18) where it stands in parallel with אִישׁ יְמִינֶךָ (*'îsh yᵉmînekā*, lit., "the man of your right hand"), and in Ezekiel (no fewer than ninety-three times, as in 2:1, 3, 6, 8, etc.) and Daniel 8:17 where the term is a term of address directed to these prophets themselves. The term בֶּן־אֱנוֹשׁ, (*ben ᵉnôsh*, lit., "a son of man") occurs in Psalm 144:3 and means the same thing as בֶּם־אָדָם, *ben 'ādhām*, standing as it does in parallel with אָדָם, *'ādhām*. The occurrence in Daniel 7:13—the one under present investigation—is the only Old Testament occurrence in an apocalyptic context.

There is virtually universal accord among Old and New Testament scholars alike on two points: first, that the Aramaic phrase בַּר אֱנָשׁ, *bar ʾᵉnāsh*, "a son of man," is a Semitic idiom for "a man"[97]; accordingly, what Daniel says is that he saw "a man-like figure" approaching the Ancient of Days; second, that by this "man-like figure" the vision intends a contrast between the first four kingdoms which are symbolized by *beasts* and the last one which is symbolized by the "*man*-like figure," the point being that as different in nature as a man is from beasts, so radically different in nature is the fifth kingdom ("the Kingdom of God") from the four kingdoms ("kingdoms of evil men") that preceded it.

Beyond these two matters of general accord, Old Testament scholars have divided over whether the "man-like figure" is symbolic of a corporate entity or an individual. Among critical scholars, there is such wide agreement, on the basis of their shared interpretation of 7:17, 22, 27, that the "man-like figure" is symbolic of a corporate entity, namely, the "saints of the Most High" (who are interpreted variously as the faithful Jews during the persecution of Antiochus IV Epiphanes, the holy angels, the "elect," or the "people of God" in general), *with no reference to an individual whatsoever*, that Hartman believes he may speak of a "consensus."[98] Porteous' opinion may be cited, for its clarity, as representative of this position:

---

[97]See, for example, C. F. Keil, *The Book of the Prophet Daniel* in *Biblical Commentary on the Old Testament*, translated by M. G. Easton (Edinburgh: T. & T. Clark, 1872), 234; Geerhardus Vos, *The Self-Disclosure of Jesus* (Reprint; Phillipsburg, New Jersey: Presbyterian and Reformed, 1978), 44; James A. Montgomery, *A Critical and Exegetical Commentary on the Book of Daniel* (ICC) (Edinburgh: T. & T. Clark, 1927), 303; Edward J. Young, *The Prophecy of Daniel* (Grand Rapids: William B. Eerdmans, 1949), 154; Vincent Taylor, *The Names of Jesus* (London: Macmillan, 1953), 25; Oscar Cullmann, *The Christology of the New Testament* (London: SCM, 1959), 138; I. Howard Marshall, *The Origins of New Testament Christology* (Downers Grove, Illinois: Inter-Varsity, 1976), 64; Louis F. Hartman, *The Book of Daniel* (AB) (Garden City, New York: Doubleday, 1978), 87; Joyce G. Baldwin, *Daniel: An Introduction and Commentary* (Leicester: Inter-Varsity, 1978), 142; Maurice Casey, *Son of Man* (London: SPCK, 1979), 28; and particularly G. Vermes, Appendix E in Matthew Black, *An Aramaic Approach to the Gospels and Acts* (Oxford: University Press, Third Edition, 1967), 310-18.

[98]Hartman, *The Book of Daniel*, 85.

> ...if the figure of one like a son of man had, in the intention of the writer, referred to an individual, it is difficult to believe that there would have been no reflection of this in the interpretation. Instead, it is clearly implied that the symbol which interests us so much because of its subsequent history was understood by the writer as signifying the saints of the Most High.[99]

Evangelicals have responded, however, by pointing out that if this is so—if it is the "saints" alone who are symbolized and who therefore receive the authority, glory, sovereign power, and religious service of all peoples, nations, and languages in 7:14, the kingdom itself forever and ever in 7:18, and the sovereignty, power, and greatness of the kingdoms under the whole heaven as an everlasting kingdom in 7:27, *it would herald an unheard-of, the first-of-its-kind kingdom without a king in human history*. Accordingly, Keil, for example, urges that the "man-like figure" must possess, in addition to its corporate character, an individualistic aspect as well:

> ...the delivering of the kingdom to the people of God does not, according to the prophetic mode of contemplation, exclude the Messiah as its king, but much rather includes Him, inasmuch as Daniel, like the other prophets, knows nothing of a kingdom without a head, a messianic kingdom without the King Messiah.[100]

Geerhardus Vos also states:

> The objection raised against [the individualizing interpretation] from verse 18, where "the saints of the Most High" are said to receive the kingdom, is by no means conclusive. If it proved anything at all, it would prove that the author was not only non-messianic but that he was pointedly anti-messianic in his eschatology [which we know he was not from Dan 9:25-26—RLR]. To allow kings for the world-powers [see 7:17 where the Aramaic reads "kings" and not "kingdoms" as the NIV reads, and 7:24] and to leave the final rule of God kingless could hardly be interpreted on any other principle. And such an anti-messianic program would have no analogy in the Old Testament.[101]

---

[99]Norman W. Porteous, *Daniel: A Commentary* (London: SCM, 1965), 112.
[100]Keil, *The Book of the Prophet Daniel*, 235.
[101]Vos, *The Self-Disclosure of Jesus*, 45-6.

Moreover, it is simply a gratuitous remark with no basis in fact for Porteous to say that there is "no reflection of [the individualizing view] in the interpretation," for in 7:17 there is indeed just this "reflection" which Porteous and others claim is lacking. Vos explains:

> ...to grant that the usage [of "son of man"] in Daniel is descriptive [of the visionary figure seen coming with the clouds of heaven] is not quite equivalent to granting that it is purely symbolical of the Kingdom of God, just as the beasts of verses 2-8 are claimed to be symbolic of the world-powers. Both contentions are inexact. *Neither the beasts nor the man-like figure directly symbolize the powers for which they stand. They do so only indirectly, through symbolizing the rulers of these several kingdoms.* Therefore it is said in the subsequent interpretation: "These great beasts, which are four, are four *kings*," (verse 17). The phrase "like a man" in like manner proximately describes the King, although this does not, of course, exclude the possibility of the thus described King symbolizing the nature of the Kingdom over which He is to rule. We may assume, then, that the Messiah is actually introduced in the passage in Daniel 7; that the phrase "like unto a man" is not a title, but a description of His appearance, and that through this description of His appearance He becomes collectively symbolical of the Kingdom of God. The collective symbolism is recognized; only it is not conceded to be an argument against the presence in the passage of a concrete figure. Nor can it be reasonably doubted that this figure is the Messiah.[102]

Vos does not stand alone in this opinion. Leupold, commenting on 7:17, also writes:

> ...just as certainly as...we may say that the beasts represent kings, just as properly...we may say that they represent kingdoms (see v.

---

[102]Vos, *The Self-Disclosure of Jesus*, 45; emphasis supplied. Vos adds this comment on the next to last sentence quoted on 45, fn. 4:

> A special reason facilitating the transition from the purely symbolic into the concretely descriptive of a single person lies in this, that the kings of the world-kingdoms are a succession of rulers and as such are incapable of being represented otherwise than symbolically, whereas the Ruler of the Kingdom of God is One, without successors, so that to depict him symbolically must mean at the same time to describe him personally. The Messiah is always One and undivided.

> 23). The approach to our verse which insists that kings may be referred to supports our interpretation of v. 13 that there, too, the king of the heavenly realm is referred to.[103]

Cullmann concurs:

> In vv. 15ff. the apocalyptic writer identifies the Son of Man as the 'saints of the Most High'. We certainly should not lose sight of this identification. Nevertheless we must ask why it is as 'man' that the nation of the saints is contrasted with the four beasts. It has been rightly pointed out [by H. Gressmann] that the explanation of the vision contains a certain inconsistency: the beasts are interpreted as kings [7:17], as *representatives*, of the world empires, but the 'man' is the nation of the saints itself. The incongruity suggests that the 'man' may also originally have been a representative of the nation of saints. Representation easily becomes identity in Judaism. According to the Jewish concept of representation, the representative can be identified with the group he represents.[104]

I. Howard Marshall, disputing Morna Hooker's view that the "Son of man" is simply a symbol of the people of God and thus a collective entity, writes:

> ...although this appears to be what the interpretation of the vision implies, it is exposed to the objection that the original vision seems to refer to a single individual and that the probable history of the figure points to it being the representation of an individual. We can square this history with the collective significance of the 'Son of man' in the interpretation by noting that a group of people can be represented by their leader...If the 'Son of man' is the leader of the 'saints of the Most High', he can properly be said to represent them, or even to be them, an identification all the more easy to make in the ancient Semitic world where 'the one' and 'the many' were more closely associated than in modern, western thinking. This individual 'messianic' interpretation of the 'Son of man' best suits the nature of the description in Daniel 7.[105]

---

[103]H. C. Leupold, *Exposition of Daniel* (Reprint; Grand Rapids: Baker, 1969), 317.

[104]Cullmann, *The Christology of the New Testament*, 140. See also E. J. Young, *The Messianic Prophecies of Daniel* (Delft: Uitgeverij Van Keulen, 1954), 43-4.

[105]Marshall, *The Origins of New Testament Christology*, 66-7.

And J. A. Motyer declares:

> ...there is a double description of the beasts who are the enemies of the saints. V. 17 says 'these four great beasts...are four kings' and v. 23 says the fourth beast 'shall be a fourth kingdom'. The figures are both individual (kings) and corporate (kingdoms). We must adopt the same preliminary reference for the 'one like a son of man'. Next, we must view the king-kingdom relationship in its OT context. The king is prior, and the kingdom is derivative. It is not the kingdom which fashions the king, but the reverse. As for the beast-kings, they are the personal enemies of the kingdom of the saints, and they involve their kingdoms with them; equally the 'one like a son of man' receives universal dominion, and in this is implicated the dominion of his people...On this ground it is urged that the 'one like a son of man' is the Messianic individual.[106]

To this point I have consciously avoided any reference to Jesus' employment of the term as a self-designation in order to underscore the fact that the "individualizing" (and thus the directly messianic) interpretation of the passage can be sustained on the basis of an exegesis of the passage itself. But it is true, as E. J. Young says, that "the conclusive proof that this [the individualizing] view is correct is the application of the title to Himself by our Lord."[107]

We will proceed, then, in our exposition on the assumption that the "man-like figure" in Daniel 7:13 is an individual—even the Messiah, the representative, of course, of the people of God—and thus that Daniel 7:13-14 is messianic to the core.

The fact having been established exegetically, then, that the "man-like figure" is Daniel's symbolic depiction of the Messiah, it necessarily follows from the details of the vision that, though "man-like" for purposes of contrast with the beast-empires and their kings, the Messiah is also other than man ("more than man" is a more accurate description) in nature, that is to say, he is a *superhuman*—let us say it frankly—even a *divine* figure. This is evident from the following data: first, there is an "unearthly" heavenly cast about the scene which lifts the entire vision out of the *natural* order of things. Second, "coming

---

[106]J. A. Motyer, "Messiah. I. In the Old Testament" in *The Illustrated Bible Dictionary* (Wheaton: Tyndale, 1980), 2, 993.

[107]Young, *The Messianic Prophecies of Daniel*, 155.

with clouds," that is, coming in connection with or "surrounded by" (Keil) clouds, as he does is a phrase descriptive of both the divine presence and activity for purposes both of executing judgment against his enemies, which is the dominant theme in Daniel 7 (see Pss 18:9-11; 97:2; 104:3; Isa 19:1; Nah 1:3; Jer 4:13), as well as of delivering and protecting his "saints" (Ex 13:21; 19:9; 1 Kgs 8:10-12; Ezek 10:4).

That such a "cloud-related coming" is descriptive of the majestic coming of a divine person is supported by an incident in the earthly ministry of our Lord. When he responded to the inquiry of the high priest as to whether he was the Messiah or not by saying: "I am ['Εγώ εἰμι, *Egō eimi*], and you will see the Son of man *sitting at the right hand of the Mighty One* and *coming on the clouds of heaven*" (Mark 14:62; Matt 26:64 [see 24:30]; Rev 1:7; 14:14), it is evident that he intended both descriptive phrases attached to "Son of man" to be taken as majestic ascriptions of deity to this individual. For evidence that the first phrase means this we have only to refer to Psalm 110:1. To sit at the right hand of God is to participate in the dignity and power of the Lord of Hosts. The scriptural bridge between the Son of man figure and the idea of his sitting at the right hand of the mighty God is provided by Psalm 80:17, in which verse, in an age of national decline, the Psalmist cries: "Let your hand rest on *the man at your right hand*, the *son of man you have raised up for yourself*." Here is a prayer that a national hero, under the good hand of God, would restore fallen, humiliated Israel to national and spiritual health once again. It can hardly be doubted that it was his reflection upon this verse which lay behind our Lord's combining the idea of Daniel's "man-like figure" and the Psalmist's "man sitting at the Lord's right hand" and applying them both to himself. Taking both descriptive phrases in Mark 14:62 together, it is apparent that he intended them both to be ascriptions of deity. His religious enemies certainly construed them to be such, because they immediately branded his statement a blasphemy, that is, an unwarranted claim to deity, which charge against him there is no indication he made any attempt to correct. Clearly, then, both exegetically and theologically, to "come with the clouds of heaven" is descriptive of the coming of a *divine* person.[108]

---

[108]Warfield, "The Divine Messiah in the Old Testament" in *Biblical and Theological Studies* (Philadelphia: Presbyterian and Reformed, 1952), 118.

There are yet two other indications in the Daniel passage of the man-like figure's divine character. First, the free access which he enjoys as he is escorted into the presence of the Ancient of Days suggests his unique supernatural character. Finally, the universal and everlasting dominion which he exercises implies that he must be in possession of divine attributes (see Pss 2, 45, 110; Isa 9:6-7; Mic 5:4, 5a). These details are all suggestive of his deity.

In his article, "The Divine Messiah in the Old Testament," after giving an overview of the critical handling of Daniel 7:13-14 by the leading Old Testament spokesmen of his day (S. R. Driver, H. Schultz, E. Riehm, J. Grill, N. Schmidt, T. K. Cheyne, P. Volz, H. Gressmann, and E. Sellin), Benjamin Warfield declared that the main result of the discussion current in his time was that

> in the "one like unto a son of man" of Dan. vii. 13, we have a superhuman figure, a figure to whose superhuman character justice is not done until it is recognized as expressly divine. It was understood to be a superhuman figure by everyone who appealed to it and built his messianic hopes upon its basis throughout the whole subsequent development of the Jewish Church. Wherever, in the Apocalyptic literature we meet with the figure of the Son of Man, it is transcendentally conceived. When our Lord Himself derived from it His favorite self-designation of Son of Man, He too took it over in a transcendental sense; and meant by applying it to Himself to present Himself as a heavenly Being who had come forth from heaven and descended to earth on a mission of mercy to lost men. On every occasion on which our Lord called Himself the Son of Man thus, He bears His witness to the transcendental character of the figure presented to Daniel. There is no apparent reason today why His judgment of the seer's meaning should be revised.[109]

No evidence has been forthcoming in the field of Old Testament studies since Warfield's day that would warrant the church to draw now another conclusion different from that which Warfield drew in

---

See also R. H. Charles, *A Critical and Exegetical Commentary on the Book of Daniel* (Oxford: Clarendon, 1929), 186.

[109]Warfield, "The Divine Messiah in the Old Testament" in *Biblical and Theological Studies*, 122-23 (Warfield's discussion of the Daniel 7 prophecy, 116-23, though dated, is still profitable reading).

his day. Indeed, when one adds to this conclusion Jesus' description of himself as the Danielic Son of man, everything that Warfield asserts here and more is borne out. As we shall see when we address the issue of Jesus' self-witness, for him the Son of man sayings, above all others, embodied his conception of Messiahship; and beyond question its associations were supernatural, even divine, in character. Evangelical Christians, as they always have, may continue to believe that Daniel intended by his "man-like figure" to confront his readers with a superhuman, indeed, just a divine Messiah and the New Testament, as we shall argue, confirms that Jesus understood himself to be this Danielic Son of man!

ZECHARIAH'S PIERCED LORD

With some seventy-one quotations and allusions from Zechariah (thirty-one from chapters 1-8, forty from chapters 9-14) appearing in the New Testament—with twenty-seven of these seventy-one found in the Gospels[110]—it is not surprising that at least one of them relates to the concern of this present essay.

In the oracle which begins at 12:1, after his promise to restore Judah and Jerusalem at some future day to world-wide prominence (12:2-9), the Lord (Yahweh), who had in 12:1 described himself as "the one who stretches out the heavens, who lays the foundations of the earth, and who forms the spirit of man within him," that is, even Yahweh, the Creator (see John 1:1-3; Col 1:16-17; Heb 1:2), declares in 12:10:

> And I will pour out upon the house of David and upon the inhabitants of Jerusalem, the Spirit of grace and supplication; and they shall look unto me whom [אֵת אֲשֶׁר, *'ēth 'ªsher*][111] they pierced, and shall mourn for him as one mourns for an only child.

---

[110]W. S. LaSor, D. A. Hubbard, and F. W. Bush, *Old Testament Survey* (Grand Rapids: Eerdmans, 1982), 499.

[111]The אֵת, *ēth*, is not to be construed "loosely [as] another preposition" as S. R. Driver suggests in his *The Minor Prophets* (Edinburgh: T. C. & E. C. Jack, 1906), 266 (so also H. G. Mitchell, *A Critical and Exegetical Commentary on Haggai and Zechariah* [ICC] [Edinburgh: T. & T. Clark, 1912], 355), but as the sign of the definite accusative before the relative pronoun to indicate that the pronoun is to be construed as the accusative after "pierced."

As we had occasion to say in our earlier discussion of Micah 5:2, for the one for whom the New Testament is an authoritative guide to the Old Testament, there can be no doubt that here we have to do with a messianic prophecy. Immediately after his recording of Jesus' death on the cross, and specifically in reference to the Roman soldiers' acts of abstaining from breaking Jesus' legs (the *crurifragium*) and instead piercing his side with a spear, John, for whom Jesus is the *divine* Agent in creation (see John 1:1-3, 18; 20:28; 1 John 5:20), writes:

> ...these things happened in order that the Scripture might be fulfilled: "Not a bone of his was broken," and again another Scripture says: "They will look unto him whom they pierced." (John 19:33-37)

Again, in Revelation 1:7, clearly referring to the glorified, divine Messiah in the person of Jesus who "freed us from our sins by his own blood" (1:5), as a thematic statement of the ensuing content of the entire Apocalypse, John writes:

> Behold, he is coming with the clouds [see Dan 7:13; Matt 26:64; Mark 14:62],
> And every eye shall see him,
> *Even those who pierced him*,
> And all the tribes of the earth shall mourn because of him.

In these references to "seeing him," "piercing him," and "mourning because of him," are unmistakable allusions to Zechariah 12:10.

All of this means, of course, in the context of Zechariah 12:10 itself only one thing: the one who is pierced there is none other than the divine Messiah himself—regarded in the prophetic vision as already having been "enfleshed" (ἐν σάρκι), for it is Yahweh who speaks in the first person throughout this segment of the oracle and accordingly who specifically states that the house of David and the inhabitants of Jerusalem "will look unto me whom they pierced."

Taken at face value, here is indeed one of the more brilliant "highlights [of the Messiah's deity] shining out brightly on the surface of a pervasive implication"—to borrow Warfield's expression once again. And as further indication of the fact—in addition to his self-identity as the Creator in 12:1—that it is the divine Messiah who is the referent here, his reference to his "pouring out the Spirit of grace and supplication upon the house of David and the inhabitants of Jerusalem" points likewise in the same direction inasmuch as the Messiah (Jesus) is specifically designated in the New Testament as the one who would baptize men with, that is, "pour out" upon them, the Spirit (see Matt 3:11 John 1:33 Acts 1:5 with Acts 2:17, 33).

Some scholars, however, are not content to take the passage as it stands but make every conceivable effort to evacuate the passage of any and all references to the Messiah and his deity. These efforts begin, not surprisingly, with the expediency of textual emendation. Despite the fact that the original Hebrew of 12:10 clearly reads "they will look unto me" and has the support of the large majority of reliable Hebrew manuscripts, the LXX, the Old Latin, the Vulgate, the Syriac Peshitta, the Aramaic Targums, and the Greek versions of Aquilla, Symmachus, and Theodotion, some scholars and modern versions such as the Revised Standard Version, the Jehovah's Witnesses' *New World Translation of the Holy Scriptures*, and Moffatt's version, have chosen to follow a minority of unreliable Hebrew manuscripts and have changed the "unto me" to "unto him."

The New English Bible, apparently following Theodotion's second-century A.D. retranslation of the Hebrew text in which the preposition εἰς, *eis*, is introduced before the relative ὧν, *hōn*, (Heb, אֲשֶׁר, *'ᵃsher*), has chosen to retain both pronouns with the resultant rather bizarre rendering: "...they shall look on me, on him whom they have pierced." In this way, the *direct* presence of the Messiah's deity is effectively removed from the verse. We must intrude the word "direct" here for I would submit that his deity is still present indirectly.

An argument adduced in favor of emending the pointing of אֵלַי (*'ēlay*, "unto me") to read simply "unto" is the fact that the third person is found five word-units farther in the text in the phrase,"they shall mourn for him." This, it is said, strongly suggests that the third person ("unto him whom they pierced") is most likely the true reading in the phrase under discussion.

Now the presence of the third-person pronoun in the following phrase is factual enough, but it is not a conclusive argument that the former first-person reference must be emended to harmonize with it.

I say this on three grounds: first is the fact that the reading "unto me," as we have already noted, is supported by the vast majority of ancient witnesses; second, the "unto me" is by far the harder reading. That is to say, it is readily conceivable why a scribe would alter "unto me" to read simply "unto," but it is not readily apparent why a scribe would change the simple "unto" to "unto me." Even though he himself prefers the easier reading and accordingly emends the text, H.G. Mitchell acknowledges the arbitrary character of this choice when he writes:

> The point may...be made, and, in fact, has been made...that ["unto]" is the easier reading; hence it is more probable that it is an error for ["unto me"] than *vice versa*. There is great force in this objection. Indeed, it so weakens the case for ["unto"] that those who feel the incongruity of the Massoretic text will have to resort to emendation.[112]

And third, the shift from the first to the third person may be an instance of either the common *enallage* (a grammatical change) of verbal number frequently met with in the speeches of Yahweh (see the many instances where Yahweh, as the first person speaker, refers to himself in a given speech in the third person as Yahweh) or the differentiation-identity pattern we have already had occasion to note for the reader (see Zech 2:10-11; MT, 2:14-15) in which the Messiah is both personally identified with God and yet, at the same time and in the same context, distinguished from him.[113]

A second expediency commonly taken to avoid the traditional view

---

[112]Mitchell, *A Critical and Exegetical Commentary on Haggai and Zechariah*, 335. Contrary to Mitchell's thinking, the fact that both of John's allusions to Zechariah 12:10 speak of the Messiah in the third person does not "point the way" in such an emendation. It is a well-known fact that the New Testament writers quote the Old Testament with a certain flexibility and freedom. Furthermore, it is easily discernible, since as John wrote the divine Messiah (surely *for John* the Messiah was divine) had already made his historical appearance with his deity beyond doubt and his "piercing" already a *fait accompli* by that time, how John could resolve the prophet's statement and the fulfillment in the now-past historical event itself by referring to the identified "divine" and "pierced" historical Jesus in the third person.

[113]Carl Friedrich Keil, *The Twelve Minor Prophets* in the *Biblical Commentary on the Old Testament*, translated by James Martin (Edinburgh: T. & T. Clark, 1871), II, 388.

is to concede the legitimacy of the first-person reading ("unto me") but to construe the meaning of "whom they pierced" in a figurative rather than a literal sense (even Calvin errs here) and to suggest accordingly that what the verse means is that the Lord was emotionally "pierced" by the insult he received through the sin and neglect of his people. A variation of this view is that the Lord was "pierced" when his *representative* (who is variously interpreted by the commentators as Zerubbabel, Onias III [assassinated in 170 B.C.], Simon the Maccabee [assassinated in 134 B.C.], or, speaking collectively, the godly remnant) was ill-treated.

Against this second view I must register three objections: first, while I am not saying that the verb could never under any circumstances bear a figurative meaning, it is nonetheless a fact that—with the just barely possible exception in Lamentations 4:9—in every other instance where it occurs outside of our present verse (Num 25:8; Judg 9:54; 1 Sam 31:4; 1 Chr 10:4; Isa 13:15; Jer 37:10; 51:4; Zech 13:3), the verb means "to pierce, thrust through" in the plain *literal* sense; second, a figurative "piercing" of the Lord as the result of his people's insults or even as the result of mistreating his representative hardly explains the deep penitence and unprecedented sorrow of the entire nation—described in the poignant terms of a comparable lamentation over the *death* of an "only son"—which ensues when the people under the conviction of the Spirit of grace and supplication reflect upon him. And third, John's specific designation of the fulfillment of this prophecy in the Roman soldier's *literal* piercing of Jesus' side (as the climactic and final event in Christ's mortal sufferings) disallows in the most decisive manner the figurative sense of the word.

Yet a third expedient has been suggested, and that is the repunctuation of the sentence thus: "And they shall look unto me. [As for] him whom they pierced, they shall mourn for him...." But this suggestion has in the main only the wish that it might be so to commend it, for while it is (barely) grammatically possible, it is hardly the first interpretation that would commend itself to one's notice. In addition, it is not supported by the Massoretic punctuation which places the major break in the sentence after "...whom they pierced," with only the disjunctive accent having a force equivalent to a English comma before the major divider in the sentence coming after "unto me." No version suggests such a punctuation either. It simply has the earmarks of a case of theological "reaching" in order to avoid the obvious and will not commend itself to the sober scholar.

The final expedient employed to deny any reference to the Messiah is the argument based upon the tenses of the two verbs involved, the first ("shall look") being future (a perfect waw consecutive), the second ("pierced") being past (a simple perfect.) Mitchell argues from these features in the sentence thus:

> ...while the effusion of the spirit and the effect produced by it ["shall look unto"] are evidently future, the act of piercing the nameless victim belongs to the past. This means that the one pierced is not the Messiah, whose advent, all will agree, was still future when these words were written, but someone who had at the time already suffered martyrdom.[114]

On the surface, this argument appears so plausible that it might convince the unwary. But only a moment's reflection will disclose the weakness of the argument. By the time that the Lord who is speaking actually pours out the Spirit of grace, which admittedly was still future when these words were written, he will have been "pierced" and hence he speaks of the "piercing"—from the perspective of the time of the Spirit's effusion—as a past event. This is obviously the intent of the verse.

I conclude, then, with the older evangelical exegetes, as a consequence of this entire line of argument, that Zechariah 12:10 is messianic in intent and as such depicts a *divine* Messiah in that the Lord (יהוה, *Yahweh*) himself—here the Creator and Baptizer of men (whom the New Testament identifies as the Son and Logos of God)—speaks of his crucifixion under the vivid imagery of "piercing."

---

[114]Mitchell, *A Critical and Exegetical Commentary on Haggai and Zechariah*, 330.

MALACHI'S MESSENGER OF THE COVENANT

In Malachi 3:1 the prophet speaks of "the Messenger of the covenant" (מַלְאַךְ הַבְּרִית, *mal'ak habb^erîth*). The setting for this reference is as follows: the backslidden priests and people of Malachi's day had been complaining against the Lord because of what appeared to them to be inequities in God's dealings with them. It seemed to them that the good men of the land (of course, they included themselves within this category) were being mistreated while evildoers prospered. Their complaint against God was being expressed in two forms: "All who do evil are good in the eyes of the Lord, and with them he is well-pleased," and "Where is the God of justice?" (2:17).

The "wearied" (that is, offended) God of Hosts responded to their vented skepticism regarding the righteousness of his character with the words of the verse under consideration:

> "Behold, I am going to send my messenger,
> and he will prepare the way before me;
> And suddenly the Lord [הָאָדוֹן, *hā'ādôn*] whom you are seeking,
> even the messenger of the covenant whom you are desiring—
> Behold, he will come!"
> says the Lord of Hosts [יהוה צְבָאוֹת, *Yahweh ṣebhā'ôth*].

A paraphrase will bring out the salient point of God's response: "You are asking, 'Where is the God of Justice.' All right, I will come to you—I, the Lord whom you are seeking; I, the Messenger of the covenant whom you are desiring."

That this is clearly the import of the divine response is evident from the following facts: first, that the Lord declares that it is he himself who would come is apparent both from the phrase "before *me*," and from the fact that *his* coming is what the people with pious hypocrisy were demanding—nothing less would satisfy their ill-founded insistence that the God of justice manifest himself; second, that "the Lord who would come suddenly to his temple" and "the messenger of the covenant who would come" are to be regarded as one and the same person is evident from the unmistakable parallelism between the phrases "whom you are seeking" (אֲשֶׁר־אַתֶּם מְבַקְשִׁים, *'^asher 'attem m^ebhaqshîm*) and "whom you are desiring"

אֲשֶׁר־אַתֶּם חֲפֵצִים, *'ªsher 'attem ḥªphētsîm*) attached respectively to the two titles; and third, that these two titles are to be construed appositionally with the "me" in the phrase "before me" is evident from the fact that it is *his* appearance that the people are demanding and that it is the Lord whom they are seeking and the messenger whom they are desiring who will come in response to their vented rage against him. This third point receives further support from the fact that הָאָדוֹן, *hā'ādôn*, is interchangeable with יהוה, Yahweh, and thus can be identical to him as proved by such verses as Zechariah 4:14; 6:5 ("the אֲדוֹן, *'ªdhôn*, of all the earth") and from the fact that הָאָדוֹן, *hā'ādôn*, in 3:1 is Yahweh as evidenced from the reference to "*his* temple" as the place to which הָאָדוֹן, *hā'ādôn*, would come.

These two facts are now clear: (1) the "me" in the phrase "before me" is further defined as "the Lord whom you are seeking," and "the messenger of the covenant whom you are desiring," that is to say, the three phrases refer to one and the same divine person; and (2) this divine person declares that, as the Lord being sought and the Messenger being desired, he would suddenly come to his temple in response to their vented unhappiness with his dealings with them. These conclusions will satisfy all except those who, perhaps anticipating the obvious conclusion, for *a priori* reasons choose to twist the passage to make it say what it does not say.

But there is another person mentioned in the verse about whom we have said nothing to this point—the servant-messenger whom the Lord announced he would send to prepare the way before him, the Lord and the greater messenger of the covenant. Who is this second person who also bears the epithet of "messenger"? If he can be identified, inasmuch as he is expressly said to be the Lord's forerunner, then the Lord himself who comes after him, whose way will have been prepared by the servant-messenger, can also be identified.

The best Old Testament clue to his identity is provided by the prophecy of Malachi itself. In 4:5-6 (MT, 3:23-24), God declares:

> Behold, I am going to send to you Elijah the prophet before the great and terrible Day of the Lord comes. And he will turn the hearts of the fathers to the sons and the hearts of the sons to the fathers, that I may not come and strike the land with a curse.

Note should be taken that here as in 3:1 the Lord speaks of his own coming *after* someone else had come, and also that this prior person was to do a work preparatory to his coming. These parallels between 3:1 and 4:5-6 clearly suggest that the messenger who was to be sent to prepare the way before the Lord in 3:1 and the "Elijah the prophet" who was to turn the hearts of the fathers to the sons in 4:5-6 are to be understood as one and the same person. Old Testament scholarship is virtually universally agreed on the validity of this connection.

For those who are willing to bow before New Testament authority, there can be no doubt regarding the fulfillment of this Elijah prophecy. Malachi's "Elijah" was John, the son of Zechariah, the six-month-older relative (cousin?) of Jesus Christ. This is clear, first, from Gabriel's declaration to Zechariah on the occasion of his announcement to the elderly priest that he and his wife Elizabeth were to have a son (Luke 1:16-17):

> Many of the sons of Israel he will turn to the Lord their God and *he will go before him* [that is, the Lord their God] *in the spirit and power of Elijah to turn the hearts of the fathers* to the children and the disobedient to the wisdom of the righteous—*to make ready for the Lord a prepared people.*

The echoes of Malachi 3:1 and 4:5-6 are inescapably apparent here: this child's "going before the Lord," this child's going "in the spirit and power of Elijah," this child's "turning the hearts of the fathers to the children," and this child's "making ready a prepared people for the Lord"—all of these expressions mirror the language of Malachi.

In his *Benedictus*, Zechariah continues this lofty theme with his words: "And you, child, will be called the *prophet* of the Most High; for *you will go before the face of the Lord to prepare his way*" (Luke 1:76)—again words reminiscent of Malachi 3:1 and 4:5-6. This is evident enough, but it is true that it is a connection drawn only because of a similarity of language. But there is testimony from three additional sources that place this connection beyond all question for the Christian.

There is first the testimony of John the Baptist who clearly saw himself as fulfilling the role of the "Elijah forerunner" to the Lord

(John 1:23).[115] Second, all three Synoptic Evangelists portray him as such (Matt 3:3; Mark 1:2-3; Luke 3:4-6), Mark's testimony to John's role relating the quotation from Isaiah 40:3 in the other two Evangelists to the reference to Malachi 3:1. Finally, there is the testimony of Jesus, who on two occasions bore testimony to the fact that John's ministry was indeed the fulfillment of Malachi 3:1 and that John was in fact the Elijah who was to come. These two instances when Jesus referred to John's ministry as the fulfillment of the Malachi 3 prophecy require further consideration.

First, in his defense of John's person and conduct as his prophet/ forerunner, who from prison had dispatched his disciples to ask Jesus: "Are you the one who is to come, or should we expect another?,"[116] Jesus included in his defense the clear statement: "This is the one about whom it is written," and he proceeded to quote Malachi 3:1

---

[115]I affirm this despite Oscar Cullmann's opinion to the contrary (see his *The Christology of the New Testament*, 26). John's denial that he was Elijah in John 1:21 means only that he denied that he was Elijah the Tishbite *redivivus*. He was *not* denying that he was the one "who came in the spirit and power of Elijah"—the sense in which Jesus identified John with Elijah. It must also be noted that those evangelical scholars who, in the interest of maintaining that all predictive prophecy *must* be *literally* fulfilled insist that Elijah the Tishbite must *literally* come to earth someday in the future, seem to fail to realize that in "literalizing" Malachi, they "spiritualize" the words of Jesus who was the the greatest Prophet of all.

[116]It would be a real advance in Gospel interpretation if, once and for all, John's questions to Jesus were understood as rising, not out of doubt on his part about the authenticity of Jesus' messiahship but rather out of his prophetic impatience with what he viewed as Jesus' slowness to accomplish what he had announced that Jesus would do when he came—namely, the destruction of the wicked. Jesus' allusions to John as "an *unswayed* reed" and as a man acclimated to difficult circumstances were intended to assure the people that John was not wavering in his role as his forerunner. It was imperative that the people should understand that John's witness to Jesus remained intact; therefore, Jesus by his question assured the people that John's confidence in him had not abated. In sum, John's question, reflecting the spirit of the Old Testament prophet which he was, was a mild rebuke because he saw no evidence in Jesus' ministry of God's righteous judgment against sinners which he had announced would be forthcoming when the Messiah appeared (see Matt 3:10-12). But, I say again, John's question was not one of doubt. See Vos, *Biblical Theology*, 337-38.

(Matt 11:10; Luke 7:27).[117] Then he declared: "This is Elijah, the one who is to come" (Matt 11:14).

On the second occasion, after his transfiguration, when it appeared to his disciples that the Lord had come *before* Elijah—reversing the order of Malachi's prophecy—since they had just seen Jesus speaking to Elijah (for it is precisely this quandary which lay behind their question: "Why do the teachers of the Law say that Elijah must come first?" [Matt 17:10; Mark 9:11]),[118] Jesus unraveled the puzzle in their minds by alluding, first, to Malachi 4:5: "Elijah, to be sure, coming first, restores all things" (Matt 17:11; Mark 9:12). This He did to buttress their confidence in the truthfulness of the Old Testament Scriptures. Then He said: "But I say to you, Elijah has already come (and they knew him not but did to him whatever they pleased), just as it has been written about him [in Mal 4:5]" (Matt 17:12; Mark 9:13). Jesus clearly intended by his mention of Elijah here to refer to John, as Matthew affirms by his concluding remark: "Then the disciples understood that he spoke to them concerning John the Baptist" (17:13).

Beyond all controversy, according to the testimonies of Gabriel, Zechariah, John himself, the Synoptic Evangelists, and Jesus, John the Baptist was the Elijah of Malachi 4:5 who was to go before the Lord to prepare the way before him (3:1).

But then this conclusion has one major implication—a further conclusion which inevitably follows from it—namely, that Jesus Christ

---

[117]Jesus' quotation of Malachi 3:1 and Mark's later citation (Mark 1:2) are both altered from the first-person to the second in the interest of making clear the messianic interpretation of the passage. See William L. Lane, *The Gospel According to Mark* (NICNT) (Grand Rapids: Eerdmans, 1974), 45.

[118]The implication for Christ's deity in the disciples' question should not be lost on the reader. Having just seen Jesus transfigured before them, his face shining like the sun and his clothes "dazzling white" as bright as a flash of lightning, and having just heard the Voice from heaven saying: "This is My Son, whom I love; with him I am well-pleased. Listen to him!", the disciples quite obviously realized that they were in the presence of incarnate deity. This is what prompted their question, for it seemed to them that Malachi had said that Elijah must first come—*before the Lord*; and yet evidently Jesus as Yahweh incarnate had appeared *before Elijah's appearance* on the Mount of Transfiguration. Peter would later write: "We were eyewitnesses of his [divine] majesty [μεγαλειότητος, *megaleiotētos*]" (2 Pet 1:16).

is the *God of judgment* of 2:17, the *Lord of Hosts* incarnate, before whom John the forerunner, as the "Elijah" of Malachi, was to go to prepare his way, even *the Lord* [הָאָדוֹן, *hā'ādôn*) who would suddenly come to his temple (see John 2:13-22; Matt 21:12-13; Mark 11:15-17; Luke 19:45-46), even the *Messenger*, or Angel, of the covenant of grace who was to come (see Jer 31:31-34; Luke 22:20; Heb 8:8-13; 9:15).

This follows from the fact that John (not to mention Gabriel, Zechariah, the Synoptic Evangelists, and Jesus himself), as the predicted messenger of Malachi 3:1, pointed with unimpeachable clarity to Jesus Christ as the one whose way it was his task to prepare (Matt 3:11-13; Mark 1:7; Luke 3:16-17; John 1:15, 26, 29-35; 3:26-36; see John 1:6-9, 5:35; Acts 19:4). It also follows from the testimony which John himself bore to Jesus' deity, which testimony is found in four passages. We will look at each in turn.

John's Witness: Jesus is the Spirit Baptizer (Matthew 3:10-12; Mark 1:7-8; Luke 3:16-17)

Even though John the Baptist's ministry is recorded in the New Testament, it is appropriate that his witness be included here inasmuch as Jesus appears to place his ministry within the Old Testament age of promise, stating: "...all the Prophets and the Law prophesied until John" (Matt 11:13). Accordingly, prior to his baptism of Jesus, John had announced to the people coming to him:

> I am baptizing you with water unto repentance. But he who comes after me is mightier than I, whose sandals I am not worthy to carry. He shall baptize you with the Holy Spirit and [judge] with fire.

In this declaration John states that the Coming One was possessed of a lofty, exalted, kingly office. But his words intend far more, for he goes on to say that the prerogatives were his to grant *eternal salvation* ("he will baptize with the Holy Spirit") and to execute *eternal judgment* ("and [judge] with fire"—see the parallelism in the three occurrences of "fire" at the end of vss 10, 11, 12, the occurrences of "fire" in Luke 3:16-17, and the fact that where Mark does not mention the "[judging] with fire," neither does he mention any other reference to fire). This, by the way, explains the reason for John's insistence in his intercourse with Jesus later that he (John) had need of being baptized (with salvation) by Jesus (Matt 3:14). Such prerogatives belong only to one with divine stature (see the parallelism between the two "this is..." statements in John 1:33 and 1:34); only God can exercise such *authority!*

John's Witness: Jesus is the One "Before" John (John 1: 15, 30)

When John was asked about his relation to the one coming after him, twice he expressed himself in the following words:

> He who comes *after* me [or, "One is coming after me who"] *was before me* [ἔμπροσθέν μου γέγονεν, *emprosthen mou gegonen*], because [ὅτι, *hoti*] He *was before me* [πρῶτός μου ἦν, *prōtos mou ēn*].

Here is a magnificent statement on John's part. BAGD suggests that the middle assertion (ἔμπροσθέν μου γέγονεν, *emprosthen mou gegonen*) has to do with status and they translate the phrase accordingly: "ranks higher than I."[119] But there are sound reasons for moving in a different direction from evidence that suggests that John is thinking *temporally*, that is, in terms of time, throughout the verse. This is certainly his intent in the first clause ("He who comes *after* me") and almost as certainly his intent in the third clause ("he *was* [ἦν, *ēn*] before me," the ἦν, *ēn*, here doubtless having as its background the three occurrences of ἦν, *ēn*, in John 1:1. These features strongly suggest that the middle clause should likewise be understood as bearing some reference to time. But what then is John saying? It is clear that he does not mean by the last two clauses the *same* thing, inasmuch as different Greek words underlie the surface similarity in the English translation above. Furthermore, the ὅτι (*hoti*, "because") suggests that the third clause provides the explanation for how it is that the thought of the middle clause can be so. I would suggest, therefore, following Vos,[120] that what John is saying is this:

---

[119]BAGD, *A Greek-English Lexicon of the New Testament*, 256, f.

[120]See Vos, *Biblical Theology*, 347. Cullmann even argues that the last phrase ("because he was before me") alludes to the "absolute time of the

"He who comes *after* me was *before me* (in his active involvement as the Angel of the Lord, indeed, as Yahweh himself in Old Testament times), and the reason I can say this of him is because he was *eternally before me* as the eternal God."

It is simply farcical in light of the biblical evidence respecting the relation of John to Jesus for Raymond E. Brown, following J. A. T. Robinson,[121] to deny that John perceived his role to be that of Malachi's "Elijah" but saw himself rather as the *forerunner* of that Elijah, and thus that he was speaking of *Elijah* when he made these statements in John 1:15, 30. In other words, on this construction, John was saying something on the order of the following: "Elijah, who comes after me, ranks higher than I, because he was before me." Brown has cleared the way, by this interpretation, to draw his further conclusion that John (incorrectly, of course) regarded *Jesus* as the Elijah to come, who *in turn* would be the forerunner of Yahweh![122] This view is easily dispelled by simply noting that nowhere does John even intimate such, but to the contrary expressly states that he was sent ahead of the Messiah Himself (John 3:28).

John's Witness: Jesus is the Son of God (John 1:34)

After he had baptized Jesus, having seen on that occasion the Spirit's descent like a dove upon Jesus and having heard the Voice from

---

Prologue"; see his "ὁ ὀπίσω μου ἐρχόμενος [*ho opisō mou erchomenos*]" in *The Early Church* (London: SCM Press, 1956), 181:

> The proposition introduced by ὅτι [*hoti*], looking at the matter from the standpoint of absolute chronology, which is that of the prologue, explains this general statement: he is before me because, being at the beginning of all things, ἐν ἀρχῇ [*en archē*], the ὁ ὀπίσω μου ἐρχόμενος [*ho opisō mou erchomenos*] is πρῶτός [*prōtos*] in an absolute way...

See also his *The Christology of the New Testament*, 28.

[121] John A. T. Robinson, "Elijah, John and Jesus" in *Twelve New Testament Studies* (London: SCM, 1962): 28-52.

[122] Raymond E. Brown, "Three Quotations from John the Baptist in the Gospel of John" in *The Catholic Biblical Quarterly* 22 (1960): 297-298; see also his *The Gospel According to John I-XII* (AB) (Garden City, New York: Doubleday, 1966), 64.

heaven declaring: "This is My Son, the Beloved; in whom I am well-pleased" (Matt 3:17; Mark 1:11; Luke 3:22), John testified: "This is the Son of God" (John 1:34).[123] Many New Testament critical scholars, understanding this title on John's lips as a functional title (what he is *for us*) and not as an ontological title (what he is *in himself* by nature), insist that John was simply saying by it that he regarded Jesus as the Messiah and nothing more. Vos, however, correctly represents the significance of John's descriptive epithet of Jesus when he writes:

> That [the title "Son of God"] can not be lower in its import than the same title throughout the Gospel follows from the position it has as the culminating piece of this first stage of witnessing, when compared with the statement of the author of the Gospel (20:31). According to this statement the things recorded of Jesus were written to create belief in the divine sonship of the Saviour. With this in view a series of episodes and discourses have been put in order. Obviously the John-the-Baptist section forms the first in this series, and therein lies the reason, why it issues into the testimony about the Sonship under discussion. That it carried high meaning also appears from [John 1:15, 30], in which nothing less than the preexistence of the Messiah had been already affirmed.[124]

In short, John intended by this epithet to ascribe nothing short of deity to Jesus, and here accordingly, at the very dawn of the New Age in the forerunner's testimony is the highest conceivable declaration made about him.

John's Witness: Jesus is the Bridegroom (John 3:27-36)

This passage falls into two sections (vss 27-30 and vss 31-36), the first of which is clearly the Baptist's testimony, the second being possibly his. In the first, John applies the epithets of "Bridegroom" to

---

[123]The variant readings, mainly Western, "the Chosen One," "the Chosen Son," and "the only Son" do not either singly or collectively have sufficient textual support to overthrow the reading "the Son," supported as it is by P^{66}, P^{75}, A, B, C, K, L, P, and corrected א. Bruce Metzger, *A Textual Commentary on the Greek New Testament*, 200, declares that both the "age and diversity" of the witnesses support "the Son" as the best reading.

[124]Vos, *Biblical Theology*, 351.

Jesus and "the friend of the Bridegroom" to himself, adding, "It is necessary that he [his light (see John 1:7-8; 3:19-21)] increase and I [my light] decrease." It is only barely conceivable that John's disciples could have heard this reference to the "bridegroom" and not have been reminded of the Old Testament descriptions of Yahweh as the Bridegroom of Israel (see Isa 62:5; Hos 2:2-23; 3:1; Jer 2:2). It is also only barely possible that John did not intend this comparison to be drawn.

In the second section, which Vos suggests *may* be "needed to round off the argument of the Baptist on the absurdity of endeavoring to rival Jesus,"[125] with which opinion the NASV and the NIV apparently concur as evidenced by their particular placing of quotation marks, Jesus is described as "the one who comes from above," "the one who comes from heaven," the one who is "above all," "the one whom God sent," "the one to whom God gave the Spirit without measure," "the Son whom the Father loves, in whose hands all things have been placed," and the one who brings eternal life to those who believe in him. In light of all of the Baptist's previous testimony which we have noted respecting Jesus (see again John 1:7, 15, 30; the details surrounding his baptism of Jesus, and Acts 19:4), there is not one single description in this second section which John could not have given of Jesus. And if it is the Baptist's testimony, then we must conclude that, for him, Jesus was the Christ, the Lord who was to come to his temple, the Messenger of the covenant who was to come, even Yahweh himself who had spoken in Malachi 3:1, and thus the Son of God. It is difficult to conceive of a higher Christology anywhere in Scripture unless it be the Christology of Jesus himself.

Without doubt, the entire relevant biblical witness supports the view then that Malachi 3:1 is messianic, and that the Messiah envisioned therein was to be none other than Yahweh himself who was to be "enfleshed" in the Virgin's womb and who was to come to his temple by means of the Incarnation in the person of Jesus of Nazareth.

---

[125]Vos, *Biblical Theology*, 352.

THE SUM OF THE MATTER

In this first part of our study, following the path that our Lord himself marked out for the Emmaus disciples when "beginning with Moses and all the prophets he explained...in all the [Old Testament] Scriptures the things concerning himself" (Luke 24:25-27), I examined several Old Testament passages which have been traditionally taken to refer to the Messiah's person and work and thus by extension to the deity and passion of Jesus Christ as well. To avoid the accusation that I was fostering only a private opinion in my exposition of them, I purposely selected passages—with the exception of the Angel of the Lord passages—which had already been earmarked by the New Testament as affirmations of such. A quick review will highlight this feature of the book:

Genesis 3:15 by Romans 16:20
Psalm 2:7 by Hebrews 1:5
Psalm 45:6-7 by Hebrews 1:8-9
Psalm 102:25-27 by Hebrews 1:10-12
Psalm 110:1 by Hebrews 1:13 *et al.*
Isaiah 7:14 by Matthew 1:23
Isaiah 9:6-7 by Luke 1:32-33
Isaiah 52:12-53:12 by Luke 22:37
Micah 5:2 by Matthew 2:5-6
Daniel 7:13 by Matthew 24:30; 26:64; Mark 13:26; 14:62 and the many self-designating "Son of man" sayings of Jesus
Zechariah 12:10 by John 19:34, 37; 20:27; Rev 1:7
Malachi 3:1 by Mark 1:2; Matthew 11:10; Luke 7:27

I concluded in each case on the basis of *exegesis* that these passages did, in fact, anticipate a Messiah who would be divine in nature and/or who would suffer at the hands of men and that the New Testament writers were entirely correct when they applied them to Jesus Christ.

We could just as quickly have chosen to expound other verses which affirm the same respecting the Messiah, such as the following:

Deuteronomy 10:17 by Revelation 17:14; 19:16
Psalm 68:18 by Ephesians 4:8-11
Joel 2:32 (MT, 3:5) by Acts 2:21 (see 2:38-39); Romans 10:13
Isaiah 6:1-10 by John 12:40-41; Revelation 4-5
Isaiah 8:13 by 1 Peter 3:14-15
Isaiah 8:14 by Romans 9:32-33
Isaiah 43:10-11 by Acts 1:8
Isaiah 44:6 by Revelation 1:17; 2:8; 22:12-13
Isaiah 45:22 by Matthew 11:28
Isaiah 45:23 by Romans 14:11; Philippians 2:10

The intriguing feature that unifies these last ten verses is the fact that in each case, where it is Yahweh who is in some way the subject of the verse in the Old Testament, the New Testament unhesitatingly applies the reference to Jesus Christ. I would suggest that the New Testament writers, in doing so, were simply reflecting both the methodology and the very data which their Lord himself had taught them when he "explained in all the Scriptures the things concerning himself."

A Pervasive Implication

The diverse spread of these Old Testament passages underscores the validity of Warfield's remark, cited earlier, that

> the testimony of the Old Testament to 'the transcendent Messiah' becomes pervasive. We no longer look for it in a text here and there...but rather see it involved in the entire drift of the eschatological expectations of the Old Testament.[126]

Three further conclusions may be drawn from our study of the first set of verses above.

---

[126]Benjamin B. Warfield, "The Divine Messiah in the Old Testament" in *Biblical and Theological Studies* (Philadelphia: Presbyterian and Reformed, 1952), 100.

The Coming Messiah's Diverse Titles of Deity

From the assertions of the Messiah's deity which we considered we may note the following: the promised Messiah is spoken of as אֵל (*'ēl*, "God"—Isa 7:14; 8:8), אֵל גִּבּוֹר, *'ēl gibbôr* ("Mighty God")–Isa 9:6), אֱלֹהִים, *'elôhîm* ("God)–Ps 45:6), and as יהוה, *Yahweh* ("Lord")–Ps 102:25-27 [see Heb 1:10-12]; Zech 12:10; and Mal 3:1 by implication from the fact that Yahweh is the speaker).

These are the more obvious terms denoting the Messiah's deity. But we must note too that the word בֵּן (*bēn*, "Son"—Ps 2:7; Isa 9:6) was intended as an ascription of deity to Jesus in light of the use made of it by the Author of Hebrews (1:4-13) who explicated the content of that "more superior name [than "angel"]" of "Son" by employing the further words θεός, *theos* (Heb: אֱלֹהִים, *'elōhîm*), and κύριος, *kurios* (Heb: יהוה, *Yahweh*), and (by implication in 1:13 from Ps 110:1) אָדוֹן, *'ādhôn*, to explicate its full significance.

I would also submit that Isaiah's titles, "wonderful counsellor," "mighty God," "everlasting father," "prince of peace" (Isa 9:6), Daniel's heavenly "man-like figure" (7:13), and the "Messenger of the covenant" (Mal 3:1)—each in its own way—ascribe the same supreme dignity of deity to the Messiah and any one of them could have served Jesus as a messianic title had he chosen to employ it.

The Differentiation-Identity Pattern: a Foreshadowing of the Trinity

Our study has also shown that a "differentiation-identity pattern" with reference to the being of God becomes ever more pronounced as God progressively revealed himself through the ages. We had occasion to call attention more than once (see the "Angel of the Lord" phenomenon; Pss 2:7; 45:6-7; 110:1; perhaps Zech 12:10) to the fact that in some contexts in which the Messiah is identified in terms falling nothing short of deity, he is at the same time distinguished in some way from the Deity, suggesting—as Vos was quoted earlier as saying—that "back of the twofold representation there lies a real manifoldness in the inner life of the Deity," these several instances lending the combined weight of their testimony to that of the still weightier revelation of the New Testament and to what was finally to become the church doctrine of the Trinity. Though he had not yet fully revealed himself as such—its full revelation necessarily awaiting the Messiah's incarnation and the Spirit's outpouring at Pentecost—the Lord God and Yahweh of the Old Testament was in fact the great Trinity in Unity and Unity in Trinity; and the sensitive Old Testament exegete, "by good and necessary consequence," will expound the Old Testament revelation of God in trinitarian terms.

Content of the Old Testament Hope

We are far from contending by our several expositions here that Old Testament saints understood these things about which the prophets spoke to the same degree that New Testament saints do (for that matter neither would *we* have been able so easily to understand them without Jesus' insights given to us in the New Testament revelation). But I believe it is true to say that they probably understood more than we are at first blush inclined to grant them. Consider the following data:

—if John the Baptist, "the prophet who was more than a prophet" (Matt 11:9), could teach the eternal pre-existence and deity of the Messiah (John 1:15, 30, 34) and proclaim that, despite his divine nature, the Messiah would die for the sins of the world (John 1:29, 36), and he could and did;

—if Isaiah before John could write that the "mighty God" as Immanuel ("God with us") was to be born a man and as the Servant of the Lord was to die for the transgressions of the unrighteous (Isa 7:14; 9:6; 53:1-12), and he could and did;

—if David before Isaiah could sing that the divine Messiah, his son "according to the flesh" and yet his Lord, as the "priest forever after the order of Melchizedek" (Ps 110:1, 4) would die and rise again (Pss 22:1-22; 16:1-11; see Acts 2:25-31; 13:32-37), and he could and did;

—if Moses before David could "regard disgrace for the sake of *the Messiah* [τοῦ Χριστοῦ, *tou Christou*] of greater value than the treasures of Egypt...because he saw him who was invisible" (Heb 11:26-27) and hence also "wrote about him" in his "writings" (John 5:46-47), and he could and did;

—if Abraham before Moses could commune with the Angel of the Lord and "rejoiced at the thought of seeing [the Messiah's] day, [who indeed] saw it, and was gladdened" (John 8:56), and he could and did;

—if all of these things are so, and they are, and if all of these men were prophets, and they were, then we may assume that they themselves not only believed these things to the degree that they understood them but also proclaimed these precious truths which had been made theirs through the revealing activity of the Spirit of the Messiah who was in them (1 Pet 1:11) both in the marketplace and—in the case of David's Psalms—in Israel's assembled worship. And we may further assume that the Holy Spirit enabled the elect, then as now, to understand these truths sufficiently and to believe them to the salvation of their souls (see *Westminster Confession of Faith*, VII/v; VIII/viii).

Of course, then as now, there would doubtless have been varying degrees of comprehension among the elect—some perhaps even grasping from these "highlights on the surface of a pervasive implication" that their God was not a simple, undifferentiated monad but rather that he existed in his inner life in some kind of real and genuine personal manifoldness. For if the Old Testament literary corpus, although "a chamber richly furnished but dimly lit" (Warfield), spoke of a divine Messiah who was at the same time distinguishable (along with the Spirit) from yet another who was also God, this means that it is not just the New Testament which is "trinitarian" but that the Old Testament revelation was latently "trinitarian" as well, with what was *latent* in the Old only becoming *patent* in the New.[127]

But it is also true that, living as the Old Testament saint did on the "yonder side" (from us) of the events of the Incarnation and Pentecost and having to content himself with the anticipatory aspects of the ever-growing body of God's revealed truth, we today are doubtless in a position to understand better than the average saint did then those things into which he and the Old Testament prophets "searched intently and with the greatest care" (1 Pet 1:10-11) because we today enjoy

---

[127]See Warfield's discussion of the latent presence of the Trinity in the Old Testament in his "The Biblical Doctrine of the Trinity" in *Biblical and Theological Studies* (Philadelphia: Presbyterian and Reformed, 1952), 29-31.

the benefit of the *historical revelation* of both the Son in his incarnation and the Spirit in his "outpouring" at Pentecost as well as the New Testament's inspired *written exposition* of the person and work of Christ.

Certainly this is true as well: that, while the messianic hope within Judaism had taken on a variety of shapes by the first century A.D,[128] increasingly the longing was deepening in the breasts of the godly "Simeons" and "Annas" of Israel (see Luke 2:25-38) for "the consolation of Israel" and "the Lord's Messiah." But as E. W. Hengstenberg wrote a century and a half ago now about the hope and longing of the elect within Israel:

> ...the more deeply the knowledge of human sinfulness, impotence, and nothingness sunk in Israel..., the less could men remain satisfied with the thoughts of a merely human redeemer, who, according to the Israelitish manner of contemplation, could do extremely little. A human king..., even of the most glorious description could never accomplish what the idea of the kingdom of God imperiously required, and what had been promised even in the first announcement respecting the Messiah, viz, the bringing of the nations into obedience, blessing all the families of the earth, and acquiring the sovereignty of the world.[129]

Consequently, as the apprehension of the inability of any man to save either himself or anyone else from their greatest enemies of sin and death increasingly pervaded the thinking of the elect of the old dispensation, increasingly did they rest their hope of salvation on one who would come to them in the "last days" *ab extra*—from outside the human condition. In the fulness of time—when God sent forth his

---

[128]Some Jews expected a Messiah in the mold of a militaristic David who would throw off the yoke of Rome by force. The Qumranites seem to have expected both a kingly Messiah and a priestly Messiah. The Samaritans looked for a Messiah like Moses who would be their teacher. Still others simply longed for a "messianic age" with no particular kind of Messiah in view. Of course, some Jews, like the Sadducees, seem to have had no messianic hope at all. See W. J. Heard, "Revolutionary Movements" in *Dictionary of Jesus and the Gospels*, 688-98.

[129]E. W. Hengstenberg, *Commentary on the Psalms* (Edinburgh: T. & T. Clark, 1854), III, Appendix, lvi.

Son, made of a woman, made under the law—that help came; and the angel of the Lord announced to the Judaean shepherds the coming of the Davidic Messiah and humankind's only Savior: "Today in the town of David a Savior has been born to you: he is Christ, *the Lord*" (Luke 2:11).

PART TWO

The New Testament Witness

In Part One I surveyed several "highlights" of the Old Testament's witness to messianism and its messianic hope. My research drove me to conclude that the Old Testament corpus holds forth a messianic vision that entails among other things the promise of a Davidic Messiah who would appear on earth as a man ("the woman's seed" of Genesis 3:15) through a virginal conception as a divine Deliverer (the virginally conceived "wonderful Child" of Isaiah 7:14 and 9:6), whose deliverance work would entail his vicarious bearing away in the stead of his people their transgressions and iniquities ("the suffering servant" of Isaiah 53), and who would come forth from death as his people's victor and intercessor at Yahweh's right hand ("the priest forever after the order of Melchizedek" of Psalm 110). Does the New Testament possess and advocate the same messianic vision?

In Part Two I have set forth the New Testament's messianism and its messianic hope. Keenly aware throughout that Jesus' questions addressed to the Pharisees, "What do you think of the Christ? Whose son is he?" (Matt 22:42), would have to be answered, I have expounded the key Christological passages of the New Testament and have attempted to allow the voice of Scripture (*ipsissima vox Scripturae*) to supply its answer to his questions.

Central, of course, to any scriptural answer to these questions is what Jesus believed and taught about himself. Therefore, in the first chapter of Part Two I set forth Jesus' self-witness, believing that what he said about himself and taught others to believe about him should first be determined since biblical scholarship should not ascribe to him opinions about himself that he did not hold or deny to him opinions about himself that he did hold.

In the chapters that then follow this basic assessment of what Jesus claimed about himself, I address in turn the rest of the New Testament witness: the Synoptic Evangelists no less than John the Evangelist, James no less than Paul, Jude no less than Peter or the Author of Hebrews—in order to discern their views of Jesus Christ.

In the chapter on pre-resurrection testimony to Jesus I consider the nativity accounts, the baptism accounts, the temptation accounts, the transfiguration accounts, and his own disciples' pre-resurrection understanding of Jesus. In the chapter on post-resurrection testimony I address the historicity and significance of Christ's resurrection itself for its witness to him, his forty-day pre-ascension ministry, the ascension event itself, and the Pentecost event. In the next chapter I consider the historicity of Paul's conversion and the massive Christology that he provides his readers in his letters. I then conclude this study by considering the remaining New Testament epistolary witness of James, Jude, Peter, the Synoptic Evangelists, and particularly the Author of Hebrews and John. Thus I have provided sufficient testimony for the reader to form a studied opinion about what the New Testament teaches about Jesus Christ. I believe that I have read these witnesses as they intended their writings to be read. The reader must judge, of course, whether I have or not.

I am quite aware, as I considered anew the New Testament witness to the Messiah, that I came to the New Testament and wrote as I have primarily as a systematic theologian. New Testament scholars may judge that I have read the New Testament witness, particularly the Gospels, "too flatly" at times and that I have left no room for genuine differences between the Messiah in the Old Testament, the Christ of the Synoptic Gospels, the Christ of John's Gospel, the Christ of Paul's witness, and the Christ of the rest of the New Testament. They may conclude that I have failed to give sufficient place to the role that a "functional Christology" played in the "development" of New Testament Christology as a whole. They may also think that I have read the Gospels "too historically" because I have not entered in any significant way into tradition criticism, a major interest in current New Testament research, in my exegesis of some relevant Gospel pericopes.

In response, let me assure my colleagues in the New Testament field that I have no brief against any "functional" Christological insights or, for that matter, against any results of New Testament scholarship which can be *exegetically* sustained. On the other hand, if some New Testament scholars become troubled because, in their opinion, I have read the Scriptures "too flatly" here or "too historically" there, I must say that I too am troubled by what I see as a willingness of at least some of them to postulate differences between and to impose "functional" Christological categories upon biblical statements where frankly I as a systematic theologian, who also have a keen interest in and a strong desire for good exegesis, find no exegetical warrant for doing so. It will be apparent where I think this has been done. I would respectfully suggest that contemporary New Testament scholarship, even some *evangelical* New Testament scholarship, may be reading the biblical writers *too developmentally and functionally* at times. I would also suggest that New Testament scholarship, as the result of form criticism, redaction criticism, and genre criticism, may be reading the Gospels today too much as mere forms of ancient secular literature and losing sight of the fact that their authors, after all is said and done, intended their accounts to be *historical* records of those aspects of the person and ministry of Jesus which were central to the apostolic witness to and proclamation of the gospel.

Of course, no knowledgeable person can or will deny that the New Testament writers expressed their Christological convictions in a variety of ways. And to the degree that their expressions and vocabularies vary, to that same degree there will be different nuances in some of their perceptions. In my opinion, however, when they are compared, the composite picture that results only makes for a richer representation of their combined apostolic voice (see 1 Cor 15:11). This is what lies, for example, behind the fact that we have four canonical portrayals of Jesus' ministry and Passion. But however much or little the New Testament writers differ in their nuanced perceptions of other things, such as the way they represent the Messiah's salvific work (ransom, propitiation, etc.), it is my conviction that they do not differ essentially in their basic perception of Jesus as the divine Messiah who came to earth to save sinners. I would argue that they all wrote out of a deep conviction that Jesus of Nazareth was in fact the Messiah promised in the Old Testament, that he was God in the same sense that Christians today would say that God the Father is God, and that they intended to communicate to others these basic perceptions of him. If I am wrong in this conviction, I want my error to be demonstrated to me by solid, careful exegesis. Such an inter-disciplinary dialogue can only result in a better, deeper, and truer understanding of Jesus.

CHAPTER THREE

JESUS' SELF-WITNESS

In his 1926 study on "the modern debate about Jesus' messianic consciousness" entitled *The Self-Disclosure of Jesus*, Geerhardus Vos analyzed the content of the Old Testament's messianic vision over against the liberal historico-critical distortion of it in his day. He isolated the following five essential elements:

1. The imposition from above of a *regal authority over men* which requires of them absolute submission (see Gen 49:10; Num 24:17-19);

2. The element of the *eschatological*, reflected in the idea that the Messiah will be "the great final King, who stands at the close of the present world order and ushers in the coming world," this new world appearing not in the natural course of events but catastrophically through a divine interposition and, when once attained, bearing the stamp of eternity, with the Messiah himself standing at the center of this eschatological complex (see Pss 2:8-12; 45:6; 110:1, 5-6; Isa 9:2-7; Dan 2:44; 7:13-14; Mal 3:2-3; 4:1-5);

3. Inseparable from the second, the *supernatural* ingredient pervading the whole vision, as it portends the creation of a new world order different in nature from the present one, in which a return to the paradisaical state which existed at the beginning of history is brought about (see Isa 11:1-9; 32:15; 65:17-25);

4. The component of the *redemptive-soteric* in which both a spiritual and a martial salvation is accomplished by the Lord through his Messiah who delivers his people from divine judgment and introduces them into the blessedness of the new world to come (see Isa 9:4-5; 11:1-16; Mic 5:4-5a; Zech 9:9-10);

5. Interwoven through it all, the *specifically religious position that the Messiah himself occupies between God and man*, entailing basically both his right to receive worship and his identification with God (biblical support for this component of Old Testament messianism is offered herein).[1]

My purpose in this chapter is to show that Jesus believed that he was the Messiah of just such an Old Testament vision. I propose to do this by setting forth precisely what Jesus thought about both himself and his mission, ascribing to him neither more nor less than what he claimed for himself. More specifically, as we consider the testimony brought before us in the four Evangelists' reported teachings of Jesus we will attempt to answer two questions: Did Jesus believe and teach that he was the promised Messiah, and did Jesus believe and teach that he was the divine Messiah?

The first New Testament datum which gives us any insight into his self-understanding is found in Luke 2:49 when Jesus, at twelve years of age, expressed an awareness of a special relationship to God as "his Father" which, he intimated, transcended in significance that familial relationship existing between himself and his earthly parents. Though it would have been with a child's comprehension, apparently Jesus had already felt his Father's pull toward the holy work which he would someday accomplish. Beyond this basic assertion we must resist the impulse to say more concerning the character of his self-understanding during the private years preceding his public ministry since we simply have no trustworthy data which would warrant such a construction. It is only from data stemming from his public ministry that we may deduce his self-understanding.

JESUS' CLAIM TO MESSIAHSHIP

The Title "Christ"

Contrary to what one might assume in light of the very frequent occurrence of the term "Christ" throughout the apostolic writings of

---

[1]Geerhardus Vos, *The Self-Disclosure of Jesus* (1926 reprint; Phillipsburg, New Jersey: Presbyterian and Reformed, 1978), 17-31.

the New Testament and in later popular Christian discourse, the title "Messiah" (מָשִׁיחַ *māshîach*, "anointed one") occurs very infrequently in the Old Testament as a reference to the future Davidic Deliverer of the people of God—only three times to be exact (Ps 2:2; Dan 9:25, 26).[2] It may also come as a surprise to learn that only on rare occasions did Jesus himself directly claim in so many words to be the "Christ" (Χριστός, *Christos*), the Greek equivalent of the Hebrew and Aramaic "Messiah":

John 4:25-26. The first of these instances occurred early in his ministry in his conversation with the Samaritan woman at the well. In response to her statement, "I know that Messiah is coming.... When he comes, he will explain everything to us," Jesus declared to her: "I who speak to you am he" (Ἐγώ εἰμι, ὁ λαλῶν σοι, *Egō eimi, ho lalōn soi*).

John 17:3. The second instance is found in his high priestly prayer where he refers to himself in the third person as "Jesus Christ, whom you [the Father] sent."

Mark 14:62. The third occurrence took place at the very end of his earthly ministry during his trial before the Sanhedrin when, in response to the high priest's adjuration, "I charge you under oath by the living God: Tell us if you are the Christ, the Son of God" (Matt 26:63; see also Mark 14:61: "Are you the Christ, the Son of the Blessed One"; Luke 22:67: "If you are the Christ, tell us"), Jesus declared unequivocally: "I am [Ἐγώ εἰμι, *Egō eimi*), and you will see the Son of Man sitting at the right hand of the Mighty One [see Ps 110:1]

---

[2]In the Old Testament, priests (Ex 29:7; 30:30-33; Lev 4:3; 6:22; 8:12, 31) and kings (1 Sam 10:1; 16:13; 24:10; 2 Sam 19:21; see 1 Sam 2:10 and Ps 89:20) were installed in their respective offices to perform their specific functions through an "anointing" ritual. In Psalm 105:15 prophets, being organs of revelation, are designated "anointed ones" by virtue of the Spirit's "anointing" visitation upon them as they prophesied. Consequently, "Messiah" or "Anointed One" came to be the most popular designation of the future Davidic Ruler who would usher in the promised eschatological Kingdom of God and represent the people before God and God before the people in that Kingdom.

and coming with the clouds of heaven [see Dan 7:13]" (Mark 14:62; see Matt 26:64; Luke 22:67-69).

To these three direct claims to messiahship we must add the two following instances when someone in Jesus' presence and to his face confessed him to be the "Christ" and he accepted, either expressly or tacitly, the assessment as correct.

Matthew 16:16 (Mark 8:29; Luke 9:20). First here of course, is Peter's famous confession in response to Jesus' inquiry concerning his disciples' understanding of him: "You are the Christ," he acclaimed (so Mark; Matt: "You are the Christ, the Son of the living God"; Luke: "The Christ of God"). While according to all three Synoptic Evangelists he would admonish his disciples not to spread this understanding of him abroad, according to Matthew, Jesus before this admonition first responded with his famous benediction: "Blessed are you, Simon bar-Jonah, for flesh and blood has not revealed this to you, but my Father who is in heaven." Clearly, Jesus accepted Peter's assessment of him as the Messiah as a true assessment.

John 11:25-27. We refer, second, to Martha's striking declaration, uttered in response to Jesus' "I am" saying and query: "I am the Resurrection and the Life. He who believes in me, even though he should die, shall live, and everyone who lives and believes in me shall never die. Do you believe this?" Martha unhesitatingly replied: "Yes, Lord; I believe that you are the Christ, the Son of God, who was to come into the world." The absence on Jesus' part of any attempt to correct her plainly implies Jesus' tacit acceptance of her description of him.

Beyond these few instances (John 4:26; 17:3; Mark 14:62; Matt 16:16; and John 11:27) nowhere else does Jesus explicitly or tacitly lay claim in so many words to the messianic investiture through the use of the title "Christ."[3] This sparing use of the term on his part was

---

[3]In my opinion, Matthew 22:42-45, 23:10, 24:5 (see Mark 13:6; Luke 21:8), 23-24, Mark 9:41, 12:35-37, 13:21-22, Luke 24:44-46, and John 10:24-25 also recount instances in which Jesus claimed by implication to be the "Christ."

due, no doubt, to the fact that the messianic idea had become distorted in one way or another away from the balanced vision of Old Testament messianism. "In circles where a quietistic priestly emphasis was strong, the Levitical character of the Messiah dominated. Where Pharisaic influence was felt, legal and prophetic elements were stressed,"[4] while for the popular imagination messianism had come one-sidedly to have strong nationalistic, racial, political, and materialistic associations. The result was that the Messiah in Jewish thought of the first century was regarded primarily as Israel's national deliverer from the yoke of Gentile oppression. Such spiritual elements in the messianic task as those delineated by Vos had been pushed so far to the rear in Jewish thought in general that had Jesus employed uncritically the current popular term as a description of himself and his mission before he had taken the opportunity to divest it of its one-sided associations and to infuse it with its richer, full-orbed Old Testament meaning, which included the work of the Messiah as the suffering Servant of Isaiah, his mission would have been gravely misunderstood and his efforts to instruct the people would have been even more difficult than it was. Consequently, evidence would suggest that he acknowledged that he was the "Christ" only when there was little or no danger of his claim being politicized, as in the case of the Samaritan woman, or in private conversation with his own disciples (at the same time, demanding that they tell no one that he was the Messiah) or in semi-private prayer or, finally, before the Sanhedrin when silence no longer mattered or served his purpose (since he had already publicly ridden into Jerusalem on a donkey in fulfillment of Zechariah 9:9 and had already cleansed the temple in fulfillment of Malachi 3:1-4, claiming by these acts to be Israel's Messiah, and since the Sanhedrin had already determined to execute him for what they regarded as his blasphemies).

But because of the somewhat oblique character of these verses, that is, because they do not register his claim to messiahship as clearly as the five I have mentioned, I will not lay stress on them at this time in making my present case that Jesus claimed to be the Messiah.

[4]Richard N. Longenecker, *The Christology of Early Jewish Christianity* (London: SCM, 1970), 65; see also M. de Jonge, "The Use of the Word 'Anointed' in the Time of Jesus" in *Novum Testamentum* 8 (1966): 132-48; E. Lohse, "υἱὸς Δαυίδ [*huios David*]" in *Theological Dictionary of the New Testament* (Grand Rapids: Eerdmans, 1972), VIII, 478-82.

But these several instances are enough, found as they are in all four Gospels (and in the case of his claim under oath at his trial, being made under the most solemn of circumstances), to satisfy most Bible students that Jesus believed himself to be and that he claimed in fact to be the Messiah.

This would be the end of the matter were it not for the fact that many form-critical scholars believe that the very infrequency of the term as a self-designation and as a term of address accepted by him renders suspect the authenticity of even these five. Accordingly, all five have been explained away by one scholar or another as fabrications (or modifications of other sayings of Jesus) by the early church.

The claim of Jesus in John 4:26 is purported to reflect a situation in which the Evangelist saw an opportunity to enhance his own declared purpose in 20:31; consequently he read into the woman's declared "messianic expectation" his own developed Christology and thus attributed to Jesus the claim to messiahship in this later and developed sense.[5] But there is nothing forced or unnatural in Jesus' claim to be the Messiah at this time and under these circumstances. It is true that John wrote his Gospel from the mature perspective of an aged Apostle (John 2:18-22; 7:37-39; 12:16; 21:18-23) and he doubtless intended that his reader should understand Jesus' claim in the maturest sense of the term. But it is not at all inappropriate to insist, if Jesus in fact made the claim, that this is what he intended as well. All the more is it appropriate to think that Jesus could make this claim to the Samaritan woman since there was little or no danger of purely political overtones being read into it inasmuch as it is a well-established fact that "the Samaritans did not expect a Messiah in the sense of an anointed king of the Davidic house," but saw him as one who would be a teacher and lawgiver rather than a king.[6]

With regard to Martha's confession of Jesus' messiahship (which we suggest Jesus tacitly approved), Bultmann believed that Wellhausen "may well be right" when he eliminated John 11:18-32 as a later

---

[5]Oscar Cullmann, *The Christology of the New Testament*, translated by Shirley C. Guthrie and Charles A. M. Hall (London: SCM, 1959), 125, fn. 4.

[6]Raymond E. Brown, *The Gospel According to John I-XII* (AB) (Garden City, New York: Doubleday, 1966), 172-73.

addition from the original form of the narrative.[7] At any rate, Bultmann believed that "it is probable that originally the sisters...were anonymous, and that their identification with Martha and Mary is secondary [that is, was made after the fact]," with verses 20-32 being the Evangelist's own composition and reflecting "the theological ideas of the Evangelist."[8] But such a major revision of the narrative is unnecessary and has nothing really to commend it but the form-critic's own biased assessment of the data. C. H. Dodd contests outright the legitimacy of a literary-critical analysis of John 11. He writes:

> In ch. xi. 1-44 we have a compact *pericope* which has the aspect of a single continuous narrative—the longest in this gospel outside the Passion-narrative.... Most significant...are the two relatively self-contained dialogues contained in xi. 7-16 and xi. 21-7 respectively, both of which deal with important theological themes...Any attempt to isolate a piece of pure narrative which may have served as nucleus soon becomes arbitrary in its treatment of the text. *There is no story of the Raising of Lazarus...separable from the pregnant dialogues of Jesus with His disciples and with Martha. On the other hand, these dialogues could not stand by themselves.* They need the situation in order to be intelligible, and they not only discuss the high themes of Johannine theology, but also promote and explain the action of the narrative.[9]

Surely Dodd's conclusion is more sober and objective than that approach which would eliminate entire blocks of Gospel material as compositions reflecting the later theological ideas of the "post-Easter" church or the Evangelist.

Against the occurrence of "Jesus Christ" as a self-designation in Jesus' high priestly prayer, it has been urged, in favor of construing the phrase as a Johannine redaction and thus the reflection of a later

---

[7]Rudolf Bultmann, *The Gospel of John: A Commentary*, translated by G. R. Beasley-Murray (Oxford: Basil Blackwell, 1971), 401, fn. 3.

[8]Bultmann, *The Gospel of John: A Commentary*, 396, fn. 4 from the previous page.

[9]C. H. Dodd, *The Interpretation of the Fourth Gospel* (Cambridge: University Press, 1954), 363, emphasis supplied; see also Leon Morris, *The Gospel According to John* (Grand Rapids: Eerdmans, 1971), 532-36, for a full and skillful defense of the historicity of the story as a whole.

Christological vision, that there is a certain anachronistic incongruity in Jesus' reference to himself in the third person by a compound title that seems only later to have acquired the character of a proper name. But there is nothing strange in our Lord's speaking of himself titularly in the third person. Indeed, it appears to be a characteristic of Jesus' manner of speaking as is evident not only by his general use of the titles "Son of Man" and "Son [of God]" as self-designations but also by his specific employment of third-person terminology in this very context as self-designations (see "your Son" in 17:1-2 and "him whom you sent" in 17:3).

As for the specific title itself, while it is a *hapax* (one occurrence) on Jesus' lips, it is just as entirely possible that its solemn employment on this occasion by Jesus "gives us the point of departure for its Apostolic use from Pentecost on" (Warfield) as it is that it is a redaction reflecting a later fixed apostolic usage. After all, this compound title as a proper name had to be employed by someone for the first time, and there is no reason why Jesus could not have been the first to employ it as a self-designation and thereby to provide the justification for the apparent propensity of the later church to develop several other similar compounds.

Finally, the symmetry in 17:3 between the explanatory clauses, "the only true God" and "[even] Jesus Christ" is lost if the compound name is eliminated from Jesus' prayer as a later redaction. Recognizing this, and to offset this loss of balance between the two phrases, many scholars, including Westcott and Plummer, propose that the former phrase should also be eliminated, with the clause in its most original form now to read: "that they may know you and him whom You sent." But there is no reason for such a critical revision of the verse. Admittedly, symmetry would suggest that the two explanatory phrases stand or fall together; but precisely because there is nothing incongruous about the former expression in this place, the latter appears to be called for as well in order to preserve the striking balance. Consequently, for these reasons, I would urge that the explanatory phrases be left intact and that "Jesus Christ" in John 17:3 be regarded as an explicit self-designation by Jesus of his messiahship.

As for the Petrine confession to which Jesus gives tacit approval in Mark and Luke and explicit approval in Matthew's account,

Bultmann treated the pericope as legend created by the "post-Easter" church by which faith in Jesus' messiahship was antedated to his lifetime. But his reasons are far from convincing.[10] Merely because Jesus took the initiative in the questioning, unlike Rabbinic discussions, is no sign that the narrative is a later creation. "One cannot argue from rabbinic practice to the practice of Jesus in this kind of way; had the initiative been taken by the disciples, one suspects that Bultmann would have claimed that the likeness of the narrative to rabbinic discussions was a sign of its artificiality."[11] As for his contention that Jesus would not have asked for information concerning a matter on which he was doubtless already as well informed as his disciples were, one is strongly tempted to judge this argument puerile. Clearly, the intention behind Jesus' question was not to gain information for himself but to force the disciples decisively to come to grips with the issue of the nature of his person and work and squarely to face whether their understanding of him had progressed beyond popular opinion, an advance essential to their spiritual development if their faith was to accept and to survive his escalating emphasis on his forthcoming execution by the leaders of *religious* Israel.

R. H. Fuller also handles the Matthean pericope form-critically in the following manner: Since Mark for him represents the more primitive tradition, Fuller declares Jesus' express approval of Peter's confession in Matthew 16:17-19 to be a "Matthean expansion" upon the historical situation and "clearly secondary...in its present position."[12] Then he argues that Mark 8:30 (the command to silence)

> is a typical Marcan theme [the so-called "Messianic secret"], and must be eliminated as a Marcan redaction. The passion prediction [8:31-32a]...did not belong originally to the scene. For it belongs to the same layer of tradition as the other passion predictions in Mark and is therefore detachable. [The Petrine rebuke in 8:32b] is clearly constructed as a link between the passion prediction and Jesus' rebuke of Peter [and should be eliminated].[13]

---

[10]See R. Bultmann, *The History of the Synoptic Tradition*, translated by John Marsh (New York: Harper & Row, 1963), 275-78.

[11]I. Howard Marshall, *Gospel of Luke—Commentary on the Greek Text* (Exeter: Paternoster, 1978), 365.

[12]Reginald H. Fuller, *The Foundations of New Testament Christology* (London: Lutterworth, 1965), 134, fn. 32.

By this reconstruction of the narrative, Fuller neatly eliminates 8:30-32 from the original form of the tradition. Jesus' rebuke of Peter comes now as his direct response to Peter's confession of him as the Messiah! Fuller's revision of the account actually represents Jesus as *rejecting* any and all claims to messiahship "as a merely human and even diabolical temptation."[14] But again, not only is this revision of the narrative unnecessary and "improbable, to say the least,"[15] but Werner Georg Kümmel brands it positively "untenable, because the first Christian community, which confessed Jesus as the Messiah, would never have transmitted unaltered an account in which Jesus rejected this confession as satanic."[16] What about Jesus' clear claim to messiahship in Mark 14:61-62? This passage as well has "felt the knife" of the form-critic. In Fuller's mind, "in view of Jesus' reaction at Caesarea Philippi," this affirmation "is unlikely to be authentic."[17] Fuller prefers to believe that at his trial Jesus in actuality either remained silent in response to the high priest's question as at Mark 14:61a and 15:5, or responded in the Matthean form: "You have said so" (Σὺ εἶπας, *Su eipas*), which Fuller interprets "either as a non-committal answer or as an outright denial. And in view of Caesarea Philippi it would have to be a denial."[18] Now it is indeed true that the other Synoptic Evangelists report Jesus' response to the high priest's question in words different from Mark. But the question we must ask ourselves is, do either Matthew or Luke contradict Mark's reported "I am"? I insist that they do not on the following grounds: Since we have already argued above that Fuller's understanding of Peter's confession at Caesarea Philippi is highly untenable, we have effectively eliminated from the debate his appeal to that incident (as revised by him) as a

---

[13]Fuller, *The Foundations of New Testament Christology*, 109.

[14]Fuller, *The Foundations of New Testament Christology*, 109. Ernst Käsemann is also convinced that Jesus did not consider himself to be the Messiah. See his *Essays on New Testament Themes* (London: SCM, 1964), 38, 43.

[15]I. Howard Marshall, *The Origins of New Testament Christology* (Downers Grove, Illinois: Inter-Varsity, 1976), 87.

[16]Werner Georg Kümmel, *The Theology of the New Testament*, translated by John E. Steely (London: SCM, 1974), 69-70.

[17]Fuller, *The Foundations of New Testament Christology*, 110.

[18]Fuller, *The Foundations of New Testament Christology*, 110.

reason to call into question the authenticity of Jesus' affirmation at his trial. Furthermore, Jesus' employment of these very words (Σὺ εἶπας, *Su eipas*) earlier in 26:25 in response to Judas' question clearly cannot have, in view of 26:14-16 and 21-24, the connotation of denial but, to the contrary, just as clearly intends an affirmative answer, as Cullmann acknowledges when he writes: "On the basis of the Greek these words [Σὺ εἶπας, *Su eipas*] would also signify an affirmative answer."[19] In his study of Jesus' answer to Caiaphas, D. R. Catchpole has convincingly shown that the phrase Σὺ εἶπας, *Su eipas*] though "circumlocutory in formula," is "affirmative in content."[20]

We have seen, then, that both Mark and Matthew (when properly understood) report an affirmative reply by Jesus to Caiaphas' question. The Lukan "If I tell you, you will not believe me, and if I asked you, you would not answer," need not, as Cullmann thinks, be interpreted as a non-committal response. It could, perhaps, have immediately preceded the affirmative response which Matthew and Mark report that Jesus gave. All the more is some solution on this order likely to reflect what actually occurred in light of the fact that when Caiaphas then asked Jesus, "Are you then the Son of God?" Luke reports that Jesus replied in the affirmative (22:70a-71), which, while it affirms more, as we shall show later, certainly includes the claim to messiahship.

There is no convincing reason then for questioning the authenticity of any one of the five passages under present scrutiny. There is equally no sound reason to doubt that Jesus did, in fact, on at least these five occasions, either directly or tacitly, claim in so many words to be the "Christ," that is, the Messiah. But though he did not regularly employ

---

[19]Oscar Cullmann, *The Christology of the New Testament*, 118.

[20]D. R. Catchpole, "The Answer of Jesus to Caiaphas (Matt. XXVI. 64)" in *New Testament Studies* XVII (1970-1971): 226. D. A. Carson, in his *Matthew* in *The Expositor's Bible Commentary* (Grand Rapids: Zondervan, 1984), 555, expresses Jesus' intent in the following words:

> Jesus speaks in this way...because Caiaphas's understanding of "Messiah" and "Son of God" is fundamentally inadequate. Jesus is indeed the Messiah and so must answer affirmatively [it is this nuance that Mark's Gospel records]. But He is not quite the Messiah Caiaphas has in mind; so he must answer cautiously and with some explanation.

the title commonly used by the people to describe himself and his mission, he did employ as his favorite self-designation another messianic title which revealed his self-understanding and underscored his claim to be the Messiah. This brings us to a discussion of the title "Son of Man."

The Title "Son of Man"

Anyone who attempts the formidable task of mastering the vast literature which has grown up around the "Son of Man" title in the Gospels will feel something of the awe that a mountain-climber experiences when standing at the foot of the Matterhorn or Mount Everest. The sheer amount of material "to scale" is truly staggering. The student who is interested in pursuing in-depth research on the title should consult the bibliographies in the surveys by A. J. B. Higgins and I. Howard Marshall.[21] Space limitations preclude a treatment of comprehensive proportions. Therefore, we will have to content ourselves with what I regard to be the pertinent data and draw the conclusions which that data warrant.

The title itself (ὁ υἱὸς τοῦ ἀνθρώπου, *ho huios tou anthrōpou*; anarthrous only in John 5:27 but this anomaly is accounted for in terms of Colwell's observation[22]) occurs sixty-nine times in the Synoptic

---

[21]See A. J. B. Higgins, "Son of Man—*Forschung* Since 'The Teaching of Jesus'" in *New Testament Essays: Studies in Memory of T. W. Manson* (Manchester: University Press, 1959), 119-35; I. Howard Marshall, "The Synoptic Son of Man Sayings in Recent Discussion" in *New Testament Studies* XII (1965-1966): 327-51; see also Marshall, "The Son of Man in Contemporary Debate" in *The Evangelical Quarterly XLII* (1970): 67-87, and his *The Origins of New Testament Christology*, 79-80, fn. 6. For the reader who desires a brief treatment of the title, three sources I would recommend are Richard N. Longenecker, *The Christology of Early Jewish Christianity*, 82-93; Marshall, *The Origins of New Testament Christology*, 63-82; and Royce G. Gruenler, "Son of Man" in *Evangelical Dictionary of Theology*, edited by Walter A. Elwell (Grand Rapids: Baker, 1984), 1034-36).

[22]See E. C. Colwell, "A Definite Rule for the Use of the Article in the Greek New Testament" in *Journal of Biblical Literature* LII (1933): 12-21. I am aware of the reserve which some New Testament scholars (for example, Nigel Turner, D. A. Carson) have expressed concerning the Colwell "rule," and I am aware of the reasons for their reserve. On the other hand, Bruce M.

Gospels, appearing in all four of the so-called earlier documentary sources (*Ur-Markus*, Q, M, L),[23] and thirteen times in the Fourth Gospel,[24] for a total of eighty-two occurrences in the Gospels.

Their Authenticity

With the exception of the three occurrences in John 12:34 (twice) and Luke 24:7 (which are not really exceptions inasmuch as in the former, in response to Jesus' teaching in 3:14, 8:28, and 12:32, the crowd merely uses the title when asking Jesus about his use of it, while in the latter the angel simply quotes Jesus' words), all of these "Son of Man" sayings occur in speeches of Jesus. Critical scholarship has called into question many if not all of the Son of Man sayings. P. Vielhauer and E. Käsemann, for example, maintain that all of them are later creations of the early church. R. Bultmann, G. Bornkamm, F. Hahn, A. J. B. Higgins, and R. H. Fuller (on the basis of Luke 12:8 and similar sayings) accept only those occurrences of the title which refer to a future coming Son of Man understood as an apocalyptic figure distinct from Jesus. And E. Schweizer accepts as most likely authentic only the sayings having to do with Jesus' earthly ministry. But on the grounds of the form-critical scholar's own "criterion of dissimilarity," their claim to authenticity is virtually unimpeachable!

Metzger endorses its general validity in his "On the Translation of John 1:1" in *The Expository Times* LXIII (1951-1952): 125-26, and in his "The Jehovah's Witnesses and Jesus Christ" in *Theology Today* (April 1953): 75. Leon Morris (*The Gospel According to John* [Grand Rapids: Eerdmans, 1971], 77, fn. 15) appeals to it as well to explain the anarthrous θεός, *theos*, in John 1:1c. C. F. D. Moule, *An Idiom Book of New Testament Greek* (Cambridge: University Press, 1953), 115-16, also endorses its general validity.

[23] *Mark:* 2:10 (Matt 9:6; Luke 5:24); 2:28 (Matt 12:8; Luke 6:5); 8:31 (Luke 9:22; 24:7); 8:38 (Luke 9:26); 9:9 (Matt 17:9), 12 (Matt 17:12), 31 (Matt 17:22); 10:33 (Matt 20:18; Luke 18:31); 45 (Matt 20:28); 13:26 (Matt 24:30b; Luke 21:27); 14:21a (Matt 26:24a; Luke 22:22); 14:21b (Matt 26:24b); 14:41 (Matt 26:45) 14:62 (Matt 26:64; Luke 22:69);

Q (the so-called "sayings-source"): Matt 8:20 (Luke 9:58); Matt 11:19 (Luke 7:34); Matt 12:32 (Luke 12:10); Matt 24:27 (Luke 17:24); Matt 24:37 (Luke 17:26); Matt 24:44 (Luke 12:40);

M: 10:23; 12:40; 13:37, 41; 16:13, 27, 28; 19:28; 24:30a, 39; 25:31; 26:2;

L: 6:22; 9:44; 11:30; 12:8; 17:22, 30; 18:8; 19:10; 21:36; 22:48.

[24] *John:* 1:51; 3:13, 14; 5:27; 6:27, 53, 62; 8:28; 9:35; 12:23, 34 (twice); 13:31.

This follows from the correlative facts that (1) "there is no evidence of a well-defined Son of man Christology in Judaism before the time of Jesus,"[25] the appearances of the term in 4 Ezra 13 and 1 Enoch 37-71 (the so-called Similitudes of Enoch) being most probably late first-century A.D. and thus "post-Jesus," and (2) apart from the Gospels, nothing to speak of is made of the Son of Man title in the sermons and writings of the first-century church.[26] F. F. Bruce writes:

> [The "Son of Man"] is a locution unparalleled in the Judaism of the period and one which, outside the Gospel tradition, was not current in the early church. Its claim to be recognized as an authentic *vox Christi* is thus remarkably strong.[27]

Royce G. Gruenler concurs:

> Since nothing in Judaism corresponds precisely to the nuances of meaning Jesus gives to the term, and as the early church makes no use of it in its own theology, attempts by radical critics to discount Jesus' originality in applying the title to himself run counter to the fact that it satisfies especially well their own criterion of dissimilarity as the basic test of authentic sayings of Jesus. Rejection of the title...may thus be seen to rest on presuppositional, not exegetical, grounds.[28]

I would urge, therefore, that we may safely conclude that behind the earliest so-called "layer of literary sources" in the still earlier so-called "layer of oral tradition" (which surely places the New Testament scholar within the period immediately after Jesus' resurrection), the church found itself in immediate possession of a fully-developed Son

---

[25]Gruenler, "Son of Man" in *Evangelical Dictionary of Theology*, 1034.

[26]The one occurrence in Stephen's defense before the Sanhedrin (Acts 7:56), the one further occurrence in Hebrews 2:6 in the quotation of Psalm 8:4, and the two allusions in Revelation 1:13 and 14:14 to Christ as the Danielic Son of Man can hardly be advanced as the reflection of a major interest in a Son of Man Christology in the early church.

[27]F. F. Bruce, "The Background to the Son of Man Sayings" in *Christ the Lord*, edited by Harold H. Rowdon (Leicester, Inter-Varsity, 1982), 52.

[28]Gruenler, "Son of Man" in *Evangelical Dictionary of Theology*, 1034. See also R. H. Stein, "Jesus Christ" in *Evangelical Dictionary of Theology*, 584:

of Man Christology, not of its own creation, but rather one created by Jesus himself!

Their Referent

The Son of Man sayings depict the Son of Man figure in three distinct situations: that of his then-current ministry, that of his suffering at the hands of men (maltreated, betrayed, executed, and buried),[29] and that of his rising from the dead and appearing in glory on the clouds of heaven.[30] Who is this Son of Man, or are these situations so disparate

---

Many attempts have been made to deny the authenticity of some or all of the Son of man sayings, but such attempts founder on the fact that this title is found in all the Gospel strata (Mark, Q, M, L, and John) and satisfies perfectly the "criterion of dissimilarity," which states that if a saying or title like this could not have arisen out of Judaism or out of the early church, it must be authentic. The denial of the authenticity of this title is therefore based not so much on exegetical issues as upon [*a priori*] rationalistic presuppositions....

See also G. M. Burge, "Sayings of Jesus" in *Evangelical Dictionary of Theology*, 977-78.

[29]*Mark:* 8:31 (Luke 9:22; 24:7); 9:12 (Matt 17:12), 31 (Matt 17:22-23); 10:33-34 (Matt 20:18-19; Luke 18:31-33); 45 (Matt 20:28); 14:21 (Matt 26:24; Luke 22:22); 14:41 (Matt 26:45);

Q: Matt 8:20 (Luke 9:58); Matt 11:19 (Luke 7:34);

M: 12:40; 26:2;

L: 9:44; 22:48;

John: 3:14; 8:28.

Ever since Wrede denied the dominical origin of Jesus' passion predictions in his *The Messianic Secret* (1901), this denial has continued to have its proponents. Bultmann, for example, in his *The History of the Synoptic Tradition* declares that the passion sayings "have long been recognized as secondary constructions of the Church" (152). But masterful defenses have been registered on behalf of the dominical origin of the passion sayings; see, for example, W. Manson, *Jesus the Messiah* (London: Hodder and Stoughton, 1956), 125-31; Vincent Taylor, "The Origin of the Markan Passion Sayings," in *New Testament Essays* (London: Epworth, 1970), 60-71; W. Zimmerli and J. Jeremias, *The Servant of God* (London: SCM, 1957), 98-104; J. A. Baird, *The Justice of God in the Teaching of Jesus* (London: SCM, 1963), 249-251; and I. Howard Marshall, *Eschatology and the Parables* (Leicester: Theological Students Fellowship, n. d.), 16.

[30]*Mark:* 8:38 (Luke 9:26); 13:26 (Matt 24:30b; Luke 21:27); 14:62 (Matt 26:64; Luke 22:69);

that we must more accurately ask, Who are these Sons of Man?

Assuming for good reason the authenticity of these sayings as containing the *ipsissima vox Jesu*, the church has traditionally understood the phrase "Son of Man" as the title Jesus chose above all others as a *self*-designation precisely because the title, although assuredly messianic (see the following discussion of Dan 7:13), was ambiguous in meaning to the current popular imagination. This feature enabled him, because of its "mysterious" character (revealing as well as concealing his messianic identity), to claim to be the Messiah with little danger of the then-current erroneous perceptions of the office being read into it before he had the opportunity to infuse it with the full-orbed content of the messianic task which was foreshadowed in and predicted by the Old Testament.

Furthermore, according to the church's traditional understanding of the title, Jesus spelled out his messianic task as the Son of Man precisely in terms of the three situations of his then-current serving (s), his suffering (S), and his future glory (G), applying all three situations to himself, the former two being fulfilled in connection with his first Advent, the third to be fulfilled first in the "lesser (typical) coming in judgment" in the destruction of Jerusalem in A.D. 70 (to which most probably Matthew 10:23; 24:27, 30 and perhaps others refer), and second in his grand and final apocalyptic revelation in eschatological glory.

That the church was correct when it understood the title as a self-designation of Jesus and when it applied these three situations of the Son of Man to Jesus is evident from the following four lines of evidence: First, where Matthew (5:11) reads "on account of me," Luke (6:22) reads "for the sake of the Son of Man"; where Matthew (10:32—G) has "I," Luke (12:8—G) has "Son of Man." Where Mark (8:27) and Luke (9:18) have "I," Matthew (16:13) reads "Son of Man," but where Mark (8:31—S and 8:38—G) and Luke (9:22—S and 9:26—G) have "Son of Man," Matthew (16:21—S and 10:33—G) correspondingly

---

Q: Matt 24:27 (Luke 17:24); Matt 24:37 (Luke 17:26); Matt 24:44 (Luke 12:40);

M: 10:23; 13:31; 16:27, 28; 19:28; 24:30a, 39; 25:31;

L: 12:8; 17:30; 18:8; 21:26;

John: 5:27; 6:27.

reads "he" and "I." Clearly the title, at least at times, was simply a periphrasis for "I" or "me," demonstrating that Jesus intended himself as its referent, although even here, as Carson notes, "always lurking in the background was the eschatological figure of Daniel 7."[31] Second, when Judas kissed Jesus, according to Luke 22:48 (see also Matt 26:23-24, 45), Jesus asked: "Judas, are you betraying the Son of Man with a kiss?" Third, as Gruenler trenchantly argues:

> Matt. 19:28 is especially instructive on the matter of who the glorified Son of man is, for Jesus promises his disciples with the authoritative "Truly, I say to you" that "in the new world when the Son of man shall sit on his glorious throne, you who have followed me will also sit on twelve thrones judging the twelve tribes of Israel." Surely Jesus, whom they have followed and in terms of whom they shall reign, will not be excluded from reigning with them. Are there then to be two enthroned central figures? The sense of the passage exegetically would imply that only one central person is assumed, namely, Jesus the Son of man.[32]

He argues further:

> ...it is likely that non-supernaturalist assumptions lie behind the refusal to allow that these sayings [which portray the Son of Man as a glorified divine being] are Jesus' own prophetic vision of his vindication and glorification in the coming judgment. Certainly there is no suggestion elsewhere in the Gospels that he anticipated any other figure to appear after him. In fact, among the Marcan sayings...9:9 [Matt 17:9; see also Mark 8:31 (Luke 9:22; 24:7); 9:31 (Matt 17:22-23); Mark 10:33-34 (Matt 20:18-19; Luke 18:31-33)] clearly refers to his own rising as the Son of man from the dead, and 14:62, the scene before the high priest, couples his "I am" confession that he is the Christ, the Son of the Blessed, with the surrogate for "I," the Son of man, "sitting at the right hand of Power, and coming with the clouds of heaven."[33]

---

[31]D. A. Carson, "Christological Ambiguities in the Gospel of Matthew" in *Christ the Lord*, 113.

[32]Gruenler, "Son of Man" in *Evangelical Dictionary of Theology*, 1035-36.

[33]Gruenler, "Son of Man" in *Evangelical Dictionary of Theology*, 1035. On Jesus' view of his own uniqueness and finality as the apocalyptic Son of Man, see also I. Howard Marshall, *The Origins of New Testament Christology*, 50-1.

Fourth, when Jesus asked the man born blind, whom he had just healed: "Do you believe in the Son of Man?,"[34] in response to the man's query: "Who is he, Lord? Tell me, that I may believe in him," Jesus replied: "You have now seen him; in fact, *he is the one speaking with you* [ὁ λαλῶν μετὰ σοῦ ἐκεῖνός ἐστιν, *ho lalōn meta sou ekeinos estin*]" (John 9:35-37).

There can be no legitimate doubt, then, that all four Evangelists, when interpreted correctly, intend their readers to understand that Jesus is the Son of Man in the roles both of suffering Servant "who came to seek and to save that which was lost" (Luke 19:10), who also came "not to be served, but to serve and to give his life a ransom for many" (Mark 10:45; Matt 20:28), and of coming Judge and eschatological King. I am not impressed by the exegesis of Luke 12:8, Mark 14:62, and Matthew 19:28 by Bultmann and others who accept the apocalyptic Son of Man sayings as authentic but only by first distinguishing between Jesus and a future apocalyptic Son of Man. Longenecker quite properly asks:

> Why should the church have been so careful to insert the title Son of Man into the words of Jesus alone, when (as the Bultmannians assert) it really represented their christology and not his? And further, why were Christians so circumspect as to preserve such a saying as that of Luke 12:8 (where Jesus supposedly distinguishes between himself and the coming Son of Man) when for them (as the Bultmannians acknowledge) there was no such distinction between Jesus and the Son of Man?[35]

Marshall also declares:

---

[34]There is a textual variant in John 9:35 ("the Son of God"), but Metzger notes that "the external support for ἀνθρώπου [*anthrōpou*]...is so weighty, and the improbability of θεοῦ [*theou*] being altered to ἀνθρώπου [*anthrōpou*] is so great, that the Committee regarded the reading adopted for the text [ἀνθρώπου, *anthrōpou*] as virtually certain" See Bruce M. Metzger, *A Textual Commentary on the Greek New Testament* (New York: United Bible Societies, 1971), 228-29.

[35]Longenecker, *The Christology of Early Jewish Christianity*, 89; see also Marshall, *The Origins of New Testament Christology*, 73.

> The evidence that [Jesus] was really speaking about somebody else rests solely on the alleged distinction found in Luke 12:8f. (*cf.* Mk. 8:38), Mark 14:62 and Matthew 19:28. None of these texts demands to be interpreted in this way, and it is clear that the early church did not think that they referred to somebody else, nor did it find them sufficiently ambiguous to need reformulation. Nor again is it conceivable that Jesus would place so much emphasis on the significance of a comparatively unknown figure in Jewish apocalyptic, when at other times he makes human destiny rest on men's response to himself. The defenders of this view have the utmost difficulty in explaining how Jesus visualized the relationship between himself and this shadowy figure, and they are compelled to reject the authenticity of the vast bulk of the Son of man sayings.[36]

And Cullmann concludes:

> Anyone who accepts these [apocalyptic] sayings as genuine but tries to explain them by the theory that Jesus designates someone other than himself as the coming Son of Man, raises more problems than he solves.[37]

An unprejudiced reading of the Gospel narratives will lead most fair-minded students to two conclusions: first, that Jesus employed the title as a self-designation and, second, that every occurrence of the title, whether describing the suffering Son of Man or the eschatological Son of Man, refers to Jesus himself.[38]

---

[36]Marshall, *The Origins of New Testament Christology*, 73.

[37]Cullmann, *The Christology of the New Testament*, 156.

[38]Even though it means that I fall into the category of what I. Howard Marshall terms the "conservative extreme" (*The Origins of New Testament Christology*, 70), I see no reason why all of the Son of Man sayings in the Gospels should not be attributed to Jesus, even the exegetically difficult one in Matthew 12:32 (Luke 12:10). I must demur here from Geerhardus Vos' admission of the possibility that Jesus, speaking Aramaic as he probably did, may actually have spoken of man generically, that is to say, he may have said "son of man" and meant simply "man," "and that through misunderstanding in the process of translation into the Greek the title Son of Man slipped in" (*The Self-Disclosure of Jesus*, 50, 231). Such a misunderstanding could only have occurred in the so-called "oral layer of tradition," in "Q" (the "sayings-source"), or on the part of the Evangelists

Their Background

There remains at this juncture of our study only the matter of considering the source of Jesus' favorite self-designation. There is no need to assume that Jesus coined a totally new term or that his source was an extra-biblical one (C. Colpe and F. H. Borsch, for example, trace its roots back to ancient mythology; others have postulated, as we have noted earlier, 4 Ezra 13 and 1 Enoch 37-41 as likely sources). For not only was the heavenly "man-like figure" of Daniel 7:13-14—personal, individual, and messianic[39]—readily available to him, but also there can be no legitimate doubt that the

---

themselves. But in any case, an error is injected into the inspired autographs of Matthew and Luke! Though Vos may regard it as "too unnatural" to commend itself, I believe the suggestion of Dalman (shared by Warfield) is valid that "Son of Man" here designates the Messiah in his humiliation, against whom blasphemy is forgivable, in distinction from a word spoken against the glorified Messiah (*The Self-Disclosure of Jesus*, 51). Warfield's opinion bears quoting:

> We cannot say...that the difference in the treatment of blasphemy against the Son of Man and against the Holy Spirit is rooted in an intrinsic difference between the two persons. It must rest on some other ground, and those seem to be led by a right instinct who seek it in the humiliation of the Son of Man in His servant-form on earth, and the culminating manifestation of the holiness of God in the Holy Spirit,—though these things rather underlie the compressed statements before us than find expression in it. It is abundantly clear at all events that there is no depreciation of the dignity of the person of Jesus in the contrast that is drawn between blasphemy against Him as forgivable and blasphemy against the Holy Spirit as unforgivable. That it is possible to blaspheme the Son of Man, itself means that the Son of Man is divine ("Misconception of Jesus, and Blasphemy of the Son of Man," *Biblical and Theological Studies* [Philadelphia: Presbyterian and Reformed, 1952], 225).

[39]There is virtually universal accord among Old and New Testament scholars on two points: first, the Aramaic phrase בַּר אֱנָשׁ (*bar 'enāsh*, "a son of man") is a Semitic idiom for "a man," so that what Daniel is saying is that he saw a "man-like figure" approaching God, the Ancient of Days; second, by this "man-like figure" the vision intends a studied contrast between the first four kingdoms which are symbolized by *beasts* and the last one which is symbolized by the "*man-like* figure," the point being that as different in nature as a man is from beasts, so different in nature is the fifth kingdom ("the Kingdom of God") from the four kingdoms ("kingdoms of evil men") that preceded it.

apocalyptic Son of Man sayings in Mark 13:26 (Matt 24:30b; Luke 21:27) and 14:62 (Matt 26:64) are squarely based on the Danielic Son of Man. Only the most radical exegesis, controlled by extra-biblical presuppositions, would advance another source for this title. There is a growing consensus that Daniel 7 is the primary source, if not among the form-critical scholars on the Continent, certainly among evangelical scholars in Britain and the United States.[40]

Beyond these two matters of general accord, Old Testament scholars have divided over whether the "man-like figure" is symbolic of a corporate entity or of an individual. Among critical scholars there is wide agreement, on the basis of 7:17, 22, 27, that the "man-like figure" is symbolic of the "saints of the Most High" alone—*with no reference to an individual whatsoever*. Evangelical scholars have noted, however, that if this is so—that the saints alone are symbolized—it would herald an unheard-of, the first-of-its-kind kingdom without a king in human history, and would suggest that Daniel was not simply non-messianic but positively anti-messianic in his eschatology, which we know from Daniel 9:25-26 he was not. They dispute the conclusion, therefore, that there is no basis in the passage for an individualizing interpretation of the "man-like figure," for Daniel 7:17 ("these great beasts, which are four, are four *kings* [not kingdoms!]") provides just this basis. Just as the four beasts symbolize "four kings," the "man-like figure," as Vos notes, "in like manner approximates the King of the fifth kingdom, although this does not, of course, exclude the possibility of the thus described King symbolizing the nature of the Kingdom over which He is to rule" (*The Self-Disclosure of Jesus*, 45). A concrete, individual figure who can hardly be anyone other than the Messiah is surely present then in the passage, and the conclusive proof that this interpretation is correct is the fact that our Lord individualized it when he applied this title to himself.

[40]Vincent Taylor writes, for example: "...Jesus's use of the title was independently derived from reflection upon the basic Old Testament passage, Dan vii. 13" (*The Names of Jesus* [London: Macmillan, 1953], 27). Many others would strongly support this position, for example, Benjamin B. Warfield, "The Person of Christ According to the New Testament" in *The Person and Work of Christ* (Philadelphia: Presbyterian and Reformed, 1950), 64; *The Lord of Glory* (Reprint; Grand Rapids: Baker, 1974), 24, 30; Vos, *The Self-Disclosure of Jesus*, 232; T. W. Manson, *The Teaching of Jesus* (Cambridge: University Press, 1951), 227; C. H. Dodd, *According to the Scriptures* (London: Nisbet, 1952), 117; C. K. Barrett, *Jesus and the Gospel Tradition* (London, SPCK, 1967), 41ff.; M. D. Hooker, *The Son of Man in Mark* (London: SPCK, 1967), 11-74; Longenecker, *The Christology of Early Jewish Christianity*, 86-7; George Eldon Ladd, *A Theology of the New*

A common objection raised against Daniel's "man-like figure" being made the source of Jesus' "Son of Man" sayings is the alleged absence of the motif of suffering in the description of this figure in Daniel 7, while the idea of suffering is often attached to the title in Jesus' usage. But this reason for denying that the Danielic "man-like figure" is the background figure for Jesus' *suffering* Son of Man is unconvincing and has not gone unchallenged. Some scholars, as Moule and Longenecker, urge that in Daniel 7:21, 25, there is the suggestion that, while the Son of Man is a transcendent and glorified figure, his glorification and vindication come through suffering.[41] It is true that Vos and Marshall are not persuaded by this proposal,[42] Vos, for example, suggesting as an alternative that the way suffering is to be joined to the Son of Man title is not by analysis but by the principle of contrast: "It is not that he must undergo humiliation, suffering and death *because* he is the Son of man, but that *although* he is the Son of man such a destiny is, paradoxically, in store for him."[43] The problem with this, of course, is how a true "joining" is derived from a "contrast"? The apocalyptic figure does not in itself imply the suffering figure. The principle of contrast is drawn simply from the fact of the two kinds of statements themselves, but says nothing about *how* suffering properly belongs to the figure. Another possibility is the suggestion of Carson that reflection by Jesus, not only on Daniel 7, but also on the other occurrences of the phrase in Psalm 8:4 and Ezekiel 2:1 *passim*, where "the chasm between frail, mortal man and God himself" are underscored, led Jesus to combine within the one title "these multiform backgrounds."[44] But it is also just possible that Dodd, Bruce, and

---

Testament (Grand Rapids: Eerdmans, 1974), 145-58, esp. 147; C. F. D. Moule, *The Origin of Christology* (Cambridge: University Press, 1977), 14 (Moule even makes the novel suggestion that the article uniformly attached to "Son of Man" in the Greek New Testament has virtual demonstrative force: "[That] Son of Man [in Daniel 7]."); F. F. Bruce, "The Background to the Son of Man Sayings" in *Christ the Lord*, 53-54; D. A. Carson, *Matthew*, 209-13; R. G. Gruenler, "Son of Man" in *Evangelical Dictionary of Theology*, 1034; R. H. Stein, "Jesus Christ" in *Evangelical Dictionary of Theology*, 584.

[41]Longenecker, *The Christology of Early Jewish Christianity*, 87-8.

[42]Vos, *The Self-Disclosure of Jesus*, 235-36; Marshall, *The Origins of New Testament Christology*, 75-6.

[43]Vos, *The Self-Disclosure of Jesus*, 236.

[44]Carson, *Matthew*, 212-13.

others are correct when they propose that the combining of both suffering and glory within the framework of the one title simply goes back to the creative insight of Jesus himself, who drew upon both Daniel's Son of Man and Isaiah's Suffering Servant and combined them together, as the Old Testament intended them to be, under the one title to describe the ministry of the Messiah.[45] I prefer this suggestion over Carson's because there is some question whether Psalm 8:4 intends to underscore man's frailty and mortality. It seems more likely that David intended to highlight man's elevated station over the work of God's creation by his statement in 8:4. And God's addressing Ezekiel as "Son of man," while it means "O Man," does not necessarily intend that the prophet's frailty and mortality are being set off over against God himself. But whatever the correct solution is, this review of proposed options points up how Jesus could have come to represent the Son of Man figure as bearing not only the apocalyptic features but the weight of suffering as well. There is no ground, then, for denying any one of the groups of sayings as authentic on the ground that it does not fit within the parameters of the Danielic "man-like figure."

I would conclude, then, that when Jesus employed the title, he was self-consciously claiming to be the Danielic "man-like figure" and hence the Messiah, uniting within the one Old Testament figure both the motif of suffering (the work of Isaiah's Suffering Servant) and the motif of apocalyptic coming to judge the earth and to complete the Kingdom of God. We shall see shortly what else Jesus was claiming for himself when he employed this Danielic title.

The Title "Son of David"

Before we turn to the second question we have posed for ourselves in this chapter—that pertaining to Jesus' understanding of his divine origin and character, there is one further title that should receive some comment in connection with the present question of Jesus' perception of his messiahship—the title "Son of David."

That the Old Testament had declared that the Messiah would be

---

[45]Dodd, *According to the Scriptures*, 108-10; F. F. Bruce, "The Background to the Son of Man Sayings" in *Christ the Lord*, 60-1.

of Davidic lineage is clear, as we have already seen, from Isaiah 9:7; 11:1, 10; 55:3; Psalms 89:3-4, 20-29, 35-37; Hosea 3:5; Amos 9:11-12; Micah 5:2 *et al*. And that the early church believed in Jesus' lineal descent from David "according to the flesh" is equally evident (1) from the genealogies in Matthew 1:6-16, 17 and Luke 3:23-31 (see also Matt 1:20 and Luke 1:27; 2:4); (2) from the Lukan report of Gabriel's message to Mary (1:32; see 2:11), Zechariah's *Benedictus* (1:69), and Peter's first sermon (Acts 2:30); (3) from Paul's letters (Rom 1:3; 2 Tim 2:8); and (4) from John's Revelation (5:5; 22:6). This fact in itself, it is true, does not prove Jesus' messiahship, inasmuch as there were doubtless other families in Jesus' time that could have claimed Davidic descent. But it is clear that it was a settled conviction of both the Old Testament Scriptures and Israel's understanding of those Scriptures that without such a lineal descent no one could have legitimately claimed to be the Messiah and thus the rightful heir to the Davidic throne (see Matt 12:23; 21:42; Mark 12:35; Luke 20:41; John 7:42). In other words, lineal descent from David did not in itself mean messiahship, but the absence of such descent would have disqualified anyone as a false Christ who would have made the claim of messiahship. The early church clearly held the conviction that Jesus met this qualification, and there is no reason whatever to question the validity of this conviction.

Because the conviction that the Messiah was to be of Davidic descent was a "commonplace" in Israel's hope, it should come as no surprise that the title "Son of David" came to be regarded in some branches of popular Judaism as a messianic title.[46] The question we wish to address now is this: Did Jesus claim to be the "Son of David" in the messianic sense? If we were to base our response solely on explicit claims, we would have to answer this question in the negative. But there is indisputable testimony from the Gospels that Jesus tacitly claimed to be the messianic "Son of David." When addressed as such by the two blind men in Matthew 9:27 and later by blind Bartimaeus and his fellow beggar in 20:30-31 (Mark 10:47-48; Luke 18:38-39), no disclaimer on Jesus' part was forthcoming. To the contrary, he healed all of them in response to their appeal to him,

---

[46]Carson, *Matthew*, 62; see also his "Christological Ambiguities in the Gospel of Matthew" in *Christ the Lord*, 104.

although it is true that in the former case, he performed the healing within the privacy of a house to dampen messianic expectations.[47] When he rode into Jerusalem on a donkey as Zechariah 9:9 had foretold, the crowds addressed him along the way and in the temple as the promised messianic "Son of David" by their cries of "Hosanna!...Blessed is the Kingdom of our Father David that is coming" (Mark 11:9-10; Matt 21:9: "Hosanna to the Son of David [see 21:15]; Luke 19:38: "Blessed is the King who comes in the name of the Lord"; John 12:13: "Blessed is he who comes in the name of the Lord, even the King of Israel"). That Jesus tacitly accepted their address is evident from the fact that when the Pharisees said, "Teacher, rebuke your disciples," he answered: "I tell you, if these were silent, the very stones would cry out" (Luke 19:39-40). Then later, when the temple leadership became indignant over the ascription of the title to him by the children, Jesus defended the children and expressed his approval of their acclamation by referring to Psalm 8:2 (Matt 21:15-16).

Without intending to suggest that those who took recourse to him under the aegis of the "Son of David" title properly comprehended all that the role entailed, I would insist that there can be no doubt that the blind men and the crowds intended by their cries to ascribe messianic stature to Jesus, and that, responding as he did, he accepted their ascription of him as proper and true. But as with the title "Christ," there was a certain reticence on his part before his triumphal entry to relate himself to the "Son of David" title, this reticence doubtless due to the same concern we noted in our discussions of "Christ" and "Son of Man," namely, the concern to avoid raising erroneous Messianic expectations.

And as with the title "Christ," this again could be the end of the discussion were it not for the fact that liberal and form-critical scholars

---

[47]Carson, *Matthew*, 233. That the title should have often been on the lips of the blind should not be surprising, as Carson notes, inasmuch as "the Messianic Age was to be characterized as a time when 'the eyes of the blind [would be] opened and the ears of the deaf unstopped,' when 'the lame [would] leap like a deer, and the tongue of the dumb shout for joy.' If Jesus was really the Messiah, the blind reasoned, then he would have mercy on them; and they would have their sight" (233). See also in this connection Jesus' response to John's question from prison in Matthew 11:4-5.

have, in one way or another, denied all of the foregoing data and the conclusions that the church has traditionally based upon that data.

For example, some have construed Jesus' famous question and comment concerning the Messiah's relationship to David in Matthew 22:41-46 (Mark 12:35-37; Luke 20:41-44), "if genuine," to be no more than "an academic discussion on Messianic doctrine." Most likely, it is urged, the pericope is "a reflection of the debate of the early church."[48] Others, following W. Wrede, understand the point of the pericope to be an outright denial on Jesus' part of the Messiah's identity with the Son of David. But if this were his point, it is incomprehensible why the Evangelists would incorporate the pericope into their Gospels when it is apparent that this identity is precisely what they wished to uphold (see Matt 1:1; Luke 18:38-39; 19:38-40). Far from this being a mere "academic discussion on Messianic doctrine" or "a reflection of the debate of the early church," and far from denying the identification of the Messiah with the Son of David, it was rather Jesus' purpose, not only to affirm the connection (the Jewish response was correct as far as it went), but also to challenge the religious leaders to rethink their messianic expectations which were too narrow and thus incapable of integrating the idea that the Messiah's sonship cannot be explained merely in terms of human descent but must embrace as well a notion of sonship involving a supernatural dignity and origin on the unprecedented scale of divine Sonship.

R. H. Fuller's thorough reworking of the accounts of the triumphal entry (an event found in all four Gospels, which fact itself strongly supports the event's authenticity and historicity) along non-messianic lines, suggesting rather that Jesus' only "intention was to go to the temple to lay down the final challenge of his eschatological message at the heart of Judaism,"[49] is highly speculative and has only the presuppositions of historical criticism to commend it.

While it is certainly not a dominant title in the Gospels, yet when it does occur (given the circumstances surrounding its occurrences), the title "Son of David" points clearly to the intention to ascribe messianic stature to Jesus; and all the evidence supports, and none weighs against, his approving acceptance of it.

---

[48]R. H. Fuller, *The Foundations of New Testament Christology*, 111.

[49]Fuller, *The Foundations of New Testament Christology*, 114.

From our cursory study of the three titles "Christ," "Son of Man," and "Son of David," we have found more than ample reason to conclude that Jesus claimed, in fact, to be the Messiah that the Old Testament had foretold. We noted that Jesus did not himself directly appeal with any frequency to the titles "Christ" or "Son of David" to describe himself in his role of Messiah (though he accepted these titles in direct address from others upon occasion). He preferred, rather, the Danielic messianic title "Son of Man." This title he preferred, as we have suggested, because it allowed him, due to its ambiguity in the public mind, to make his messianic claims with a minimum of interference from the recalcitrant religious leadership and from those among the populace who, embued with the vision of a Messiah only with political associations who would deliver the nation from the yoke of Gentile oppression and extend the nation's political influence throughout the world, would have attempted to declare him Israel's king in opposition to Rome (see John 6:15). Because of its ambiguity in the minds of the people, Jesus' preferred self-designation also possessed a certain "openness" about it which permitted him to shape its significance as a messianic designation by his own teaching and work.[50] This concern to avoid terminology which would raise inappropriate and misleading messianic expectations is doubtless what lay behind Jesus' command that demons (Mark 1:25, 34; 3:12; Luke 4:35, 41), those whom he healed (Matt 8:4; 9:30; 12:16; Mark 1:44; 5:43; 7:24, 36; 9:30; Luke 5:14; 8:56), and his own disciples (Matt 16:20; 17:9; Mark 8:30; 9:9; Luke 9:21) remain silent and tell no one that he was the Messiah before he was ready to reveal himself publicly (we may properly speak in this sense of the "Messianic secret" over against the contrived

---

[50]See Vos' comment, *The Self-Disclosure of Jesus*, 253-54: "...there must have existed in our Lord's mind a potent reason why He preferred this way of designating Himself to all others. Other names He might acknowledge, or at least not repudiate, but this name stands alone as the name that was His favorite, and as a result became in His use almost eliminative of other names, the name Son of God only excepted, though even the latter did not attain to the same frequency as Son of man upon His lips. If we see correctly, this potent reason lay in the fact that the title Son of man stood farthest removed from every possible Jewish prostitution of the Messianic office.... It moves in an altogether different sphere from the kingdom which the spirit of Judaism favored and expected."

[and erroneous] view of Wrede that Mark created this theme in order to explain why [so Wrede thought] Jesus was never recognized as the Messiah during his lifetime). This is doubtless also the reason behind his practice of teaching the crowds about the Kingdom of God in parables (Matt 13:10-17; 34-35; Mark 4:10-12, 33-34; Luke 8:9-10). But as far as his claim to be the Messiah is concerned, we have seen enough to conclude that this he most assuredly did! And claiming that role, as we shall now see, he laid claim to its requisite corollary—that is, to unabridged deity—as well!

JESUS' CLAIM TO DEITY

The Old Testament prophets, with increasing clarity, had spoken of a Messiah who would possess divine titles (Isa 7:14; 9:6) and whose coming to his people was to be in some sense just the coming of God himself to them (Pss 45:6; 96:13; 98:9; Zech 12:10; Mal 3:1) in the person of his Son the King (Ps 2:7; Isa 9:6).

When we turn to our Lord's self-estimation of his own person and work as that may be discerned from teachings authenticated to be his own even by the form-critic's own criteria of authenticity, we discover that everything that Old Testament revelation anticipated the Messiah to be, Jesus believed himself to be. Consider first his self-designation, the title "the Son of Man," and his teaching concerning himself as the Son of Man.

The Implications of Deity in Jesus' "Son of Man" Sayings

Commenting upon the significance of the "Son of Man" title in his *The Self-Disclosure of Jesus*, Vos writes:

> In close adherence to the spirit of the scene in Daniel from which it was taken, it suggested a Messianic career in which, all of a sudden, without human interference or military conflict, through an immediate act of God, the highest dignity and power are conferred. The kingship here portrayed is not only supernatural; it is "transcendental."[51]

---

[51]Vos, *The Self-Disclosure of Jesus*, 254.

Even a cursory examination of the Daniel 7 passage and Jesus' Son of Man sayings will bear out all that Vos asserts here and more. The "man-like figure" in the Daniel 7 passage[52] —said to be "man-like" only in order to highlight the contrast between himself and the beast-empires and their kings—is assuredly more if not other than man in nature. He is depicted there as a *superhuman*—let us say it frankly—even a *divine* figure. This is evident from the following data: to begin, there is an "unearthly," heavenly cast about the scene which lifts the entire vision out of the *natural* order of things. And his "coming with clouds," that is, in connection with or "surrounded by" (Keil) clouds, as he does, is a phrase descriptive of both divine presence and divine activity in the execution of judgment against his enemies (see Pss 18:9-11; 97:2; 104:3; Isa 19:1; Nah 1:3; Jer 4:13) and in the deliverance and protection of his saints (Ex 13:21; 19:9; 1 Kgs 8:10-12; Ezek 10:4). Then the free access which he enjoys as he is escorted into the presence of the Ancient of Days suggests the supernatural character of his person. Finally, both the universal and everlasting dominion which he receives from God and the universal and everlasting worship which he receives from men imply that he is in possession of divine qualities (see Pss 2, 45, 110; Isa 9:6-7; Mic 5:4, 5a).

On Jesus' lips this title in the Fourth Gospel, as Vos remarks, "connotes the heavenly, superhuman side of Jesus' mysterious existence,"[53] expressing what is commonly called his pre-existence. To Nicodemus Jesus declared: "No one has ever gone into heaven except the One who came from heaven—the Son of Man" (John 3:13). And to his own disciples he exclaimed: "What if you see the Son of Man ascend to *where he was before* (ὅπου ἦν τὸ πρότερον, *hopou ēn to proteron*]" (6:62). Jesus also claimed as the Son of Man to have the authority to forgive sins (Matt 9:6; Mark 2:10; Luke 5:24)[54] and to regulate *even* the observance of the divine ordinance

---

[52]See footnote 39 again for my reasons for understanding the "man-like figure" individualistically as well as corporately.

[53]Vos, *The Self-Disclosure of Jesus*, 239.

[54]To those scholars who insist that the "Son of Man" phrase in these verses means simply "man as such" because of the presence of the word "man" in Matthew 9:3 and Mark 2:7 and because of Matthew's statement in 9:8, Vos' comment (*The Self-Disclosure of Jesus*, 51) is a sufficient response:

of the Sabbath (Matt 12:8; Mark 2:28; Luke 6:5)[55]—clearly prerogatives of deity alone. To speak against the Son of Man, he said, although forgivable, is blasphemy (Matt 12:32; see Mark 3:28). The

---

> These reasons can avail little in the face of the indisputable fact that, according to the common Christian and Jewish faith, the forgiveness of sins was exclusively a divine prerogative. How can we impute to Jesus the monstrous idea that every man has the authority to forgive sin? A modern Jesus, assimilating man to God, without principial difference, might perhaps have thought so, but scarcely the historical Jesus. If He actually proceeded to forgive sin on the basis of the 'rights of men,' then all we can say is that the scribes were right in their insinuation, and Jesus was wrong in His religious usurpation. Surely, what our Lord laid claim to cannot have been this, but only that the Son of Man possessed this right.

Vos' entire discussion (51-53) may be read with great profit.

[55]The καί, *kai*, in Mark 2:28, to be translated "*even* [or "also"] of the Sabbath," suggests that *in addition to* other things "of relatively lesser importance, to which the authority of the Son of Man extended, it covers also such an important matter as the Sabbath" (Vos, *The Self-Disclosure of Jesus*, 53; see also Warfield, *The Lord of Glory*, 99).

To those who would urge that the "Son of Man" phrase here means simply "man as such" because the phrase must have the same sense in the ὥστε (*hōste*, "therefore") clause as ἄνθρωπος (*anthrōpos*, "man") has in the premise clause, it is again sufficient to point out, with Vos, that "the argument is just as conclusive when Son of Man is understood of the Messiah. This Messianic name suggested to Jesus...that all things affecting the interests of man lay particularly within His jurisdiction. Inasmuch as the Sabbath partook of this character to a high degree ("made for man"), He possessed the right to regulate its observance." (*The Self-Disclosure of Jesus*, 53)

It is prejudiced exegesis that imputes to Jesus here the monstrous intention to relegate such a venerable religious sanctity as the Old Testament Sabbath to the area of "things indifferent" by insisting that what he meant by his statement is that the observance of the Sabbath should be left to the free choice of men. To the contrary, as Vos asserts,

> the general law underlying Jesus' reasoning seems to be that in the service of the Theocracy the lower must give way to the higher, and provision for the special servants of God and the performance of their functions must take precedence over the ordinary routine of religious duty; the ceremonial must give way to the ethical. But the decision about such things is not left to the free choice of men; the Son of Man is sovereign over it. (*The Self-Disclosure of Jesus*, 53)

angels are his (Matt 13:41), he said, clearly implying thereby his own super-angelic status and lordship over them. He said, it is true, that he would know, as the Son of Man, a period of humiliation, having no place to lay his head (Matt 8:20; Luke 9:58) and finally even dying the cruel death of crucifixion; but he would suffer and die, he declared, only to the end that he might ransom many (Matt 20:28; Mark 10:45). A man's eternal destiny would turn on his relationship to the Son of Man, he taught, for unless the Son of Man gives a man life, there is no life in him (John 6:53). As the Son of Man, he would rise from the dead and "sit at the right hand of power," and "come in clouds with great power and glory" (Matt 24:30; Mark 13:25; Luke 21:27)—coming with all his holy angels in the glory of his Father, true enough (Matt 16:27; Mark 8:38), but coming in his own glory as well (Matt 25:31). And when he comes, he declared, he would come with the authority to execute judgment upon all men precisely *because* (ὅτι, *hoti*) he is the Son of Man (John 5:27). Clearly, for Jesus the Son of Man sayings, above all others, embodied his conception of messiahship; and beyond question its associations were supernatural, even divine, in character. Warfield can hardly be accused of overstating the matter then when he writes:

> ...in the picture which Jesus Himself draws for us of the 'Son of Man'...we see His superhuman nature portrayed. For the figure thus brought before us is distinctly a superhuman one; one which is not only in the future to be sitting at the right hand of power and coming with the clouds of heaven...; but which in the present world itself exercises functions which are truly divine,—for who is Lord of the Sabbath but the God who instituted it in commemoration of His own rest (2:28), and who can forgive sins but God only (2:10, see verse 7)? The assignment to the Son of Man of the function of Judge of the world and the ascription to Him of the right to forgive sins are, in each case, but another way of saying that He is a divine person; for these are divine acts.[56]

---

[56]Warfield, *The Lord of Glory*, 41. We must conclude from this entire discussion of the significance of the Son of Man sayings that such early Fathers as Ignatius (*Ephesians*, 20:2), the anonymous author of *The Epistle of Barnabus* (12:10); Irenaeus (*Against Heresies*, 3:16. 7; 17:1), and Justin Martyr (*Dialogues*, 76: 1; 100) were in error when they taught that "Son of God" referred to Jesus as God and "Son of Man" designated him simply as man.

The Implications of Deity in Jesus' "Son [of God]" Sayings in the Synoptic Gospels

More can be said—a great deal more—in favor of Jesus' claim, as the Messiah, to deity. It is interesting to note that on two of the five occasions when he openly acknowledged himself to be the "Christ," explaining the significance of that title in terms of the Danielic Son of Man (Peter's confession, Matt 16:16-21; Mark 8:29-31; Luke 9:20-22, and his trial before the high priest, Matt 26:64; Mark 14:62; Luke 22:67-70), he claimed as well to be the Son of God, not in an ethico-religious, in an official or functional, or in a nativistic sense of the title,[57] but in what the church would later come to describe as the Sonship of the intra-trinitarian relation denoting essential oneness and sameness with the Father. This was clearly the case at his trial, for when he acknowledged that he was the "Son of God" (or "Son of the Blessed"), his judges accused him of blasphemy worthy of death (Matt 26:65-68; Mark 14:63-64; Luke 22:71), the basis of which judgment Jesus made no attempt to repudiate.

This claim on his part to divine Sonship opens for us an entirely new area of investigation—that of the significance of the titles, "the Son" and, more fully, "the Son of God." We shall contend in the next two sections of this chapter as we develop this current point that by them he was registering a claim tantamount to the claim of possessing essential divine oneness with God.

Jesus claimed by his "Son" sayings essential divine oneness with God in the Synoptic Gospels in Matthew 11:27 (Luke 10:22); 21:37-38 (Mark 12:6; Luke 20:13); 24:36 (Mark 13:32); and 28:19; and in the Gospel of John in (at least) 5:17-29; 6:40; 10:36; 11:4; 14:13; 17:1. To these must be added those instances in the Fourth Gospel when he claimed that God was his Father in such a unique sense that the Jewish religious leadership correctly perceived that he was claiming a Sonship with God of such a nature that it constituted essential divine oneness

---

[57]By "ethico-religious," I refer to the sense in which the term may designate the Christian (or, for that matter, anyone else) simply as a "child of God"; by "official," I mean the sense in which it describes "office," not essential nature; and by "nativistic," I refer to the sense in which (some scholars argue) the Messiah is the Son of God as the direct, supernatural work of God in the virginal conception. See Vos, *The Self-Disclosure of Jesus*, 141-42.

and equality with God and thus, from their perspective, was the committing of blasphemy deserving death (John 5:17-18; 10:24-39, especially verses 25, 29, 30, 32-33; 37, 38; see also 19:7). To an exposition of the more significant occurrences of this title we will now turn.

The "Son" in Matthew 11:25-27 (Luke 10:21-22): "The Four Great Parallels"

This passage, judged by Vos to be "by far the most important seat of the testimony which Jesus bears to his sonship" and "the culminating point of our Lord's self-disclosure in the Synoptics,"[58] brings us face to face with some of the most wonderful words Jesus ever spoke. Because of their clear, unmistakable, and forthright testimony to Jesus' self-advocacy of his own divine nature and Sonship, it is not surprising—even though, recorded as it is by both Matthew and Luke, it is in "the supposedly most ancient source of the sayings of Jesus,"[59] that is, in "Q" (which on source-critical grounds assures its existence to within a score or less of years from the time when our Lord presumably had uttered these words, hardly sufficient time for a radical reshaping of a more original saying to have occurred and to have gained the acceptance of the disciples who had actually been with Jesus personally)—it is not surprising, I repeat, because of its content that its authenticity has been vigorously assailed from that theological quarter which *a priori* has rejected the ontological deity of Jesus Christ.

The difficulties which these scholars have with the passage are three in number: (1) the passage has a "Johannine ring" to it (recall here K. A. von Hase's oft-quoted description of the passage as a "thunderbolt [a meteor] from the Johannine heaven"); (2) both its form and content suggest that it is a "product of late Christian Hellenization"; and (3), as David Hill candidly acknowledges: "The greatest barrier to the acceptance of the genuineness of [Matt 11:27] is the supposition that Jesus could not have made such an absolute claim for himself"[60] because (it is said) the simple title "the Son" was

---

[58]Vos, *The Self-Disclosure of Jesus*, 143.

[59]Vos, *The Self-Disclosure of Jesus*, 144.

[60]David Hill, *The Gospel of Matthew* (London: Oliphants, 1972), 206.

not a common title for the Messiah until after Easter.

These problems, more imagined than real, have been ably answered by such scholars as John Chapman, A. M. Hunter, I. Howard Marshall, and D. A. Carson, to name a few.[61] But before I consider the passage itself, it will be in order to review the responses to these so-called difficulties.

Its "Johannine" Ring

There is no question that our Lord's words in this context have a "pronounced Johannine sound" to them (see John 3:35; 5:20-21; 6:46; 8:19; 10:15, 30; 14:6, 9). But this fact in no way invalidates its authenticity, "unless" as A. M. Hunter writes, "we make it a canon of criticism that any saying in the Synoptics with a parallel in John must *ipso facto* be spurious."[62] The fact is that, regardless of its "tone," on grounds recognized by the critical scholar, the pericope is still an

---

[61]John Chapman, "Dr. Harnack on Luke X 22: No Man Knoweth the Son," in *The Journal of Theological Studies* X (1909): 552-66; A. M. Hunter, "Crux Criticorum—Matt. XI. 25-30—A Re-Appraisal," in *New Testament Studies* VIII (1962): 241-49; I. Howard Marshall, "The Divine Sonship of Jesus," in *Interpretation* XXI (1967): 91-4; D. A. Carson, *Matthew*, 276-77.

[62]Hunter, "Crux Criticorum—Matt. XI. 25-30—A Re-Appraisal," in *New Testament Studies* VIII: 245; see also O. Cullmann, *The Christology of the New Testament*, 287, for a similar conclusion. Hunter in the same context points out that instead of the pericope being spurious, "the precise opposite might indeed be argued: that if we find in John a logion with parallels in the Synoptics, John either depends on the Synoptics or else draws upon an independent tradition." G. B. Caird says virtually the same thing:

> Many scholars have doubted whether Jesus could really have made the claims attributed to him in this passage [Luke 10:21-22]. Hase described it as 'an aerolite from the Johannine heaven', the implication being that such a theological affirmation has no place in the more terrestrial narrative of the Synoptic Gospels, that the historical Jesus could not have used the terms Father and Son in this absolute fashion (cf. Mark 13:32). Modern scholars would be a little more hesitant about the assumption that sayings found in John's Gospel are necessarily unhistorical. If we find a 'Johannine' saying in Q, the oldest strand of the Synoptic tradition, the natural inference is, not that Q is untrustworthy, but that John had access to a reliable sayings source. (*The Gospel of Luke* [London: Adam & Charles Black, 1968], 146)

integral part of their so-called "Q," and, as Jeremias points out, is not a precise parallel to anything that John writes.[63]

Its Late Christian Hellenization

As for the second difficulty—that its form and content reflect a late Hellenistic rather than a Jewish milieu, Hunter's judgment again is worthy of note:

> Still less is it permissible to dismiss the saying blandly as a Hellenistic 'revelation word'. The Hellenistic parallels to it...were never impressive, and...the discovery of the Dead Sea Scrolls has altered the whole picture. So large a role does 'knowledge' play in the Scrolls that it is quite 'unnecessary to go outside a Jewish milieu to account for our passage'.[64]

G. B. Caird concurs:

> The whole passage abounds in Semitic turns of phrase and follows the rhythms of Hebrew verse, so that it cannot be regarded as a theological product of the Greek-speaking Church.[65]

Increasingly today, the scholarly consensus is that the provenance of the passage is Palestinian.

Leon Morris, in fact, has cogently argued that John did not allow his theological interests to warp his view of the facts which he reported ("The Fourth Gospel and History," in *Jesus of Nazareth: Saviour and Lord* [London: Tyndale, 1966], 123-32), a conclusion that I infinitely prefer to James D. G. Dunn's regrettable declaration as a professing evangelical that "despite the renewal of interest in the Fourth Gospel as a historical source for the ministry of Jesus, *it would be verging on the irresponsible to use the Johannine testimony on Jesus' divine sonship in our attempt to uncover the self-consciousness of Jesus himself*" (*Christology in the Making*, 31, emphasis original).

[63]Joachim Jeremias, *The Prayers of Jesus*, translated by John Bowden and Christoph Buchard (London: SCM, 1967), 48.

[64]Hunter, "Crux Criticorum—Matt. XI. 25-30—A Re-Appraisal," in *New Testament Studies* VIII: 245. See also Alan Richardson, *An Introduction to the Theology of the New Testament*, 43.

[65]G. B. Caird, *The Gospel of Luke*, 146.

The Presence of the So-called Late Title "the Son"

This objection must assume that this title is spurious everywhere else it occurs in the Synoptic tradition (Matt 24:36 and the Marcan parallel in 13:32, and Matt 28:19), which assumption the radical form-critic, in fact, does affirm. But in light of Jesus' frequent reference to God as *Abba* ("[the] Father"), there is no reason to doubt that he referred to himself as "the Son," particularly in light of the Old Testament references (in messianic contexts) to the "Son" in 1 Chronicles 17:13, Psalm 2:7, and Isaiah 9:6, and the "great acknowledgement" from heaven in Matthew 3:17 (Mark 1:11; Luke 3:22): "This is my Son, whom I love; with him I am well pleased." Hunter's final estimate of the matter, in light of this data, certainly seems justified:

> ...if men reject this logion, they reject it not because they have proved it a Hellenistic revelation word, or because its Johannine ring condemns it, but because they have made up their minds, *a priori*, that the Jesus of history could not have made such a claim.[66]

But such a basis for rejecting the saying, the arguments for the authenticity of which are exceedingly strong, only underscores the bias with which the radical form-critic approaches the biblical text. I am not convinced that any evidence or argument advanced to date compels one to doubt its authenticity; therefore, I will proceed to the exposition of the passage, assuming that Matthew 11:25-27 (as well as its parallel in Luke 10:21-22) confronts us with one of Jesus' authentic sayings.

Its Four Great Parallels

My exposition of this saying will focus on the four parallels which Jesus drew between God as "the Father" and himself as "the Son" of Matthew 3:17 (Mark 1:11; Luke 3:22). The unique and intimate nature of the Father-Son relationship asserted here by Jesus, higher than which it is impossible to conceptualize unless it be in certain of the utterances of the Fourth Gospel, finds its expression precisely in terms of these parallels.

The first parallel has to do with the *exclusive, mutual knowledge each has of the other.* Jesus declares in 11:27: "No one knows

---

[66]Hunter, "Crux Criticorum—Matt. XI. 25-30—A Re-Appraisal," in *New Testament Studies* VIII: 245.

[ἐπιγινώσκει, *epiginōskei*] the Son except the Father, and no one knows [ἐπιγινώσκει, *epiginōskei*] the Father except the Son." The first point to note here is Jesus' emphasis upon the exclusiveness of this mutual knowledge ("no one knows except").[67] But even more striking, as a moment's reflection will show, is the inference that the nature of this knowledge which Jesus claims to have lifts Jesus above the sphere of the ordinary mortal and places him "in a position, not of equality merely, but of absolute reciprocity and interpenetration of knowledge with the Father."[68] Vos observes:

> That essential rather than acquired knowledgc is meant follows...from the correlation of the two clauses: the knowledge God has of Jesus cannot be acquired knowledge [it must, from the fact that it is God's knowledge, be direct, intuitive, and immediate—in a word, divine—knowledge, grounded in the fact that the Knower is divine[69]]; consequently the knowledge Jesus has of God cannot be acquired knowledge either [it too must be direct, intuitive, and immediate—in a word, divine—knowledge, grounded in the fact that Jesus as God's Son is divine], for these two are placed entirely on a line. In other words, if the one is different from human knowledge, then the other must be so likewise.[70]

The only conclusion that is warranted from this correlation of the two clauses is that God has this exclusive and penetrating knowledge of the Son because he is the Father of the Son, and that Jesus has this exclusive and penetrating knowledge of the Father because he is the Son of the Father. And inasmuch as the knowledge Jesus here claims for himself could not possibly have resulted from the investiture of the messianic task but must have originated in a Sonship which, of necessity, would have been *antecedent* to his messianic investiture, it

---

[67]The exclusiveness of Jesus' knowledge is not invalidated by his following remark, "and to whomever the Son wills to reveal him," since the very point of his statement is that men must acquire their saving knowledge of the Father *from him.* They can acquire it *in no other way* (John 14:6), whereas his knowledge of the Father is intrinsic to the filial relationship he sustains to the Father.

[68]Benjamin B. Warfield, "The Person of Christ According to the New Testament" in *The Person and Work of Christ*, 65.

[69]See George Eldon Ladd, *A Theology of the New Testament*, 166.

[70]Vos, *The Self-Disclosure of Jesus*, 149

is plain that Jesus' Sonship and the messianic task with which he had been invested are not descriptive of identical relationships to the Father. To the contrary, the former must have preceded the latter and provided the ground for it.

The second parallel, which rests upon the first, comes to focus in Jesus' assertion of *the mutual necessity of the Father and the Son each to reveal the other* if men are ever to have an acquired saving knowledge of them. This parallel is highlighted in Jesus' thanksgiving to the Father, Lord of heaven and earth, that he, the Father, had hidden (ἐκρύψας, *ekrupsas*] the mysteries of the Kingdom which are *centered in the Son* (for it was he whom that generation [11:19] and the cities of Korazin, Bethsaida and Capernaum [11:20-24] were rejecting) from the "wise" and had *revealed* (ἀπεκάλυψας, *apekalupsas*] them to "babies" (that is, to men like Peter; see Matt 16:17) (11:25), and his later statement that "no one knows the Father except the Son and to whoever the Son wills *to reveal* [ἀποκαλύψαι, *apokalupsai*] him" (11:27).

The reason that the messianic task was invested in the Son becomes even plainer, if that is possible, from this parallel: Not only does the Son alone know the Father with the depth of understanding (that is, to infinity) necessary to a true revelation of him, but also, and precisely because he alone has such knowledge, the Son alone can be the revelatory channel of salvific blessings leading to a saving knowledge of the Father (John 14:6). Therefore, the messianic investiture had to repose in him.

The third parallel is that of the *mutual absolute sovereignty each exercises* in dispensing his revelation of the other. The Father's sovereignty is displayed in Jesus' words: "for this was your *good pleasure* [εὐδοκία, *eudokia*]" (11:26); the Son's is displayed in his words: "to whomever the Son *wills* [βούληται, *boulētai*] to reveal him" (11:27).

A higher expression of parity between the Father and the Son with respect to the possession of the divine attributes of knowledge and sovereignty in the dispensing of that saving knowledge is inconceivable. Warfield is surely justified when he writes concerning this "in some respects the most remarkable [utterance] in the whole compass of the four Gospels":

> ...in it our Lord asserts for Himself a relation of practical equality with the Father, here described in most elevated terms as the "Lord of heaven and earth" (v. 25). As the Father only can know the Son, so the Son only can know the Father: and others may know the Father only as He is revealed by the Son. That is, not merely is the Son the exclusive revealer of God, but the mutual knowledge of Father and Son is put on what seems very much a par. The Son can be known only by the Father in all that He is, as if His being were infinite and as such inscrutable to the finite intelligence; and His knowledge alone—again as if He were infinite in His attributes—is competent to compass the depths of the Father's infinite being. He who holds this relation to the Father cannot conceivably be a creature.[71]

Such a parity of which we have been speaking is surely the basis upon which our Lord grounds his great invitation to the weary—and

---

[71]Warfield, *The Lord of Glory*, 82-3; see also 118-19. Ned B. Stonehouse in his *The Witness of Matthew and Mark to Christ* (Philadelphia: Presbyterian Guardian, 1944), 212, similarly declares:

> Here [in Matt 11:25-27] Jesus claims such an exclusive knowledge of the Father, and a consequent exclusive right to reveal the Father (both corresponding with the Father's exclusive knowledge and revelation of the Son), that nothing less than an absolutely unique self-consciousness, on an equality with that of the Father, is involved. To summarize Zahn's comment on this passage, the Son is not only the organ of revelation but is himself a mystery to be revealed; the knowledge of the Father and the knowledge of the Son are two sides of the same mystery, which is now revealed, and so the Father and the Son in fellowship with one another are both subject and object of revelation.

In his *The Witness of Luke to Christ* (London: Tyndale, 1951), 167, Stonehouse writes:

> Most clearly of all, perhaps, the claim to divine Sonship in a form excluding subordination altogether is found in Luke x. 22, which closely parallels Mt. xi. 27. The Son's knowledge of the Father and the Father's knowledge of the Son are set forth with such exact correspondence and reciprocity, and are moreover made the foundations of their respective sovereign revelational activity, that all subordination is excluded, and the passage constitutes an unambiguous claim of deity on the part of the Son.

this is the fourth parallel—which follows this utterance, an invitation to come not to the Father but *to himself* as the Revealer of the Father. Surely this would have been an unholy usurpation of divine place and privilege if he were not himself deity. And it is not without significance, I would urge, that Jesus' invitation, in its all-encompassing comprehensiveness ("*all* you who are weary and burdened") and his unqualified promise of blessing ("I will give you rest"), finds its parallel in form to the divine invitation in Isaiah 45:22, as is plain if one places the two invitations in their several parts beside each other as follows:

Isaiah 45:22: "Turn to me, all the ends of the earth, and be saved [that is, I will save you]."

Matthew 11:28: "Come to me, all you who are weary and burdened, and I will give you rest."

Clearly, by his promise to succor *all* who come to him, Jesus was asserting for himself a place of power and privilege as the Son of the Father altogether on the level of deity.

The "Son" in Jesus' Parable of the Wicked Farmers (Matthew 21:37-38; Mark 12:6; Luke 20:13)

In this parable Jesus tells the story of a landowner who leased his vineyard to some farmers and then went into another country. When the time arrived for him to receive his rental fee in the form of the fruit of the vineyard he sent servant after servant to his tenants, only to have each one of them beaten, or stoned, or killed. Finally, he sent his son (Luke: his "beloved son"; Mark: "yet one [other], a beloved son" which evokes the earlier words of the Father from heaven [1:11; 9:7]), saying: "They will respect my son." But when the tenants saw the landowner's son, they said: "This is the heir; come, let's kill him and take his inheritance." This they did, throwing his body out of the vineyard. When the landowner came, he destroyed the tenants and leased his vineyard to others. The hermeneutical equivalents of the parable, as Carson notes,[72] are obvious on the face of it: the landowner is God, the vineyard the nation of Israel (Isa 5:7); the farmers the nation's leaders, the servants the prophets of the theocracy (Matt

[72]D. A. Carson, *Matthew*, 451.

23:37a); and the son is Jesus himself, the Son of God.

As with all the other passages which we have considered, in which a high Christology is present, this passage has also suffered at the hands of the form-critic. W. G. Kümmel in particular has argued that the parable in its present form is a creation of the first-century church.[73] Since I. Howard Marshall, however, has demonstrated quite adequately its essential authenticity in the form in which it appears in the canonical Gospels, concluding that "we may...add this saying to the texts...which throw light on the mind of Jesus,"[74] I will proceed to the elucidation of its Christology.

The central teaching of the parable is obvious, as it was to its original audience (Matt 21:45): after having sent his prophets repeatedly to the nation and its leaders to call the nation back to him from its sin and unbelief, only to have them rebuffed and often killed, God, the Owner of Israel, had in Jesus moved beyond sending mere (human) servants. In Jesus God had *finally* sent his beloved Son, that is, his "one and only" Son, who was to be similarly rejected. But *his* rejection, unlike the rejections of those before him, was to entail, neither a continuance of dealing with a recalcitrant nation on God's part nor a mere change of politico-religious administration, but "the complete overthrow of the theocracy, and the rearing from the foundation up of a new structure in which the Son [the elevated Cornerstone] would receive full vindication and supreme honor."[75]

The parable's high Christology—reflecting Jesus' own self-understanding I am suggesting—finds expression in the finely-arranged

---

[73]W. G. Kümmel, *Promise and Fulfilment* (London, SCM, 1957), 82f.

[74]I. Howard Marshall, "The Divine Sonship of Jesus" in *Interpretation* XXI (1967): 97-8. Cullmann, *The Christology of the New Testament*, 289, also supports the authenticity of Jesus' reference to himself as "the Son" in this parable. The opinion of A. B. Bruce, *The Parabolic Teaching of Jesus* (Fifth revised edition; New York: George H. Doran, 1886), 457, may be cited as representative of the prevailing interpretative understanding of the "one beloved Son" of the parable: "...it is natural to suppose that as that son represents the Speaker, He claims for Himself all that He ascribes to the former. In that case this text must be associated with the remarkable one in the eleventh chapter [11:27] of Matthew as vindicating for Jesus a unique position in relation to God."

[75]Vos, *The Self-Disclosure of Jesus*, 162.

details of the story. Vos brilliantly elucidates the following aspects of that Christology:[76]

1. By virtue of his Sonship, Jesus possesses "a higher dignity and a closer relation to God than the highest and closest official status [prophets, priests, kings] known in the Old Testament theocracy."[77] This is apparent from the highly suggestive "beloved" attached to the title "Son," not to mention the title "Son" itself over against the word "servant."

2. The Son's exalted status in the salvific economy of God is apparent from the *finality* of the messianic investiture which he owns. From the word ὕστερον (*husteron*, "finally") (see Mark: "He had yet *one* other" and his ἔσχατον, *eschaton*, "finally"; also Luke: "What shall I do?"), it is clear that Jesus represents himself as the *last*, the *final* ambassador, after whose sending none higher can come and nothing more can be done. "The Lord of the vineyard has no further resources; the Son is the highest messenger of God conceivable" (see Heb 1:1-2).

3. The former two points cannot be made to answer merely to an official "messianic" sonship, as some theologians would like to believe. This is apparent from the two facts that Jesus represents himself as the Son *before his mission*, and that he is the "beloved Son" *whether he be sent or not!* "His being sent describes...his Messiahship, but this Messiahship was brought about precisely by the necessity for sending one who was the highest and dearest that the lord of the vineyard could delegate.... The sonship, therefore,

---

[76]Vos, *The Self-Disclosure of Jesus*, 161-63.

[77]See Jesus' "greater than" teaching in this connection. He is "greater than" Abraham (John 8:56; see 8:53), Jacob (John 4:12-14), David (Matt 22:41-45), Solomon (Matt 12:42), Jonah (Matt 12:41), and the temple (Matt 12:6). For the demonstration that Jesus rather than worship, the love command, or the kingdom is the subject-referent of the neuter "one greater than" in Matthew 12:6, that Jesus rather than his deliverance from death is the subject-referent of the neuter "one greater than" in Matthew 12:41, and that Jesus is the subject-referent of the neuter "one greater than" in Matthew 12:42, see Carson, *Matthew*, 281-82, 296-97.

existed antecedently to the Messianic mission." And because he was, as the Son, the "heir" (in all three Synoptics; see also Ps 2:8; Heb 1:2, where the Son is the heir of all things prior to his creating the world), his Sonship is the underlying ground of his messiahship.[78]

It is impossible to avoid the strong suggestion here, on Jesus' part, of his pre-existence with the Father as the latter's "beloved Son," James D. G. Dunn's opinion to the contrary.[79] Here his divine station in association with his Father prior to his messianic commitment in space-time history is confirmed. The "Son" in this parable of Jesus, a self-portrait one may say with ample justification, is clearly divine.

The "Ignorant" Son in Mark 13:32 (Matthew 24:36)

Already in his 1901 article entitled "Gospels" appearing in *Encyclopaedia Biblica*, Paul Wilhelm Schmiedel had included Mark 13:32 among his nine "foundation-pillars for a truly scientific life of Jesus," meaning by this entitlement that they "prove that in the person of Jesus we have to do with a completely human being [that "he really did exist, and that the gospels contain at least some absolutely trustworthy facts concerning him"]," and that "the divine is to be sought in him only in the form in which it is capable of being found in a man."[80] For Schmiedel, these nine passages (Mark 3:21; 6:5; 8:12, 14-21; 10:17; 13:32; 15:34; Matt 11:5; 12:31) could serve as a base for "a truly scientific life of Jesus" because each in its own way affirms of him something which would be appropriate to a human Jesus but which would be *impossible* for a divine Jesus. The reason, of course, for the inclusion of Mark 13:32 among his nine "pillar passages" is Jesus' admission of his ignorance of the day and hour of his return in glory. But does this passage affirm, as clearly as Schmiedel and a host of other writers since him have believed, that Jesus was clearly a man who truly existed, but just as clearly, because of his professed ignorance, also the impossibility of his being divine? I would say no and would urge the following as the basis for my negative response.

---

[78]Vos, *The Self-Disclosure of Jesus*, 162-63.

[79]James D. G. Dunn, *Christology in the Making*, 28, 280, fn. 106.

[80]P. W. Schmiedel, "Gospels" in *Encyclopaedia Biblica*, 1881. For Warfield's response, see his "Concerning Schmiedel's 'Pillar-Passages'" in *Christology and Criticism*, 181-255.

First, with respect to its authenticity, I believe we must conclude because there is no significant textual variant at Mark 13:32 that in Mark the saying is textually secure. I would myself affirm the same for Matthew 24:36 because, although the phrase "not even the Son" is lacking in the majority of the Matthean witnesses, including the late Byzantine text, "on the other hand," as Metzger declares:

> the best representatives of the Alexandrian, the Western, and the Caesarean types of text contain the phrase. The omission of the words because of the doctrinal difficulty they present is more probable than their addition by assimilation to Mk 13.32. Furthermore, the presence of μόνος [*monos*, "alone"] and the cast of the sentence as a whole (οὐδὲ...οὐδέ [*oude...oude*, "not even...not even"] belong together as a parenthesis, for εἰ μὴ ὁ πατὴρ μόνος [*ei mē ho patēr monos*, "except the Father alone"] goes with οὐδεὶς οἶδεν [*oudeis oiden*, "no one knows"]) suggest the originality of the phrase.[81]

I believe we may conclude, second, against Marshall's cautious reserve,[82] that it is highly unlikely that anyone in the early church, not even to offset the influence of apocalyptic enthusiasts who were claiming that they knew the time of his coming, would have invented such a saying in which the Son is made to confess his ignorance. I believe that one must accept the saying in both Matthew and Mark as authentic (however much we might prefer to have it otherwise because of the doctrinal difficulty it poses for us) and treat it as another authentic saying that reveals to us something of the mind of Jesus respecting himself as the Son of the Father. But what does it reveal?

It is too facile an answer to assume, as did Schmiedel, because of Jesus' assertion of ignorance with respect to this specific datum[83]

---

[81]Bruce M. Metzger, *A Textual Commentary on the Greek New Testament*, 62.

[82]I. Howard Marshall, *The Origins of New Testament Christology*, 116. He seems to be not as cautious in his earlier article, "The Divine Sonship of Jesus" in *Interpretation* XXI (1967): 94-5. Cullmann, *The Christology of the New Testament*, 288-89, supports the authenticity of this saying. R. H. Fuller, *The Foundations of New Testament Christology*, 114, thinks it was originally a "Son of Man" saying. Fuller's proposal I reject because there is no textual evidence for his conjecture, but even if it were the case, it would make no substantial difference to my basic conclusion as to the meaning of the saying.

that it clearly places the Son entirely within the category of the *merely* human. This fails to take into account Jesus' equally plain claim in Matthew 11:27 to a knowledge all-encompassing in character—equal to that of the Father himself. (The fact that this claim is found in Matthew 11:27 might explain why a scribe would have omitted "not even the Son" from Matthew 24:36 but would have allowed it to remain in Mark 13:32 since Mark does not contain the so-called "thunderbolt from the Johannine heaven.") It is equally too facile a handling of the text simply to declare, as does the Roman Catholic decree, *Circa quasdam propositiones de scientia animae* (1918), that Christ does not mean here that as man he did not know the day of judgment, that the idea of any limitation to the knowledge of Christ cannot possibly be taught in view of the hypostatic union of the two natures.[84] Clearly it is dogmatic bias that is governing Roman Catholic exegesis here. What then is one to say who is committed to "hearing" the text as Mark gives it?

That Jesus speaks here as one with divine self-consciousness is apparent, I would urge, for three reasons: first, this is the meaning of the simple "the Son" when it is associated as it is here with "the Father," as we have already had occasion to observe in Matthew 11:27 and will observe in Matthew 28:19; second, it is of his coming as *the Son of Man* in glory that Jesus speaks in this passage (verse 37; 25:31), which Danielic figure, as we have noted earlier, is

---

[83]With respect to Jesus' acknowledgement of ignorance of some matters, Warfield, "The Foresight of Jesus" in *Biblical and Theological Studies*, 180, writes:

> We may wonder why the 'day and hour' of his own return should remain among the things of which our Lord's human soul continued ignorant throughout his earthly life. But this is a matter about which surely we need not much concern ourselves. We can never do more than vaguely guess at the law which governs the inclusions and exclusions which characterize the knowledge-contents of any human mind, limited as human minds are not only qualitatively but quantitatively; and least of all could we hope to penetrate the principle of selection in the case of the perfect human intelligence of our Lord; nor have the Evangelists hinted their view of the matter.

[84]See G. C. Berkouwer, *The Person of Christ*, 211-15, for his discussion of the Roman Catholic exegesis of this passage.

supernatural, even divine in character; and third, coming as the phrase "not even the Son" does *after* the reference to angels, Jesus places himself, on an ascending scale of rank, above the angels of heaven, the highest of all created beings, who are significantly marked out here as supramundane (see Matthew's "of heaven," Mark's "in heaven"). Clearly, he classifies himself with the Father rather than with the angelic class, inasmuch as elsewhere he represents himself as the Lord of the angels whose commands the angels obey (Matt 13:41, 49; 24:31; 25:31; see Heb 1:4-14). If this be so, and if for these two Synoptic Evangelists, Jesus is not merely superhuman but superangelic, "the question at once obtrudes itself whether a superangelic person is not by that very fact removed from the category of creatures."[85]

But if Jesus is speaking here out of a divine self-consciousness, as we believe we have just demonstrated is the case, how can he say of himself that he is ignorant of the day and hour of his coming in glory? In response, I would submit that in both Jesus' statements about himself and those of the later New Testament writers about him a theological construction, quite common in their language, governs his and their speech about him. To grasp the precise point I have in mind, it will be necessary to provide the reader a little doctrinal background.

In light of all of the biblical data concerning Christ's person (which we even now are in the process of reviewing), the church has seen it doctrinally appropriate to affirm that Jesus, "being the eternal Son of God, became man, and so was, and continueth to be, God and man in two distinct natures, and one person, forever" (*Westminster Shorter Catechism*, Question 21). This means that the eternal Son of God, without in any way divesting himself of his divine attributes (which is just to say, his deity), took human nature into union with his divine nature in his one divine person. In sum, he continued to be God when he became a man. But, of course, this means that he possessed two whole and entirely distinct complexes of attributes—the divine and the human. Now in Scripture—and this is the theological construction to which I referred a moment ago—because of the union of the two distinct natures in the one person, the person of Christ is sometimes in

[85]Warfield, *The Lord of Glory*, 37; see 81. See also David F. Wells, *The Person of Christ* (Westchester, Illinois: Crossway, 1984), 44.

Scripture *designated* in terms of what he is by virtue of one of his natures when what is then *predicated* of him, so designated, is true of him in virtue of what he is because of his other nature. As the *Westminster Confession of Faith* says (VIII, vii):

> Christ, in the work of mediation, acts according to both natures, by each nature doing that which is proper to itself; yet, by reason of the unity of the person that which is proper to one nature *is sometimes in Scripture* attributed to the person denominated by the other nature. (Emphasis supplied)

This means that, regardless of the designation which Scripture might employ to refer to him, it is always the *person* of the Son, and not one of his natures, who is the *subject* of the statement. To illustrate: when what is predicated of Christ is true of him by virtue of *all* that belongs to his person as essentially divine and assumptively human, for example, "that he might become a...high priest" (Heb 2:17), it is the *person* of Christ (the "he" of the text), as both divine and human, and not one of his natures, who is the subject. Then when what is predicated of Christ, designated in terms of what he is as human, is true of him by virtue of his divine nature, for example, he is "the man [he may be designated here "the man" because he possesses our human nature] from heaven [it may be predicated of him that he is "from heaven" because he is divine]" (1 Cor 15:47-49), again, it is the *person* of Christ and not his human nature who is the subject. And again, when what is predicated of Christ, designated in terms of what he is as divine, is true of him by virtue of his human nature, for example, "they crucified [it may be predicated of him that he was "crucified" because he possesses our human nature] the Lord of Glory [he may be designated "the Lord of Glory" because he is divine]" (1 Cor 2:8), yet again it is still his *person* and not his divine nature who is the subject.

What is the application of all of this to Mark 13:32? As in the case of the last category above, I would submit that we find Christ designating himself in terms of what he is as divine ("the Son" of "the Father"), but then what he predicates of himself, namely, ignorance as to the day and hour of his return in heavenly splendor, is true of him in terms of what he is as human, though it is not true of him in terms of what he is as divine. As the God-man, he is simultaneously omniscient as God (in company with the other persons of the Godhead) and ignorant of some things as man (in company with the other persons of the human race). Warfield has quite properly assessed the governing conditions in this present regard when he writes:

> When He speaks of "the Son" (who is God) as ignorant, we must understand that He is designating Himself as "the Son" because of His higher nature, and yet has in mind the ignorance of His lower nature; what He means is that the person properly designated "the Son" is ignorant, that is to say with respect to the human nature which is as intimate an element of His personality as is His deity.[86]

So what we have in Mark 13:32, contrary to Schmiedel's "pillar for a truly scientific life of Jesus" as a mere man, is as striking a witness by our Lord himself as can be found anywhere in Scripture both to his supremacy as God over the angels—the highest of created personal entities—and at the same time to his creaturely limitations as a man as well as to the unity of both complexes of attributes—the divine and the human—in the one *personal* subject of Jesus Christ. I would conclude, then, that in this saying which brings before us the "ignorant" Son, Jesus, as "the Son," places himself outside of and above the category even of angels, that is, outside of and above *creatures* of the highest created order, and associates himself as the divine Son with the Father while testifying at the same time to his full, unabridged humanity.[87]

The "Son" of the Triune "Name" in Matthew 28:19

Sometime between his resurrection and his ascension to the right hand of his Father forty days later, our Lord gathered with his eleven disciples (perhaps here is the occasion when he appeared also to the

---

[86]Warfield, "The Person of Christ According to the New Testament" in *The Person and Work of Christ*, 63.

[87]In arriving at this conclusion, in addition to employing exegesis, I employed the hermeneutical "key" which the Reformed world believes explains the way that Scripture speaks about Jesus Christ. But I am aware that the question still remains how a person can be simultaneously both omniscient and finite in knowledge. For this reason I am in entire sympathy with Vos (*The Self-Disclosure of Jesus*, 168) when he writes:

"more than five hundred brethren" whom Paul mentions in 1 Corinthians 15:6) and commissioned them to "go and make disciples of all the nations."

As a prelude to the Commission itself, our Lord declared that all authority in heaven and on earth had been given to him, words reminiscent of Daniel 7:13-14, claiming thereby an all-encompassing, unrestricted *sovereignty* over the entire universe. In his postlude to

---

> As to how this matter-of-fact ignorance is to be explained in One who elsewhere claims for Himself a knowledge of God equal to God's knowledge of Himself (Matt. 11:27), cannot...be indicated on the basis of this passage alone. Of course it is necessary to maintain that whatever ignorance existed in the Son must have existed only within the limits of His human nature. But this is no more than a statement—highly valuable, indeed, as such—by which we guard the vital doctrine of the two natures of Christ. It does not really elucidate the problem psychologically, if we may so speak. In reality it only leads us to the threshold of the ulterior problem as to how the interaction of the two natures possessed by one subject, and that particularly in the matter of knowledge, is to be understood.

The "ulterior problem" to which Vos alludes is usually addressed by the systematic theologian, and some solution such as the likely presence of different levels of consciousness within Jesus is proposed. But it was necessary to say this much here in order to reach the conclusion that I believe the entire tenor of Scripture would have us reach regarding "the ignorant Son" saying.

As for the second problem for Vos and others in this saying—how, that is, our Lord can issue here an avowal of unqualified ignorance as to the day and hour of his coming and yet earlier have made some rather definite prediction "to some extent...concerning its hour of coming" (since Vos gives no Scripture references, I can only assume that he has reference to such earlier passages in Matthew as 10:23; 24:4-8, 9-14, 15-31, and, most particularly, 32-34), I would suggest that the problem is more imagined than real. If one will only recognize that Matthew 10:23 and that part of the Olivet Discourse found in 24:4-35 both have to do with Jesus' "coming" in judgment at the destruction of Jerusalem in A.D. 70, which did occur before that generation passed from the scene while 24:36-25:46 is dealing with his coming in eschatological glory at the end of the age, all becomes clear. Jesus did know about the time of his coming in judgment against Jerusalem in A.D. 70 (this he could have known being both divine and the Controller of events and/or by the Spirit's prophetic enabling); he did not know as man, by prior divine decree, the day or the hour of his advent in global glory.

it, he declared he would be with his church ("I am with you"), words reminiscent of the Immanuel title of Isaiah 7:14 and Matthew 1:23 and implying that the attributes of *omnipresence* and *omniscience* were his. In the additional words ("always, even to the end of the age"), he implied his possession of the attribute of *eternality.* Between the prelude and the postlude—both pregnant, as we have just seen, with the suggestion of deity—comes the Commission itself (Matt 28:19-20a). In its words, "all nations...teaching them to observe all that *I have commanded* you," his universal *Lordship* is affirmed. Sovereignty, omnipresence, omniscience, eternality, and Lordship—if we were to say no more, we will have already said enough to demonstrate that the risen Christ claimed to be in possession of the complement of divine attributes. But more can and must be said.

Before we look at the "the Son" saying, which is our central concern here, we must say something respecting the widely-held opinion that what we have in Matthew 28:16-20 is "a Matthean redaction of a [more] primitive apostolic commissioning."[88] Of course, for those radical form-critical followers of Bultmann, such as are some of *The Myth of God Incarnate* scholars, for whom the resurrection of Christ is only an existential (non-historical) experience ("myth"), this saying must necessarily be the later creation of Matthew, reflecting the developing theological attitudes and practices of the early church. But even among the less radical form-critics who actually accept the historicity of the resurrection of Jesus (for example, Robert Gundry[89]) the saying has been regarded as a Matthean creation and not the actual words of the risen Christ. The reasons for rejecting its authenticity are mainly two in number: first, the resistance to the Gentile mission on the part of the Jewish church, it is said, is inexplicable if Jesus had actually enjoined his disciples to evangelize the world; and second, Christian baptism throughout the New Testament (Acts 2:38; 8:16; 10:48; 19:5; see Gal 3:27; Rom 6:3) is uniformly administered not in the name of the Trinity but in the name of Jesus alone.

With respect to the first difficulty, that of the disciples' hesitancy

---

[88]I have borrowed the phrase from B. J. Hubbard's study by the same name (Missoula, Montana: The Society of Biblical Literature and Scholars' Press, 1974).

[89]Robert H. Gundry, *Matthew: A Commentary on His Literary and Theological Art* (Grand Rapids: Eerdmans, 1982), 596.

about evangelizing and receiving Gentiles into the church if they had really been charged by Christ to embark on the evangelization of the world, R. V. G. Tasker writes:

> ...it was surely not to be expected that they would be able to grasp all at once the full implication of their commission, or that a 'catholic' church would immediately emerge from what was originally a movement within Judaism. Many difficulties had to be overcome, and many adjustments had to be made, before it was fully understood that 'in Christ Jesus there is neither Jew nor Gentile'.[90]

Surely Tasker's perception of the situation shows a greater sensitivity to the inbred "Jewishness" which controlled the first disciples in much of their early reflections on the task before them. Luke records Jesus' same universal commission (Acts 1:8), and yet only a few chapters later, in spite of Christ's commission, he must report Peter's reticence to "eating anything common or unclean," that is, to Gentile evangelism, (Acts 10:9-16) and God's insistence that Peter must be about the job of discipling the nations, beginning with Cornelius and his household (see also Gal 2:11-12). I say again, to expect those first Jewish disciples to understand instantaneously the implications of Christ's commission to them and thus to submit to that commission with no psychological resistance is simply to evince an insensitivity to the position in which the first Jewish disciples found themselves.

Concerning the second difficulty, that such a commission to baptize in the triune Name must be an anachronism in Jesus' mouth in light of the reported Christian baptisms in Acts and elsewhere, two things can be said. First, there is nothing irregular, abnormal, or unexpected about our Lord mentioning all three persons of the Godhead here in what appears to be something of a summary of his teaching. He had made repeated mention of "the Father" and "the Son" previously, as we have already seen (Matt 11:27; 24:36; see also his *Abba* references in the Sermon on the Mount and his references to "the Father" and "the Son" in the Fourth Gospel). And he had referred to "the Spirit" in an extended fashion in John 14:25-26; 15:26; 16:7-15. Moreover, reference to "the Spirit" are found in both the Lukan and Johannine

---

[90]R. V. G. Tasker, *The Gospel According to St. Matthew* (Leicester: Inter-Varsity, 1961), 275.

versions of the Commission (Luke 24:49 and Acts 1:4-5, 8; and John 20:22). So there is no biblical-theological reason why the mention of all three persons could not have occurred on this occasion. Second, it is just as possible that Acts gives only an abbreviated form of the words actually used in the baptismal ceremony, highlighting by the employment of Jesus' name the fact that the persons mentioned were being admitted to the *Christian* church, as it is that Matthew reflects a later redactional form of the baptismal formula. Alfred Plummer suggests that Jesus in Matthew 28:19 might not have been giving primarily a formula to be used as much as an explanation of "what becoming a disciple really involves: it means no less than entering into communion with, into vital relationship with, the revealed Persons of the Godhead." He concludes:

> If, then, in this important passage our Lord was explaining the import of Christian baptism rather than enjoining a particular mode of administration, the difficulty of believing that He uttered this saying is greatly diminished, if it does not vanish altogether.[91]

I see no compelling reason, then, to conclude that this saying must be a Matthean redaction, and every reason to believe that here we are afforded further entrance into the mind of the risen Jesus with respect to his own self-understanding. My exposition will proceed accordingly.

We are particularly interested at once in calling attention to the precise form of the so-called "baptismal formula." Jesus does not tell his church to baptize

1. "...into the *names* [plural] of the Father and of the Son and of the Holy Spirit," or what is its virtual equivalent:

2. "...into the name of the Father, and into the name of the Son, and into the name of the Holy Spirit," "as if we had to deal with three separate Beings."[92] Nor does he state that the church is to baptize

---

[91] Alfred Plummer, *An Exegetical Commentary on the Gospel According to S. Matthew* (London: Robert Scott, 1915), 433-34.

[92] Benjamin B. Warfield, "The Biblical Doctrine of the Trinity" in *Biblical and Theological Studies* (Philadelphia: Presbyterian and Reformed, 1952), 42.

3. "...into the name of Father, Son, and Holy Spirit," (omitting the three recurring articles), "as if 'the Father, Son, and Holy Ghost' might be taken as merely three designations of a single person."[93] What he does state is that the church is to baptize

4. "...into the name [singular] of *the* Father, and of *the* Son, and of *the* Holy Spirit," first "[asserting] the unity of the three by combining them all within the bounds of the single Name, and then [throwing] into emphasis the distinctness of each by introducing them in turn with the repeated article."[94]

To comprehend fully the import of Jesus' statement, one must appreciate the significance of the term "the Name" for the Hebrew mind. In the Old Testament, the term does more than serve as the mere external designation of the person. Rather, it refers to the essence of the person himself. "In His name the Being of God finds expression; and the Name of God—'this glorious and fearful name, Jehovah thy God' (Deut. xxviii. 58)—was accordingly a most sacred thing, being indeed virtually equivalent to God Himself"[95] (See Isa 30:27; 59:19). "So pregnant was the implication of the Name, that it was possible for the term to stand absolutely...as the sufficient representation of the majesty of Jehovah"[96] (see Lev 24:11). Warfield's conclusion is worthy of quotation in full:

> When, therefore, our Lord commanded His disciples to baptize those whom they brought to His obedience "into the name of..." He was using language charged to them with high meaning. He could not have been understood otherwise than as substituting for the Name of Jehovah this other Name "of the Father, and of the Son, and of the Holy Ghost", and this could not possibly have meant to His disciples anything else than that Jehovah was now to be known to

---

[93]Warfield, "The Biblical Doctrine of the Trinity" in *Biblical and Theological Studies*, 42.

[94]Warfield, "The Biblical Doctrine of the Trinity" in *Biblical and Theological Studies*, 42.

[95]Warfield, "The Biblical Doctrine of the Trinity" in *Biblical and Theological Studies*, 42-3.

[96]Warfield, "The Biblical Doctrine of the Trinity" in *Biblical and Theological Studies*, 43.

> them by the new Name, of the Father, and the Son, and the Holy Ghost. The only alternative would have been that, for the community which He was founding, Jesus was supplanting Jehovah by a new God; and this alternative is no less than monstrous. There is no alternative, therefore, to understanding Jesus here to be giving for His community a new Name to Jehovah and that new Name to be the threefold Name of "the Father, and the Son, and the Holy Ghost."[97]

What are the implications for his deity in a saying, as Warfield declares elsewhere, that places him as "the Son," along with the Father and the Holy Spirit and equally with them, "even in the awful precincts of the Divine Name itself"?[98] The answer is obvious: Jesus is affirming here his own unqualified, unabridged deity! And that this is unquestionably his intent may be seen, still further, from an analysis of just that portion of his statement that precedes his mention of "the Son," namely, the phrase "the name of the Father." Clearly, in this abbreviated context, the phrase "the name" must carry the highest connotation, even that of deity itself inasmuch as it is the Father's name and thus the Father's nature which is so designated. But it is precisely this same "name" which the Son (along with the Holy Spirit) possesses and to which the Son (along with the Holy Spirit) stands related, evincing his equality with the Father insofar as his deity is concerned.

Our examination of the occurrences of "the Son" in the Synoptic Gospels is now completed. The significance of the title, "the Son," for the Synoptic Evangelists is consistent and pervasive: as "the Son" of "the Father" Jesus Christ is deity incarnate!

The Implications of Deity in Jesus' "Son [of God]" Sayings in the Fourth Gospel

When we press our investigation of the meaning of Jesus' "Son [of God]" sayings into the Fourth Gospel, we find no new doctrinal content in them respecting his person but rather only a more pervasive testimony, if that is possible, to the same doctrine of Jesus' divine

---

[97]Warfield, "The Biblical Doctrine of the Trinity" in *Biblical and Theological Studies*, 43-4.

[98]Warfield, *The Lord of Glory*, 156.

Sonship which we discovered in the Synoptic Gospels. While it is true that the Synoptic Gospels only infrequently report Jesus' use of "the Son" as a self-designation (we have just reviewed the instances), preferring to preserve for the church the memory that Jesus favored the title "Son of Man" as his public self-designation (which fact, of course, John does not ignore, as for example, see his mention of that title in 1:51; 3:13; 5:27; 6:62; and 9:35, and which, as we have seen, connotes through its association with the Danielic "Son of Man" a *divine* Messiah), John informs us that on certain occasions our Lord employed with great frequency and as a self-designation the title "the Son" in direct association with "the Father," and used "the Father" by itself some seventy additional times and "my Father" by itself almost thirty more times.

I intend to consider the implications in the more significant occurrences of this title in a moment, but it is again necessary to say something first about the authorship of John's Gospel in order to validate my conclusions.

My studied opinion is that John the Apostle wrote the Gospel which bears his name. When I say this, I do not, of course, intend to suggest that I believe that every single word came from his pen. For example, appended to 21:24 is the non-Johannine "validation": "and we know that his [the author's] witness is true."[99] But B. F. Westcott's massive argument for the over-all authorship of the Gospel by John son of Zebedee, I believe—with Leon Morris—"has not so much been confuted as bypassed."[100] Westcott argues first from what he terms "indirect evidence" (Carson speaks of his argument as moving "in concentric circles from circumference to centre") that the author was a Jew, then a Jew of Palestine, then an eye-witness, then an Apostle, and finally John the Apostle. Then from what he construes

---

[99]I am also aware of the widely-held view that John 21 in its entirety is a later supplement, but see Grant R. Osborne, "John 21: Test Case for History and Redaction in the Resurrection Narratives" in *Gospel Perspectives*, edited by R. T. France and David Wenham (Sheffield: JSOT, 1981), II, 293-328.

[100]Leon Morris, *The Gospel According to John* (Grand Rapids: Eerdmans, 1971), 9. For Morris' sustained defense of Westcott's argument for John the Apostle's authorship of the Gospel of John, see his "The Authorship of the Fourth Gospel" in *Studies in the Fourth Gospel* (Grand Rapids: Eerdmans, 1969), 215-92.

to be "direct evidence" (1:14: 19:35; 21:24) he reaches the same conclusion. Finally, he shows that this conclusion is supported by early patristic evidence.[101] This means, of course, if Westcott is correct, that the Gospel was written by one who had been an eye- and ear-witness to Christ's ministry from the very beginning, his passion, his empty tomb, and his post-resurrection appearances, which in turn implies that its author would have needed no assistance when he wrote the Fourth Gospel from the Synoptic Gospels or from the so-called Synoptic literary sources of "*Ur-Markus*" or "Q," "M" or "L." Nor would he have needed to rely on other literary or oral sources for the content of his Gospel. The facts about Jesus, surely the major concern of John himself as he composed his Gospel (19:35), are certified to us simply by his own pen as one of the original Twelve. How his Gospel should be viewed in relation to the Synoptic Gospels, I would then urge, is as a supplement to them.[102] Surely aware of their existence and their content, John wrote his Gospel self-consciously as a climactic supplement to the other three. And although John's supplementary depiction of Christ differs from those of the Synoptic Gospels in that it takes on the decided character of a Christology "from above," beginning as it does with the intra-Trinitarian relations between the Father and the Son in eternity and tracing the "descent" of the divine Word to his enfleshment as Jesus of Nazareth, *there is no evidence that John ascribes to Jesus anywhere a self-understanding which is not already implicit , if not explicit, in the Synoptics.* It has been argued that John allowed the later faith of the church and his own more mature theological reflections to distort Jesus' true self-understanding. But this is hardly likely in light of the fact that John himself will often carefully distinguish between something Jesus said and the meaning of that statement which he and the other disciples only later after the resurrection comprehended (see 2:18-22; 7:37-39; 12:16; 21:18-23; see also 20:9).

---

[101]B. F. Westcott, *The Gospel According to St. John* (London: John Murray, 1908), ix-lxvii.

[102]James D. Dvorak, "The Relationship Between John and the Synoptic Gospels" in *JETS* 41/2 (June 1998): 201-13, also argues that John "wrote his gospel literarily independent of the synoptics but that he knew them and their tradition(s)" (213). See also D. A. Carson, *The Gospel According to John* (Grand Rapids: Eerdmans, 1991), 49-58.

But precisely because John's high Christology is unacceptable to much of current New Testament critical scholarship, his authorship has been rejected, and the Gospel that bears his name has been traced to other sources—Jewish Wisdom, Hellenistic, Gnostic, and so on. The general opinion today is that the Fourth Gospel is probably literarily independent of the Synoptics but, like the Synoptics, is ultimately dependent upon a hazy "layer" of oral tradition about Jesus which lies behind the "literary sources" which were used in the composition of John's Gospel as we have it today. Now it goes without saying that if these postulated literary sources cannot be isolated from each other, neither can they be analyzed for the historical authenticity of the events they report or for the philosophico-theological influences which they bring to bear on the total composite make-up of the "Johannine" Christology. Consequently, a great amount of effort has been and is being expended on the source-criticism of the Fourth Gospel. R. Bultmann in his commentary on John postulated that underlying the Fourth Gospel are a "signs source," a revelatory discourse source (originally in Aramaic and based on Gnostic material), a passion and resurrection narrative (which is independent of the tradition of the Synoptics), plus contributions from the Evangelist and a later editor. While his particular view has not found general acceptance among New Testament scholars, it has spawned a number of other theories, among them being those of J. Becker, R. Schnackenburg, W. Nicol, R. Fortna, H. Teeple, and S. Temple. But these have faired no better in attracting a following. D. A. Carson has critically analyzed these attempts to discover the literary sources for John, only to conclude that "it is doubtful if [these attempts] are demonstrable, even in the limited sense of commanding sustained assent to their probability." He concludes his survey of them with "an appeal for probing agnosticism in these matters."[103]

In a more recent article, in which he critically analyzes C. H. Dodd's form-critical study of John entitled *Historical Tradition in the Fourth Gospel* and the responses of a number of reviewers of

---

[103]D. A. Carson, "Current Source Criticism of the Fourth Gospel: Some Methodological Questions" in *Journal of Biblical Literature* 97 (1978): 428. Morris had earlier reached the same conclusion (*The Gospel According to John*, 58):

that work, Carson reaches a similar conclusion,[104] making the point along the way that the form-critical scholar's presuppositions, rather than the method itself which he uses, all too often are the determining factors in the conclusions which he reaches, and he calls upon those engaged in the method to exercise more objectivity than they have in the past.[105] I could not agree more since my own research bears out both the highly subjective nature of the form-critic's application of his so-called "criteria of authenticity" and (at times) his failure to see the "forest of meaning" for the "trees of minutia" which engross his attention. With both Morris and Carson, therefore, I am not persuaded that any argument against the Johannine authorship of John's Gospel has to date been forthcoming which compels one to abandon the view which until more recent times enjoyed virtually universal acceptance in the church. I will turn then to the exposition of Jesus' "Son of God" sayings in John's Gospel with the studied opinion that it is eye- and ear-witness testimony which we are considering.

In his *The Christology of the New Testament* Oscar Cullmann declares that, beginning and ending his Gospel as John does with the description of Christ as θεός, *theos* (1:1; 20:28), if there is merit in

---

> If John did take sources he has so re-worked them and made them his own that in the judgment of many competent scholars it is now impossible to discern which were sources and which was John's own material. What B. H. Streeter said about a particular view has a much wider application: "if the sources have undergone anything like the amount of amplification, excision, rearrangement and adaptation which the theory postulates, then the critic's pretence that he can unravel the process is grotesque. As well hope to start with a string of sausages and reconstruct the pig." It seems much safer to take the Gospel as it stands and assume it comes from the Evangelist.

See also C. S. Lewis, "Modern Theology and Biblical Criticism" in *Christian Reflections*, edited by Walter Hooper (London: Geoffrey Bles, 1967), 152-66, who, as only Lewis can do, points up the weaknesses of the Bultmannian source critical and form critical methods of New Testament analysis.

[104]D. A. Carson, "Historical Tradition in the Fourth Gospel: After Dodd, What?" in *Gospel Perspectives*, edited by R. T. France and David Wenham (Sheffield: JSOT, 1981), II, 112-14, 135.

[105]Carson, "Historical Tradition in the Fourth Gospel: After Dodd, What?" in *Gospel Perspectives*, 121, 135.

the literary device known as inclusion (*inclusio*), "there can be no doubt that for him all the other titles for Jesus which are prominent in his work...ultimately point toward this final expression of his Christological faith."[106] Even a cursory examination of the Johannine occurrences of the Christological titles, "the Son" and "the Son of God," bears out the accuracy of Cullmann's assertion.

The Divine Son of John 5:17-29

That the title "the Son of God" is, for John, at least messianic is borne out from its appearance in his Gospel along side of the clearly messianic titles of "the King of Israel," "the Christ," and "he who was to come into the world" (1:49; 11:27; 20:31). But that it connotes more than the messianic office *per se* is clear from its occurrences in several of the rich discourses of Jesus in the Gospel. In John 5:17-29, after healing the lame man on the Sabbath day, Jesus justified his act before the offended religious hierarchy by claiming both the ability and prerogatives of "seeing" and "doing" as "the Father" does:

> "My Father is working still, and I am working" (5:17);

> "The Father loves the Son, and shows him all that he himself is doing" (5:20).

Therefore,

> "The Son does...what he sees the Father doing" (5:19a).

Indeed,

> "Whatever he does, that the Son does *likewise* [ὅμοίος, *homoiōs*]" (5:19b).

Furthermore, as "the Son," Jesus claimed to have the "Father-granted" sovereign right to give life: "The Son gives life to whom he is pleased to give it" (5:21b; see Matt 11:27). There is no contextual consideration that warrants our placing any limitation on the denotation he intends here, either to spiritual or to physical life, for as *spiritually* dead men hear the voice of "the Son of God," they "live" (5:24-25;

---

[106]O. Cullmann, *The Christology of the New Testament*, 308.

see also 6:40a), and as *physically* dead men someday hear his voice, they will come forth from their graves (5:28-29; see also 6:40b). And when they do the latter, he declared, they do so only to stand before *him* in the Final Judgment inasmuch as the Father has committed all judgment to him (5:22-27). These are clearly activities within the province and powers of deity alone to perform, and in making these claims Jesus laid claim to his coordinate engagement in every work of the Father. In short, in this one brief passage, Jesus claimed, as "the Son," to be—coordinate with "the Father"—the Sovereign of life, of salvation, of the resurrection, and of the Final Judgment. But perhaps his most emphatic claim to equality with the Father comes in 5:23 when he makes one's honoring of "the Father" turn on the issue of whether one honors "the Son," that is, Jesus himself. With these words Jesus laid claim to the right to demand, equally with the Father, the honor (that is, the devotion and worship) of men!

Is it any wonder, given the assumption of the religious leaders concerning him (that is, that he was only a man) that they thought him, under Jewish law (see Lev 24:16), to be worthy of death? By the unique relationship which he was declaring existed between himself and "the Father," he was making himself "equal [ἴσον, *ison*] with God" (5:18).

In view of Jesus' express statements that "the Son can do nothing by himself; he can do only what he sees his Father doing" (5:19), and "By myself I can do nothing" (5:30), not to mention his later declaration that "the Father is greater than I" (14:28), one might on first consideration conclude that the charge that he was making himself "equal with God" was both unfounded and one which, by these words, he was expressly disavowing, that is to say that in declaring himself to be "less than the Father" he was explicitly making himself "less than God." There can be no doubting the fact that in making these statements, our Lord was asserting in some sense a subordination to the Father. But *in what sense?* In the ontological, the covenantal, or the functional sense? This is the issue that must be addressed. Warfield sensitizes us to the problem and offers words of caution here:

> There is, of course, no question that in "modes of operation," as it is technically called—that is to say, in the functions ascribed to the several persons of the Trinity in the redemptive process, and, more

> broadly, in the entire dealing of God with the world—the principle of subordination is clearly expressed...The Son is sent by the Father and does His Father's will (Jn. vi:38)...In crisp decisiveness, Our Lord even declares, indeed: 'My Father is greater than I' (Jn. xiv.28)....But it is not so clear that the principle of subordination rules also in "modes of subsistence," as it is technically phrased; that is to say, in the necessary relation of the Persons of the Trinity to one another. The very richness and variety of the expression of their subordination, the one to the other, in modes of operation, create a difficulty in attaining certainty whether they are represented as also subordinate the one to the other in modes of subsistence. Question is raised in each case of apparent intimation of subordination in modes of subsistence, whether it may not, after all, be explicable as only another expression of subordination in modes of operation. It may be natural to assume that a subordination in modes of operation rests on a subordination in modes of subsistence; that the reason why it is the Father that sends the Son...is that the Son is subordinate to the Father.... But we are bound to bear in mind that these relations of subordination in modes of operation may just as well be due to a convention, an agreement, between the Persons of the Trinity—a "Covenant" as it is technically called—by virtue of which a distinct function in the work of redemption is voluntarily assumed by each. It is eminently desirable, therefore, at the least that some definite evidence of subordination in modes of subsistence should be discoverable before it is assumed.[107]

Here are words of wisdom which we would do well to ponder since in the very context which we are considering it is not at all evident, in "subordinating" himself to "the Father," that he was denying that he was in essence one with the Father. When the charge of blasphemy for making himself "equal with God" was leveled against him, a charge by the way which hounded him to the very end of his life and which became finally the basis for the sentence of death against him (see John 8:58-59; 10:33; 19:7; and in the Synoptics, Matt 26:65-66; Mark 14:61-62; Luke 22:70-71), he said nothing to allay the hardened suspicions of the religious leaders concerning him, but followed their charge with the very discourse we have been considering

[107]Warfield, "The Biblical Doctrine of the Trinity" in *Biblical and Theological Studies*, 53-4.

in which he laid claim to the powers and privileges which belong to deity alone!

The Unity of "the Son" and "the Father" in John 10:22-39

In his "Good Shepherd" discourse, Jesus asserted that the security of his sheep is grounded in their mutual keeping by both the Father and himself (10:28, 29). Then our Lord explained that this *coordinated* keeping on their part was grounded in turn in the essential oneness of "the Father" and "the Son." "I and the Father *are one* [ἕν ἐσμεν, *hen esmen*]," he declared (10:30; see also 12:45; 14:9, 23), concerning which declaration B. F. Westcott writes:

> It seems clear that the unity here spoken of cannot fall short of unity of essence. The thought springs from the equality of power (*my hand, the Father's hand*); but infinite power is an essential attribute of God; and it is impossible to suppose that two beings distinct in essence could be equal in power.[108]

When he was confronted by the religious leaders who took up stones to kill him, charging him again with blasphemy because he "being a man, make yourself God" (10:33), if they were hoping that some word from him would relieve their suspicions concerning him, they were to be disappointed, for instead of declaring that they had misunderstood him, to the contrary, arguing *a minori ad majus* ("from lesser to greater"), he insisted that if human judges, because they had been made recipients of and were thus the responsible administrators of the justice of the Word of God, could be called "gods" (see Ps 82:6), how much greater right did he—"the one whom the Father sanctified and sent into the world" (10:36)—have to call himself "the Son of God." The fact that Jesus' claim to be "the Son of God," both here (10:36) and earlier (5:25), invoked on both occasions the same response from the Jewish opposition, namely, the charge of blasphemy, points up how wrong the modern popular perception is that concludes that Jesus' claimed "Sonship" intended something less than the claim of deity. "He is not God; he said he was the *Son* of God," the saying

---

[108]B. F. Westcott, *The Gospel According to St. John* (Reprint of 1881 edition; Grand Rapids: Eerdmans, 1958), 159.

goes. Such a perception completely overlooks the fact that the religious leadership of his day understood his claim to have just the opposite intention, namely, the precise claim to deity, which understanding Jesus did nothing to correct. And that his answer intended the claim to deity is evident also from the fact, as Vos trenchantly notes with respect to the word order of "sanctified" and "sent" in Jesus' explanation of his right to the title "the Son of God," that "he places the sanctifying before the sending into the world, because it preceded the latter, and a suggestion of pre-existence accompanies the statement."[109] Jesus clearly asserts for himself here, as "the Son," a transcendent character—he is not "the Son" because he was sent, but rather was "the Son" and was "sanctified" (that is, was "set apart" through the investiture of the messianic task) *before he was sent;* and he was sent precisely because only one such as himself as "the Son" could complete the task which the messianic investiture entailed.

The Eternal Pre-existence of the Son In the Fourth Gospel

Vos' observation catapults us into the center of a controversy which is raging today around the person of Christ: Did Jesus claim for himself pre-existence, and if so, in what sense? In the ontological (eternal) or in the ideal ("foreknown") sense?[110] For one who takes Jesus' words at face value, it is evident that Jesus affirmed of himself as "the Son," not just ideal pre-existence but pre-existence of an *eternal* kind: "Glorify me, Father," he prayed, "with yourself, with the glory which I had with you before the world was" (17:1, 5), indeed, with "my glory which you have given me because you loved me before the foundation of the world" (17:24).

This particular claim on Jesus' part to an eternal pre-existence with his Father is not an aberration on the surface of John's Gospel, for he speaks elsewhere, though in somewhat different terms, of that same pre-existence:

---

[109]Vos, *The Self-Disclosure of Jesus*, 198.

[110]See R. G. Hamerton-Kelly, *Pre-Existence, Wisdom, and the Son of Man* (Cambridge: University Press, 1973), and the numerous short discussions of the issue of Christ's pre-existence throughout James D. G. Dunn, *Christology in the Making* (see Dunn's index) for the questions which are being raised and the critical answers which are being offered.

"No one has ascended into heaven but he who descended from heaven, even the Son of Man" (3:13);

"I have come down from heaven, not to do my own will, but the will of him who sent me" (6:38; see 6:33, 50, 58);

"[No one] has seen the Father except him who is from [παρά, *para*, with genitive; that is, from the side of] the Father" (6:46);

". . . what if you were to see the Son of Man ascending where he was before [τὸ πρότερον, *to proteron*]?" (6:62);

"You are from below, I am from above; you are from this world, I am not from this world" (8:23);

"I speak of what I have seen with the Father" (8:38);

"...I came out and came forth from [ἐκ, *ek*, with genitive] God" (8:42); and finally,

"I came out from [ἐκ, *ek*, παρά, *para*] the Father, and have come into the world" (16:28; see 9:39; 12:46; 18:37).

Jesus' "I Am" Sayings

Perhaps the greatest assertion among all of his claims not only to eternal pre-existence but also to actually being the Yahweh of the Old Testament is that which is found in his "I am" saying of John 8:58: "Before Abraham was, I am" (see Ex 3:14: "This is what you are to say to the Israelites: 'I AM [the personal name of God] has sent me to you").

Most of Jesus' "I am" sayings,[111] it is true, he supplied with a subjective complement of some kind, such as the following:

"I am the bread of life" (John 6:35, 48, 51 [or, "the living bread who came down from heaven"]);

---

[111]Jesus "I am" sayings, in which he is the referent of the "I", in the Synoptic Gospels are found only once in Matthew (14:27), twice in Mark (6:50; 14:62), and twice in Luke (22:70; 24:39). Most by far, some 26 times, are found in the Fourth Gospel (4:26; 6:20, 35, 41, 48, 51; 8:12, 18, 23 (2), 24, 28, 58; 10:7, 9, 11, 14, 25; 13:19; 14:3, 6; 15:1, 5; 18:5, 6, 8).

"I am the light of the world" (John 8:12);

"I am from above" (John 8:23)

"I am the door of the sheep" (John 10:7, 9);

"I am the good shepherd" (John 10:11, 14);

"I am the resurrection and the life" (John 11:25);

"I am the way, the truth, and the life" (John 14:6); and

"I am the vine" (John 15:1, 5).

But I agree with D. A. Carson that "two are undoubtedly absolute in both form and content...and constitute an explicit self-identification with Yahweh who had already revealed himself to men in similar terms (see especially Isa. 43:10-11)."[112] The two instances Carson refers to are in John 8:58 and 13:19, but there could well be other instances as well, such as Jesus' "I am" usages in John 6:20; 8:24, 28; and 18:5-8.

In the case of John 8:58, standing before men who already regarded him as demonic and who had told him as much, Jesus declared as we have already noted: "Before Abraham was, I am," invoking not only the term which Yahweh in the Old Testament had chosen as his own special term of self-identification but claiming also in the process a

---

[112]D. A. Carson, "'I Am' Sayings" in *Evangelical Dictionary of Theology*, 541. Carson goes on to say in the same article that "these two occurrences of the absolute 'I am' suggest that in several other passages in John, where 'I am' is *formally* absolute but a predicate might well be supplied from the context (e.g., 4:26; 6:20; 8:24, 28; 18:5, 6, 8), an intentional double meaning may be involved" (541). I personally believe that, with the exception of the single occurrence in 4:26, all of the other "I am" statements which Carson cites, because of some detail(s) in the context, should be regarded as absolute in form and content, reflecting Jesus' ascription to himself of deity through the utilization of the great Old Testament "I am" language. See C. H. Dodd, *The Interpretation of the Fourth Gospel* (Cambridge: University Press, 1953), 345 on 6:20; 95 on 8:28 (see also Isa 43:10 LXX); Leon Morris, *The Gospel According to John*, 447 on 8:24; 743-44 on 18:5, 6, 8; G. C. Berkouwer, *The Person of Christ*, 168 on 8:24.

For other general discussions of Jesus' "I am" sayings, see Raymond E. Brown, *The Gospel According to John I-XII*, Appendix IV, 533-38; G.

pre-existence appropriate only to one possessed of the nature of Yahweh. Unbiased exegesis of these words, Henry Alford reminds us, "must recognize in them a declaration of the essential pre-existence of Christ."[113] His meaning was not lost on his audience, for "they took up stones to throw at him" (8:59). "They understood that Jesus ascribed divine existence to himself and made himself equal with God."[114] In the case of his "I am" in John 13:19 Jesus himself explicated its implications for his unity with the Father and in turn his own Yahwistic identity when he declared in the following verse: "...he who receives me receives him who sent me." Perhaps these absolute "I am" sayings are the background to Jesus' prayer to the Father in John 17:26: "I have manifested your name to those whom you gave me out of the world." But it must also be remembered that in all these declarations "the subject of the affirmation is the actual person speaking; it is of himself who stood before men and spoke to them that Our Lord makes these immense assertions,"[115] making "I am" also his own name and leading his audiences in the Gospels either to believe in him or to accuse him of blasphemy.

In John 6:20, by his "I am, be not afraid" saying, Jesus admittedly might have been simply identifying himself to his terrified disciples, yet, as Carson notes, "...not every 'I' could be found walking on water."[116] And Mark's "He was about to pass them by" (6:48) is reminiscent of Yahweh's theophany in Exodus 33:22.

Then in John 8:24, following immediately as it does his declaration that he was "from above" and "not from this world," Jesus' "I am" statement, "If you do not believe that I am, you will die in your sins," surely carries with it divine implications.

Braumann and H.-G. Link, "I Am" in *The New International Dictionary of New Testament Theology*, edited by Colin Brown (English edition; Grand Rapids: Zondervan, 1976), 2.278-83; and G. M. Burge, "'I Am'" Sayings" in *Dictionary of Jesus and the Gospels*, edited by Joel B. Green, Scot McKnight, and I. Howard Marshall (Downers Grove, Illinois: InterVarsity, 1992), 354-56.

[113]Henry Alford, *The Greek Testament* (Cambridge: Deighton, Bell, 1868), I, 801.

[114]G. C. Berkouwer, *The Person of Christ*, 165.

[115]Warfield, "The Person of Christ According to the New Testament" in *The Person and Work of Christ*, 60.

[116]D. A. Carson, "'I Am' Sayings" in *Evangelical Dictionary of Theology*, 541.

Finally, in the case of his "I am" in 18:5-8, as soon as he uttered these words, his would-be captors "drew back and fell to the ground." It is difficult to avoid the conclusion that John intended to suggest by this "eye-witness touch" in his account of Jesus' arrest that his readers were to recognize in Jesus' acknowledgment that he was the one whom the arresting officals sought also his implicit self-identification with Yahweh.[117]

Jesus' Divinity in his Teaching, Works, and Attributes

Returning from his conflict with "the strong man," that is, Satan (see Matt 12:29), Jesus, "in the power of the Spirit" (Luke 4:14), began his public ministry as the Messiah. Having called Andrew, Simon, Philip, and Nathaniel to be his disciples while in Judea (John 1:35-51), he journeyed to Cana in Galilee where he performed his first "miraculous sign"—the changing of the water into wine (John 2:1-11). After a brief stay in Capernaum (John 2:12), Jesus returned to Jerusalem and drove the money-changers out of the temple (John 2:13-14), the first of two such "temple-cleansings," the second occurring during the Passion Week. As a result of this "act of zeal" (John 2:19), he invoked the opposition of the religious leaders whose antipathy toward him would follow him throughout his ministry and which would finally lead at their instigation to his crucifixion at the hands of the Roman procurator.

It is interesting to note in connection with this first temple-cleansing his reference, even at this early stage of his ministry, to God as "my Father" (John 2:16), surely an indication of his awareness of that unique and personal divine Sonship which he had already implied was his at the age of twelve, which Sonship only weeks before the heavenly Voice had confirmed at his baptismal "commissioning," and which forty days later Satan himself had had to acknowledge was his essential station. On this occasion, Jesus also spoke of his resurrection although his disciples did not comprehend his meaning.

It was during this early Judean stage of his ministry that he spoke too with Nicodemus (John 3:1-15). And it is not unrelated to our entire

---

[117]Burge, "'I Am'" Sayings" in *Dictionary of Jesus and the Gospels*, states: "The mere uttering of this name creates a powerful revelation which leaves the arresting party prostrate before God" (355a).

study to note in passing, in his "new birth" discourse, the features which would surface again and again throughout his teaching ministry—references, for example, to "the kingdom of God" (3:5, 8), to the Spirit as a distinct person of the Godhead (3:5, 8), his early use of "the Son of Man" title (3:13, 14; see 1:51), and even a veiled allusion to his death by crucifixion ("the Son of Man must be lifted up"). Such early references serve to highlight the sustained continuity of the content of his teaching ministry.

After only a brief ministry in Jerusalem (John 3:23) and in the surrounding countryside (3:22), Jesus returned to Galilee (John 4:3). On his way he ministered to the woman at the well of Samaria, evidencing in his conversation with her his supernatural awareness of her past (4:17), and expressly claiming in the privacy of that conversation to be the Messiah (4:25-26). Arriving in Galilee and calling James and John, he launched what has come to be known by New Testament scholars as his "great Galilean ministry," proclaiming that the kingdom of God was "near" (that is, had come in its "mystery" form) (Matt 4:17), and giving evidence of the same by "healing every disease and sickness among the people" (Matt 4:23-25). Wherever he went the supernatural was present in both his words and deeds—and in both his divine character was manifested.

His Teaching

As illustrations of his general teaching, one may cite (1) his Sermon on the Mount (Matt 5-7), at the end of which, we are told, "the crowds were amazed at his teaching, because he taught as one who had authority and not as the teachers of the law" (Matt 7:28-29), (2) his lesson on the nature of the kingdom of heaven (Matt 13) which he sovereignly related in parable form because, so he informed his disciples, "The knowledge of the secrets of the kingdom of heaven has been given to you, but not to them," that is, to the people at large (Matt 13:11), (3) his Bread of Life Discourse (John 6:25-59) in which he repeatedly claimed, as "the Bread of Life," that he had come down from heaven (6:33, 38, 51, 58), (4) his Good Shepherd Discourse (John 10:1-18, 25-30) in which he claimed that he and the Father were one (10:30) and that he was "the Son of God" (10:36), (5) his Olivet Discourse (Matt 24–25) in which he foretold the destruction of

Jerusalem in A.D. 70 and his own future coming in power and great glory to consummate the kingdom of God, and (6) his Upper Room Discourse in which he revealed the most intimate details concerning the relations obtaining within the very Godhead itself (14:10, 16, 18, 26-15:26; 16:12-15).

The Law of God

Admittedly, it is only an indirect indication that Jesus understood himself to be divine but it is a fact that never anywhere in his general deliverances to the people does he claim the Spirit's inspiration as the origin of his teaching. Never does he say: "Thus the Lord says." Always he taught as if he were himself the divine Oracle. Take, for example, the authoritative manner in which he expounded the Law of God to his contemporaries. He claimed to know the will and true intention of God which lay behind the Law (see his "I say to you," Matt 5:22, 28, 32, 34, 39, 44, and his many sayings introduced by ἀμήν [*amēn*, "Truly"], Matt 6:2, 5, 16). In speaking the way he did, writes Marshall, he

> made no claim to prophetic inspiration; no 'thus says the Lord' fell from his lips, but rather he spoke in terms of his own authority. He claimed the right to give the authoritative interpretation of the law, and he did so in a way that went beyond that of the prophets. He thus spoke as if he were God.[118]

The Kingdom of God

His teaching concerning the kingdom of God, acknowledged on all sides as the central theme of his teaching ministry, also suggests that Jesus' self-understanding included the self-perception of deity. According to Jesus, while the kingdom or rule of God will come some day in the future in power and great glory in conjunction with his own return (Matt 25:31-46, particularly 25:34), it had already invaded history in the soteric/redemptive sense (its "mystery" form) *in his own person and ministry* (see Matt 11:2-6 against the background of Isa

---

[118]I. Howard Marshall, *The Origins of New Testament Christology*, 49-50. Marshall's entire chapter 3, "Did Jesus Have a Christology?" (43-62), can be read with real profit, for he defends, on grounds that pass radical criteria of authenticity, the unique authority of Jesus and Jesus' claim to messiahship.

35:5-6; 12:28; 13:24-30, 36-43). *In him* God's Kingdom had invaded the realm of Satan, and he had bound the "strong man" himself (Matt 12:29; Mark 3:27), a claim clearly caring *messianic* implications. But Jesus was equally explicit that the Kingdom of God is both supernatural in nature and supernaturally achieved. George E. Ladd explains:

> As the dynamic activity of God's rule the kingdom is supernatural. It is God's deed. Only the supernatural act of God can destroy Satan, defeat death (I Cor. 15:26), raise the dead in incorruptible bodies to inherit the blessings of the kingdom (I Cor. 15:50ff.), and transform the world order (Matt. 19:28). The same supernatural rule of God has invaded the kingdom of Satan to deliver men from bondage to satanic darkness. The parable of the seed growing by itself sets forth this truth (Mark 4:26-29). The ground brings forth fruit *of itself.* Men may sow the seed by preaching the kingdom (Matt. 10:7; Luke 10:9; Acts 8:12; 28:23, 31); they can persuade men concerning the kingdom (Acts 19:8), but they cannot build it. It is God's deed. Men can receive the kingdom (Mark 10:15; Luke 18:17), but they are never said to establish it. Men can reject the kingdom and refuse to receive it or enter it (Matt 23:13), but they cannot destroy it. They can look for it (Luke 23:51), pray for its coming (Matt. 6:10), and seek it (Matt. 6:33), but they cannot bring it. The kingdom is altogether God's deed although it works in and through men. Men may do things for the sake of the kingdom (Matt. 19:12; Luke 18:29), work for it (Col. 4:11), suffer for it (II Thess. 1:5), but they are not said to act upon the kingdom itself. They can inherit it (Matt 25:34; I Cor. 6:9-10, 15:50), but they cannot bestow it upon others.[119]

Jesus, so declares David F. Wells in this connection, clearly saw himself as the Messiah and as bringing in this supernatural kingdom. But "if Jesus saw himself as the one in whom this kind of Kingdom was being inaugurated, then such a perception is a Christological claim which would be fraudulent and deceptive if Jesus was ignorant of his Godness."[120] Warfield would surely have concurred with Wells, concluding as he did about Jesus' teaching that "in its insight and foresight it was as supernatural as the miracles themselves...The

---

[119]George Eldon Ladd, "Kingdom of Christ, God, Heaven" in *Evangelical Dictionary of Theology*, 609.

[120]David F. Wells, *The Person of Christ*, 38.

theme of his teaching was the kingdom of God and himself as its divine founder and king."[121]

Claims from the Passion Week

Coverage of the last week[122] of our Lord's life occupies a major portion of the four Gospels. If sheer amount of material is any indication, one may safely conclude that for the Evangelists that last week was the most significant week of Jesus' entire ministry. And, of course, it was—since its events were to bring him directly to "the hour" for which he had come (John 12:23-27), and to the "cup" which his Father had ordained that he should drink (Matt 26:39, 42).

Much of his time that week was spent teaching in the temple courts (F. L. Godet says he "resided in the temple, as if in his palace, and exercised there a sort of Messianic sovereignty."[123]) (Luke 19:47), debating in conflict-situations with those who were plotting his death and communing with his small band of disciples whose spirits he sought to fortify against the fears and disappointments which were to overwhelm them as a result of the events of that approaching first "Good Friday." But in the course of events that week he did and said certain things that require the exegete to conclude that he be understood as laying claim both to an essential divine Sonship over against a functional sonship and to the messianic investiture which in its own way implied the former. Due to space limitations I must restrict myself to only the more significant items of evidence in this regard, grouping that evidence according to the days of the passion week for facility of presentation.

---

[121]Warfield, "The Historical Christ" in *The Person and Work of Christ* (Philadelphia: Presbyterian and Reformed, 1950), 31.

[122]T. W. Manson's suggestion in his "The Cleansing of the Temple" in *Bulletin of the John Rylands Library* 33 (1951): 271-82, which suggestion receives some support in William L. Lane, *The Gospel According to Mark* (Grand Rapids: Eerdmans, 1974), 390-91, 489, that the traditional "week" commencing with the entrance of Jesus into Jerusalem may, in fact, have been a period of approximately six months extending from the Feast of Tabernacles the previous Fall to the Passover in the Spring is, in my opinion, expressly precluded by John's explicit statements that date Jesus' Jerusalem entry five days before the Passover (John 12:1, 12-15).

[123]F. L. Godet, *Commentary on the Gospel of John* (Reprint of the 1893 third edition; Grand Rapids: Zondervan, 1968), II, 216.

"Palm Sunday": Matthew 21:1-11; Mark 11:1-11; Luke 19:28-44; John 12:12-19

The one major event of the first day of that momentous week was, of course, Jesus' entry into Jerusalem riding on a young donkey with the crowds of pilgrims on their way to the Passover festivities hailing him as "the Son of David" and "the King of Israel." Jesus, quite clearly, intended that this act, in accordance with Zechariah 9:9, be regarded as his public announcement that he was Israel's messianic King; and coming as he did—not on a military charger with armies behind him but on a donkey—he came as the Prince of Peace of Isaiah 9:6 (see Matthew 21:5: "gentle"; John 12:15: "Do not be afraid").

There can be little doubt that the crowds did not grasp the significance of the symbolism in the humble means of entry which he had arranged. In their hailing him as "the Son of David" (Matt 21:9), "the King who comes in the name of the Lord" (Luke 19:38), and "the King of Israel" (John 12:13), they doubtless were thinking of him for the most part, if not exclusively, in terms of a political Messiah. In fact, John informs us that even his disciples did not understand the real significance in the symbolism of this aspect of his messianic announcement until after his resurrection (John 12:16). They too were still capable of thinking of his messiahship in nationalistic and political terms. But there can be no legitimate doubts regarding Jesus' intention. Notwithstanding Bultmann's view that the opinion which I am espousing here is "absurd," Jesus, I would submit, intended his entrance into Jerusalem on the unridden young ass, in accordance with and in fulfillment of Zechariah 9:9, to be his formal and public proclamation to Jerusalem that he was the Old Testament's promised Messiah. The time for messianic secrecy was past.[124] Nor can there

---

[124]C. E. B. Cranfield, *The Gospel According to Saint Mark* (Cambridge, University Press, 1966), 352-54, argues that certain details in the Gospel records—for example, the fact that Jesus' entry on the donkey and the accompanying demonstration are not mentioned at the Jewish trial, the crowd's designation of Jesus as (only) "the Prophet" (Matt 21:11), John's remark in 12:16, and Mark's "incredibly quiet ending" to the demonstration (11:11)—indicate that, while Jesus was fulfilling Zechariah 9:9, he intended to do so "in circumstances so paradoxical as to make the meaning of his action hidden. It was a veiled assertion of his Messiahship.... The messianic hiddenness is still maintained." William L. Lane, *The Gospel According to*

be any legitimate questioning of the fact that both the crowds and the disciples perceived Jesus' act to be a messianic act. Finally, there are no legitimate grounds to deny the historicity of the event.

It is not my intention to argue here that Jesus (1) was exercising the attributes of divine prescience and omnipotence over the actions of men in his acquisition of the donkey, (2) was asserting divine lordship over the ordinary laws of nature when he rode the unbroken animal, or (3) was intending by his use of "the Lord" (ὁ κύριος, *ho kurios*) (Matt 21:3; Mark 11:3; Luke 19:31) to refer to himself as "the (real) owner" of the colt over against οἱ κύριοι (*hoi kurioi*, "the owners") (Luke 19:33) since one may propose alternative interpretations which are within the bounds of reason. I will only say that I believe that a reasonable case can be made in each of the above situations for a supernaturalist interpretation.

The one point I wish to underscore here is this: in presenting himself as Zechariah 9:9's promised King by consciously arranging the circumstances of his entry to conform to the Old Testament prophecy (see Matt 21:4-5; John 12:14-15), Jesus was claiming by implication to be the fulfiller of every other Old Testament Messianic prophecy—

Mark, 393-94, concurs. I vigorously disagree with this interpretation of the event. Jesus was *unambiguously* claiming to be the Messiah—and the biblical evidence indicates that the crowds perceived this fact (see John 12:13)—but in terms the *full* significance of which only the spiritually illumined, such as Mary (John 12:7; see Matt 26:12), would understand. After all, to present oneself publicly as the King in Zechariah 9:9's terms is to claim, *unambiguously and publicly*, to be the Messiah. John does not intend by his remark in 12:16 to say that no one perceived "the fact" of his Messiahship. As I have just said, he expressly implies otherwise by his report of the crowd's exclamations in 12:13. And the disciples had realized for some time that he was the Messiah (John 1:41, 49; Matt 16:16). What John intends by the remark in 12:16 is that the disciples "did not understand the real significance of these events. They did not comprehend the nature of Jesus' kingship.... John is not affirming that the multitude correctly evaluated the Person of the Lord. They thought of him as King in the wrong sense. After the glorification the disciples thought of him as King in a right sense" (Morris, *The Gospel According to John*, 588). But publicly and unambiguously declare himself by his Jerusalem entry to be the Messiah—this Jesus most assuredly did though it is true that neither the crowds nor the disciples perceived that the Cross yet stood between him and the Crown.

simple consistency requires that we say this much. That is to say, he was claiming to be the "Shiloh" of Genesis 49:10, the "star" and "scepter" of Numbers 24:17, the "King" and "Son" of Psalm 2:6-7, the "mighty one" and the "God" of Psalm 45:3-6, David's "Lord" and the "priest forever in the order of Melchizedek" of Psalm 110:1-4, the "Immanuel" and the "wonderful counsellor, the mighty God, the enduring father, and the prince of peace" of Isaiah 7:14 and 9:6, the "Son of Man" and the "Messiah" of Daniel 7:13-14 and 9:25-26, the suffering "servant" of Isaiah 53, "the one whom they pierced" of Zechariah 12:10, and the "Lord who would suddenly come to his temple" of Malachi 3:1. In fact, it is specifically in fulfillment of this last prophecy that he would act the following day.

"Monday: the Day the Lord Came": Matthew 21:18-19, 12-17; Mark 11:12-19; Luke 19:45-58

Leaving Bethany the following morning, where he had spent the night (Mark 11:11), Jesus cursed the barren fig tree on his way into the city, then entered the temple and drove out the merchants and the money changers,[125] healed the blind and the lame who came to him there, and accepted the praise of the children over the protests of the chief priests and teachers of the Law, citing Psalm 8 as his justification for doing so. Then he returned to Bethany for the night.

Each of his recorded acts that day was clearly messianic and in one way or another gave evidence of his deity. His cursing of the barren fig tree symbolically underscored his divine prerogative to judge and gave symbolic prominence to the truth he was to express the following day in his parable of the wicked farmers that the Kingdom of God was to be taken from fruitless Israel and to be given to a people (the Gentiles) who would produce its fruit (Matt 21:43). Which is just to say that as Israel's God he was going to reject ("curse") the nation and turn to the Gentiles for praise. With regard to his actions at the temple that day, Malachi's words need to be recalled:

---

[125] I am following Mark's arrangement of events here. Matthew gives the impression that the cleansing of the temple occurred on Sunday, immediately after Jesus entered the city, but he is doubtless following here his practice of arranging material topically rather than chronologically. See, for another illustration of this, Matthew 21:18-20 and Mark 11:12-14, 20-21.

> Behold, I will send my messenger, who will prepare the way before me, Then suddenly the LORD you are seeking ["the God of justice," from 2:17] will come to his temple; the messenger of the covenant, whom you desire, will come, says the LORD of Hosts. But who can endure the day of his coming? Who can stand when he appears? For he will be like a refiner's fire or a launderer's soap. He will act as a refiner and purifier of silver; he will purify the Levites and refine them like gold and silver. Then the LORD will have men who will bring offerings in righteousness, and the offerings of Judah and Jerusalem will be acceptable to the LORD, as in days gone by, as in former years. So I will come near to you for judgment. I will be quick to testify against sorcerers, adulterers and perjurers, against those who defraud laborers of their wages, who oppress the widows and the fatherless, and deprive aliens of justice, but do not fear me, says the LORD of Hosts. (3:1-5)

There really can be little doubt that this awesome prediction saw at least the initiation of its fulfillment when Jesus—the Lord whose temple it was—walked into the temple that day and drove them out who had turned it into a house of dishonest merchandising. It is significant that Jesus here does not refer to the temple as "my Father's house," as he had done in John 2:16 at the time of his first temple cleansing. Citing Isaiah 56:7 and Jeremiah 7:11, he speaks of it as "*my* house." And his work did have the salutary effect not too long after, as Malachi had predicted, of "purifying the Levites," for we read in Acts 6:7: "A large number of priests became obedient to the faith."

That he was thinking of himself as he so acted in terms of one with divine authority is brought out, not only by his reference to the temple as "my house," but also by what immediately followed his acts of healing. Some children who had heard the cries the day before of "Hosanna to the Son of David," having just witnessed the authority by which he cleansed the temple and the power by which he healed the blind and lame, began to repeat the cries of their elders of the day before. The chief priests and teachers of the law insisted that he silence their cries of praise to him. But Jesus defended their praise of *him* by appealing to Psalm 8:2 (Heb, 8:3), which speaks of *God* ordaining that children should praise him. The point of the Psalm is that God has ordained that he would receive praise from children, and the point of Jesus' citation of Psalm 8 is clear. As Carson writes:

> The children's 'Hosannas' are not being directed to God [in heaven, in this instance] but to the Son of David, the Messiah. Jesus is therefore not only acknowledging his messiahship but justifying the praise of the children by applying to himself a passage of Scripture applicable to God alone.[126]

It is clear from his citation of Psalm 8:2 that Jesus not only viewed himself as divine, but also that he believed that he was acting throughout that day as the divine Messiah!

"Tuesday: Jesus' Last Day of Public Ministry": Matthew 21:20-25:46; Mark 11:20-14:37; Luke 20:1-21:27; John 12:20-36

Tuesday was to be not only Jesus' final day of public ministry but perhaps also his busiest. It was filled with conflict but it concluded with God's confirming voice coming to him from heaven for the third time in the recorded accounts of his public ministry, the previous two times being at Jesus' baptism and at his transfiguration.

On his way into Jerusalem that morning, passing the fig tree that had withered (Mark 11:20), Jesus delivered a short homily to his disciples on the need for and power of faith in prayer. Then entering the temple again, he engaged himself throughout the day in teaching the people and debating the religious opposition. Against the chief priests and teachers of the Law who questioned his authority for acting as he had been doing he raised the issue of their attitude toward John's baptism. Then against their stubbornness and hardness of heart, he delivered his parables of "the two sons," "the wicked farmers," and "the wedding banquet." Then he found himself in debate with the Pharisees and the Herodians over the question of whether Jews should pay taxes to Caesar. Then the Sadducees accosted him with their casuistic question concerning the resurrection. Finally, the Pharisees confronted him again over the question of which is the greatest commandment.

Jesus, having either amazed them or put them to silence with his answers in each of these conflicts, then asked them his questions concerning the sonship of the Messiah: "Whose Son is he?" "If David...calls him 'Lord,' how is he his son?" Turning then to the crowds and to his disciples, he issued his stinging discourse of warnings

---

[126]D. A. Carson, *Matthew*, 443.

and woes against the teachers of the Law and the Pharisees, just as Malachi had said he would (see Matt 23 and Mal 3:5). Following this and his commendation of the widow for her great act of love in "giving all she had," he delivered his Olivet Discourse.

Sometime, probably on that day in light of John's remark in 12:36, and perhaps just before he departed from the temple for the Mount of Olives where he delivered his Olivet Discourse, some Greeks who had come to Jerusalem for the Passover celebration, expressed their desire to see Jesus.[127] It was on this occasion, as he was reflecting on his imminent death, that the Father spoke from heaven, assuring him that he would glorify his name in his Son's forthcoming death. When Jesus had delivered his Olivet Discourse, he returned to Bethany, his public ministry completed, to spend Wednesday in Bethany with his disciples, and to await the events of Thursday.

There are so many details indicative of Jesus' divine Sonship and messianic investiture in the reports of this day's events that it is not an overstatement to say that one could write a chapter on them alone. I, of course, can only note the more obvious ones, and for convenience will simply itemize them.

1. The fact that the fig tree by Tuesday morning had withered at his previous day's word of imprecation is indicative of the power which was his and which was present in all of his mighty works including those of the previous day. These, in turn, he himself had said were indicative of both his supernatural, divine origin (see John 2:11; 5:36; 10:24-25, 37-38, 14:11) and his messianic investiture (see Matt 11:4-5; Luke 7:22).

2. His question about John's baptism is significant for our present interest in that if the Pharisees had said John's baptism (i.e., his ministry) had been authorized by heaven, he would have said, as they themselves rightly surmised: "Then why did you not believe

---

[127]Another proposal is that this event occurred on Sunday, immediately after Jesus had entered the city and had arrived at the temple "to look around," because of the connection suggested by John's reference to the "crowd" in 12:17 and 12:19. See Raymond E. Brown, *The Gospel According to John I-XII*, 469. Morris does not commit himself in *The Gospel According to John*, 596.

him?" But why did Jesus ask them this specific question about John when obviously he could have asked them any number of questions? The answer is clear and plain: because John had publicly identified Jesus as "the one mightier than I, whose sandals I am not worthy to remove," in whose hands resided the sovereign prerogatives of salvation and judgment (heaven and hell), whose baptism of salvation John had said that he himself needed, and who was in fact the pre-existent Son of God and the one in whom all men should place their trust (Matt 3:11-12, 14; John 1:15, 30, 34; Acts 19:4).

3. In his parable of the wicked farmers, as we have already demonstrated, he portrayed himself as the "only beloved Son" and the "heir" of the landowner (God) of the vineyard (Israel), who existed *before he was sent* and who was loved *whether he be sent or not.* And in his application of the parable, he applied the messianic passage in Psalm 118:22-23 to himself and taught thereby that he was the "chief cornerstone" of God's "true temple" (the church) which Israel was in the process of rejecting and by so doing was sealing its own fate (Matt 21:42-44).

4. In his parable of the wedding banquet Jesus represented himself as the "king's son," the title denoting, at the very least, his messianic dignity but more likely bearing the full significance for him that the titular "Son" had in his previous parable.

5. In his conflict-situations with the Pharisees, Herodians, and Sadducees he displayed special insight into the Scriptures, even explicating a previously unrecognized implication in one of the Old Testament titles for God and demonstrating that divine wisdom "that comes down from above" (Jas. 3:15). Not only did his wisdom amaze his opposition and often silenced them but also in every instance in which he employed or interpreted Scripture he acted as if he knew the very will and mind of God respecting the meaning of Scripture.

6. By his question concerning the Messiah's sonship (Matt 22:41-46; Mark 12:35-37; Luke 20:41-44), although he did not say so in so

many words, he intimated that the person of the Messiah is not fully explained if one says he is only David's son inasmuch as David by the Spirit of God called him "Lord," thus assigning a superior status to him (Ps 110:1). This can properly be understood within the context of the theology of the New Testament to mean only one thing: that while the Messiah was to be traced on his human side back to his father David, he, as David's "Lord," was on the divine side the Son of God as well (see Rom 1:3-4).

Critical scholars have written much on this pericope and the intention behind Jesus' question: "If David then calls [the Messiah] 'Lord,' how is he his son?" As for the issue of its authenticity, over against such scholars as F. Hahn who contend that the pericope and specifically the question arose in the Hellenistic church, Marshall neatly summarizes the arguments against the pericope's authenticity and rebuts them.[128] For example, it is highly unlikely that the later church created a story in which Jesus is represented as calling into question the Messiah's Davidic sonship because Jesus' Davidic sonship was being denied by the church's detractors. This is so, first, because the Messiah's Davidic descent is too clearly taught in both the Old Testament and Judaism (see Matt 1:1, 6-17; Luke 3:23-31), and second, because there is no evidence that such a denial was being registered against Jesus' ancestry. But if Jesus in this pericope is not calling into question the Messiah's Davidic descent but is in some sense affirming the Messiah's lordship over his father David, and if the church had created the pericope, because it surely saw the point of the question as applying to Jesus (why else would *his* church have "created" it?), it is exceedingly strange that the church did not make the manner of its application to Christ more explicit and obvious. The very fact that Jesus is portrayed as leaving its point "hanging" lends the ring of authenticity to Jesus' question. Marshall concludes that there is simply no convincing *Sitz im Leben* for the pericope in the later early church.

We may assume then for good reason that the pericope is authentic and that Jesus was not denying the Messiah's Davidic descent, but the question still remains: "How is it that David would

---

[128]I. Howard Marshall, *The Gospel of Luke*, 744-47.

call his son his 'Lord'?" There can be no question that part of the answer must be found in David's knowledge that God would raise his son, the Messiah, from the dead (Psalm 16:8-11; see Acts 2:25-31) and exalt him to his own right hand (Psalm 110:1 [the verse Jesus cites]; see Acts 2:32-36). In other words, the Messiah's "functional" Lordship over David, according to Luke (the author of Acts) and Peter (the preacher in Acts 2), is found in the exaltation of the Messiah to the Lord's right hand through the instrumentality of his resurrection and ascension. But can nothing more be said? Can a case not be made for the Messiah being *intrinsically*, that is, ontologically, David's Lord, apart from and, indeed, prior to his resurrection? I submit that this question can be answered affirmatively, and for the following reasons: David understood that the Messiah would be divine. According to the author of Hebrews (1:5), when David wrote Psalm 2:7 he was ascribing such super-angelic dignity to the Messiah that the further supreme titles of "God" and "Lord" (the Yahweh of Psalm 102), with all the attributes and functions which these titles connote, could also be rightly ascribed to him. And still further, according to the same author (Heb 1:13), when David wrote Psalm 110:1 it was this *divine* Son of whom he was speaking when he asserted his superangelic dignity.

The Author of Hebrews is only affirming what Jesus himself taught before him. For while it is true that Jesus did not apply the citation to himself in a direct way in this pericope, he did do so in Matthew 26:64 and the synoptic parallels, and he did so in such a fashion that it is clear that he understood his Lordship over David as entailing more than his exaltation through resurrection. This is evident for four reasons: first, his claim that he would shortly be sitting at the right hand of God (an allusion to Psalm 110:1) immediately followed his claim to be the Son of God which denotes divine status; second, to "sit on the right hand of the Mighty One" implies not only *occupancy* of the place of highest honor in the heavens but also *participation* in the very dignity and power of that Mighty One; third, to "come on clouds of heaven," an allusion to Daniel's transcendent "man-like figure" which he also employs in the later pericope, is descriptive not of human but of divine activity (Nah 1:3); and fourth, all of the Synoptic Evangelists record that the Sanhedrin clearly branded his claim to Sonship in such terms as blasphemy worthy of death.

When all of this data is taken into account it cannot be validly questioned that Jesus by his question concerning the Messiah's sonship was speaking of his own Sonship and that he was thinking of that Sonship as essentially divine and as entailing divine attributes.

7. In his denunciation of the teachers of the Law and the Pharisees (Matt 23), in addition to the general fact that his pronouncement of woes is reflective of that prophetic prerogative which transcended the prophets themselves (never did he say "Thus the Lord says") and which was his by virtue of his being the divine Messiah (Deut 18:15), several other very significant features in the denunciation itself underscore the fact that he was speaking with a consciousness that he was the very Son of God as well. By implication he declared himself to be the Christ, and as such the *only* legitimate "Teacher" and "Master" of men (23:8-10).[129] He declared that it was he, "the Wisdom of God" (see Luke 11:49),[130] who "sends prophets to you" (23:34). When one recalls that according to Old Testament teaching a man could only be a true "prophet" (נָבִיא, *nābhî'*) if God stood behind him as his authority (Ex 4:15; 7:1) and that it was Yahweh who commissioned and sent the prophets to Israel, one can hardly find a more explicit claim to deity anywhere in Jesus' teaching (in this same regard, see John's exposition of Isaiah 6:1-7 in 12:39-41 where we learn that it was the pre-incarnate Son, whose glory Isaiah saw, who commissioned Isaiah on behalf of the Godhead). When Jesus then cried: "O Jerusalem, Jerusalem, you who kill the prophets and stone those sent to you, how often I longed to gather your children together...," the immediate context

---

[129]See Warfield, *The Lord Of Glory*, 67-8. Vos, *The Self-Disclosure of Jesus*, 133, writes: "The uniqueness of even the teacher-dignity of Jesus, and the admixture of religious reverence evoked by it, are recognizable in the saying of Matt. 23:8.... This uniqueness is no less than that [uniqueness] of the religious fatherhood, when predicated of God... (Matt. 23:9)."

[130]"That Jesus could be and actually was identified with the Wisdom of the Old Testament is inferred from Matt. 23:34-36 (Luke 11:49-51)." So Vos, *The Self-Disclosure of Jesus*, 146.

suggests that the temporal extent of his expressed longing should not be restricted to the years of his personal ministry but embraced the Old Testament economy as well. What lay behind his judgment against *his* generation that placed the guilt of the blood of all the prophets upon it was the fact that his generation (descendants of the "fathers who murdered the prophets") was not simply rejecting the prophets whom he had sent to them but was dismissing *the very one who had sent all of the prophets throughout all past generations.*

He concluded his denunciation against them by applying the messianic passage in Psalm 118:26 to himself, declaring that they would not see him after the events of the next few days until they said: "Blessed is he who comes in the name of the Lord." Throughout the warp and woof of the entire denunciation are strong intimations of his divine consciousness and messianic dignity.

8. It is quite likely that it was at this time that the Greeks expressed a desire to see him (John 12:20-36). From his reaction it is evident that Jesus saw in this desire on the part of Gentiles for an audience with him a "sign" that his death was imminent. Morris observes:

> Jesus recognizes in their coming an indication that the climax of his mission has arrived.... The fact that the Greeks had reached the point of wanting to meet Jesus showed that the time had come for Him to die for the world. He no longer belonged to Judaism, which in any case has rejected Him.[131]

And so Jesus began to contemplate the cross work which lay before him in a fresh and vivid way, so much so that his contemplation created in him "a foretaste of Gethsemane," evoking from him the cry: "Now is my soul troubled. And what shall I say? 'Father, save me from this hour'? But for this purpose I came to this hour! Father, glorify your name!" (12:27-28)

At that moment, a voice, audible even to the crowds which were present, came from heaven: "I have glorified it, and will

---

[131] Morris, *The Gospel According to John*, 590. Bengel calls their coming "a prelude of the transition of God's kingdom from the Jews to the Gentiles." See the words of the Pharisees in 12:9 and John's illustration of it in 12:20.

glorify it again" (12:28). Responding directly to the prayer which Jesus prayed to his Father, the voice speaking in the first person was clearly the voice of God the Father. Here then is the third instance when the Father confirmed to Jesus and/or attested to others the unique filial relationship in which Jesus as "the Son" stood with respect to God as "the Father," and surely by this heavenly affirmation his claim to messianic investiture received fresh confirmation as well.

9. In his Olivet Discourse one can find a sustained emphasis on Jesus' consciousness of both his divine Sonship and messianic prerogatives and functions. By contrasting himself with the "false Christs" who would come in *his* name, he declared himself to be the *true* Christ (24:5). By placing his reference to himself as "the Son" in the particular order that he did in Matthew 24:36 (see Mark 13:32), he implied that his was a superangelic existence. By foretelling both the destruction of Jerusalem in A.D. 70 and his own second advent in power and great glory, he demonstrated his possession of supernatural prescience. He spoke of sitting someday on his glorious throne with all the angelic hosts behind him and all the nations before him (25:31). And as "the King" (who speaks of God as "my Father," 25:34, 40), he declared that he would judge the nations and decide their eternal destinies. The criterion of his division among men would be ultimately their relationship to him (25:40, 45), and the outcome of his judgment would mean either eternal life or eternal punishment (25:46). The portrait he draws of himself in this final judgment scene is so awesome and majestic that it is simply moral perversity that prevents one from viewing him here in terms of his full divine character as God and in terms of his messianic investiture as one conducting the awesome affairs of his Father.

"Thursday: The Last Passover": Matthew 26:17-75; Mark 14:12-72; Luke 22:7-65; John 13:1-18:27

Having spent Wednesday in Bethany with his disciples, with the day following (Friday) being "the first day of Unleavened Bread when the Passover lamb was being sacrificed" (Mark 14:12), Jesus made preparations to eat his last Passover with his disciples in Jerusalem. When it was evening (which by Jewish reckoning would have been the day of Passover), Jesus gathered with his disciples in the upper room and ate the Passover with them. At that time he instituted the Lord's Supper, washed his disciples' feet, and said his farewell to them (John 13-16), closing the meal with his great high priestly prayer (John 17). Then he went to the Garden of Gethsemane to pray. There he was arrested and taken for trial first before Annas and then before Caiaphas.

The accounts of these events are so filled with intimations of Jesus' understanding of himself as the divine Messiah that I can only mention the more significant ones. Again, I will itemize them according to the events in which they are found for facility of presentation.

1. At the Passover meal, the arrangements for which may well have been carried out in accordance with details known to Jesus by divine prescience (Mark 14:13-16; Luke 22:8-13), Jesus gave several indications that he regarded himself as the Messiah. He declared that what was about to befall him was coming to pass "just as it had been written" (Matt 26:24; Mark 14:21; Luke 22:22). He cited the following specific Old Testament verses in this regard: Psalm 41:9 (John 13:18), Psalm 69:4 (John 15:25), and Isaiah 53:12 (Luke 22:37), declaring in connection with this last citation: "This which has been written must be fulfilled in me: 'And with the transgressors he was numbered'; yes, what concerns me is reaching its fulfillment" (Luke 22:37). This last citation is most significant in that it is the one occurrence of record where we find Jesus himself explicitly relating his messianic work to the Servant of Isaiah 53, no doubt a major reason why the New Testament writers later felt at liberty to do so (see Matt 8:17; John 12:38; Acts 8:32-33; Rom 15:21; 1 Pet 2:22).[132] And as the Servant who would "bear the sin

---

[132]Because of the connection which Jesus makes here between his messianic work and the sacrificial work of the Servant of Isaiah 53, this saying has been viewed by many modern form-critical scholars as a product of the early church's over-all efforts to give scriptural support to its representation of Jesus' death as sacrificial. If Jesus' authority could be added to everything else favoring this view, so the argument goes, this representation of his death would be greatly enhanced. Donald Guthrie in

of many," Jesus saw himself as the Mediator of the New Covenant of Jeremiah 31:31-34, his own life being offered in sacrifice for the sins of many (Luke 22:20). And with messianic authority Jesus declared: "I confer on you a kingdom, just as my Father conferred one on me, so that you may eat and drink at my table in my kingdom..." (Luke 22:29-30). Then in his high priestly prayer (John 17:3), he actually refers to himself in the third person as "Jesus *Christ*, whom you have sent."[133]

His perception of himself as divine is brought out plainly in connection with his revelation of Judas' forthcoming betrayal. Citing Psalm 41:9 as the Old Testament prediction of it, he asserted: "I am telling you now before it happens, so that when it does happen you will believe that *I am*" (John 13:19; emphasis supplied). "The ["I am"] expression almost certainly has overtones of deity as in 8:28," declares Morris.[134] Divine prescience is evident also in Jesus' prediction down to minute detail concerning Peter's denial—"before

---

his *New Testament Theology* (Leicester: Inter-Varsity, 1981), 261-62, defends the authenticity of the saying and argues that Jesus' citation of Isaiah 53:12 raises the "strong probability that he saw himself as fulfilling the whole role [of the Servant] including the vicarious suffering." Many students of the Gospels have detected other references to Isaiah 53 in single words in the sayings of Jesus, for example, "rejected" in Mark 9:12 (see 53:3) and "taken away" in Mark 2:20 (see 53:8). Furthermore, Isaiah 53:7 appears to be reflected in Jesus' deliberate silence before his judges (Mark 14:61; 15:5; Luke 23:9; John 19:9), 53:12 in his intercession for his executioners (Luke 23:34), and 53:10 in his "laying down his life" for others (John 10:11, 15, 17). Martin Hengel, in fact, in his *The Atonement: The Origin of the Doctrine in the New Testament*, translated by John Bowden (London: SCM, 1981), 33-75, argues that Isaiah 53 and Jesus' understanding of it lies behind both his "ransom sayings" (Matt 20:28; Mark 10:45) and his "supper sayings" (Matt 26:26-28; Mark 14:22-24). The later New Testament uses of Isaiah 53 (53:1 in John 12:38; 53:4 in Matt 8:17; 53:5, 6, 9, 11 in 1 Pet 2:22-25; 53:7-8 in Acts 8:30-35; 53:12 in Phil 2:7) surely go back to the mind of Jesus himself.

[133]See Warfield, *The Lord of Glory*, 183-86, for his extended defense of the phrase "Jesus Christ" in John 17:3 as an authentic self-designation on Jesus' part.

[134]Leon Morris, *The Gospel According to John*, 623. T. W. Manson proposed that the formula ἐγώ εἰμι (*egō eimi*, "I am") really means, "The Messiah is here." But Raymond E. Brown writes: "...there is not much in the context of the Johannine passages that would incline us to think that Jesus

the cock crows *twice*, you will deny me *three* times."

In his words of farewell in John 14-16 and in his prayer of John 17 his essential divine Sonship is acutely evident. So sustained is Jesus' emphasis on his Sonship here that I can do little more than mention the recurring themes. He speaks, for instance, of his pre-temporal eternal pre-existence with his Father (14:24; 15:21; 16:27, 28; 17:5, 24), of his coming out from his Father into the world to do his Father's will (14:10, 31; 15:10, 15; 16:5, 28; 17:3, 8, 18, 21, 23, 25) and of his return to his Father (14:2, 12, 28; 16:5, 10, 28; 17:13). He speaks of the fellowship which was his with the Father and of the love which he had continued to know by virtue of his union with the Father throughout his earthly sojourn among men (14:10, 11, 20; 15:10; 17:11, 21, 22, 23). Clearly, here is the "stuff" of which the church's incarnational Christology is made!

With the celebration of the Passover completed, after singing a concluding psalm, Jesus left the upper room and went to the Garden of Gethsemane.

2. In the garden Jesus agonized before his Father in prayer over "the cup" which his Father had placed before him to drink. On the way there he cited Zechariah 13:7 as foretelling what was about to happen to "the Shepherd" and his "sheep" (Matt 26:31; Mark 14:27)—further evidence that Jesus perceived that the way he was going was the way which had been foretold for the Messiah. And during his stay in Gethsemane, if the text is original, an angel from heaven came to strengthen him (Luke 22:43), further evidence that he was walking in the way the Father had willed for him.

Then his arresters came, led by Judas. Stepping forward, in reply to their declaration that they were seeking Jesus of Nazareth, He declared: "I am!" (John 18:5)[135] At this, we are informed by John that they retreated and fell to the ground. Surely both in his

---

is speaking of messiahship. A more common explanation...is to associate the Johannine use with ἐγώ εἰμι [*egō eimi*] employed as a divine name in the OT and rabbinic Judaism" (*The Gospel According to John I-XII*, 533).

[135]Morris, *The Gospel According to John*, 743: "...the answer is in the style of deity." Brown, *The Gospel According to John I-XII*, 534, observes: "...the fact that those who hear it fall to the ground when he answers suggests a form of theophany which leaves men prostrate in fear before God."

words and their reaction to them is further evidence of his deity. Then after Peter, impulsively trying to protect Jesus, had cut off Malchus' ear, Jesus healed Malchus, asserting to Peter: "Do you think I cannot call on my Father and he will at once put at my disposal more than twelve legions of angels? But how then would the Scriptures be fulfilled that say it must happen in this way" (Matt 26:53-54). In this remark are clear suggestions of his consciousness of his unique Sonship and his messianic investiture. Then he submitted to his captors, saying again: "This has all taken place that the writings of the prophets might be fulfilled" (Matt 26:56; Mark 14:49).

3. At his trial before Caiaphas, in response to the high priest's question, he affirmed that he was both "the Christ" and "the Son of God," both Daniel's "Son of Man who would come on clouds of heaven" and David's "Lord, the one who would sit at the right hand of God." Here are unmistakable claims both to deity and to messiahship, for which claim to deity they judged him a blasphemer and worthy of death.

Throughout the recorded events of this day, our Lord testified to his deity in so many ways that to deny this testimony and to explain it away as the later "mythical" creation of the church, appears to be, to say the least, a radical expedient. More likely, something deeper than mere scholarly reserve or the "assured results of scholarly research" underlies this denial by much modern scholarship.

"Friday: The Hour When Darkness Reigned": Matthew 27:1-61; Mark 15:1-47; Luke 22:66-23:56; John 18:28-19:42

At daybreak, the council of elders decided to put Jesus to death for blasphemy (Luke 22:66-71). But because the Jewish religious authorities did not have the authority to execute criminals (John 18:31), they determined to hand Jesus over to Pilate, the Roman procurator, on the trumped-up charge that he opposed paying taxes to Caesar and that he, by claiming to be the Messiah, posed a political threat to Rome (Luke 23:2). After Herod and Pilate had examined him, however, they both concluded that there was no substance to these charges.

So Pilate sought to have him released. But he finally capitulated to their protests and turned him over to the soldiers to be crucified. After six hours on the cross, Jesus died, making the practice of *crurifragium* unnecessary in his case, thus fulfilling the Scriptures once again (John 19:33, 36). His body was then taken down from the cross by friends and placed in the tomb of Joseph of Arimathea.

While the intimations of Jesus' deity are not as many, they were still present on this day up to the very end. At his final early morning trial before the Sanhedrin Jesus again affirmed that he was, indeed, both the Danielic "Son of Man" who would sit at the right hand of the Mighty God and the Son of God (Luke 22:69-70), further attestation by Jesus that he was the divine Messiah.

Before Pilate Jesus affirmed that he was the "King of the Jews," but not in the sense that his accusers had represented him to Pilate (Matt 27:11; Mark 15:22; Luke 23:3; John 18:33-37). Concluding that his claim was no apparent threat to Caesar, Pilate attempted to have him released. It was then that the Jews admitted their real reason for hostility toward him: "We have a law [a reference probably to Leviticus 24:16] and according to that law he must die, because he claimed to be the Son of God" (John 19:7). From this acknowledgment by his enemies we learn again that Jesus had, in fact, claimed to be the Son of God, and that claiming to be such he was in their opinion making a claim tantamount to the claim to deity.

Claiming no responsibility for his death Pilate released Jesus to the soldiers who took him away and crucified him.

Even on the cross, Jesus gave expression to his consciousness of (1) his Sonship ("*Father*, forgive them"; "*Father*, into your hands..."),[136] (2) his assurance that he was going to his Father ("Today, you will be *with me* in paradise"; "*Father, into your hands* I commit

---

[136]There is ground for legitimate doubt respecting whether the "first saying from the cross" ("Father, forgive them") is a part of the original Gospel of Luke. Found as it is only in Luke 23:34, it is absent even there in such early and diverse witnesses as P^{75}, B, the original hand of D, W, *Th*, and several significant versions, a "most impressive" group of witnesses (Metzger). But the textual support for its retention is not weak either, being found in the original hand of ℵ, A, C, L, N and several other versions. Harnack, Schlatter, Zahn, and a host of fine commentators support the authenticity of this prayer, as does the editorial committee of the UBS Greek New Testament who consider

my spirit"); (3) his need as the Messiah to fulfill all Scripture ("I thirst"; see John 19:28 and Ps 69:21), and (4) his having completed the objective requirements of the Messianic task which had been assigned him by the Father ("It is finished").

His Works

His Miracles

"The purport of [Jesus'] miracles was that the kingdom of God was already present in its King."[137] The following specific healing miracles by Jesus are mentioned in the Gospels:

1. the royal official's son (John 4:46-54)
2. Peter's mother-in-law (Matt 8:14-17; Mark 1:29-31; Luke 4:38-40)
3. the woman with a hemorrhage of blood (Matt 9:20-22; Mark 5:25-34; Luke 8:43-48)
4. the centurion's servant (Matt 8:5-13; Luke 7:1-10)
5. the man suffering from dropsy (Luke 14:1-6)
6. the blind (Matt 9:27-31; John 9:1-7; Matt 20:29-34; Mark 10:46-52; Luke 18:35-43)
7. the deaf (Mark 7:31-37)
8. the paralyzed and lame (Matt 9:1-8; Mark 2:1-12; Luke 5:17-26; John 5:1-15; Matt 12:9-13; Mark 3:1-5; Luke 6:6-10; 13:10-17)
9. lepers (Matt 8:1-4; Mark 1:40-45; Luke 5:12-16; 17:11-19), and
10. Malchus' ear (Luke 22:49-51).

One must also mention here both his exorcisms of demons which, in the mastery they exhibited over the forces of Satan, signalized in a unique way his divine authority over and messianic assault against

---

the logion as dominical in origin even though, writes Metzger, it is "probably not a part of the original Gospel of Luke" (*A Textual Commentary on the Greek New Testament*, 180).

[137]Warfield, "The Historical Christ" in *The Person and Work of Christ*, 31; see also David F. Wells, *The Person of Christ*, 40.

the cosmic kingdom of evil and sin (Matt 8:28-34; Mark 5:1-20; Luke 8:26-39; Mark 1:23-27; Luke 4:33-37; Matt 15:21-28; Mark 7:24-30; Matt 17:14-21; Mark 9:14-29; Luke 9:37-43) and the resuscitating or raising again to life of Jairus' daughter (Matt 9:18-19, 23-26; Mark 5:22-24, 35-43; Luke 8:41-42, 49-56), the widow's son (Luke 7:11-16), and Lazarus (John 11:1-54).

In addition to these specific examples of healing—against which much effort has been expended to explain them away—we have several general narrative statements found in all of the Synoptic Gospels which are not so easily explained away:

> Jesus went throughout Galilee,...healing every disease and sickness among the people. News about him spread all over Syria, and people brought to him all who were ill with various diseases, those suffering severe pain, the demon-possessed, the epileptics and the paralytics, and he healed them. (Matt 4:23-24)

> When evening came, many who were demon-possessed were brought to him, and he drove out the spirits with a word and healed all the sick. (Matt 8:16)

> Jesus went through all the towns and villages,...healing every disease and sickness. (Matt 9:35)

> When Jesus landed and saw a large crowd, he had compassion on them and healed their sick. (Matt 14:14)

> People brought all their sick to him and begged him to let the sick just touch the edge of his cloak, and all who touched him were healed. (Matt 14:35-36)

> Great crowds came to him, bringing the lame, the blind, the crippled, the dumb and many others, and laid them at his feet; and he healed them. The people were amazed when they saw the dumb speaking, the crippled made well, the lame walking and the blind seeing. (Matt 15:30-31)

> ...the people brought to Jesus all the sick and demon-possessed. The whole town gathered at the door, and Jesus healed many who had various diseases. He also drove out many demons. (Mark 1:32-34)

> So he traveled throughout Galilee,...driving out demons. (Mark 1:39)

> He had healed many, so that those with diseases were pushing forward to touch him. (Mark 3:10)
>
> And everywhere he went—into villages, towns or countryside—they placed the sick in the marketplaces. They begged him to let them touch even the edge of his cloak, and all who touched him were healed. (Mark 6:56)
>
> When the sun was setting, the people brought to Jesus all who had various kinds of sickness, and laying his hands on each one, he healed them. (Luke 4:40)
>
> A large crowd of his disciples was there and a great number of people from all over Judea, from Jerusalem, and from the seacoast of Tyre and Sidon, who had come to hear him and to be healed of their diseases. Those troubled by evil spirits were cured, and the people all tried to touch him, because power was coming from him and healing them all. (Luke 6:17-19)
>
> ...the crowds...followed him. He welcomed them and spoke to them about the kingdom of God, and healed those who needed healing. (Luke 9:11)

Matthew and Luke also report Jesus' own general description of his ministry in his response to John the Baptist's query:

> The blind receive sight, the lame walk, those who have leprosy are cured, the deaf hear, and the dead are raised. (Matt 11:4-5; Luke 7:22)

He furthermore declared that if his "powers" which had been done in Chorazin, Bethsaida, and Capernaum had been done in Tyre, Sidon, and even Sodom, those ancient cities would have repented (Matt 11:20-24; Luke 10:12-13). Even his enemies acknowledged his authority over demons (Matt 12:22-32; Mark 3:20-30; Luke 11:14-23).

In addition to his own miraculous works, Jesus gave to his twelve disciples the authority to "drive out evil spirits and to cure every kind of disease and sickness" (Matt 10:1), including even the authority to raise the dead (Matt 10:8); and Mark informs us that "they went out and...drove out many demons and anointed many sick people with oil and healed them" (Mark 6:13). Then later he commissioned seventy(-two) other disciples to do the same thing (Luke 10:1, 9, 17, 19). With pardonable over-statement, Warfield writes: "For a time disease and death must have been almost banished from the land."[138]

To these "signs and wonders" having to do with the alleviation of human suffering, one can add the following so-called "nature miracles".

1. the changing of water into wine (John 2:1-11)
2. the two miraculous catches of fish (Luke 5:1-11; John 21:1-14)
3. the stilling of the storm (Matt 8:23-27; Mark 4:35-41; Luke 8:22-25)
4. the feeding of the five thousand (Matt 14:15-21; Mark 6:34-44; Luke 9:12-17; John 6:5-14)
5. the walking on the sea (Matt 14:22-27; Mark 6:45-52; John 6:16-21)
6. the feeding of the four thousand (Matt 15:32-39; Mark 8:1-10)
7. the four-drachma coin in the fish's mouth (Matt 17:24-27) and
8. the cursing of the fig tree (Matt 21:18-22; Mark 11:12-14, 20-21).

If the New Testament record is reliable here—and there is no reason to doubt its reliability and many reasons to accept it—never had any other age of the world witnessed such a dazzling display of "wonders," "signs," "powers," and "works" of God. Of course, much effort has been expended through the centuries, as I have already said, to explain away Jesus' works of power, some explanations more speculative, some more crassly rationalistic than others, but all having as their chief aim the reduction of Jesus to manageable "human" dimensions. Baruch Spinoza (1632-1677), the Dutch rationalist philosopher of Jewish parentage, for example, argued in his *Tractatus Theologico-politicus* (1670) that God was a God of such unchangeable order that were he to work a miracle, since that miracle would then be as much God's law as the law of nature it violated, he would

[138]Warfield, "The Historical Christ" in *The Person and Work of Christ*, 31.

violate the unchangeable order he had decreed for the laws of nature and thus contradict himself. David Hume (1711-1776), the Scottish philosopher of the Enlightenment,[139] argued in his "Essay on Miracles," one section of his *Philosophical Essays Concerning Human Understanding* (1748), that the only case in which the evidence for a miracle could prevail over the evidence against it would be that

---

[139]David Hume has been often characterized as a religious skeptic and an enemy of the Christian faith. He was a philosophical skeptic, true enough. But he was not a philosophical skeptic in the sense of one who despairs of all knowledge from any and every source. And he was certainly not a religious skeptic. He simply did not think that mere unaided human reason could arrive at truly significant truth which was the position of his deistic opponents. As a biblical presuppositionalist he restricted the foundation of all knowledge to Scripture, and his "surface skepticism" must be read in this light. I too am a philosophical skeptic in this sense. Hume sought to reserve the source of truth to the one religion which he regarded as true, even to Christianity. For example, in his *History of England*, he writes:

> This interested diligence of the clergy [to teach anything they want] is what every wise legislator will study to prevent; because in every religion, *except the true*, it is highly pernicious, and it has even a natural tendency to pervert the true, by infusing into it a strong mixture of superstition, folly and delusion. (emphasis supplied)

In his *Natural History of Religion* he writes in his discussion of Islam which he thought contained contradictions:

> Nothing indeed would prove more strongly the divine origin of any religion, than to find (and happily this is the case with Christianity) that it is free from a contradiction so incident to human nature.

In his essay "On Suicide," he refers to Holy Scripture as "that great and infallible rule of faith and practice which must control all philosophy and human reasoning." In his *Dialogues Concerning Natural Religion*, he writes:

> A person, seasoned with a just sense of the imperfections of natural reason, will fly to revealed truth with the greatest avidity, while the haughty dogmatist, persuaded that he can erect a complete system of theology by the mere help of philosophy, disdains any farther aid, and rejects this adventitious instructor [revealed truth]. To be a philosophical skeptic is, in a man of letters, the first and most essential step towards being a sound, believing Christian.

situation in which the falseness or error of the affirming witnesses would be a greater miracle than the miracle which they attest. Friedrich Schleiermacher (1768-1834), often called the father of liberal Protestant theology, contended in his *The Christian Faith* (1821) that Christ's "miracles" were such only for those in respect to whom they were first done but not miracles in themselves, being but the anticipation of the discoveries of the laws which govern in the kingdom of nature. Christ, it seems, by the providence of God, simply possessed a deeper acquaintance with the laws of nature than any other man before or after him and was able to evoke from the hidden recesses of nature those laws which were already at work therein and to employ them for others' benefits. Another German theologian of the same period, Heinrich Paulus (1761-1851), in his *Exegetical Handbook Concerning the First Three Gospels* (3 vols., 1830-1833) argued that the Evangelists did not intend their reports to be understood as miracles but only as ordinary facts of everyday experience. Thus Christ

---

Toward the end of his essay, "On Miracles," he writes:

> We may conclude that the Christian religion not only was first attended with miracles, but even at this day cannot be believed by any reasonable person without one. Mere reason is insufficient to convince us of its [Christianity's] veracity: and whoever is moved by faith to assent to it, is conscious of a continued miracle in his own person, which subverts all the principles of his understanding, and gives him a determination to believe what is most contrary to custom and experience.

In "A Letter from a Gentleman to His Friend in Edinburgh," he writes:

> In Reality, whence comes all the various Tribes of Hereticks, the *Arians*, *Socinians*, and *Deists*, but from too great a Confidence in mere human Reason, which they regard as the *Standard* of every Thing, and which they will not submit to the superior Light of Revelation? And can one do a more essential Service to Piety, than by showing them that this boasted Reason of theirs, so far from accounting for the great Mysteries of the Trinity and Incarnation, is not able fully to satisfy itself with regard to its own Operations, and must in some Measure fall into a Kind of implicite Faith, even in the most obvious and familiar Principles?

See also *The Letters of David Hume*, Vol. 2, Ltr. 509, for his advocacy letter, written shortly before his death, on behalf of one Professor Wight, who was a Reformed Christian, to William Strahan.

> did not heal an impotent man at Bethesda, but only detected an imposter; He did not change water into wine at Cana, but brought in a new supply of wine when that of the house was exhausted; He did not multiply the loaves, but, distributing his own and his disciples' little store, set an example of liberality, which was quickly followed by others who had like stores, and thus there was sufficient for all; He did not cure blindness otherwise than any skilful occulist might do it;—which, indeed, they observe, is clear; for with His own lips He declared that He needed light for so delicate an operation—'I must work the works of Him that sent me, while it is day; the night cometh, when no man can work' (John 9:4); He did not walk on the sea, but on the shore; He did not tell Peter to find a stater in the fish's mouth but to catch as many fish as would sell for that money; He did not cleanse a leper, but pronounced him cleansed; He did not raise Lazarus from the dead, but guessed from the description of his disease that he was only in a swoon, and happily found it as He had guessed.[140]

David Strauss (1808-1874), another German theologian, under the influence of Hegelian thought, in his famous *Life Of Jesus, Critically Examined* (2 vols., 1835-1836), argued that the supernatural elements in the Gospels, including the miracles of Jesus, were simply Hellenistic "myths," created between the death of Christ and the writing of the Gospels in (so he thought) the second century. R. Bultmann also espoused a position not too different in its final conclusion from that of Strauss. And Joachim Jeremias, in his *New Testament Theology* (I) (ET 1971), after critical literary and linguistic analyses, comparisons with Rabbinic and Hellenistic miracle stories, and form-critical analyses of the individual miracle stories, contends that one is left with only a "historical nucleus" of "psychogenous" healings (exorcisms) and healings through "overpowering therapy"—in short, healings produced by psychic powers. G. Vermes in his *Jesus the Jew* (1973) takes a different approach, categorizing Jesus as a "charismatic" similar to other "Galilean charismatics" such as Honi the Circle-Drawer and Hanina ben Dosa. Another view is that of Morton Smith, the title of whose book, *Jesus the Magician* (1978), leaves little to guesswork respecting his estimate of Jesus. A. E. Harvey's *Jesus and the*

---

[140]Cited by Richard C. Trench, *Notes on the Parables of Our Lord* (London: SPCK, 1904), 82-3.

Constraints of History (1982) is not as radical in its denials as the former two books, but he reduces the authentic miracles of Jesus to eight in number—those dealing with healings of the deaf, dumb, blind, and lame.

A detailed response in support of the historicity and authenticity of Jesus' mighty works would require far more space than is possible here. Suffice it to say that this has been done, ably and often when the need arose, by such men as R. C. Trench in his *Notes on the Miracles of our Lord* (see Chap. V, "The Assaults on the Miracles"), J. B. Mozley in his *Eight Lectures on Miracles*, J. Gresham Machen in his *Christianity and Liberalism* (see Chap. V, "Christ,"), C. S. Lewis in his *Miracles*, Bernard Ramm in his *Protestant Christian Evidences* (see Chap. V, "Rebuttal to Those Who Deny Miracles"), H. van der Loos in his *The Miracles of Jesus*, *Gospel Perspectives: The Miracles of Jesus*, edited by David Wenham and Craig Blomberg, and Craig L. Blomberg, *Gospel Truth: Are the Gospels Reliable History?* (see Chap. III, "Miracles"). It has been shown time and again that every assessment of Christ's miracles as spurious or rationally explicable results from the antagonist making his own *a priori* judgment of the nature of God or of the world the touchstone of what is and is not possible. The Christian, of course, acknowledges that he places the question of the historicity and authenticity of Jesus' miracles, first, within the total context of Christian theism *per se:* "Once admit," Machen writes, "the existence of a personal God, Maker and Ruler of the world, and no limits, temporal or otherwise, can be set to the creative power of such a God. Admit that God once created the world, and you cannot deny that he might engage in creation again."[141] The Christian, secondly, places the question of the historicity and authenticity of Jesus' miracles in the more narrow context of the specific requisite occasion of the reality of sin. He realizes that man's only hope of conquest over it is in the coming to him of supernatural aid from outside the human condition .[142] He believes this exigency is fully met in the supernatural Savior who gave evidence of his supernatural origin and character through, among other means, the

[141]J. Gresham Machen, *Christianity and Liberalism* (Grand Rapids: Eerdmans, 1923), 102.

[142]Machen, *Christianity and Liberalism*, 104-06.

working of miracles. Grant, in other words, the fact of the infinite, personal God and the exigency of human sin and no philosophical or historical barrier stands in the way of the historicity of any of the miracles of Scripture. The distinct likelihood of the miracles of the Gospels follows as a matter of course.

Now within the context of biblical theism, the weight of Jesus' miracles, separately and collectively, point, according to Jesus' own testimony, to a two-fold conclusion. They testified to the coming of the Messianic Age in the person of the Messiah (Matt 12:28), and they testified also to his own divine character as the Son of God who visited this poor planet on a mission of mercy (Matt 20:28; Mark 10:45) to seek and to save that which was lost. Consider Jesus' own testimony regarding the significance of his miraculous works.

John 5:36

In the John 5 context, where may be found his most amazing series of claims to equality with God, in addition to John the Baptist's witness (5:33-35), the Father's witness (doubtless including but not to be restricted to the confirmation from heaven at the time of his baptismal "commissioning") (5:37), and the witness of the Old Testament Scriptures (5:39, 46), he said: "...the works that the Father has given me to finish, the very works which I am doing, testify concerning me, that the Father sent me" (5:36). These unique works—unique because they were "works...which no one else did" (15:24), unique because they "bear upon them the hallmark of their divine origin"[143]—underscored, Jesus said, his uniqueness as one not of human origin but as one whom "the Father sent" from heaven.

John 10:24-25, 37-38

In these verses, in direct response to the demand from the religious leaders, "If you are the Messiah, tell us plainly," Jesus replied: "I did tell you, but you do not believe. The miracles I do in my Father's name speak for me." He then said: "Do not believe me unless I do what my Father does. But if I do it, even though you do not believe me, believe the miracles, that you may learn and understand that the Father is in me and I in the Father." By these remarks, Jesus asserts

[143]Morris, *The Gospel According to John*, 328.

that his miracles witnessed both to his messianic investiture and to that intimate union between the Father and himself which he describes in terms which some theologians have urged come nothing short of a mutual indwelling or interpenetration of the persons of the Father and the Son.

John 14:11
In his Upper Room Discourse, after making the marvelous claims that "anyone who sees me has seen the Father" (14:9) and that he and the Father were in personal union one with the other (14:10-11), Jesus urged his disciples to believe him for his own words' sake, but if they had any hesitancy in believing his words, then "at least," he said, "because of the works themselves believe." Again, his works, he declared, testified to his divine nature and mission.

Matthew 11:4-5; Luke 7:22
As confirmation to John the Baptist that he was indeed the "one who was to come," that is, the divine Messiah, Jesus said to John's disciples: "Go back and report to John what you hear and see: the blind receive sight, the lame walk, those who have leprosy are cured, the deaf hear, the dead are raised, and the good news is preached to the poor." Clearly, Jesus implies that his miracles validated and authenticated the fact that the Messianic Age had come in his own person as the divine Messiah.

Matthew 9:1-8; Mark 2:1-12; Luke 5:17-26
As we noted earlier in our discussion of the Son of Man title, Jesus vindicated his right to forgive sin—a prerogative of God alone—by healing the paralytic.[144]

---

[144]We are considering Jesus' self-witness here, but the reader might note the testimony of John and Peter in this connection. By his first miracle, John informs us in 2:11, Jesus "revealed his glory." And what glory was that? Just "the glory of the one and only [Son] who came from the side of his Father" (John 1:14). What is it, then, that John says this miracle, as a "sign," signified but just Jesus' glory as the divine Son of God! Then Peter's opening remark (Acts 2:22) in his sermon on the Day of Pentecost is also quite revealing: "Jesus of Nazareth, a man attested to you by God with miracles and wonders and signs which God performed through him in your midst...." (see Acts 10:38-39). Here Peter attests to the authenticating value of Jesus miracles—

We can only conclude that Jesus' miraculous works, when viewed as Jesus doubtless intended that they should be viewed, both authenticated his teachings and were themselves direct and immediate indications of the presence of the Messianic Age and his own divine character as the Messianic King.

In addition to his mighty miracles ("powers") which were designed to authenticate his messianic claim (Matt 11:2-6; John 5:36; 10:25; 38; 14:11; Acts 2:22) and to reveal his divine glory (John 2:11), instances of Jesus' exercise of other divine prerogatives (like his public claims to deity itself, as we have seen) occur with sufficient frequency to warrant our notice of them.

The Forgiving of Sins

We have already noted that Jesus claimed, as the Son of Man, to have the authority to forgive sins (Matt 9:6; Mark 2:10; Luke 5:24) and, in fact, did forgive men of their sins against God both by the spoken word (Matt 9:2; Mark 2:5; Luke 5:20; 7:48) and by his attitude in eating meals with sinners (Luke 15:1-2). This authority, as the teachers of the Law who were present on the occasion of Jesus' healing of the paralytic rightly judged, is the prerogative of God alone. The one fact which they did not recognize but which would have explained his act to them is the fact of his deity. It is true, of course, that a man may forgive the transgressions of another man against him, but Jesus forgave men of their sins against God! Only one who is himself divine has the right to do that.

The Hearing and Answering of Prayer

In a remarkable passage in John's Gospel, Jesus declared that he would answer the prayers of his disciples (14:13), but equally significant for our purpose, he represents himself as one to whom prayers may properly be addressed. Morris writes on 14:14: "The true text appears to be 'if ye shall ask me anything in my name.' Prayer may be addressed to the Son as well as to the Father."[145] In

---

they testified to God's approval of the "man" Jesus. But then this means that God approved of his teaching as well. And in that teaching he claimed to be the Son of God, one with the Father, and in possession of the rights and privileges of deity.

[145]Morris, *The Gospel According to John*, 647.

verse 14, Jesus stated again that he himself would answer his disciples' prayers, surely an implicit claim to deity. While many other examples might be cited, the instances of prayer addressed to Jesus in Acts 1:24; 7:59; 9:10-17; and 2 Corinthians 12:8 bear out the literalness with which the disciples understood Jesus' promise and speaks also of the immediacy of their recognition of his divinity.

The Receiving of Men's Adoration and Praise

Immediately after his triumphal entry into Jerusalem, when asked by the indignant chief priests to silence the children who were praising him (Matt 21:16), Jesus defended their praise of him by appealing to Psalm 8:2 (Heb, 8:3), which speaks of children praising *God.* On this appeal to Psalm 8:2, Carson writes:

> God *has* ordained praise for himself from "children and infants"...Jesus' answer is a masterstroke...1. It provides some kind of biblical basis for letting the children go on with their exuberant praise.... 2. At the same time thoughtful persons, reflecting on the incident later (especially after the Resurrection), perceive that Jesus was saying much more. The children's "Hosannas" are not being directed to God but to the Son of David, the Messiah. Jesus is therefore not only acknowledging his messiahship but justifying the praise of the children by applying to himself a passage of Scripture applicable only to God.[146]

Later, on the occasion of his second appearance to the disciples a week after his resurrection, he accepted Thomas' adoring ascription of him as his "Lord and God." There can be no doubt, in light of these clear instances when Jesus accepted and approved the adoration and praise of men, that he was endorsing the notion of his own deity. R. T. France believes that New Testament Christology "was first perceived functionally" and was expressed in the worship of Jesus. This functional Christology "was then necessarily worked out in ontological terms" by the later church, this later ontological Christology, of course, describing what was already true about Jesus from the beginning.[147] I applaud France's forthright defense of the doctrine of Christ's full

---

[146]D. A. Carson, *Matthew*, 443.

[147]R. T. France, "The Worship of Jesus: A Neglected Factor in Christological Debate," in *Christ the Lord*, 17-36.

deity on the ground that he was regarded by the Christian community as a proper object of worship, but I feel quite strongly that we must insist that virtually from the beginning, even prior to his resurrection, in concert with the "functional" aspects of its Christology, the disciples also held to an ontological Christology which had been taught by Jesus himself, which was the basis for Thomas' belated confession only a week after Jesus' resurrection and which provides the only ground upon which a Jewish worshiping community could have *worshiped* Jesus as early as it did as in Acts 1.

His Portrayal of Himself as the Proper Object of Men's Faith

In the familiar saying of John 14:1, whether the two occurrences of πιστεύετε εἰς (*pisteuete eis*, "believe in [with unreserved trust]") are both to be rendered indicatively ("You believe in") or imperatively ("Believe in"), or whether the former is to be translated indicatively with only the latter to be rendered imperatively (or vice versa), makes no difference relative to our present purpose. The outcome is exactly the same: Jesus places himself on a par with the Father as *equally* with him the proper object of men's trust. If Jesus was not in fact divine, such a saying would constitute blasphemy of the first order. The only ground upon which his goodness may be retained in the light of such teaching is to affirm his Godness. He cannot be a mere man and at the same time be good while teaching men to trust him as they would trust the Father.

His Attributes

Jesus, in addition to exercising divine powers and claiming divine prerogatives, claimed to possess and exhibited divine attributes. Before we consider them individually, a word is in order concerning what I mean by "attribute." I mean simply a "characteristic" of the nature of a person or thing. A person's nature is just the sum total of the complex of attributes or characteristics which are necessary to his being what he is. Put another way, one may say that it is precisely in the sum total of his attributes that the nature of a person subsists. This is what we mean by "attribute." Now we say that God has a nature. We speak accordingly of the "divine nature" and intend by the phrase the ascription to God of that complex of attributes, whatever and however many they might be, that are essential to his being God. When I say, then, that Jesus claimed to possess divine attributes, I intend by the statement to suggest that Jesus, of necessity, would have had to think of himself as divine in order to do so. I do not mean to imply that a claim in so many words to every divine attribute may be found in Jesus' discourses. But a sufficient number may be elicited from his statements to warrant the conclusion that he believed himself to be divine and thus in possession of them all.

We have had occasion already to take note of certain of Jesus' claims to the possession of divine attributes. What we intend here is simply to list them as a group for the benefit of the reader with brief comments on each.

Eternal Pre-existence

The reader is referred to our earlier discussions of Matthew 28:20, John 8:58, and 17:5 for our reasons for ascribing this attribute to Jesus.

Sovereignty and Omnipotence

In claiming the authority to reveal the Father to whomever he chose (Matt 11:27) and to give life to whomever he chose (John 5:21), in claiming both the prerogative and the power to call all men someday from their graves (5:28-29) and the authority to judge all men (John 5:22, 27), in claiming the authority to lay down his life and the authority to take it up again (John 10:18), in declaring he would return someday "in power and great glory" (Matt 24:30), and in claiming that all authority in heaven and on earth had been given to him by the Father (Matt 28:18)[148], Jesus was claiming, implicitly and explicitly, an absolute sovereignty and power over the universe, claims, were they to be

---

[148]It would be a major mistake theologically to infer from the ἐδόθη, *edothē* in Matthew 28:18 (or for that matter the ἔδωκεν [*edōken*] in John 5:26) that Jesus was given authority to exercise universal dominion for the first time *as God's Son* only at his resurrection. As we shall argue later, when Jesus declared here that authority "was given" to him, we must understand him as saying this about himself in his mediatorial role as the divine-human Messiah. But as the *divine* Messiah and being as such the eternal Son of God, Jesus continued as he always had done to exercise over his creation the powers and lordly rights which were intrinsically his as God the Son (see John Calvin, *Institutes*, II. 13. 4).

made by any other man, that would deserve only the rightful judgment of psychological madness but made by him deserving men's adoration and praise.

Omnipresence

When Jesus promised that "where two or three gather together in my name, there am I with them [ἐκεῖ εἰμι ἐν μέσῳ αὐτῶν, *ekei eimi en mesō autōn*]" (Matt 18:20), and when he promised "I am with you always [ἐγὼ μεθ' ὑμῶν εἰμι πάσας τὰς ἡμέρας, *egō meth humōn eimi pasas tas hēmeras*]" (Matt 28:20), not only was he invoking thc language of the Immanuel title but he was also claiming that he is himself personally always with his own, not just in the power and presence of his Holy Spirit but present with them himself as the omnipresent Savior.

Omniscience

When Jesus surprised Nathaniel with his comment: "I saw you while you were still under the fig tree before Philip called you" (John 1:48), "it is difficult," as Morris observes,

> to explain Jesus' knowledge of the incident on the level of merely human knowledge. Nathaniel had never met Him before this moment. We are required to understand that Jesus had some knowledge not generally available to the sons of men.[149]

When Jesus claimed for himself the prerogative to hear and to answer the prayers of his disciples, he was making the implicit claim to the possession of omniscience. One who can hear the innumerable prayers of his disciples, offered to him night and day in virtually all of the languages of the world, day in and day out throughout the centuries, keep each request infallibly related to its petitioner, and answer each one in accordance with the divine mind and will would need himself to be omniscient.[150]

When Jesus claimed to have not only an *exclusive* knowledge of

---

[149]Morris, *The Gospel According to John*, 167.

[150]This is one of the insuperable difficulties inherent within the Roman Catholic dogma of the supreme veneration (*hyperdulia*) of Mary because of

the Father but also a knowledge whose object is just God the Father himself in all the infinite depths of his divine being (Matt 11:27), he was again claiming to be in possession, as "the Son," of a degree of knowledge falling nothing short of just omniscience itself.

We conclude then that not only in the specific titles which he employed but also in the explicit claims which he made and the works which he did, Jesus *believed* himself to be and *claimed* to be in possession of attributes normally the property of God alone, and in making this claim he was claiming to be God incarnate.

An objection: Jesus' alleged confession of sin

Before we draw this section of our study to a close, lest we be accused of ignoring a piece of Jesus' self-witness which flies in the face of this conclusion, I feel it imperative that we say something about a statement of Jesus alleged by Arians in the fourth century and by liberals in our own day to be a disclaimer on his part of being in any sense of the word divine. I refer to Jesus' response to the rich young ruler's strange[151] address ("Good Teacher," διδάσκαλε ἀγαθέ, *didaskale agathe*, Mark 10:17; Luke 18:18; see Matt 19:16) to him: "Why do you call me good? No one is good except one, even God" (τί με λέγεις ἀγαθόν; οὐδεὶς ἀγαθὸς εἰ μὴ εἷς ὁ θεός, *ti me legeis agathon? oudeis agathos ei mē eis ho theos*, Mark 10:18; Luke 18:19; see Matt 19:17). From the contrast which these theologians infer that Jesus drew between himself (see the enclitic με, *me*) on the one hand and God on the other, it has been urged that Jesus not only disclaimed being divine but that he even confessed creaturely moral imperfection.

But does Jesus' response intend the contrast between himself and God which is the core of this interpretation? The enclitic (unemphatic)

---

her supposed mediation for the earthly petitioner. In allowing her to hear the prayers of Christians on earth, that communion regrettably is ascribing to her a knowledge and an ability found only in God, and in so doing virtually divinizes her.

[151]Warfield, "Jesus' Alleged Confession of Sin," in *The Person and Work of Christ*, 156-57, citing Edersheim, Plummer, and Dalman, says of the young man's address that it is "apparently unexampled in extant Jewish literature," throwing into relief "the levity with which the young man approached Jesus of whom he knew so little, with so remarkable a demand" (157).

με, *me,* which Jesus employs to refer to himself simply will not bear the weight of this inferred contrast. Nor will its position in the sentence support the weight of this inferred contrast either, given the fact, as Blass-Debrunner observes, that "the old rule, observable in Greek and cognate languages, that unemphatic (enclitic) pronouns and the like are placed as near the beginning of the sentence as possible..., applies also to the NT (they are not, however, placed first)."[152] Moreover, such an inferred contrast "throws into chief prominence a matter which lies quite apart from the main subject under discussion,"[153] the main subject of the interchange being the contrast not between God and Jesus but between God as the only true standard of goodness and any and all others who would attempt to prescribe standards for the acquisition of eternal life. Warfield explains:

> The whole emphasis is absorbed in the stress laid upon God's sole right to announce the standard of goodness. The question of the relation of Jesus to this God does not emerge: there is equally no denial that He is God, and no affirmation that He is God. The young man is merely pointed to the rule which had been given by the good God as a witness to what it is requisite to do that we may be well-pleasing to Him. He is merely bidden not to look elsewhere for prescriptions as to life save in God's revealed will. The search for a master good enough to lead men to life finds its end in God and His commandments.[154]

That this is the contrast intended by Jesus and not a contrast between himself and God is borne out by the fact that immediately after his opening response he declared: "You know the commandments" (Mark 10:19); "If you would enter life, keep the commandments" (Matt 19:17). So this saying which has been alleged to be a rejection on Jesus' part of any thought of being divine in

---

[152]Blass-Debrunner, *A Greek Grammar of the New Testament and Other Early Christian Literature* (Translation of ninth and tenth German edition; Chicago: University of Chicago Press, 1961), 249, sec. 473 (1).

[153]Warfield, "Jesus' Alleged Confession of Sin," in *The Person and Work of Christ*, 161.

[154]Warfield, "Jesus' Alleged Confession of Sin," in *The Person and Work of Christ*, 158-59. So also Alexander, Swete, Lagrange, Plummer, *et al.*

actuality does not address the issue one way or the other.[155] Agreeably, neither should it be construed as a confession of sin on Jesus' part.

* * * * *

This first first phase of our study is completed. I would remind the reader that we set for ourselves at the beginning of this chapter the task of discovering the answers to two questions:

1. Did Jesus believe himself to be—and teach others to believe—that he was the promised Old Testament Messiah?

2. Did Jesus believe himself to be—and teach others to believe—that he was more than a man, that he was, in fact, also divine?

It is of paramount importance to determine the answers to these questions at the outset of our study since we would not want to ascribe to the personal subject of any study a teaching which he rejected out of hand or to deny to him a claim that he made for himself before the full evidence for that claim is considered. To arrive at our answers to these two questions, we restricted ourselves in this chapter to a consideration of only Jesus' teaching and the things he did. At this stage we ignored the testimonies of God himself, of angel, of disciple (unless expressed in his presence), of Evangelist, or of Apostle (the task addressed in the next four chapters), being concerned as we were to discern Jesus' *self*-understanding.

From our examination of the occurrences of the messianic titles "Christ," "Son of Man," and "Son of David," we found more than ample reason to conclude that Jesus did, in fact, claim to be the promised Messiah of the Old Testament. We noted too the significant fact that Jesus preferred "Son of Man" over the other messianic titles as his favorite public self-designation because it stood at the farthest remove from the purely political associations with which the messianic concept and hope had been debased in and by the popular imagination.

---

[155]Warfield's article should be read in its entirety by any who remain unconvinced that this is the proper construction which should be placed on Jesus' remarks.

This brought us to our second concern. From our examination of Jesus' "Son of Man" and "Son [of God]" sayings, we felt compelled to conclude that he believed himself to be divine and taught men so. As the "Son of Man," Jesus claimed to possess both attributes and prerogatives of deity (John 3:13; 6:62; Matt 9:6; 12:8). As "the Son" of "the Father," he claimed to possess an exclusive, direct, intuitive, and absolute knowledge of "the Father," and the exclusive, sovereign right to reveal "the Father" to whomever he chose (Matt 11:27). He further claimed as "the Son" to be the highest and final messenger from God (Matt 21:37-38), placing himself outside of and above the angelic order (Mark 13:32), indeed, within the "awful precincts of the Divine Name itself" (Matt 28:19), which is just to say within the venue of deity. Jesus claimed as the Son of God to exercise, in conjunction with "his own Father," sovereign Lordship over life, the eternal destinies of men, the eschatological resurrection, and the Final Judgment (John 5:17-29), claims which his enemies understand, quite correctly, as claims to equality with God himself (John 5:18; 10:33). He claimed, as the Son of God, furthermore, to be in essential union with the Father (John 10:30). Indeed, he laid claim to being just the eternal "I am" of the Old Testament (John 8:58 *et al.*), insisting upon his own eternal pre-existence, omnipotence, omnipresence, and omniscience, and representing himself as the one who forgives men of their sins, who hears and answers their prayers, and who deserves their adoration and praise, their honor and worship, as well as their trust.

With respect to the relationship between Christ's divine Sonship and his messiahship, all indications are that the former is *ontologically anterior* to the (covenantally grounded) functional, or economical, messiahship with which he was invested. That is to say, he received from his Father the messianic investiture precisely because he is the Son of God; he is not the Son of God because he received the messianic investiture.

Many critical scholars, of course, do not like this verbal portrait which Jesus drew of himself. Yet they wish, nevertheless, quite possibly in order to meet their own religious needs, to cleave to him still as in some sense the Man for all men (J. A. T. Robinson), universally significant but not universally perceived yet as such. So while they explain away his high claims to deity by applying their form-critical analyses and the "criteria of authenticity" to his teachings in a highly subjective way, they are solicitous to leave themselves with some form of functional Christology. But the issue which every purely functional Christologist must squarely face, as I have suggested earlier, is that a functional Christology alone cannot sustain the uniqueness and universal significance for Christ which its advocate desires for him.

Much more consistent are those who, offended at his claims, simply dismiss his claims as the claims of one suffering delusions of grandeur, to put it as mildly as possible. They seem to have grasped much better the point which C. S. Lewis made in the third of his famous BBC radio broadcasts on "What Christians Believe":

> ...there suddenly turns up a man who goes about talking as if He was God. He claims to forgive sins. He says He has always existed. He says He is coming to judge the world at the end of time. Now let us get this clear...I'm trying here to prevent anyone from saying the really silly thing that people often say about Him: "I'm ready to accept Jesus as a great moral teacher, but I don't accept His claim to be God." That's the one thing we mustn't say. A man who was merely a man and said the sort of things Jesus said wouldn't be a great moral teacher. He'd either be a lunatic—on the level with the man who says he's a poached egg—or else he'd be the Devil of Hell.
>
> You must make your choice. Either this man was, and is the Son of God: or else a madman or something worse. You can shut Him up for a fool, you can spit at Him and kill Him as a demon; or you can fall at His feet and call Him Lord and God. But don't let us come with any patronising nonsense about His being a great human teacher. He hasn't left that open to us. He didn't intend to.

CHAPTER FOUR

THE PRE-RESURRECTION WITNESS TO JESUS

In the last chapter we investigated whether Jesus understood himself to be and whether he claimed in fact to be the Messiah which the Old Testament had promised. We found a great deal of evidence which supports the classic Christian insistence that he did, and that, in the process of doing so, he claimed to be divine as well.

It is now our intention to turn to the larger New Testament witness and to consider in this and the following chapters the major lines of testimony on the basis of which the Christian church confessed, with Jesus, from the beginning that he is both the Messiah and God incarnate (*vere Deus vere homo*). In this chapter, we will consider pre-resurrection testimony (assuming for the present time the fact of Jesus' resurrection), presenting it under five heads: the nativity accounts, the baptism accounts, the temptation accounts, the transfiguration accounts, and the disciples' understanding of Jesus.

TESTIMONY FROM THE NATIVITY ACCOUNTS

"...before him," "...before the Lord" (Luke 1:17, 76)

As we noted in Chapter Two the word-revelation aspect of the Old Testament epoch had come to a close with the prophetic word of Malachi holding forth the promise of the two (related) comings of the Lord's "forerunner" (whom Yahweh describes both as "my messenger who will prepare the way *before me*" [Mal 3:1a] and "the prophet Elijah" [Mal 4:5]) and of the Lord of Hosts himself (who describes himself as "the Lord you are seeking" and "the messenger of the covenant" [3:1]). Four hundred years of revelatory silence then ensued, to be finally broken by the announcement of the angel Gabriel to Zechariah, that he and his barren wife Elizabeth were to have a son in their old age (Luke 1:11-17).[1]

What is quite remarkable about this first revelatory disclosure of the New Testament age is the fact that embedded in Gabriel's description of this child's future ministry are the words: "And he will go *before him* in the spirit and power of Elijah" (1:17), clearly a collated allusion to both Malachi 3:1a and 4:5, words with which the revelatory aspect of the Old Testament epoch had concluded, marking out John the Baptist as the promised forerunner of the Lord. The word-revelation aspect of the New Testament epoch, in other words, is represented as beginning precisely where the Old Testament word-revelation aspect had terminated. From the New Testament perspective, all of history now stood on the brink of its most stupendous moment—the Lord of Hosts himself was about to make his long-promised coming a space/time reality.

To whom do the words "before him" (ἐνώπιον αὐτοῦ, *enōpion autou*) in 1:17 refer? It is possible that their referent is "the Lord their God" in Luke 1:16, referring then simply to God in the unspecified totality of his majestic being and not necessarily to the Messiah directly. Inasmuch as the phrase "the Lord their God" is the closest possible antecedent, a case can be made for this interpretation. But because the "Elijah"-forerunner, who we are now informed was John the Baptist, was to be, according to Malachi 3:1, the forerunner of none other than the Lord of Hosts who was himself to "come to his temple" and about whom Zechariah specifically speaks later when he says of his son that he was to be the "prophet of the Most High...[who] shall go before the Lord [ἐνώπιον κυρίου, *enōpion kuriou*] to prepare

---

[1]See J. Gresham Machen, *The Virgin Birth of Christ* (Second edition; London: James Clarke, 1932), 44-61, for his valuable demonstration that Luke 1:5-2:52, which he describes as "probably the most markedly Semitic section of the whole New Testament" (46) and "a strikingly Jewish and indeed Palestinian narrative" (62), is an original part of Luke's Gospel. his defense of the textual integrity of the Lucan birth narratives (119-68), particularly 1:34-35, is still unparalleled though naturally dated somewhat by the passage of time. I. Howard Marshall's defense of Luke 1:5-25 in his *The Gospel of Luke* (Exeter: Paternoster, 1978), 50-1, although it moves in the same direction, is, in my opinion, too cautious and not to be preferred over Machen's defense. The latter's book is still one of the best on the subject to be found anywhere in print. I would also highly recommend Robert G. Gromacki's *The Virgin Birth: Doctrine of Deity* (Grand Rapids: Baker, 1974).

his way" (1:76; again an allusion to Malachi 3:1a), it is much more likely that by his words "before him" Gabriel intended to refer to the one before whom John actually went in the temporal sense, whose coming he actually announced, namely, the Messiah.

If this is so, and it certainly is the most natural implication of the words of 1:76,[2] then inasmuch as the reference to "the Lord" in the Lukan passages alludes to the God of the Malachi prophecy who is just Yahweh himself who, as "the Lord you are seeking," speaks of his own coming which will follow the coming of "my messenger who will prepare the way before me" (Mal 3:1a), it follows that we are given here in the very first revelatory disclosure of the New Testament era a clear intimation of Jesus' identity as Yahweh incarnate. This conclusion receives additional support from (1) Gabriel's announcement to Mary which follows immediately (1:30-37), (2) Elizabeth's greeting (1:43), and (3) the angel's announcement to the shepherds (2:11).

Gabriel's Announcement to Mary (Luke 1:30-37)

In connection with the first of these, the support to which I refer comes in a three-fold form: first, in the name which Mary is instructed to give her Son (1:31; Matt 1:21), second, in the fact of Jesus' virginal conception itself (1:34-35), and third, in the two titles which Mary's Son would bear (1:32, 35).

The Name "Jesus" (Luke 1:31; Matthew 1:21)

Mary was instructed that she should name her Son "Jesus." Although Luke does not draw attention to its significance, Matthew does (1:21). (It can hardly be the case, however, that Luke was unaware of its significance in light of the fact that he alone of the Synoptic Evangelists employs σωτήρ [*sōtēr*, "Savior"] as a Christological title [2:11].) Matthew records that Joseph was instructed to name Mary's Son Jesus, "for he will save his people from their sin." According to W.

---

[2]F. Godet's comment on Luke 1:76 in *A Commentary on the Gospel of St. Luke* (Fifth edition; Edinburgh: T. & T. Clark), I, 114, is pertinent: "In saying *the Lord* Zacharias can only be thinking of the Messiah...but he could not designate him by this name, unless, with Malachi, he recognized in his coming the appearing of Jehovah."

Foerster, the name "Jesus" in its full form is a "sentence name, in which the subject comes first and represents a form of the divine name יהוה [*Yahweh*] and in which the verb is a subsidiary form of the verb [ישׁע, *ysh'*] which...means 'to help.'"[3] The name "Jesus" means then "Yahweh saves" and its essence is captured by Luke's "Savior." This fact in itself, it is true, does not need to mean that the one who bears this name is identical with Yahweh; others bore the name under the Old Testament economy to symbolize the fact that Yahweh was at work in the salvation of his people. But I would suggest that in Jesus' case it is to be understood as connoting more than a mere symbol, inasmuch as

> some intimation of the identity between Jehovah and the Messiah seems to be contained in the words of the angel (Matt. 1:21). here the name Jesus, to be given to the child, is understood in its etymological sense: "Jehovah is Salvation."...Jesus bears the name...because he (Jesus) saves his (Jesus') people from their sins. We have, therefore, in close succession the statements, that Jehovah is salvation, and that Jesus saves, that Israel (Jehovah's people) are Jesus' people.[4]

---

[3]W. Foerster, "Ἰησοῦς [*Iēsous*]"in *Theological Dictionary of the New Testament* (Grand Rapids: Eerdmans, 1965), III, 289.

[4]Geerhardus Vos, *Biblical Theology* (Grand Rapids: Eerdmans, 1948), 331-32; see also his *The Self-Disclosure of Jesus*, edited and rewritten by J. G. Vos (Phillisburg, New Jersey: Presbyterian and Reformed, 1978), 182, where he writes:

> The very words of the annunciation in 1:21 suggest the Deity of the child, in the form of equivalence to Jehovah. Of course the appointment of the name Jesus—"Jehovah is salvation"—does not of itself affirm this, for as before under the Old Covenant, so now also the name might have been borne by the child as a standing witness to the fact that Jehovah is salvation, without thereby meaning that the child is Jehovah. In reality, however, the context here makes the situation far more concrete than would be the case under general circumstances. When after the appointment of a name meaning "Jehovah is salvation" there is immediately added the explanatory statement, "For it is he that shall save his people from their sins," no other interpretation remains possible than that Jesus will function as Jehovah, and that this truth is conveyed by his name. Still even this does not go to the extent of putting the close

The suggestion is quite strong, then, because of this close succession of ideas, and particularly because of the pronoun "his" in the expression "*his* people," that this "Jesus" who saves *his* people is just Yahweh himself. Agreeing with this interpretation, Warfield writes:

> ...here [in Matt 1:21] [the simple name "Jesus"] is represented as itself a gift from heaven, designed to indicate that in this person is fulfilled the promise that Jehovah shall visit his people,—for it is he [Jesus] who, in accordance with the prediction of the Psalmist (130:8), shall save his people—*his* people, although, in accordance with that prediction, they are Jehovah's people—from their sins.[5]

When one adds to this compelling data first the fact that Yahweh again and again in the Old Testament declares that he alone is Israel's "Savior" (Isa 43:3, 11; 45:21; 49:26; 60:16; Hos 13:4; see 1 Sam 10:19; 14:39; 2 Sam 22:3; Pss 7:10; 17:7; 106:21; Isa 45:15; 63:8; Jer 14:8) and then the fact that Jesus is often declared (along with God the Father) to be "the Savior" in the New Testament (Luke 2:11; John 4:42; Acts 5:31; 13:23; Eph 5:23; Phil 3:20; 1 Tim 4:10; 2 Tim 1:10; Tit 1:4; 2:13; 3:6; 2 Pet 1:1, 11; 2:20; 3:2, 18; 1 John 4:14), it is difficult to avoid the conclusion that when Jesus was named "Yahweh saves," the name was intended to connote more than the mere fact that he stood as one more in the long line of "saviors" (see Judg 3:9, 15; 6:36; 2 Kgs 13:5; Neh 9:27), but rather that in him, as himself Yahweh incarnate, the line of "saviors" had now been consummated in a transcendent manner. If there is some lingering doubt that this is an appropriate deduction to draw from the name he bore, it should be dispelled as we consider the next aspect of the angel's announcement to Mary—namely, the momentous and unique truth that this one, so named, was to be *virginally* conceived. What are the implications of this fact for our present purpose?

---

identification with God in the form of Jesus' being the Son of God. It is not rash to infer, however, that this latter lay actually in the mind of the Evangelist, since it is hard to tell how he could have conceived the identification in "saving" with Jehovah on any other principle than that of sonship.

[5]Warfield, *The Lord of Glory* (Reprint; Grand Rapids: Baker, 1974), 91.

The Virginal Conception of Jesus (Luke 1:34-35; Matthew 1:18-25)

I would like to say at the outset of my comments on "the miracle of Christmas," using the words of Machen, that "it is perfectly clear that the New Testament teaches the virgin birth of Christ; about that there can be no manner of doubt. There is no serious question as to the *interpretation* of the Bible at this point."[6] Clear indications that the Bible teaches the doctrine of Jesus' virginal conception are to be found in Isaiah 7:14 ("the virgin will be with child"), Matthew 1:16 ("out of whom [fem.] was born Jesus"), Matthew 1:18 ("before they came together, she was found to be with child through the Holy Spirit), Matthew 1:20 ("that which has been begotten in her is through the Holy Spirit"), Matthew 1:22-23 ("All this happened *in order that* [ἵνα, *hina*] the utterance [τὸ ῥηθὲν, *to rhēthen*] of the Lord through the prophet might be fulfilled: 'Behold, the virgin will be with child, and shall bear a son, and they shall call his name "Immanuel"'—which means, 'God is with us'"), Matthew 1:25 ("he knew her not until she gave birth to a son."), Luke 1:27 ("to a virgin...and the virgin's name was Mary"), Luke 1:34 ("How shall this be, since I know not a man?"), Luke 1:35 ("The Holy Spirit will come upon you, even the Power of the Most High will overshadow you. Wherefore, the one to be born will be called holy. [After all, he is] the Son of God"), and Luke 3:23 ("being the son, so it was supposed, of Joseph"). The reader is also referred to Mary's musings in Luke 2:19 and 2:51b, to the snide intimations that something (illegitimacy?) was unusual about his birth in Mark 6:3 when compared with its parallels in Matthew 13:55 and Luke 4:22, as well as in the suggestions of John 8:41 and 9:29, and to Paul's "made of a woman" reference in Galatians 4:4. In light of this biblical data, the most indisputable fact about the tradition respecting Jesus' conception is that his conception occurred out of wedlock. We have, in other words, to do with either a virginal conception or an illegitimate conception. And the Bible clearly endorses the former as the basis for the rumors of the latter.

We must acknowledge, it is true, that only two New Testament writers—Matthew and Luke—directly mention the virginal conception of Jesus, but then it is equally true that they are the only two to record his birth at all. As to whether other New Testament writers knew of

[6]Machen, *The Virgin Birth of Christ*, 382.

his virginal conception, it certainly seems likely that Paul, working as closely as he did with Luke and being familiar with Luke's Gospel as he was (see 1 Tim 5:18 and Luke 10:7), would have known about it. And it is also most likely that John, writing his Gospel after Matthew and Luke, would have known about it as well. He certainly understood that "the Word became flesh" (John 1:14) by human birth (John 19:37) and that he had a human mother (John 2:1; 19:25). And in the light of his recurring statements that Jesus "came from above," "came down from heaven," "came into the world," and "was sent by the Father," John would have had to believe that some form of supernatural intervention intruded itself at the point of Jesus' human conception if all of these features which he reports about Jesus are to be harmonized. This much is clear: *no New Testament writer says anything which would contradict the Matthean and Lukan testimonies.*

Furthermore, with respect to the question of how the church has understood the Matthean and Lukan birth narratives, there is no doubt that Jesus' literal virginal conception has been uniformly seen in them. This is evidenced by the united testimonies of Irenaeus (Asia Minor and Gaul), Ignatius (Antioch of Syria), Tertullian (North Africa), Justin Martyr (Ephesus and Rome), and the Old Roman Baptismal Symbol in the second century[7] right down through the great creeds of the church to the present day (see the Apostles' Creed, the present "Nicene Creed," the Definition of Chalcedon, the so-called "Athanasian Creed"[*homo est ex substantia matris*, that is, "he is man from the substance [nature] of his mother"], the *Augsburg Confession*, Article III, the *Belgic Confession*, Article XVIII, the *Westminster Confession of Faith*, Chapter VIII, and the *Thirty-Nine Articles*, Article II). The current suggestion of some modern scholars that Matthew (in particular) was writing "midrash" (the expansion and embellishment of actual history with the "non-historical") is simply unproven. There is, in fact, a real question whether midrash was a

---

[7]For specific references in the writings of these early Fathers, see Machen, *The Virgin Birth of Christ*, 2-43 (the first chapter, "The Virgin Birth in the Second Century"). There were, of course, some sects which dismissed the story of Christ's virginal conception (the Jewish Ebionites, the heretic Marcion), but they clearly understood what the birth narratives intended to report, namely, history and not myth.

common literary genre at the time when Matthew wrote. At any rate, the early church fathers did not understand Matthew's birth narrative as a midrash. So when men like E. Brunner and W. Pannenberg, whatever their reasons and however well-intentioned they might be, deny the fact of the virginal conception of Jesus, it is not only the New Testament witness but also the consistent, universal testimony of the church that they reject—no small departure from Christian doctrine on the part of any single man. For myself, I accept the fact of the virginal conception of Jesus[8] and am simply concerned here to draw out the implications of it for the nature of Jesus' person. Given then the fact of his virginal conception, what was its purpose relative to Jesus himself?

---

[8]My reasons for believing in Christ's virginal conception in the womb of the Virgin Mary through the power of the Holy Spirit are as follows: In addition to (1) the *biblical* teaching which, of course, is paramount and (2) the weight of the church's *historical* testimony that is set forth in its creeds (which I reviewed in a cursory way above), there is (3) the *Christian theistic* reason: Jesus' virginal conception is simply one aspect of the total supernaturalism of Scripture and of Christian theism in general; if one can believe, for example, the assertion of Genesis 1:1, or that God speaks to men in Scripture, or in Jesus' miracles, or that he rose from the dead and ascended to his Father, it is asking of one very little more to believe that Jesus was virginally conceived; (4) the *psychological* reason: only the virginal conception can explain Mary's willingness to be included in the company of those who *worshiped* Jesus as the Son *of God* (Acts 1:14); it taxes one's credulity to accept that Mary could have believed that her Son died for her sins and was her *divine* Savior deserving of her worship if she knew in her heart that his origin was like that of every other man; (5) the *theological* reasons: (a) the virginal conception of Jesus is the Bible's explanation for the Incarnation, and (b) while the virginal conception is not necessarily the total explanation for Jesus' sinlessness, it is a fact that if Jesus had been the offspring of the union of a human father and mother, such a natural generation would have entailed depravity (John 3:6) and implicated Jesus in Adam's first sin (Rom 5:12, 19); and (6) the *apologetic* or *polemical* reasons: (a) if Jesus was not virginally conceived, then the Bible is in error and ceases to be a trustworthy guide in matters of faith (See Machen, *The Virgin Birth of Christ*, 382-87); (b) if Jesus was not virginally conceived, serious gaps are left in any effort to understand the person of Christ and the Incarnation (*The Virgin Birth of Christ*, 387-95); and (c) if Jesus was conceived like all other men, then he stood under the Adamic curse like the rest of us who descend

Perhaps we should begin our answer to this question by underscoring two things that we must not say its purpose was. First, we must not understand the birth narratives as teaching that Mary's virginal conception of Jesus through the power of the Holy Spirit was the efficient cause or source of his deity. Vos quite properly declares that while "there is truth in the close connection established between the virgin birth of our Lord and his Deity," it would be "a mistake to suspend the Deity on the virgin birth as its ultimate source or reason." To do so "would lead to a lowering of the idea of Deity itself."[9] What we mean to highlight here is the obvious fact that "neither sinful nor holy human parents could produce an offspring *who is God.* That is beyond their humanity. And neither could a virgin human mother do this!"[10] If our understanding of New Testament Christology is correct, another ground exists for believing that Jesus Christ is God, namely, the fact that as God the Son, he was God prior to and apart from his virginal conception. So we say again, his virginal conception in Mary's womb must not be viewed as the ultimate cause or source of his deity. Nor did the virginal conception, we must say in this same connection, produce a hybrid or a sort of demi-god, an offspring of the union between a god (the Holy Spirit) and a human woman, who was neither fully god nor fully man but only half-god and half-man. This is simply mythology for which there is *no* scriptural warrant.

---

from Adam by natural generation and this in turn means that he would not have been an acceptable Savior of men before God. But this would mean in turn the end of Christianity as the religion of redemption of men from their sins since there would then be no one who could offer himself up to God as an acceptable, unblemished sacrifice to satisfy divine justice and to reconcile God to man. I fully realize that this last point assumes a particular doctrine of sin ("original and race sin") and a particular view of the atonement ("satisfaction"), but then it is a fact that the Bible teaches this doctrine of sin (Rom 5:12-19) and that it was this kind of atonement that Jesus accomplished by his sinless life and substitutionary death on the cross. The reader is referred to Warfield's brief but magnificent article, "The Supernatural Birth of Jesus" in *Biblical and Theological Studies* (Philadelphia: Presbyterian and Reformed, 1952), 157-68, for further argument in behalf of the salvific necessity of the virgin birth of Christ.

[9]Vos, *The Self-Disclosure of Jesus*, 191, fn. 15.

[10]Kenneth S. Kantzer, "The Miracle of Christmas" in *Christianity Today* 28, 18 (December 14, 1984): 15.

Another purpose, as we hope to show, underlay the virginal conception of Jesus.

Second, the virginal conception of Jesus by Mary through the power of the Holy Spirit was probably not the efficient cause of Jesus' sinlessness (see 2 Cor 5:21; Heb 4:15). At least, it is most unlikely, for the reason that one occasionally hears espoused, that Jesus' virginal conception was essential to his sinlessness because "original [or race] sin" is transmitted through the *male* line. Women, as well as men, share in the sinfulness of the human race and are corrupted by it, and this pervasive sinfulness encompassed Mary who possessed a sinful nature, committed sins, and confessed her need of a Savior (Luke 1:47). All the biblical, not to mention the biological, evidence suggests that the woman contributes equally to the total physical, spiritual, and psychic make-up of the human offspring which comes from natural generation. It is striking, for example, that in his great penitential Psalm, it is specifically his mother whom he mentioned when David traces his sinful deed back to his sinful nature: "With sin," he declares, "did my *mother* conceive me" (51:5). There is reason to assume, therefore, that, apart from a special divine work of preservation beyond the virginal conception itself, Mary would have transmitted the human bent to sin to her firstborn. John Calvin was even willing to assert as much:

> ...we make Christ free of all stain not just because he was begotten of his mother without copulation with man, but because he was sanctified by the Spirit that the generation might be pure and undefiled as would have been true before Adam's fall.[11]

Luke 1:35, to be discussed in a moment, also suggests as much, if we construe ἅγιον (*hagion*, "holy") as a predicate and understand it in the moral/ethical sense. John Murray also entertains the same possibility although he does so with a certain amount of discretionary reserve:

> [Jesus' preservation from defilement] may reside entirely in the supernatural begetting, for it may be that depravity is conveyed in

---

[11]John Calvin, *Institutes of the Christian Religion*, translated by Ford Lewis Battles (Philadelphia: Westminster, 1960), II.13.4.

> natural generation. [Note that he does not place the transmission of racial sin in the male line *per se* here but rather in the "natural generation" that involves the union of male *and* female.] In any case, natural generation would have entailed depravity (John 3:6). Yet it may not be correct to find the whole explanation of Jesus' sinlessness in the absence of natural begetting. So it may well be that preservation from the stain of sin (see Psalm 51:5) required another, supernatural factor, namely, the preservation from conception to birth of the infant Jesus from the contamination that would otherwise have proceeded from his human mother.[12]

Obviously, great care should be expended in any explanation of the ground of Jesus' sinlessness. But until we know a great deal more than we do about natural generation and human reproduction, we would be wise to refrain from suspending Jesus' sinlessness simply and solely on the obvious fact that in the virginal conception the male factor had been eliminated in his human generation. In any event, it seems quite safe to say, even if Jesus' sinlessness is an indirect effect of the virginal conception, that his sinlessness was not the effect that his virginal conception was primarily intended to bring about.

What then was the primary purpose of Jesus' virginal conception? Before I respond directly to this question, it is appropriate that I point out that Jesus' conception in a *human* mother's womb, although virginal in nature, followed by his normal development in that human mother's womb, and his altogether normal passage at birth from that human womb into the world, as recorded in both Matthew and Luke, are features of his human origination which insure and guarantee to us that Jesus was and is truly and fully human. The Bible is quite adamant that Jesus' full and true humanity was in no way threatened or impaired by the miracle of his virginal conception, but just to the contrary, by being conceived by a human mother he "shared" our humanity (Heb 2:14), and was "like" us in every way (Heb 2:17). To the objection of some that a virginal conception precludes at the outset the possibility of our Lord being truly and fully man, I would simply say that such an

---

[12]John Murray, "The Person of Christ" in *The Collected Writings of John Murray* (Edinburgh: Banner of Truth, 1977), II, 135; see also J. Oliver Buswell Jr., *A Systematic Theology of the Christian Religion* (Grand Rapids: Zondervan, 1962), I, 251; II, 57.

objection is simply hypothetical and indemonstrable.

When we then penetrate to the mysterious and marvelous primary purpose of the Christmas miracle, I think we must conclude that both Evangelists intend that we should understand before everything else that it was by means of the virginal conception that "the [pre-existent] Word *became flesh*" (John 1:14)! Mary's virginal conception, in other words, was the means whereby God became man, the means whereby he who "was rich for our sakes became poor, that through his poverty, we might become rich" (2 Cor 8:9). It is the Bible's answer to the question which naturally arises in the minds of men as soon as they learn that Jesus Christ is the both God and man: "How did this occur?" The virginal conception is the effecting means of the "Immanuel event" (Isa 7:14; Matt 1:22-23) which made God man with us without uniting the Son of God to a second (human) person which would have surely been the effect of a *natural* generation. But by means of Mary's virginal conception, God the Son, without ceasing to be what he is—the eternal Son and Word of God—took into union with his divine nature in his divine person our *human nature* (not a *human person*) and so came to be "with us" as "Immanuel." Any other suggested purpose for the virginal conception of Jesus as reported in the Matthean and Lukan birth stories, whatever truth it may contain, pales into insignificance in the glorious light of this clear reason for it. And when this is clearly perceived, one will acknowledge that the Matthean and Lukan birth narratives take their rightful place along with the other lines of evidence in the New Testament—grander no doubt than some—for the deity of Jesus Christ and thus for the classical doctrine of an incarnational Christology.

The Two Titles Jesus Is To Bear (Luke 1:32, 35)

Many scholars today argue that the pericope in which the first of these two titles is found (1:26-33) and the pericope in which the second is found (1:34-37) represent two oral traditions, the second being an interpolation, either by Luke or an earlier hand, introducing the motif of the virginal conception into an earlier story in which it was absent. As we noted in our first footnote to this chapter, Machen defended, first, the birth narrative as an original part of Luke's Gospel, second, its genuinely primitive and Palestinian character, and third, the textual integrity of the Lukan birth narrative as a whole. I. Howard Marshall also has more recently demonstrated from an analysis of the two purported traditions the high probability of the narrative's unity against the views of such scholars as G. Schneider and J. Geweiss.[13] I will therefore proceed to the exposition with the assumption that Gabriel's announcement is an original and single unit, reflecting accurate, authentic information which Luke acquired, probably from Mary herself, in the course of investigating the evidence for the composition of his Gospel (see 1:1-4).

The two titles which Gabriel employs descriptively of Mary's offspring are "the Son of the Highest" (1:32) and "the Son of God" (1:35), titles obviously intended to be virtual equivalents in meaning. It is commonly held by scholars of all theological persuasions that both are to be understood in this context in the nativistic sense, that is to say, that Jesus "will be called" (that is, "will be") "the Son of the Highest" and "the Son of God" *because* the origin of his human nature is directly traceable to a *paternal* act on the part of God. In other words, it is suggested that with respect to Jesus' humanity, while Mary was to be his mother, God was to be his "Father," and accordingly Jesus was to be "the Son of God." Luke 1:35, in fact, is cited more than any other New Testament verse as biblical support for the presence of this nativistic sense of the title in Scripture. It is not too much to say that it is virtually the only verse that *can* be cited in support of Jesus' "nativistic" Sonship.[14]

With regard to the title in 1:32, given the fact that Jesus' birth is not connected with the title as the causal explanation of the title,[15] and the fact that the virginal conception had as its primary purpose the marvelous design of the enfleshing of the eternal Son of God, it seems

---

[13]I. Howard Marshall, *The Gospel of Luke*, 63.

[14]See, for example, Vos, *The Self-Disclosure of Jesus*, 142, 209, and L. Berkhof, *Systematic Theology* (Grand Rapids: Eerdmans, 1941), 92. A number of modern scholars, including Zahn, Blass, Loisy, R. Seeberg, and Burney, in addition to Vos and Berkhof, also cite John 1:13 in support of the nativistic sense of Jesus' sonship, but this interpretation of John 1:13 seems forced. The singular ("he who was born") is a very poorly attested reading, while the plural ("who were born") is attested by all the Greek manuscripts as well as the versions and most patristic witnesses.

altogether inadequate to suggest that the significance of the title in 1:32 is exhausted by a nativistic sonship if it is even present at all. There is simply no evidence in the context of 1:32 to warrant the conclusion that the title is to be construed in the so-called nativistic sense.

It is, of course, true that the διὸ καὶ (*dio kai*, literally, "because of which also") in 1:35 might appear to bring the child's supernatural conception into causal connection with his "Son of God" title. But does it? Are we to understand Gabriel to mean, at least here if not in 1:32, insofar as this specific announcement is concerned that Mary's offspring "would be called" (that is, "would be") "the Son of God" because of God's "fatherly" act in effecting his virginal conception—that the significance of the title, in other words, at least in this context, is exhausted by his nativistic sonship? I would suggest not. Indeed, I would urge that the title is not directly related to the διὸ καὶ, *dio kai*, at all, and that for two reasons. First, the Christological title, "the Son of God," most uniformly designates Jesus in his essential relationship to the Father, and his claim to be "the Son of God" in this sense became, in fact, the ground of his enemies' charge of blasphemy against him in all four Gospels (Matt 26:63-66; Mark 14:61-64; Luke 22:69-71; John 10:33-39; 19:7). But mention of the *Father* is conspicuous by its absence in both the Matthean and Lukan birth accounts as the divine person effecting the miraculous conception. Rather, both Evangelists uniformly trace the virginal conception to the activity or agency of the Holy Spirit (see Matt 1:18, 20; Luke

---

[15]Vos explains the absence of a connection between Mary's bearing a son and Jesus' being called "the Son of the Highest" on the ground that "in the first greeting the mode of birth is not yet defined as supernatural, it simply being stated that she has found grace with God, and will conceive and bear a son" (*The Self-Disclosure of Jesus*, 182-83). But this suggestion is not very convincing. The motif of a supernatural birth is clearly present in the allusions in 1:31 to the virginal conception of Isaiah 7:14 and in 1:32 to the divine Son of Isaiah 9:6-7. It is precisely the implicit suggestion of an irregularity about the birth in 1:31, which provokes the question that Mary, as a virgin (1:27, 34), asks. Besides, there was nothing to prevent Gabriel, who certainly was aware that the birth would be supernatural, from making the causal connection between the birth and the title in this context if such a connection existed.

1:35).[16] It should be carefully noted that the words in 1:35, "the Power of the Highest," placed as they are in synonymous parallelism with "the Holy Spirit," denote a *title* of the Holy Spirit and not a reference to the creative power of the Father. In other words, Jesus' virginal conception is uniformly represented in Scripture as a miracle wrought by the Holy Spirit. If one person of the Godhead rather than another is to be regarded as the "father" of Jesus in the nativistic sense, it would seem that it should be the Holy Spirit, with Jesus in turn to be regarded, again in the nativistic sense, as the Son of the Holy Spirit. But such a representation of the matter is out of accord with the uniform representation of Jesus as "the Son of God," that is, as the Son of the Father.[17] Because it is precisely the Father's activity, however, which is absent in the birth accounts, I would urge this as the first reason for understanding "the Son of God" in 1:35 in a sense other than the so-called nativistic one.

Second, there is a syntactical reason to question whether "the Son of God" phrase is to be construed as a predicate with "will be called." Κληθήσεται (*Klēthēsetai*, "will be called"), the future passive of καλέω, *kaleō*, when introducing a title or description (but not a proper name), regularly *follows* in word order the word which stands in the predicate position to it (see Matt 2:23; 5:19 [twice], 21:13; Mark 11:12; Luke 1:32, 76; 2:23; see Matt 5:9; Rom 9:7; Heb 11:18). But in 1:35 it *precedes* the title of "the Son of God" (see the punctuation in *The Greek New Testament* [UBS], RV, RSV, NEBmg, NIVmg). This would strongly suggest that the anarthrous ἅγιον (*hagion*, "holy") which κληθήσεται, *klēthēsetai*, does follow in word order is alone the predicate, underscoring what we had earlier suggested, namely,

---

[16]It is true that the words "Holy Spirit" appear anarthrously each time they occur in these verses, but this fact means nothing. C. F. D. Moule, *An Idiom Book of New Testament Greek* (Cambridge: University Press, 1960), 112-13, writes: "...it seems to me rather forced to interpret the anarthrous uses [of πνεῦμα ἅγιον, *pneuma hagion*] (e.g., in the Gospels) as uniformly meaning something less than *God's Holy Spirit*." I concur.

[17]See Kantzer, "The Miracle of Christmas," 15: "Jesus Christ is not the son of the Holy Spirit as to his humanity. Rather, Jesus Christ, with respect to his humanity, *had no father*. We have here no mythological mating of a divine being with a human mother...." (emphasis supplied).

that through the Holy Spirit's sanctifying influence the Child would be preserved from all defilement from sin while in the womb, and intimating that the title following the verb is intended as the ultimate reason for his being preserved "holy": "[After all, he *is*] the Son of God!"[18] By this construction, the title "the Son of God" would not describe what he would become (or be) as the result of the virginal conception but would rather specify the ultimate reason for his humanity being preserved from sin's defilement from the moment of his conception to the time of his birth—because, in other words, it was the eternal Son of God who was taking otherwise sinful flesh into union with himself. Accordingly, I would urge that the title in 1:35, as in 1:32, does not refer to what he would be by virtue of his virginal conception; rather, it speaks of his personal and eternal relationship to the Father in the trinitarian sense. In my opinion, this accords more nearly with the central message of the angel which was his announcement of the staggering, *ultimate* aim of the virginal conception, namely, the effecting of the Incarnation itself, not the creating of a manchild through supernatural agency. Consequently, I would urge that these two titles are more properly to be interpreted as designations of Jesus' divine Sonship, and that they should be allowed to add their testimony to the New Testament's incarnational thinking.

Elizabeth's Greeting (Luke 1:43)

Having been informed by Gabriel, as a confirmation of his word to her that God can do the impossible (1:36-37), that Elizabeth, her relative, was also to bear a child in her old age, Mary hurried to the home of Elizabeth in the hill country of Judea and greeted her older relative. At her greeting, the unborn John leaped in his mother's womb for joy—"the beginning of John's witness to Jesus" (Marshall) (1:41, 44). Elizabeth, responding under prophetic inspiration from the Holy Spirit (1:41), exclaimed: "Blessed are you above all other women, and blessed is the child you bear! Why has this high favor been granted to me, that the mother of my Lord should come to me?" (1:43)

---

[18]See Buswell, *A Systematic Theology of the Christian Religion*, I, 106, for the suggestion that the proper translation of Luke 1:35 is "...that which is born will be called holy. [He is] the Son of God."

The high evaluation which Elizabeth places here on Mary she makes entirely dependent upon the nature of the one Mary carries in her womb as indicated by her description of Mary as the mother of "my Lord." That Elizabeth is speaking by divine illumination (1:41) when she addresses Mary follows from the fact that nothing had been said to her previously respecting the momentous thing that had happened to her young relative. In fact, apart from divine illumination, she had no way of knowing Mary was even pregnant, if indeed at that moment she was.

Elizabeth calls Jesus here "my Lord" (τοῦ κυρίου μου, *tou kuriou mou*). Speaking most likely in Aramaic or Hebrew, she probably actually described him as מָרַנִי, *māranî*, or as אֲדֹנַי *'ᵃdhōnay*. But assuming that Luke's κύριος (*kurios*) captures the dynamic equivalency of her word, it is hardly likely that she intended to ascribe to Mary's unborn infant simply messianic status and sovereignty (this, even so, would carry divine implications, as we have seen). Rather, it is virtually certain that she intended more, for just as Zechariah had doubtless instructed her (through writing) concerning the name to be given to her own son (see 1:13, 60), he most likely would also have informed her that John was to be the Elijah-forerunner of the "Lord" of Malachi 3:1 who was to be just Yahweh himself, a fact which Zechariah expressly states later (1:76). So under the Holy Spirit's illumination, she immediately perceived through the sign of John's leaping in her womb for joy that Mary's Son was "the Lord" before whom her own son was to go in order to prepare his way. Furthermore, it is extremely doubtful, to say the least, from Luke's repeated employment of κύριος (*kurios*) to denote the Deity throughout his account of Jesus' birth (see 1:6, 9, 11, 15, 16, 17, 25, 28, 32, 38, 45, 46, 58, 66, 68, 76; 2:9 [twice], 11, 15, 22, 23 [twice], 24, 26, 39) that he could have failed to realize that this is the meaning which his readers would most naturally attach to the word he put in Elizabeth's mouth.

When all these features of Luke's narrative are taken into account, it would appear that Elizabeth's remark intended, certainly not the veneration of Mary (which is where modern Roman Catholicism inappropriately places the emphasis), but the ascription of deity to Mary's Son with special emphasis on the Lordship which is intrinsic to his deity.

The Angel's Announcement to the Shepherds (Luke 2:11)[19]

Addressing the shepherds in the Judean fields on the night of our Lord's birth, the angel of the Lord (Gabriel perhaps; see 2:9 with 1:11, 19, 26) declared: "Today in the town of David a Savior has been born to you, who is Christ the Lord" (2:11). There are some textual variants to the *hapax* "Christ [the] Lord" (Χριστὸς κύριος, *Christos kurios*), but Metzger explains: "It was to be expected that copyists, struck by the unusual collocation [instead of the more frequent Χριστὸς κυρίου [*Christos kuriou*]—"the Lord's Messiah" (see for example, Luke 2:26)], should have introduced various modifications, none of which has significant external attestation."[20] The phrase does, in fact, then, intend to describe the newborn Savior as "the Messiah [and] the Lord" or as "the Messiah [who is] the Lord."

At this moment we are concerned to discover the meaning of κύριος (*kurios*, "[the] Lord"). The suggestion of some scholars that it is merely a Lukan elucidation of "Messiah" to aid non-Jewish readers is admittedly a possibility, but two contextual features make it most likely that κύριος (*kurios*) as the climactic term in the angel's description of Jesus, was intended to *add* significantly to the meaning of the person designated Χριστὸς (*Christos*). If this is so, since "Christ" already entails kingly sovereignty and overtones of deity, then what remains to be added can hardly be anything other than the direct ascription itself of deity to the Messiah. What are these two considerations?

First, the angel, it should be carefully noted, describes the newborn Savior, not as "Christ *your* Lord," but as "Christ, [the] Lord"—the Sovereign, in other words, not just of men but of angels as well, "for it is an angel who speaks these words."[21] This feature of the angel's declaration—that this one is the Lord in the unqualified sense of Sovereign over both men *and* angels—implies that the term is intended

---

[19]For a defense of the integrity of Luke 2:1-20 as an original *Christian* story and not an adaptation of a pre-Christian legend, see Machen, *The Virgin Birth of Christ*, 317-79, particularly 348-63, and Marshall, *The Gospel of Luke*, 97.

[20]Bruce M. Metzger, *A Textual Commentary on the Greek New Testament*, 132.

[21]Warfield, *The Lord of Glory*, 108.

to ascribe a dignity superceding even the dignity of the angels to the Savior/Messiah, which is just to say that "the adjunction of 'Lord' is intended to convey the intelligence that the 'Christ' now born is a divine Christ."[22]

Second, we must not overlook the fact that Luke employs κύριος (*kurios*) three times in this very context to designate Yahweh (2:9: ἄγγελος κυρίου (*angelos kuriou*, "an angel of the Lord") and δόξα κυρίου (*doxa kuriou*, "the glory of the Lord") and 2:15: ὅ ὁ κύριος ἐγνώρισεν (*ho ho kurios egnōrisen*, "which the Lord made known"). As we said earlier, it is difficult, if not impossible, to believe that Luke would fail to realize, if the angel or if he (if it is his elucidation) had actually intended something less than deity by this term, that his readers would nonetheless make a connection between his references to the angel of *the Lord* and the glory of *the Lord*, on the one hand, and Christ *the Lord*, on the other, and would ascribe such superangelic majesty and glory to Christ by this connection as to justify an assessment of him rising to the level of just deity itself as his essential character. Not only would his readers make this connection and draw this conclusion, but, I would submit, the angel and/or Luke intended that they should. This view alone comports with the *aim* of the virginal conception itself which in this very context is brought to its consummation—namely, the bringing of God the Son into the world as a man. Can any lesser meaning be attached to this word κύριος (*kurios*) and still do justice to the miraculous and unique character of the birth event itself? I think not.

In the preceding pages we have discussed the pertinent passages in the nativity stories which affirm the deity of Christ and the fact of the Incarnation. We have demonstrated that Matthew and Luke intend their readers to learn that Jesus was Yahweh incarnate, the one before whom John, his "Elijah-forerunner," was to go temporally as the "preparer of his way." It only remains to highlight, from this same block of material, the fact that the two Evangelists also intend their readers to learn that Jesus, as God incarnate, is also the promised Messiah. This is clear from the following passages:

---

[22]Warfield, *The Lord of Glory*, 144.

1. Luke 1:32-33, in which Gabriel declared that "the Lord God will give him the throne of his father David, and he will reign over the house of Jacob forever; his kingdom will never end".
2. Mary's song (1:46-55), in which Mary affirmed that God "has helped his servant Israel, remembering to be merciful to Abraham and his descendants forever, even as he said to our fathers".
3. Zechariah's song (1:68-76; see 1:69-70, and the references to "salvation from our enemies" and the "forgiveness of sins").
4. The angel's explicit identification of Jesus as "the Messiah" (2:11).
5. Simeon's song (2:29-32, see 2:26) and his prophetic oracle (2: 33-35).
6. Anna's proclamation (2:38; see Isa 52:9).
7. Matthew 1:16 (see 1:18) wherein Jesus is described as the one "who is called Christ" (ὁ λεγόμενος Χριστός, *ho legomenos Christos*).
8. The Magi's description of Jesus as the "king of the Jews" (Matt 2:2) and their presentation of gifts to him (2:11).
9. Herod's question concerning the place of "the Messiah's birth" (Matt 2:4).
10. The reference to Jesus in the Micah prophecy as "[the] ruler who shall shepherd my people Israel" (Matt 2:6).
11. Matthew's application to him of Old Testament passages (2:15, 23).

Just as we saw when we examined his self-understanding that Jesus claimed to be both the divine Son and the Messiah, the former the ultimate antecedent ground of the latter, so also here in the Matthean and Lukan birth narratives we see these same two themes: that Jesus is God incarnate and that he, as such, is the promised Messiah of the Old Testament.

TESTIMONY FROM THE ACCOUNTS OF JESUS' BAPTISM

All four Gospels record something of the ministry of John the Baptist leading up to Jesus' baptism. In all four he is either represented by the Evangelists as "a voice crying in the wilderness to prepare the way for the Lord" (Matt 3:3; Mark 1:2-3; Luke 3:4) or he represents himself in that role (John 1:23). All four Gospels record his warning of the coming after him of one more powerful than he whose sandals "I am not fit to carry" (Matt 3:11) or "stooping down, to untie" (Mark 1:7; Luke 3:16; John 1:26). All four Gospels record John's description of Jesus as the "Spirit-Baptizer" (Matt 3:11; Mark 1:8; Luke 3:16; John 1:33). And all four Evangelists (John by allusion) know of Jesus' baptism at the hand of John (Matt 3:13-17; Mark 1:9-11; Luke 3:21-22; John 1:32-34). These corroborating literary facts put beyond reasonable doubt the historicity of the baptismal event *per se*.

Those (for example, Bultmann) who insist that early Hellenistic Jewish Christians added the miraculous features in the accounts (the Spirit's descent and the Father's voice from heaven) to an earlier non-messianic tradition in order to interpret the event messianically offer as support for their view mainly the form-critical conclusion that the *Sitz im Leben* of the pericope is Hellenistic. But there is nothing particularly Hellenistic about the account—indeed, I would suggest that the accounts simply report quite accurately what occurred. As Edwin Hoskyns and Noel Davey declare: "At no point is the literary or historical critic able to detect in any stratum of the synoptic material evidence that a Christological interpretation has been imposed upon an un-Christological history."[23] And Marshall, more recently, has asserted: "When the narrative can be fully understood on its own terms, it is doubtful whether we are entitled to press back to a conjectural earlier form and function by which we may hope to explain it more amply."[24]

The view of some that the baptism narratives intend to record God's "adoption" of Jesus as his "Son" has nothing ultimately to

---

[23]Edwin Hoskyns and Noel Davey, *The Riddle of the New Testament* (Second edition; London: Faber and Faber, 1958), 145.

[24]I. Howard Marshall, *The Gospel of Luke*, 151.

commend it either. Against the background of the birth narratives in both Matthew and Luke in which the clear purpose of the virginal conception as the means by which the Son of God became flesh is set forth and of Matthew 2:15 ("Out of Egypt I have called my Son.") where Matthew *before* Jesus' baptism represents him as *already* God's Son, it simply makes no sense to view the baptism story as an "adoption" story marking the point when Jesus was "adopted" as "the Son of God." It should be apparent that at least for Matthew and Luke the baptism story cannot be an "adoption" story but is rather Jesus' "commissioning" to public ministry by personal confirmation (see Luke 3:22; Mark 1:11) and public attestation (Matt 3:17) of his messiahship and divine Sonship.

Because Mark says nothing about Jesus' supernatural entrance into the world, unlike Matthew and Luke, it has been urged by Wellhausen, Bultmann, and others that at least in Mark the baptism narrative suggests an adoptionist Christology, that, as Wellhausen writes, "[Jesus] descended into the water a simple man and comes out of it as Son of God." But Stonehouse correctly declares:

> The conception that Jesus, according to Mark, became the Son of God at the moment of his baptism, that is, that he then received appointment as Messiah and underwent a certain transformation, presupposes that the reference to the fact of God's choice in the second clause, "on thee my choice has fallen," explains the appellation "Son" in the first clause, "Thou art my beloved Son." The divine voice declares then that Jesus becomes the Son of God because he has been chosen as Messiah. The chief difficulty of such an interpretation is, however, that the utterance then becomes tautological. It understands the first clause in the sense: "thou has now become my Son," or "thy name has now become Son." But this presumes a past tense where the present is employed, and substitutes the idea of *becoming* for the expressed thought of *being*. As the text stands, however, there is a contrast between the two clauses, the former describing an essential relationship, a relationship conceived without reference to its origin, and the latter a past choice for the performance of a particular function. That the present tense cannot envisage an historical act receives powerful confirmation from the use of similar language in the transfiguration scene in Mark 9:7. Jesus did not any more become the Son of God at the baptism

> through the pronouncement of the words, "Thou art my beloved Son," than he became Son again at the transfiguration when the divine voice declared, "This is my beloved Son." He is seen to be the divine Son quite apart from the word spoken to him. The essential relationship...is clearly a completely distinctive relationship. The relationship of the second clause to the first in 1:11, while not expressed, is therefore by implication more properly viewed as resultative: *because* of the unique filial relationship of Jesus he has been chosen to the task upon which he is about to enter.[25]

If Jesus' earthly ministry was, in fact, messianic, and we have already itemized the evidence given in the accounts prior to his baptism for such an understanding of his life's purpose, then there is nothing incredible about an event, similar in character to a "prophetic commission," that "set him apart" and authenticated him as divine and his work as messianic. This, I would suggest, is the main purpose of his baptism and the intent behind the heavenly manifestations.

Before we consider the significance of the two heavenly manifestations which accompanied Jesus' baptism, something should be said first about the Baptist's Christology. John's testimony concerning Jesus is found in four contexts in particular. We will look at each in turn.

The Baptist's Testimony (Matt 3:10-12; Mark 1:7-8; Luke 3:16-17)

Prior to his baptism of Jesus John had announced to the people coming to him at the Jordan River:

> I am baptizing you with water unto repentance. But he who comes after me is mightier than I, whose sandals I am not worthy to carry. He shall baptize you with the Holy Spirit and [judge you] with fire.

In this declaration John states that the coming one was more powerful than he, whose sandals he was not worthy to carry. These features of his pronouncement imply at least that for John the Messiah was possessed of a lofty, exalted, kingly office. But they intend more

[25]Ned B. Stonehouse, *The Witness of Matthew and Mark to Christ* (Philadelphia: Presbyterian Guardian, 1944), 18-19.

for he goes on to say that the coming one's functional prerogatives entail both eternal salvation ("he will baptize you with the Holy Spirit") and eternal judgment ("and [judge you] with fire"). There is a parallelism in the three occurrences of "fire" at the end of Matthew 3:10, 11, and 12 and the occurrences of "fire" in Luke 3:16-17. It is true that Mark does not mention the "[judging] with fire," but neither does he mention any other reference to "fire." The prerogatives in the possession of the Messiah explain the reason for John's insistence in his intercourse with Jesus later that he (John) had need of being baptized (with salvation) by Jesus (Matt 3:13). Such prerogatives belong only to one with divine stature (see the parallelism between the two "this is..." statements in John 1:33 and 34); only one who is God can exercise such authority!

The Baptist's Testimony (John 1:15, 30)

When John was asked about his relation to the one coming after him, twice he expressed himself in the following words:

> He who comes after me [or, "A Man is coming after me who"] was before me [ἔμπροσθέν μου γέγονεν, *emprosthen mou gegonen*], because he was before me [πρῶτός μου ἦν, *prōtos mou ēn*].

Here is an enigmatic statement on John's part. What does he mean? BAGD suggests that the middle assertion has to do with status and translates the phrase: "ranks higher than I."[26] But there are sound reasons for moving in a different direction. The evidence would suggest that John is thinking *temporally*, that is, in terms of time, through the verse. This is certainly his intent in the first clause ("He who comes *after* me"), and almost as certainly it is his intent in the third clause ("he *was* [ἦν, *ēn*] before me"), the ἦν, *ēn*, here doubtless having as its background the three occurrences of ἦν, ē*n*, in John 1:1. These features strongly suggest that the middle clause should also be construed as bearing some reference to time. But what then is John saying? It is clear that he does not mean by the last two clauses the same thing, inasmuch as different words underlie the surface similarity

---

[26]BAGD, *A Greek-English Lexicon of the New Testament*, 256, f.

in the English translation above. Furthermore, the ὅτι (*hoti*, "because") suggests that the third clause provides the explanation for how it is that the thought of the middle clause can be so. I would suggest, therefore, following Vos,[27] that what John is saying is this: "He who comes *after* me was *before* me [in his active involvement as the Angel of the Lord, indeed as Yahweh himself, in Old Testament times], because he was *eternally before* me [as the eternal God]."[28]

It is simply farcical in light of the biblical data reviewed thus far for Raymond E. Brown, following J. A. T. Robinson,[29] to suggest that John did not perceive his role to be that of Malachi's "Elijah" but saw himself rather as the forerunner of the promised Elijah, and thus he was speaking of Elijah when he made these statements in John 1:15, 30. That is to say, John was saying something on the order of the following: "Elijah, who comes after me, ranks higher than I, because he was before me." By this construction Brown cleared the way to suggest the further conclusion that John regarded Jesus as the Elijah who was to come, who in turn was to be the forerunner of Yahweh.[30] This view is easily dispelled by simply noting that nowhere does John even remotely intimate such but to the contrary expressly states that he was sent ahead of the Messiah himself (John 3:28).

---

[27]Vos, *Biblical Theology*, 347.

[28]Oscar Cullmann, "Ὁ ὀπίσω μου ἐρχόμενος [*ho opisō mou erchomenos*]" in *The Early Church* (London: SCM, 1956), 181, also argues that the last phrase alludes to the "absolute time of the prologue":

> The proposition introduced by the ὅτι [*hoti*], looking at the matter from the standoint of absolute chronology, which is that of the prologue, explains this general statement: he is before me because, being at the beginning of all things, ἐν ἀρχῇ [*en archē*], the ὁ ὀπίσω μου ἐρχόμενος [*ho opisō mou erchomenos*] is πρῶτος [*prōtos*] in an absolute way.

See also his *The Christology of the New Testament*, 28.

[29]John A. T. Robinson, "Elijah, John and Jesus" in *Twelve New Testament Studies* (London: SCM, 1962), 28-52.

[30]Raymond E. Brown, "Three Quotations from John the Baptist in the Gospel of John" in *The Catholic Biblical Quarterly* 22 (1960): 297-98; see also his *The Gospel According to John I-XII* (AB) (Garden City, New York: Doubleday, 1966), 64.

The Baptist's Testimony (John 1:34)

After he had baptized Jesus, having seen on that occasion the Spirit's descent upon Jesus and having heard the voice from heaven declaring, "This is my beloved Son, in whom I am well-pleased," John testified of Jesus: "This is the Son of God."[31] The significance of the Baptist's epithet at this time is insightfully elucidated by Vos:

> That [the title "Son of God"] can not be lower in its import than the same title throughout the Gospel follows from the position it has as the culminating piece of this first stage of witnessing, when compared with the statement of the author of the Gospel (20:31). According to this statement the things recorded of Jesus were written to create belief in the divine sonship of the Saviour. With this in view a series of episodes and discourses have been put in order. Obviously the John-the-Baptist section forms the first in this series, and therein lies the reason, why it issues into the testimony about the Sonship under discussion. That it carried high meaning also appears from [John 1:15, 30], in which nothing less than the preexistence of the Messiah has already been affirmed.[32]

In sum, John intended by this epithet to ascribe nothing short of deity to Jesus, and here accordingly at the very dawn of the New Age in the Forerunner's testimony is the highest conceivable declaration about him.

The Baptist's Testimony (John 3:27-36)

This passage falls into two sections (3:27-30 and 3:31-36), the first of which is clearly the Baptist's testimony, the second possibly his. In the first, John applies the epithets of "Bridegroom" to Jesus and "the friend of the Bridegroom" to himself, adding, "It is necessary that he

---

[31]The variant readings at this point in the Greek text—mainly Western—"the Chosen One," "the Chosen Son," and "the only Son," do not either singly or collectively have sufficient textual support to overthrow the reading "the Son," supported as it is by P[66], P[75], A, B, C, K, L, P, and corrected א. Metzger (*A Textual Commentary on the Greek New Testament*, 200) declares that both the "age and diversity" of textual witnesses support "the Son."

[32]Vos, *Biblical Theology*, 351.

[his light (see John 1:7-8; 3:19-21)] increase and I [my light] decrease." It is only barely conceivable that John's disciples could have heard this reference to the "Bridegroom" and not have been reminded of the Old Testament references to Yahweh as the Bridegroom of Israel (see Isa 62:5; Hos 2:2-23; 3:1; Jer 2:2). It is also just barely possible that John did not intend this comparison to be drawn.

In the second section, which Vos suggests just may be "needed to round off the argument of the Baptist on the absurdity of endeavoring to rival Jesus,"[33] with which opinion the NASV and the NIV apparently concur as evidenced by their placing of quotation marks, Jesus is described as "the one who comes from above," "the one who comes from heaven," the one who is "above all," "the one whom God sent," "the one to whom God gave the Spirit without measure," "the Son whom the Father loves, into whose hands all things have been placed," and the one who brings eternal life to those who believe in him. In light of the Baptist's other testimony respecting Jesus (see again John 1:15, 30; the details surrounding Jesus' baptism itself; and Acts 19:4) there is not one single description in this second section which the Baptist could not have expressed concerning Jesus although it is true that this section may be the Apostle John's testimony after all. But if it is the Baptist's testimony, we must conclude that for John Jesus was the Christ, the Lord who was to come to his temple, the messenger of the covenant who was to come, indeed, just Yahweh himself who spoke in Malachi 3:1, and thus the divine Son of God. It is difficult to imagine a higher Christology anywhere in Scripture unless it be the Christology of Jesus himself.

Having reviewed the Baptist's perception of Jesus, we are now in a position to consider the implications for the nature and office of Jesus in the two heavenly manifestations which accompanied Jesus' baptism.

The Spirit's Descent (Matt 3:16; Mark 1:10; Luke 3:22; John 1:33)

All four Gospels refer to the fact that at Jesus' baptism the Holy Spirit descended upon him in the form of a dove. John describes this

[33]Vos, *Biblical Theology*, 352.

as an indication that the Spirit had been given to him without limit (1:34), and Jesus would say later, referring to the whole event: "On [the Son of Man] God the Father has placed his seal of approval" (John 6:27). Luke, describing Jesus immediately thereafter as "full of the Holy Spirit" (4:1), tells his readers (as do Matthew in 4:1 and Mark in 1:12) that Jesus was "led by the Spirit" into the wilderness (4:1), and that he then "returned to Galilee in the power of the Spirit" (4:14). In Nazareth on the Sabbath day, Luke reports, Jesus went to the synagogue and read in the hearing of the assembly there the words of Isaiah 61:1-2:

> The Spirit of the Lord is on me, because he *has anointed me* [ἔχρισέν με, *echrisen me*: note the allusion in the verb to the lexical meaning of "Messiah"] to preach good news to the poor. He *has sent me* to proclaim freedom for the prisoners and recovery of sight for the blind, to release the oppressed, to proclaim the year of the Lord's favor. (emphasis supplied)

"Today," Jesus declared, "this Scripture is fulfilled in your hearing" (4:21). Many healing and nature miracles then issued forth from his hand (Matt 4:23-24; 9:35; see Acts 10:37-38), which, he states in Matthew 12:28 (see Luke 11:20), at least in regard to demonic exorcisms he performed "by the Spirit of God." What is the meaning of the Spirit's descent upon Jesus and his empowering him to perform these mighty works? To every enlightened Jew the meaning was obvious: the Messianic Age had dawned! David F. Wells aptly remarks:

> Jews knew that the coming of the messianic age would be signaled by the Spirit's outpouring...That Jesus realized that he was bringing with him the age of Messiah was, from the time of the baptism at least, beyond question. It was visibly signaled [the Spirit's descent] and audibly declared [the voice from heaven]. And the Synoptic authors plainly wanted their readers to understand this.[34]

What then is the meaning of the Spirit's descent upon or anointing

---

[34]David F. Wells, *The Person of Christ* (Westchester, Illinois: Crossway, 1984), 38-39.

Spirit of God, then the kingdom of God has come upon you" (Matt 12:28). In other words, the Spirit's descent upon Jesus visibly designated him as the Messiah and indicated the inauguration of the Messianic Age![35]

The Voice from Heaven (Matt 3:17; Mark 1:11; Luke 3:22)

Accompanying the Spirit's descent upon Jesus was the Father's (inferred from the words, "my Son") personal confirmation: "You are my Son, the Beloved, in whom I am well-pleased" (Mark and Luke). Matthew represents the heavenly Witness as *publicly* attesting Jesus' Sonship by rendering the divine statement in the third person: "*This is* my Son...."[36] It is doubtful that both renderings were actually spoken. It is more likely the case that Matthew, interested as he was in "interpreting" Jesus for his readers as God's Son and Messiah (see 1:23), while certainly retaining the substance of the divine oracle, took the next step beyond the *confirmation* in the "You are" of Mark and Luke and represented the oracle as an *attestation* to or *proclamation* of Jesus as Son and Messiah. But it is, of course, possible that the Father did say both things.

The oracle itself consists of two parts. The first is "You are my Son," universally acknowledged as a reminiscence of the divine oracle in Psalm 2:7 with this one difference—that the word order has been altered by the Evangelists away from the LXX (which reflects the Hebrew word order) "to stress the fact that it is Jesus who is God's Son rather than that the dignity of Sonship has been conferred on the

---

[35]See Vos, *Biblical Theology*, 344-46, for his insightful discussion of the significance of the Spirit's descent upon Jesus. He states that it represented God's designation of Jesus as the Messiah and his equipping "for the execution of his Messianic task."

[36]The additional words, "Today I have begotten you," following the phrase, "You are my Son," at Luke 3:22 are found in one fifth-to-sixth-century Greek manuscript (D) and a few Western readings. It is clearly an assimilation to Psalm 2:7 and thus secondary, but the fact that it was "widely current during the first three centuries" (Metzger, *A Textual Commentary*, 136) and found in such church fathers as Justin, Origen, Hilary, and Augustine, illustrates how apparent the words, "You are my Son," are as an allusion to Psalm 2:7.

person addressed."[37] There are those who insist that "Son" here is simply the messianic title given to Jesus on the occasion of his "institution into the office of the eschatological king"[38] and that no ontological overtones are to be read into it. But there are six compelling reasons to understand the title otherwise, that is, as entailing, beyond its messianic implication, also a pre-existent *personal* relationship to God which preceded his messiahship and which served as the basis of both it and that self-understanding of his as "the Son" which is present in such passages as Matthew 11:27, Mark 14:61-62, and Luke 20:13.

First, if even in other situations the idea of personal Sonship is present and represented as antecedently behind the messianic Sonship, it seems totally unlikely, on the only two occasions in the Gospel accounts (the transfiguration is the second) when heaven itself bore witness to Jesus' Sonship, that the sense of "Son" therein was solely official and non-personal.[39]

Second, "Beloved" (ὁ ἀγαπητός, *ho agapētos*) is probably to be construed adjectivally rather than as a second title, leaving us with the full phrase, "You are my *beloved* Son." But whether it is construed this way or as a second title, against the LXX background of Genesis 22:2, 12, 16, in which verses Isaac is described in precisely the same terms as Abraham's "beloved son" (ὁ υἱός σου ὁ ἀγαπητός, *ho huios sou ho agapētos*) and where ἀγαπητός, *agapētos*, translates the Hebrew יָחִיד, *yāḥîd*, meaning "one and only" and where, quite obviously, Isaac's sonship must be understood in an *intensely* personal way, it is virtually certain that the phrase means the same

---

[37]Marshall, *The Gospel of Luke*, 155.

[38]E. Schweizer, "υἱός [*huios*] (in the New Testament)" in *Theological Dictionary of the New Testament* (Grand Rapids: Eerdmans, 1972), VIII, 368. James D. G. Dunn writes: "Mark thought of Jesus' sonship as from his anointing with the Spirit at Jordan and in terms particularly of his suffering and death" (*Christology in the Making*, 50; See also 47). So too must be mentioned here R. W. Lyon who states in his article, "Baptism of Jesus" in *Evangelical Dictionary of Theology*, 120: "The significance here of the sonship is service to the Father rather than any particular reference to Jesus' divine nature. The expression [the Father's confirmation] is teleological rather than ontological."

[39]Vos, *The Self-Disclosure of Jesus*, 186.

thing in the heavenly allocution. Vos declares: "A sonship so unique [that is, a Sonship grounded in the Father's love for his *only* Son] does not permit us to restrict its meaning to that of a bare figure for Messiahship."[40]

Third, the phrase "my beloved Son" (τὸν υἱόν μου τὸν ἀγαπητόν, *ton huion mou ton agapēton*) is found in Jesus' parable of the wicked farmers (Luke 20:13) which we considered in the last chapter in connection with Jesus' self-understanding. There we saw that Jesus portrays himself as "the beloved Son" *before his mission* and as enjoying a pre-existent relationship with the Father *whether he be sent or not.* Jesus' representation of himself in Luke 20:13 strongly suggests that the similar phrase in Luke 3:22 means the same thing—pre-existent, personal Sonship.

Fourth, it more accords with the backgrounds of the birth narratives in Matthew and Luke and the titles in Matthew 2:15 and Luke 1:32, 35 (not to mention Jesus' youthful reference to God as "my Father" in Luke 2:49), in which the referent in every case is to his antecedent personal Sonship, to understand the heavenly utterance in the ontological, divine sense rather than in a messianic sense.

Fifth, John the Baptist testified that his vision of the divinely appointed sign of the Spirit's descent had brought him to two conclusions: first, that the one coming after him, who would baptize with the Spirit, was as to his identity Jesus, and second, that Jesus was "the Son of God" (John 1:34). If John *saw* the Spirit descending as a dove (John 1:33-34), there is no reason to question the likelihood that his testimony about Jesus as "the Son of God" reflects the fact that he *heard* the divine oracle as well. And, as we have already noted, his witness to Jesus as "the Son of God" cannot be lower in its import than the same title throughout the Gospel, which is that of identity with God as to nature and distinction from the Father as to person. This simply means, if John the Baptist meant by "Son" *divine* Sonship (and all that John the Evangelist says suggests he did), and if he was correct in this assessment of Jesus (and John implies that he was), and if he deduced this in this historical context on the basis of what he had heard from heaven, then it follows that it was *divine* Sonship which the prior heavenly oracle had in view.

---

[40]Vos, *The Self-Disclosure of Jesus*, 187.

Sixth, according to the Author of Hebrews, the title "Son" in Psalm 2:7, to which the heavenly utterance at the baptism alludes, ascribes to Jesus a Sonship to God that entails such super-angelic dignity that the supreme titles of "God" (1:8) and "Lord" (1:10), with all the dignity, attributes, and functions that these two titles connote, may also rightly be ascribed to him—not, however, as titles additional to "Son" but rather as explications of the content of that *one* "more superior name [than "angel"]" of "Son." If the Author of Hebrews may be allowed to serve as a legitimate commentator on the meaning of the title of "Son" in Psalm 2:7 and by extension to the heavenly oracle under consideration, then it is evident that "the Son, the Beloved" in the heavenly oracle goes beyond messianic Sonship and embraces the super-official, personal, divine Sonship lying behind it.

For these six reasons—compelling, in my opinion—I would conclude that by his statement "You are my Son," the Father's design was to attest to Jesus' antecedent, personal, and eternal Sonship which lay behind his messianic investiture and which provided the ground and presupposition of it.[41]

This is not to suggest that no allusion whatever to Jesus' messianic role is to be found in the heavenly utterance, for indeed there is. The second part of the heavenly witness is "in whom I delight [εὐδόκησα, *eudokēsa*]." This appears to be a reference to a phrase in Isaiah 42:1: "my chosen one, in whom my soul delights." While it reflects a Greek translation unknown to us in the LXX tradition, it does accord

---

[41]See Vos' entire discussion of the divine testimony at Jesus' baptism in *The Self-Disclosure of Jesus*, 186-87. See also Warfield, *The Lord of Glory*, 80 (also fn. 29), and 139:

> It is by the term 'my Son' above all that God himself bore witness to him on the two occasions when he spoke from heaven to give him his testimony...—adding to it moreover epithets ["the Beloved, in whom I am well-pleased" and "the Chosen One" (in the case of Luke 9:35 at the transfiguration)] which emphasized *the uniqueness of the Sonship* thus solemnly announced. It would seem quite clear, therefore, that the title 'Son of God' stands in the pages of the Synoptics as the supernatural Messianic designation by way of eminence, and represents the Messiah *in contradistinction from children of men as of a supernatural origin and nature.* (emphasis supplied)

with the translation of Isaiah 42:1-4 in Matthew 12:18-21 which reflects the influence of the LXX but with various alterations for the sake of closer conformity to the Hebrew or to bring out more clearly the messianic application. Vos even argues, because εὐδόκησα, *eudokēsa*, in the traditional rendering is both tautological and anti-climactic relative to the preceding "Beloved," that it means in the aorist something akin to "upon whom my good pleasure has *settled*" or "whom I have *chosen* in my good pleasure." (He cites the statement in 1 Maccabees 10:47: "Having the choice between Alexander and Demetrius, they chose [εὐδόκησαν ἐν, *eudokēsan en*] Alexander," in support of his contention.[42]) If this is so, this points even more strongly to Isaiah 42:1 as the Old Testament background to the divine statement, for it becomes the dynamic equivalent to the fuller statement in the Hebrew: "my *chosen* one, in whom my soul *delights.*"

Since Isaiah 42:1 is the introduction to the first of the four Servant Songs in Isaiah, I would infer from this that the second half of the divine utterance *does* allude to Jesus' messianic investiture, and, if so, it would suggest that when Jesus later ascribed to himself both intra-divine Sonship and the servant task spoken of in the four Servant Songs of Isaiah (see Matt 11:27a, 29b; 20:28; Mark 10:45; Luke 22:37), he was only following the pattern established by the heavenly oracle at the time of his messianic commissioning. In sum, there is sound justification for seeing in the divine utterance at Jesus' baptism the attestation to and confirmation of both Jesus' divine Sonship and his messiahship.

TESTIMONY FROM THE ACCOUNTS OF JESUS' TEMPTATION

All three Synoptic Gospels report that immediately following his "baptismal commissioning," Jesus, upon whom the Spirit was now "remaining" (John 1:33), was led by the Spirit into the desert to be tempted by the devil (Matt 4:1-11; Mark 1:12; Luke 4:1-13). The primary accounts are those of Matthew and Luke. These two accounts are quite uniform in reporting the incident, with the single exception that Luke reverses the order of Matthew's second and

---

[42]Vos, *The Self-Disclosure of Jesus*, 186, and fn. 12 on the same age.

third temptations. But even in doing so, Luke retains the substance of the temptations. The Evangelists obviously reserved to themselves the right to arrange their material to suit their own plan and purpose for their respective Gospels (a legitimate observation of "redaction criticism"), but this is in no way intended to suggest that they took liberties with history and created events out of thin air.

As with so many other events in the Gospel accounts, the advocates of the school of form-criticism see in the temptation narratives evidence of later Hellenistic influence which, they argue, indicates that the story was created by the Hellenistic Christian community. But Marshall observes that

> the narrative displays such a strong combination of Jewish features that it is impossible to assume that it went through a preliminary Hellenistic stage before receiving its present Jewish form. In particular, the objection that the use of the LXX here (and elsewhere in the Gospels) betrays a Hellenistic origin should be forgotten once and for all; the evidence implies nothing more than that when the story was told in Greek the narrator made use of the current Greek translation of the OT. Finally, it must be insisted that it is one thing to show how a narrative was used in the early church [an exercise which the form-critic claims that he is very good at doing but whose conclusions have been shown all too often to be erroneous], and quite another thing to claim that because it was used for a particular purpose in the church, it must have been created by the church without any historical basis.[43]

It has often been noted that there must have been a single definite historical event lying behind Jesus' statement in Matthew 12:29 concerning his "binding the strong man" (see also Mark 3:27; Luke 11:21-22) as the explanation for his statement. Such a necessary antecedent is most admirably met by the temptation event.[44] The Evangelists represent Jesus' demonic exorcisms as occurring in the objective world of space and time, and "there can be no doubt that Jesus regarded the demons as actually existing supernatural beings, who could be spoken to and give answer, and [who] exercised a wide

---

[43]Marshall, *The Gospel of Luke*, 167-68.
[44]See Vos, *Biblical Theology*, 355-56.

sphere of baneful power."[45] And the reason he was able to exercise the authority and power he did over them was to be traced, he said, to the fact that he had "first tied up the strong man" of the "house" which he was now plundering, thereby enabling him to plunder that "strong man's house" at will. That "binding" would of necessity have had to happen also in and through an objective, historical event, and this occurred most naturally at the temptation.

Those who take exception to the spiritual phenomenon of a personal Satan as being distasteful to the modern mind must, of course, find all the references in the New Testament, indeed, in the whole Bible, to Satan and his demons as unhistorical reflections of ancient and/or pagan mythology. But these references are too deeply embedded in the very warp and woof of Scripture and particularly in the Gospel accounts of Jesus' healing miracles, both in number and significance, to be cavalierly dismissed on the *a priori* assumption that they are mythological.

We are not told in what form—whether tangible and visible or not—Satan came to Jesus after his fast of forty days, but "an encounter between persons, especially in the supersensual world, can be perfectly objective without necessarily entering into the sphere of the corporeally perceptible."[46] To decide such a question is not pertinent to our present purpose. The point that we want to underscore is that when Satan employed the title "[the] Son of God" in his conversation with Jesus (Matt 4:3, 6; Luke 4:3, 9),[47] he intended to acknowledge Jesus' divine Sonship.

Now it is true that the title occurs on each occasion in the temptation accounts in the protasis of a conditional sentence (the "if" clause), but in each case the protasis according to Greek syntax is a "first-class condition" which means that the condition expressed is regarded, from the perspective of the speaker, as real and factual. An English

---

[45]Vos, *Biblical Theology*, 357.

[46]Vos, *Biblical Theology*, 356.

[47]The anarthrous υἱός, *huios*, coming before the copula, is to be regarded as definite in accordance with Colwell's observations in his "A Definite Rule for the Use of the Article in the Greek New Testament" in *Journal of Biblical Literature* LII (1933), 20. See also Moule, *An Idiom Book of New Testament Greek*, 115-16.

translation on the order of "*Since* you are the Son of God" will make clear what I mean here, although I am not suggesting that the εἰ, *ei* ("if") should necessarily be so rendered by the English versions of the Bible. Supporting factors for urging this are primarily three in number.

First, the near juxtaposition of Satan's employment of the title to the preceding occurrence of the title in the heavenly oracle during Jesus' baptism, highlighted by the Matthean "then" (4:1) and the Marcan "at once" (1:12), can hardly be accidental. By this juxtaposition the Evangelists surely intended that the fact itself of Jesus' Sonship and the meaning of the title in the immediately preceding event are to extend themselves to govern the universe of fact and meaning for the occurrences in the latter event. And since the Father had just attested in Jesus' hearing that he *was* the Son of God, it is hardly likely that Satan only days later believed it to be contrary to fact and was seeking proof of Jesus' Sonship by suggesting ways that Jesus might demonstrate his divine Sonship both to himself and to Satan. But then, if Jesus' Sonship is not to be understood in the "if" clauses as a condition contrary to fact, it must be assumed that Satan was not questioning the status of Jesus but, to the contrary, was assuming that Jesus was the Son of God and was devising the forms of the several temptations accordingly. This is just to suggest that it was precisely in the recognition on his part that Jesus was the Son of God that the force and intent of the temptations are to be perceived. A paraphrase of them will bring out my meaning here. It is as if he were saying: "One who enjoys such inherent station and rank as is resident in your status as God's eternal Son should not have to endure such deprivation as hunger or have to walk the servant's road in order to win the right to govern the kingdoms of the world; therefore, repudiate the messianic investiture which entails such humiliation and exercise the powers and functions native to the Sonship which God himself has confirmed is yours and achieve the same end." The assumption by Satan that Jesus' Sonship is fact and *not* contrary to fact, I would submit, more clearly meets the demands which the temptations call for.

Second, all three Synoptic Evangelists inform us that "whenever the unclean spirits [demons] saw him, they fell down before him and cried out: 'You are the Son of God'" (Mark 3:11; see Luke 4:41[48]) or that they addressed him as "Son of God" (Matt 8:29) or "Son of the Most High God" (Mark 5:7; Luke 8:28). From other things that they say in these contexts, there is clearly no uncertainty in *their* understanding as to who he was: he was deity incarnate. Whence the source of *their* understanding? It is *theoretically* possible that Satan had informed his demonic cohorts of the fact, but it is *theologically* highly unlikely that such was the source of his demons' knowledge of Jesus' Sonship. Such a representation of the origin of their understanding is probably too crassly literalistic to be truly reflective of the supernaturally-charged conditions present in the intercourse among spirits. Rather, while theirs was certainly not an understanding reflecting in any sense an omniscient apprehension of things, their understanding would have been an intuitive, supernatural kind of awareness. Because they were themselves supernatural spirit beings, they would have "scented," to use Wrede's picturesque characterization, the supernatural in Jesus. As Vos aptly comments: "It was a case of spirit recognizing spirit."[49] And if this is what lay behind the demons' awareness of Jesus' station, it would follow that it would surely be equally true for Satan himself. Therefore, to Satan's likely awareness of the heavenly oracle's witness to Jesus' Sonship

---

[48]Regarding Luke's comment following the demons' cries: "You are the Son of God," to the effect that Christ would not allow them to say more "because they knew he was the Christ" (4:41), Marshall writes (*The Gospel of Luke*, 197):

> Luke's elucidation of the title in terms of the Messiah does not mean that he has down-graded "Son of God" to become merely an attribute of the Messiah; this is impossible in the light of 1:32-35 [Marshall's view of the earlier passage accords with my own that the titles in the Lucan birth narrative refer to Jesus' personal rather than a nativistic or a messianic sonship; see *The Gospel of Luke*, 67, 68, 71]. Rather the term "Messiah" is seen to be applicable a more-than-earthly figure, able to exorcise demons, and on a different level from political saviours. At the same time, Luke's purpose may be to indicate that "Son of God" must not be understood in purely Hellenistic categories as a reference to a charismatic, semi-divine figure, but must be seen in the light of Jewish messianic expectations.

[49]Vos, *The Self-Disclosure of Jesus*, 171.

must be added the likelihood that lying behind Satan's "Since you are the Son of God" was his "scented" recognition of the fact and reality of Jesus' Sonship. All this is more likely his meaning than the possibility that the opposite perception of Jesus was governing the choice of his words, namely, the perception on his part of the non-factuality and non-reality of Jesus' Sonship.

Third, by the form of the temptations themselves, Satan implied a recognition that Jesus possessed the *power* to work miracles (turning stones to bread), a *special right* to divine care, and the *entitlement to the kingdoms of this world*. Why, otherwise, in the last case, for example, does he offer the kingdoms of the world then and there *to him* rather than to someone else if he would only worship the Tempter? Clearly, here is an acknowledgement of powers, privileges, and prerogatives in Jesus' possession which are messianic in character, but "a type of Messiahship lifting him far above the level of the natural."[50] But this is just to say that the prior Sonship which in this context governs the universe of these messianic privileges is supramundane as well and is thus just a divine Sonship. I would submit, therefore, that here we find the arch-demon of all dark spirits himself affirming the divine Sonship of the Son of God.

TESTIMONY FROM THE ACCOUNTS OF JESUS' TRANSFIGURATION

Peter's great confession at Caesarea Philippi that Jesus was "the Christ, the Son of the living God" (Matt 16:16; see Mark 8:29; Luke 9:20) marked the beginning of a new emphasis in Jesus' instruction of his disciples. Now that they were fully convinced that he was the Messiah, Jesus began (ἤρξατο, *ērxato*) to emphasize the necessity of his death and resurrection[51] (which latter event, as the instrumental means to his enthronement at the Father's right hand, he apparently thought of in "shorthand" fashion for his resurrection *and* ascension since he says nothing about the latter event but rather assumes it when later he speaks about his Parousia) (Matt 16:21; Mark 8:31; Luke 9:22). Assured by Peter's confession, it was now both possible and needful for him to infuse the messianic concept with the content

[50] Vos, *The Self-Disclosure of Jesus*, 172-73.

of the Servant Song of Isaiah 52:13-53:2 and to correct the purely nationalistic associations which still lingered in the disciples' minds (see Matt 16:22-23; Mark 9:32-33; 10:35-37; Luke 9:46). So from that moment on to the end of his ministry, even though his disciples did not understand him (Mark 9:32; Luke 18:34), he kept constantly and prominently before them the fact of his "departure which he was about to accomplish at Jerusalem" (Matt 17:22-23; 20:17-19, 22, 28; 21:39; 26:2, 11-12, 24, 28; Mark 9:31; 10:32-34, 38, 45; 12:8; 14:8, 21, 24; Luke 9:51, 53; 13:33; 17:11; 18:31-33; 22:20).

But he not only began to speak more often than he had before about *his* suffering and death; in this context he also informed them that they, his disciples, must be prepared to die as well and that they must never be ashamed of him, else "the Son of Man will be ashamed of [such a one] when he comes in his glory and in the glory of his Father and of the holy angels" (Luke 9:23-26; see Matt 16:24-27;

---

[51]This incident at Caesarea Philippi should not be regarded as marking the point of emergence of a totally new *doctrine* in Jesus' teaching. Rather, it pinpoints only the beginning of a new *emphasis* upon a doctrine which may be found in his earliest teaching. For example, he had spoken earlier of his death (John 3:14; by implication also in Matt 9:15; Mark 2:20; Luke 5:35) and resurrection (John 2:19-22). And his earlier warnings that his disciples would be persecuted (Matt 5:11, 44; 10:16-39) because of him assumes that he will be persecuted as well. Vos, *The Self-Disclosure of Jesus*, 278-79, writes:

> Our Lord simply takes for granted that there will be a breach between his followers and the world. And, since the cause of this breach is placed in their identification with him, the underlying supposition doubtless is that the same conflict is in store for the Master himself, only after a more principial fashion. And there is no point in Jesus' life where this mental attitude can be said to have first begun. The "sunny" and untroubled days of "fair Galilee" are, when exploited in such a sense, a pure fiction. There never was in the life of Jesus an original optimistic period followed later by a pessimistic period. As the appoaching of the dread crisis did not render him despondent towards the end, so neither did its comparative remoteness render him sanguine at the beginning. The intrusion of such a terrifying thought as the thought of his death, in the specific form belonging to it, must have been, could not have failed to leave behind it the evidence of a sudden shock. But there is no evidence of any such sudden shock in the Gospels.

Mark 8:34-37). Solemn words these—both those concerning his own passion and those concerning his demand from his disciples for unflagging loyalty to him. All three Synoptic Evangelists report that, following immediately upon this reference to his return in glory (which is in itself an implicit claim to the messianic investiture), our Lord then cryptically declared: "Some who are standing here shall not taste death before they see the Son of Man coming in his kingdom" (Matt 16:28),[52] words which I cannot help but think were intended to be words of encouragement to counterbalance the apprehension which his previous words concerning martyrdom must have invoked in the minds of those present with him on that occasion. The cryptic saying implicitly enjoined them to view his passion and their own persecution against the background of his and (by extension) their own ultimate and eternal glory.

C. E. B. Cranfield neatly summarizes seven suggestions which have been proposed for the fulfilling referent of this saying,[53] any one of which, I would submit, is infinitely to be preferred to the widely-

---

[52]The other Synoptists report this "Son of Man" saying in essentially the same way. Luke's account reads simply: "...until they see the kingdom of God" (9:27), which I take to mean, because in all the Gospels the Kingdom of God and the person of Jesus as the Messiah are integrally and inseparably bound together, "until they see the kingdom of the divine Messiah"; Mark's account reads: "until they see the kingdom of God having come in power" (9:1), which adds the idea that the Messiah's kingdom will have come with accompanying manifestations indicative of the presence of divine omnipotence. See Gruenler, "Son of Man" in *Evangelical Dictionary of Theology*, 1036, for the view that Jesus employs the title in a *corporate* sense both here and in Matthew 10:23.

[53]C. E. B. Cranfield, *The Gospel According to Saint Mark* (Cambridge: University Press, 1966), 285-88. The seven, briefly, are as follows: (1) Dodd's use of it in support of his view of "realized eschatology"; (2) the view that "shall not taste of death" refers to spiritual death, from which faithful disciples will be exempted; (3) Michaelis' view that the meaning is that there will be some at least who will have the privilege of not dying before the Parousia, but that it is not said when these will live and not implied that they must belong to Jesus' contemporaries; (4) the destruction of Jerusalem in A.D.70; (5) Pentecost; (6) Vincent Taylor's view that Jesus was referring to a visible manifestation of the Rule of God displayed for men to see in the life of the Elect Community; and (7) the transfiguration.

held view that Jesus mistakenly expected his Parousia to take place within the lifetime of that generation of disciples. For myself, with Cranfield,[54] William L. Lane,[55] and (I would suspect) most evangelicals, I believe that Jesus was referring to his transfiguration which took place a week later and which all three Synoptic Gospels place immediately after the saying. Such a fulfillment meets the following four requirements of the saying:

1. The phrase, "*some* who are standing here," would refer to his "inner circle" of disciples, Peter, James, and John, who alone were present at the transfiguration.

2. The phrase, "shall not taste of death," that is, "shall not die," finds the explanation for its presence in the reference which our Lord had just made to the need for the disciple to "take up his cross" and "lose his life for me." The argument of some that if Jesus' transfiguration is made the fulfilling referent of his remark, then the "some" in the first phrase would imply that at least some if not all of the others there present *would* die in the next few days, is surely a *non sequitur*. For while Jesus' remark implies that the majority of those present would not see this thing themselves in their lifetime, it does not mean that they must necessarily die before *some* did see it.

3. The phrase, "before they *see*," fits well with the sustained emphasis in the transfiguration narrative on this inner circle of disciples *seeing* him in his "unearthly" radiance (see the phrases "transfigured *before* them" and "what you have *seen*" in Matt 17:2, 9; the phrases "transfigured *before* them," "there *appeared* before them," and "what they had *seen*" in Mark 9:2, 4, 9; and the phrases "they *saw* his glory" and "what they had *seen*" in Luke 9:32, 36).

4. The phrase, "the Son of Man coming in his kingdom" (Mark: "with power"), as Cranfield notes, "is a not unfair description of what

[54]Cranfield, *The Gospel According to Saint Mark*, 287-88.

[55]William L. Lane, *The Gospel of Mark* (Grand Rapids: Eerdmans, 1974), 313-14.

the three saw on the mount of Transfiguration,"[56] for Jesus' transfiguration was, although momentary, nonetheless a real and witnessed manifestation of his sovereign power and glory which pointed forward, as an anticipatory foretaste, to his Parousia when his kingdom would come "with [permanent] power and glory" (Mark 13:26).

Before we comment on the event of the transfiguration itself, I need to say something about its historicity in view of the assaults upon it. Regarding the view of Bultmann, which continues to find steady support to this day, that "it is an Easter-story projected backward into Jesus' life-time,"[57] that is, a legendary resurrection appearance mistakenly displaced and put in the pre-resurrection material, it needs only to be said that G. A. Boobyer[58] and C. H. Dodd[59] have convincingly demonstrated that nothing about it resembles the later resurrection appearances. For example, all of the accounts of the resurrection appearances in the Gospels begin with Jesus being absent while here he is present from the beginning. Again, in all of the accounts of Jesus' resurrection appearances, Jesus' spoken word is prominent where here he is silent as far as any encouragement or instruction to his disciples is concerned. he speaks, but to Moses and Elijah about his *future* death (Luke 9:31). And again, the presence of Moses and Elijah here is strange if this is a resurrection appearance since no figure from the beyond ever appears at the same time with him in the resurrection appearances. Finally, this account contains none of the features that one might have expected if it is an appearance in the context of which Peter is present as a guilt-ridden disciple (see John 21). Consequently, Dodd declares:

---

[56]Cranfield, *The Gospel According to Saint Mark*, 288.

[57]R. Bultmann, *Theology of the New Testament*, translated by Kendrick Grobel (London: SCM, 1952), I, 26, 27, 30, 45, 50.

[58]G. H. Boobyer, *St. Mark and the Transfiguration Story* (Edinburgh: T. & T. Clark, 1942), 11-16.

[59]C. H. Dodd, "The Appearances of the Risen Christ: An Essay in Form Criticism of the Gospels" in *Studies in the Gospels*, edited by D. E. Nineham (Oxford: Basil Blackwell, 1955), 9-35. See also J. Schiewind, *Das Evangelium Nach Markus* (Göttingen: Vandenhoeck & Rurecht, 1949), 123.

> To set over against these points of difference I cannot find a single point of resemblance. If the theory of a displaced post-resurrection appearance is to be evoked for the understanding of this difficult *pericope*, it must be without any support from form-criticism, and indeed in the teeth of the presumption which formal analysis establishes.[60]

Against the view of Lohmeyer[61] and others that it is a non-historical, symbolical expression of a "theological conviction" concerning Jesus derived from imagery drawn from the Old Testament Feast of Tabernacles (see Peter's referencc to "booths"), Cranfield marshalls details in the account which are very strange if the pericope was only a theological statement created by the early church, such as Mark's "after six days" and Peter's use of "Rabbi" and his absurd statement about the "booths." This title of Jesus and Peter's thoughtless statement are hardly likely to have been put in the mouth of a chief apostle if the post-Easter church was creating a symbolic narrative with a theological statement about Jesus as its purpose.[62] The fairer analysis will conclude that Mark was relating something that really happened.

Finally, Matthew's τὸ ὅραμα (*to horama*, "the vision") (17:9), which I translated earlier by "what you have seen," need not mean that what is reported here occurred merely in a vision which the disciples had. Three facts register tellingly against the view that Jesus' transfiguration was simply a visionary experience shared by the three disciples. First, a single vision is not shared, at least normally, by a plurality of persons at the same time. Second, ὅραμα, *horama*, may be used of what is seen in the ordinary way (see Deut 28:34). And third, Luke expressly declares that the disciples "had been very sleepy," but it was when "they became fully awake" that "they saw his glory and the two men standing with him" (9:32).

Everything about the Gospel accounts suggests that the Evangelists intended to report an event that actually happened, that could have

---

[60]Dodd, "The Appearances of the Risen Christ: An Essay in Form Criticism of the Gospels," 25.

[61]E. Lohmeyer, *Das Evangelium des Markus* (Göttingen: Vanderhoeck & Rurecht, 1937), 173-81.

[62]Cranfield, *The Gospel According to Saint Mark*, 293-94.

been seen by others had they been present; and no argument has been advanced by solid scholarship to date that overthrows the traditional view of the church that represents the transfiguration as an actual occurrence in the life of Jesus and the lives of the three disciples. Therefore, I will presume the historicity of the event and proceed to its exposition.

The "Metamorphosis" Itself

The Synoptic accounts[63] all begin by informing the reader that a week after Jesus' cryptic prophecy,[64] Jesus took Peter, James, and John up into a mountain.[65] Luke alone adds, "to pray." And while he was praying, we are told, Jesus was "transfigured" (μετεμορφώθη, *metemorphōthē*) before them. We are not left to wonder about the nature of this "metamorphosis." Two aspects of his physical appearance in particular are singled out for comment: his face (but this probably included his entire body as well because of the reference to his garments) and his clothing. While Luke simply states that "the appearance of his face was changed" (9:29), Matthew writes: "his

---

[63]One can only guess why John, as interested as he obviously was in proving the deity and messiahship of Jesus, does not mention the transfiguration of Jesus, particularly since he was one of only three disciples who witnessed it. There may be a veiled allusion to it in John 1:14: "We have seen his glory, the glory of the one and only Son, who came from the Father, full of grace and truth," and knowing that the other Evangelists had mentioned it perhaps he considered this statement a sufficient reference to it.

[64]Matthew's and Mark's "after six days" could place the event on the seventh day, especially if it occurred at night after the close of the sixth day, whereas Luke's "some eight days after," by inclusive reckoning, as in John 20:26, also means "on the seventh day." In any event, Luke's ὡσει; (*hōsei*, "about") suggests that he was conscious that his number of days was an approximation to the figure in the other Gospels.

[65]See Walter L. Liefeld, "Theological Motifs in the Transfiguration Narratives" in *New Dimensions in New Testament Study*, edited by R. N. Longenecker and M. C. Tenney (Grand Rapids: Zondervan, 1974), 167, fn. 27, for an interesting defense of Mt. Meron, rather than the more traditional Mt. Tabor or Mt. Hermon, as the most likely site of the transfiguration. I mention this fact merely to underscore the space/time historical character of the transfiguration.

face shone like the sun" (17:2). And while Matthew simply states that "his clothes became as brilliant as the light" (17:2), Mark adds that they became "dazzling white, whiter than any cleaner on earth could bleach them" (9:3), and Luke writes that they were "gleaming as lightning" (9:29). If this transformation took place at night, as some details in the Lukan account suggest (see 9:32, 37), the scene unfolding before the disciples must have been all the more fearsomely awesome (Mark 9:6), beyond the capacity of words fully to describe.

This "transfiguration" in Jesus' appearance Luke characterizes in two words: it was a revelation of "his glory" (9:32), a momentary substantiation of the essence of his prophecy in Luke 9:26 where he makes mention of "his glory." Because Luke declares that Moses and Elijah, whose appearances are mentioned by all three Synoptics, also appeared in "glorious splendor" (9:31), one might at first be disinclined to make too much of Jesus' transfiguration so far as that feature in the accounts indicating anything unique about him is concerned and conclude that the combined glory of all three is simply indicative of the "supernaturalism" of the occasion. But Peter would declare later that, in seeing what they saw, the disciples were made "eyewitnesses of [Jesus'] μεγαλειότης [*megaleiotēs*]" (2 Pet 1:16), that is, his "grandeur," "sublimity," or "majesty." He says nothing about Moses and Elijah. This word is used on only two other occasions in the New Testament—as an attribute of God in Luke 9:43 and of the goddess Diana of Ephesus in Acts 19:27, a word which can and does clearly designate the glory of deity. For Peter the word took up into itself the idea also of divine power (see δύναμις, *dunamis*, 2 Pet 1:16). So Jesus' "metamorphosis" was a visible manifestation, we may safely conclude, of his divine "glory" (Luke 9:32) and "majesty" (2 Pet 1:16), revealed in "power" (2 Pet 1:16).

The Voice From the Cloud

In response to Peter's thoughtless statement invoked by this awesome sight: "Rabbi, it is good for us to be here. Let us put up three shelters—one for you, one for Moses and one for Elijah" (Mark 9:5), God, in order to remove even the remotest notion that these three "glorious" figures should be regarded in any sense "equal in power and glory," appeared theophanically in the form of a bright cloud that enveloped them, and a terrifying voice from the cloud said: "This is my beloved Son, in whom I am well pleased. Listen to him." (Matt 17:5-6) Whereas the Father's voice from heaven at his baptism *confirmed to Jesus* his rightful claim to Sonship, here it *attests to his disciples* his unique station as the Son of God. Here, as there, these words signalized Jesus' personal and essential divine Sonship as the antecedent ground and presupposition of his messianic investiture which is alluded to in the final words, "Listen to him," words reminiscent of those in Deuteronomy 18:15: "The Lord your God will raise up for you a Prophet like me [that is, Moses; recall his presence here on this occasion] from among your brothers. *You must listen to him.*" Peter was later to confirm that the voice was that of God the Father and that the Father's attestation "honored" and "glorified" the Lord Jesus Christ (2 Pet 1:17). Here, then, in the Father's attestation to his Son, in addition to the feature of the transfiguration itself, do we find the second indication in the transfiguration accounts of Jesus' essential deity.

The Disciples' Question

Coming down from the mountain the next day (Luke 9:27), the disciples asked Jesus: "Why, therefore, do the teachers of the Law say that Elijah must come first?" (Matt 17:10; Mark 9:11). Their mention of Elijah, of course, was prompted by the fact that they had just seen him. But what lay behind their question about him? There can be no doubt that it was something in Malachi's prophecy that now was perplexing them. Malachi had said that "Elijah" would come *before* the Lord came (3:1), *before* the great and terrible day of the Lord (4:5), which they had just seen "in miniature." The implications of their question for the identity of Jesus must not be lost on the reader. The only conclusion that one can fairly draw from it is that for them Jesus—just attested as such by the glory of his deity shining through his humanity and by the heavenly Voice—was Malachi's "Lord who was to come," the Yahweh of the Old Testament, but the order of their historical appearances—Jesus had first appeared, then Elijah—seemed to them to be the reverse of what Malachi had predicted.

This seeming inversion of the prophet's order was what was creating for them the quandary which provoked their question. Jesus solved their problem for them by informing them that "Elijah" (in the person of John the Baptist) had indeed come first, whom Jesus had then followed as that "Elijah's" Lord. By his exposition of Malachi's prophecy here, Jesus laid unmistakable claim to being the Lord of Hosts, the messenger of the covenant, who had promised he would come *after* "Elijah," his messenger, had come.

The entire account of the transfiguration is replete—resplendent might be the more appropriate word—with indications of Jesus' essential divine Sonship. It is not surprising that those who deny his deity are so solicitous to reduce this event to legend or myth. But the accounts stand, unfazed by the attempts of critical scholarship to make them into something which they are not, and thus they lend their combined voices to the larger witness of Scripture to Jesus' essential divine Sonship in the Godhead.

TESTIMONY FROM THE DISCIPLES' UNDERSTANDING OF JESUS

In our last area of investigation in this chapter we shall examine the disciples' pre-crucifixion understanding of Jesus for the light that their understanding sheds on Jesus' person and work. It is, of course, theoretically possible that they could have been mistaken in their understanding of him and, indeed, the Scriptures indicate that they often were mistaken. But when they express their understanding of him in his presence and are not corrected or rebuked by him but, to the contrary, are actually encouraged to continue in their expressed perception of him, we may safely conclude that their understanding received his endorsement and coincided with his own. It is this kind of testimony that I intend now to consider.

We have already called attention to Jesus' many mighty works. But what we did not mention earlier is the impact which his "glorious deeds" (ἐνδόξοις, *endoxois*) (Luke 13:17) made on the crowds that swarmed around him almost daily. Not only do the Evangelists report that the crowds, as a result of his miracles, "marveled" (Mark 1:27), "wondered at" (Mark 5:20; Luke 9:43), were "amazed" (Mark

2:12; Luke 8:56), were "utterly astonished" (Mark 7:37), were "overcome with fear" (Luke 8:37; see 5:26; 7:16), and "rejoiced" (Luke 13:17); but they also report the crowds' following direct comments:

"What is this? A new teaching with authority! He commands even the unclean spirits, and they obey him!" (Mark 1:27)

"What is this word, that with authority and power he commands the unclean spirits, and they obey!" (Luke 4:36)

"We have never seen anything like this!" (Mark 2:12)

"Nothing like this was ever seen in Israel!" (Matt 9:33)

"He has done all things well! He makes even the deaf to hear and the dumb to speak!" (Mark 7:37)

"We have seen marvelous things today!" (Luke 5:26)

"A great prophet has appeared among us!" (Luke 7:16)

"God has visited his people!" (Luke 7:16)

Now if his miracles impacted upon the crowds in this fashion, we should not wonder then that the disciples who were with him almost constantly throughout his earthly ministry and who saw virtually all of his "powers" (δυνάμεις, *dunameis*) (Matt 11:20-23; Luke 10:13) were also deeply affected by what they beheld and formed certain definite opinions about him, several of which they openly expressed in his hearing on certain occasions. We shall consider eight of these expressions of belief.

Nathaniel's Testimony (John 1:49)

We will pass over Andrew's designation of Jesus as "the Messiah" (1:41) and Philip's description of him as the object of Old Testament prophecy ("the one about whom Moses wrote in the Law, and about whom the prophets spoke") (1:45) simply because they were not spoken in Jesus' presence. But I would like to make one observation about them nonetheless. It is this: These early testimonies should not be entirely discounted as "reflections of a later theological development" merely because the Synoptic Gospels suggest that it took some time for the disciples to come to a deeply-held conviction with respect to the nature of his *person*. It is one thing to call Jesus "Messiah" and to do so in a "dawning" way, and it is quite another to have anything like an adequate understanding of the messianic concept and how Christ's person is to be related to it. But both are legitimate stages in the growth process, and both stages represent degrees of *true* awareness—the later stages, of course, entailing the greater degrees of knowledge. True, the evidence indicates that there was many a "false start" in the disciples' understanding and a good many "ebbs and flows" as well before they finally came to a settled conviction about him (see Mark 4:41; 6:51-52; 8:32; 10:31-32). But these testimonies, even though they appear in the early days of Christ's public ministry, should be allowed nonetheless to stand as authentic statements and as two "true starts," and to add their weight, however minor, to the overall New Testament witness to Jesus' messiahship.

Now to the matter before us. At Philip's invitation, Nathaniel came to Jesus to investigate for himself the question of Jesus' messiahship (1:45-47). We know nothing about Nathaniel, outside of this single incident, beyond the fact that he was from Cana in Galilee and was with six other disciples when Jesus appeared to the seven of them by the Sea of Galilee in one of his post-resurrection appearances (21:2). This latter fact surely indicates that he was a disciple of Jesus, but whether he was one of the original Twelve is another question. It has been suggested that Nathaniel is the Bartholomew of the Synoptics (for the reasons, see the commentaries), but it is entirely possible that he was not one of the original Twelve. Jesus, after all, had many disciples besides the twelve Apostles. But whatever the actual case in this regard, "there is no evidence that Nathaniel is a purely symbolic figure."[66]

Before we actually consider the titles Nathaniel employed to describe Jesus, it is important that we note Nathaniel's response to Philip's invitation to come to Jesus, for in it we can detect a glimpse of his attitude toward the messianic hope *per se*. Even though his question, "Can anything good come out of Nazareth?" (1:46), may be

---

[66]Raymond E. Brown, *The Gospel According to John I-XII* (AB) (Garden City, New York: Doubleday, 1966), 82. See Leon Morris, *The Gospel According to John* (Grand Rapids: Eerdmans, 1972), 164.

a local proverb reflecting the rivalry often existing between small towns in close proximity to one another, it still describes his estimation of the messianic hope as something "good." Then when we find Jesus addressing Nathaniel later as a "true Israelite [literally, "truly an Israelite," but the adverb has the equivalent force here of an adjective] in whom there is no guile" (1:47; see Gen 27:35), we may conclude, since Jesus was not one to pander to men's egos with empty flattery, that Nathaniel, like Simeon and Anna, was waiting for the "consolation of Israel" (see Luke 2:25-38). And because he later applies both "Son" and "King" to Jesus, it is a virtual certainty that he knew the prophetic Scriptures and had the words of Psalm 2:6-7 in mind in his titular descriptions of Jesus. Furthermore, the entire report clearly suggests that, in his thinking, the Messiah would do just such works as Jesus did here, that is, would display *supernatural* abilities, for as a result of only the briefest exchange between them, in which he was confronted with the fact of Jesus' supernatural knowledge of his heart (1:47-48),[67] he concluded that Jesus, far from being clairvoyant, was his "Rabbi" (literally, "my Teacher"), and exclaimed: "*You* [emphatic] are the Son of God; *You* [emphatic] are the King of Israel" (1:49).

Now in reaching a correct interpretation of these two latter titles, it must be kept constantly in mind that *both* titles reflect conclusions gained from Nathaniel's apprehension of Jesus' supernatural insight into the very thoughts of his heart. Consequently, although the latter title is tantamount to a confession of Jesus' messiahship,[68] it must be seen, because it was provoked spontaneously by Jesus' supernatural insight into his inmost thoughts, to be a confession "on a higher plane than that of the Messiah in vs. 41."[69] It is thus entirely possible that even this title indicates that Nathaniel's perception of Jesus' kingship included the attribution of deity to him, for here was someone who

---

[67]See Morris, *The Gospel According to John*, 167: "It is difficult to explain Jesus' knowledge of the incident on the level of merely human knowledge. Nathaniel had never met him before this moment. We are required to understand that Jesus had some knowledge not generally available to the sons of men (See 2:24f.)."

[68]C. H. Dodd, *The Interpretation of the Fourth Gospel* (Cambridge: University Press, 1953), 88; C. K. Barrett, *The Gospel According to St. John* (London: SPCK, 1955), 155.

[69]Brown, *The Gospel According to John I-XII*, 87.

could read his heart, "here was someone who could not be described in ordinary human terms."[70] And that the title "the King of Israel" could be descriptive of deity is clear from Isaiah 44:6 where it serves as a title of Yahweh. But whatever the real case may be, by this second title Nathaniel clearly confessed faith (1:50) in Jesus as "the King of Israel" and thus as *his* Messiah inasmuch as *he* was a "true Israelite."

With regard to his first title for Jesus—"the Son of God," for two reasons I would suggest that by it Nathaniel was confessing that he stood in the presence of deity. First, whatever experience in Nathaniel's past it was to which Jesus alluded when he said, "I saw you while you were still under the fig tree before Philip called you," it was clearly an experience which was so *intimate* and so *private* that only *God* could have known about it, for Nathaniel's reaction to Jesus' comment was such that it suggests that it was an experience known to no *man* other than himself. And the fact that Jesus alluded to it implies that he knew this to be the case, indeed, this was his reason for alluding to it. But for *Jesus* to know about it (and recall that Nathaniel was so amazed by Jesus' knowledge that he *immediately* confessed faith in Jesus' messiahship) could only mean for Nathaniel that Jesus stood in the closest possible relationship to God—that filial relationship ascribed to the Messiah in Psalm 2:7 (see Heb 1:5) and elsewhere, a Sonship of essential oneness with God. In other words, as the dove descending on Jesus, by divine appointment, was the sign to John the Baptist that Jesus was the Son of God, so Jesus' knowledge of his very private past became, under the Spirit's illumination, the sign to Nathaniel that Jesus was not only the Messiah but also the Son of God in a supra-natural sense.

My second reason is the same one I employed earlier in connection with John the Baptist's attestation of Jesus as the Son of God: The title here cannot be lower in its import than the same title in John's statement of purpose for writing his Gospel (20:31), which, because of its proximity to Thomas' confession in 20:28, indicates both identity with God as to his nature and distinction from the Father as to his person. To suggest that John knowingly incorporated a pericope in which the title occurs but where its user (Nathaniel) meant less by it

[70] Morris, *The Gospel According to John* , 168.

than its import in his overall purpose is to raise a serious question about his authorial integrity and to vitiate to some degree the validity of his entire argument for Christ's divine Sonship. To suggest that he did it unknowingly is to call into question his competence as a writer and as a witness to Christ. But the former possibility is most unlikely in light of both his stated concern for truth in reporting (19:35) and the validation which his Gospel receives from those who knew both him and the facts he reports (21:24). And the latter possibility is excluded both by the literary skill and by the rich theological insights which even the most radical critics acknowledge are present in every sentence John wrote.

Against this title meaning essential Sonship with God two objections have been raised. It is urged, first, that the juxtaposition of the title before "the King of Israel" suggests that it too carries messianic import rather than denoting essential Sonship with God the Father. I would urge, however, that this juxtaposition is one of the strongest arguments against it simply meaning a messianic "sonship." We have already seen that the latter title—"the King of Israel"—does signify messiahship. To make the former also signify messiahship results in the following harsh tautology of meaning: "You are the Son of God [that is, the Messiah]; You are the King of Israel [that is, the Messiah]." If the two were intended to be synonymous for "Messiah," the second could have been connected as a simple apposition. As it is, the occurrences of σὺ ει, *su ei* ("You are"), with both titles precludes the synonymy of the titles. It is urged, second, that if the former title denotes essential rather than messianic sonship, since the former title would then be the more significant of the two titles, the order would be anticlimactic. But this does not follow if the former title is being treated as the ground of the latter with the latter being viewed as the covenantal consequence of the former (see the same order in Psalm 2:7; Matt 3:17; 17:5).

Now it is exceedingly important for our present purpose that we note Jesus' reaction to Nathaniel's attestations. Jesus did not register any objections to either of Nathaniel's descriptions of him. To the contrary, Jesus assured Nathaniel that he would see even greater things than Jesus' disclosure of the thoughts of his heart. Adding solemn certainty to his next words by introducing them with his authoritative "Truly, truly I say to you," Jesus declared that Nathaniel would see heaven opened and the angels ascending and descending on the Son of Man (1:51), doubtless an allusion to the words in Genesis 28:12-13). Employing the Danielic "Son of Man" figure, Jesus here confirmed Nathaniel in his estimation of him as the Messiah; and by the *apocalyptic* imagery he employed (the heavens opened and the Son of Man surrounded by the angels of God), he spoke prophetically of his future glorious return,[71] underscoring thereby both his supernatural character as the divine Son of God and his role as Israel's Messiah.

Consequently, I conclude that Nathaniel confessed faith in both Jesus' divine Sonship and his messianic investiture, and that Jesus confirmed his confession to be correct. I also submit that Nathaniel's confession resulted from his awareness of Jesus' supernatural ability to know that which only God could have known. And because Jesus did nothing to correct either his confession or the ground upon which he was basing it, we have another instance where the New Testament affirms the deity of Jesus.

Peter's Confession of Jesus as "Lord" (Luke 5:8)

On the occasion of Jesus' addressing the crowds from the haven of Peter's boat (Luke 5:1-11), after he had finished speaking Jesus invited Peter to put out into deep water and to let down his nets for a catch. Although Peter mildly protested that it would do no good inasmuch as he had been fishing all night and had caught nothing, nevertheless, addressing Jesus as "Master" (Ἐπιστάτα, *Epistata*), he agreed to do as he was instructed. Immediately upon carrying out Jesus' order he caught so many fish that his nets began to break, and when the second boat came alongside to render assistance the catch was so plentiful that both boats began to sink!

Before we consider the implications of Peter's response in words and actions to his catch, something should be said about the historicity of the incident. Because certain details in the story resemble the miracle in John 21:1-14, Bultmann and his school have urged that

---

[71]See J. H. Bernard, *A Critical and Exegetical Commentary on the Gospel According to St. John* (ICC) (Edinburgh: T. & T. Clark, 1928), I, 68.

Luke has ante-dated a post-Easter story,[72] but again, C. H. Dodd has shown that the account lacks the essential "form" of a resurrection story and must be placed in the pre-resurrection period.[73] The mere fact that the two accounts of the two incidents resemble one another in some details does not necessarily mean that they both reflect one original story in the "tradition." There are numerous examples in the Gospels of pairs of similar but distinct incidents (see Matt 9:27-31 and 20:29-34; Luke 7:37-38 and John 12:1-3). There is no reason to deny either the historicity or the authenticity of the Lukan account.

At the evident display of not only Jesus' supernatural knowledge of but also his supernatural power over the creatures of nature, and apparently overcome with the numinous[74] awareness of his own sinfulness in the presence of Jesus' majestic holiness,[75] Peter fell at Jesus' knees, crying: "Depart from me, because I am a sinful man, O Lord!" Although Marshall states that "no precise connotation (e.g., of divinity) can necessarily be attached to [Peter's use of κύριος (*kurios*, "Lord")],[76] Peter's act of prostrating himself at Jesus' knees, accompanied as it is with his acknowledgement of his sinfulness, can only be properly viewed as an act of religious worship. Whereas godly men and angels always condemned such prostration when it occurred in reference to them as an act of misplaced devotion, indeed, as an act of idolatry (see Acts 10:25-26; 14:11-15; Rev 19:9-10), it is significant that Jesus issued no such prohibition to Peter. To the

---

[72]R. Bultmann, *Theology of the New Testament*, I, 45.

[73]Dodd, *The Interpretation of the Fourth Gospel*, 88.

[74]By "numinous" here I refer to that sense of religious awe that is aroused in the soul when one is suddenly confronted by the presence of the Holy. See Rudolf Otto's *The Idea of the Holy* and J. D. Spiceland, "The Numinous" in *Evangelical Dictionary of Theology*, 783.

[75]Vos, *The Self-Disclosure of Jesus*, 110, writes: "The disciples came into awesome contact with [Jesus' holiness] through the miracle of the great draft of fishes and the perspective it opened to them of the supernatural Messianic potencies stored up in the Person of Jesus (Luke 5:1-11). The experience made Peter exclaim: 'Depart from me, for I am a sinful man, O Lord.' [His holiness] also explains, to some extent, the atmosphere of mystery enveloping Jesus as he walks through the Gospels. And it is one of the channels through which the apperception of *that which was even higher than Messiahship* broke in upon his followers" (emphasis supplied).

[76]Marshall, *The Gospel of Luke*, 204.

contrary, he endorsed Peter's adoration by calling him to follow him as a "fisher of men." (The parallel between Peter's attitude and action here and Isaiah's attitude and action in Isaiah 6:1-7 is quite remarkable.) And concerning Peter's address of Jesus as "Lord" (κύριε, ***kurie***), Warfield remarks that it

> seems to be an ascription to Jesus of a majesty which is distinctly recognized as supernatural: not only is the contrast of "Lord" with "Master" here expressed (see v. 5), but the phrase "Depart from me; for I am a sinful man" (v. 8) is the natural utterance of that sense of unworthiness which overwhelms men in the presence of the divine [see Job 42:5-6; Isa 6:5; Dan 10:16; Luke 18:13; Rev 1:12-17], and which is signalized in Scripture as the mark of recognition of the divine presence.[77]

There can be no legitimate doubt that Peter here regards Jesus as divine and addresses him accordingly as "Lord."

---

[77]Warfield, *The Lord of Glory*, 142. See also F. Godet, *A Commentary on the Gospel of St. Luke* (Edinburgh: T. & T. Clark, 1870), I, 257: "Peter here employs the more religious expression *Lord*, which answers to his actual feeling"; Alfred Plummer, *A Critical and Exegetical Commentary on the Gospel According to St. Luke* (ICC) (Edinburgh: T. & T. Clark, 1896), 145: "The change from' Επιστάτα [*Epistata*] "Master" to "Lord" is remarkable, and quite in harmony with the change of circumstances. It is the 'Master' whose orders must be obeyed, the 'Lord' whose holiness causes moral agony to the sinner..."; William Hendriksen, *The Gospel of Luke* (Grand Rapids: Baker, 1978), 284: "Peter stands in awe of his Master and confesses him to be his 'Lord.' Astonishment and fear had seized him, and not only him but also his men...and his partners, James and John. They have become aware of the fact that Jesus is superhuman; in fact, that he is God! Again and again in the Septuagint...the title *Lord* is used as an equivalent of God. Instantaneously, under the impression of the astounding miracle, Simon Peter knew in his heart that his 'Master' was at the same time his 'Lord,' truly worthy of worship and adoration. Over against this 'Lord' Peter was nothing but a 'sinful man'"; Marshall, *The Gospel of Luke*, 204-05: "What Simon expressed was the sense of unworthiness...and fear...which men should feel in the presence of the divine.... The revelation of Jesus' divine power in this epiphany sufficed to demonstrate to Simon that he was in the presence of the Holy One...and to make him aware of his own inadequacy."

The Disciples' Confession of Jesus as "the Son of God" (Matthew 14:33)

It had been an awe-inspiring day for the disciples—they had just witnessed Jesus' miraculous feeding of "about five thousand men, not counting women and children" with only five loaves and two fish (Matt 14:13-21). But now, only hours later, they were on the Sea of Galilee some three to three and a half miles from shore (John 6:19); and with a strong wind against them, they found themselves in "rough sea." And it was night. Suddenly, they saw Jesus walking toward them on the sea's surface, unhindered by the strong winds which were causing them such difficulty. And until Jesus reassured them that it was he, the disciples, terrified, imagined that they were seeing a ghost (a sea-demon of some kind?). Peter requested that he might be allowed to go to Jesus, and with Jesus' permission and by his power Peter walked, not without a lapse of faith, on the sea's surface as well. As soon as they both were received into the boat, the wind died (another demonstration of Jesus' sovereignty over nature?). All of this could not but make a great impression on the disciples. So much so, as Matthew informs us, that "those who were in the boat worshiped him, and said: 'You are truly the Son of God'" (14:33).[78]

Before we consider the meaning of this exclamation, it is again necessary to deal with the question of the historicity of the incident. We must insist at the outset that there is no real ground for seeing this pericope as another displaced story of a resurrection appearance. Cranfield writes:

> The close connection between this section and the preceding makes [this] most unlikely. The character of the detail with which the section abounds makes it also unlikely that the narrative is a pious legend or a symbolical story; it suggests rather the memory of an actual

---

[78]According to Zahn, the "truly" should be construed not as the indicator that the statement is an asseveration, that is: "Truly, you are...," but should rather be taken adverbially with εἶ, *ei*, that is to say, "You are truly...," underscoring the nature of this one in whose presence they were. This accords, says Zahn, with the fact that Matthew does not use' Ἀληθῶς, *Alēthōs*, (as Luke does in 12:44; 21:3) like ἀμήν, *amēn*. See BAGD, *A Greek-English Lexicon of the New Testament*, 36, no. 1.

> incident. When the third person is changed to the first person plural, the section reads like the vivid reminiscence of one of the Twelve.... It seems very likely that we have here Petrine reminiscence.[79]

As for the disciples' confession itself, because neither Mark (6:45-51) nor John (6:16-21) mention it, it is commonly held by critical scholars that Matthew has taken redactional liberties, in line with his purpose, and created this feature of the story. This is all the more likely, it is argued, in light of the fact that Mark declares that the reaction of the disciples was not what Matthew suggests—one of faith—but one of amazement (6:51), a statement interpreted to mean incomprehension because of the words which follow: "for they had not understood about the [miracle of the] loaves, but their hearts were hardened" (6:52). But Mark's words do not need to be interpreted in such a manner. It is quite plausible that the disciples' amazement should not be interpreted in terms of utter lack of comprehension but rather in terms of "dawning apprehension [which makes room for Matthew's account of their confession], a sign that the hardening of their hearts was now to some extent passing away."[80] Mark's point would then be that if they had grasped earlier the significance of the miracle of the loaves (which had occurred the previous day), they would have realized *then* "the secret of Jesus' person" (Cranfield) and not later, after the frightening experience they had just experienced.

We are left, then, with Cullmann's two difficulties with the pericope: first, he judges that "within Matthew itself it has no special significance whatsoever," and second, "it seems inconsistent that this recognition should come in Matt. 14.33, when, according to the structure of the Gospel of Matthew, the disciples first recognized Jesus in Matt. 16.16."[81] As for the first, I would suggest that it is a reckless (if not perverse) remark on Cullmann's part to say that the pericope "has no special significance whatsoever." That is not for Cullmann to say;

---

[79]Cranfield, *The Gospel According to Saint Mark*, 224; see also Lane, *The Gospel of Mark*, 234.

[80]Vos, *The Self-Disclosure of Jesus*, 178, citing Weiss.

[81]Oscar Cullmann, *The Christology of the New Testament* (London: SCM, 1959), 277, and on the same page, fn. 3.

Matthew apparently thought otherwise. If it reports a miracle that actually occurred, that is a significant fact in itself. And if it reports a miracle whose effect was that the disciples were brought to a fresh and deeper appreciation of Jesus' superhuman character and were led to affirm that fact, that too is indeed significant—both for themselves and for the guidance and instruction of the church throughout all subsequent generations.

As for Cullmann's second problem, it is based upon a false assumption. Nowhere in the pericope itself or in the structure of the Gospel itself is there the remotest suggestion that it was at Caesarea Philippi that the disciples "first recognized Jesus." The actual case is quite different. The earliest of the disciples, including Peter himself, from the beginning concluded that Jesus was the Messiah (John 1:41, 49). But because he proceeded to act differently from what they had anticipated in light of their preconceptions concerning the messianic hope, they were often perplexed about his messiahship. But again and again, some new miracle or some new discourse would persuade them afresh of his messianic investiture and give them clearer insight into the nature of his person. This is what we have here in Matthew 14:33 and which we will see occurring later in John 6:69 and in a most significant way in Matthew 16:16.[82] But even after Caesarea Philippi,

---

[82]Ned Stonehouse, *The Witness of Matthew and Mark to Christ*, 126-28, writes in this regard:

> It is necessary to insist...that the situation [in Matthew 16:16-17] is not [to be construed as a totally new disclosure of the messiahship of Jesus], in spite of the conspicuous reference to the divine revelation. If Mt. 16:17 is viewed in the persective which Mt. 11:27 provides, as well as in the light of the entire previous record of the activity of Christ, it will appear that no new objective revelation of the moment can be in mind. Rather, the entire history of Christ has been in the nature of a divine revelation which the disciples, with greater or lesser clarity, and with admixture of doubt and bewilderment, have come to comprehend. In Peter's confession we are invited to observe then, not a new objective revelation, but genuine subjective apprehension. And even this apprehension is not clearly intimated to be a completely new apprehension. The fundamental contrast of the narrative is not between the disciples' previous lack of apprehension and their suddenly bestowed understanding, but between the inadequate and erroneous estimates of men, who held that he was at

the disciples had difficulty taking in his teaching about his impending cross (see John 12:16). It would not be until after Jesus' resurrection that all that he said to them came together in a comprehensive, coherent fashion. But even the later "false starts" after Matthew 16 in no way invalidate the legitimacy and the significance of their earlier expressions of faith. Cullmann's difficulties, I must conclude, are more created than real and are not really substantive problems.

Taking the Matthean account, then, just as it stands as an authentic report of the event, it is apparent from their act of worship and their confession that the disciples realized afresh the supernatural character of the one who was capable of such works. Their act of worship may be deduced from the Matthean word προσεκύνησαν, *proskunēsan*, which means "they [fell down and] worshiped, did obeisance to, prostrated themselves before, did reverence to." At the very least the word connotes an attitude of reverence but because of the character of the miracle itself (see Pss 89:9; 106:9; 107:23-30 which Jewish sailors and fishermen must surely have known by heart), the word must certainly be given its maximum allowable sense of worship. As for their confession, "You are truly the Son of God," is it not plain that their earlier question, "What kind of [Ποταπός, *Potapos*]

---

best one of the prophets, and the evaluation of his disciples who belonged to the inner circle and who had eyes to see and ears to hear.

From this perspective no difficulty is presented by the acknowledgment of Jesus as God's Son which appears in Mt. 14:33. If the confession of Peter in Mt. 16:16 represented a turning point in the attitude of the disciples, grounded in a completely new revelation of the person of Jesus to them, the acknowledgment of Jesus' sonship which Matthew records in the narrative of the walking upon the sea might appear to introduce confusion and inconsistency into Matthew's delineation of the historical developments. Since, however, the whole of the ministry of Jesus is viewed as constituting a divine revelation, the apprehension of the revelation expressed in the words, "Of a truth thou art God's Son," does not imply that Matthew is reading back into an earlier stage of the disciples' experience an estimate of Christ's person which actually emerged at a later juncture. In fact, the confession of Mt. 14:33 is fully as intelligible as that in 16:16 since in the context the response is called forth by the miraculous action of Jesus in walking upon the water, rescuing Peter from the deep, and apparently also quieting the wind, besides Jesus' words of challenge to faith and of rebuke for doubt (Mt. 14:24-32).

man is this? Even the winds and the waves obey him!" (Matt 8:27), which question is concerned with the *kind* of person he is, receives here its answer: "You are truly the Son of God!" This can only mean that they believed that they were in the presence of one who was supernatural and divine. Vos can even remark that in respect to its momentary dissociation from the idea of messiahship, the confession of Matthew 14:33 stands even higher than Peter's famous confession at Caesarea Philippi "for through it, the disciples for a moment caught a vision of this [superhuman] character of Jesus as such, apart from its reflection in the Messiahship."[83] Again, it is significant that Jesus does nothing to disabuse his disciples of their perception of him as the Messiah or to correct their apprehension of him as a proper object of worship. And so this confession adds the weight of its testimony to the larger New Testament witness to Jesus' divine nature and thus to the church's doctrine of an incarnational Christology.

Peter's Confession of Jesus as "the Holy One of God" (John 6:69)

If the last few days had been a period of acute significance for the disciples with regard to the question of Jesus' person, all the more so had it been for Peter since it had been he who had actually walked with Jesus on the Sea of Galilee. Certainly Peter must be included in that small group of seamen who had on that occasion acknowledged him by deed and word to be the divine Son of God. Now on this occasion presently under scrutiny, presumably only some hours or days later, certainly not weeks (see John 6:22), Peter had just listened to his Lord's discourse on the Bread of Life in which Jesus had claimed that he had come down from heaven (6:33, 38, 51, 62), was the giver of eternal life to the *world* (6:33, 40, 50, 51, 53, 54, 57, 58), and was the Lord of resurrection (6:39, 40, 44, 54). Because of these exalted, exclusive, and universal claims and his insistence on man's inherent inability to believe on him (6:44-45, 65), many of his followers departed and no longer followed him. At this defection, Jesus turned to the Twelve and asked: "You do not want to leave too, do you?" Although the question was put to all of them, not surprisingly (in view of the last

---

[83]Vos, *The Self-Disclosure of Jesus*, 178-79.

few days' proceedings), Peter answered for the group: "Lord, to whom shall we go? You have words of eternal life. And we have believed and we know that you are the Holy One of God" (6:68-69).[84]

Since there is no miracle to get in their way in this pericope, most critical scholars concede the general authenticity of Peter's remarks. But some critical scholars do insist that this is the Fourth Gospel's variant account of Peter's confession at Caesarea Philippi, taken out of its historical setting and placed here against the betrayal that was growing in Judas' heart (see 6:70-71). Against such an identification, however, may be arrayed the differences of place, Jesus' approach, the circumstances, and the wording of the confession itself.[85] There is no reason for taking this confession as anything other than a separate, distinct, and earlier confession on Peter's part, and that is the way in which I intend to approach it.

In light of the several indications in the Gospels of Peter's growing appreciation of the deity of Christ, though it is true that his term of address here ("Lord") "could mean much or little" in itself, in this context, Morris seems to be correct when he writes: "There can be no doubt that the word has the maximum, not the minimum meaning" of the ascription of deity to Jesus.[86]

As for his statement: "You are the Holy One of God," while it is, at the very least, a messianic title,[87] several things can be said with cumulative force in favor of viewing it as including the further affirmation, by implication, of Jesus' divine origin and character. The first factor favoring the notion that the title carries with it divine implications is just the fact itself of Peter's growing appreciation of who Jesus was. We noted earlier his confession of Jesus as his "Lord"

---

[84]With the manuscript support in its favor (P^{75}, ℵ, B, the original hand of C, D, L, W, and others), "the Holy One of God" is surely the original reading. The variants can all be explained as assimilations to John 1:49; 11:27; and Matthew 16:16. The editors of *The Greek New Testament* (UBS) give it an "A" rating. See also Metzger, *A Textual Commentary on the Greek New Testament*, 215.

[85]See Morris, *The Gospel According to John*, 388, fn. 155.

[86]Morris, *The Gospel According to John*, 389.

[87]So Bernard, *Commentary on the Gospel According to St. John*, 223; Vincent Taylor, *The Names of Jesus* (London: Macmillan, 1953), 80; C. K. Barrett, *The Gospel According to St. John*, 253.

(and that in the divine sense) on the occasion of his call to become a "fisher of men" in Luke 5 when, awed by Jesus' supernatural knowledge and power over nature, he acknowledged his own sinfulness over against the majestic and ethical holiness of Jesus. We also just noted his confession (along with the other disciples) of Jesus in view of Jesus' miracle of the loaves and his walking with Jesus on the sea, as "truly the Son of God." And we have just noted that his title of address here ("Lord") suggests deity. I would submit, once a man has begun to apprehend that Jesus is divine, that no title (with the exception of those that clearly mark him out as a true man) he ever employs in referring to him can be totally void of intending the ascription of deity to him. This is the first thing I would say.

Second, while this title ("the Holy One of God") is applied to Jesus on only one other occasion, leaving little room for extensive comparative study of the title, that one other occasion does cast some light on its meaning here. The title occurs in the mouth of the demoniac in the synagogue at Capernaum, clearly revealing the demon's intuited awareness of who Jesus was (Mark 1:24; Luke 4:34). The demon was obviously fearful of Jesus and implied that he had the power to cast it into hell, suggesting thereby that Jesus possessed divine authority and power, but it was as "the Holy One of God," it should be noted, that the demon attributed to him this authority.

Third, the stress on holiness in the title is significant. It reminds us of the frequently occurring title for God, "the Holy One of Israel," in the Old Testament. In this connection, Morris writes: "There can be not the slightest doubt that the title is meant to assign to Jesus the highest possible place. It stresses his consecration and his purity. It sets him with God and not man."[88]

Finally, C. H. Dodd calls attention to the similarity between Peter's words here, "we have *believed* and we have come to *know*" and Yahweh's words, "that you may *know* and *believe* that I am he" (LXX, Isa 43:10). Dodd writes:

> The combination [in Peter's confession] πιστεύειν καὶ γινώσκειν [*pisteuein kai ginōskein*] follows Isaiah closely; but for ὅτι ἐγώ εἰμι [*hoti egō eimi*, "that I am"] is substituted ὅτι σὺ εἶ ὁ ἅγιος

---

[88]Morris, *The Gospel According to John*, 390.

τοῦ θεοῦ [*hoti su ei ho hagios tou theou*, "that you are the Holy One of God"]. The content of knowledge is the unique status of Christ himself, which is an equivalent for knowledge of God.[89]

For these reasons it appears not unlikely that Peter's confession, stressing as it does Jesus' inward character of holiness, marks him out not only as the Messiah, but also, by virtue of his possessing a majestic and ethical holiness identical to that of God himself (see Luke 5:8), as being just divine himself. And it is hardly necessary to point out again that Jesus accepted Peter's tacit assessment of him as the Messiah and his implied identification of him as divine.

Peter's Confession of Jesus as "the Christ, the Son of the Living God" (Matthew 16:16)

Following (1) the disciples' united confession of him as "truly the Son of God," and after (2) a brief trip into the region of Tyre and Sidon where he healed a Canaanite woman's daughter of demon possession (Matt 15:21-28), (3) a brief time around the region of the Sea of Galilee where he continued his healing ministry (Matt 15:29-31) and fed about four thousand men, not counting women and children, with seven loaves and a few fish (Matt 15:32-37), and (4) a brief journey to the region of Magadan, probably an area on the western side of the Sea of Galilee (Matt 15:39-16:4), Jesus journeyed with his disciples northeast to Caesarea Philippi, healing on his way there a blind man at Bethsaida (Mark 8:22-26). While at Caesarea Philippi, Jesus through questioning the disciples drew from Peter, the self-appointed spokesman for the group, his great confession: "You are the Christ, the Son of the living God" (Matt 16:16; see Mark 8:29; Luke 9:20).

In the last chapter, in connection with our discussion of Jesus' self-understanding, we addressed the views of Bultmann who regarded the whole episode as a legend of the early church to undergird its "Easter faith" in Jesus' messiahship and of R. H. Fuller who regards Matthew 16:17-19 as a "Matthean expansion" and thus "clearly secondary" and Mark 8:30-32 as both Marcan redaction and later tradition, the end result being that Jesus is represented as positively

---

[89]Dodd, *The Interpretation of the Fourth Gospel*, 168.

rejecting all claims to messiahship as a "diabolical temptation." We will not repeat here the arguments we registered there against their revision of this significant pericope but would simply refer the reader to the earlier discussion and to Marshall's refutation in his commentary on the Greek text of Luke's Gospel.[90] Suffice it to say that there is no legitimate ground to question either the historicity of the event or the authenticity of Jesus' recorded response.

Given the fact, then, that all three Synoptic Evangelists report that Peter confessed faith in Christ's messiahship (Matthew and Mark: "You are the Christ"; Luke: "You are the Christ of God"), and that in Matthew Jesus gives express approval and in Mark and Luke tacit approval to this confession, I must conclude that here is a clear and incontrovertible instance when Jesus claimed to be the Messiah.

But as we have seen, Matthew reports Peter's confession as containing a second part: "You are...the Son of the living God." We have no way of knowing why Mark and Luke do not report this second part; we can only assume that it did not serve their respective purposes. It has been suggested that the second part is only a further elucidation or synonym for Peter's "the Christ," and that the two Evangelists saw no need for the elucidation. But there are four cogent reasons for insisting that Peter did not intend the second description to be viewed merely as a synonym of the first, and that he intended by it to go beyond the ascription to Jesus of messianic investiture and to confess him as the "super-messianic Son" both as to nature and origin. Those reasons are as follows:[91]

First, we argued earlier from the fact of the disciples' act of worship in Matthew 14:33 that their united confession on that occasion of Jesus as "truly the Son of God" ascribed divine Sonship to him. The title, "the Son of the living God" in 16:16 can hardly carry lower import on this later occasion than the same phrase did on the former occasion. In fact, the additional word "living" in this latter expression, if anything,

---

[90]Marshall, *The Gospel of Luke*, 364-65.

[91]I am indebted for some of the thoughts in the following paragraphs to Vos, *The Self-Disclosure of Jesus*, 179-81, where he himself is following Zahn's exposition for the most part. But his second and third points of argument, which the interested reader may assess for himself, appears too abstruse to me and decidedly weak.

adds weight to the import of Peter's confession, in that it particularizes the God whose Son Jesus is and by extension particularizes him as well.

Second, if the second part does not intend *more* than the ascription of messiahship to Jesus then it follows that all that Peter was confessing here is just Jesus' messiahship. But such a confession, expressed both by Peter and others on other occasions (see John 1:41, 49; 6:69), hardly explains Jesus' unusual response to Peter's confession here. Why would Peter's confession of the mere fact of Jesus' messiahship elicit Jesus' declaration on *this* occasion that Peter's confession was the result of a special, supernatural revelation when "the ordinary means of self-disclosure during our Lord's long association with Peter would have sufficed for the basis of a mere confession of Jesus' Messiahship"[92] The question cannot be intelligently answered on the assumption that Peter's confession entailed simply the recognition of Jesus' messiahship.

Third, the two facts—(1) that the two Evangelists who do not report the second part of Peter's confession do not report Jesus' response to Peter either, whereas Matthew reports both, and (2) Peter's reference to Jesus as "the Son" in his second part and Jesus' reference to God in his response to Peter not as "God," which would have been appropriate in light of Peter's reference to "the living God," but as "my Father"—strongly suggest that Jesus' benediction was not primarily a response to the first part (although the first part cannot be divorced from the universe in which Jesus' response is to be interpreted) but was rather his response primarily to the second part. Now if it is true that *any* correct assessment of Jesus must be finally traced to the Father's "teaching" (John 6:45), especially is it true that the Father's "teaching" is necessary with respect to the essential Sonship of Jesus. Jesus expressly declared this to be so in Matthew 11:25-27: "No one knows *the Son* except *the Father*," he said, and if one is to know "the Son," he also stated, such knowledge will come through the Father's act of revelation and by his good pleasure. Now Jesus declares Peter's confession to be the result of just such a supernatural revelation (16:17); and by his reference to "my Father"

---

[92]Vos, *The Self-Disclosure of Jesus*, 180.

in 16:17, it is apparent (1) that Jesus regarded Peter's confession of his Sonship as just such an instance of the revealing activity by the Father which he had spoken of in 11:25-26, and (2) that the disclosure made to Peter had reference to the paternal ("Father") and filial ("Son") relationship between God and Jesus and not simply to the messianic investiture *per se*.

Fourth, the juxtaposition of the two occurrences of σῦ ει ("You are") in this context should not be overlooked: Peter's "*You are* the Christ, the Son of the living God" (vs 16), and Jesus' "*You are* Peter" (vs 18). They are very significant in determining the intent of Peter's confession, the pointed correspondence between them being highlighted very strongly by Jesus' words: "And I, on my part, say also to you" (16:18). The import of Jesus' "You are" lifts Peter as "Simon bar Jonah" by this new title to an altogether *new* and *higher* category, even that of being—as the representative of all of the Apostles—the very foundation of the church which Jesus was erecting (Eph 2:20; Rev 21:14). The correspondence then, to which we just alluded between Peter's "You are" and Jesus' "You are" strongly suggests that Peter's prior confession be construed similarly, that is, as moving in its intention beyond the purely *official* interpretation of Jesus in which Jesus' supernatural nature and origin, although not absent, remain somewhat in the background to a supra-messianic ascription in which the anterior supernatural nature and origin of Jesus receive special stress. And as a matter of historical record, it is a fact that the church which Jesus erected on the foundation of the Apostles and prophets as authoritative teachers of doctrine has never confessed Jesus simply as the Messiah but has also declared him to be the divine Son of God with respect to both nature and origin.

For these reasons I would urge that by his confession Peter self-consciously intended, as the result of the Father's revelatory activity, to ascribe full, unabridged deity to Jesus as "the Son" of "the Father," and that Jesus, by declaring him in making such a confession to have been directly blessed by his Father, tacitly claimed to be God incarnate.

The Inner Circle's "Elijah" Question (Matthew 17:10; Mark 9:11)

We have already discussed in connection with the transfiguration accounts the significance of the disciples' question for Jesus' identity as Yahweh: "Why then do the teachers of the Law say that Elijah must come first?" We do not intend to repeat the points we made there. We only mention the fact again here in the interest of giving a complete list of the most significant instances when, by something the disciples say in Jesus' presence, the point is directly made or implied that Jesus is divine. By their question concerning Elijah, the disciples were suggesting that Jesus was the Yahweh who had promised to come. What prompted their question was that they could not understand why he had come *before* rather than *after* Elijah whom they had just seen conversing with Jesus. It was this inversion of the prophet Malachi's order of appearances for them that was for the disciples the problem. Their quandary Jesus proceeded to resolve by making it clear that the "Elijah" who was to come was John the Baptist, his forerunner. The obvious conclusion of his interpretation of Malachi's "Elijah" prophecy is that, if he believed the Baptist was the Elijah-forerunner, he also believed himself to be the Yahweh of Malachi 3:1.

Martha's Great Confession (John 11:27)

After Lazarus died, with Jesus' consoling "I am" saying, "I am the resurrection and the life. He who believes in me will live, even though he dies; and whoever lives and believes in me will never die," flooding her thoughts with comfort, Jesus asked her: "Do you believe this?" With no hesitancy whatever, Martha replied: "Yes, Lord, I believe that you are the Christ, the Son of God, who was to come into the world" (John 11:27)—surely her finest hour of record, who should be remembered quite as much, if not more so, for this great confession as for some of the lesser things with which the church is accustomed to associate her name.

Because of the complexity of the problems raised by radical critical scholars with regard to the historicity of the entire incident recorded in John 11:1-54, it would take us far afield from our present purpose were we to enter deeply into a defense of its historicity. For example, it is said that the fact that the miracle of raising Lazarus from the dead is not mentioned in the Synoptic Gospels is inexplicable if it had really had the effect that John ascribes to it of setting in motion the chain of events that led to Jesus' crucifixion (see John 11:46-53). The Synoptic Evangelists, the same critics argue, suggest that it was the "triumphal entry" and the cleansing of the temple that initiated the events which issued in the crucifixion. I would respond by saying that these two grounds for the hostility of the religious leadership need not be viewed as contradictory but should be seen rather as complementing one another. After all, the conflict between Jesus and the Sanhedrin had been seething for quite some time, and many things which Jesus had said and done—not just these things—had provoked them to the point of plotting his execution. Full defenses of the historicity of this miracle—competent and comprehensive—have been made and are available, such as those of Raymond E. Brown[93] and Leon Morris.[94] It will have to suffice to refer the reader to these defenses and to state that I am convinced that what we have in John 11:1-54 is real history and that what we have in 11:27 is an authentic response by Martha to Jesus' query.

So we turn to Martha's confession: "Lord," "the Christ," "the Son of God, who was to come into the world." What did Martha intend by this rich multi-titular description of Jesus?

As for her title of address, "Lord," since theoretically it could have been nothing more than a title of respect with the equivalent meaning of our "Sir," the sense in which she intended it will in large measure turn on the meanings to be assigned to the titles that immediately follow it. But I will assert, in light of what I hope to show she meant by her following titles, that by it she was attributing to Jesus' unabridged *Lordship* over her life—that lordship which properly belongs only to God himself. I say this not only because of the following titles but because of her unhesitating "Yes" and her "I have believed," the significance of which might be lost on the reader of John's Gospel as

---

[93]Brown, *Gospel According to John I-XII*, 427-30.

[94]Morris, *The Gospel According to John*, 532-36. I prefer Morris' remarks over Brown's inasmuch as the latter scholar is willing to question the historicity, if not of the basic story itself, of at least some of its details.

his attention is drawn, by their power to attract the mind, to the following titles themselves. These two features in her answer indicate that she had placed her confidence—"once given and permanently remaining"[95] (for this is the force of πεπίστευκα, *pepisteuka*—"I have and still do believe")—explicitly in Jesus. He was her "Lord" in the full, unqualified sense of the word.

By "the Christ," of course, she was acknowledging Jesus to be the Messiah of Old Testament promise and of enlightened Jewish hope. And it is important to note, even if by the following words she intended nothing more than this, that she still at least ascribes to Jesus here messianic stature, which ascription Jesus did nothing to correct. Clearly, here is an instance where, by the absence of any word of correction, Jesus tacitly claimed to be the Messiah.

But I believe that she did intend more by the next title. For four reasons I would urge that Martha, by her title, "the Son of God," intended the attribution of deity to Jesus. My first two reasons have engaged the reader's attention before in earlier contexts:

First, if the title here is simply an additional ascription of messianic stature to Jesus as Barrett, for example, and a good many other scholars would insist, it reduces the "Son of God" title to a tautology. Barrett, in fact, suggests that even the words, "he who is to come into the world," should be construed this way as well, so that we have "three parallel titles" all intending messiahship.[96] But this is to heap tautology on top of what is already tautology, if the first words, "the Son of God," is construed only as a title denoting messiahship.

Second, Martha's words, "the Christ, the Son of God," are precisely parallel to John's words in his stated purpose in 20:31. Because of its proximity to Thomas' full, unqualified ascription of deity to Jesus in his confession in John 20:28, John's term, "the Son of God," while it distinguishes Jesus as the Son from the Father, does not distinguish him from God. If then "the Son of God" in 20:31 includes the ascription of deity to Jesus, it is highly unlikely that the same title means less than that anywhere in his Gospel (see 1:34, 49; 5:25; 10:36; 11:4, 27; 19:7; 20:31). We have already argued in this section that this is precisely its import in 1:34, 1:49, and 20:31; and even those who would not

---

[95]Morris, *The Gospel According to John*, 555.

[96]Barrett, *The Gospel According to St. John*, 330.

agree with everything I have said in these earlier expositions must admit, as we have also argued elsewhere, that its occurrence in 5:25, 10:36, and 19:7 must convey this meaning. In these contexts Christ's enemies accuse Jesus of blasphemy in employing the term the way he did, for, they argue, in doing so, he was "making himself God." And certainly the occurrences of the unqualified title, "the Son," and the fuller title, "the one and only Son," throughout John's Gospel connote essential equality with the Father as to nature. All this being so, it seems highly unlikely that either Martha or John intended the title in Martha's confession to have intended less. In fact, I would urge that this is precisely the reason behind John's decision to report her confession—he knew what she intended and he knew that it accorded with the purpose of his Gospel.

Third, Martha must have heard Jesus speaking about himself on other occasions as the Son of God. Where else would she have gained such an assessment of him if not from his teaching? But, and here I am indebted to Hendriksen for the thought,

> ...if *others* [that is, his enemies] understood this to mean that he claimed full equality with the Father..., *why not Martha?* She had heard the claims of Jesus, and *she* had believed them.... *Others* had heard the same claims, but had rejected them, calling Jesus a blasphemer.[97]

She doubtless knew, as did his enemies, what Jesus intended by the title when he used it of himself. And since she believed him, this requires that her use of the title be allowed to carry the same import of deity as his own use of it.

Fourth, whether her last words, ὁ εἰς τὸν κόσμον ἐρχόμενος, *ho eis ton kosmon erchomenos*, are to be construed as a third title or appositionally,[98] her words εἰς τὸν κόσμον(*eis ton kosmon*, "into the world"), coming between the article and the participle, clearly affirm of "the Son of God" a heavenly origin. These words are equivalent in meaning to the ἄνωθεν (*anōthen*, "from above") coming in precisely the same place in ὁ ἄνωθεν ἐρχόμενος, *ho anōthen erchomenos*, in John 3:31 (see also 9:39; 12:46). Furthermore, Jesus

---

[97]William Hendriksen, *A Commentary on the Gospel of John* (London: Banner of Truth, 1959), 151-52.

himself declares in John 16:28 that for him to have "come into the world" involved *first* his coming "from [the side of] the Father," clearly claiming thereby the attribute of pre-existence.

For all these reasons, I agree with Morris who seems not to have overstated the case when he writes of Martha's affirmations: "[They] give us as high a view of the person of Christ as one well may have."[99] And Warfield declares.

> There is no reason to doubt that here, too...'Son of God' carries with it the implication of supernatural origin and thus designates the Messiah from a point of view which recognized that he was more than man.[100]

This text, then, joins the many others we have considered which attest to the deity of Christ.

The Disciples' Upper Room Confession (John 16:30)

On the last evening before his crucifixion Jesus met in the upper room with the Twelve, and there he delivered what has come to be known as his Upper Room or Farewell Discourse(s) (John 14-16). At the end of his discourse, the disciples declared: "Now we know that you know all things, and you have no need that anyone should ask you anything. By this we believe that you came from God" (16:30).

Here is a remarkable "confession of faith."[101] Each of the three clauses deserves some comment. By their first statement, "Now [that you speak plainly and no longer in 'dark sayings'] we know that you

---

[98]The reason it is regarded by some as a third title is its "fixed form" appearance as in Matthew 11:3, Luke 7:19-20, 19:38. But in these contexts there is no preceding noun either, to which the articular participle could point as an antecedent. But where there is an immediately preceding noun which can serve as an antecedent as in John 11:27, and because the article and the participle are broken apart by the intervening words "into the world" (literally, "the one into the world coming," thereby disrupting the fixed form, it is quite possible that the words are to be construed appositionally, that is, "[he] who was to come into the world."

[99]Morris, *The Gospel According to John*, 552.

[100]Warfield, *The Lord of Glory*, 195.

[101]Dodd, *The Interpretation of the Fourth Gospel*, 410, 416.

know all things," they plainly ascribe to Jesus the attribute of omniscience. Barrett concedes that this clause may be taken in this way ("you have all knowledge"), but he suggests that the universe of intent should more likely be restricted to the immediate subject in 16:19-28.[102] But this interpretation the next clause expressly precludes. The second clause reads: "and you have no need that anyone should ask you [anything]." What do they mean? On first reflection, one might think that they should have said: "and [as a result of your knowing all things] *you* have no need to ask anyone anything." But they say the reverse: "You have no need that anyone ask you anything." What do they mean? One possibility is that they were saying, "Because of your knowledge, you have no need that anyone should ply you with questions in order to stimulate you to new and deeper levels of understanding." But it could mean also that they were ascribing such knowledge to him as the reader of the thoughts and intents of men's hearts that he did not need men even to ask him questions in order for him to discern what it was that was troubling them. It is this latter meaning that receives the endorsement of the passage itself for we are told in 16:17-18 that some of his disciples were asking one another: "What does he mean by saying: 'In a little while you will see me no more, and then after a while you will see me,' and 'Because I am going to the Father'?" They kept asking one another: "What does he mean by 'a little while'? We don't understand what he is saying." But they were not asking *Jesus* these questions! Then what do we read in 16:19? "Jesus knew that they were wanting to ask" these very questions! And so he answered their questions even before they asked him. So the disciples by this second clause were saying that he had read their very thoughts. The *Jerusalem Bible* captures their meaning in this second clause quite nicely with its "...you do not have to wait for questions to be put into words." And a man who can do this must "know all things."

Their third statement gives us their final deduction from their realization of his omniscience: "By this [that is, because we know you are omniscient], we believe that you came out from God." And by this statement they affirm his divine origin. But why do they declare that his knowledge had convinced them of his divine origin? One

[102]Barrett, *The Gospel According to St. John*, 414-15.

possibility is that they reasoned thus: Only God is omniscient. Jesus is omniscient. Therefore, he came out from God. But this is not what they should strictly have concluded by such a process of deduction. Rather, they should have concluded: Therefore, Jesus is God. So we still lack the missing premise in their thinking that led them to the specific conclusion which they drew. So we ask again, why did they single out this feature of his person and declare that his omniscience had convinced them that he had come from God? Jesus himself provides the answer: only a few moments before (16:28), in responding to *their* unasked questions, Jesus had given them a "simple and precise recapitulation of all the mysteries of his past, present, and future existence"[103] : "I came out from the Father and have come into the world; again, I am leaving the world and going to the Father." And in saying this, he affirmed his own divine origin. Here is the missing piece. He had affirmed that he was "from the Father," and his evident attribute of omniscience gave evidence of that fact to them. Their process of thinking then was as follows: Jesus says he is from God. How do we know he is? Jesus is himself omniscient; this we know from the fact that he has read our very hearts. Therefore if he knows all things, he must have come from God as himself just said.

Now why some men say that the faith they now confessed lacked depth (Lightfoot), or "had not advanced as far as the Baptist" (Westcott), or was "inadequate" (Morris), because it was grounded in what Barrett calls the "slight foundation" of Jesus' display of divine knowledge escapes me.[104] What better foundation for his faith can anyone find than Jesus' omniscient word about himself? Does not his possession of omniscience guarantee that he knows all truth, and is truth not the ground of all healthy faith? And even if Jesus' following words be construed as a question ("Do you now believe? Behold, the hour is coming and has come that you will be scattered...."), his intention could have been to dampen an enthusiasm stemming from

---

[103]F. Godet, *Commentary on the Gospel of John* (Reprint of the 1893 third edition; Grand Rapids: Zondervan, 1969), II, 321.

[104]R. H. Lightfoot, *St. John's Gospel* (Oxford: Clarendon, 1956), 290; B. F. Westcott, *The Gospel According to St. John* (London: John Murray, 1890), 235-36; Morris, *The Gospel According to John*, 712; Barrett, *The Gospel According to St. John*, 415.

their confessed apprehension of him which had not yet comprehended the cross work that still lay ahead of him. But he does not deny that they have faith; indeed, he had expressly stated earlier: "You have believed that I came out from [the side of] God" (16:27). Nor does he deny the content of their faith, but, in fact, had himself affirmed *that very content* only moments before about himself (16:28). And it is entirely possible grammatically to construe his words as a statement: "Now you believe!" If this was the import of his words, then even with sharper lines does Jesus emphasize their faith in his divine origin. But in either case, it is clear from the entire episode that in this last confession of the Eleven before the crucifixion of their Lord, they confessed *in his presence* their belief in his divine origin and, by implication, also in his pre-existence; and he did nothing to correct their statement of faith but had, in fact, declared the same thing about himself only moments before.

Here, then, is an eighth occasion when, through our examination of the disciples' understanding of Jesus, we find them asserting something that implied his deity, and on each occasion we discovered that he either expressly or tacitly acknowledged that what they were saying about him was so.

The Centurion's Confession (Matthew 27:54; Mark 15:39)

During his crucifixion, God attested to the fact that Jesus was his Son by causing darkness to come upon the land for three hours—the length and extension of the darkness and the time of the month precluding this being merely an eclipse of the sun. And at the moment of his death, God ripped the curtain in the temple in two from top to bottom and caused the earth to shake. Jesus' utterances from the cross and the darkness and the earthquake evoked from the centurion (and the watching crowd) the one exclamation the Jewish leaders did not want to hear: "*This was truly the Son of God*" (Matt 27:54; Mark 15:39).

What did the Roman centurion mean by this utterance, and on what ground should we consider his confession—hardly the confession of one who was a disciple in the same sense that the others we have been considering were disciples—a credible witness to the identity of Jesus? I would respond to these questions by suggesting that one may presume from the fact itself that Mark reported his confession that what the centurion had witnessed had brought him to an understanding of Jesus' Sonship. In accordance with Colwell's studied observation that "definite predicate nouns which precede the verb usually lack the article" while "a definite predicate nominative has the article when it follows the verb,"[105] the word order in the centurion's exclamation—specifically the fact that the predicate nominative ("Son of God") precedes the copula ("was")—suggests that his intention was to affirm Christ as "*the* Son of God." There is no justifiable reason to reduce the intent in his confession simply to an affirmation of Christ as one of many Hellenistic "divine men." He had just heard the jeers and taunts of the crowd: "He said, 'I am the Son of God'" (Matt 27:43) and "Come down from the cross, if you are the Son of God" (Matt 27:40). He had just heard Jesus address God from the cross as "Father" (Luke 23:34, 46). And even if he had been in Judea only a matter of days—much more if he had spent some years there, we cannot imagine that he was wholly ignorant of Christ's own claims and his authenticating deeds. And having just witnessed the serene, courageous manner in which Jesus endured his execution and the frightening natural phenomena of the three hours of darkness and the earthquake that occurred at the moment of Jesus' death, it is difficult to believe that the centurion intended to attach no more meaning to his words than that suggested by the mythology of his pagan background.

It is true that Luke reports the centurion as saying: "Surely, this man was righteous" (23:47), this comment intended as a judgment against the whole sordid treatment which Jesus had received at their hands. But it need not be taken to mean that the other Synoptic Evangelists' "Son of God" expression intended nothing more than that Jesus was a good man. If his confession amounted to no more than that, one might well wonder why Mark and Matthew were inspired to record for all time to come his confession in the manner in which they did. It would seem that to interpret the centurion's statement to mean less in its import than we have suggested is to impute a literary ineptitude to Mark and Matthew, for it suggests that they permitted

---

[105]Colwell, "A Definite Rule for the Use of the Article in the Greek New Testament" in *Journal of Biblical Literature* LII [1933]: 13, 22.

the driving thrust of their respective Gospels' testimony to Jesus as "the Son of God" in the high, supernatural, divine sense which the other occurrences of this title in their Gospels intend (see Mark 1:1 [?], 11; 3:11; 5:7; 9:7; 12:6; 13:32; 14:61-62; Matt 2:15; 3:17; 8:29; 11:27; 14:33; 16:16; 17:5; 21:7; 28:19) to culminate in a climactic testimony which was one in word only but which, in intention, meant less than they themselves intended. It seems appropriate, therefore, to understand Luke's statement as supplementary to, not explanatory of, the other Synoptic Evangelists' report. And accordingly it seems equally appropriate to suggest that the centurion was confessing that Jesus was "the Son of God" in the same sense that the Evangelists' earlier uses of that title intended.

* * * * *

As I bring this chapter to a close, let me remind the reader what it was that I set out to do. I attempted to set forth major lines of pre-resurrection evidence which corroborate the church's confession—in concert with Jesus himself—that he is both God and man and thus God incarnate. We considered five broad areas of testimony: the nativity accounts, the baptism accounts, the temptation accounts, the transfiguration accounts, and the disciples' pre-resurrection understanding of Jesus. I grant the selectivity here, but I have not knowingly avoided a passage which would require a position other than the one which I have urged in my expositions. The over-all witness of the combined testimony of these areas in the Gospel accounts—each area arguably and demonstrably historically reliable and trustworthy—is overwhelmingly supportive of the historic view of the church that the Christ of the Gospels is supernatural, indeed, both divine and human, and thus God manifest in the flesh. The virginal conception was the means whereby God the Son became man. God the Father testified both at Jesus' baptism and at his transfiguration that he is the Son of God. The Devil gave similar testimony at his temptation. And while his disciples were sometimes slow to come to a full appreciation of all that was implied in their confessions, the evidence indicates that from the beginning of his public ministry, they confessed him (with varying degrees of apprehension, no doubt) to be divine, their Lord, and their Messiah.

It is true that he was crucified as a criminal under Roman law. But his death must not be viewed as the one event that puts the lie to the church's confession. For, as we shall see in the next chapter, on the third day after death the Arimathean's tomb was empty and the world had a resurrection on its hands.

CHAPTER FIVE

THE POST-RESURRECTION WITNESS TO JESUS

Jesus was crucified by Roman authorities at the instigation of the Jewish religious leaders. But in Paul's words he "was raised on the third day according to the Scriptures" (1 Cor 15:4). This quotation highlights not only a major theme of both the New Testament and church proclamation; more immediately, it also states the presupposition behind the title of this chapter. So before I continue my investigation of the New Testament data regarding Jesus' identity, I feel I must say something to justify this presupposition.

Christians should admit, given the first-century Jewish milieu in which Christ's resurrection occurred, that it was not at all what the nation expected. I do not mean to suggest by this comment that Jews of the first century did not believe in the resurrection of the dead since it is a well-known fact that many if not most Jews did indeed believe in the resurrection (see Acts 23:6-8). But they believed that the resurrection of the dead would occur in the future at the end of time. But suddenly here was a small group of men proclaiming, not in some out-of-the-way place like Azotus but in Jerusalem itself—the politico-religious center of the nation—that God had raised Jesus from the dead. Not only was this very strange teaching to the Jewish ear, it was also exceedingly offensive teaching to the majority of them, including Saul of Tarsus, because Jesus had been executed as a blasphemer with the sanction of the nation's highest court, the Sanhedrin.

The disciples of Jesus believed, however, that there were compelling reasons for such a proclamation, for they continued to preach in the face of threats, bodily persecution, and martyrdom that he had risen from the dead. What were their reasons? I would submit that two great interlocking strands of evidence convinced them beyond all reasonable doubt that Jesus had risen from the dead just as he said he would.[1] These strands of evidence are the empty tomb and the fact and character of his numerous post-crucifixion physical appearances. Each of these calls for comment.

EVIDENCE FOR JESUS' RESURRECTION FROM THE DEAD

The First Great Strand of Evidence: the Empty Tomb

All four Gospels report that on the third day after Jesus had been crucified and entombed his disciples discovered that his body had disappeared from the tomb in which it had been placed and that his tomb was empty (Matt 28:6; Mark 16:5-6; Luke 24:3, 6, 22-24; John 20:5-8). Almost immediately, as we have said, the disciples began to proclaim their conviction that Jesus had risen from the dead. Now if the tomb, in fact, had still contained his body—the women and later Peter and John all having gone to the wrong tomb (a most unlikely eventuality in light of Matt 27:61; Mark 15:47; Luke 23:55)—we may be sure that the authorities, both Jewish and Roman, would have corrected the disciples' error by guiding them to the right tomb and to the fact that the tomb still contained Jesus' physical remains.

Many critical scholars over the years who have not accepted the historicity of Jesus' resurrection have felt it necessary to concede that the tomb was undoubtedly empty, but they have blunted the edge of their concession at the same time by advancing such explanations as the stolen body explanation and the swoon explanation to explain why it was empty.

---

[1]Jesus spoke of his resurrection in John 2:19-21; Matthew 12:40; 16:21 (Mark 8:31; Luke 9:22); 17:9 (Mark 9:9); 17:23 (Mark 9:31); 20:19 (Mark 10:34; Luke 18:33); see also Matthew 27:63; Mark 14:58; Luke 24:6-7. Certainly, the veracity of everything that Jesus taught is called into question if he did not rise from the dead as he said he would. Indeed, it is not saying too much to insist that if Christ rose from the dead as he said he would, the gospel is true; if he did not rise from the dead, the gospel is false. And the faith that would believe that he did rise from the dead, if in fact he did not do so, would be vain and futile (1 Cor 15:17).

The "Stolen Body" Explanation

With regard to the former explanation, we may safely conclude that if Jesus' body had been removed by human hands, they were the hands of either his disciples, his enemies, or professional grave robbers. Now if his disciples had stolen his body, which was the explanation first concocted to explain his body's disappearance (Matt 28:12-15), one must still face the question how his disciples could have gotten past the Romans guards (who, according to Matthew 27:62-66, had been posted there for the express purpose of preventing his disciples from stealing his body) and how they could have rolled the stone away without being detected. The only possible explanation is that the entire Roman watch must have fallen asleep, which again was the first explanation offered.

Now it is most unlikely that disorganized, fearful disciples would have even attempted such an exploit. And it is even more unlikely that *all* the Roman guards would have fallen asleep on duty since to do so would have meant certain and severe punishment. Nevertheless, both of these "unlikelihoods" would have to have occurred simultaneously if this explanation for the fact of the empty tomb is to be sustained. Furthermore, with respect to the first explanation which was offered, it should be patently clear that any tough-minded hearer would have immediately rejected the guards' explanation concerning what happened, for if in fact they all had fallen asleep they would not have known who had stolen the body (see Matt 28:13). There is one more problem that this explanation must face: If Jesus' disciples had been responsible for his body's disappearance—a most unlikely prospect in light of their reaction to everything that had just happened to Jesus (see John 20:19), one must then believe that they then went forth and proclaimed as historical fact a mere fiction which they knew they had contrived, and then, when faced by persecution and threats of execution as many of them were, not one of them, even when facing martyrdom, revealed that it was all a hoax. I would submit that this scenario is not probable, indeed, it is highly improbable; liars and hypocrites are not the stuff from which resolute martyrs are made.

Now if the religious leaders arranged for his body's removal, one must surely wonder why they did the one thing which would have contributed as much as anything else to the very idea which they were solicitous to prevent from happening (see Matt 27:62-66). And if they, in fact, had his body in their possession or knew of its whereabouts, one must wonder why they did not produce either it or reliable witnesses who could explain the body's disappearance and prove the disciples wrong when they began to proclaim that Jesus had risen from the dead.

To attribute the fact of the empty tomb, finally, to grave robbers is the least likely possibility of all. For it is to intrude on the story an explanation for which there is not a shred of evidence in the record. Not only would thieves have been prevented from doing so by the Roman guards but also, even if they could have somehow avoided detection and had proceeded to plunder the tomb, they would have hardly, having first unwrapped it, taken the *nude* body of Jesus with them, leaving his grave wrappings behind and essentially intact (John 20:6-7).

The "Swoon" Explanation

As for the swoon theory, if we may accept Albert Schweitzer's judgment (see his *Vom Reimarus zu Wrede* [1906], entitled *The Quest of the Historical Jesus* in the English translation), David Strauss dealt the "death-blow" to this view over one hundred and sixty years ago. But one occasionally hears it advanced as a possibility in popular discussions today. This discredited theory maintains that Jesus had not actually died on the cross but had only slipped into a coma-like state and that in the tomb he revived and somehow made his way past the guards to his disciples who then concluded that he had risen from the dead. He died shortly thereafter.

To believe this pushes the limits of credibility beyond all legitimate boundaries. It requires one to believe that those responsible for his execution by crucifixion were woefully incompetent as executioners and then as judges of the state of the crucified victims when they performed the *crurifragium* (the breaking of the legs of the victim; see John 19:31-33). It also requires one to believe that Jesus, though suffering from the excruciating pain of wounded hands and feet not to mention the loss of blood, the physical weakness which would have naturally ensued from the horrible ordeal of the crucifixion itself, and the lack of human care and physical nourishment, somehow survived the mortal wound in his side and the cold of the tomb without human aid or succor and then pushed the huge stone away from the entrance of the tomb with wounded hands and made his way on wounded feet past Roman guards into the city and to the place where his disciples were hiding and there convinced his followers that he—the emaciated shell of a man—was the Lord of Life! Such a scenario is surely beyond all possibility and is undeserving of any thinking man's assent. Such books as Hugh Schonfield's *The Passover Plot* and Donovan Joyce's *The Jesus Scroll* are only variations on this same theme and are not taken seriously by the scholarly community.

But if some critical scholars have acknowledged the fact of the empty tomb and have attempted (unsuccessfully) to offer explanations for it, others have simply declared that the empty tomb was not an essential part of the original resurrection story, that the church only later created the "fact" in order to fortify its stories of the resurrection appearances. This is not true. The empty tomb was part of the church's proclamation from the outset (see Acts 2:31; 1 Cor 15:4). It is simply erroneous teaching that asserts that the first disciples believed that one can have a real resurrection without an empty tomb. G. C. Berkouwer has correctly observed:

> Not the empty grave but the resurrection of Christ is the great soteriological fact, but as such the resurrection is inseparably connected with the empty tomb and unthinkable without it. It is absolutely contrary to Scripture to eliminate the message of the empty tomb and still speak of the living Lord. The Gospels picture his resurrection in connection with historical data, moments, and places of his appearance. Scripture nowhere supports the idea of his living on independently of a corporeal resurrection and an empty tomb.[2]

The conclusion is self-evident: the theologian who dismisses the empty tomb as irrelevant to the Christian message but who still speaks of "the resurrection of Jesus" does not mean by Jesus' "resurrection" what the New Testament means or what the church has traditionally

---

[2]G. C. Berkouwer, *The Work of Christ*, translated by Cornelius Lambregste (Grand Rapids: Eerdmans, 1965), 184.

meant by it. It has become more a saving "idea" than a saving event. But such a view of the resurrection would have been rejected out of hand by the early church as no resurrection at all.

We have defended to this point the fact of the "empty" tomb. But now we must point out that such a description is not entirely accurate since the tomb was not completely empty. For not only did angels appear to the women in the tomb and announce to them that Jesus had risen (Mark 16:5-7; Luke 24:3-7) but also both Luke (24:12) and John (20:5-7) mention the presence of his empty grave clothes. The strips of linen in which Jesus' body had been wrapped were still there with the cloth that had been around his head folded and lying by itself, separate from the linen. The empty grave linens suggest that not only had Jesus' body not been disturbed by human hands (for it is extremely unlikely that friends or foe would have first unwrapped the body before taking it away) but also that the body which had been bound within the wrappings had simply disappeared, leaving the wrappings behind like an empty chrysalis. It is highly significant, according to John's own testimony (John 20:3-9), that it was when he saw the empty grave wrappings within the empty tomb that he himself came to understand that Jesus had risen from the dead.

The Second Great Strand of Evidence: Jesus' Numerous Post-Crucifixion Appearances

The second great strand of evidence, after the fact of the empty tomb, is the many post-crucifixion appearances which our Lord made under varying circumstances and in numerous places to his disciples. The New Testament records at least ten such appearances, five of them occurring on that first "Easter," and the remaining five occurring during the following forty days leading up to and including the day of his ascension.

He appeared first to the women who had left the tomb (Matt 28:8-10),[3] and then to Mary Magdalene who had returned to the tomb

---

[3]Mark 16:9 states that Jesus "appeared first to Mary Magdalene," and this may well be the case. But appearing as it does in the longer ending of Mark 16, there is some question as to the authenticity and veracity of this statement. The appearance accounts, in my opinion, are more easily

after telling Peter and John what she and the other women had seen (John 20:10-18). Then he appeared to Cleopas and the other (unnamed) disciple on the road to Emmaus (Luke 24:13-35), and then to Peter, no doubt sometime that same afternoon (Luke 24:34; 1 Cor 15:5). His last appearance on that historic day was to the "Twelve" (actually ten in number since Judas and Thomas were not present) in the upper room (Luke 24:36-43; John 20:20-28; 1 Cor 15:5). What is of great significance on this last occasion is the fact that Jesus invited the disciples to touch him in order to satisfy themselves that it was really he who stood among them, and he ate a piece of broiled fish in their presence as proof that his body was materially real and not merely a phantasy.

A week later he appeared again to his disciples, Thomas this time being present with the other ten disciples (John 20:26-29). Again Jesus encouraged confidence in the reality and factuality of his resurrection by inviting Thomas to do precisely what the doubting disciple had said earlier would be necessary if he was ever to believe that Jesus had risen, namely, to put his fingers into the wounds in Jesus' hands and side. Then Jesus appeared to seven disciples by the Sea of Galilee—"the third time Jesus appeared to his disciples"—and he prepared and ate breakfast with them (John 21:1-22). Then he appeared to the Eleven on a mountain of Galilee (Matt 28:16-20), this occasion quite possibly being the same occasion when he appeared to more than five hundred disciples at one time, many of whom were still alive at the time Paul wrote 1 Corinthians (1 Cor 15:6). Then he appeared to James, his half-brother (1 Cor 15:7), and finally to the Eleven again on the occasion of his ascension into heaven (Luke 24:44-52; Acts 1:4-9; 1 Cor 15:7). (We should also remind the reader of his appearance to Saul of Tarsus some time later.)

Viewed as "evidence," it is true, of course, that the fact of the empty tomb alone does not prove that Jesus rose from the dead but it does indicate that something had happened to his body. The numerous

---

harmonized if one has Jesus appearing first to the women as they hurried away from the tomb (Matt 28:8-9), and then to Mary who followed Peter and John back to the tomb after informing them that the tomb was empty (see John 20:1-18). But a harmonization is still possible even if Jesus did appear first to Mary Magdalene.

post-crucifixion appearances of Jesus best explain what had happened to his body: *he had risen from the dead.* And the fact that the appearances occurred (1) to individuals (Mary, Peter, James), to a pair of disciples, to small groups, and to large assemblies, (2) to women and to men, (3) in public and in private, (4) at all hours of the day—in the morning, during the day, and at night, and (5) both in Jerusalem and in Galilee, removes any and all likelihood that these appearances were simply hallucinations. An individual may have a hallucination, but it is highly unlikely that entire groups and large companies of people would have the same hallucination at the same time!

One more highly significant feature about the Gospel accounts of the appearances of Jesus must be noted: they lack the smooth "artificiality" that always results when men of guile have conspired to make a contrived story plausible. One immediately encounters numerous difficulties in harmonizing the four accounts of the several post-resurrection appearances. Furthermore, according to the Gospel record it was women who first discovered the empty tomb and it was to women that Jesus first appeared after his resurrection. Given the fact that the testimony of women was virtually worthless in that day and time, it is highly unlikely, if the disciples had conspired together to concoct the stories of the empty tomb and Jesus' several "post-resurrection" appearances, that they would have begun their account with a significant detail which almost certainly would have discredited it at the outset. So in spite of the fact that it might have been more desirable from the disciples' point of view—in order to make their proclamation more plausible—to be able to say that men had first discovered the empty tomb and that it was to men that Jesus had first appeared, this feature as it stands in the Gospel accounts compels the conclusion that it simply did not happen that way, and concerned to report what in fact had happened, the disciples reported the event accordingly. This feature of the Gospel record gives the account the ring of truth.

These two great strands of New Testament data—the empty tomb and Jesus' numerous post-crucifixion appearances—put beyond all legitimate doubt, I would urge, the factuality and the historicity of Jesus' resurrection from the dead.

In addition to these two lines of argument, one may also mention, for their inferential value for the historicity of Jesus' resurrection, (1) the disciples' transformation from paralyzing discouragement to faith and certainty a few days after his death, (2) the later conversion of Saul of Tarsus, and (3) the change of the day of worship for Christians from the seventh to the first day of the week, each of these facts requiring for its explanation just such an event behind it as is provided by the resurrection of Christ.

Critical Views Answered

For many critical scholars today the appearance stories recorded in the Gospels are legends. But what is intriguing is that, while these same scholars are not prepared to admit that Jesus actually rose bodily from the dead, most by far, if not all of them, will acknowledge the historicity of Jesus' death by crucifixion under Pontius Pilate, the subsequent despair of his disciples, their "Easter" experiences which they understood to be appearances to them by the risen Jesus, their resultant transformation, and the later conversion of Saul. In short, for many scholars today, while the resurrection of Jesus is not to be construed as a *historical event*, the disciples, they will admit, had some *subjective experiences* on the basis of which they proclaimed that Jesus had risen from the death and had appeared to them. What should we think about this contention?

Regarding the contention that the appearance stories are later legendary creations of the early church, it is significant that New Testament scholars in increasing numbers are advocating that Paul's statements in 1 Corinthians 15:3-5 (the first written account of the resurrection appearances since 1 Corinthians was written prior to the canonical Gospels) reflect the contents of a quasi-official early Christian creed much older than 1 Corinthians itself (which letter was written probably in the spring of A.D. 55 from Ephesus) which circulated within the *Palestinian* community of believers.[4] This

---

[4]Günther Bornkamm, for example, refers to Paul's enumeration of the appearances of the risen Christ in 1 Corinthians 15:3-7 as "the oldest and most reliable Easter text...formulated long before Paul." He says of this "old form" that it "reads almost like an official record" (*Jesus of Nazareth* [New York: Harper and Brothers, 1960], 182). See also Wolfhart Pannenberg, *Jesus—*

assertion is based upon (1) Paul's references to his "delivering" to the Corinthians what he had first "received," terms suggesting that we are dealing with a piece of "tradition," (2) the stylized parallelism of the "delivered" material itself (see the four ὅτι, *hoti*, clauses and the repeated κατὰ τὰς γραφὰς, *kata tas graphas*, phrases in the first and third of them), (3) the Aramaic "Cephas" for Peter, suggesting a Palestinian milieu for this tradition, (4) the traditional description of the disciples as "the Twelve," and (5) the omission of the appearances to the women from the list. If Paul, in fact, had "received" some of this "tradition," for example, that concerning Jesus' appearances to Peter and to James (referred to in 15:5, 7; see also Acts 13:30-31) directly from Peter and James themselves during his first visit to Jerusalem three years after his conversion (see Acts 9:26-28; Gal 1:18-19), which is quite likely, then this pericope reflects what those who were the earliest eye-witnesses to the events that had taken place in Jerusalem were teaching on *Palestinian* soil within *five to eight years* after the crucifixion. This clearly implies that the material in 1 Corinthians 15:3b-5 is based on *early Palestinian eye-witness testimony* and is hardly the reflection of legendary reports arising much later within the so-called Jewish Hellenistic or Gentile Hellenistic communities of faith. There simply was not enough time, with the original disciples still present in Jerusalem to correct false stories that might arise about Jesus, for legendary accretions of this nature to have risen and to have become an honored feature of the "tradition." The presence of this "early confession" raises serious questions in turn concerning whether the appearance stories in the canonical Gospels are "legendary" stories based upon non-Palestinian sources, as many Bultmannian scholars have insisted. The facts strongly suggest otherwise—that the appearance stories in the Gospels are not legendary accounts as Bultmannians contend.

God and Man (Philadelphia: Westminster, 1968), 90-1. Excellent treatments of this generally accepted view may be found in George E. Ladd, "Revelation and Tradition in Paul" in *Apostolic History and the Gospel*, edited by W. Ward Gasque and Ralph P. Martin (Exeter: Paternoster, 1970), 223-30, particularly 224-25; Grant R. Osborne, *The Resurrection Narratives: A Redactional Study* (Grand Rapids: Baker, 1984), 221-25; and Gary R. Habermas, *Ancient Evidence for the Life of Jesus* (Nashville: Thomas Nelson, 1984), 124-27.

Now it is significant that virtually all critical scholars today, as we have already noted, are prepared to admit that the disciples very shortly after Jesus' death—for some reason—underwent a remarkable transformation in attitude, with confidence and certainty suddenly and abruptly displacing their earlier discouragement and despair. Even Bultmann admits the historicity of their "Easter experience"[5] and concedes that it was this newborn confidence that created the church as a missionary movement. What effected this transformation? If one replies, as some scholars do, that it was their belief that they had seen Jesus alive that effected this transformation from fear to confidence, I must point out that this is tautological: one in the final analysis is simply saying that their *belief* that they had seen Jesus alive gave rise to their *faith* in Jesus' resurrection. We are still left with the question: What gave rise to their belief that they had seen Jesus alive and in person? Some prior event had to effect their belief that they had seen the risen Lord. What was it? If one replies that a visionary experience, that is, a hallucination, was the event which gave rise to their Easter faith, it must be asked, what caused this visionary experience? Opinions vary, of course. Some scholars (Lampe, Schweizer, and Bornkamm, for example) have held that the resurrection appearances were mental images which the spiritual ego of the disembodied Jesus actually communicated back to his disciples from heaven, that is to say, that the resurrection appearances were real activities on the part of a "spiritualized" Jesus in which he entered

---

[5]Rudolf Bultmann writes: "The resurrection itself is not an event of past history. All that historical criticism can establish is the fact that the first disciples came to believe in the resurrection" ("New Testament and Mythology" in *Kerygma and Myth*, edited by Hans-Werner Bartsch [London: SPCK, 1972], I, 42). Donald Guthrie, however, is quite right to insist at this point upon an explanation for their "Easter faith": "The more pressing need at once arises for an explanation of the 'event of the rise of the Easter faith.' The fact is that the skepticism of Bultmann over the relevance of historical enquiry into the basis of the Christian faith excludes the possibility of a satisfactory explanation of any event, whether it be the actual resurrection or the rise of Easter faith. The one is in no different position from the other. The rise of faith demands a supernatural activity as much as the resurrection itself, especially since it arose in the most adverse conditions" (*New Testament Theology* [Leicester: Inter-Varsity, 1981], 183).

into genuine personal intercourse with his disciples. Others have held that the experience of seeing Jesus after his crucifixion was a purely natural phenomenon—simply the work of auto-suggestion. Bultmann, for example, suggests that Jesus' "personal intimacy" with them during the days of his ministry among them began to nourish such fond memories in them that they began to experience "subjective visions" of him and to imagine that they saw him alive again.[6] Michael Goulder, in the first of his two contributions to *The Myth of God Incarnate*, traces belief in Jesus' resurrection back to Peter who, belonging to that psychological type, he says, whose beliefs are rather strengthened than weakened the more apparently refuted they are, underwent a "conversion experienced in the form of a vision" and imagined that he saw Jesus on that first Easter morning. That night he told the other disciples of his experience, and

> so great is the power of hysteria within a small community that in the evening, in [the hypnotic spell (?) of] the candlelight, with [the highly charged emotional situation of] fear of arrest still a force, and hope of resolution budding in them too [but on what ground?], it seemed as if the Lord came through the locked door to them, and away again. So [now note how effortlessly Goulder moves to his conclusion]...the experience of Easter fused a faith that was to carry Jesus to divinity, and his teachings to every corner of the globe.[7]

Now in addition to the fact that all such views leave the fact of the empty tomb unexplained (it is not too much to say that they are scuttled on the "rock" of the empty tomb and fail to come to terms with the variety of objective details in the several accounts of the appearances themselves, George E. Ladd has quite correctly pointed out that

> visions do not occur arbitrarily. To experience them requires certain preconditions on the part of the subjects concerned, preconditions

---

[6]Bultmann's actual words are as follows: "The historian can perhaps to some extent account for that faith from the personal intimacy which the disciples had enjoyed with Jesus during his earthly life, and so reduce the resurrection appearances to a series of subjective appearances" (*Kerygma and Myth*, 42).

[7]Michael Goulder, "Jesus, The Man of Universal Destiny" in *The Myth of God Incarnate*, edited by John Hick (Philadelphia: Westminster, 1977), 59.

> that were totally lacking in the disciples of Jesus. To picture the disciples nourishing fond memories of Jesus after His death, longing to see Him again, not expecting Him really to die, is contrary to all the evidence we possess. To portray the disciples as so infused with hope because of Jesus' impact on them that their faith easily surmounted the barrier of death and posited Jesus as their living, risen Lord would require a radical rewriting of the Gospel tradition. While it may not be flattering to the disciples to say that their faith could result only from some objectively real experience, this is actually what the Gospels record.[8]

Even G. Bornkamm, one of Bultmann's most influential students, has to admit that "the miracle of the resurrection does not have a satisfactory explanation in the inner nature of the disciples," for as he himself acknowledges:

> The men and women who encounter the risen Christ [in the Gospels] have come to an end of their wisdom. Alarmed and disturbed by his death, mourners, they wander about the grave of their Lord in their helpless love, trying with pitiable means—like the women at the grave—to stay the process and odor of corruption, disciples huddled fearfully together like animals in a thunderstorm (Jn. xx. 19 ff.). So it is, too, with the two disciples on the way to Emmaus on the evening of Easter day; their last hopes, too, are destroyed. One would have to turn all the Easter stories upside down if one wanted to present these people in the words of Faust: "They are celebrating the resurrection of the Lord, for they themselves are resurrected." No, they are not themselves resurrected. What they experience is fear and doubt, and what only gradually awakens joy and jubilation in their hearts is just this: They, the disciples, on this Easter day, are the ones marked out by death, but the crucified and buried one is alive.[9]

He goes on to say that by no means was "the message of Jesus' resurrection...only a product of the believing community," and concludes that "it is just as certain that the appearances of the risen Christ and the word of his witnesses have in the first place given rise

---

[8]George E. Ladd, "The Resurrection of Jesus Christ" in *Christian Faith and Modern Theology*, edited by Carl F. H. Henry (Grand Rapids: Baker, 1964), 270-71.

[9]G. Bornkamm, *Jesus of Nazareth*, 184-85.

to this faith."[10] I concur, and would insist that the "objectively real experience" of the disciples, of which Ladd spoke earlier, came to them as the result of the "many convincing proofs" (Acts 1:3) of his resurrection afforded them by Jesus' numerous material post-resurrection appearances to them. Nothing less than his actual resurrection can explain both the empty tomb and the disciples' transformation from doubt and gloom to faith and the martyr's joy. And neither should we nor need we look for another explanation as the ground of their Easter faith.

Having set forth our reasons for affirming the historicity of Jesus' resurrection—*the* epochal event in the history of the world—we will now continue with our investigation of the New Testament witness to Jesus' identity.[11] In this chapter we will consider the evidence that four major historical events yield up: Christ's resurrection itself, his pre-ascension ministry, his ascension, and the Pentecost event. Our investigation of the New Testament epistolary witness will then follow in the two following chapters.

TESTIMONIAL SIGNIFICANCE OF CHRIST'S RESURRECTION

At his resurrection Jesus' ministry entered a new and momentous phase. By it his state of *humiliation*, consisting in his being "born, and that in a low condition, made under the law, undergoing the miseries of this life, the wrath of God, and the cursed death of the cross; in being buried, and continuing under the power of death for a time"

---

[10]Bornkamm, *Jesus of Nazareth*, 183. The reader should recall, however, that Bornkamm espouses the view that Jesus' resurrection appearances were visions sent from heaven and not physical in nature.

[11]I would refer those who care for more argumentation for the historicity of Jesus' resurrection as a central validating event of the Christian faith to Bernard Ramm, *Protestant Christian Evidences* (Chicago: Moody, 1953), 184-207; Daniel P. Fuller, *Easter Faith and History* (Grand Rapids: Eerdmans, 1965); George E. Ladd, *I Believe in the Resurrection of Jesus* (London: Hodder & Stoughton, 1975); Donald Guthrie, *New Testament Theology*, 375-91; G. R. Habermas, "Resurrection of Christ" in *Evangelical Dictionary of Theology*, edited by Walter A. Elwell (Grand Rapids: Baker, 1984), 938-41; John Wenham, *Easter Enigma* (Exeter: Paternoster, 1984).

(*Westminster Shorter Catechism*, Question 27), came to an end. Also by it he entered into his state of *exaltation*, consisting in his "rising again from the dead on the third day, in ascending up into heaven, in sitting at the right hand of God the Father, and in coming to judge the world at the last day" (*Shorter Catechism*, Question 28). I speak intentionally of Jesus' *ministry* entering a new and momentous phase at his resurrection, for nothing could be farther from the truth than the view that suggests that at his ascension to the Father's right hand Jesus' ministry came to an end and that it is now the Holy Spirit who is at work. While it is true that the Holy Spirit is at work today (but there was never a time when the Holy Spirit was not at work), the Son of God is as active now as he always was both in the providential upholding of all things and in the salvation of men. But this awaits our discussion of the meaning of his ascension and Pentecost.

As we shall see in connection with our discussion of Jesus' ascension, both his resurrection and ascension (and the glory attendant particularly upon the latter) are made central in early apostolic preaching (see Acts 1:21-22; 2:24-36; 3:15, 21; 4:2, 10-11, 33; 5:30; 7:56; 10:40-41; 13:30-37; 17:3, 31; see also the ascended Jesus' glorious appearance to Paul in Acts 9:3-9, and Paul's later accounts of that incident in Acts 22:6-15 and 26:12-23). Indeed, it is not an overstatement to suggest that it was not so much the preaching to unbelievers about the significance of the cross as much as it was the proclamation to them of Christ's resurrection and the implications implicit in and attendant upon his subsequent exaltation to the Father's right hand that "turned the [first-century Roman] world upside down" (Acts 17:6; AV, RSV)! Those implications we will consider in due course. Virtually all of the New Testament writers expound upon and apply in some fashion the significance of Jesus' resurrection for the edification of believers.[12] But one passage in particular highlights with

[12]See Gal 1:1; 1 Thes 1:10; 4:14; 5:10; Rom 4:24-25; 5:10; 6:3-11; 7:4; 8:11; 1 Cor 9:1; 15:3-8, 12-23, 56; 2 Cor 4:14; 5:15; Eph 1:19-22; 4:7-12; Phil 2:5-11; 3:10, 21; Col 2:11-12; 3:1; 1 Tim 3:16; 2 Tim 1:10; 2:8, 11. Note that the Author of Hebrews sustains emphasis on Christ's present session at the Father's right hand, which presupposes his resurrection; see Heb 4:14;7:24; 131:20. See 1 Pet 1:3, 11, 21; 3:18, 21-22; Rev 1:5, 17-18, and the signal demonstration throughout John's Revelation on Jesus' glory and final triumph over death and Hades (20:14).

singular clarity the significance of Christ's resurrection for his divine Sonship.

Romans 1:3-4

In these early verses of Paul's great theological treatise to the church at Rome, he informs us of certain characteristics of the gospel. He tells us that it is *God's* gospel, that it had been *promised in the Old Testament Scriptures*, and that it "concerned *his Son*." It is what he then says in 1:3-4 concerning Jesus as "God's Son" which concerns us. A literal rendering of these verses is as follows:

> concerning his Son,
> *who came* [or "came to be," that is, "was born"] of the seed of David, according to the flesh,
> *who was marked out* the Son of God in power, according to the spirit of holiness, by the resurrection from the dead,
> Jesus Christ, our Lord.

Before we say anything about the passage itself it should be noted that these verses are not only found in the salutation of one of the four critically undisputed letters in the Pauline corpus, written around A.D. 57, but also that they comprise what many scholars regard as a *pre-Pauline* church confession.[13] This suggestion was first made by

---

[13]Oscar Cullmann, *The Earliest Christian Confessions*, translated by J. K. S. Reid (London: Lutterworth, 1949), 55. See also V. H. Neufeld, *The Earliest Christian Confessions* (Grand Rapids: Eerdmans, 1963), 50; O. Betz, *What Do We Know About Jesus?* (London: SCM, 1968), 85; and the bibliography in F. Hahn, *The Titles of Jesus in Christology* (Reprint; New York: World, 1969), 268-69. Rudolf Bultmann, *Theology of the New Testament* (London: SCM, 1952), I, 49, views the passage as a "handed-down formula" that probably read, before Pauline syntax and additions, as follows:

> (Jesus Christ) the Son of God,
> Come from the seed of David,
> Designated Son of God in power by his resurrection from the dead.

C. E. B. Cranfield, *A Critical and Exegetical Commentary on the Epistle to the Romans* (ICC) (Sixth revised edition; Edinburgh: T. & T. Clark, 1975), I, 57, also regards the suggestion that Romans 1:3-4 is an early confessions as "highly probable." See G. R. Habermas, *Ancient Evidence for the Life of Jesus*, 123.

J. Weiss in his *Das Urchristentum* (1917), and the diction and the careful parallelism of the phrases admittedly do give a creedal ring to the passage. If this is so, and it may well be, it only underscores the primitive character of the doctrine we find set forth therein. This is the reason behind my decision to introduce at this time a Pauline statement, written some twenty-five years after Christ's resurrection, in order to assess the significance of the event itself for Jesus' sonship. It may not have been originally "Pauline" at all but rather a confessional reflection of the faith of the original apostles and the first Christians in Jerusalem. At any rate, we may be sure that it accurately reflects what the earliest Christians believed on the basis of the apostles' testimony.

The "Bracketing" Phrases

The first thing that I wish to call the reader's attention to is the fact that the two participial clauses which I have indented in the translation above for easy identification (the participles are italicized) are "bracketed" between the two phrases: "his Son" and "Jesus Christ, our Lord." Were it the case that Paul had omitted the intervening participial clauses entirely we would still have here the highest kind of incarnational Christology. The former phrase ("his Son") indicates both the relationship in which Jesus, as God's Son, stands with God the Father and what he is in himself, while the latter phrase ("Jesus Christ, our Lord") designates what he is, as such, to us. In view of several contexts where Paul employs the title "Son," specifically those in which he speaks of God "sending [πέμψας, *pempsas*] his own Son" (Rom 8:3), "sparing not his own Son" (Rom 8:32), and "sending forth [ἐξαπέστειλεν, *exapesteilen*] his Son" (Gal 4:4), the implication is clear that for Paul the Son enjoyed an existence with God the Father prior to his being sent and that in this pre-existent state he stood in a relation to the Father as the Father's *unique* Son (see also Col 1:13, 16-17 where the Son is said to be "before all things").[14] The reflexive

[14]Paul uses the term "Son" 17 times of Jesus: Rom 1:3, 4, 9; 5:10; 8:3, 29, 32; 1 Cor 1:9; 15:28; 2 Cor 1:19; Gal 1:16; 2:20; 4:4, 6; Eph 4:13; Col 1:13; 1 Thes 1:10. Concerning Christ's pre-existence which Paul presupposes in Galatians 4:4 and Romans 8:3, H. N. Ridderbos, *Paul: An Outlines of His Theology*, translated by John R. DeWitt (Grand Rapids: Eerdmans, 1975), 68, writes:

pronoun and possessive adjective respectively in Romans 8:3 and 8:32 (ἑαυτοῦ, ***heautou***, and ἰδίου, ***idiou***), in the words of John Murray, also highlight

> the uniqueness of the sonship belonging to Christ and the uniqueness of the fatherhood belonging to the Father in relation to the Son...In the language of Paul this corresponds to the title *monogenēs* ["only one of a kind"] as it appears in John (John 1:14, 18; 3:16, 18; 1 John 4:9). It is the eternal sonship that is in view and to this sonship there is no approximation in the adoptive sonship that belongs to redeemed men. The same applies to the fatherhood of the first person. In the sense in which he is the eternal Father in relation to the Son he is not the Father of his adopted children.[15]

This being so, Murray is justified when he also writes concerning the phrase "his Son" in Romans 1:3:

> There are good reasons for thinking that in this instance the title refers to a relation which the Son sustains to the Father antecedently to and independently of his manifestation in the flesh. (1) Paul entertained the highest conception of Christ in his divine identity and eternal preexistence (*see* 9:5; Phil. 2:6; Col. 1:19; 2:9). The title "Son"

> This pre-existence of Christ with the Father so emphatically declared by Paul underlies his whole Christology and makes it impossible to conceive of all the divine attributes and power that he ascribes to Christ exclusively as the consequence of his exaltation. It is true that he often speaks in this sense of the *Kyrios* exalted by God.... But this "exaltation Christology" is at the same time not for a moment to be divorced from the significance of Christ's person as such.

Hengel, *The Son of God* (Philadelphia: Fortress, 1976), 7-15, following Schweizer, *Theological Dictionary of the New Testament* (Grand Rapids: Eerdmans, 1948), 8, 382ff., urges the interesting thesis that Paul reserves the "Son [of God]" title "for exceptional usage, at the climax of certain theological statements" about Jesus (14). One cannot dogmatize here but if Hengel is correct it would explain the rarity (and the location of certainly some) of the occurrences of "Son" in Paul's letters.

[15]John Murray, *The Epistle to the Romans* (Grand Rapids: Eerdmans, 1960), I, 279. See also Benjamin B. Warfield, *The Lord of Glory* (Reprint; Grand Rapids: Baker, 1974), 251.

> he regarded as applicable to Christ in his eternal preexistence and as defining his eternal relation to the Father (8:3, 32; Gal. 4:4). (2) Since this is the first occasion in which the title is used in this epistle, we should expect the highest connotation to be attached to it. Furthermore, the connection in which the title is used is one that would demand no lower connotation than that which is apparent in 8:3, 32; the apostle is stating that with which the gospel as the theme of the epistle is concerned. (3) The most natural interpretation of verse 3 is that the title "Son" is not to be construed as one predicated of him in virtue of the process defined in the succeeding clauses but rather identifies him as the person who became the subject of this process and is therefore identified as the Son in the historical event of the incarnation. For these reasons we conclude that Jesus is here identified by that title which expresses his eternal relation to the Father and that when the subject matter of the gospel is defined as that which pertains to the eternal Son of God the apostle at the threshold of the epistle is commending the gospel by showing that it is concerned with him who has no lower station than that of equality with the Father.[16]

C. E. B. Cranfield concurs:

> It is clear that, as used by Paul with reference to Christ, the designation, 'Son of God' expresses nothing less than a relationship to God which is 'personal, ethical and inherent', involving a real community of nature between Christ and God. The position of the words τοῦ υἱοῦ αὐτοῦ [*tou huiou autou*, "his Son"]—...they are naturally taken to control both participial clauses—would seem to imply that the One who was born of the seed of David was already Son of God before, and independently of, the action denoted by the second participle.[17]

The latter phrase ("Jesus Christ, our Lord") Paul obviously intends as explanatory of the former phrase. That is to say, he who stands in relation to God the Father as his own unique Son and who is himself the pre-existent Son of God is also as to his historical identity just

---

[16]Murray, *The Epistle to the Romans*, I, 5. See also Warfield, "The Christ That Paul Preached" in *The Person and Work of Christ* (Philadelphia: Presbyterian and Reformed, 1950), 77.

[17]C. E. B. Cranfield, *A Critical and Exegetical Commentary on the Epistle to the Romans* (Edinburgh: T. & T. Clark, 1975), I, 58.

"Jesus" of Nazareth who because of his antecedent Sonship received the messianic investiture ("Christ") and as such is not only "Lord," the one who has been exalted to the Father's right hand (Ps 110:1; Phil 2:9-11) and who exercises there all authority in heaven and on earth (Matt 28:18), but also "*our* Lord," the one to whom we owe absolute obedience and who properly exercises such Lordship over the creature as is the prerogative only of one who is himself the divine Creator.

We have then in the two bracketing phrases a pregnant summary statement of Paul's Christology: for Paul the Son in his pre-existent state is both equal with the Father as God and distinguishable from the Father as his Son. This one, in keeping with the terms of his messianic investiture, became man, and by virtue of his work as the incarnate Son was exalted to the highest place of honor in the heavens and was given a name above every name ("Lord"), "that at the name of Jesus, every knee should bow, in heaven and on earth and under the earth, and every tongue confess that Jesus Christ is Lord, to the glory of God the Father" (Phil 2:10-11).

The "Bracketed" Clauses

As we turn now to the participial clauses between the bracketing phrases, it is imperative that we keep constantly in mind that what the Apostle now tells us about Christ by them is "thrown up against the background of his deity"[18] implicit in the "bracket" phrases. This backdrop must be allowed to serve as a governing control over all of our subsequent exegesis. For example, we should realize immediately that something is amiss in our exegesis if, in determining the meaning intended by the second participle, we conclude that Paul teaches that at his resurrection Jesus was "constituted" or "appointed" as "Son of God." Such an adoptionistic Christology is precluded at the outset by Paul's representation of his subject as *being* the Son of God prior to and independently of either his "being born" of the seed of David or his being "marked out" as the Son of God. Whatever one makes of Paul's second clause, the "bracket" phrases preclude any form of

---

[18]Warfield, "The Christ That Paul Preached" in *The Person and Work of Christ*, 78.

adoptionism. With this caveat, we turn now to the clauses in question.

With regard to the first clause, "who came [that is, "came to be" or "was born"] of the seed of David, according to the flesh," there is little dispute among recognized students of Romans regarding its meaning. Paul simply intended that his reader understand that in one sense, that is, "according to the flesh," the Son of God had a *historical beginning* as the Son of David. He says essentially the same thing in Galatians 4:4 when he writes: "When the time had fully come, God sent forth his Son, born [the same word he employs in Rom 1:3] of a woman," only in Romans 1:3 he specifies the lineage out of which he came, namely, the Davidic line. Of course, by making specific mention of Jesus' Davidic lineage, Paul intended by it to do more than simply offer his reader a brief account of Jesus' human genealogy. He obviously desired that it should be clearly understood that Jesus, standing as he does in the Davidic line on his human side, was the promised Messiah, and, even more, "in declaring the Messiahship of Jesus, Paul adduces his royal dignity."[19]

But as we have already noted but not yet highlighted Paul does not simply say that Jesus was born of the seed of David, and then end his description of Jesus' historical beginning with that announcement. He adds the qualifying phrase "according to the flesh." What does he intend by this additional thought attached to the clause as a whole? As in Romans 9:5, here as there the phrase intends a specificity and limits the sense in which it may be said that Jesus had a historical beginning as the seed of David. There can be no question, of course, that the word "flesh" denotes Christ's human nature in its entirety. According to New Testament usage σάρξ (*sarx*, "flesh"), when applied to Christ (see John 1:14; 6:51; Rom 8:3; 9:5; Eph 2:14; Col 1:22; 1 Tim 3:16; Heb 5:7; 10:20; 1 Pet 3:18; 4:1; 1 John 4:1; 2 John 7), denotes not simply the material or physical aspect of his human nature over against the non-material aspect, that is, over against his human spirit. Rather, it uniformly refers to him in the totality of his humanness as a man. Accordingly, when Paul says that Jesus had a historical beginning "according to the flesh," he intends, as Cranfield well states,

---

[19]Warfield, "The Christ that Paul Preached" in *The Person and Work of Christ,* 79.

> that the fact of Christ's human nature, in respect of which what has just been said is true, is not the whole truth about Him. 'Son of David' is a valid description of Him so far as it is applicable, but the reach of its applicability is not coterminous with the fullness of His person.[20]

The sense in which the lineal description of him as the Son of David ceases to be applicable as a full description of Jesus Paul had already implicitly stated in the first of the "bracket" phrases—he is not only David's son but he is also "his ["God's"] Son." As we shall now see, Paul makes this explicit in the second participial clause.

The second clause reads: "who was marked out the Son of God in power according to the spirit of holiness by the resurrection from the dead." This clause has proven to be more difficult than the former for exegetes, but it seems to me that, whereas the former clause speaks of Jesus' *historical beginning* as "the Son of David" on his human side, this latter clause speaks of Jesus' *historical establishment*, by his resurrection from the dead, as the Son of God on his divine side.[21] My reasons for this conclusion follow.

The participle ὁρισθέντος, *horisthentos*, the aorist passive of ὁρίζω, *horizō*, I suggest, should be translated "was marked out," "was delineated," or "was designated." The verb is used in the

---

[20]C. E. B. Cranfield, *A Critical and Exegetical Commentary on the Epistle to the Romans*, I, 60. Charles Hodge, *Commentary on the Epistle to the Romans* (Reprint; Grand Rapids: Eerdmans, 1968), 18, well says:

> The limitation...obviously implies the superhuman character of Jesus Christ. Were he a mere man, it had been enough to say that he was of the seed of David, but as he is more than man, it was necessary to limit his descent from David to his human nature.

I find extremely interesting but do not agree with Richard B. Gaffin, Jr., *Resurrection and Redemption* (Philadelphia: Westminster Student Services, 1978), 113-21, that σάρξ, *sarx* ("flesh") refers to the "aeon" or "world order" from which Jesus was delivered by the resurrection. In my opinion, this construction fails to do justice to the New Testament usage of σάρξ, *sarx*, when applied to Christ, particular in Romans 9:5 where it clearly denotes Christ's human nature. H. N. Ridderbos, *Paul: An Outlines of His Theology*, 66-7, also maintains that the "flesh-Spirit" contrast in Romans 1:3 refers to "aeons" but I must withhold my endorsement of his view for the same reason.

[21]The italicized terms are from Warfield, *The Lord of Glory*, 259.

Septuagint in the sense of "fixing" or "marking out" or "delineating" boundaries (see Num 34:6; Josh 13:27; 15:12; 18:20; 23:4), and the noun ὅρια, *horia*, is used in both the Septuagint and the New Testament for "boundaries" or "borders" (see Matt 2:16; 4:13; 8:34; 15:22, 39; 19:1; Mark 5:17; 7:24, 31; 10:1; Acts 13:50).

In accordance with its uniform usage as a periphrasis for the adverb "powerfully" (see Mark 9:1; Col 1:29; 1 Thes 1:5; 2 Thes 1:11),[22] I would construe the phrase ἐν δυνάμει (*en dunamei*, "in power"), in concert with Meyer, Hodge, Sanday and Headlam, Alford, Godet, and Warfield, with the participle rather than with "the Son of God" and translate the participle and the prepositional phrase accordingly by "was powerfully marked out" or "was powerfully delineated."

The preposition ἐκ, *ek*, introducing the phrase "the resurrection from [ablative use of the genitive] the dead," I would submit, has a nuance different from the ἐκ, *ek*, in the former clause. Whereas the preposition ἐκ, *ek*, in the former clause, after the participle of "begetting," clearly denotes "origin," that is, "came to be [or "was born"] *out of* [or "*from*"] the seed of David," in the second clause, after the passive participle "was marked out," ἐκ, *ek*, I would urge, denotes "instrumentality" or even "result" (on the analogy of its use in Heb 11:35). Accordingly, I would render the last phrase of the clause by "through the instrumentality of [or "as the result of"] the resurrection from the dead." This can be, of course, and probably should be, reduced to the simpler "*by* the resurrection from the dead."

The final phrase to be discussed is "according to the spirit of holiness." It is universally agreed that the phrase stands in contrast to "according to the flesh" in the first clause. I would urge, since "flesh" in the former clause, as we have already stated, denotes Christ's humanity *in its totality*, including both corporeal and non-corporeal aspects of his human nature, that "spirit" in the latter clause cannot refer to the human spirit of Jesus. His human spirit is already included within the Davidic "flesh" which he assumed at his birth. Its referent must be sought outside of his humanity. Many, if not most, modern commentators assume that the phrase refers to the Holy Spirit, but I

---

[22]BAGD, *A Greek-English Lexicon of the New Testament and Other Early Christian Literature* (Second edition; Chicago: University of Chicago, 1979), 261, III.2.

would urge that it does not refer to him. On every other occasion in the New Testament where the word "holy" is attached to the noun "spirit" to refer to the Holy Spirit, the adjective ἅγιος, ***hagios***, is employed. But here, precisely to avoid reference to the Holy Spirit, I would suggest, Paul employs the genitive form of the noun ἁγιωσύνη, ***hagiōsunē***, "the spirit *of holiness*." If "spirit" does not refer to Christ's human spirit or to the Holy Spirit then to what does it refer? I would suggest that it refers to Christ's divine nature, to what he is, as the Son of God on his divine side and for the following two reasons: first, because it stands in contrast to "flesh" in the former clause which refers to what Christ, as the Son of David, is on his human side, the implication is that "spirit" in the latter clause must also refer to something intrinsically inherent in Christ. But standing as it does in such close correlation to the title "the Son of God" in the same phrase which denotes Christ in terms of his Godness, it follows that its referent here is to what he is, as the Son of God, on his divine side, that is, to his deity. Second, in this letter some chapters later (9:5) Paul refers again to Christ as "from the fathers, specifically according to the flesh," intimating that something more can and must be said about him. In this later context what this "something more" is Paul himself provides us in the phrase "who is over all, God blessed forever." In other words, in Romans 9:5 Paul declares that Christ is "of the fathers according to the flesh," but in the sense that he is not "of the fathers" and not "flesh" he was and is "over all, God blessed forever." Similarly, I would argue, in Romans 1:3-4 Paul informs us that Christ is "of David, according to the flesh," but in the sense that he is not "of David" and not "flesh," he was and is, as the Son of God, "the spirit of holiness" (see 1 Cor 15:45), that is, divine spirit, intending by this phrase what he explicitly spells out in the later Romans 9:5 context. Warfield explains:

> [Paul] is not speaking of an endowment of Christ either from or with the Holy Spirit....He is speaking of that divine Spirit which is the complement in the constitution of Christ's person of the human nature according to which He was the Messiah, and by virtue of which He was not merely the Messiah, but also the very Son of God. This Spirit he calls distinguishingly the Spirit of holiness, the Spirit the very characteristic of which is holiness. He is speaking not

> of an acquired holiness but of an intrinsic holiness; not, then, of a holiness which had been conferred at the time of or attained by means of the resurrection from the dead; but of a holiness which had always been the very quality of Christ's being [see Luke 1:35; 5:8; John 6:69]...Evidently in Paul's thought of deity holiness held a prominent place. When he wishes to distinguish Spirit from spirit, it is enough for him that he may designate Spirit as divine, to define it as that Spirit the fundamental characteristic of which is that it is holy.[23]

Putting all these features together now, I would suggest that the entire clause can be paraphrased as follows: "who was powerfully marked out the Son of God in accordance with his divine nature by his resurrection from the dead."

Now while it is true that the verb ὁρίζω, *horizō*, can also mean "appoint" or "constitute," Paul cannot mean that Jesus was "appointed" or "constituted" the Son of God at the point of or by reason of his resurrection from the dead inasmuch as he had already represented Jesus by the first "bracket" phrase as the Son of God prior to and independent of not only his resurrection but also his birth of the seed of David in Bethlehem. John Murray (Cranfield as well) is persuaded that the verb, nonetheless, means "appoint" or "constitute" in this context and connotes, as does the former clause, a new "historical beginning" of some kind commencing with the resurrection. Accordingly, he regards the two clauses, in relation to one another, as depicting the "two successive stages" of *humiliatio* and *exaltatio* in the historical process of Jesus' incarnate messianic state.[24] He carefully avoids what would otherwise be an adoptionist Christology

---

[23]Warfield, "The Christ That Paul Preached" in *The Person and Work of Christ*, 87-88. C. Hodge, *Systematic Theology*, I, 472, R. Haldane, Liddon, Bengel, Lagrange, Alford, Vincent, Denney, R. L. Dabney, *Lectures in Systematic Theology* (Reprint; Grand Rapids: Zondervan, 1972), 208, and many other eminent theologians concur that "the spirit of holiness" refers to Christ's divine nature.

[24]Murray, *The Epistle to the Romans*, I, 7, is following here the suggestion of Geerhardus Vos, "The Eschatological Aspects of the Pauline Conception of the Spirit" in *Biblical and Theological Studies* (New York: Charles Scribner's Sons, 1912), 228-30. See also Vos, *The Pauline Eschatology* (Princeton: University Press,1930),155, n. 10, for the same exegesis.

by affirming that in the second of the two stages what was "constituted" was not Jesus as the Son of God *per se* but Jesus as the Son of God "in power." This addition, he writes, "makes all the difference."[25] The successive stages stand in Murray's construction, then, in a certain kind of *antithesis* with each other, the former clause denoting what Jesus was *before* his resurrection, the latter clause denoting what he was *after* his resurrection. In other words, in the former stage, having been "born of the seed of David according to the flesh," Jesus, as the Son of David, was in a state of apparent *weakness;* but with his resurrection, Jesus entered a new stage of messianic existence, one of powerful "pneumatic endowment" (according to Murray this is the meaning of "according to the spirit of holiness") commensurate with his messianic Lordship, a Lordship "all-pervasively conditioned by pneumatic powers."[26] To assure the reader that I have not misrepresented Murray, I offer his own words: "The relative *weakness* of his pre-resurrection state, reflected on in verse 3, is *contrasted* [note his projection of antithesis between the two clauses] with the *triumphant power* exhibited in his post-resurrection lordship."[27]

While I deeply appreciate Murray's reverent scholarship and the interpretative sentiment which seeks to avoid at all costs any taint of an adoptionist Christology, I am persuaded that my (and the traditional) view is correct that avers that what Paul intended to teach in the second clause is that Jesus was powerfully marked out as the Son of God in accordance with what he is on his divine side (that is, "according to the spirit of holiness") by his resurrection from the dead. My reasons follow:

Murray's view, representing the two clauses as "successive stages," injects a contrast between the clauses (what Jesus was *before*, and what he was *after* his resurrection) which I fail to find in the text. Murray implies that being "the Son of David according to the flesh" meant for Jesus a certain state of lowliness and weakness, this former clause (vs 3) needing to be read, at least to a degree, depreciatingly or concessively ("although he was born..."). But as Warfield says of the former clause:

---

[25]Murray, *The Epistle to the Romans*, I, 10.

[26]Murray, *The Epistle to the Romans*, I, 11.

[27]Murray, *The Epistle to the Romans*, I, 11, emphasis supplied.

> To say "of the seed of David" is not to say weakness; it is to say majesty. It is quite certain, indeed, that the assertion "who was made of the seed of David" cannot be read concessively, preparing the way for the celebration of Christ's glory in the succeeding clause. It stands rather in parallelism with the clause that follows it, asserting with it the supreme glory of Christ.[28]

In other words, while there is, of course, the intimation of the idea of a second successive stage within the second clause itself simply because of the mention of the resurrection, it is not the dominant idea in the passage. As for succession between the clauses, it is absent from the context. The two clauses, as is evident from the parallelism of the two genitive participles (τοῦ γενομένου, *tou genomenou*, τοῦ ὁρισθέντος, *tou horisthentos*) with no connecting particle, stand parallel to one another as together representing all that the Son of God is in his incarnate state. This is also made clear by Paul's similar statement in 2 Timothy 2:8 where he writes as an encouragement to Timothy: "Remember Jesus Christ, having been raised out of the dead, is of the seed of David, according to my gospel." Clearly Christ's descent from David was, in Paul's mind, a truth which should cause the beleaguered Christian to rejoice for it speaks of Christ's messianic majesty. It in no way speaks of weakness and it is not to be set off over against his state inaugurated by his resurrection for it is precisely Jesus Christ as the One who "has been raised" (the same theme as in Romans 1:4) and who "is of the seed of David" (the same theme as in Romans 1:3) who is in *both* aspects to be remembered by the Christian in distress. The relation of the second participial clause to the first in Romans 1:3-4 is not then one of opposition or contrast but rather one of climax, not one of *supersession* but one of *superposition.* This is obvious from the fact that Jesus did not cease to be either "the Son of David" or "flesh" at his resurrection; indeed, the resurrection insured that he would continue to be both (a fact which Murray recognizes, of course). So what Paul is saying by the first clause is that the Son of God was born as the Davidic Messiah with all the glories that such an investiture entails; what he is saying by the second clause is that

---

[28]Warfield, "The Christ that Paul Preached" in *The Person and Work of Christ*, 81.

> the Messiahship, inexpressibly glorious as it is, does not exhaust the glory of Christ. He had a glory greater than even this. This was the beginning of His glory. He came into the world as the promised Messiah, and He went out of the world as the demonstrated Son of God. In these two things is summed up the majesty of His historical manifestation.[29]

I would offer this (following Warfield) as a respectful corrective to Murray and conclude by saying that Paul offers us in these two verses a magnificent Christology: the eternal Son of God, who was born of the seed of David according to his manhood, was also the Son of God according to his deity. And this latter fact was powerfully marked out or displayed by his resurrection from the dead, as not only he himself exercised that divine power which he had often displayed in raising others from the dead by raising himself from the dead (John 2:19; 10:18) but also his Father placed his stamp of approval on all that his Son had done by raising him from the dead "in accordance with the working of the might of his strength which he exerted in Christ when he raised him from the dead" (Rom 4:24; 6:4; 8:11; Eph 1:19-20).

Our exposition of Romans 1:3-4 is completed. What we have been concerned to highlight by our exposition of what may well be a portion of an early Christian confession is the significance of his resurrection for Jesus' divine Sonship. And I would submit that Romans 1:3-4 does this in a matchless fashion. In it we are clearly informed, if we will have ears to hear it, that Jesus' resurrection from the dead was both his and his Father's powerful witness to the fact that Jesus of Nazareth was both Messiah and God incarnate and not simply a man like other men.

EVIDENCE FROM CHRIST'S PRE-ASCENSION MINISTRY

During the forty days the risen Christ spent with the apostles between his resurrection and ascension, during which time, as we have already shown, he gave "many convincing proofs" (NIV) that he was alive (Acts 1:3), he continued to make either tacitly or expressly the same

---

[29]Warfield, "The Christ that Paul Preached" in *The Person and Work of Christ*, 80.

exalted claims which he began to make in increasing clarity and number prior to his Passion. These, of course, were made in conjunction with his resurrection appearances.

When Jesus appeared to the women returning from the tomb on the morning of his resurrection, Matthew informs us that the women "clasped his feet and *worshiped* [προσεκύνησαν, *prosekunēsan*] him" (28:9). We are not told what form this worship took. Because of Jesus' calming "Do not be afraid," it appears that it included that numinous awe that overwhelms the human spirit when it is suddenly made aware of the presence of the "transcendentally holy." Whatever else it involved Matthew's statement makes it clear that the women did something beyond and in addition to their act of grasping him by the feet, which act implies that they were already in a kneeling or prostrate position before him at the time that they performed whatever it was that Matthew intended by his second verb. There can be little doubt that Matthew intended that this additional act on their part should be understood as involving the going out of their *religious* affections toward him, which is just to say that it was a religious activity in which they were involved, constituting what any fair-minded person would acknowledge to be the activity of worship. And the point to be made here, in conjunction with their worship of him, is that Jesus did not reject their worship nor did he rebuke them for their devotion but he seems rather to have accepted it as proper and right. This means in turn that from the perspective of his own self-understanding he viewed himself as divine and thus worthy of their worship.

In his appearance then to Mary Magdalene (John 20:10-18), he informed her that he had not yet "returned to the Father," this saying indicating that that unique filial relationship in which he stood to God had in no way been violated or affected negatively by his Passion. Then he instructed her to inform "his brothers" that he was returning "to my Father and your Father and to my God and your God" (20:17). It is significant that nowhere in the teaching of Jesus did he ever speak of God to his disciples as "our Father" or "our God." Throughout his ministry he consistently spoke of the Father as "the Father" or "my Father" but never as "our Father." (The "Our Father" of the so-called "Lord's Prayer" is not an exception to this inasmuch as there Jesus is instructing his disciples concerning how *they* should corporately address God in prayer.) In keeping then with his established pattern of speech, he continued to avoid the obviously shorter form of expression ("our") and chose to remain with the longer form ("my" and "your"). I would suggest that his concern here was to maintain and not to obliterate the distinction between the sense in which he is God's Son by nature and by right and the sense in which his disciples are God's sons by grace and by adoption.[30]

In his appearance to the two disciples on the road to Emmaus (Luke 24:13-35), Jesus declared that "these things" (24:26; see, for the referent of "these things," 24:20) which *he* had just endured were only what "all the prophets" had said must happen to the Messiah before he entered his glory (24:26). By linking the events of the previous three days to the prophetic vision of the Old Testament respecting the Messiah's work, Jesus laid claim again to the messianic investiture. And Luke the Evangelist adds his comment at this point: "And beginning with Moses and all the Prophets, he explained to them what was said in all the Scriptures *concerning himself*" (24:27).

That evening he appeared to the disciples in the upper room (Luke 24:36-49; John 20:19-23), and after greeting them and proving to them that it was really he by showing them his wounded hands, side, and feet, and by eating a piece of fish before them, he said to them: "This is what I told you while I was still with you: Everything must be fulfilled that is written *about me* in the Law of Moses, the Prophets and the

---

[30]Donald Guthrie, *New Testament Theology*, 313, writes:

> The uniqueness of the sonship of Jesus is supported by the clear statement of the risen Christ in John 20:17, when he made a distinction between 'my Father and your Father' and 'my God and your God.' The distinction is of great importance because it rules out the view that Jesus' sonship was of the same kind as man's but developed to a greater intensity. Others may be given power to become sons of God (1:12), but Jesus has no need for this since he is Son of a different kind, *i.e.*, he is essentially a son.

See also here Leon Morris, *The Gospel According to John* (Grand Rapids: Eerdmans, 1971), who writes: "It seems as though He is of set purpose placing Himself in a different relationship to the Father from that which His followers occupy" (842). He also affirms: "The most natural way of taking the words is to see a difference between Jesus' relationship to God and that of the disciples." (842, fn 42).

Psalms" (Luke 24:44). Then he opened their minds that they might understand the Scriptures (this act itself being a divine act) and said to them: "This is what is written: The Messiah will suffer and rise from the dead on the third day, and repentance and forgiveness of sins will be preached *in his name* to all nations, beginning at Jerusalem. You are witnesses of these things. I am going to send you what my Father has promised but stay in the city until you have been clothed with power from on high" (24:45-47). His claim again to messiahship is apparent and needs no comment. But it is worthy of note that he informs them that their witness is to be self-consciously Christocentric, that is, the blessings they promise men are to be related directly to him ("in *my* name"). Surely, were any other to insist that a world-wide message should have his person made so integrally central to all that is proclaimed we would conclude that it constituted the gravest form of self-worship and idolatry. But all of this seems perfectly natural, and rightly so, coming from the lips of Jesus.

Then, after having commissioned them to be his witnesses, Jesus did a very significant thing: he breathed upon them and said to them: "Receive the Holy Spirit" (John 20:22). Now it is true that he had just said that he was going to send them the Holy Spirit but it is equally true that he implied that it would be some days later before he did so. What is the significance then of this act at this time on his part? It is my opinion that on this occasion he did not actually impart nor did they actually receive the Holy Spirit in the "empowering" sense he had just spoken about. I say this, first, because the text does not state that they did, and second, because there is no indication of any kind that they immediately assumed their role as witnesses. To the contrary, in the words of E. C. Hoskyns: "The disciples still remain in secret, behind closed doors."[31] If Jesus did not impart the Spirit to them on this occasion then what is the significance of this act? I would submit that it was a symbolic act, analogous to his act of breaking the bread prior to his crucifixion, a visible depiction of the spiritual reality which was to occur only days later at Pentecost. On that occasion, when the Spirit was poured out upon them, with the image of Jesus' symbolic act of "on-breathing" a recent memory indelibly etched upon their

---

[31]E. C. Hoskyns, *The Fourth Gospel* (London: Faber and Faber, 1947), 2.653.

minds, they would become aware in a powerful way by their recollection of this symbolic breathing that it was the ascended Lord who was "breathing" upon them at Pentecost, that it was the life-infusing power of his "breath" that was present with them in their proclamation and witness. In other words, he was preparing them, in a tangible way, for the event of Pentecost, insuring them that though he was to be absent from them in one sense (physically) he was to be present with them in the person and power of his "breath"—the Holy Spirit. And they would be conscious, even as he was to say himself during a subsequent appearance to them, that he was indeed "with [them], even to the end of the age" (Matt 20:28). We shall say more about the significance of Pentecost later, but it is important, I feel, that Jesus' act on this occasion be understood as a symbolic foreshadowing of what was to take place then. Also, by this construction the so-called "discrepancy" is eliminated that many critics insist exists between John and Acts over precisely when the Spirit was given.

A week later Jesus appeared to his disciples again, this time Thomas also being present with them. After showing Thomas his hands and side, Thomas exclaimed: "[You are] my Lord and my God!" (John 20:28) Not only did Jesus not correct Thomas' response as a misconception but, just to the contrary, Jesus declared of Thomas that he had finally "believed" (20:29). There can be no doubt that Jesus gives evidence here by his tacit acceptance of Thomas' assessment of him that he was in his self-understanding their *Lord* to be served and their *God* to be worshiped.

Thomas' Use of Θεός as a Christological Title (John 20:28)

John 20:28, in the words of Raymond E. Brown, is a critically secure text "where clearly Jesus is called God."[32] As such, Thomas' confession of Jesus as his "Lord [κύριος, *kurios*] and God [θεός, *theos*]" is the "supreme christological pronouncement of the Fourth Gospel."[33] Here only a week after Jesus' resurrection, in the presence

---

[32]Raymond E. Brown, "Does the New Testament Call Jesus God?" in *Theological Studies* 26, no. 4 (1965): 561.

[33]Raymond E. Brown, *The Gospel According to John XIII-XXI* (Anchor Bible; Garden City, New York: Doubleday, 1970), 1047.

of the other disciples who would surely have learned from Thomas' words and Jesus' favorable response to them the appropriateness of doing so, a disciple for the first time employs θεός, *theos*, as a Christological title. This would suggest that there is no basis in fact for the view of some form-critical scholars that the church only gradually came to the view of an incarnational Christology. Christians from the beginning believed that in Jesus they had to do with the Son of God incarnate.

No modern scholar has shown any interest in following the opinion of Theodore of Mopsuestia (c. A.D. 350-428) that Thomas' words do not refer to Christ "but having been amazed over the wonder of the resurrection, Thomas praised God who raised the Christ."[34] This opinion was rejected by the Second Council of Constantinople in A.D. 553. The closest one comes to finding the idea expressed today is in the insistence of Jehovah's Witnesses that the first title was addressed to Jesus while the second was addressed to Jehovah. But Bruce Metzger is justified when he writes:

> It is not permissible to divide Thomas' exclamation.... Such a high-handed expedient overlooks the plain introductory words, "Thomas said *to him:* 'My Lord and my God!'"[35]

Moreover, the fact that both appellations appear to be nominative in form should occasion no difficulty for the view that the terms are addressed to Jesus. The so-called articular nominative with vocative force is a well-known idiom in classical, Septuagint, and New Testament Greek. Thomas' confession is an exceptionally wonderful exclamation, but it is all the more amazing when one reflects, first, on the incongruity of a confession of this magnitude coming from probably the least likely of the Twelve to utter it—one given to melancholy and gloom (John 11:16) and to theological dullness (John 14:5), and, second, on the fact that "Thomas...makes clear that one may address Jesus in the same language in which Israel addressed Yahweh"[36] (see Pss

---

[34]See H. Denzinger and A. Schönmetzer, *Enchiridion Symbolorum* (Freiburg: Herder, 1976), 150, sec. 434.

[35]Bruce M. Metzger, "The Jehovah's Witnesses and Jesus Christ" in *Theology Today* (April 1953): 71, fn. 13.

[36]Brown, *The Gospel According to John XIII-XXI*, 1047.

35:23; 38:15, 21). John doubtless intended his report of Thomas' ascent from skepticism to full faith in Jesus as Lord and God under the impact of the historical reality of the resurrection to illustrate what he thought should be the response of everyone when informed of Jesus' resurrection.

Two contextual features of Thomas' confession are worthy of note. The first is that only a week earlier Jesus in his conversation to Mary had spoken of his Father as "my God," using precisely the same words that Thomas used later of him. He also said on that occasion that *his* God was also his disciples' God. And yet now, only a week later, he accepts Thomas' description of *himself* as his disciple's God! Clearly, in Jesus' mind there was a personal manifoldness in the depth of the divine being which would permit his Father to be regarded as their God and also himself to be regarded as their God. Here is certainly the biblical material from which the church was later to formulate its doctrine of the Trinity.

The other interesting contextual feature is that Thomas' confession is followed immediately by John's stated intention for writing his Gospel, namely, that his readers "may believe that Jesus is the Christ, the Son of God" (20:31). If John had intended by the title "Son of God" in his stated purpose for his Gospel something other than or less than an ascription of full deity to Jesus, one can only impute unforgivable ineptitude to him for bringing this lesser title into such close proximity to Thomas' confession of Jesus' unabridged deity. Clearly, the only adequate explanation for the near juxtaposition of the two titles is that, while "Son of God" distinguishes Jesus as Son from the the Father, it does not distinguish him as God from God the Father. To be the Son of God in the sense John intended it of Jesus is just to be God the Son.

Continuing our overview of the post-resurrection witness to Jesus we note that on the occasion of his early morning appearance to the seven disciples by the Sea of Galilee, he demonstrated his supernatural lordship over nature by effecting the miraculous catch of fish. On that same occasion he called the church "*my* sheep," applying to himself again the Old Testament imagery of Yahweh as the Shepherd of Israel, and then with divine foresight he predicted the kind of death that Peter would die.

On the mountain of Galilee (Matt 28:16-20), his next appearance, Jesus accepted his disciples' worship (28:17) and then made the stupendous claim that "*all authority* in heaven and on earth" had been given to him. He followed this claim to universal sovereignty by commanding his followers to make *all* the nations *his* disciples. Beyond all legitimate debate such universal authority and lordship is the rightful prerogative only of one who is himself equal with God. And if this conclusion should be thought to be premature, it needs only to be said that it is fortified by Jesus' next utterance, "baptizing them into the name of the Father and of the Son and of the Holy Spirit," for by this statement he assigned himself a place as "the Son" within "the awful precincts of the divine name" and represented himself as a co-sharer with the Father of the single ineffable divine "name." He followed this by the claim to the "Immanuel" attributes of omnipresence ("I will be with you"; the "you" is plural) and eternality ("always, even to the end of the age"). Here is testimony replete with both overt claims to and implicit overtones of deity.

Finally, on the day of his ascension, he declared again that his disciples were to be witnesses unto him throughout the whole world, which commission can only be regarded as blasphemous idolatry on both his and their parts, in light of Isaiah 43:10 and 44:8, if he were not himself the Yahweh of these Old Testament declarations. Then having blessed them, he ascended to heaven, sending them the promise immediately that he would return someday just as he had ascended. In that context, we are told, his disciples worshiped him (Luke 24:52),[37] the significant thing about this act of worship being that he was no longer with them, their religious affections in worship now needing to be directed to him in heaven just as they would have worshiped the God of Israel. Accordingly, we find them referring to Jesus as "the Lord" in Acts 1:21,[38] and praying to him as both the proper recipient

---

[37]The words, "...worshiping him," supported as they are by weighty manuscript evidence, are textually secure. See Bruce M. Metzger, *A Textual Commentary on the Greek New Testament* (New York: United Bible Societies, 1971), 189-90, for sound reasons for retaining the longer ending of Luke here.

[38]R. T. France, "The Worship of Jesus: A Neglected Factor in Christological Debate?" in *Christ the Lord*, edited by Harold H. Rowdon (Leicester: Inter-Varsity, 1982): 29, writes:

of their prayers and "the knower of all men's hearts."[39]

It is not an overstatement to say that Jesus' pre-ascension ministry is replete with testimony to the effect that he is properly to be regarded as God, the Yahweh of the Old Testament, the divine Son of God, the Lord of the universe, and the promised Messiah.

TESTIMONIAL SIGNIFICANCE OF CHRIST'S ASCENSION

Both in his Gospel and in Acts Luke records that Jesus, upon completing his forty-day pre-ascension ministry, bodily "ascended into heaven." He employs three verbs to describe this momentous event: ἀνεφέρετο, *anephereto*, "was led up" (Luke 24:51), ἀνελήμφθη, *anelēmphthē*, "was taken up" (Acts 1:2, 11; see ἀναλήμψεως, *analēmpseōs*, in Luke 9:51), and ἐπήρθη, *epērthē*, "was lifted up" (Acts 1:9). Of the four Gospel writers, Luke alone records the historical account of Jesus' ascension,[40] but he is by no means the only New

---

> ...the vocative *kurie* addressed to a living person need have no superhuman connotations, but when a man is described after his death as *ho kurios*, this is a different matter altogether, especially when those references are to his present rather than his past status.... Such uses immediately bring into view the associations which *ho kurios* inevitably carried for a Greek-speaking Jew, in that it was the standard LXX translation for the name of God. He could no more use *ho kurios* without thinking of its divine connotations than we could use "the Lord" of a human leader today. And this title springs into prominence immediately after the resurrection.

[39]See also Acts 7:56; 9:14; 1 Cor 1:2; 2 Cor 12:8-9. That it is Jesus that the church in the upper room is addressing by κύριε, *kurie*, is evident both from its proximity to ὁ κύριος 'Ιησους, *ho kurios Iēsous*, in Acts 1:21 and from the fact that the very thing they request—"Show us which of these two you have chosen to take over this apostolic ministry"—is what Jesus had done with reference to them earlier (Acts 1:2: "the apostles whom he chose"). In both 1:2 and 1:24-25 the same Greek words are employed. This being so, we have in their description of him as the "knower of the hearts of all men" a further evidentiary datum of the early church's perception of the ascended Lord Jesus as divine (see also John 2:24-25). See also here Warfield, *The Lord of Glory*, 208.

[40]The longer ending of Mark (16:19-20) records that Jesus "was taken up

Testament writer who refers to the event. Peter, Luke reports, referred to it in the upper room shortly after it occurred (Acts 1:22) and mentioned it in his sermons later (2:33-35; 3:21; 5:31); he also writes of it directly in 1 Peter 3:22. Stephen's statement in Acts 7:56 presupposes the past occurrence of it. Paul presupposes its historical actuality in his references to Christ's session at the Father's right hand in Romans 8:34 and Colossians 3:1, alludes to it in his words of Ephesians 1:20-22, 2:6, and Philippians 2:9-11, and expressly mentions it in Ephesians 4:8-10 and 1 Timothy 3:16. The Author of Hebrews presupposes it in 1:3, 13, 2:9, 8:1, 10:12, and 12:2, and expressly refers to it in 4:14, 6:20, and 9:24. John informs us that Jesus himself often alluded to it (John 6:62; 7:33-34; 8:21; 13:33; 14:2, 28; 16:7-10; 20:17), and that he "knew that...he had come from God and was returning to God" (13:3). Finally, it is clear that Jesus presupposed it in his testimony before the Sanhedrin at his trial when he said: "...you will see the Son of Man sitting at the right hand of the Mighty One" (Matt 26:64; Mark 14:62; Luke 22:69).

Its Historicity

The Bultmann school, not surprisingly, relegates Christ's ascension to the realm of legend, Bultmann himself writing:

> According to 1 Cor. 15:5-8, where Paul enumerates the appearances of the risen Lord as tradition offered them, the resurrection of Jesus meant simultaneously his exaltation; not until later was the resurrection interpreted as a temporary return to life on earth, and this idea then gave rise to the ascension story.[41]

This construction reflects his overarching aversion to the "intrusion" of the supernatural into the realm of space-time history, the ascension particularly mirroring for him the so-called "mythological" (non-scientific) "three-story universe" concept of the ancient world. But

---

[ἀνελήμφθη, *anelēmphthē*] into heaven and he sat at the right hand of God." This section is textually suspect, but it does reflect a tradition that accords with the Lukan report. It appears, in fact, to have been based mainly on the Lukan testimony.

[41]Rudolf Bultmann, *Theology of the New Testament*, translated by Kendrick Grobel (London: SCM, 1971), 1, 45.

as Donald Guthrie states, this is not the construction which should be placed on the ascension data:

> The upward movement [of Jesus' physical figure] is almost the only possible method of pictorially representing complete removal. The OT instances of Enoch and Elijah present certain parallels. Inevitably a spatial notion is introduced, but this is not the main thrust of the Acts description. The focus falls on the screening cloud, precisely as it does in the transfiguration account.... The reality of the ascension is not seen in an up-there movement, so much as in the fact that it marked the cessation of the period of confirmatory appearances.[42]

B. F. Westcott, likewise, aids us by sensitively commenting on the nature of the ascension in these words:

> [Jesus] passed beyond the sphere of man's sensible existence to the open Presence of God. The physical elevation was a speaking parable, an eloquent symbol, but not the Truth to which it pointed or the reality which it foreshadowed. The change which Christ revealed by the Ascension was not a change of place, but a change of state, not local but spiritual. Still from the necessities of our human condition the spiritual change was represented sacramentally, so to speak, in an outward form.[43]

In other words, the "heavenly places" of Scripture expression are not to be conceived in spatio/temporal dimensions as "up there," but in spiritual dimensions to which Jesus' *glorified* corporeal existence was capable of adapting without ceasing to be truly human as evidenced by his activity described in Luke 24:31, 36 and John 20:19, 26. Therefore, Berkouwer quite properly declares:

> Only severe Bible criticism can lead one to a denial of the ascension and even to its complete elimination from the original apostolic *kerygma*.... To the Church it has always been a source of comfort

---

[42]Donald Guthrie, *New Testament Theology* (Leicester: Inter-Varsity, 1981), 395. See also Gordon H. Clark, "Bultmann's Three-Storied Universe" in *A Christianity Today Reader*, edited by Frank E. Gaebelein (New York: Meredith, 1966), 173-76.

[43]B. F. Westcott, *The Revelation of the Risen Lord* (London: Macmillan, 1898), 180.

> to know that Christ is in heaven with the Father. And over against the denial of both the *ascensio* and *sessio* as being contrary to the "modern world conception," the Church may continue on the basis of Holy Scripture to speak of these facts in simplicity of faith.[44]

Still other critical scholars contend that the earliest ascension tradition in the church had Christ ascending to heaven directly from the cross with no intervening resurrection and pre-ascension ministry. Traces of this are purportedly to be found in the early Christian hymn cited by Paul in Philippians 2:6-11, for there Christ's humiliation and exaltation are contrasted with no mention of his burial and resurrection. John's Gospel also is supposed to reflect this "ascension from the cross" teaching—with no room for the resurrection or pre-ascension ministry—in such verses as 12:23 and 13:21 where John quotes Jesus to the effect that his hour of death would also mean his glorification. The Author of Hebrews is also said to have favored the idea that Jesus ascended to heaven from the cross because of such statements as the one in 10:12: "But when this priest had offered for all time one sacrifice for sins, he sat down at the right hand of God." Again, the point is made, there is no mention here of Christ's resurrection or pre-ascension ministry.

Several things may be said about this effort to explain the ascension in non-literal, non-historical terms. First, apparently the operative (but erroneous) canon of exegesis here is this: if a New Testament writer does not mention Christ's resurrection in every context where he mentions Christ's exaltation or his session at the right hand of his Father, one may conclude that either he himself was unaware of the resurrection and the subsequent pre-ascension ministry or that the tradition he is citing was unaware of these events. But this is a *non sequitur*, and it imposes the highly artificial requirement upon the New Testament writer, if he believed in them, always to mention the resurrection, pre-ascension ministry, and ascension whenever he mentions Christ's session at the right hand of God. Second, such a contention completely ignores the fact that all of these New Testament writers refer elsewhere—indeed, in the very works where the so-called "ascension from the cross" is supposedly taught—to the post-

---

[44]Berkouwer, *The Work of Christ*, 206, 234.

crucifixion resurrection of Christ: by *Paul*, for instance, in Galatians 1:1, 1 Thessalonians 1:10, 4:14, Acts 17:31, 26:23, 1 Corinthians 15:4, 12-20, Romans 1:4, 4:25, 6:4, 5, 9, 7:4, 8:11, 34, Ephesians 1:20, Philippians 3:10, Colossians 1:18, 2:12, 3:1, 2 Timothy 2:8; by *John* in John 2:19-21, 20:1-29, 21:1-22; and by the Author of *Hebrews* in Hebrews 13:20. Moreover, Paul makes mention of the "many days" intervening between Christ's resurrection and ascension (Acts 13:31). Third, what Berkouwer says in defense of the Author of Hebrews, namely, that the only way these critical scholars can interpret the work in this way is to proceed with the following formula: "The glory of Christ in Hebrews minus Hebrews 13:20 equals the ascension 'from the cross,'"[45] may be said in defense of all of the New Testament writers: the only way they can be used to support the idea that Christ ascended to heaven from the cross and not some weeks later is to ignore all of the references in their writings to Christ's resurrection, his post-resurrection appearances, and his pre-ascension ministry.

One can only conclude that these scholars have very little confidence in the trustworthiness of the Gospels and epistles. For myself, I am aware of no reason advanced to date which can justify the wholesale abandonment of Luke's account of the ascension. Accordingly, I will turn to the significance of Christ's ascension both for men and for himself.

Its Significance

The ascension of Christ meant, of course, for those first disciples and also for every other disciple since then, in a word, his *separation* from them, not "with respect to his Godhead, majesty, grace and Spirit" (*Heidelberg Catechism*, Ques 47; see also Ques 46), of course, for his spiritual communion with them remains unbroken and undisturbed as a genuine and even enhanced spiritual reality but only with respect to his physical presence among them. This separation Christ himself spoke about in such places as Luke 5:35; John 7:33; 12:8; 13:33; 14:30; and 16:10 (see also 1 Pet 1:8; 1 John 3:2).[46]

---

[45]Berkouwer, *Work of Christ*, 208.

[46]The trained theologian will recognize by my formulation here that I am following the Reformed rather than the Lutheran tradition, which latter

With respect to Christ himself, the Scriptures virtually exhaust available "triumphalist" language, images, and metaphors, to describe the significance of Christ's ascension for him. At this time I can only enumerate some of these descriptions. As his resurrection was the means to his ascension, and so a significant aspect of his total exaltation, so his ascension in turn was the means to his climactic exaltation and enthronement (*sessio*) at the Father's right hand as Holy One, Lord, Christ, Prince, and Savior of the world (Acts 2:27, 33-36; 5:31; Rom 8:34; Col 3:1; Phil 2:9-11; Heb 1:3). And what an exalted enthronement it is! If his ascension was "in [ἐν, *en*] glory" (1 Tim 3:16), exalting him thereby "higher than all the heavens" (Eph 4:10; Heb 7:26), he is also now "crowned with glory and honor" (δόξῃ καὶ τιμῇ ἐστεφανωμένον, *doxē kai timē estephanōmenon*, Heb 2:9) "with angels, authorities, and powers in submission to him" (1 Pet 3:22), with "everything under his feet," the Father alone excepted (1 Cor 15:26; Eph 1:22a), sitting "far above all rule and authority, power and dominion, and every title that can be given, not only in the present age but also in the one to come" (Eph 1:21). God has also "given" (ἔδωκεν, *edōken*) him to be "head-over-everything for the church, which is his body, the fullness of him who fills everything in every way" (Eph 1:22-23), indeed, who fills "the whole universe" (τὰ πάντα, *ta panta*) with his power and lordship (Eph 4:10). In sum, he now occupies the "highest place" (Phil 2:9) of glory and honor (Heb 2:9) which heaven can afford, and to him belongs *de jure* and *de facto* the titles "Lord of all" (Acts 10:36; Rom 10:12) and Lord above all other lords (Acts 2:36; Phil 2:9b; Rev 19:16), "that at the name of Jesus, every knee should bow in heaven and on earth and under the earth, and every tongue confess that Jesus Christ is Lord" (Phil 2:10-11a). The nature of his lordship entitles him sovereignly to bestow gifts of every and of whatever kind upon men as he pleases (Eph 4:7-8, 11).

There can be no question, in light of such undeniably transparent language, that upon his resurrection and ascension (these two events

---

tradition maintains, because of its peculiar doctrine of the *communicatio idiomatum*, that Christ is by virtue of the union of the two natures in the one person of Christ *physically* ubiquitous and therefore physically present "in, with, and under" the elements of the Lord's Supper.

may be construed quite properly together, even though the former preceded the latter by forty days, as the collective two-stage means to his exaltation to lordship), and as the fruit and reward for his labors on earth, Jesus as the Messiah was granted supreme lordship and universal dominion over men. This is also suggested (1) by his own statement in Matthew 28:18: "All authority in heaven and on earth has been given to me," where he speaks of that messianic lordship which he received *de jure* at his resurrection but which he actually began to exercise *de facto* universally from heaven upon his ascension and present session at the Father's right hand (I would suggest that his references in Matthew 11:27 and John 17:2 to a possessed "delegated" dominion should be understood against the background of the covenant of redemption in the councils of eternity.); (2) by Peter's statement "God made [ἐποίησεν, *epoiēsen*, "appointed," "constituted"] him both Lord and Christ" (Acts 2:36) following upon his resurrection and ascension—another declaration, surely, of his *de facto* assumption of mediatorial reign as the God-man since Jesus was obviously both Lord and Messiah by divine appointment from the moment of his incarnation; and (3) by Paul's statement: "because of which [διὸ καὶ, *dio kai*] [his earthly work] God exalted him to the highest place and gave him the name, the 'above everything' name," that is, the name of "Lord" (Phil 2:9).

It would be a fatal mistake theologically to deduce from any of this that Jesus as the Son of God, who (though in union with our flesh) continued infinitely to transcend all creaturely limitations, became "Lord" only at his exaltation and acquired *as God's Son* only then *de jure* and *de facto* universal dominion. We must never forget that, for Peter, it was "our God and Savior Jesus Christ" who "sprinkles us with his blood" (2 Pet 1:1; 1 Pet 1:2). For Paul, likewise, it was "the Lord of Glory" (ὁ κύριος τῆς δόξης, *ho kurios tēs doxēs*), this expression meaning "the Lord to whom glory belongs as his native right," who was also just both "God over all" (Rom 9:5) and "our great God" (Tit 2:13), who was crucified for us (1 Cor 2:8). As God the Son, then, Jesus, of course, continued as he always had done to uphold all things by the word of his power (Heb 1:3) and to exercise the powers and lordly rights which were intrinsically his as the divine Being (see John Calvin, *Institutes*, II.13.4). Consequently, when these apostles tell us that Christ Jesus was "appointed" Lord or was "exalted" and "given" authority and the title of "Lord" at his ascension, it is necessary that we understand that these things were said of him in his mediatorial role as the Messiah. It is appropriate to say these things about him but only because he, "the Son," who is intrinsically and essentially "rich," who is "Lord" by right of nature, had *first* deigned to take into union with himself our "flesh," becoming thereby "poor" (2 Cor 8:9). It was as the divine-human Messiah, then, that he "acquired" or "was given" at his ascension *de facto* authority to exercise mediatorial dominion. It was not then his exaltation but his prior "humiliation" which was the "strange experience"[47] to the Son *as God.* Conversely, it was not his humiliation but his "exaltation" which was the "new experience" to the Son *as the divine-human Messiah.* If we are to take history and specifically New Testament history seriously we must say this. We must be willing to say that, in a certain sense, the exaltation entailed for the Son an experience which had not been his before. This "new experience" was universal dominion, not as God *per se*, of course, but as the divine-human Messiah and as the divine-human Mediator between God and man. We even learn elsewhere that this mediatorial dominion is a temporarily-delegated authority. When he and his Father have subjugated finally all his and our enemies, then he will yield up not his Sonship[48] but this delegated authority as the Messiah to God, even the Father, and his special mediatorial dominion will be "re-absorbed" into the universal and eternal dominion of the triune God (1 Cor 15: 24-28). But in sum the ascension meant for the Son, as the divine-human Messiah, the assumption of the prerogatives of the messianic investiture on a universal scale, rights which were already his by right

---

[47]The phrase is Benjamin B. Warfield's (Reprint; *The Lord of Glory* [Grand Rapids: Baker, 1974], 225).

[48]Herman Ridderbos observes that "where there is mention of the consummation of Christ's work of redemption, in the words of 1 Corinthians 15:28 (when the Son has subjected all things to the Father, then will he himself be subject to him, that God may be all in all), this cannot mean the end of the Sonship. One will rather have to judge the 'post-existence' of the Son intended here in the light of what is elsewhere so clearly stated of his pre-existence" (*Paul: An Outline of His Theology*, translated by John Richard DeWitt [Grand Rapids: Eerdmans, 1975], 69).

of nature as God the Son but which he "won" or was "awarded" as the incarnate Son for fulfilling the obligations pertaining to the estate of humiliation intrinsic to the messianic investiture.

It was this Christ, in precisely the terms of this his glorious messianic lordship, who was made central to all early apostolic preaching. The apostles were solicitous to draw out the implications of Christ's exclusive lordship over the world for their audiences. None of the modern clamor for religious pluralism was present in their preaching. For them there was an exclusivity and finality about God's revelation to men in Jesus Christ (Matt 21:37; Mark 12:6; Heb 1:1). For them, because of who Christ is, the work he did, the place he presently occupies, and the titles he bears, "salvation is in no one else, for there is no other name given among men by which we must be saved" (Acts 4:12). For them, as Jesus Himself said, he alone is the way, the truth and the life (John 14:6). For them, he is the only Mediator between God and man (1 Tim 2:5). He is also the one who, as Lord, will judge the living and the dead at his appearing (Acts 10:42; 17:31; Rom 14:9; 2 Tim 4:1). And he is the one whose once-for-all offering up of himself as a sacrifice to satisfy divine justice is alone acceptable to God the Father, the "legal" representative of the Godhead, in the "great transaction" of redemption and the canceling of sin (Heb 9:24-26), and whose high priestly intercession alone meets with the Father's approval (Rom 8:34; Heb 7:24-25; 1 John 2:1). In light of their exclusive claims for him, it is not surprising that the blessing and power of God rested upon the Apostles' evangelistic efforts.

TESTIMONIAL SIGNIFICANCE OF PENTECOST

It is not my intention, as we address the meaning of the event that took place on the day of Pentecost, to weary the reader with a detailed refutation of the view of E. Zeller, A. Loisy, and E. Haenchen that the event recorded in Acts 2 is wholly the dogmatic construct of Luke's theological genius, his own redactional adaptation of an early Jewish legend about the law-giving at Sinai in which God's voice is divided into seventy languages, which adaptation he intended as an explanation of the origin of the church. Suffice it to say, there is no evidence to suggest that Luke adapted a Jewish legend to serve this purpose and every reason to believe that Luke was simply recording under inspiration the occurrence of an event the historicity of which we have no reason to doubt. As a historian, Luke, we may assume, was reporting an incident that had roots deep in the earliest common Christian tradition concerning the first days of the church after Christ's resurrection and ascension.

As for the still-popular hypothesis associated with the name of E. von Dobschütz that the Pentecost event is actually a variant account of the resurrection appearance to the five hundred brethren which Paul mentions in 1 Corinthians 15:6 but stripped of its appearance features by Luke himself in order to highlight the distinctive significance of Pentecost, I would only say in response that it has nothing to commend it beyond the hypothesis itself. The most that one can say about it is that it is an interesting hypothesis that has no real supporting evidence beyond the powers of the imagination that would have it so.

Regarding the source-critical analysis of the event that would insist that Luke (or his source) took an account of an experience of ecstatic glossolalia from the primitive church and, under the influence of the Babel legend or his own theological interest to portray symbolically the church's universal embrace from its very inception, transformed it into a miracle of speaking foreign languages, it must be said again that such an approach lacks evidence, is highly subjective, and smacks of being an attempt to explain on purely rationalistic grounds what Luke clearly intended as a supernatural event of deep and abiding significance.

Finally, the modern attempts to explain the Acts account psychologically on the basis of what is known about and is still being learned from the modern Pentecostal movement, in my opinion, reverses the true order of things by making the modern movement the norm for determining the nature of the Pentecost event rather than making the Acts account the norm for evaluating the validity of the current occurrences of glossolalia.

Finding nothing in these proposals which commends them as a truer, more apparently real, historical accounting of what actually occurred on the day of Pentecost than the Lukan account itself, I propose to take the Acts account as a straight-forward narrative rendition of what actually occurred and set forth the evidence contained in it in support of the exalted and divine character of Christ.[49]

The Contextual Setting of Pentecost

The events that occurred on the Day of Pentecost are set in the context of Jesus' statement, made just prior to his ascension, that he would baptize his disciples with the Holy Spirit "in a few days" (Acts 1:5). In light of the teaching of Matthew 3:11, Mark 1:8, Luke 3:16, 24:49, and John 1:33, there can be no doubt that Jesus' statement, "you will be baptized" (Acts 1:5), when transposed from the passive into the active voice, means: "*I* will baptize you." (The reader should recall here also our earlier exposition of Jesus' act of breathing upon his disciples which is reported in John 20:22).

This fact—that *Jesus* baptized his church on that occasion—provides the hermeneutical paradigm for understanding the event of Pentecost, as I hope to show shortly.

The Facts of Pentecost

The facts of the event that took place that day are clear enough—the disciples waiting, in accordance with Christ's instruction, in Jerusalem for the empowering gift of the Holy Spirit; the sudden "sound from heaven like the rush of a strong wind" (may we say the sudden "amplified" sound of the "expulsion of breath" in view of John 20:22?); the "tongues" of fire that came to rest upon each of the disciples; and

---

[49]See James D. G. Dunn, *Jesus and the Spirit* (London: SCM, 1975), 136-52, for a detailed form-critical defense of the likelihood of the occurrence of the ecstatic speech on the day of Pentecost, in the course of which defense Dunn refutes the views mentioned above. It is regrettable that Dunn concludes that one can say no more, on the basis of Acts 2, than that a group of Jesus' disciples were suddenly caught up in a "communal experience of ecstatic worship," that others thought they recognized the words of praise to God in other languages (152), and that Luke is "only of marginal help" in providing an answer to the question of how the early Christians related the risen Christ to the Spirit as the source of their experience (156). Luke provides all the help one needs in coming to a conclusion on this matter if his account is only taken at face value.

the Spirit-wrought capacity to "declare the wonders of God" (2:11) in the "native languages" of the Jews present from the territorial regions of the then-known world (2:8-11)[50]—all these phenomena being interpreted by Luke himself as evidence that they had been "filled with the Holy Spirit" (2:4), this filling, it should be recalled, being described earlier by Christ as his "baptism" of them with the Holy Spirit.

What is not so clear, or perhaps more accurately, what is often misunderstood is the *meaning* of the event because men have tended to concentrate their attention either on the Holy Spirit who was "poured [or "breathed"] out" and/or on the empirical phenomena accompanying his "out-pouring"—rather than on the "Baptizer" himself, the one who did the "pouring."

And yet its meaning is patently clear, inasmuch as Peter, with enviable clarity, explained its meaning and significance in his sermon that followed in response to the people's query: "What does this mean?" (2:12). I propose now to "walk" the reader through Peter's sermon, that he may see for himself precisely what Peter said the events of Pentecost meant for the first disciples and what it should mean for the church as a whole.

The Meaning of Pentecost

The "Spirit-filling" meant, of course, for the disciples their "empowering" as witnesses—this we know from our Lord's own statements to that effect (Luke 24:49; Acts 1:8) and from Peter's sermon which as a Christian sermon classically illustrates the effect of this "empowering." But from the perspective of the history of redemption, it meant something else, and it is this "something else" that Peter brings out in his sermon.

Peter begins by citing Yahweh's promise in Joel 2:28-32a (he alludes later at the end of his sermon to Joel 2:32c) that in the last

---

[50]Luke's list of regions in Acts 2:9-11 is supposed by some scholars to reflect "the whole world" through his mention of nations and lands purportedly assigned to the twelve signs of the zodiac. But the evidence is nil that Luke has any interest in astrological matters. See Bruce M. Metzger, "Ancient Astrological Geography and Acts 2:9-11" in *Apostolic History and the Gospel*, 123-33.

days he would pour out his Spirit on all kinds of "flesh"—sons and daughters, young men and old men, and men and women servants (2:16-21). By his "This is that which was spoken by the prophet Joel" (2:16), Peter identifies the events of Pentecost as the inaugural fulfillment of that prophecy. Then he launches into his argument. I use the word "argument" here by studied choice, for that is precisely what the remainder of his discourse comprises—one grand, sustained argument from the event of Pentecost for the lordship and messianic investiture of Jesus Christ! There is hardly a word of teaching with respect to the person and work of the Holy Spirit! There is no word of exhortation on Peter's part to the effect that his audience should seek a glossolalic experience similar to that which the disciples were presently experiencing. Virtually everything he says focuses on the person and character of the work of Jesus Christ, even his closing appeal in 2:38-39 which includes a reference to the gift of the Holy Spirit whom all who repent and are baptized in the name of Jesus Christ will receive.

That his remarks are a sermonic "apologetic" in behalf of the lordship and messiahship of Jesus is apparent from the outset—from his opening remark after quoting the Joel prophecy to his concluding statement in 2:36. Three times in the course of his sermon he refers to "this Jesus." Let us hear him: first, "Men of Israel, listen to this: *Jesus* of Nazareth, a man who was *accredited* by God to you by powers, wonders, and signs which he did through him in your midst, as you yourselves know—*this one*...you killed, whom God raised, loosing the bonds of death..." (2:22-23a); second, "*This Jesus* God has raised..." (2:32); and third, "Therefore, let all the house of Israel know for certain that God has made him both Lord and Christ—*this Jesus* whom you crucified" (2:36). Further indication that Peter intended his remarks as an apologetic underscoring Jesus' lordship and messiahship may be seen in his reference to God's having *accredited* him by doing authenticating miracles through him, in his insistence that his audience knew of Jesus' mighty works, and in his concluding "therefore" statement in 2:36. All of these features indicate that Peter's remarks prior to his "therefore" are to be regarded as an argument intended to buttress the conclusion which he himself draws in 2:36. The implication is clear that Peter believed that he had said enough about Jesus prior to 2:36 to warrant such a conclusion as the one he draws for his listeners. What specifically had he said to warrant this conclusion?

To discover the answer to this question let us follow Peter's argument from the point of his remark in 2:24 to the effect that God had raised Jesus from death. Why had God so acted? "Because [καθότι, *kathoti*]," Peter says, "it was not possible for him to be held by it [that is, by "death"]." And why not? Because (γὰρ, *gar*), Peter declares, David had prophesied concerning Jesus' resurrection in Psalm 16:8-11. But how do we know that David was not speaking of himself when he wrote Psalm 16 since, after all, the Psalm is written in the first person? First of all, Peter says, because David died and was buried and his tomb is "with us to this very day" (2:29). In other words, because David died and his body saw decay. (Paul will use this same argument later in Acts 13:35-37.) And second, Peter says, because David, "being a prophet, and knowing that God had sworn with an oath to seat one of his descendants on his [that is, God's] throne—knowing this beforehand, he spoke concerning the resurrection of the Messiah that 'he was not abandoned to the grave, nor did his body see decay'" (2:30-31). In short, Peter's argument is as follows: David was obviously speaking of the Messiah's resurrection and not his own in Psalm 16 because he died and was not raised to life, and because, as an inspired prophet, he had been informed of the Messiah's resurrection and enthronement and thus, under inspiration, had written about these matters.

Before we proceed further with Peter's argument, it is imperative that I call the reader's attention to the fact that I purposely emphasized in my translation the "throne" as God's throne. I did this because it is evident when David spoke of the Messiah's glory that he was laboring under no illusion that the Messiah was to be raised from death to sit upon his (David's) earthly throne. Rather, "being a prophet," he knew that God was going to raise his descendant, God's Messiah, from the dead to sit on his (God's) heavenly throne. How do we know this? First, because, and here we use Peter's own argument from history, upon his resurrection the Messiah did not mount an earthly throne of David. Rather, he ascended to heaven and sat down on God's throne. And in the sense that any throne upon which the messianic Son of

David sat would become by that very act the Davidic throne, God's throne itself became the "Davidic throne." And second, because David, according to Peter, made it perfectly clear that this heavenly enthronement is what he had in mind. He did so by implication in Psalm 16 itself when he has the resurrected Messiah say: "...you will fill me with joy *in your presence*, with eternal pleasures *at your right hand"* (16:11), and he did so expressly in Psalm 110:1 where he reports that Yahweh said to his Messiah: "Sit at my right hand" (see Matt 26:64 and parallels).

Let us now return to our "walk" through Peter's discourse, intercepting his thought at the point where we left it at 2:33: "Having been exalted to the right hand of God...." Here Peter refers to Jesus, with David's description of his exaltation in Psalm 110 in mind. But how do we know that David was speaking of the Messiah's exaltation in Psalm 110? How do we know that he was not reflecting upon his own exaltation in the third person? Because, Peter says, "David did not ascend to heaven" (2:34)—here Peter employs the same form of argument that he had used earlier, even the argument from history—"and yet he said, 'The Lord said to my Lord, sit [the same root as the one Peter had employed earlier in 2:30] at my right hand.'" The conclusion is clear: David was not speaking of himself in Psalm 110:1 but of the Messiah, not only his descendant "according to the flesh" but also his Lord, who would be exalted to the right hand of God, every detail of which prophecy had been accomplished in Jesus.

To this point, with consummate skill, Peter has demonstrated that all that had come to pass with respect to "this Jesus" David had forecast of the Messiah, and accordingly, that David had prophesied that "this Jesus" as the Messiah would be raised from the dead (Ps 16:10) and would be exalted to God's right hand (Pss 16:11 and 110:1). But now we must ask, how does all of this relate to the event of Pentecost itself? Why did Peter use this occasion to argue the case for the messiahship of Jesus? There can be no doubt concerning the answer: Peter is transparently clear about the connection between the events that had just occurred and their meaning for Jesus himself: "Having been exalted to the right hand of God, and having received the promise of the Holy Spirit from the Father [note the implication in his reference to "the Father" that the Messiah is at the right hand of "the Father" as "the Son"], he [that is, Jesus] has poured out this which you now see and hear" (2:33). What is the significance of this? When we recall the "accrediting" character of his previous miracles—the point that Peter had underscored at the outset of his discourse—it becomes clear that for Peter the event of Pentecost is to be viewed as a further tangible, concrete, miraculous self-attestation on Jesus' part that he was the Messiah. This is why Peter believed that he could conclude his remarks with his ringing "therefore": "*Therefore*, [that is, in light of (1) the attesting miracles which God performed through him during his years of earthly ministry, which miracles you, my listeners, cannot deny, (2) David's Old Testament prophecies concerning him, and (3) now Jesus' present miraculous self-attestation from heaven that it is he who is the Spirit-Baptizer of men], let all the house of Israel know for certain that both Lord and Christ God has made him—*this Jesus* whom you crucified."

Peter's argument is complete, and he has driven home the meaning of that event. What then is the significance of the event that occurred on the Day of Pentecost? It is not to be found primarily in the fact that the Holy Spirit had been manifested in a unique and striking fashion but rather in the fact that Jesus, the exalted Lord and Messiah, by this further display of his authority and power had attested once again to his lordship and messianic investiture before the nation of Israel by "breathing upon" ("baptizing") his disciples. C. H. Dodd's insight is to the point in this regard, capturing the significance of Pentecost in these simple words: "...the Holy Spirit in the Church is the sign of Christ's present power and glory."[51] Jesus was also demonstrating to Israel by the particular character of this miracle that resident with him, as the Baptizer, was the authority to bless and to curse, to make alive and to kill, to save and to damn, as John the Baptist had earlier said. And in light of the force of the present participle in John's statement in John 1:33 ("this one is *the one who baptizes* with the Holy Spirit"), the Pentecostal "outpouring" simply illustrates the fact that it ever had been so in the past as well as for the present and the

---

[51]C. H. Dodd, *The Apostolic Preaching and Its Developments* (London: Hodder and Stoughton, 1936), 42. See also I. Howard Marshall's comment in *Luke: Historian and Theologian* (Exeter: Paternoster, 1970), 161-62: "The main theme is not so much the Spirit as the Lord."

future: *this Jesus* was, is, and always will be the Lord of Salvation!

But because men's minds have tended to focus on the empirical phenomena of Pentecost rather than on the Baptizer himself, the church's understanding today of the significance of Pentecost has become warped and distorted, with the point which Scripture itself emphasizes now being forgotten or minimized. The point of emphasis today has shifted away from viewing the miracle as a self-attestation to Israel of Christ's saving Lordship and has come to rest all too often and in too many quarters upon the person and work of the Holy Spirit. Thus the true significance of the event has been well-nigh lost or marginalized. But when it is kept clearly in mind as one reads and studies Acts 2 that it was the risen Christ who was actively engaged that day in attesting once again in a grand, climactic way to his saving prerogatives as Israel's Lord and Messiah, it will become evident both how erroneous it is, on the one hand, to represent Christ's present session at the Father's right hand as a state of relative inactivity save for his intercessory work, with the Holy Spirit now setting about the task of applying the benefits of Christ's accomplished work of redemption to men, and how perceptively correct the framers of the *Westminster Confession of Faith* were, on the other hand, when, representing the work of the risen Christ, they wrote:

> To all those for whom Christ hath purchased redemption, *he doth certainly and effectually apply and communicate the same*, making intercession for them, and revealing unto them, in and by the Word, the mysteries of salvation; effectually persuading them by his Spirit to believe and obey; and governing their hearts by his Word and Spirit; overcoming all their enemies by his almighty power and wisdom, in such manner and ways as are most consonant to his wonderful and unsearchable dispensation. (VIII, viii, emphasis supplied)

The Westminster divines are here, of course, only stating in a different fashion what they confess elsewhere when they affirm that Christ executes the offices of prophet, priest, and king, not only in his estate of humiliation but also in his estate of exaltation (*Shorter Catechism*, Questions 23-28).

Here then, in a sentence, is the real significance of Pentecost in the history of redemption: *It was Jesus' further self-attestation to the truth that he was Israel's Lord and Messiah.* And the non-repeatable so-called "Samaritan Pentecost" (Acts 8:14-17) and the non-repeatable so-called "Gentile [or, "ends of the earth"] Pentecost" (Acts 10:44-46) are to be viewed in the same light: both were Jesus' self-attestations to the church and to the people involved, at the critical junctures of the missionary endeavor which he himself had delineated in Acts 1:8, of his messiahship and saving lordship over the nations (see 8:14; 11:17-18).

Implications for Jesus' Deity

In explaining the significance of Pentecost, Peter also said certain things that carry implications with respect to Jesus' divine character. To these features of his discourse—four in number—we now want to turn.

First, the very fact of his ascension and, more particularly, of his session at his Father's right hand suggests that Jesus is divine, for he who would sit as "Lord" over all the nations on the throne of God must himself be God.[52] Certainly, his session on the throne of God attests to his super-angelic nature, for "to which of the angels did God ever say, 'Sit at my right hand until I make your enemies a footstool for your feet'"? F. F. Bruce has well commented here:

> The most exalted angels are those whose privilege it is to "stand in the presence of God" like Gabriel (Luke 1:19), but none of them has ever been invited to sit before Him, still less to sit in the place of unique honor at His right hand.[53]

---

[52]Warfield, *The Lord of Glory*, 211, writes:

> In Peter's Pentecostal sermon Jesus is conceived as sitting at the right hand of God (2:34) and as having been constituted "both Lord and Christ," where the conjunction is significant (2:36): and more explicitly still He is designated in a later discourse of the same Peter, "Lord of all" (10:36), that is to say, universal sovereign, a phrase which recalls the great declaration of Rom. 9:5 to the effect that He is "God over all," *as indeed He who sits on the throne of God must be.* (emphasis supplied)

[53]F. F. Bruce, *Commentary on the Epistle to the Hebrews* (Grand Rapids: Eerdmans, 1964), 24.

To the divine Son alone, the Author of Hebrews affirms, this honor has been accorded (Heb 1:4, 13).

Second, the fact that it was the ascended *Jesus* who poured out the Spirit (2:33) moves in the same direction, for the connection between what Peter expressly emphasized in 2:17 by his deliberate insertion of the words "God says" into the Joel prophecy ("'In the last days,' *God says*, '*I will pour out* my spirit'") and his later statement in 2:33 ("*he* [the ascended Jesus] *has poured out* this which you now see and hear") can not have been unintentional or lost on Peter. Clearly, Peter connects the God and Yahweh of Joel 2 who promised to pour out his Spirit to the ascended Jesus of Acts 2 who poured out his Spirit.

Third, the fact that the authority to apply the benefits of his redemption by his Spirit to whomever he pleases in his role as Baptizer of men by his Spirit (salvation) and by fire (judgment) means nothing less than that the prerogatives and functions of deity are his to exercise, but then this means that he himself is God.

Fourth, when Peter, in response to his listeners' query: "Brothers, what shall we do?," urged them to "repent and be baptized *in the name of Jesus Christ*"(2:38), it is difficult to avoid the conclusion that he was simply urging them to avail themselves of the remedy which Joel himself had prescribed in his prophecy when he said: "And everyone who calls on *the name of the Lord* will be saved" (Acts 2:21). But then this means, in turn, that for Peter Jesus was the Lord of Joel 2:32a (see Rom 10:9-13) which means in turn that Jesus was the Yahweh who spoke through Joel.[54]

We discover from these features, then, that the event of Pentecost in its own striking way adds its testimony to the combined and consentient witness of Scripture to Christ's messianic investiture and his divine nature.

* * * * *

---

[54]Marshall, *Luke: Historian and Theologian*, 163, writes: "Peter spoke in Joel's words...of the need to call upon the name of the Lord in order to be saved. The effect of the argument is to show that Jesus is the Lord in the prophecy of Joel."

In this chapter we have considered four historical events—Jesus' resurrection, his pre-ascension ministry, his ascension, and Pentecost—for the light they throw on the nature of his Sonship and messianic status. Each in its own way provided data which the church has employed in confessing Jesus to be the Christ and both very God and very man and thus God incarnate.

Along the way we considered alternative interpretations to the church's historic understanding of Jesus' resurrection and found them wanting in that they fail to explain the story itself, Easter faith, or the church which emerged from the story. We saw that virtually from the moment of his resurrection the church confessed him as Son of God in the divine sense, Thomas even employing the noun θεός, *theos*, itself as a Christological title for Jesus a week after his resurrection. Both his ascension and the Pentecost event also highlighted his status as both Lord of the universe and Lord of the church.

We will now turn to the New Testament letters for the light which they shed on Jesus' identity. We will take up Paul's testimony in the next chapter and then address the remaining non-Pauline New Testament witness to Jesus in the final chapter of our study.

CHAPTER SIX

PAUL'S WITNESS TO JESUS

After the events of the Day of Pentecost, the risen Christ continued to display his divine power in the recorded events of Acts (see Luke's suggestive phrase in this regard, "all that Jesus *began* to do" in Acts 1:1), for example, in the healing of the crippled man at the temple gate called Beautiful (3:6, 12-13, 16; 4:9-10), in the many miracles performed through the Apostles among the people (Acts 5:12), in his self-revelation to Stephen as "the Son of Man standing at the right hand of God" in that first Christian martyr's moment of death (7:55-56), and in the so-called "Samaritan Pentecost" (Acts 8:14-17). But it is surely arguable that no post-ascension act by the risen Christ has ever rivaled in the significance of its effect on the on-going world-wide life of the church for all time to come his post-ascension appearance to his arch-foe, Saul of Tarsus, on the road to Damascus, sometime between A.D. 32 and A.D. 35, the record of which is found in Acts 9:3-18; 22:6-16; 26:12-18 (see also 1 Cor 9:1; 15:8).

THE HISTORICITY OF PAUL'S CONVERSION

So significant is Saul's conversion that it is not too much to say that if he was not converted as the Acts accounts report not only is Luke/ Acts, taken together as a corporate whole, rendered immediately and directly a false witness to history, but the Pauline literary corpus, in whole and in part, is also rendered invalid as a trustworthy rule for faith and practice because Paul claimed in all of his letters to be a legitimate Apostle, meeting all of the requirements of one who would be an Apostle, particularly the one Peter mentions in Acts 1:22: "a witness of his resurrection." Paul claimed to have "seen Jesus our Lord" (1 Cor 9:1). He claimed that Jesus "last of all,...appeared unto me also" (1 Cor 15:8). He claimed that he had received his commission as an Apostle "not from men nor by [any] man, but by Jesus Christ"

(Gal 1:1). And he claimed that he neither received his gospel from nor was he taught his gospel by any man, but to the contrary, and I quote him directly: "I received it by revelation from Jesus Christ" (ablative use of the genitive) (Gal 1:12). So I repeat, it is not overstating the case to say that if Paul was *not* converted as Acts reports his conversion, then the Pauline corpus is no longer a trustworthy guide in matters of faith and practice, and also the church itself, honoring Paul as it so self-consciously does as a true Apostle of Jesus Christ, is a false witness to God. But no less certain is it that if Paul *was* converted as Acts reports his conversion, then this single event in a unique way establishes and validates not only the divine character of the Son of God but also the heavenly origination of Paul's teaching and the authenticity of the church's other teachings.

It should surprise no one, then, to learn that a vast literature, both pro and con, has grown up around the man Paul and the origin of his message. In fact, the literature on Paul's conversion along with its implications for his ministry is so absolutely enormous that I can do little more than recommend a few of the better evangelical treatments of the subject.[1] Moreover, I can do little more than mention the kinds of negative theories that have been advanced to explain on naturalistic grounds this extremely important event in the life of Saul of Tarsus and of the church which reveres his memory, and offer a few remarks by way of rebuttal.

Three extreme rationalizations of the event are that Saul either suffered an epileptic seizure of some kind or suffered a sun stroke or, seeing a flash of lightning which blinded him and being thrown from

---

[1] I would recommend James Stalker, *The Apostle Paul* (Edinburgh: T. & T. Clark, 1889), J. Gresham Machen, *The Origin of Paul's Religion* (Reprint; Grand Rapids: Eerdmans, 1965), H. N. Ridderbos, *Paul and Jesus*, translated by David H. Freeman (Nutley, New Jersey: Presbyterian and Reformed, 1957); Richard N. Longenecker, *Paul, Apostle of Liberty* (New York: Harper & Row, 1964) and his *The Ministry and Message of Paul* (Grand Rapids: Zondervan, 1971); F. F. Bruce, *Paul: Apostle of the Free Spirit* (Reprint; Grand Rapids: Eerdmans, 1996); S. Kim, *The Origin of Paul's Gospel* (Second edition; Tübingen, Mohr, 1984); and Ben Witherington III, *The Paul Quest: The Renewed Search for the Jew of Tarsus* (Downers Grove, Illinois: InterVarsity, 1998)); Those readers interested in further reading are advised to consult the extensive bibliographies provided in these works.

his horse when the horse became startled and bolted at the same flash of lightning from under him, struck his head on the ground and in the daze that resulted imagined that he had seen the Lord. But these explanations have not commended themselves generally even to the critical mind. More popular is the view that, under the stress of his fanatical persecution of the church, Saul suffered a mental breakdown on the road to Damascus and in this broken mental state imagined that the Lord of the very ones he was persecuting had called upon him to desist in his persecution and instead to serve him. But probably the most popular naturalistic explanation is that Saul was sub-consciously being conditioned by the logic of the Christian position plus the dynamic quality of the Christians' lives and their fortitude under oppression. Then, it is said, when he underwent that "mood-changing" crisis experience on the road to Damascus, the precise nature of which we are now unable to recover, he became convinced because of this prior sub-conscious pre-conditioning of mind and psyche that he should become a follower of Christ rather than his persecutor. But such psychologico/psychoanalytic solutions leave too many questions unanswered. In addition to the impossibility of psychoanalyzing a person who lived almost two thousand years ago with any degree of clinical accuracy, what real evidence is there that Saul suffered a mental breakdown? And what was the nature of the crisis experience that triggered it? Such questions as these, and many more besides, must be answered satisfactorily before any credence can be given to these theories.

Then there is Rudolf Bultmann who believed that all such depictions of "biblical supernaturalism" are actually reflections of ancient "mythology," but his own explanation of Saul's conversion is wholly unsatisfactory in that it fails to come to terms to any degree with the historical character of the Acts narrative itself: "Not having been a personal disciple of Jesus, *he was won to the Christian faith by the kerygma of the Hellenistic church*."[2] But neither is James D. G. Dunn's view much better when he concludes that it is impossible to know for sure whether Jesus was "'out there,' alive and making himself known to Paul." All that one can say with any certainty, Dunn

---

[2]Rudolf Bultmann, *Theology of the New Testament* (London: SCM, 1952) I, 187; emphasis original.

continues, is that "Paul himself was convinced that what he saw was external to him" but it may have been "after all, all 'in the mind.'"[3]

Krister Stendahl has even argued that Saul's experience of meeting the glorified Christ on the Damascus Road, since it involved no change of religion or change of Gods but only a change in assignments, was not a conversion at all but rather a new call.[4] In fact, says Stendahl, the traditional understanding of Saul's Damascus Road experience as a conversion experience is due more to the West's introspective readings of Augustine and Luther than to the New Testament documents.[5]

---

[3]James D. G. Dunn, *Jesus and the Spirit* (Philadelphia: Westminster, 1975), 107-08.

[4]Krister Stendahl, *Paul Among Jews and Gentiles and Other Essays* (Philadelphia: Fortress, 1976), 7-23.

[5]Is Stendahl correct when he contends that it is doubtful whether Paul was ever stricken with guilt, that his conscience was robust, both before and after the Damascus Road experience, and that Western theology has introspectively read the conversion experiences of Augustine and Luther back into Luke's Acts and Paul's letters? I would urge that not only has the Western church not read Augustine and Luther back into Paul; neither Augustine nor Luther read their own conversion experience directly and singularly in the light of Paul's.

While it is true that Augustine in his *Retractations* of A.D. 396 argued that Saul's "fierce, savage, and blind will" was suddenly "turned from [its] fierceness and set on the right way towards faith," and then in his *Confessions* of c. A.D. 400 saw himself in his new evaluation of Paul, it must be noted that what he found in common between himself and Paul was not a troubled conscience but a vanquished will. Interpreting Romans 7:14-25 as he did as the experience of Paul the Christian, not Saul the persecutor, the previous comparison was not open to him.

Not even Martin Luther, with whom Paul's conversion has been so often compared in modern church history, was converted to Christ the way Paul was. There was much time and distance between the lightning bolt that drove Luther into the Augustinian monastery at Erfurt and his later "tower experience" at Wittenberg in which he came to understand the meaning of the "righteousness of God" in Romans 1:17 and thus was finally delivered from his hostility toward God. Luther himself seems to have had relatively little interest in Paul's conversion as a topic of reflection and preaching, nor does he draw an analogy between his own spiritual struggle with a "troubled conscience" and Paul's experience. His view of Romans 7:14-25, holding as he did Augustine's interpretation of the passage, would not permit him to do so.

Such conclusions, as I have said, frankly fail to come to terms with Luke's historical narrative (in the third person) in Acts 9 or with Paul's later accounts (in the first person) in Acts 22 and 26, given on the formal occasions of defending his office and actions under the auspices of the Roman commander and before high government dignitaries respectively. There are pertinent data which indicate that his conversion was simply not merely mentally induced. We are expressly informed that, while Saul alone saw Jesus, the men who were traveling with him both heard a voice (9:7), though they did not understand the words (22:9), and saw the brilliant light (22:9; 26:13-14). And while it is true that Paul would later call the event a "vision from heaven" (26:19), which description itself imputes an *ab extra* character to it ("*from* heaven"), the accounts make it clear that his conversion was not subjectively self-induced in the sub-conscious mind of Saul but, rather, that it resulted from an initiating action external to him (9:3-4; 22:6-7; 26:13-14). Indeed, the ascended Christ represents *himself* as the Initiator in 26:16: "I have appeared to you" (ὤφθην σοι, *ōphthēn soi*). And Ananias will say later that God had chosen Saul "to see the Righteous One and to hear words from his mouth" (22:14). When all the facts in Acts 9, 22, 26, and 1 Corinthians 15 are taken into account, Longenecker's judgment seems clearly justified:

> Only the Damascus encounter with Christ was powerful enough to cause the young Jewish rabbi to reconsider the death of Jesus; only his meeting with the risen Christ was sufficient to demonstrate that God had vindicated the claims and work of the One he was opposing. Humanly speaking, Paul was immune to the Gospel. Although he was ready to follow evidence to its conclusion, he was sure that no evidence could overturn the verdict of the cross; that is, that Christ died the death of a criminal. But...the eternal God "was pleased," as Paul says by way of reminiscence, "to reveal his Son to me" (Gal 1:16). Thus Paul was arrested by Christ, and made His own (Phil 3:12).[6]

---

[6]Richard N. Longenecker, *The Ministry and Message of Paul*, 34-5. I must add to Longenecker's suggested reason for Saul's immunity to the gospel the additional reason that faith in Christ's obedience for salvation was surely for him incompatible with his Judaistic inclination to rely upon his own obedience to the law for salvation (see Jacques Dupont, "The Conversion of Paul, and Its Influence on His Understanding of Salvation by

As for Stendahl's view, Saul would later describe his experience much more radically than simply the receiving of a new assignment. In 1 Corinthians 15:8 he speaks of it as of the nature of an "irregular birth"—he was "one abnormally born" (an ἔκτρωμα,[7] *ektrōma*). In Philippians 3:12, he speaks of it as an "arrest"—he "was apprehended [κατελήμφθην, *katelēmphthēn*] by Christ Jesus." In Galatians 1:13 he speaks of his "*previous* [ποτε, *pote*] life in Judaism,"[8] setting his former religious experience off over against "the church *of God* [τὴν ἐκκλησίαν τοῦ θεοῦ, *tēn ekklēsian tou theou*," implying by this contrast that the one living and true God was in the church but not in Judaism. In Philippians 3:4-8 he declares that he had come to regard his prior "Judaic" reasons for confidence in the flesh as "rubbish" (σκύβαλα, *skubala*), which suggests a radical and complete break with his "Judaic" past. And in transferring his confidence as he did, in

---

Faith" in *Apostolic History and the Gospel*, edited by W. Ward Gasque and Ralph P. Martin (Exeter: Paternoster, 1970), 178-94. E. P. Sanders has argued in his *Paul and Palestinian Judaism* (Philadelphia: Fortress, 1977) that Palestinian Judaism was not a religion of legalistic works-righteousness wherein right standing before God was earned by good works in a system of strict justice. It is true, of course, as Sanders points out, that one can indeed find references in the literature of the period to God's election of Israel and to his grace and mercy. But Sanders makes too much of these facts since Palestinian Judaism also taught that the elect man was obligated, even though he would do so imperfectly, to obey the law in order to *remain* in the covenant. Thus the legalistic principle was still present and ultimately governed the soteric status of the individual. But Paul rightly saw that any obligation to accomplish a "works-righteousness" on the sinner's part would negate the principle of *sola gratia* altogether (Rom 11:6). For a detailed critical analysis of Sanders' thesis, see Karl T. Cooper, "Paul and Rabbinic Soteriology" in *Westminster Theological Journal* 44 (1982): 123-139.

[7]Bruce (*Paul*, 86) understands Paul's descriptive term to mean "an abortion." George Eldon Ladd (*A Theology of the New Testament* [Grand Rapids: Eerdmans, 1974], 367-68) takes it to mean "an abnormal birth" in the sense that Christ appeared to Saul "after [he] had ceased to appear to the other disciples").

[8]The term Ἰουδαϊσμος ("Judaism") only occurs twice in the New Testament—in Galatians 1:13-14. It first appears in 2 Macabbees 2:21; 8:1; 14:38, apparently having been coined to express opposition to "Hellenism" (2 Mac 4:13). In every instance it denotes the national Jewish religion and way of life.

his search for personal righteousness before God, away from personal obedience to the Mosaic law and the temple ritual to the cross-work of Jesus Christ who was the fulfillment and embodiment respectively of these two central features of the Old Testament, Saul in fact created a new religious pattern for others to follow. For while it is true that Saul continued to think of himself as a Jew, his radical reinterpretation of the Mosaic covenant and its Law as a "glorious anachronism (2 Cor 3; see Gal 4)"[9] and his rejection of the Gentile's need for circumcision for salvation did in fact constitute for him a religious conversion—a conversion away from Second Temple "Judaism," the man-made deconstruction of Old Testament Yahwism (see Mark 7:6-8), to New Covenant Yahwism, the fulfillment of Old Testament religion, which fulfillment later came to be called "Christianity."[10] Of course, his conversion at first was more principial than substantive since it originally amounted in content to little more than his new conscious faith in Jesus Christ as the Son of God and Jewish Messiah (Acts 9:20, 22) plus the logical implicates of that new faith, and since the maturation of his thought as a Christian apostle had to await the spiritual struggles and controversies of the mission field for its fullest development. And, of course, his conversion to Christ was also

---

[9]The phrase is Ben Witherington III's, found in his *The Paul Quest: The Renewed Search for the Jew of Tarsus*, 78.

[10]Bible students should draw a distiction between the religion of the Old Testament and Judaism. The former is rightly designated Yahwism—the worship and service that Yahweh required in the Abrahamic and Mosaic covenants—while Judaism is the postexilic deconstruction of Old Testament Yahwism that the rabbinic schools erected around the law in such sources as the Babylonian Talmud in order to make Yahwism compatible with and applicable to the Jews' lack of access to land and to Temple. The two are *not* the same and are *not* compatible, as Jesus so clearly declared (Mark 7:6-8), the former urging "the commands of God," the latter urging "the traditions of men" which nullified (ἀκυροῦντες, ***akurountes***) the Word of God (7:13; see also his condemnation of Judaism's handling of the Word of God in Matt 15:3-9 and Matt 23). On the other hand, "new covenant" Christianity is simply the administrative extension and unfolding of the Abrahamic covenant, which is just to say that the spiritual blessings which Christians enjoy today under Jeremiah's "new covenant" (31:31-34) are founded on the Abrahamic covenant.

accompanied by his call to be the apostle to the nations.[11]

In support of the "revealedness" and truth-character of his own apostleship and the gospel he proclaimed we can produce no better argument than the one which Paul himself adduced in Galatians 1:13-2:10 when he was defending his apostolic calling. The issue that he tacitly raised there and that we must now face is, in one sentence: What was the ultimate origin of Paul's gospel and his apostolic commission? It is evident that he could have obtained his gospel and the authority to preach it from only one of three possible sources. Let us look at each of these possibilities in turn.

His Judaistic Training?

Did Paul obtain the gospel he was preaching after his conversion from his previous life in Judaism? To ask the question is to answer it. Certainly not! Paul himself describes his experience in Judaism for us five different times:

> For you have heard of my previous way of life in Judaism, how intensely I persecuted the church of God and tried to destroy it. I was advancing in Judaism beyond many Jews of my own age and was extremely zealous for the tradition of my fathers (Gal 1:13-14).

> I am a Jew, born in Tarsus of Cilicia, brought up in this city at the feet of Gamaliel, thoroughly trained in the law of our fathers, being zealous for God (Acts 22:3).

> The Jews all know the way I have lived ever since I was a child, from the beginning of my life in my own country, and also in Jerusalem. They have known me for a long time and can testify, if they are willing, that according to the strictest sect of our religion, I lived as a Pharisee (26:4-5).

> If anyone else thinks he has reasons to put confidence in the flesh, I have more: circumcised on the eighth day, of the people of Israel, of

---

[11]See Janet Meyer Everts, "Conversion and Call of Paul" in *Dictionary of Paul and His Letters*, edited by Gerald F. Hawthorne, Ralph P. Martin, and Daniel G. Reid (Downers Grover, Ill.: InterVarsity, 1993), 156-63.

> the tribe of Benjamin, a Hebrew of the Hebrews; in regard to the law, a Pharisee; as for zeal,[12] persecuting the church; as for legalistic righteousness, faultless (Phil 3:4-6).

> I was once a blasphemer and a persecutor and a violent man (1 Tim. 1:13).

---

[12]In these biographical sketches of his life in Judaism Paul speaks in the following ways of the zeal that he had then: he was "extremely zealous" for the traditions of the fathers, he was "zealous for God," and "as for zeal, [I was] persecuting the church." But as far as we know Saul was never involved in the political movement of the Jewish Zealots who sought Rome's overthrow, so what did he mean when he described himself as a "zealot"? Rooted in the consciousness of the Jewish zealot as Paul seemed to use the term was the conviction that Israel's God, whose very name is "Zealot" (קַנָּא, *qannā'*, Ex 34:14), was a "jealous" or "zealot" God (Ex 20:5; 34:14; Deut 4:24; 5:9; 6:15; the Hebrew word underlying our English "jealous" in these verses [קַנָּא, *qannā'*], as is true also of the Greek, means both "jealous" and "zealous"). Then in Israel's history certain "heroes of zeal" were singled out by Israel's God for their "zeal" in preserving Yahweh's honor: (1) Yahweh commends Phinehas who, seeing an Israelite man bring a Midianite woman into his tent, ran them both through with his spear: "he was zealous [בְּקַנְאוֹ, *ḇᵉqan'ô*]...for my honor [קִנְאָתִי, *qin'āthî*] among them, so that in my zeal [בְּקִנְאָתִי, *bᵉqin'āthî*] I did not put an end to them...he was zealous [קִנֵּא, *qinnē'*] for the honor of his God" (Num 25:6-13; see Ps 106:30-31; Sir 45:23-24; 1 Macc 2:54); (2) Yahweh commended Jehu for his "zeal [בְּקִנְאָתִי, *bᵉqin'āthî*] for the Lord" in killing Ahab's descendents (2 Kgs 10:16-17, 30). Later Jewish tradition commended Simeon and his brothers for avenging the rape of their sister Dinah (Gen 34:25-26) even though Jacob condemned their treachery (Gen 34:30; 49:5-7): "thy beloved sons burned with zeal for you [O Yahweh] and abhorred the pollution of their blood" (Judith 9:2-4; for its commendation of Levi's zeal in the same incident, see Jub 30:8 and Test. of Levi 6:3), and it commended Elijah for the zeal he displayed in the slaying of the prophets of Baal (1 Kgs 18:40; see Sir 48:2-3; 1 Macc 2:58). These men were commended for their violent deeds, especially against *fellow Jews* who in some way had dishonored God. In sum, whereas for Christians today zeal is what propels one to prayer or to evangelism or to works of charity, to the first-century Jew zeal was what one showed with a knife against an infidel Jew. It was this kind of zeal that Paul most likely intended when he referred to his life in Judaism as the life of a "zealot" who burned "beyond measure" (καθ' ὑπερβολὴν, *kath hyperbolēn*, Gal 1:13) with "persecuting zeal" for the honor of "the tradition of the fathers" against its enemies.

It is evident from these autobiographical descriptions that Paul was not proclaiming as the Christian Apostle what he had learned from his life in Judaism. As the Christian Apostle, just to the contrary, he directed men's trust away from personal law-keeping where his own had resided as a Pharisee and toward Jesus Christ.

Apostolic Training and Authorization?

Did he obtain the gospel he was preaching after his conversion, if not at the feet of Gamaliel, at the feet of the Apostles? Listen to Paul again:

> ...when God...was pleased to reveal his Son to me..., I did not consult any man nor did I go up to Jerusalem to see those who were apostles before I was, but I went immediately into Arabia and later returned to Damascus (Gal 1:15-17).

In this connection, there is separate evidence, if Paul intended by this reference to Arabia to refer to the Nabataean Kingdom, that Paul did not simply devote himself to a life of quiet contemplation in Arabia after his conversion but in fact immediately began to missionarize the populace there. Paul informs us in 2 Corinthians 11:32-33 that "the governor under King Aretas guarded the city of Damascus in order to seize me," but one does not stir up the kind of trouble he alludes to in the Corinthians passage merely by meditation. This would suggest that long before he made any contact with the Jerusalem Apostles Paul had already engaged himself in Gentile evangelism.

Then Paul informs us under a self-imposed oath (see 1:20: "I assure you before God that what I am writing to you is no lie.") that three years passed after his conversion before he finally met any of the Apostles, and then it was only Peter and James he met, and even then it was for only the space of fifteen days (Gal 1:18-19). This was doubtless the visit Luke records in Acts 9:26-28, and while it is likely that it was at this time that he "received" the precise details about Jesus' post-resurrection appearances, particularly those to Peter and James, that he later "delivered" to the Corinthians in 1 Corinthians 15:5-7, it is evident, since they had no opportunity, that the Apostles conferred no authority on him at that time. Furthermore, Paul assures his reader, "I was personally unknown to the churches of Judea" (Gal 1:22). Then Paul declares that another eleven years passed (I am assuming the correctness of the South Galatia theory here) before he saw the Apostles again, this time on the occasion of his so-called "famine-relief" visit to Jerusalem recorded in Acts 11:27-30. On this second occasion, Paul informs us, "I set before [the Apostles] the gospel that I preach among the Gentiles" (Gal 2:2). The outcome of this presentation, which surely would have included his view of Christ himself, was that the Apostles "added nothing to my message" (2:6), but to the contrary, they saw "that I had been entrusted with the gospel" (2:7), that "God who was at work in Peter as an Apostle to the circumcision was also at work in me [as an Apostle] to the Gentiles" (2:8), and they "gave me the right hand of fellowship" (2:10). In other words, they again conferred no authority to preach on him but rather only acknowledged the authority which was already his by virtue of which he had been engaged in his apostolic ministry among the Gentiles for many years. We conclude, then, that throughout this entire fourteen-year period (Gal 2:1)—during the three-year period preceding his first visit to Jerusalem and during the eleven-year period preceding his second visit to Jerusalem—beginning immediately (Acts 9:20), Paul was "proclaiming Jesus, that this One is the Son of God" (Acts 9:20), "proving that this One is the Messiah" (9:22), and "preaching the faith that he once tried to destroy" (Gal 1:23)—a ministry that was only much later to be personally and directly acknowledged as authentic by the other Apostles.

Divine Call and Authorization!

Now if Paul was not preaching what he had learned during his life in Judaism, it is also clear from his summary of the first fourteen years of his apostolic ministry that he was not preaching what he had learned from the original Apostles either. Nor had they conferred authority on him to execute his ministry as an Apostle. But then this means that the gospel he was proclaiming he received neither from his Judaistic training *before* his conversion nor from apostolic indoctrination *after* his conversion. The only remaining alternative is that he was proclaiming a gospel which he received, as he says, in and from his conversion experience itself—"by revelation from Jesus Christ" (Gal 1:12)!

This does not mean, of course, that Saul had known nothing before his conversion about Jesus Christ or about the church's doctrinal teaching concerning him. He knew some of these matters well enough, for he had confronted them often enough. What it does mean is that Jesus' post-ascension appearance to Saul on the Damascus Road forced upon him an entirely new "hermeneutical context" into which he had to place not only his understanding of Jesus' person and work but also his previous Judaistic instruction concerning law and grace.[13]

Nor does it mean that Paul did not grow in his understanding of Christ during those fourteen years, for indeed, he continued to grow in his knowledge of Christ to the very end of his life (Phil 3:10-14). What it does mean is that in all his "growing up" and maturation in the faith he never "grew away" from that first clear "vision from heaven," as Stalker so poignantly suggests when he writes: "His whole theology is nothing but the explication of his own conversion."[14]

Given then the fact and historicity of Jesus' post-ascension appearance to Saul and the details which we have rehearsed regarding his ministry, there is no legitimate reason to question (1) Paul's apostolic calling which he declared he received "not from men, nor through man, but through Jesus Christ and God the Father" (Gal 1:1)—an expression which many New Testament scholars suggest, because of the contrast Paul draws between "men" and "man" on the one hand and "Jesus Christ and God the Father" on the other is itself an implicit assertion of Christ's divine character, (2) the Lord's continuing leading throughout his ministry (see Acts 13:2-3; 16:6-10; 18:9-11; 20:22; 22:17-21 [see 9:28-30]; 23:11; 27:23-24; see also 2 Cor 12:1-10), (3) his exercise of the signs of an Apostle (2 Cor 12:11-12; see Acts 14:3, 8-10), or (4) his role as a unique organ of revelation in the history of redemption (1 Thes 2:13; 1 Cor 2:13; Eph 3:2-11; 2 Pet 3:15-16). All this being so, we can assume as we turn now to the Pauline corpus that in it we possess a trustworthy mine of information

---

[13]See J. Gresham Machen, *The Origin of Paul's Religion*, 144ff.

[14]James Stalker, *The Life of St. Paul* (Edinburgh: T. & T. Clark, 1889), 40. See particularly here Margaret E. Thrall, "The Origin of Pauline Christology" in *Apostolic History and the Gospel*, 304-316.

about him who called Paul that day out of his life of legalism on his way to Damascus. Of course, given the restrictions of space, we cannot pretend that we are going to exhaust the wealth of truth to be found therein. We must content ourselves with notices and expositions of only the more apparent lines of evidence—the "high lights on the surface of a pervasive implication" (Warfield)—that run throughout the great Apostle's writings respecting the supernatural person of Jesus Christ.

PAUL'S CHRISTOLOGY

As we begin to consider the writings of Paul, we must not allow to slip from our thinking the recognition that Paul was, first and foremost, a missionary and the fact that his letters were written for the most part to churches which he had founded (Romans is the exception here) and to pastors of those churches (Philemon is the exception here). In these letters Paul affords us a glimpse of the content of the message which he proclaimed when first he arrived in a city to evangelize it as the "Apostle to the Gentiles." Not surprisingly, we find that his message centered upon Christ. To be specific, the historical events of Christ's death, burial, and resurrection formed the "cutting edge" of his proclamation (1 Cor 15:3-5). To the Galatians he wrote: "Before your very eyes Jesus Christ was portrayed as crucified" (3:1). To the Thessalonians he declared that he had "shared the gospel of God" with them (1 Thes 2:8), the content of which concerned "the living and true God" and the coming of "his Son from heaven, whom he raised from the dead—Jesus, who rescues us from the coming wrath" (1:9-10; see 2 Thes 2:5). Among the Corinthians, Paul informs us, he had resolved to know nothing "except Jesus Christ and him crucified" (1 Cor 2:2; see 1:23), which focus of concentration he then described as his work of "laying a foundation" (3:10-11). Later, in the same letter, he spoke of "the gospel which I preached to you" (15:1), the content of which he spells out in the following terms:

> that Christ died for our sins according to the Scriptures, and
> that he was buried, and
> that he was raised the third day according to the Scriptures, and
> that he appeared to Cephas, then the Twelve (15:3-5).

In his letter to the Romans, as we saw in the preceding chapter, he declared that the "gospel of God," having been "promised through his prophets in the holy Scriptures,"

> concerned his Son,
> who was born of the seed of David according to the flesh,
> who was powerfully marked out the Son of God according to [his] spirit of holiness by the resurrection from the dead,
> Jesus Christ our Lord" (Rom 1:1-4).

In the same letter he wrote of "the word of faith which we are proclaiming," and he described that "word" in this fashion: "...if you confess with your mouth, 'Jesus is Lord,' and believe in your heart that God raised him from the dead, you will be saved" (10:9-10). In 2 Corinthians 1:19 Paul declares that he had preached among his readers "the Son of God, Christ Jesus" as God's "Yes" to men, and in 2 Corinthians 4:5, Paul writes: "We preach Christ Jesus as Lord." In Colossians 1:28, he simply writes: "Christ we proclaim."

Luke, as he had done earlier in Acts with reference to Peter's discourse on the Day of Pentecost, gives us also an account of one of Paul's missionary sermons to a Gentile audience (13:16-41). In the synagogue at Pisidian Antioch Paul began by rehearsing for his listeners God's care for Israel in times previous (13:16-22) and then quickly focused their attention on the "Savior Jesus," the one whom John the Baptist had served as forerunner (13:23-25). Then, following the format which he outlined in 1 Corinthians 15:3-4, he informed them that the rulers of Jerusalem "fulfilled the words of the prophets which are read every Sabbath" (13:27) and "carried out all that had been written concerning him" (13:29) by condemning Jesus and having him crucified (under Pilate's orders) and buried. Then Paul declared: "But God raised him from the dead" (13:30), eliciting as evidence for Christ's resurrection the fact "that for many days he was seen by those who had traveled with him from Galilee to Jerusalem" (13:31) and employing Psalm 2:7, Psalm 16:10 and Isaiah 55:3 to show that his resurrection was "according to the Scriptures."[15] Having

---

[15]It is noteworthy that Paul employed Psalm 16 in precisely the same manner as Peter had done on the Day of Pentecost to make the point that David, when he died, was buried and saw decay with his fathers; hence, he

proclaimed, then, that Jesus died according to the Scriptures, was buried, and rose again according to the Scriptures, Paul applied his proclamation to his audience: "Therefore, I want you to know...that through *this one* the forgiveness of sins is proclaimed to you; and from all which you were unable to be justified by the law of Moses, everyone who believes in *this one* is justified" (13:38-39). Here we have the apostolic model of a Christ-centered evangelistic sermon (see also 17:2, 22-31; 18:5; 20:21).

It is clear from this biblical data that when we consider Paul's Christology we are addressing what for him was central to everything else. And he is not silent with regard to who Christ is. We intend to elicit evidence from Paul's letters that will put beyond all legitimate doubt that he regarded Jesus both as the Christ and as very God as well as very man.

Jesus as "the Christ"

Beyond all doubt, Jesus was, for Paul, the promised Messiah. This we may assume as a "given." Not only does "Christ" become a proper name for Jesus in Paul's writings, indeed, even his favorite designation for him, occurring (more often with than without the article) around 210 times by itself in this sense and many more times in conjunction with other designations,[16] but also Paul affirms that it was of Jesus that the Old Testament Scriptures spoke (see, for example, Acts 13:27-36; 17:2-3; 26:22-23; Rom 1:1-3; 1 Cor 15:3-4). And precisely because of its employment in conjunction with the term "Lord" ("the Lord Christ" in Rom 16:18; Col 3:24; "the [or, "our"] Lord Jesus Christ"; "Christ Jesus, the [or, "our," or "my"] Lord"; "Jesus Christ, our Lord"), it is clear that for Paul "Christ" was a title of great dignity, compatible as we shall see in every way with the implicates of deity which are often suggested by the title combinations in which it is found and the predicative statements surrounding it (see, for example, the statements in Col 3:24: "The Lord Christ you are serving," and Rom 9:5: "...Christ...who is over all, God blessed forever").

---

was not writing of himself in Psalm 16 but of Jesus.

[16]Leon Morris, *New Testament Theology* (Grand Rapids: Zondervan, 1986) states that Paul uses "Christ" 379 times in his letters, 72 percent of the total New Testament occurrences.

Jesus as "the Lord"

It is plainly in his description of Jesus as "the [or, "our" or "my"] Lord" (κύριος, ***kurios***) that Paul brings out most clearly his assessment of Jesus as divine. From the five distinct facts that Paul

1. prayed to Christ as "the Lord" (2 Cor 12:8-9);
2. declared "the name of our Lord Jesus Christ" to be the name to be "called upon" in the church (1 Cor 1:2; Rom 10:9-13; see Joel 2:32a);
3. coupled "the Lord Jesus Christ" with "God our Father" as the co-source of those spiritual blessings (grace, mercy, and peace) which God alone has the power to grant (Gal 1:3; 1 Thes 1:1; 2 Thes 1:1-2; Rom 1:7; 16:20; 1 Cor 1:3; 2 Cor 1:2; Eph 1:2; Phil 1:2; 1 Tim 1:2; 2 Tim 1:2; Tit 1:4; see 1 Thes 3:11; 2 Thes 1:12; Eph 6:23);
4. applied to Christ the very term (κύριος, ***kurios***) that in the Septuagint is employed to translate the sacred name of Yahweh; and more specifically,
5. applied Old Testament passages in which God (Yahweh) is the subject directly to Jesus (see Isa 8:14 and Rom 9:32, 33; Joel 2:32 and Rom 10:12-13; Isa 40:13 and 1 Cor 2:16; Ps 24:1 [LXX, 23:1] and 1 Cor 10:26 [see 10:21-22]; Ps 68:18 and Eph 4:8-10; Isa 45:23 and Phil 2:10),

there can be no legitimate doubt that as "the Lord," Jesus was, for Paul, divine and rightly to be regarded by others as such. When it is further noted that it is as "the Lord" that Paul speaks of Jesus in his "trinitarian" passages (Rom 15:30; 1 Cor 12:4-6; 2 Cor 13:14; Eph 4:4-6), it is not too much to say that the title "Lord" was for Paul the Christological title which both equates and distinguishes him from the Father and the Spirit, and that it is the heavenly triad that is his presupposition when he speaks of Jesus as "Lord."[17] Magnificently does Warfield capture the essence of the meaning of "Lord" as a Christological title in Paul's writings when he writes:

---

[17]So also Benjamin B. Warfield, *The Lord of Glory* (Reprint; Grand Rapids: Baker, 1974), 231.

> 'Lord' to [Paul] is not a general term of respect which he naturally applies to Jesus because he recognized Jesus as supreme, and was glad to acknowledge Him as his Master (Eph 6:9, Col 4:1), or even in the great words of Col 2:19 as the 'Head' of the body which is His Church (see Eph 4:15). It is to him the specific title of divinity by which he indicates to himself the relation in which Jesus stands to Deity. Jesus is not 'Lord' to him because He has been given dominion over all creation; He has been given this universal dominion because He is 'Lord,' who with the Father and the Spirit is to be served and worshipped, and from whom all that the Christian longs for is to be expected.[18]

The Pre-existence of "the Son"

A further line of evidence suggesting that Jesus Christ, for Paul, was divine is the catena of verses that implies his pre-existence as God's Son (see 2 Cor 8:9; Rom 8:3; Gal 4:4; Phil 2:6-7; Col 1:15-16; Eph 4:8-9). It has been suggested that such statements need reflect no more than an "ideal" pre-existence, and do not require Christ's personal pre-existence. But such a contention will fail to persuade any but the gullible once the passages have been carefully examined. Consider: The Apostle will appeal for Christian generosity on the ground that Christ, the Christian's example, "though he was rich, yet for your sakes became poor "(2 Cor 8:9). He urges Christians to live as sons of God should live because "God sent forth his Son" to make us his sons (Gal 4:4). He grounds his argument for Christian self-effacement in the fact that "though [Christ] was in the form of God,...he poured himself out, having taken [λαβών, *labōn*] the form of a servant" (Phil 2:6-7). He insists that the Colossians must not find in the pagan πλήρωμα (*plērōma*, "fullness") their fullness because it is Christ, God's Son (see vs 13), who is "before all things" and "by whom and for whom all things were created" (Col 1:16-17). To bring about such practical ends as are here envisioned by the Apostle, it is highly doubtful that he would have grounded his pastoral appeals in a mere speculative "ideal" pre-existence. Much more likely is it that such appeals were based upon a familiar, treasured, foundational truth central to the Christian faith—namely, that Christ as God's Son had personally pre-

---

[18]Warfield, *The Lord of Glory*, 231.

existed with the Father from eternity and had come to earth on a mission of mercy.

The foregoing material makes it abundantly clear, then, that for Paul the One who apprehended him on the Damascus Road was indeed God in his own right and the proper recipient of man's worship and service. Consequently, Paul can move easily into a complete linguistic identification of Christ with Yahweh:

> If Yahweh is our sanctifier (Ex. 31:13), is omnipresent (Ps. 139:7-10), is our peace (Judg. 6:24), is our righteousness (Jer. 23:6), is our victory (Ex. 17:8-16), and is our healer (Ex. 15:26), then so is Christ all of these things (1 Cor. 1:30; Col. 1:27; Eph. 2:14). If the gospel is God's (1 Thess. 2:2, 6-9; Gal. 3:8), then that same gospel is also Christ's (1 Thess. 3:2; Gal. 1:7). If the church is God's (Gal. 1:13; 1 Cor. 15:9), then that same church is also Christ's (Rom 16:16). God's Kingdom (1 Thess. 2:12) is Christ's (Eph. 5:5); God's love (Eph. 1:3-5) is Christ's (Rom. 8:35); God's Word (Col. 1:25; 1 Thess. 2:13) is Christ's (1 Thess. 1:8; 4:15); God's Spirit (1 Thess. 4:8) is Christ's (Phil. 1:19); God's peace (Gal. 5:22; Phil. 4:9) is Christ's (Col. 3:15; see Col. 1:2; Phil. 1:2; 4:7); God's "Day" of judgment (Isa. 13:6) is Christ's "Day" of judgment (Phil. 1:6, 10; 2:16; 1 Cor. 1:8); God's grace (Eph. 2:8, 9; Col. 1:6; Gal. 1:15) is Christ's grace (1 Thess. 5:28; Gal. 1:6; 6:18); God's salvation (Col. 1:13) is Christ's salvation (1 Thess. 1:10); and God's will (Eph. 1:11; 1 Thess. 4:3; Gal. 1:4) is Christ's will (Eph. 5:17; see 1 Thess. 5:18). So it is no surprise to hear Paul say that he is both God's slave (Rom. 1:9) and Christ's (Rom. 1:1; Gal. 1:10), that he lives for that glory which is both God's (Rom 5:2; Gal. 1:24) and Christ's (2 Cor. 8:19, 23; see 2 Cor. 4:6), that his faith is in God (1 Thess. 1:8, 9; Rom. 4:1-5) and in Christ Jesus (Gal. 3:22), and that to know God, which is salvation (Gal. 4:8; 1 Thess. 4:5), is to know Christ (2 Cor. 4:6).[19]

Such linguistic identification is pervasive throughout Paul's writings and one may observe it by ranging freely through the Pauline corpus. But there are eight contexts in particular, in addition to the one we considered in the previous chapter (Rom 1:3-4), where Paul makes explicit his view of Christ—the great Christological passages in

[19]David F. Wells, *The Person of Christ* (Westchester, Illinois: Crossway, 1984), 64-5.

Colossians 1:15-20, 2:9, Philippians 2:6-11, Ephesians 4:9-10, 1 Timothy 1:15, and 3:16, Romans 9:5, and Titus 2:13. The remainder of this chapter will address them in turn.

Jesus, as God's Divine Son, Supreme Over Creation and the Church (Colossians 1:15-20)

Apparently in the Colossian church some teachers, under a kind of Jewish folk religion, Phrygian folk religion, and some basic Christian ideas[20] were teaching the existence of angelic intermediaries (see "thrones, powers, rulers, authorities" in 1:16) between the Creator and the material universe, among which intermediaries was Jesus. It was to oppose this Christological representation that Paul incorporates this hymn to Christ in his letter to the Colossians.

In this pericope, beginning in 1:15 with the words "who is," the antecedent of which is "the Son of his [that is, "the Father's"; see 1:12] love" in 1:13, Paul gives us a magnificent description of the person of our Lord. So sublime is it that it bears quoting in full:

Jesus is Lord of the Natural Creation:

...who is
the Image of the invisible God,
the Firstborn of all creation,
because by him were created all things in heaven and upon earth,
things visible and things invisible—
whether thrones or dominions,
whether rulers or authorities—
[because] all things through him and for him have been created,
and he is before all things, and all things by him endure.

Jesus is Lord of the Spiritual Creation:

And he is the Head of the body, the church,
who is
the Beginning,
the Firstborn from the dead, in order that he might come to have first place in all things,

because in him he [God] willed all the fullness to dwell, and
[because] through him [he willed] to reconcile all things for him,
by making peace through the blood of his cross—
through him,
whether things upon earth,
or things in heaven.

Paul scales such breathtaking heights in this sublime ascription of divine qualities to Christ that it is not surprising that a vast literature has emerged over the years around this passage of Scripture. Also not surprising, given the spirit of the times in which we live, is the amount of literature devoted to explaining its Christology in terms that eliminate all ontological overtones.

It is a virtual "given" today among critical scholars that what we have in this section of Colossians is a pre-Pauline "hymn" which Paul (or another writer) adapted for his purpose.[21] But there is no consensus among these scholars on how the hymn is to be "strophed" or concerning the nature of its pre-Pauline background. For example, regarding its strophic arrangement, E. Nordern urged that the "hymn" should be divided into two strophes of unequal length, each to begin with "who is" (1:15-18a; 18b-20).[22] E. Lohmeyer divided the passage into two strophes of seven lines each (1:15-16e; 18:20), with a connecting section of three lines (1:16f-17).[23] E. Käsemann argues

---

[20]See my *Paul: Missionary Theologian* (Ross-shire, Scotland: Mentor, 2000), 232-34.

[21]By the word "hymn" is not necessarily intended what is sung today in the Christian church as a congregational song. It is, rather, a quasi-technical term, used broadly like that of "creed," to include dogmatic, confessional, liturgical, or doxological material. The criteria employed to identify "hymnic" material in the New Testament are both *stylistic* (rhythm, parallelism of lines, meter, alliteration, antithesis, chiasm) and *linguistic* (unusual vocabulary such as words that occur only once or that seem different from the language of the context) in nature. See R. P. Martin, *Carmen Christi* (Cambridge: University Press, 1967), 1-13; see also his *Colossians: The Church's Lord and the Christian's Liberty* (Exeter: Paternoster, 1972), 39-40.

[22]E. Nordern, *Agnostos Theos* (Darmstadt: Wissenschaftliche Buchgesellschaft, 1956), 250-54.

[23]E. Lohmeyer, *Die Briefe an die Kolosser und an Philemon* (Göttingen: Vandenhoeck & Ruprecht, 1953), 40-68.

for two strophes of six lines each (1:15-16; 18b-20), connected by 1:17-18a; but in his arrangement he discards the phrase "the church" in 1:18a, and the phrase "through the blood of his cross" in 1:20b as later interpolations.[24] And E. Schweizer divides the material into three strophes (1:15-16; 17:18a; 18b-20), but in order to secure the "original symmetry," with each stanza consisting of three lines, he omits the phrases, "things visible and things invisible—whether thrones or dominions, whether rulers or authorities" in 1:16, the phrases "the church" and "in order that he might come to have first place in all things" in 1:18, and the phrases "by making peace through the blood of his cross—through him, whether things upon earth or things in heaven" in 1:20.[25]

With regard to its background Käsemann argues that it was originally a pre-Christian Gnostic text dealing with the Gnostic Redeemer myth which the church adapted to form part of a baptismal liturgy.[26] But R. P. Martin has pointed out that the absence of any pre-Christian non-Christian parallel to the portrayal of the redeemer-figure as one who achieves reconciliation between God and man raises a serious question concerning the correctness of Käsemann's view.[27]

C. F. Burney and W. D. Davies suggest the pericope should be viewed against the background of Wisdom in Proverbs 8:22 and Genesis 1:1 as the latter is interpreted by Rabbinic Judaism with reference to Wisdom.[28] While this is a more attractive hypothesis

---

[24]E. Käsemann, "A Primitive Christian Baptismal Liturgy" in *Essays on New Testament Themes*, translated by W. J. Montague (Naperville: Alec R. Allenson, 1964), 149-68.

[25]E. Schweizer, *The Churches as the Body of Christ* (Richmond, Virginia: John Knox, 1964), 64-73; see also his "The Church as the Missionary Body of Christ" in *New Testament Studies* 8 (1961-1962): 1-11, particularly 6-7, and his *The Letter to the Colossians*, translated by Andrew Chester; London: SPCK, 1982), 55-88. In the last work he speaks of "two strophes" but 17-18a still "form a link" between them.

[26]E. Käsemann, "A Primitive Christian Baptismal Liturgy" in *Essays on New Testament Themes*, 149-68.

[27]R. P. Martin, *Colossians*, 41-2.

[28]C. F. Burney, "Christ as the APXH [*ARCHE*] of Creation" in *Journal of Theological Studies* 27 (1926): 160-77; W. D. Davies, *Paul and Rabbinic Judaism. Some Rabbinic Elements in Pauline Theology* (London: SPCK, 1955), 150-52.

than Käsemann's, seeking as it does to locate the hymn's background in the Old Testament, it is based upon the assumption that Paul's opposition at Colossae was mainly from a Jewish source which is not at all evident.[29]

E. Schweizer urges that its background must be sought in the Wisdom understanding of Hellenistic Judaism. He also believes that the hymn's theology has been corrected, both by later insertions and by the commentary that follows (1:21-23).[30] But P. T. O'Brien, granting Schweizer's understanding of the theology of the author of Colossians for the sake of making his point, has argued that there still seem to remain in the hymn certain elements which are different from his theology which fact is, to say the least, strange as long as the author was correcting the hymn's theology anyway. Moreover, it is not at all certain that the author has varied the hymn's theology by his commentary that immediately follows.[31]

For myself, while I do not question the possibility that we may well have an early Christian hymn in this passage (there certainly appear to be "hymnic" characteristics in the pericope), I prefer to divide the pericope according to its content into two main sections (1:15-17, 18-20), the former treating Christ's supreme lordship over all of the natural creation and the latter treating his supreme lordship over God's spiritual creation, the church. As for the original composition of the hymn, with O'Brien I see no reason why Paul himself could not have been the author of an earlier hymn originally written for another occasion and circumstance, but here modified and adapted to the present situation, "expressing in an exalted hymnic style his beliefs about Christ in view of the situation of his readers."[32] If so, it appears from the

---

[29]Martin, *Colossians*, 43.

[30]Schweizer, *Letter to the Colossians*, 55-88.

[31]Peter T. O'Brien, *Word Biblical Commentary: Colossians, Philemon* Vol. 44, (Waco, Texas: Word, 1982), 39. See 32-42 for an extended discussion of current critical views of Colossians 1:15-20. In R. P. Martin, *Colossians*, 40-4, and in Donald Guthrie, *New Testament Theology* (Leicester: Inter-Varsity, 1981), 352-55, may be found similar discussions in briefer compass.

[32]P. T. O'Brien, *Colossians, Philemon*, 41-2. See also C. F. D. Moule, *The Epistles of Paul the Apostle to the Colossians and to Philemon* (Cambridge: University Press, 1962, 60-2, for his defense of the Pauline authorship of the passage.

vocabulary in the hymn (ἀρχή, *archē*, πλήρωμα, *plērōma*) that he made use of some of their language. But whether it was originally Pauline or not does not affect in any way our final exposition since it is the hymn as it comes to us in what I would suggest we have reason to regard as Paul's *inspired letter* to the Colossians that is the basis of our remarks.

The first thing that Paul tells us is that Christ, as the Father's Son, is "the Image of the invisible God." What does he mean by this description? In view of Paul's equation of "*the light of* the gospel of *the glory of Christ*, who is the *Image* of God" (2 Cor 4:4) with "*the light of the glory of God [imaged] in the face of Jesus Christ*" (2 Cor 4:6), we may conclude that when Paul called Christ "the Image of God" both in 2 Corinthians 4:4 and Colossians 1:15, he was saying "nothing less than that in him the glory of God, indeed God himself, becomes manifest."[33] When one recalls, in addition, that the Author of Hebrews also described God's Son as "the radiance of God's glory and the exact representation of his being" (1:3), and that James described "our Lord Jesus Christ" as just "the Glory" of God (2:1; see Zech 2:5), there can be little doubt that Paul, with the New Testament writers in general, intended by his description of Jesus as "the Image of the invisible God" to assert that Jesus is "just the invisible God made visible."[34]

This understanding that Paul intended by this description of Jesus to assert among other things his divine nature receives further support by the hymn's accompanying descriptions of him. Four times Paul employs the phrase τὰ πάντα, *ta panta*, once πάσης, *pasēs*, once πάντων, *pantōn*, once πᾶσιν, *pasin*, and once πᾶν, *pan* (all to be translated "all [things]") to express Christ's exaltation over anything which would pretend to be his equal. Paul first declares that Christ is

---

[33]H. N. Ridderbos, *Paul: An Outline of His Theology*, translated by John R. DeWitt (Grand Rapids: Eerdmans, 1975), 70.

[34]Warfield, *The Lord of Glory*, 254. F. F. Bruce, *Commentary on the Epistles to the Ephesians and the Colossians* (London: Marshall, Morgan & Scott, 1957), 193, comments on "the Image of the invisible God": "What is this but to say that the very nature and being of God have been perfectly revealed in Him—that in Him the invisible has become visible?" R. P. Martin, *Colossians*, 45, commenting on "Image," writes: "He is the objectivization of God in human life, a coming into visible expression of the invisible God."

"the Firstborn of *all* creation" (πρωτότοκος πάσης κτίσεως, *prōtotokos pasēs ktiseōs*). This is to be understood in the Hebraic sense of the ascription of priority of rank to the firstborn son who enjoys a special place in the father's love and who accordingly is the primary heir of the father (see Heb 1:2). Clearly the ὅτι, *hoti,* clause of 1:16 and the πρὸ πάντων, *pro pantōn*, in 1:17 disallows the Arian insistence that the genitive ("of all creation") is to be construed as a partitive genitive.[35] Moreover, with the exception of its occurrence in Luke 2:7, no special emphasis is placed on the -τοκος element in the word anywhere else in the New Testament.

The Son, Paul tells us further, enjoyed pre-existence with the Father prior to the creation of the entire universe: He is ("exists") "before *all things*"[36] (1:17; see John 1:15, 30; 8:58). Furthermore, God created "*all things* in heaven and on earth—things visible and things invisible—whether thrones or dominions, whether rulers or authorities" by (ἐν, *en*) him, through (διά, *dia*) him, and for (εἰς, *eis*) him (1:16, τὰ πάντα, *ta panta*, occurs twice in this verse). Upon the Son all things are dependent for their *continuance* in existence: "*all things* by him endure [or "hold together"]" (1:17; see Heb 1:3). He was raised from the dead "in order that he might have the preeminence in *all things*" (1:18). And finally—and this has to do with the fact that he carried out the responsibilities of the messianic task—through him, Paul declares, God has been pleased "to reconcile to himself *all thing*, whether on earth or in heaven" (1:20).

From these clear statements respecting the Son's pre-existent and preeminent relationship to the Father and his involvement in the creation, preservation, and reconciliation of all created things, it is apparent that Dunn's recent attempt to empty Paul's description of

---

[35]See J. B. Lightfoot, *St. Paul's Epistles to the Colossians and to Philemon* (Reprint; Grand Rapids: Zondervan, 1959), 147; Bruce, *Epistles to the Ephesians and Colossians*, 194; Moule, *The Epistles of Paul the Apostle to the Colossians and to Philemon*, 63-64; R. P. Martin, *Colossians*, 45-6; P. T. O'Brien, *Colossians, Philemon*, 44; Larry R. Helyer, *The Prototokos Title in the New Testament* (dissertation; Fuller Theological Seminary, 1979), and his "Arius Revisited: The Firstborn Over All Creation" in *Journal of the Evangelical Theological Society* 31/1 (March 1988): 59-67.

[36]See C. F. D. Moule, *The Epistles of Paul the Apostle to the Colossians and to Philemon*, 66-7.

all references to the Son's *personal* pre-existence and to make his words mean nothing more than that the power which God exercises in creation is now fully revealed and embodied in Christ falls far short of its full import.[37] Furthermore, Paul's intention behind his description of Jesus as "the Firstborn of all creation" is light-years away from the Arian interpretation of the Jehovah's Witnesses that would insist that the word shows that the Son was the "first" of all *other* created things. As we have said, the entire context cries out that the term is to be understood otherwise, namely, in the Hebraic sense as an ascription of priority to the firstborn son who enjoys a special place in the father's love. It is, therefore, sheer theological perversity which leads the Jehovah's Witnesses in their *New World Translation* to insert the bracketed word "other" ("all [other] things") throughout the passage in order to justify their Arian view of the Son as being properly part of the created order.

That the Son is also preeminent over the church is stated in Paul's description of him as "the Head of the body, the church," "the Beginning [of the new humanity]," "the Firstborn from the dead, that he might come to have first place [as the Father's exalted Son] over all things" (1:18a, b, c; see Rom 8:29) and the One through whose peacemaking "cross work" God is finally to reconcile all things for his [Christ's] glory (1:20).

It is difficult to find any other biblical passage that more forthrightly affirms the full and unabridged deity of Jesus Christ than Colossians 1:15-20, spelling out as it does on a scale of cosmic dimensions his role in creating and preserving all things and his divine preeminence over all created things as Creator and Redeemer. Here, in plain, explicit language, Paul declares that Jesus Christ, as God's Son, was existing with the Father prior to the creation of the universe, was himself God's agent in creation, and as the Image of the invisible God, that is, as God himself, by his incarnation made the invisible God visible to men. Then, as the exalted "Firstborn from the dead," his eschatological preeminence is implied in Paul's assertion that God willed to reconcile all things for his (Christ's) glory (εἰς αὐτόν, *eis auton*), which is finally to be fulfilled in the Eschaton.

---

[37]See James D. G. Dunn, *Christology in the Making* (London: SCM, 1980), 187-94.

Jesus as "the Incarnate Plenitude of Deity" (Colossians 2:9)

I purposely postponed the discussion of Paul's phrase in 1:19, "all the fullness" (πᾶν τὸ πλήρωμα, *pan to plērōma*), to this point inasmuch as he uses the same phrase in 2:9 with even greater clarity as to his meaning if that is possible. The phrase almost certainly means the same thing in both contexts and to discuss it in connection with 2:9 avoids reduplication of comment.

In Colossians 1:19 Paul had written: "In him [God] willed all the fullness to dwell." Here in Colossians 2:9 Paul says virtually the same thing but he specifies the nature of the "fullness" and the manner in which the "fullness" dwells in Jesus. To see this, let us follow his thought. In the last verses of Colossians 1 Paul discussed the "mystery" of God, which, he says, is "Christ in you, the hope of glory" (1:27). A few verses later, Paul affirmed again that God's "mystery," only recently fully revealed (it had been anticipated in the Old Testament revelation), is Christ (2:2) "in whom *all* the treasures of wisdom and knowledge are deposited" (2:3). This is striking enough in that it highlights the uniqueness of Christ as the sole true repository and integrating point of all knowledge. But then a few verses later, Paul excels even himself in his exaltation of his Lord, for in 2:9 he says something even more striking. While he does not in so many words, as we shall observe him doing in Romans 9:5 and Titus 2:13, describe Christ directly as "God" (θεός, *theos*), his statement comes as close to it without doing so as is humanly imaginable[38] and gives the reason his readers are to "walk" in Christ and to "be on guard" that no one should take them captive through the pursuit of knowledge which springs from human philosophy and tradition. Translated literally, 2:9 reads as follows: "because [ὅτι, *hoti*] in him [Christ] dwells all the fullness of deity bodily."

To assess Paul's intention here, it will be necessary to give some attention to three of his words. By "fullness" (πλήρωμα, *plērōma*), which is perhaps an example of his employment of his opponents' terminology (scholars differ on what precisely was the nature of the

---

[38]See Oscar Cullmann's remark in *The Christology of the New Testament* (London: SCM, 1959), 311-13: "...such a text...is just a step from directly designating Jesus 'God.'"

Colossian heresy), Paul means plainly and simply "completeness," "totality," or "sum-total."[39] To insure that no one would miss his intention, Paul qualifies this noun with "all" (πᾶν, *pan*), that is, "*all* [not just some of] the fullness."

If it is an allusion to his opponents' language, this phrase already carries overtones of "fullness of *deity*," but Paul clarifies his intention by the following defining genitive "of deity" (θεότητος, *theotētos*). The word for "deity" here is θεότης, *theotēs*, the "abstract noun from θεός,"[40] meaning "the being as God," or "the being of the very essence of deity." Putting these two words together, Paul is saying something about the "totality of all that is essential to the divine nature."

Concerning this "totality of divine essence" Paul affirms that it "dwells [permanently]" (for this is the force of the preposition κατά, *kata*, prefixed to the verb and the present tense of the verb κατοικέω, *katoikeō*, in Jesus.

Precisely how it is that this totality of the very essence of deity "permanently dwells" in him, Paul specifies by the Greek adverb σωματικῶς, *sōmatikōs*. Some scholars suggest that the word means "essentially" or "really" (as over against "symbolically"; see the contrast in 2:17 between "shadow" [σκιά, *skia*] and "reality" [σώμα, *sōma*]) but much more likely it means "bodily," that is, "in bodily form," indicating that the mode or manner in which the permanent abode of the full plenitude of deity in Jesus is to be understood is in incarnational terms. In short, Paul intends to say that in Jesus we have to do with the very "embodiment" or incarnation of deity, or as he says elsewhere, Christ is God "manifest in the flesh" (1 Tim 3:16). Here we come very close in a Pauline equivalent to the Johannine ὁ λόγος σάρξ ἐγένετο (*ho logos sarx egeneto*, "the Word became flesh"). Finally, to underscore Jesus' uniqueness as such, Paul throws the "in him" forward in the sentence to the position of emphasis,

---

[39]See C. F. D. Moule, *The Epistles of Paul the Apostle to the Colossians and to Philemon*, 164, and his articles, "Pleroma" in *The Interpreter's Dictionary of the Bible* (Nashville: Abingdon, 1962), III, 826-28; and "'Fullness' and 'Fill' in the New Testament" in *Scottish Journal of Theology* 4 (1951): 80. See also Lightfoot, "On the meaning of πλήρωμα [*plerōma*] " in *St. Paul's Epistles to the Colossians and to Philemon*, 257-73.

[40]BAGD, *A Greek-English Lexicon of the New Testament* (Chicago: University of Chicago, 1957), 359.

implying by this, against his opponents' claim that "fullness" could be found elsewhere, that "in him [and nowhere else]" permanently resides in bodily form the very essence of deity!

To interpret Paul so is clearly in keeping with his earlier "hymn" to Christ in Colossians 1:15-20, as virtually every commentator acknowledges.[41] This view alone coincides with the rich language of the earlier hymn where, as we have already seen, Christ is described as the "Image of the invisible God," who was "before all things" and by, through, and for whom God created all things, and in whom all things "hold together."

Some modern scholars believe that Paul's language should be construed, both in 1:15-20 and in 2:9, as functional language but such an interpretation fails to take seriously the nature of the salvation envisioned in 2:10, its import only being meaningful if the Savior who effects it is the one in whom resides the fullness of deity. As O'Brien remarks: "If the fullness of deity does not reside in him then the Colossians' fullness would not amount to much at all—the very point Paul is making over against the errorists' teaching on fullness."[42]

Jesus as the Divine and Exalted Lord (Philippians 2:6-11)

The amount of literature on Philippians 2:6-11, as anyone can testify who has ever taken the time to find out, is absolutely staggering.[43] I have no intention, therefore, to interact with it here in a manner approaching comprehensiveness. It is safe to say, however, that on at least one issue all the scholarly literature agrees since Lohmeyer's

---

[41]See the commentaries of Olshausen, Endicott, H. A. W. Meyer, J. B. Lightfoot, Abbot (ICC), H. C. J. Moule, A. L. Williams, E. F. Scott, L. B. Radford, K. Wuest, C. F. D. Moule, Carson, Baggott, Hendriksen, Johnston, E. Lohse, R. P. Martin, Rogers, Lucas, O'Brien, and Patzia. See also the writings of such theologians as Liddon, Hodge, Warfield, D. Guthrie, I. H. Marshall, *et al.*

[42]O'Brien, *Colossians, Philemon*, 112.

[43]For a bibliography on the pericope, see Gerald F. Hawthorne, *Word Biblical Commentary: Philippians (Volume 43)* (Waco, Texas: Word, 1983), 71-5; R. P. Martin, *Carmen Christi*, 320-39. See also Robert B. Strimple, "Philippians 2:5-11 in Recent Studies: Some Exegetical Conclusions" in *Westminster Theological Journal* 41 (1979): 247-268, for a listing and summary of studies since 1963 to the approximate date of his article.

epochal 1928 study, *Kyrios Jesus, Eine Untersuchung zu Phil. 2:5-11* which is substantially reproduced in his commentary, *Der Brief an die Philipper* (1930), and that is that in Philippians 2:6-11 we have to do with (at least a fragment of?) an early Christian hymn.[44] Scholars disagree as to whether the hymn is Paul's own composition[45] or whether it was originally pre-Pauline and employed by Paul because it suited his purpose. If it is Pauline, one must acknowledge that he employed some uncustomary language (μορφή, *morphē*; ἁρπαγμός, *harpagmos*). There is also very little scholarly consensus on how the hymn is to be versified.[46] But, I repeat, they all agree that Philippians 2:6-11 is "hymnic" with respect to literary genre. This may very well be so since certain stylistic and lexical characteristics usually associated with hymnic material, such as various kinds of parallelism of thought, inversions, unusual vocabulary, and elevated style, are present in the pericope. But I would register mild reservation as to the number of hymns which are present in the passage. Whereas contemporary New Testament scholarship proposes the presence of one hymn which incorporates the whole of the material in these verses, I would propose the possibility that what we may actually have are (portions of?) two hymns—the first comprising 2:6-9 and based on

---

[44]R. P. Martin, *Carmen Christi*, 21, 28. Martin himself speaks of the hymn specifically as a "piece of early Christian kerygmatic confession" (21), and devotes Part III of his highly-regarded study to the support of this description.

[45]I. Howard Marshall, "The Christ-Hymn in Philippians 2:5-11: A Review Article" in *Tyndale Bulletin* 19 (1968), 104-27, and Morna D. Hooker, "Philippians 2:6-11" in *Jesus und Paulus: Festschrift für Werner Georg Kümmel zum 70 Geburtstag*, edited by E. Earle Ellis and Erich Grasser (Göttingen: Vandenhoeck & Ruprecht, 1975), 151-64, both express an openness to Pauline authorship, as does Hawthorne, *Philippians*, 78.

[46]For four proposed versifications, see E. Lohmeyer, *Der Brief an die Philipper* (Twelfth edition; Göttingen: Vandenhoeck & Ruprecht, 1964), 90; Joachim Jeremias, "Zur Gedankenführung in den paulinischen Briefen: Der Christushymnus, Phil. 2:6-11" in *Studia Paulina*, edited by J. N. Sevenster and W. C. van Unnik (Haarlem: DeErven R. Bohn, 1956), 152-54; Charles H. Talbert, "The Problem of Pre-existence in Philippians 2:6-11" in *Journal of Biblical Literature* 86 (1967), 141-53; M. D. Hooker in *Jesus und Paulus* even comments: "I myself have produced six or seven different analyses—and found each of them convincing at the time!" (157).

Genesis and Isaianic material, the second comprising 2:9-11 and based mainly on Isaianic material. I would submit the following structural arrangement of the two proposed hymns as a possibility, preferable, I believe, to arrangements I have seen to date inasmuch as virtually all of them either eliminate (as interpolations) or rearrange entire lines and phrases in order to bring strophic symmetry to the hymn. My arrangement has in its favor two considerations: it leaves intact the text as it comes to us in Paul's letter, and it allows the content of the material to govern the strophic arrangement and division. I would tentatively suggest, then, that the first "hymn" be strophed as follows:

Who [refers antecedently to "Christ Jesus" in 2:5],

Strophe 1:

though in the form of God existing,
  did not regard equality with God a thing to be seized,
  but himself he poured out,
having taken the form of a servant."

It should be noted, by this arrangement, that there are four lines in this strophe, the first and the fourth being participial clauses, separated by the second and third lines which set up a contrast ("did not regard" and "but poured"). That the first and fourth lines appear to belong together strophically is evident from the occurrence of μορφή (*morphē*, "form") in both and the occurrence of participles in both, suggesting also that they are to be viewed as "bracketing" clauses, tieing these four lines together.

Strophe 2:

In the precise likeness of men having been born,
  and having been found by external appearance to be a man,
  he humbled himself,
Having become obedient unto death—

Climactic addendum:

even the death of the cross.

Postponing for the moment any discussion of what I am calling the climactic addendum which may have been an original short choral refrain at the end of the hymn or Paul's own addendum intended to highlight the shameful character of the death which our Lord died, I would like to point out that again we have a strophic arrangement of four lines, and again the first and the fourth are participial clauses separated by the second and third lines. (These inner lines do not stand in contrast to one another as do the inner lines of the former strophe.) That these four lines appear to form a natural and single strophe is evident from the fact that the aorist participles in the first and fourth lines are the same in both (γενόμενος, *genomenos*) although it is true that their nuance of meaning is different and that they appear in inverted word order—in last place in the first line, in first place in the last line. Again, I would suggest that these participial clauses serve as "brackets" to set the strophe apart from the preceding strophe and that which follows. Further evidence that these lines are to be construed together strophically is the climactic parallelism of thought between the first and second lines and the occurrences of the word for "man" in the first and second lines (though it is true that they differ in number, being plural in the first line and singular in the second line).

With the two strophes clearly distinguished from each other before us, we may now note the following parallels that exist between them which suggest that they, taken together, form a single hymn:

1. The two strophes have the same number of lines.
2. Both first lines begin with the preposition ἐν (*en*, "in"), which is then followed in each case with a dative noun, then a genitive noun, concluding with a participle.
3. The first lines of the two strophes contain an antithetic parallelism: "form of God" and "likeness of men."
4. The third line in both strophes ascribes to Christ a reflexive action, the relation of the reflexive pronoun ἑαυτὸν (*heauton*, "himself") to the verb appearing in inverted order: in the former, "*himself* he poured out," in the latter, "he humbled *himself*." This striking similarity suggests that the two actions mean essentially the same thing, a possibility that receives further support from the distinct

likelihood that the former phrase has Isaiah 53:12 as its background while the latter phrase echoes the thought of Isaiah 53:8 (LXX) which is quoted in Acts 8:33 ("In his *humiliation* he was deprived of justice"), both Isaianic statements, of course, describing the suffering Servant.

5. Postponing the reason for my interpretation until later, but assuming its validity here for the sake of grouping together the several parallels between the strophes, the hymn moves from the idea of "death" ("poured himself out") in strophe 1, line 3, to "servitude" ("he humbled himself") in strophe 2, line 3; but it moves in reverse order from the idea of "servitude" ("the form of servant") in strophe 1, line 4, to "death" ("obedient unto death") in strophe 2, line 4.
6. In strophe 1 the word "God" occurs in the first and second lines; in strophe 2 the word "man" occurs in the first and second lines, suggesting an antithetic parallel between these lines of the two strophes.
7. Both strophes deal with the same subject: Jesus' state of humiliation.

The second "hymn" is to be strophed as follows:

Therefore [because of Christ's "servant work"],

Strophe 1:

God has highly exalted him,
and he has given to him the name,
    the 'above everything' name."

These lines are separated both from the preceding hymn by the "Therefore" (διὸ καὶ, *dio kai*) preceding them (a Pauline connecting word) and from the lines which follow them by the following purpose particle ἵνα (*hina*, "in order that") which introduces the purpose behind the divine action of this strophe. Further evidence that these lines are to be strophically distinguished from the preceding strophes is, of course, the shift in the subject of the actions from Christ in the earlier strophes to the God the Father here. But the most obvious indication to me that these lines may be *hymnically* distinguished from the previous two strophes is the fact that in this strophe we find only three lines, as over against four in the previous strophes. The three lines here follow the pattern of "independent line, independent line, dependent line."

As evidence that these lines are to be construed together strophically, we may cite the undeniable synonymous parallelism in thought between the first two lines, and the three internal lexical parallels, namely, the repeated "him" (αὐτὸν, *auton*, and αὐτῷ, *autō*) in lines 1 and 2 (in both cases in the emphatic position), the repeated preposition ὑπέρ (*huper*, "above") in lines 1 and 3, and the repeated reference to "the name" (τὸ ὄνομα, *to onoma*) in lines 2 and 3.

Strophe 2:

"in order that

at the name of Jesus
every knee should bow in heaven and on earth and under the earth,
and every tongue should confess that Jesus Christ is Lord—

Climactic addendum:

to the glory of God the Father!"

Postponing again for the time being any discussion of the climactic addendum, we are immediately conscious that we have again only three lines to consider. But it is also immediately apparent that in strophe 2 the structural arrangement is the precise reverse of strophe 1: where earlier we had the arrangement "independent line, independent line, dependent line," here we find the arrangement "dependent line, independent line, independent line."

Within the strophe itself, again we have an undeniable synonymous parallelism in thought between lines 2 and 3. This parallelism is underscored by the presence of the word "every" in both lines, the aorist subjunctive verb form in both lines, and the adverbial modifying phrase in both lines, the former anticipating the question "where?" or "whose?" and the latter anticipating the question "what?" There is also a lexical connection between lines 1 and 3 through the repetition of the proper name "Jesus," found here and nowhere else in the hymn.

Having distinguished between the two strophes, we may now note the following parallels between them:

1. The phrase "the name" is found in the dependent line of both strophes.
2. The word "every" is found in line 3 of both strophes.
3. Both strophes are concerned with the same subject: Jesus' state of exaltation, the former stating the fact itself, and the latter stating the Father's design behind the fact.

A word now concerning the climactic addenda. "Even the death of the cross" and "to the glory of God the Father" may have been either original to both hymns or Pauline additions to both. But it is apparent that a marked antithesis lies between them, each of them beautifully capturing the mood of its respective hymn. The former, by designating the particular kind of death Christ died, underscores the depth of the humiliation which Christ voluntarily underwent. The latter highlights the Father's glory which Christ's exaltation entailed. The former concentrates our attention on the death of Jesus; the latter focuses our attention on the glory of the Father. The former brings the first hymn to a close by focusing on the cross; the latter brings the second hymn to a close by focusing on the glory that followed. These addenda, I would submit, neatly summarize for us the essential flow of the apostle's thought: from humiliation to exaltation, from cross to crown.

This, I would suggest, is the likely structural arrangement of the hymns and the relationship between them. Together the two hymns appear then as follows:

Though in the form of God existing,
    he did not regard equality with God a thing to be seized,[47]
    but himself he poured out,[48]
the form of a servant having taken.[49]

---

[47]This translation construes ἁρπαγμὸν, *harpagmon*, as a *res rapienda* ("a thing to be seized") rather than a *res rapta* ("a thing to be held onto") for reasons which will be forthcoming in the exposition.

In the precise likeness of men having been born,
and having been found by external appearance to be a man,
he humbled himself,
having become obedient unto death—even the death of the cross.

Therefore, God has highly exalted him,
and he has given him the name,
the "above everything" name,

that at the name of Jesus,
every knee should bow in heaven and on earth and under the earth, and
every tongue should confess that Jesus Christ is Lord—to the glory of God the Father.

Now it should be obvious that the very first line of the first strophe is directly related to the concern of this present study. What does Paul mean when he declares that Christ Jesus was "existing in the form of God"?[50] Those who are advocates of what is called today the "Adam Christology" insist that it is the equivalent to the Genesis description of Adam as created in the image of God—the meaning here then being that Christ, as was Adam, was truly a man. Now it is true that the two Greek words εἰκών (*eikōn*, "image") and μορφή (*morphē*, "form") are both employed to translate the same Semitic root in the Septuagint, εἰκών, *eikōn*, translating the Hebrew noun צֶלֶם, *tselem*, in Genesis 1:26 and μορφή, *morphē*, translating the Aramaic noun צְלֵם, *tsᵉlem*, in Daniel 3:19. But this is hardly sufficient evidence to warrant the conclusion that εἰκών, *eikōn*, and μορφή, *morphē*, are interchangeable or are synonymous. And the fact must be squarely faced that μορφή, *morphē*, is not the word used in the Septuagint to render either "image" (צֶלֶם, *tselem*) or "likeness" (דְּמוּת, *dᵉmûth*) in Genesis 1:26-27. Moreover, this ignores the occurrence

---

[48]The reason for this rendering of ἑαυτὸν ἐκένωσεν, *heauton ekenōsen* (literally, "himself he emptied"), will be given in the exposition.

[49]For the reason for this rendering of the aorist participle λαβών, *labōn*, as a participle denoting action antecedent to that of the main verb, see fn. 65.

[50]For a summary of the most commonly-held views, see Hawthorne, *Philippians*, 81-4.

of μορφή, *morphē*, three lines later, for clearly Jesus did not assume the mere "image" of a servant. To the contrary, he became in very fact the Servant of Yahweh. The connection between Adam as the "image of God" and Christ as the "form of God" simply cannot be made on the basis of such slim linguistic evidence.

Others urge that the meaning of μορφή, *morphē*, should be established on the basis of its usage in the Septuagint, but the problem here is that it is used only four times in the Septuagint, and each time it is the translation of a different Hebrew word (see Judg 8:18; Job 4:16; Isa 44:13; Dan 3:19), none of them being, I would point out, the Hebrew word צֶלֶם, *tselem*. At best, taken together, the idea of μορφή, *morphē*, as the translation of the four words seems to be that of "visible form," but the number of samples is just too small and too diverse to draw any hard and fast conclusions on the basis of the occurrences of the term in the Septuagint. Besides, if it means "visible form," it is questionable whether this meets the conditions of the first occurrence in Philippians 2:6, for there Christ is not said to *be* "the μορφή [*morphē*] of God" but that he is in "the μορφή [*morphē*] of God." "In the 'visible form' of God" would be Scripturally inappropriate inasmuch as God is "invisible" as Colossians 1:15 reminds us.

R. P. Martin maintains that μορφή, *morphē*, in 2:6a is equivalent in meaning to δόξα (*doxa*, "glory"), and he presents a very interesting case for it,[51] but it can hardly be argued that this same equivalency is appropriate for μορφή, *morphē*, in the phrase, "form of servant," three lines later.

In light of these problems, I must conclude that the weight of linguistic evidence is still on the side of J. B. Lightfoot who demonstrated from a study of both its usage throughout the history of Greek thought and the occurrences of the μορφ- (*morph*-) root in the New Testament that μορφή, *morphē*, refers to the "essential attributes" of a thing, and that Christ's being *in* the form of God, while not the linguistic equivalent, is the connotative equivalent to the Pauline description of Christ in 2 Corinthians 4:4 and Colossians 1:15 as the "[essential] image of the [invisible] God."[52] Warfield concurs:

---

[51]R. P. Martin, *Carmen Christi*, 108-19.

[52]J. B. Lightfoot, *Saint Paul's Epistle to the Philippians* (Reprint; Grand Rapids: Zondervan, 1953), 110. See also Lightfoot's extended note on "the

> "Form" is a term which expresses the sum of those characterizing qualities which make a thing the precise thing that it is. Thus, the "form" of a sword (in this case mostly matters of external configuration) is all that makes a given piece of metal specifically a sword, rather than, say, a spade. And the "form of God" is the sum of the characteristics which make the being we call "God," specifically God, rather than some other being—an angel, say, or a man. When our Lord is said to be in "the form of God," therefore, he is declared, in the most express manner possible, to be all that God is, to possess the whole fulness of attributes which make God God.[53]

John Murray concurs, describing Lightfoot's exposition on 2:6a as "yeoman service in the exposition of the first clause of verse 6,"[54] while David Wells declares that it "appears inescapable that by 'form' we are to understand that Paul meant the essence or essential characteristics of a thing."[55] Another fact in its favor, in addition to the evidence from usage, is that this understanding of the term fits both occurrences in 2:6: "form of God" and "form of servant." When the force of the present participle is then also taken into account which conveys the idea of "continually [beforehand] subsisting,"[56] which in turn excludes any intimation that this mode of subsistence came to an end when he assumed the form of servant, we have here as bold and unqualified assertion of both the pre-existence and the full unabridged deity of Jesus Christ as one could ever hope to find in the pages of the New Testament.

But having affirmed that here in Philippians 2:6a is yet another indisputable confession by Paul that the incarnate Christ is just deity

---

synonymes μορφή [*morphē*] and σχήμα [*schēma*]" at 127-33.

[53]Warfield, "The Person of Christ According to the New Testament" in *The Person and Work of Christ*, 39. See his *The Lord of Glory*, 236; and his sermon "Imitating the Incarnation" in the former volume, 566-68.

[54]John Murray, *Collected Writings of John Murray* (Edinburgh: Banner of Truth, 1982), III, 359.

[55]David F. Wells, *The Person of Christ*, 64.

[56]Lightfoot, *St. Paul's Epistle to the Philippians*; 110; Warfield, "The Person of Christ According to the New Testament" in *The Person and Work of Christ*, 40. R. P. Martin, *An Early Christian Confession* (London: Tyndale, 1960), 17, translates ὑπάρχων, ***huparchōn***, "was originally possessing." The sharp contrast between the present tense of this participle and the four aorist participles that follow should not go unnoticed.

itself, we are now faced with a difficulty. The classical evangelical interpretation of the entire pericope contends that, when properly understood, these verses depict a great "parabola,"[57] starting with God the Son in the glory of his pre-existent condition of sharing the divine essence with God the Father ("in the form of God existing"), then tracing his "downward" movement by means of the Incarnation ("himself he emptied") to his "cross work" as the Father's servant, and then recording his "upward" movement by means of the Father's exaltation through resurrection and ascension to his present session at his Father's right hand as "Lord." No evangelical, of course, will take exception either to the sentiment behind or to the high Christology itself which is thus extracted from these verses by such an exposition. Certainly I do not. Nor do I for a moment have any intention of denying to our Lord in the slightest degree his rightful claim to full unqualified deity or to equality with the Father in power and glory. This I have already shown from my exposition of 2:6a. Nor am I unaware of the fact that the New Testament does set forth the work of Christ in precisely these terms of "descent–ascent" (κατάβασις–ἀνάβασις, *katabasis–anabasis*) in some contexts.[58] But it is precisely this "descent–ascent" motif, purported to be present in Philippians 2:6-11, which has created for evangelical scholars in this particular context the difficulty of which I spoke earlier. To be more precise, I should speak of two difficulties.

The first difficulty is this: if we understand the beginning point of the "flow" of the passage, as the classic evangelical view does, as the pre-existent state of the Son of God ("in the form of God being") and take the phrases, "himself he emptied, taking the form of a servant," as the metaphorical allusion to the 'downward" event of the Incarnation, it is only with the greatest difficulty, because of the intervening clause (to be discussed in a moment), that the conclusion can be avoided that the "emptying" involved his surrender of the "form"

---

[57]The term is from Emil Brunner, *The Mediator*, translated by Olive Wyon (London: Lutterworth, 1934), 561-63.

[58]See John 3:13; 6:62; Rom 10:6-7; Eph 4:8-10; 1 Tim 3:16; Heb 4:14-10:8; 1 Pet 3:18-22; see also 2 Cor 8:9. The reader may refer to Richard N. Longenecker, *The Christology of Early Jewish Christianity* (London: SCM, 1970), 58-62, for a helpful brief treatment of the theme.

("very nature"– NIV) of God. I grant that the verb κενόω, ***kenoō***, may have a metaphorical meaning, as in its other occurrences in the New Testament (Rom 4:14; 1 Cor 1:17; 9:15; 2 Cor 9:3), and that it need not be literally rendered "emptied" in Philippians 2:6. I too in the end attach a non-literal meaning to it. But even a metaphor has a literal meaning when it is divested of its metaphorical "wrapping." What does this metaphor mean literally when it is "unpacked" in the interest of interpretation? The ready answer, of course, is that it refers to the event of the Incarnation ("he made himself of no reputation, by means of taking the form of a servant"). But it is just here that the difficulty arises for the classical view. For according to this view, the intervening clause ("he did not regard..."), in the "flow" of the hymn, has to mirror an attitude in the *pre-existent Son* that comes on the "prior side" of the event of Incarnation. But if this clause describes what the pre-existent Son of God as God the Son "thought" (ἡγήσατο, *ēgēsato*, of his equality with God, it does not matter, I would suggest, whether ἁρπαγμὸν, *harpagmon* (from the root ἁρπάζω, *harpazō*, meaning "to seize") is construed *res rapta*, that is, "a thing to be held onto," or *res rapienda*, that is, "a thing to be seized"[59]—neither is appropriate as a description of what the Son "thought" with regard to his "equality with God." The former is theologically suspect for it implies that the Son was willing to and did in fact divest himself of his deity ("the form of God") when he took the "form of a servant," for that is what "equality with God" means lexically, contextually, and according to John 5:18 and 10:28-33.[60] The latter is also theologically suspect for it suggests that the Son did not already possess equality

---

[59]The variation of the *res rapienda* view, known as *res retinenda* ("a thing to be retained") and espoused by Martin, *Carmen Christi*, 143-49, in my opinion is too subtle a distinction to assume that the first-century reader of Paul's letter would have caught it.

[60]See G. Stählin, "ἴσος [*isos*]" in *Theological Dictionary of the New Testament* (Grand Rapids: Eerdmans, 1965), III, 353: "In [John] 5:18 ἴσος [*isos*] expresses...the equality of dignity, will and nature which the later ὁμοούσιος [*homoousios*] was designed to defend...it denotes an equality which is both essential and perfect. This is also the meaning of ἴσα [*isa*] in the famous and difficult verse Phil 2:6...." See also "ἴσος [*isos*]," 353, fn. 52: "At Phil. 2:6 the ἴσα [*isa*] has all the significance of the concept of equality in Jn. 5:18."

with God; but this introduces confusion into the passage in light of the fact that it is clearly affirmed in the first clause of 2:6, as we have seen, that the Son was God and was thus as such "equal with God." If one should reply that the reason it is said that the Son did not "grasp after" equality with God is because he already had it as the first clause affirms (and as I have just indicated), I would respond that this now introduces a certain theological barrenness, if not an exegetical inanity, into the text at the very point where, obviously, a highly significant insight is intended, for one does not need to be informed of the obvious—that the Son did not seek after something which was already in his possession. Accordingly, I would submit, from the perspective of the classical interpretation of the pericope, that it is only the *res rapta* interpretation of ἁρπαγμὸν, *harpagmon*, that circumvents this barrenness of meaning, but then it is only with the greatest difficulty that the evangelical scholar can escape, if escape at all, the conclusion that the Son is represented, by the implication in his willingness to forego his "equality with God," that is, his essential divine attributes, as having divested himself of his "very nature" character of God when he became a man. (We are not debating at this moment what all admit is the impossibility of one who is God doing such a thing. We are only concerned here with interpreting the text in a meaningful fashion.) One has only to peruse the evangelical literature on these verses to discover there what can only be described as "hermeneutical gymnastics" being resorted to to affirm, on the one hand, that the Son did not regard equality with God ("the form of God") a thing to be held onto, and that he accordingly "emptied himself" (or, "made himself nothing") by becoming a man, and yet, on the other hand, that he still retained all that he essentially is and was from the beginning. For example, it is said: "He did not divest himself of his divine attributes but only the independent use of his attributes." But when did the Son ever exercise his attributes independently? Or, "He did not divest himself of his deity but only the glory of his deity." But is not the "divine glory" just the sum and substance of the Deity? And how does one square this interpretation with John 1:14 and 2:11 *et al*? Or, "He did not divest himself of his deity but only his rights as the Deity." But what rights did he forego as God when he became a man? While I do not for a moment agree with the "kenotic" theologians who teach just this—that the Son, according to the teaching of this passage, divested himself of at least something that was essentially his as God when he became a man, I can appreciate their fearless willingness, given the presumption that the passage begins with the Son in his pre-existent state, to take the passage at face value and to conclude that here we have to do with a "kenotic Christology"—with the fact that the Son, in some essential way, divested himself of his "form of God" in the course of his taking the "form of servant."

The second difficulty about which I spoke is this: If the "flow" of the passage commences, as the classical view maintains, with God the Son in his pre-existent state, then he is obviously the Primary Subject throughout the unfolding drama of the "great parabola." But then we must ask, what meaning can his later exaltation possibly have meant to him? It seems to me, if exaltation is to have any meaning at all, it must involve elevation to a state not in one's prior possession. But such an elevated state is simply non-existent with regard to God the Son as God. If one should reply that his later exalted state involved his being elevated, as the second hymn declares, to the position of *lordship* over all things, I must ask, does Scripture permit us to believe that God the Son, often identified by Scripture itself as the God and Yahweh of the Old Testament, was not already *de jure* and *de facto* Lord over creation, nature, religious institutions such as the Law and the Sabbath, and, most significantly, over the lives of men prior to the exaltation spoken about in Philippians 2:9-11? Does not careful reflection on simply what is entailed in being God the Son preclude this notion and force one to conclude that the Son as God the Son continued ever, even during the days of his earthly ministry, to be the Lord which he was from the beginning? I must ask again then, what meaning can be attached to an exaltation of one who cannot be exalted more highly than he already is? It is only with the greatest difficulty that the evangelical scholar can escape, if escape at all, the conclusion, if he insists that the exaltation was still indeed the exaltation of the pre-existent Son of God *per se*, that the Son's former state was lower in dignity than his latter state, and that the Son's latter state elevated him to a state which was above the state which he enjoyed when "existing in the form of God" prior to his incarnation. But Scripture simply will not permit such a conclusion.

These two difficulties with the classical interpretation—(1) giving satisfactory meanings to the clauses, "he did not regard equality with God a thing to be held onto [or, "grasped after"]" and "himself he emptied, taking the form of a servant," while at the same time avoiding a kenotic Christology; and (2) giving intelligible sense to an exaltation of God the Son *per se*—these two difficulties, I would urge, ought to make us willing to consider another interpretation that avoids both problems and at the same time affirms the *vere deus vere homo* doctrine of classical Christology.

The key to the solution of both of these difficulties, but more important, simply to the proper interpretation of the verses themselves, in my opinion, is to perceive that it is not God the Son in his preincarnate state as the Second Person of the holy Trinity *per se* who is the subject throughout the first two strophes and to whom reference is made by the "him" in verse 9 of the third strophe, but rather it is *Christ Jesus* (see 2:5 and references to "Jesus" and "Jesus Christ" in 2:10-11 respectively)—God the Son certainly, for this is the meaning of "though in the form of God existing" but God the Son *already incarnately present* with men as himself the God-man—who is the subject of the hymns.[61] The hymn, in other words, does not begin with the Son in his *pre-existent* state. It begins with "Christ Jesus," and affirms that, as God incarnate, he refused to follow an alternative path to glory to that one which his Father had charted for him. Nor does it refer to the "downward" movement (the κατάβασις, *katabasis*) of the Incarnation event itself, so vital a part of the classical view, save as an event that had already taken place, presupposing it in its affirmation that he, "though existing as God," had "taken the form of servant." By this construction, all that is said of him is said then of him as the Messiah, the Son-already-dispatched-on-his-mission. It is possible, but this is only a conjecture, that the first hymn has been "decapitated," and that a previous strophe dealt with his pure pre-existent state as God the Son, eternal Son of the eternal Father.

Now, quite properly, it can be asked, how does this elimination of the Son's pre-existent state and his κατάβασις, ***katabasis***, from

[61] I do not deny that in other contexts, for example, 1 Timothy 1:15, "Christ Jesus," as a titular description, does designate the Son of God in his pre-incarnate state.

the hymn's "flow" circumvent the two difficulties earlier highlighted? The answer is that now we are no longer interacting at the point of Philippians 2:6 with the Incarnation as a future or occurring event, but are now interacting with the Incarnation as from the outset the incarnate God's existing state of being. Accordingly, the clauses under discussion may now be interpreted within the context of the Incarnation as a *fait accompli* and not within the context of the Incarnation as a *fait anticipè*. But are meaningful interpretations ready at hand? To this I would reply in the affirmative. With respect to the clause, "he did not regard equality...," I would urge that it may now be meaningfully construed *res rapienda*, that is, "he did not regard equality with God a thing to be seized," and that it should be interpreted against the background of his temptation recorded in Matthew 4. We know that Paul is willing to contrast Adam and Christ in Romans 5:12-19 and 1 Corinthians 15:45-49, actually referring to Christ in the latter passage as the Last Adam and the Second Man. I would suggest that this phrase in the Philippians hymn draws a further contrast between the respective temptations of Adam and Christ. Unlike Adam, the first man, who did "regard equality with God [τὸ εἶναι ἴσα θεῷ, *to einai isa theō*] a thing to be seized" (see Gen 3:5 where the Serpent's temptation is framed in the words: "...you will be like [the *k*, *k*, translated by ἴσα, *isa*, in the LXX at Deut 13:6; Job 5:14; 10:10; 13:28; 15:16; 24:20; 27:16; 29:14; 40:10; Isa 51:23] God, knowing good and evil"), Christ, the Last Adam and Second Man, when urged to "seize equality with God" (see Matt 4:3, 6: "Since you are the Son of God,...") by taking matters into his own hands and asserting his rights as the "Son" *per se* and not as the Son-already-dispatched-on-his-messianic-mission as the Servant of the Lord refused to do so. That is to say, this "thought" of "seizure of equality," that is, the temptation to walk no longer in the path of the Servant but rather to achieve lordship over "all the kingdoms of this world" (Matt 4:8) by a route (a "self-willed" act of "exaltation") not charted for the Servant in the economy of salvation Christ Jesus steadfastly resisted, refusing to succumb to the Tempter's suggestion.

There is another Old Testament motif beyond the Adam-Christ contrast that assists us when we address the meaning of "himself he emptied," and that is the "Servant" motif of Isaiah's "Servant Songs."

In what I have called the second hymn, clearly lines 1 and 2 of strophe 1 borrow a sentiment from Isaiah 42:1-8, and lines 2 and 3 of strophe 2 directly reflect the language of Isaiah 45:23. And in what I have called the first hymn, Paul's references to the "servant" in strophe 1, line 4, and to Christ's "self-humbling" and "obedience unto death" in lines 3 and 4 of strophe 2 are general allusions to the "servant" motif of Isaiah's songs (see Isa 53:8 [LXX] and Acts 8:33). (By the way, Paul also relates Christ to both Adam and the "servant" motif in Romans 5:12-19.) All this being beyond doubt, can there be any substantive objection to the suggestion of H. Wheeler Robinson, J. Jeremias[62] and others,[63] that the phrase, "himself he emptied," is the non-literal Greek dynamic equivalent to the Isaianic phrase, "he poured his soul out [which means, "he poured himself out"] unto death," which means, "he voluntarily died," in Isaiah 53:12, climactically descriptive of the Suffering Servant's self-sacrificing work so often referred to elsewhere in the New Testament (see, for example, Matt 8:17; Luke 22:37; Acts 8:32-35; 1 Pet 2:21-25). The phrase, thus interpreted, derives its meaning against the backdrop of the *high-priestly ministry* of our Lord rather than against the backdrop of his *pre-existence*, referring, as Jeremias writes, "to the sacrifice of his life and not to the self-emptying of his incarnation."[64] I would suggest, then, that the aorist participle λαβών, *labōn*, in the first hymn, strophe 1, line 4, is to be construed as a participle denoting antecedent action ("having taken"),[65] thus placing Christ's "self-emptying" subsequent in time to the "taking." That is to say, the participle does not explain

---

[62]H. Wheeler Robinson, *The Cross of the Servant* (London: SCM, 1926), 72-4; Jeremias, "Zur Gedankenführung in den paulinischen Briefen: Der Christushymnus, Phil. 2:6-11" in *Studia Paulina*, 154, fn. 3, and his article, "παις" [*pais*] " in *Theological Dictionary of the New Testament*, V, 711-12.

[63]For example, C. H. Dodd, *According to the Scriptures* (London: Nisbet, 1952), 93.

[64]Jeremias, "Zur Gedankenführung in den paulinischen Briefen: Der Christushymnus, Phil. 2:6-11" in *Studia Paulina*, 154, fn. 3.

[65]I construe the aorist participle λαβών, *labōn*, here as referring to action antecedent to the action denoted in ἐκένωσεν, *ekenōsen*, according to the common rule of Greek syntax that an aorist participle generally denotes action antecedent to that of the main verb.

The fact that the participle follows the main verb in the word order does

the manner of the "self-emptying" ("emptied, by taking") but rather denotes a prior action which was the necessary precondition to the "self-emptying." A paraphrase of the first strophe will assist the reader in understanding what we are advocating.

---

not require that it be construed as denoting coincident or subsequent action. As Moulton states in *A Grammar of New Testament Greek: Prolegomena* (Third edition; Edinburgh: T. & T. Clark, 1930), I, 132: "There are a good many NT passages in which exegesis has to decide between antecedent and coincident action, in places where the participle stands second."

Incidentally, while we are treating this subject, lest Moulton be quoted against himself, it is imperative that A. T. Robertson's inaccurate citation of Moulton to the effect that "Moulton (*Prol.*, p. 131) observes that when the verb precedes the aorist participle it is *nearly always* the participle of coincident action" (*A Grammar of the Greek New Testament in the Light of Historical Research*, 1113; emphasis supplied) be once and for all corrected. What Moulton actually writes is: "...the [aorist] participle naturally came to involve past time relative to that of the main verb. Presumably this would happen *less completely* when the participle stood second.... In many cases, especially in the NT, the participle and the main verb denote *coincident* or *identical* action" (*Prolegomena*, 131). It should be apparent to all that there is a great deal of difference between what Moulton actually said ("less completely [antecedent action]...many") and what Robertson quotes him as saying ("nearly always" [coincident action]). Moulton's final conclusion, as I quoted him previously, is that exegesis must decide in "a good many NT passages" what the writer intended. Frankly, I would modify even Moulton's statement and say that exegesis must finally decide in every case the time relation between the action of the participle and that of the main verb. In other words, one can never merely ascertain the word order (that is, whether the aorist participle appears before or after the main verb) and automatically deduce from that that the participle denotes antecedent, coincident, or subsequent action.

An interesting sidelight to this whole issue, but one which generally supports my construction here is the fact that C. F. D. Moule, in his *An Idiom Book of New Testament Greek* (Cambridge: University Press, 1959 [second edition]), 99-100, suggests as a "principle" that it is still the aorist or present tense of the participle that mainly determines antecedent or coincident action. He says not one word regarding the significance of the position of the participle relative to the main verb (before or after), stating rather: "...it often turns out that a Present Participle alludes to an action with which the action of the main verb coincides..., while an Aorist Participle refers to action previous to what is referred to in the main verb. This 'schoolboy' rule is even safer for N.T. Greek than for the Classical writers" (99-100).

> Though Christ Jesus was and is God [of course, God incarnate],
> he [unlike Adam] did not regard equality with God a thing to be
> seized [at his temptation by a self-willed exercise of power],
> but poured himself out [unto death],
> having taken the form of the servant [of Isaiah 53].

By this construction we have both precluded at the outset a kenotic Christological interpretation and the first difficulty I mentioned earlier and have been able to give substantive meaning to 2:6-7b, something we had earlier suggested the classical view is able to do only with the greatest exegetical ingenuity.

We are now also in a position to give substantive meaning to the act of exaltation asserted in the second hymn, for now we may refer it, not directly to God the Son *per se* but to God the Son in his incarnate state as the Messiah. It is, in other words, the divine-human Messiah, Christ Jesus, who is exalted. And because we are compelled by the historical fact itself to describe the Son, now incarnately existent in Jesus Christ, as "the divine-human Messiah," we can boldly say, without fear of denigrating his divine honor, that the Father's exaltation of Jesus Christ entailed for the Son, *as the Messiah*, a new and genuine experience of exaltation. Precisely because we must use the word "human" as part of our description of him now, we can also say that something truly new and unique occurred at the resurrection and ascension of Jesus Christ: the man Christ Jesus—the Last Adam and Second Man—assumed *de facto* sovereignty over the universe, over all of the principalities and powers in heavenly places, and over all other men, demanding that they submit to the authority of his scepter. That King's name is Jesus, at the mention of whose name some day every knee will bow and every tongue will confess that *Jesus Christ*—the divine-human Messiah—is Lord!

We have completed our consideration of Philippians 2:6-11. Our concluding comments can be brief. Beyond controversy, this pericope, regardless of its precise hymnic structure, when fairly interpreted ascribes deity to "Christ Jesus." It does so in three ways: first, by its description of Jesus as "in the form of God [continually] being"; second, by its indirect ascription to him of "equality with God" when it affirmed that he did not "seize" this station in the sense, as I have suggested, that at the time of his temptation he did not assert himself or exploit his filial ranking in a self-willed show of power commensurate with his divine station; and third, by the very nature of the lordship which the Father delegated to him, the entail of his exaltation. It is true that this lordship was "delegated" to him in his role as Messiah as the result of his labors (see the "because" of Isa 53:12 and the "therefore" of Phil 2:9). But the specific character of this lordship, described as it is in terms of Isaiah 45:23 where such lordship is declared by Yahweh to be his prerogative alone, requires that we not lose sight of the fact that the conventional or covenantal basis upon which it was determined that he should "receive" this specific kind of lordship as the Messiah upon the completion of his suffering was his own divine Sonship, the antecedent condition to the messianic investiture. Said another way, it is because he was, as the Messiah, "obedient unto death, even the death of the cross" that he was exalted to lordship, but it is also because he is "in the form of God" and "equal with God," as the *divine* Messiah, that the lordship he was delegated could assume the proportions which it does and involve the universal obligation of men to worship him.

In addition to the Pauline passages which we have considered to this point in behalf of Christ's deity (Rom 1:3-4; Col 1:15-20; 2:9; Phil 2:6-11), there is a variety of other expressions in the Pauline corpus which clearly suggest that Christ, for Paul, was pre-existent and thus by logical extension, the *divine* Son of God. I want to look at three of these briefly.

"He descended...He ascended" (Ephesians 4:9-10)

These verses occur in a context in which Paul asserts Christ's sovereign right to distribute spiritual gifts to his church as he deems fitting and proper. He cites Psalm 68:18 as the explanation of this privilege: "Ascending on high, he led captives in his train, and gave gifts to men." The allusion in this striking metaphor is to Christ's ascension as the vindicating exhibition of his triumph over the spiritual powers of darkness arrayed against him (Col 2:15): having been triumphant "in the field" as he was, he now, "back in the camp," exercises the hard-won privilege of "dividing the booty," that is, "engifting" his own as he deems appropriate.

Now it is at this point that Paul, never one to miss the opportunity to declare again who this Victor is, injects the parenthetical words which are the subject of our present interest:

> Now this "he ascended"—what does it mean except that also he descended to the lower, earthly regions.[66] He who descended is also the one who ascended higher than all the heavens, in order that he might fill all the universe [with his kingly power and dominion].

It has been often noted that, insofar as what is actually expressed in these words is concerned, something is lacking in the Pauline logic inasmuch as an ascent *per se* neither necessitates nor implies a prior descent. Elijah's ascension to heaven is a case in point (2 Kgs 2:11). On what basis does Paul say this then? He obviously is assuming something about the subject of his remarks—a fact so well-known and so widely received among the Christians to whom he is writing that it does not need to be spelled out at every turn in his exposition. What is this datum that does not require even the stating because Paul is assured in his own mind that his readers will be able to provide it? Paul is obviously assuming that the subject of the ascent existed *prior* to his earthly existence, and that in order to "ascend" he first would have had to "descend"! When this datum is factored into the Pauline statement—the supposition of Christ's pre-existence as the Son of God—what otherwise would be a flaw in his logic is cleared up and the statement makes perfect sense. And there can be no doubt that if he pre-existed as the Son of God (see Rom 8:3; Gal 4:4), then his "descent" effectively resulted in what classical Christologists intend by the doctrine of the Incarnation. Even Bultmann, although he traces the "descent-ascent" metaphor here to the Gnostic Redeemer mythology, acknowledges that what Paul had in mind here is "the pre-existent Son's journey to earth."[67]

---

[66]See Charles Hodge, *A Commentary on the Epistle to the Ephesians* (Reprint; Grand Rapids: Eerdmans, 1954), 220-21, for reasons for understanding τὰ κατώτερα [μέρη] τῆς γῆς, *ta katōtera* [*merē*] *tēs gēs*, as just the earth itself. For the evangelical view that it should also include Christ's death on the cross, see William Hendriksen, *New Testament Commentary: Exposition of Ephesians* (Grand Rapids: Baker, 1967), 192, fn. 111.

[67]Bultmann, *Theology of the New Testament*, 175.

"Christ Jesus came into the world" (1 Timothy 1:15)

In Paul's statement in 1 Timothy 1:15: "Christ Jesus came into the world—sinners to save"—the first of the five "faithful sayings" in his pastoral letters—again Christ's pre-existence is implied and, as a corollary to his pre-existence, his divine Sonship as well.

But just as the "he ascended" in Ephesians 4:8 does not in itself require a prior descent, so it is also true that the phrase "came into the world" does not necessarily contain within itself the notion of pre-existence *per se* (see Rom 5:12; 1 Tim 6:7). But George Knight trenchantly observes at this point:

> It is one thing to point out that the phrase ἦλθεν (ἔρχεσθαι) εἰς τὸν κόσμον, *ēlthen [erchesthai] eis ton kosmon*, itself does not imply preexistence and it is another to make this evaluation of the phrase when it is used by Christians with Christ Jesus as the subject. Is it not, as a matter of fact, evident that the uniform usage of that phrase *with* reference to Christ Jesus is to both his preexistence and also his incarnation...?[68]

He then proceeds to show from an analysis of the six occurrences of the phrase in John's Gospel (1:9; 3:19; 11:27; 12:46; 16:28; 18:37)—the only other book of the New Testament where the expression is found[69]—that when the phrase is applied to Christ Jesus, it "demands

---

[68]George W. Knight, III, *The Faithful Sayings in the Pastoral Letters* (Nutley, New Jersey: Presbyterian and Reformed, n.d.), 36-37.

[69]Warfield, "The Saving Christ" in *The Person and Work of Christ*, 550-551, writes:

> ...the very language in which [the purpose of the incarnation] is expressed is startling, meeting us here in the midst of one of Paul's letters. For this is not Pauline phraseology that stands before us here; as, indeed, it professes not to be—for does not Paul tell us that he is not speaking in his own person, but is adducing one of the jewels of the Church's faith? At all events, it is the language of John that here confronts us, and whoever first cast the Church's heart-conviction into this compressed sentence had assuredly learned in John's school. For to John only belongs this phrase as applied to Christ: "He came into the world." It is John only who preserves the Master's declarations: "I came forth from the Father, and am come into the world...." It is he only who, adopting, as is his wont,

the understanding of preexistence as well as incarnation."[70] This conclusion enjoys virtually universal support among commentators, and it is only the hyper-critical scholar who refuses to concede the obvious.

A Digest of the Christological Mystery (1 Timothy 3:16)

With the aid of a succinct compendium of the great "mystery of Godliness" (that is, the "revealed Secret" of the Faith, even Jesus Christ; see Col 1:27; 2:2-3) in the form of a "quotation from an early Christian hymn,"[71] Paul elaborates his Christology—the Great Mystery—in six phrases:

who[72] [that is, Christ Jesus]
was manifested in the flesh,
was vindicated in the spirit,
was seen by angels,
was proclaimed among the nations,
was believed on in the world,
was taken up in glory."

---

the very phraseology of his Master to express his own thought, tells us in his prologue that "the true Light—that lighteth every man—was coming into the world."

William Hendriksen, *New Testament Commentary: Exposition of the Pastoral Epistles* (Grand Rapids: Baker, 1957), 77, offers the alternative opinion that Paul is not reflecting a "Johannine" phrase as much as he is "simply making use of the Savior's own way of speaking about himself, and is employing language which, having been adopted from his lips by the earliest disciples, had been spread far and wide." But if Hendriksen is correct, it is strange that John alone of all the gospel writers retains the phrase. Moreover, Hendriksen seems to ignore the fact that Paul expressly declares that it is a "faithful saying" which he is citing here and not a remark original to himself.

[70]Knight, *The Faithful Sayings in the Pastoral Epistles*, 38.

[71]Robert H. Gundry, "The Form, Meaning and Background of the Hymn Quoted in 1 Timothy 3:16" in *Apostolic History and the Gospel*, 203.

[72]Of the textual variants there is little doubt that the masculine relative pronoun Ὅς, *Hos*, is to be preferred to the neuter relative pronoun ὅ, *ho*, and the θεός, *theos*, of the Textus Receptus. For the reasons, see Bruce M. Metzger, *A Textual Commentary on the Greek New Testament*, 641.

As with the other Christological hymns we have considered, this one as well has undergone considerable analysis with regard to its strophic arrangement. Some see strict chronological progression throughout the six lines, with each line therefore receiving independent treatment. Others see two strophes of three lines each (or two strophes of two lines and a refrain). And still others—the majority view today—divide the quotation into three couplets.

It appears to be a finely crafted piece of poetry with not one but two patterns of internal relationships that bind the six lines together in a remarkable literary unit. There are first the six dative nouns—flesh, spirit, angels, nations, world, and glory—which almost certainly are intended to be construed both antithetically and chiastically, that is to say, the hymn moves from that which is earthly ("flesh") to that which is heavenly ("spirit"), then from that which is heavenly ("angels") back to that which is earthly ("nations"), then back again from that which is earthly ("world") to that which is heavenly ("glory"). This being so, it seems that the poet was thinking in terms of the couplets following an a/b, b/a, a/b pattern, with the hymn's movement being not primarily chronological but spatial, emphasizing the truth that both spheres—the earthly and the heavenly—find their center in Christ as he unites both heaven and earth.[73]

Gundry has observed that when the six lines are considered individually in their entirety, there seems also to be a synthetic parallelism between lines 2 and 3—"vindicated, seen"—and lines 4 and 5—"proclaimed, believed on," both of which are framed between line 1 commemorating the Lord's "descent" and line 6 commemorating the Lord's "ascent." The first of these synthetic parallels (lines 2 and 3) takes place in the realm *invisible* to men; the second of these parallels (lines 4 and 5) takes place in the realm *visible* to men, while the third (lines 1 and 6) begins in the *visible* realm and passes into the *invisible*.[74] The pattern here would be a, bb, aa, b.

This strophic analysis or one very similar to it has large currency among most commentators today.[75] So now we turn to a consideration of the individual lines themselves.

---

[73]See E. Schweizer, *Lordship and Discipleship* (London: SCM, 1960), 64-6.

[74]Gundry, "The Form, Meaning and Background of the Hymn Quoted in 1 Timothy 3:16" in *Apostolic History and the Gospel*, 208-09.

[75]See, for example, W. Hendriksen, *Exposition of the Pastoral Epistles*,

Line 1: "was manifested in the flesh."

With respect to the meaning of the first line it is commonly acknowledged that "was manifested in the flesh" refers to the Incarnation and by the constative aorist speaks of Christ's entire incarnate life as a *revelation* of the divine Son "in the sphere of *human* being." That it has reference to the Incarnation, implying as well Christ's pre-existence as the Son of God,[76] is evident not only from the fact that we do not speak this way about an ordinary man but also from the fact that the New Testament speaks elsewhere of Jesus' *incarnate* life in terms of "manifestation" (John 1:31; Heb 9:26; 1 Pet 1:20; 1 John 1:2; 3:5, 8; see John 1:14; Col 2:9).[77]

Line 2: "was vindicated in the spirit."

Opinions vary concerning the meaning of this line. Because σάρξ (*sarx*, "flesh") in the preceding line, as we similarly urged in connection with our exposition of Romans 1:3-4, when applied to Christ has

---

138-139, and J. N. D. Kelly, *A Commentary on the Pastoral Letters* (London: Adam and Charles Black, 1963), 90-2, the latter of whom makes the insightful comment that the parallelism "makes it practically certain that the hymn is really arranged in three couplets, each containing a carefully designed antithesis. First, Christ incarnate and thus in the form of a servant is seen vindicated at his resurrection. Secondly, Christ receives the worship of angels and is preached to the nations of mankind, i.e., he is brought to the knowledge of all rational beings, celestial and terrestrial. Thirdly, he is accepted both throughout the entire created universe (cf. Col. i.23) and in the heavenly realm itself." (92)

[76]Walter Lock, *A Critical and Exegetical Commentary on the Pastoral Letters* (ICC; Edinburgh: T. & T. Clark, 1936), 45, speaks of this "manifestation" as an "unveiling of a previous existence."

[77]I. Howard Marshall, "Incarnational Christology in the New Testament" in *Christ the Lord*, edited by Harold H. Rowdon (Leicester: Inter-Varsity, 1982), 10, writes:

> Incarnational language is found in 1 Timothy 3:16 which describes how 'he [Jesus] was manifested in the flesh'. Although no subject is expressed (the AV 'God was manifest' follows a late text), the language is based on that used elsewhere to describe how the Son of God was incarnate. The thought is of an epiphany in human form, and the implication is that a divine or heavenly subject is intended. The reference is certainly to the earthly life of Jesus and not to his resurrection appearances.

reference to Christ's human nature in its entirety, including his human spirit, it is most unlikely (*contra* Gundry) that his human spirit is the intended referent of πνεῦμα (*pneuma*, "spirit") here. The choice, it seems to me, really lies between understanding the referent to be the Holy Spirit or Christ's divine nature. Are there any indications as to which is intended? I think so. If it refers to the Holy Spirit, the preposition ἐν, *en*, must be construed instrumentally ("by"), and while this is certainly possible, it does violence to the symmetry present in the uniform locative sense of the ἐν, *en*, in the other lines of the poem. Therefore, since Paul has already instructed us in Romans 1:3-4, as we have seen, that Christ was "powerfully marked out the Son of God according to the spirit of holiness [not the Holy Spirit but his own holy divine spirit] by the resurrection from the dead," his resurrection there clearly being represented as a *vindicating* event, I would urge that the verb "was vindicated" here refers to that same vindicating event, and that "in the spirit," as the antithesis to "in the flesh," that is, "in the sphere of *human* being," means "in the sphere of *divine* being." A paraphrase of the line would then be "was vindicated [as the Son of God by the resurrection] in the sphere of [his divine] spirit."[78]

Line 3: "was seen by angels."

Since this line contains no ἐν, *en*, "angels" is probably to be construed as a true rather than an instrumental dative.[79] This means in turn that ὤφθη, *ōphthē*, which "nearly always means the *self*-exhibition of the subject,"[80] quite probably means "appeared" rather than "was seen." The upshot of these two points is that the phrase means something on the order of "appeared to angels," which is not substantively different from the traditional translation.

---

[78]So also such commentators as Charles Hodge, *Commentary on Romans* (Reprint of 1886 edition; Grand Rapids: Eerdmans, 1955), on 1:3-4, and J. N. D. Kelly, *Commentary on the Pastoral Letters*, 90-1.

[79]See A. T. Robertson, *A Grammar of the Greek New Testament in the Light of Historical Research* (Nashville: Broadman, 1934), 534; M. R. Vincent, *Word Studies in the New Testament* (New York: Charles Scribner's Sons, 1900), IV, 241; and BAGD, *A Greek-English Lexicon of the New Testament* (Third edition), 581-82, 1, a, *d*.

[80]Gundry, *Apostolic History and the Gospel*, 214.

There is little question that this line refers both to Christ's triumph over the angelic forces of evil by his cross and to his exaltation over all the angelic powers at his ascension (see Eph 1:21; Col 2:15; Phil 2:9-11; Heb 1:4-14; 1 Pet 3:22; Rev 5:8-14). It certainly implies his super-angelic dignity.[81]

Lines 4, 5, and 6.

There is little substantive disagreement among scholars over the meanings of lines 4, 5, and 6. Line 4, "was proclaimed among the nations," reflects the church's conviction that Christ is properly the subject of world-wide proclamation and also the fact that the church was in the process of proclaiming him as such. Line 5, "was believed on in the world," reflects the church's confidence in the outcome of that proclamation—the nations of the world will become his disciples. And line 6, "was taken up in [not "into"] glory," brings the hymn to a close with the imagery of Jesus' ascension to heaven *in* the glory *attendant upon* him on that occasion (see the "glory cloud" in Acts 1:9; see also Acts 1:11 and Matt 24:30; 26:64; Mark 14:62).

From beginning to end this hymnic confession of faith (see the adverb ὁμολογουμένως, *homologoumenōs*, in Paul's prefatory introduction to the hymn[82]) extols Christ—as the pre-existent Son who became "enfleshed," who was then "vindicated" as the divine Son of God by his resurrection from the dead, who, having "ascended," is properly the acknowledged Lord among the "angels" and the "proclaimed" Lord in the world of men. Here is, indeed, a high Christology, found in the confessional framework of an early Christian hymn, which is in accord with that high Christology to be found throughout the Pauline corpus which confesses a Messiah who is Deity incarnate!

---

[81]Donald Guthrie in *New Testament Theology*, 359, only slightly more cautiously, writes: "This [line 3] may well have been a variant way [to that of Heb 1:4] of expressing the superiority of Christ [to angels]."

[82]Walter Lock, *Commentary on the Pastoral Epistles*, 44, suggests that it means something on the order of "by common agreement" or "by common profession." Kelly, *Commentary on the Pastoral Letters*, 88, states that it means "by common consent."

Paul's Two Usages of Θεός As a Christological Title

Romans 9:5

This Pauline statement reads: "...from whom came the Messiah according to the flesh, who is over all, God blessed forever. Amen." The debate surrounding this verse arises not from a divergence of opinion over textual variants or the meaning of words. The debate is rather over the question of punctuation. The most natural way to punctuate the verse is to place commas after both "flesh" and "all" and a period after "forever" as above. This is supported by both the context and the grammatical and implicatory demands of the verse itself.

No one expresses the significance of the context for the meaning of Romans 9:5 with greater depth of insight than E. H. Gifford:

> St. Paul is expressing the anguish of his heart at the fall of his brethren: that anguish is deepened by the memory of their privileges, most of all, by the thought that their race gave birth to the Divine Saviour, whom they have rejected. In this, the usual interpretation, all is most natural: the last and greatest cause of sorrow is the climax of glory from which the chosen race has fallen.[83]

As for the grammatical demand of the verse, it can hardly be denied that the most natural way to handle ὁ ὢν (*ho ōn*, the definite article and present participle) is to view the phrase as introducing a relative clause and to attach it to the immediately preceding ὁ Χριστὸς, *ho Christos*.

The implicatory demand of the verse flows from the presence of the words τὸ κατὰ σάρκα (*to kata sarka*, "insofar as the flesh is concerned"[84]). This expression naturally raises the question: in what sense is the Messiah not from the patriarchs? The second half of the

---

[83]E. H. Gifford, *The Epistle of St. Paul to the Romans* (London: John Murray, 1886), 168-69.

[84]See F. Blass and A. Debrunner, *A Greek Grammar of the New Testament and Other Early Christian Literature* (Chicago: University of Chicago Press, 1961), 139, para. 266.2, on Romans 9:5: the "addition of the art. [before κατὰ σάρκα, *kata sarka*]," they say, "strongly emphasizes the limitation."

implied antithesis is supplied in the words which follow: "who is over all, God blessed forever." This treatment of the verse, of course, ascribes full, unqualified deity to the Messiah.

James D. G. Dunn, after acknowledging that the "punctuation favours a reference to Christ as 'god,'" immediately blunts the force of his concession by saying: "Even if Paul does bless Christ as 'god' here, the meaning of 'god' remains uncertain...[It] is by no means clear that Paul thinks of Christ here as pre-existent god."[85] Anxious to demonstrate his thesis that early Christological thinking developed from a non-incarnational kind to the incarnational Christology of John and maintaining accordingly that Paul could not yet have reached the heights which John was later to scale, Dunn fails to do justice to the significance of the descriptive phrases on either side of θεὸς, *theos*: "who is over all" and "blessed forever." The former ascribes supreme lordship over the universe to the Messiah while the latter acknowledges his right to that everlasting adoration and praise which in other contexts is reserved for God the Creator (Rom 1:25) and God the Father (2 Cor 11:31). These striking locutions, once θεὸς, *theos*, is allowed to refer to the Messiah, rule out the possibility of regarding him, as Dunn does here, as "god" with a lower-case g.

This natural, straightforward rendering of Romans 9:5—"which every Greek scholar would adopt without hesitation, if no question of doctrine were involved" (Gifford)—has enjoyed not only the support of "a not inconsiderable number of early Fathers"[86] and the large majority of commentators,[87] but also the primacy of choice in the AV (1611), RV (1881), ASV (1901), NASV (1971), NIV (1978), and the NKJV (1982).

Some scholars (see RSV [1946] and NEB [1970]), because they judge it to be an "un-Pauline locution" to refer to Christ as "God," have proposed two alternative punctuations, the first detaching the last expression, θεὸς εὐλογητὸς εἰς τοὺς αἰῶνας, *theos*

[85]James D. G. Dunn, *Christology in the Making* (London: SCM, 1980), 45.

[86]Bruce M. Metzger, "The Punctuation of Rom. 9:5" in *Christ and Spirit in the New Testament* (Cambridge: University Press, 1973), 102.

[87]Even John A. T. Robinson in *Wrestling With Romans* (London: SCM, 1979), 111, admits that "grammatically, there is almost everything to say for [construing θεός, *theos*, in Romans 9:5 as a Christological title]."

eulogētos eis tous aiōnas (construing it as a doxology), from the preceding, the second detaching the entire expression after σάρκα, *sarka*, from the preceding, again construing the clause as a doxology.

It is a clear case of "begging the question" to declare it "un-Pauline" for Paul to refer to Christ as "God" in a Pauline letter where all the syntactical evidence indicates that this may well be the very time that he has done so. Can a writer never express a theological *hapax legomenon* ("said one time")? And to assert that he does so nowhere else requires the additional judgment (which these scholars are willing to make) that Titus 2:13 is at best "deutero-Pauline," that is, non-Pauline in authorship though "Pauline-like" in style and essential substance. Furthermore, it is to ignore the words of Colossians 2:9, not to mention the profusion of exalted terminology throughout Paul's writings which ascribe deity to Jesus.

What about the two alternative proposals? Can their sponsors justify them? The first, as we indicated, suggests that these last words of 9:5 be construed as a disconnected doxology ("May God be blessed before!"). But Metzger is correct when he writes: "Both logically and emotionally such a doxology would interrupt the train of thought as well as be inconsistent with the mood of sadness that pervades the preceding verses."[88] Furthermore, if this detached clause is a doxology to God, it reverses the word order of the subject and the predicate present in every other such doxology in the Bible (over thirty times in the Old Testament and twelve times in the New) where the verbal adjective always *precedes* the noun for God and never follows it as it is reputed by this proposal to do in Roman 9:5. It is difficult to believe that the Apostle, whose ear for proper Hebraic linguistic and syntactical formulae was finely tuned, would violate the established form for expressing praise to God which even he himself observes elsewhere (see Eph 1:3; 2 Cor 1:3). Finally, if this clause is an ascription of praise to God, it differs in another respect from every other occurrence of such in Paul's writings. Invariably, when Paul would ascribe blessedness to God, he connects the expression either by some grammatical device or by direct juxtaposition to a word which precedes it. There is, in other words, an antecedent reference to God in the

---

[88]Metzger, "The Punctuation of Rom. 9:5" in *Christ and Spirit in the New Testament*, 108.

immediately preceding context. For example, he employs ὅ ἐστιν (*ho estin*, Rom 1:25), ὁ ὢν (*ho ōn*, 2 Cor 11:31), ᾧ (*hō*, Gal 1:5; 2 Tim 4:18), αὐτῷ (*autō*, Rom 11:36; Eph 3:21), and τῷ δὲ θεῷ (*tō de theō*, Phil 4:20; 1 Tim 1:17) to introduce ascriptions of praise to God. In the cases of Ephesians 1:3 and 2 Corinthians 1:3, even here there is an antecedent reference to God in the immediately preceding contexts. Thus all of Paul's doxologies to God are connected either grammatically or juxtapositionally to an immediately preceding antecedent reference to God. Never is there an abrupt change from one subject (in this case, the Messiah in 9:5a) to another (God in 9:5b) as suggested by this proposal. Consequently, this proposal has nothing to commend it grammatically and much to oppose it.

The second proposal—the one preferred by most of the scholars who reject the natural view and which is also commended by the *Greek New Testament* (UBS), the RSV, and the NEB—has even less to commend it, for not only do the objections against the former proposal tell equally against it as well, but an additional objection may be registered. By disconnecting everything after σάρκα, *sarka*, and construing the disconnected portion as an independent ascription of praise, it denies to the participle ὢν, *ōn*, any real significance. Metzger highlights this failing:

> If...the clause [beginning with ὁ ὢν, *ho ōn*] is taken as an asyndetic [unconnected] doxology to God,...the word ὤν, *ōn*, becomes superfluous, for "he who is God over all" is most simply represented in Greek by ὁ ἐπὶ πάντων θεός [*ho epi pantōn theos*; and also "he who is over all" is most simply represented by ὁ επὶ πάντων, *ho epi pantōn*—RLR]. The presence of the participle suggests that the clause functions as a relative clause (not "he who is..." but "who is..."), and thus describes ὁ Χριστός, *ho Christos*, as being "God over all."[89]

Nigel Turner also points out that detaching the words beginning with ὁ ὢν, *ho ōn*, from the preceding clause "introduces asyndeton and there is no grammatical reason why a participle agreeing with

[89]Metzger, "The Punctuation of Rom. 9:5" in *Christ and Spirit in the New Testament*, 105-06. The best brief treatment of Romans 9:5 that I am aware of is Metzger's discussion in *A Textual Commentary on the Greek New Testament*, 520-23.

'Messiah' should first be divorced from it and then be given the force of a wish, receiving a different person as its subject."[90] One must surely wonder at the strange facility of some scholars to recognize the presence and natural force of the relatival ὁ ὢν, *ho ōn*, in 2 Corinthians 11:31 where we find precisely the same syntactical construction ("God..., who is blessed forever") as that here in Romans 9:5 and to fail to recognize its presence and force in Romans 9:5.

I would conclude that there can be no justifiable doubt that Paul, by his use of θεός, *theos*, as a Christological title here—surrounding it with the particular descriptive phrases that he does, ascribes full deity to Jesus Christ who is and *abides as* (the force of the present participle) Lord over the universe and who deserves eternal praise from all.

Titus 2:13

The debate surrounding this verse relative to our present interest is whether the Apostle Paul[91] intended to refer to one person (Christ) or to two persons (the Father and Christ) when he wrote: "...while we wait for the blessed hope, even the appearing of the glory [or, glorious appearing] of the great God and Savior of us, Jesus Christ." The issue, more pointedly put, is this: Are the two words "God" and "Savior" to be construed as referring to one person or are they to be divorced from one another because of the demands of exegesis and referred to two persons? In my opinion, there are five compelling reasons for understanding Paul to be referring to Christ alone throughout the verse and to translate the relevant phrase: "the appearing of our great God and Savior, Jesus Christ."

---

[90]Nigel Turner, *Grammatical Insights Into the New Testament* (Edinburgh: T. & T. Clark, 1965), 15.

[91]In this section I am assuming that Paul wrote Titus just as the letter claims (1:1). No one in antiquity seems to have questioned Paul's authorship of Titus, it being only in comparatively recent times that his authorship has been called into question. The reader may consult Donald Guthrie, *The Pastoral Epistles* (London: Tyndale, 1957), 212-28; Everett F. Harrison, *Introduction to the New Testament* (Revised edtion; Grand Rapids: Eerdmans, 1971), 351-63; and George W. Knight III, *The Pastoral Epistles* (Grand Rapids: Eerdmans, 1992), 4-6, for general defenses of Paul's authorship of Titus.

First, it is the most natural way to render the Greek sentence as numerous commentators and grammarians have observed. Indeed, more than one grammarian has noted that there would never have been a question as to whether "God" and "Savior" refer to one person if the sentence had simply ended with "our Savior."[92]

Second, the two nouns both stand under the regimen of the single definite article preceding "God," indicating (according to the Granville Sharp rule) that they are to be construed corporately, not separately, or that they have a single referent. If Paul had intended to speak of two persons, he could have expressed this unambiguously by inserting an article before "Savior" or by writing "our Savior" after "Jesus Christ."

Third, inasmuch as "appearing" is never referred to the Father but is consistently employed to refer to Christ's return in glory, the *prima facie* conclusion is that the "appearing of the glory of our great God" refers to Christ's appearing and not to the Father's appearing.

Fourth, note has often been made of the fact that the terms θεὸς καὶ σωτήρ (*theos kai sōtēr*, "god and savior") were employed in combination together in second and first century B.C. secular literature to refer to single recipients of heathen worship. James Hope Moulton, for example, writes:

> A curious echo [of Titus 2:13] is found in the Ptolemaic formula applied to the deified kings: thus GH 15 (ii/B.C.), τοῦ μεγάλου θεοῦ...καὶ σωτῆρος [*tou megalou theou...kai sōtēros*].... The phrase here is, of course, applied to one person.[93]

Walter Lock writes in the same vein:

> The combination σωτὴρ καὶ θεός [*sōtēr kai theos*] had been applied to Ptolemy I, θεὸς ἐπιφανής [*theos epiphanēs*] to Antiochus Epiphanes, θεὸν ἐπιφανὴ καὶ...σωτῆρα [*theon epiphanē kai ...sōtēra*] to Julius Caesar [Ephesus, 48 B. C.]....[94]

---

[92]Murray J. Harris, "Titus 2:13 and the Deity of Christ" in *Pauline Studies: Essays presented to Professor F. F. Bruce on his 70th Birthday* (Edited by Donald A. Hagner and Murray J. Harris; Grand Rapids: Eerdmans, 1980), 266.

[93]James Hope Moulton, *A Grammar of New Testament Greek* (Third edition; Edinburgh: T. & T. Clark, 1930), I, 84.

[94]Lock, *Commentary on the Pastoral Epistles*, 145; see W. Dittenberger,

It is difficult to avoid the conclusion in light of this data, as Murray Harris writes, that "one impulse behind this particular verse was the desire to combat the extravagant titular endowment that had been accorded to human rulers."[95]

Fifth, contrary to the oft-repeated assertion that the use of θεός, *theos*, as a Christological title is an "un-Pauline locution" and thus the noun cannot refer to Christ here, I would simply say that our exposition of Romans 9:5 has demonstrated that this simply is not so. Grammatically and biblically, the evidence would indicate that Paul intended in Titus 2:13 to describe Christ as "our great God and Savior."[96]

If we could look no further for Paul's Christology than to these two texts—Romans 9:5 and Titus 2:13—we would have to conclude that his was a Christology of the highest kind. The one who had identified himself to Paul on the Damascus Road as "Jesus of Nazareth" (Acts 22:8), who as his Lord had called Paul to himself and whom Paul now served, was "over all things, the ever-blessed God" (Rom 9:5) and his "great God and Savior" (Tit 2:13). And if this was Paul's Christological vision, considering the extensiveness of his missionary travels and the significance of the church (Rome) and the man (Titus) to whom he wrote these letters, we may assume that this same high Christology would have become widely revered and regarded as precious by those for whom Paul's apostolic authority was not a matter of debate. In sum, for Paul and his churches, theirs would have been a high, ontological , incarnational Christology.

* * * * *

We have completed our survey of the Pauline corpus—written over approximately a seventeen-year period during the late fifth, sixth, and seventh decades of the first century—with regard to the Christology

---

Sylloge Inscriptionum Graecarum (Third edition; Hildesheim: Georg Olms, 1960), 760.6=Second edition, 347.6.

[95]Murray Harris, "Titus 2:13 and the Deity of Christ" in *Pauline Studies*, 267; see Nigel Turner, *Grammatical Insights*, 16.

[96]Four alternative translations have been offered for the entire verse. I would refer the reader to Murray Harris' definitive article, referred to above, for these alternatives and their respective rebuttals.

to be found therein. In the course of our review, in addition to the scores of verses which we have noted in a general way, we have considered in some detail Romans 1:3-4; 9:5; Colossians 1:15-20; 2:9; Philippians 2:6-11; Ephesians 4:9-10; 1 Timothy 1:15; 3:16; and Titus 2:13.

We have seen that from his first days as a Christian Paul regarded Christ as the Messiah and the incarnate Son of God (Acts 9:20, 22). In his letters he portrays Christ as the pre-existent Creator and Yahweh of the Old Testament (Col 1:15-17), and the co-source with the Father of all spiritual blessings, whose name is to be called upon in the church, at whose name every knee is to bow and whom every tongue is to confess is Lord (Rom 10:12-13; Phil 2:9-11). As the Son of God incarnate, he is the visible "Image of the invisible God" (Col 1:15), who "being in the form of God," possesses all the essential attributes of God and is "equal with God" (Phil 2:6-7). "In [Christ] dwells all the fullness of deity bodily" (Col 2:9), the result of the Son of God having become "enfleshed" within the line of David as a man like other men (Rom 1:3; Phil 2:7; 1 Tim 3:16), who as a man died for other men's sins and was buried, but who rose on the third day and ascended some days later to the right hand of God, assuming *de facto* mediatorial sovereignty over the universe. He is, for Paul, just Lord "over all, God blessed forever" (Rom 9:5) and "our great God and Savior" (Tit 2:13).

Now it would appear to be a subterfuge unbecoming to scholarship to claim that all of this is only functional language. While it is undoubtedly true that some of Paul's descriptions of Jesus are quite rightly to be viewed as "functional" (for example, Christ, Servant, Head of the church, even Lord in the mediatorial sense), many are not (for example, Son, Son of God, Lord in the Yahwistic sense, Image of the invisible God, and God). And it is only being sensitive to the nuances of Scripture and true to our own deepest instincts when we acknowledge that even the functional descriptions of Jesus derive their power to evoke our religious interest and devotion ultimately from the ontological descriptions of Christ which surround them and lie behind them.

Nor will it satisfy all of the data which we have considered to acknowledge on the one hand that Jesus was for Paul both *vere deus* and *vere homo,* but to assert on the other that his Christology was an anomaly in the thinking of the first-century church. What Warfield wrote almost a century ago is still true today:

> Paul is not writing a generation or two [after the generation of those who had companied with Jesus in His life], when the faith of the first disciples was a matter only of memory, perhaps of fading memory; and when it was possible for him to represent it as other than it was. He is writing out of the very bosom of this primitive community and under its very eye. His witness to the kind of Jesus this community believed in is just as valid and just as compelling, therefore, as his testimony that it believed in Jesus at all. In and through him the voice of the primitive community itself speaks, proclaiming its assured faith in its divine Lord.[97]

If anything has changed since Warfield wrote these words, it is that there would seem to be even more evidence today than there was in his time that his insight accords with the actual situation then existing, for, as we have noted elsewhere, there is a general consensus today among both critical and evangelical scholars that in Colossians 1:15-20, Philippians 2:6-11, and 1 Timothy 3:16 we have in hymnic form reflections of the primitive Christology of the early church that may very well antedate the letters of Paul in which they appear respectively. By these hymns Christ was worshiped. Then in 1 Corinthians 15:3-5 and Romans 1:3-4 we have what may well be reflections of primitive church confessions, while in 1 Timothy 1:15 we have, beyond doubt, an early church confession in the form of a "faithful saying" which Paul endorsed when he declared it to be "worthy of acceptance." When taken at face value—and there is *no* compelling reason why they should not be—all of these pericopes reflect the highest kind of Christology in which Jesus is regarded as the divine, pre-existent Son of God who through "descent" became "flesh" for us men and for our salvation and who through "ascent" assumed mediatorial headship over the universe and the church. And in the case of 1 Timothy 1:15 it is significant that here we have the spokesman of the so-called "Pauline community" commending what is now commonly recognized as a piece of teaching framed in the wording of the "Johannine community." So instead of there being

---

[97]Warfield, *The Lord of Glory*, 257.

competing communities in the early church, each headed up by a specific Apostle and each vying with one another for the minds of the masses, here is indication that the primitive church, at least that majority portion of it which followed the lead of the Apostles and for whom the Apostles were authoritative teachers in the church, was one in its essential understanding of Christ. When one also takes into account that the Jerusalem Apostles approved Paul's gospel (which surely would have included an account of who Jesus was for Paul) when he informed them of it on his second visit to Jerusalem (Gal 2:2, 6-9), plus the fact that for both the (Palestinian?) Aramaic-speaking and (Hellenistic?) Greek-speaking Christians in the primitive church Jesus was "Lord" (see the occurrence of both κύριος [*kurios*, "Lord"] and μαρανα θα [*marana tha*, Aramaic meaning either "Our *Lord* has [or will] come" or "Our *Lord*, come"] in 1 Cor 16:22), we must conclude that such strict distinctions as have been drawn by some modern scholars between an early Christology of the Jewish Palestinian church, a later Christology of the Jewish Hellenistic church (or mission), and a still later Christology of the Hellenistic Gentile church (or mission) (all stages of development before Paul) exist more in the minds of those who espouse the view than in the actual first-century church itself.[98] Paul's testimony, reflected throughout his letters, gives evidence of the fact that for Christians generally who lived at that time, Jesus was, as Warfield avers,

> a man indeed and the chosen Messiah who had come to redeem God's people, but in His essential Being just the great God Himself. In the light of [Paul's] testimony it is impossible to believe there ever was a different conception of Jesus prevalent in the Church: the mark of Christians from the beginning was obviously that they looked to Jesus as their 'Lord' and 'called upon His name' in their worship.[99]

---

[98]F. Hahn, *The Titles of Jesus in Christology* (Reprint, 1963 German edition; New York: World, 1969), and Reginald H. Fuller, *The Foundations of New Testament Christology* (London: Lutterworth, 1965). are two prominent scholars who sponsor such distinctions. But see I. Howard Marshall, "Palestinian and Hellenistic Christianity: Some Critical Comments" in *New Testament Studies* 19 (1972-1973): 271-87, and his *The Origins of New Testament Christology* (Downers Grove, Illinois: Inter-Varsity, 1976), 24-8, 29, 32-9, for an excellent evangelical response to this theory.

[99]Warfield, *The Lord of Glory*, 255-56.

CHAPTER SEVEN

THE REMAINING NEW TESTAMENT WITNESS TO JESUS

In this last chapter we propose to listen to the remaining voices of the New Testament concerning the person of Jesus—who he was in himself and who he was for others. I refer to James, Jude, Peter, the synoptic Evangelists, and particularly the Author of Hebrews and John.

JAMES' WITNESS TO JESUS

Although Paul would write the larger portion of what we know today as the New Testament he was not the first to write a letter which would become a part of the New Testament canon. That honor goes to James. The James who authored the epistle which bears this name, which was written quite probably around A.D. 45-48,[1] refers to himself as "James ['Ιάκωβος, ***Iakōbos***], a servant of God and of

[1]Since there is no reference in this letter, written expressly to the "twelve tribes which are in the Diaspora," to the destruction of Jerusalem which occurred in A.D. 70, it almost certainly was written before A.D. 70. Since James was martyred, according to Josephus, in A.D. 63, it surely had to be written before that year. Since James, if he had written *after* the Jerusalem conference (c. A.D. 49), most likely would have avoided even the *appearance* of contradiction between his epistolary teaching on justification and the decision (which he himself probably drafted) reached by the Jerusalem Conference over which he presided , it seems most likely that he wrote his letter *before* that date. Evidence within the epistle itself also suggests a pre-Conference date since the recipients still met in synagogues (probably those in which Christians had control) (2:2), and since the question of admission of Christian Gentiles into their assemblies—the burning question after Paul's first missionary journey and at the Jerusalem Conference—seems not to have been a matter of concern for James' readers. The description of his addressees suggests a time of composition before the effects of Paul's mission labors in that it appears that he can address the entire church as "the twelve

[the] Lord Jesus Christ" (1:1), is almost certainly James, "the Lord's [half-] brother" (Gal 1:19),[2] who, as one of the three "pillars" of the church of the circumcision (the other two were Peter and John, Gal 2:9, 12), presided over the mother church of Christendom in Jerusalem (Acts 12:17; 15:13; 21:18).

I would offer the following reason for urging that James, "the Lord's brother," authored this letter: If we ask ourselves which one of the four men named James in the New Testament—James, the son of Zebedee and brother of John, one of the Twelve who was martyred by Herod (Matt 4:21; 10:2; 17:1; Mark 10:35; 13:3; Luke 9:54; Acts 1:13; 12:2); James the younger, the son of Alphaeus, one of the Twelve (Matt 10:3; 27:56; Mark 3:18; 15:40; Luke 6:15; 24:10; Acts 1:13); James, the father of Judas "not Iscariot" (Luke 6:16; Acts 1:13); or James, the Lord's brother (Matt 13:55; Mark 6:3)—could expect to be recognized and identified when he called himself simply "James, a servant of God and of the Lord Jesus Christ" and could speak with such massive authority to Judaic Christianity as he does in this writing, simple reflection on what we know of the first three—which is virtually nothing—should convince us that the last James alone attained the special leadership among Jewish Christians generally which could justify its author making the broad appeal that we find in this letter.

Among modern critical scholars who support a pre-Pauline date

---

tribes of the Diaspora." Therefore, a date around A.D. 45-48 seems most likely.

See the definitive argument for the early date of James in J. B. Mayor, *The Epistle of St. James* (Third edition; London: Macmillan, 1913), cxliv-clxxvii, clxxviii-ccv. Donald Guthrie, *New Testament Introduction* (London: Inter-Varsity, 1970), 736-58, 761-64, may also be consulted for arguments in support of an early date for James.

[2]Over against the *Epiphanian* view which holds that Jesus' "brothers" and "sisters" were Joseph's sons and daughters by a former marriage, and the *Hieronymian* view—the established view of the Roman Catholic Church—which holds that these people were Jesus' "cousins," that is, the children of Clopas and Mary the sister of Jesus' mother, I would urge as more probable the *Helvidian* view, espoused in the latter half of the fourth century, that contends that Jesus' "brothers" and "sisters" were the actual sons and daughters of Joseph and Mary.

for the letter, the opinion is commonly expressed that James' "unobtrusive Christology"—A.M. Fairbairn spoke in 1893 of "the poverty of [James'] Christology"[3]—reflects "an important type of Christianity overshadowed by and misinterpreted through the figure and influence of Paul."[4] The fact that he makes no mention of Jesus' death and resurrection, for example, is interpreted to mean that "the author did not realize the importance of them."[5] For those scholars who urge that James was written contemporaneously with the Pauline corpus, the same silence respecting Jesus' death and resurrection is interpreted to mean that its author wrote "to provide a counterblast to Pauline Christianity in the interests of Judaistic Christianity."[6]

But James' Christology is neither "ante-Pauline" nor, as we shall see, "anti-Pauline" in content. Adamson notes:

> ...evidence such as that from the Dead Sea and Nag Hammadi has almost miraculously revealed or confirmed...the continuity preserved in the distinctive Jewish character, thought, and language of early Christian theology. We can now see that the Jewish first Christians had grown up in a wealth of ancient but lively tradition of messianic Christology, so that James, writing to Jewish converts who had accepted the Christian message, "This is he," was able to give most of his Christian letter not to Christian theology but to Christianity in everyday life.[7]

In other words, we may assume that James takes for granted the great saving events that centered in the historical person of Jesus as he set about the task of writing his guide to Christian behavior. Whatever reasons lay behind his decision not to speak directly of Jesus' death and resurrection (and any number of other things as well, such as his supernatural conception in Mary's womb, his mighty

---

[3]A. M. Fairbairn, *The Place of Christ in Modern Theology* (Tenth edition; London: Hodder and Stoughton, 1902), 328.

[4]E. M. Sidebottom, *James, Jude and 2 Peter* (Camden, New Jersey: Thomas Nelson, 1967), 24.

[5]Sidebottom, *James, Jude and 2 Peter*, 24.

[6]G. R. Beasley-Murray, *The General Epistles: James, 1 Peter, Jude, 2 Peter* (Nashville: Abingdon, 1965), 21.

[7]James Adamson, *The Epistle of James* (Grand Rapids: Eerdmans, 1976), 23.

miracles, his ascension, and his present session at the right hand of his Father), it certainly goes beyond the evidence to conclude that he was unaware of these things and their significance—witness his own response in faith to Jesus' resurrection appearance to him—or that he opposed Paul's Christology—witness his approval of Paul's gospel in Galatians 2:9 and his judgment at the Jerusalem council after listening to the testimonies of Peter and Paul. In fact, if we had no more than his one letter to draw upon, we would still have to conclude that James' Christology in no way contradicts and in every way is consistent with that which we learn about Christ either from Jesus' self-testimony or from the other New Testament writers.

There is sufficient evidence from parallels between the Sermon on the Mount and verses, clauses, and phrases in James' letter to warrant the assumption that James had heard his half-brother preach on numerous occasions (see Matt 5:3 and James 2:5; 5:7 and 2:13; 5:11-12 and 1:2; 5:34-37 and 5:12; 6:11 and 2:15-16; 6:19 and 5:2-3; 6:22 and 4:4, 8; 6:34 and 4:13-14; 7:1 and 4:11-12; 7:7-8 and 1:5; 7:16 and 3:10-13, 18; 7:21-23 and 1:26-27; 7:24 and 1:22-25). And while it is true that he speaks of Jesus by name only twice (1:1; 2:1), on both occasions he not only speaks of him as "the Lord Jesus Christ"—"designations expressive of marked reverence"[8] speaking as they do of both his Messiahship and Lordship—but also in each case this exalted designation is enhanced by a contextual feature that places Christ on a par with God the Father. In the former case (1:1), James describes himself as a "servant of God and of the Lord Jesus Christ"—a genitival coordination of God and Jesus that implies the latter's equality with God. In the latter case (2:1), James appositionally describes Jesus as "the Glory,"[9] undoubtedly intending by this term to describe Jesus as the manifested or "Shekinah" ("dwelling") Glory of God (see John 1:14; 2 Cor 4:4; Heb 1:3; Rev 21:3). Warfield quite correctly observes:

> The thought of the writer seems to be fixed on those Old Testament passages in which Jehovah is described as the "Glory": e.g., "For I,

---

[8]Warfield, *The Lord of Glory*, 263.

[9]In my opinion Mayor, *The Epistle of St. James*, 79-82, provides still the fullest and finest exposition of τῆς δόξης, *tēs doxēs* (2:1) in English.

> saith Jehovah, will be unto her a wall of fire round about, and I will be the Glory in the midst of her" (Zech 2:5). In the Lord Jesus Christ, James sees the fulfillment of these promises: He is Jehovah come to be with His people; and, as He has tabernacled among them, they have seen His glory. He is, in a word, the Glory of God, the Shekinah: God manifest to men. It is thus that James thought and spoke of his own brother who died a violent and shameful death while still in His first youth![10]

James also speaks of Jesus as "the Lord" (which title from New Testament usage elsewhere presupposes his resurrection and ascension) who, as such, is the one in whose name Christians are to pray and who answers their prayers (5:13-14), who heals and forgives (5:14-15), and whose coming Christians are patiently to await (5:7-8). And while it is true that James also refers to the Father as "the Lord" (see 1:7; 4:15; 5:10-11), precisely because he can pass back and forth between the Father and Jesus in his use of κύριος, *kurios*, applying it now to one, now to the other, he implies the fitness of thinking of Jesus in terms of equality with God. There is even sound reason for believing that it is Jesus who is before his mind when he speaks in 4:12 of the Lawgiver and Judge (see particularly 5:9).

As Jesus' half-brother, James surely knew of Jesus' death. And inasmuch as he had experienced first-hand an encounter with the glorified Christ, we may be assured that James knew of and believed in Jesus' resurrection and that he had some appreciation for the significance of Jesus' death. From his references to Christ as "Lord" and to Christ's coming (παρουσία, *parousia*) in 5:7-8, we may surmise that James was also aware of his ascension and present session at the Father's right hand, since such a state is the necessary prerequisite to his return. Therefore, it is not going beyond the available data to insist that James knew about and accepted the great objective central events of redemption.

So while James' declared Christology is hardly an exhaustive Christology, what he does say about Jesus is explicit and exalting, falling nothing short of implying what would come to be known later as the metaphysical Sonship of Jesus.

---

[10]Warfield, *The Lord of Glory*, 265.

JUDE'S WITNESS TO JESUS

The Epistle of Jude was written by Jude, the brother of James (1:1) and also, with James, a younger half-brother of Jesus himself (see Matt 13:55; Mark 6:3). There is no reason to doubt the authenticity of the letter as from the pen of Jesus' younger half-brother inasmuch as it is highly improbable that any forger would have selected a name comparatively so obscure as that of Jude under which to shelter himself. When all of the evidence is taken into account, a date for its composition around A.D. 65-80, or perhaps even somewhat earlier, seems appropriate.[11]

In this short letter of only twenty-five verses Jude refers to Jesus no less than six times by name and always in conjunction with one or more additional titles: "Jesus Christ" (vs 1 [twice]), "our Lord Jesus Christ" (vss 17, 21), "Jesus Christ, our Lord" (vs 25), and "our only Master and Lord, Jesus Christ" (vs 4). All ascribe to Jesus both the messianic investiture and Lordship, while the contexts in which they occur suggest that for Jude Christ's was a station not below the Father himself insofar as divine status is concerned. For if it is in God the Father that the called are loved, it is in or for Jesus Christ that they are kept (vs 1). If they are to keep themselves in the Father's love, they are no less to wait for the mercy of our Lord Jesus Christ to grant them eternal salvation (vs 21). If it is the Father who is to be glorified for the final salvation of the called, it is through Jesus Christ, our Lord, that such praise is to be mediated (vs 25). If it is the Father who is the "only God" (vs 25), it is Jesus Christ who is "our only Master and Lord" (τὸν μόνον δεσπότην καὶ κύριον, *ton monon*

---

[11] While it is true that his reference to the apostles (17) might suggest that they are no longer on the scene, his statement also suggests that his readers actually heard the apostles. So there is no need to postulate a second century date for the letter's composition. Since Jude makes no reference to the destruction of Jerusalem, which would have been a prime example of the destruction which befalls the ungodly (see 5-7, 14-15), it is unlikely that the letter was written after A.D. 70. A date around 67 or 68 A.D., is probably a safe "guesstimate." See Donald Guthrie, *New Testament Introduction*, 906-12, for a reasoned argument for both the traditional view of the letter's authorship and a first-century rather than a second-century date of composition.

despotēn kai kurion) (vs 4). And if Jude sees himself as a servant, it is as a servant of Jesus Christ (vs 1) precisely because it is Jesus Christ who is "our only Master and Lord" (vs 4).

There is some debate, it must be admitted, as to whether the full title in verse 4 refers only to Christ ("our only Master and Lord, Jesus Christ") or to both the Father ("the only Master") and to Jesus ("our Lord Jesus Christ"). Many commentators argue that the latter is the more likely interpretation, but mainly on *a priori* theological grounds. In my opinion, two factors militate against this view in favor of the former interpretation. First, both nouns ("Master" and "Lord") stand under the regimen of the single article before "Master," suggesting that they are to be construed together as characterizations of the same person. While it is certainly true that κύριος (*kurios*, "Lord") does not require the article, it is also true that had Jude intended to refer both to God the Father and to Jesus, he could have made that intention explicit either by placing "our Lord" after "Jesus Christ" as he does in verse 25, or by employing a second article before "our Lord Jesus Christ" as he does in the other two places where he refers singly to Jesus by that title (vss 17, 21). Second, 2 Peter 2:1, with a similar statement, evidently refers to Jesus as the Master. These two factors place it beyond all reasonable doubt that Jude intended to describe Jesus as both our Master and our Lord. Since it is doubtful that the two titles are a pleonasm or tautology, what did Jude intend to imply by the former title? In addition to the fact that Jesus is "our Lord," Jude by this title highlights the fact that Jesus is the "Owner" of Christians by virtue of his messianic work with the right that inheres in such ownership to command and to expect his followers' immediate and humble response.

But there is still more that Jude implies about Jesus. For in addition to the six direct references to Jesus by name, there is sound reason to think that he may well have had Jesus in mind when he refers to "the Lord" in verses 5 and 14. Consider the latter context first. Can there really be any doubt, regardless of who the referent is in 1 Enoch 1:4-9, that Jude intended to refer to Jesus in verse 14 when he wrote: "Behold, the Lord will come [ἦλθεν, *ēlthen*, an aorist with prophetic (future) intention] with his myriad holy ones" (see Matt 16:27; 25:31; Mark 8:38; Luke 9:26; 1 Thes 3:13; 2 Thes 1:7-10)? In light of consentient Christian testimony, no other referent will suffice. But then, this being so, Jude here ascribes the divine prerogative of eschatological judgment to Jesus.

In the former verse (vs 5), apart from the fact that "Jesus" may well be the original reading instead of "Lord,"[12] even with the reading "the Lord," there is every reason to believe that Jesus may still have been Jude's intended referent. Consider the following facts. First, there is no question that Jude employed "Lord" to refer to Jesus four times (vss 4, 17, 21, 25). Second, we have just seen that the almost certain referent of "Lord" in verse 14 is Jesus. And third, this occurrence of "Lord" in verse 5 comes hard on the heels of Jude's certain reference to Jesus in the immediately preceding verse as "our only Master and Lord, Jesus Christ." So it is not only possible but also virtually certain that it is to Jesus, in his preincarnate state as the Yahweh of the Old Testament, that he ascribes, first, the deliverance of Israel from Egypt and then the destruction of those within the nation who rebelled; second, the judgment of the angels at the time of their primeval fall; and third, the destruction of Sodom and Gomorrah. And if all this is true, Jude was clearly thinking of Jesus Christ in terms that encompass the Old Testament Deity. But however one interprets this last verse, it is apparent from the others that, for Jude, Christ was the sovereign Master and Lord of men, who at his coming will exercise the prerogative to dispense eschatological salvation and judgment as the Savior and Judge of men. There can be no doubt, in light of these facts, that for him Christ was divine.

---

[12]Bruce M. Metzger, *A Textual Commentary on the Greek New Testament*, 725-26, explains with respect to the reading ὁ κύριος, *ho kurios*, in the UBS *Greek New Testament* that "a majority of the Committee was of the opinion that the reading ['Ιησοῦς, *Iēsous*] was difficult to the point of impossibility, and explained its origin in terms of transcriptional oversight." But Metzger himself and Allen Wikgren affirm that "Critical principles seem to require the adoption of 'Ιησοῦς, *Iēsous*, which admittedly is the best attested reading among Greek and versional witnesses [e.g., A, B, 33, Vulgate, and some significant church fathers]. Struck by the strange and unparalleled mention of Jesus in a statement about the redemption out of Egypt (yet compare Paul's reference to Χριστός, *Christos*, in 1 Cor 10.4) copyists would have substituted *[ὁ]* κύριος [*[ho] kurios*] or ὁ θεός [*ēo theos*]." In short,'Ιησοῦς, *Iēsous*, is both the best supported reading textually and

PETER'S EPISTOLARY WITNESS TO JESUS

Peter wrote his two letters most probably during the seventh decade of the first century (the first about A.D. 62-64 during Nero's reign and the second shortly before the end of his life around A.D. 68).[13] As we consider Peter's epistolary witness to Jesus, we should bear in mind that from numerous experiences as one of the original twelve disciples he had gained first-hand insight into the character and work of his Lord. We may mention, by way of review, that on the occasion of the first miraculous catch of fish, he had expressed a numinous awe of Jesus, calling him "Lord" and worshiping him (Luke 5:4-10). Later, moved by Jesus' discourse on the Bread of Life, as the spokesman for the disciples Peter had confessed that Jesus alone was the wellspring of words of eternal life as the Holy One of God (John 6:68-69). Then after he and Jesus had walked on Sea of Galilee, he joined the other disciples in the united confession: "You are truly the Son of God" (Matt 14:33). And, of course, it was Peter who registered the great confession at Caesarea Philippi: "You are the Christ, the Son of the living God" (Matt 16:16). In addition to seeing the miracles which Jesus performed publicly, Peter was among that inner circle of disciples who also witnessed his transfiguration and who heard the Father's attestation to Jesus' unique Sonship (Matt 17:2-6). He was also the private beneficiary of one of Jesus' post-resurrection appearances (he probably was the first apostle to see him) (Luke 24:34; 1 Cor 15:5), and he saw him on several other occasions, specifically hearing Thomas' confession of Jesus of "Lord and God" during one of them (John 20:28). He witnessed Jesus' ascension into heaven, and it was Peter who preached the sermon on the Day of Pentecost in which he acclaimed both the messiahship

---

undoubtedly the hardest of the variant readings—canons of criticism which, when both are true of a given reading, normally carry the field.

[13]See Guthrie, *New Testament Introduction*, 773-90, 795-96, 820-48, 850-51, for a reasoned defense of the Petrine authorship of both letters and the arguments for placing them in the seventh decade of the first century. See also Gleason L. Archer, Jr., *Encyclopedia of Bible Difficulties* (Grand Rapids: Zondervan, 1982), 425-27, for a brief but substantive defense of the Petrine authorship of 2 Peter.

and mediatorial lordship of the divine Jesus.[14] Finally, we should not overlook the fact that Peter was surely aware of Paul's Christology and was approving in his assessment of it (Gal 1:19; 2:1-9; 2 Pet 3:15-16). Consequently, one should not be surprised to find Peter espousing the highest kind of Christology "from above" in his letters. Indeed, it would be exceedingly strange were one to find it in any way otherwise.

---

[14]Peter said the following four things in his Pentecost sermon that carry implications concerning Jesus' divine character.

1. The very fact of Christ's ascension and, more particularly, of his session at his Father's right hand suggests that Jesus is divine, for he who would sit as "Lord over all" the nations on the throne of God must himself be God. Certainly, his session on the throne of God attests to his superangelic nature, for "to which of the angels did God ever say, 'Sit at my right hand until I make your enemies a footstool for Your feet'" (Heb. 1:5)?

2. The fact that it was the ascended *Jesus* who poured out the Spirit (2:33) moves in the same direction. The connection between what Peter expressly emphasized in 2:17 by his deliberate insertion of the words "God says" into the Joel prophecy ("'In the last days,' *God says*, '*I will pour out* my Spirit'") and his later statement in 2:33 ("*He* [the ascended Jesus] *has poured out* this which you now see and hear") cannot have been unintentional or lost on Peter. Clearly, Peter connects the God and Yahweh of Joel 2 who promised to pour out his Spirit with the ascended Jesus of Acts 2 who poured out his Spirit.

3. The fact that the authority to apply the benefits of his redemption by his Spirit to whomever he pleases in his role as Baptizer of men by his Spirit (salvation) and by fire (judgment) means nothing less than that the prerogatives and functions of deity are his to exercise, but then this means that he himself is God.

4. When Peter, in response to his listeners' query: "Brothers, what shall we do?," urged them to "repent and be baptized *in the name of Jesus Christ*" (2:38), it is difficult to avoid the conclusion that he was simply urging them to avail themselves of the remedy which Joel himself had prescribed in his prophecy when he said: "And everyone who calls on *the name of the Lord* will be saved" (Acts 2:21). But then this means, in turn, that for Peter Jesus was the Lord of Joel 2:32a (see Rom 10:9-13), which means in turn that Jesus was the Yahweh who spoke through Joel.

These four features in Peter's exposition of the Pentecost event indicate that Pentecost in its own striking way adds its testimony to the combined and consentient witness of Scripture to Christ's messianic investiture and his divine nature.

First Peter

In his first letter Peter refers to Jesus as "[the] Christ"—his most common designation for him (1:11, 19; 2:21; 3:15, 16, 18; 4:1, 13, 14; 5:1, 10[15], 14), "Jesus Christ" (1:1, 2, 3, 7, 13; 2:5; 3:21; 4:11), "[the] Lord" (2:3, 13; 3:15; perhaps also in 1:25; 3:12), and "our Lord Jesus Christ" (1:3). What Peter says about Jesus in these contexts reveals a fully-developed incarnational Christology. He implies his pre-existence with the Father (1:20a),[16] affirming that it was Christ's Spirit who had inspired the prophets in Old Testament times (1:11) and that he had been "manifested" in these last times (1:20b). In accordance with Old Testament prophecy (1:11), as our sinless substitute (2:22, a citation of Isaiah 53:9) he suffered death vicariously on the cross (1:2, 11, 19; 2:21, 23, 24; 3:18; 4:1, 13; 5:1), was raised from the dead (1:3, 21; 3:18, 21), ascended to the right hand of God and to glory (1:11, 21; 3:22), and will be revealed in the Eschaton (1:7, 13; 5:1, 4). He is the Mediator between God and man (1:21; 2:5; 4:11; 5:10, 14) and the one in whom men must trust for salvation (2:6).

In the course of setting forth his Christology not only does Peter place Christ in the trinitarian context of the Father and the Spirit (1:2,

---

[15]See Metzger, *A Textual Commentary on the Greek New Testament*, 697, for the reasons for the preference for the shorter reading "Christ" over the longer reading "Christ Jesus."

[16]Ernest Best, *1 Peter* (London, Oliphants, 1971), 91, declares that "the pre-existence of Christ is implied here through the additional words *was made manifest*, i.e., at the incarnation," and this is, of course, true. But then, if this is so, it would follow that the immediately preceding words, "foreknown before the foundation of the world," *when applied to Christ*, would imply the same as well. For as James Moffatt, *The General Epistles: Peter, James and Judas* (London: Hodder and Stoughton, 1928), 107, observes: "In i. 2... Christians are *predestined* [his translation of προγινώσκειν, *proginōskein*] but here the conception of a personal pre-existence is extended to the personality of Christ." I. Howard Marshall, "Incarnational Christology in the New Testament" in *Christ the Lord*, 11, also notes:

> The writer also speaks of [Christ] as One who was predestined before the foundation of the world, but made manifest at the end of the times (1:20). This appears to be a remnant of incarnational language; Peter does not lay stress on it, but simply makes use of a stereotyped traditional terminology which reflects an existing incarnational theology.

3, 11; 4:14) but three times he refers to Old Testament passages in which Yahweh is the subject and uses them of Christ in a way that suggests that Christ is to be equated with the Yahweh of the Old Testament Scriptures. In 2:3, alluding to Psalm 34:8 ("Taste and see that the LORD is good"), he writes with reference to Christ: "if you tasted that the Lord is good."[17] In 2:8, citing Isaiah 8:14b, he equates

---

[17]That ὁ κύριος, *ho kurios*, in 2:3 refers to Christ and implies his identity with the Yahweh of Psalm 34:8 is evident from the immediately following phrase in 2:4, "to whom coming, as to a living stone" (a further echo of Ps 34:5 [LXX]), where the relative pronoun and the "stone" metaphor clearly refer to Christ as the entire context makes clear.

C. E. B. Cranfield, *I & II Peter and Jude* (London: SCM, 1960), 62, comments on 2:3: "[This clause] is a quotation from Ps. 34.8 (slightly modified). That by THE LORD...Christ is meant is indicated by the following verse." He further declares (34-35):

> With regard to the significance which the title had for the primitive Church, the following facts are of decisive importance: in the LXX *Kyrios* ('Lord') represents the Divine Name or Tetragrammaton...more than six thousand times; the New Testament writers had no scruple about applying Old Testament texts in which *Kyrios* is so used to the exalted Jesus (e.g. Rom. 10.13; 1 Thess 5:2; I Peter 2.3; 3.15); and the first Christians, men brought up in Judaism in a religious tradition for which such texts as Ex. 20.3 and Deut. 6.4 were of utterly fundamental importance, prayed to Jesus (e.g. Acts 7:59f.; 9:14; I Cor. 1.2). In view of these facts it can hardly be denied that the confession 'Jesus is Lord' was a confession that the exalted Jesus was in the fullest sense divine.

Best, *1 Peter*, 99, likewise comments on 2:3:

> Lord: in Ps. 34:8 the 'Lord' is God. Our author in common with the other NT writers regularly understands the 'Lord' of the OT to refer to Christ...; this is made clear by the beginning of verse 4 where 'him' refers back to 'Lord' in verse 3.

He even suggests that Peter deliberately substituted "Lord" for "our God" in 1:25, when citing Isaiah 40:6-8, to link the word to Christ, who is the "Lord" of 2:3 (96).

Moffatt, *The General Epistles: Peter, James and Judas*, 114, comments on 2:3:

> Any mention of *the Lord* in the O.T. naturally suggested the divine Christ to an early Christian, and this sent Peter off again...to expatiate upon the vital value of Christ to Christians.

the LORD of Hosts there, who would become "a stone that causes men to stumble, and a rock that makes them fall" with Christ, the "stone laid in Zion" (2:6, citing Isa 28:16), and the "stone the builders rejected [who] has become the capstone" (2:7, citing Psa 118:22). And in 3:14-15, alluding to Isaiah 8:12-13, he equates the LORD of Hosts who is to be sanctified there in Isaiah with Christ ("Sanctify Christ as Lord in your hearts").[18]

There can be no doubt that, for Peter, Christ as God's Son was essentially divine in nature and to be regarded as God incarnate.

Second Peter

In his second letter[19] Peter refers to Jesus as "Jesus Christ" (1:1), "[the] Lord" (3:8, 9, 10, 15; perhaps 2:9), "the Lord and Savior" (3:2), "our Lord and Savior Jesus Christ" (1:11; 2:20; 3:18), and finally, "our God and Savior Jesus Christ" (1:1).

Finally, J. N. D. Kelly, *The Epistles of Peter and Jude* (London: Adam & Charles Black, 1969), 86, comments on 2:3: "In the original [Hebrew] 'the Lord' of course denotes Yahweh, but the Christian understanding of the Psalter naturally transferred the title to Christ."

[18]The reading Χριστὸν, *Christon*, is textually secure, supported as it is both by "early and diversified external evidence" and by the transcriptional probability that "the more familiar expression [κύριον τὸν θεόν, *kurion ton theon*]' replaced "the less usual expression [κύριον τὸν Χριστόν, *kurion ton Christon*]." So Metzger, *A Textual Commentary on the Greek New Testament*, 691. On the significance of the verse for Christ's divine nature, Kelly, *The Epistles of Peter and Jude*, 142, writes: "The verse has a bearing on I Peter's Christology, for as in ii. 3 the title 'the Lord', which in the Hebrew original denotes God, is unhesitatingly attributed to Christ."

[19]I am assuming that Simon Peter bar Jonah wrote this letter. The author identifies himself as "Simon Peter, a servant and apostle of Jesus Christ" (1:1), he declares that the Lord had spoken to him about his death (1:14; see John 21:18-19), he claims to have been an eye- and ear-witness of Christ's transfiguration (1:16-18), he claims to have written his readers a previous letter (3:1), and he implies that he knows "our dear brother Paul" (3:15-16). All of this provides exceptionally solid internal evidence for accepting the Petrine authorship of 2 Peter. See E. M. B. Green's *Second Peter Reconsidered* (London: Tyndale, 1960), an admirable monograph of original scholarship, which ably combats today's prevailing liberal contention that 2 Peter is a spurious "pious forgery."

This last reference is very important, for now we find Peter—like Thomas and Paul before him—employing θεός, *theos*, as a Christological title. This assertion, of course, has not gone unchallenged, the alternative suggestion being that by θεός, *theos*, Peter intended to refer to the Father. As earlier with Titus 2:13 the issue turns on the question whether by the phrase, "the righteousness of our God and Savior Jesus Christ," Peter intended to refer to two persons (God the Father and Jesus) or to only one person, Jesus alone. It is my opinion, as well as that of the KJV, RV, RSV, NASV, NEB, NIV, and the NKJV, that Peter intended to refer only to Christ. I would offer the following six reasons for my conviction:

First, it is the most natural way to read the Greek sentence. If Peter had intended to speak of two persons, he could have expressed himself unambiguously to that effect, as he does in the very next verse ("knowledge of God and of Jesus our Lord"), by placing "our Savior" after "Jesus Christ" or by simply inserting an article before "Savior" in the present word order. Bigg rightly observes: "...if the author intended to distinguish two persons, he has expressed himself with singular inaccuracy."[20]

Second, both "God" and "Savior" stand under the regimen of the single article before "God," linking the two nouns together as referents to a single person.[21] Bigg again rightly states: "It is hardly open for anyone to translate in I Pet. 1.3 ὁ θεὸς καὶ πατὴρ [*ho theos kai patēr*] by 'the God and Father,' and yet here decline to translate ὁ θεὸς καὶ σωτήρ [*ho theos kai sotēr*] by 'the God and Saviour.'"[22]

Third, five times in 2 Peter, including this one, Peter uses the word "Savior." It is always coupled with a preceding noun (the other four times always with κύριος, *kurios*) in precisely the same word order

---

[20]Charles Bigg, *A Critical and Exegetical Commentary on the Epistles of St. Peter and St. Jude* (ICC) (Edinburgh: T. & T. Clark, 1902), 251.

[21]See A. T. Robertson, *A Grammar of the Greek New Testament in the Light of Historical Research*, 785-86; also Blass-Debrunner, *A Greek Grammar of the New Testament*, 144-45, para. 276, and Bruce M. Metzger, "Jehovah's Witnesses and Jesus Christ" in *Theology Today* (April 1953), 78-9.

[22]Bigg, *A Critical and Exegetical Commentary on the Epistles of St. Peter and St. Jude*, 251; see Warfield, *The Lord of Glory*, 270.

as in 1:1. Here are the last four uses in their precise word order:

> 1:11: "...kingdom of the Lord of us and Savior Jesus Christ"
> 2:20: "...knowledge of the Lord of us and Savior Jesus Christ"
> 3:4: "...commandment of the Lord and Savior"
> 3:18: "...knowledge of the Lord of us and Savior Jesus Christ"

In each of these four cases, "Lord" and "Savior," standing under the regimen of the single article before "Lord," refer to the same person, a fact recognized by all grammarians, commentaries, and Bible versions. If we simply substitute the word θεός, *theos*, for κύριος, *kurios*, we have precisely the word order in 1:1: "...righteousness of the God of us and Savior Jesus Christ." In other words, the phrases in these verses are perfectly similar and must stand or fall together. The parallelism of word order between the phrase in 1:1 and the other four phrases, where only one person is intended, puts it beyond all reasonable doubt that Peter intend one person in 1:1 as well.

Ernst Käsemann's contrary opinion that "our Lord and Savior" in the four occurrences reflects a "stereotyped" Christological formula and that therefore the employment of θεοῦ, *theou*, in 1:1 stands outside of the stereotype, the phrase thus referring to two persons,[23] is unconvincing. There is no reason why a variant of a stereotyped formula could not occur. And when the grammar clearly indicates that it has occurred then the interpreter should feel it necessary to be led by the grammar.

Fourth, the doxology to "our Lord Jesus Christ" in 3:18 ascribes "glory both now and forever" to him, an ascription suggesting a Christology in which Christ may be glorified in the same way that God is glorified. There would be, then, nothing incongruous in describing Christ as God in 1:1.

Fifth, Peter was surely present on the occasion of Thomas' confession of Jesus as both Lord and God (John 20:28), which confession had received Christ's approval. The memory of that confession, not to mention his own confession in Matthew 16:16, would have dissolved any reticence on Peter's part to refer to Jesus as

---

[23]Ernst Käsemann, "An Apologia for Primitive Christian Eschatology" in *Essays on New Testament Themes* (London: SCM, 1964), 183, fn. 2.

θεός, *theos*. Such a description of Jesus here as God is simply in line with those earlier confessions and does not go one centimeter beyond them.

Sixth, since Peter was almost certainly aware of the content of Paul's letter to the Roman church (he seems to allude to it in 2 Peter 2:19 and 3:15 (compare 2:19 with Rom 6:16, and 3:15 with Rom 2:4; 9:22-23, 11:22-23), he would have been aware that Paul in Romans 9:5 had referred to Christ as "over all, the ever-blessed God." According "scriptural status" to Paul's letters as he does (3:16), he would have seen nothing inappropriate or "unscriptural" about his own description of Christ as God just as his "dear brother Paul" had done some years earlier.

We conclude then that 2 Peter 1:1 takes its place alongside John 20:28, Romans 9:5, and Titus 2:13 as a fourth verse in which Jesus is described as being God by the Christological title of θεός, *theos*.

While Peter's Christology in 2 Peter is not as full with respect to detail as in his first letter it is still the same high Christology "from above" which we observed there. That Jesus is God incarnate is attested, as we have just argued, by Peter's description of him as "our God" (1:1) and by his being, with the Father, the co-source of grace and peace (1:2). He also assigns to him divine power (ἡ θεῖα δύναμις, *hē theia dunamis*), divine essence (θεῖα φύσις, *theia phusis*), and divine majesty (μεγαλειότης, *megaleiotēs*) (1:3, 4, 16).[24] His is an eternal kingdom (1:11), into which Christians will be welcomed when he comes in power (1:16) on his "Day" (3:10), which

---

[24]It is exegetically possible that either "God" or "Jesus our Lord" in 1:2 could be the antecedent of the αὐτοῦ (*autou*, "his") in 1:3, but the preponderance of evidence leans toward the latter. It is the nearest possible antecedent, and having just designated Christ as "our God" in 1:1, it would not be at all strange were Peter to refer to Christ's "divine power." Moreover, inasmuch as Christ is the object of knowledge in 1:2, 8; 2:20; 3:18, it is most likely the case that he is the referent of the phrase "him who called" in 1:3, although effectual calling is usually assigned to God the Father in Scripture (but see Matt 9:13; Mark 2:17; 3:13). (There is no difficulty, considering the rhetorical style of the passage, in referring "his" and "him who called" to the same person.) If this is so, and I would suggest that it is, then both a unique (see "his own") glory and the divine nature are ascribed to him in addition to divine power (so Bigg, Lenski, Barclay, Bauckham). Note: One last comment

is "the Day of God" (3:12), to destroy the heavens and earth with fire (3:10-12). He is the Owner (δεσπότης, *despotēs*) of men (2:1) whose commands they are to obey (3:2) and through the knowledge of whom all spiritual blessing and Christian virtue come (1:2, 8; 2:20; 3:18). Finally, to him is directed the doxology in 3:18 ("To him be the glory both now and forever"), a doxology not unlike those addressed both to him (2 Tim 4:18; Heb 13:20-21; 1 Pet 4:11; Rev 1:5b-6) and to the Father (1 Pet 5:11; Jude 24-25) elsewhere.[25] And yet he is distinct from his Father as the Son of the Father who in his mediatorial role receives honor and glory from his Father (1:17). Peter's epistolary witness comports with what we have seen elsewhere in his witness to Jesus and simply adds the weight of its testimony to the New Testament's depiction of the full unabridged deity of Jesus Christ.

THE SYNOPTISTS' WITNESS TO JESUS

It was most likely during the seventh decade of the first century—the decade in which several of the New Testament letters were written and also in which Peter and Paul were martyred—that the Synoptists wrote their Gospels.[26] In their accounts of Jesus' life and ministry, not only do they report what we have already treated under the topic

---

is in order: Christians do not become "sharers of his divine nature" in the sense that they become "divinized" but in the sense that they become incorruptible and immortal in Christ's eternal kingdom.

[25]That the doxology is addressed to Christ in 3:18 is beyond question. That the doxologies in 1 Peter 4:11 and Hebrews 13:21 are also directed to Christ seems apparent from the collocation of words in these respective verses. Bigg, *A Critical and Exegetical Commentary on the Epistles of St. Peter and St. Jude*, 176 (on 1 Pet 4:11), has rightly pointed out: "It is hardly to be supposed that any serious writer would lay himself open to misunderstanding on so grave a point, when by merely throwing back the words διὰ Ἰησοῦ Χριστοῦ [*dia Iēsou Christou*, "through Jesus Christ"] he could have prevented all possibility of mistake."

[26]See D. A. Carson, *Matthew*, 19-21; Walter W. Wessel, *Mark*, 607-08; Walter L. Liefeld, *Luke*, 807-09, all to be found in *The Expositor's Bible Commentary* (Grand Rapids: Zondervan, 1984), Volume 8, for the reasons for this approximate dating. Donald Guthrie, *New Testament Introduction*, 45-6, 72-6, 110-15, seems to be open to even earlier dates for Matthew and Mark than are Carson and Wessel.

of Jesus' self-witness but also, in doing so, since it can hardly be maintained that they wrote as disinterested biographers,[27] they revealed what they themselves believed regarding Jesus. Thus it can be said at the outset of this section of our study that Jesus' reported *self*-witness reflects also *their* understanding of him—which is just to say that for all three Jesus was the divine Son of God who, being co-equal and co-essential with the Father as to his deity, was dispatched as the Son of the Father on the messianic errand and thus became man and died for man's sins, but who then rose from the dead the third day after death and who now sits at the right hand of God, awaiting the time when he will return in power and great glory to judge the world.

But there are also certain authorial distinctions between the Evangelists, and these are equally important to note in a study such as this present one.

Mark's Witness

If Matthew and Luke are in some ways more explicit than Mark regarding their views of Christ, it is still the case that for Mark Jesus is no less divine than he is for the other two Synoptists (assuming for the time being that he is divine for them). The title "Son of God" as a Christological title occurs in 3:11 and 15:39, with the variants "Son of the Most High God" and "Son of the Blessed" occurring in 5:7 and 14:61 respectively.[28] Beside these stand the simple "a son" (12:6), "the Son" (13:22), and "my Son" (1:11; 9:7). In earlier analyses of these passages we demonstrated that in each of these instances the title intends the ascription to Jesus of a unique filial relationship to the Father, this unique Sonship being ultimately grounded in his transcendent co-essentiality with the Father.

---

[27]This is not to suggest for a moment that because they were, as Jesus' followers, *interested* biographers that their accounts are in any way distortions of the history of his life.

[28]See Metzger, *A Textual Commentary on the Greek New Testament*, 73, and William L. Lane, *The Gospel According to Mark* (Grand Rapids: Eerdmans, 1974), 41, fn. 7, for the text-critical arguments respectively for the textual uncertainty and for the presumptive certainty of "the Son of God" in 1:1.

Mark's "Son of Man" sayings also indicate that, although Jesus as the Danielic "Son of Man" would suffer and be betrayed into the hands of sinners and be killed (8:31; 9:31; 10:33-34; 14:21, 41), he is, as that same Son of Man, also a superhuman, super-angelic figure of transcendent dignity who does mighty works, is the Lord of the Sabbath (2:28), has the authority to forgive sins (2:10), who actually *gives* his life as a ransom for many (10:45) in accordance with the prophetic Scriptures (14:21), but who rises from the dead (8:31; 9:9, 31; 10:34), sits on the right hand of the Mighty One (14:62), and will return in clouds with the holy angels and with great power and glory to judge the world (8:38; 13:26-27).

E. Lohmeyer's assessment of Mark's Jesus is clearly on target when he declares that, as the Son of God, Jesus for Mark is

> not primarily a human but a divine figure.... He is not merely endowed with the power of God, but is himself divine as to his nature; not only are his word and work divine but his essence also.[29]

William Lane notes in this same connection that "it is widely recognized that the figure of Jesus in Mark's Gospel is altogether supernatural."[30]

Matthew's Witness

For Matthew, as for Mark, Jesus is the Son of God (2:15; 3:17; 4:3, 6; 11:27; 14:33; 16:16; 17:5; 21:37-38; 22:2; 24:36; 26:63-64; 27:54; 28:19), by which title he intends all that Mark means by it—that Jesus stands in a unique filial relationship to the Father because, as the Father's Son, he is divine. But Matthew makes explicit at some points what Mark takes for granted. Matthew reports Jesus' supernatural entrance into the world as "Immanuel"—"God with us" (1:18-25). In the "embryonic Fourth Gospel" in 11:27 he brings out the truth that Jesus' knowledge of the Father is on a par with the Father's reciprocal knowledge of him, and his sovereign disposition of that knowledge to men is also on a par with the Father's reciprocal sovereign disposition of his knowledge of the Son (11:27). And it is in Matthew's account

---

[29]E. Lohmeyer, *Das Evangelium des Markus* (Twelfth edition; Göttingen: Vandenhoeck & Ruprecht, 1953), 4 (my translation).

[30]Lane, *The Gospel According to Mark*, 44, fn. 23.

of the Great Commission that we see Jesus placing himself even in the "awful precincts of the divine Name" (Warfield) as the co-sharer with the Father and the Spirit of the one ineffable Name or essence of God (28:19).

As the messianic Son of Man, Matthew's Jesus undergoes a period of humiliation as he serves men (20:28) and suffers all kinds of indignities—even death—at their hands (12:40; 17:12, 22-23; 20:18-19, 28; 26:2, 24, 45). But as the same Son of Man he possesses the authority to forgive sins (9:6) and is the Lord of the Sabbath (12:8). Although he is killed, according to Matthew his death was a self-sacrifice—"a ransom for many" (20:28)—in accordance with prophetic Scripture (26:24), but he rises from the dead (12:40; 17:9, 23; 20:19), assumes authority at the right hand of the Mighty One (26:64), and will return on the clouds with *his* angels (16:27; 24:31) in power and great glory to judge the nations of the world (19:28; 24:27, 30, 39, 44; 25:31-46; 26:64).

There can be no doubt that Matthew's Jesus—a man surely—is also of supernatural origin, and is superhuman, superangelic, indeed, equal with the Father in essential nature though submissive to the Father's will in his mediatorial role as the Messiah.

Luke's Witness

Luke's witness to Jesus' divine Sonship is just as transparent as the other Synoptists (1:32, 35; 3:22; 4:3, 9, 41; 8:28; 9:35; 10:22; 20:13; 22:70). With Matthew he reports Jesus' supernatural birth, and with Matthew he also records Jesus' claim to a knowledge of the Father equivalent in every way—"complete, exhaustive, and unbrokenly continuous" (Warfield)—with the Father's knowledge of him, by virtue of which he also is the only adequate revealer of the Father to men just as the Father is the only adequate revealer of the Son to men (10:21-22).

With the other Synoptists, Luke's Jesus, as the Danielic Son of Man, suffers for a time at the hands of men "in order to seek and to save that which was lost" (9:22, 44; 18:31-32; 19:10) as it had been predicted in Scripture (18:31; 22:22). But then he rises from the dead (9:22; 18:33; 24:7), ascends to the right hand of the Mighty God

(22:69), and will return in a cloud with power and great glory (9:26; 21:27) to determine the destinies of men—surely a divine prerogative and function (9:26; 12:8; 21:36). Again, as in the other Synoptic Gospels, Luke's Jesus, as the Son of Man is a figure of transcendent proportions.

But Luke's Gospel contains a feature which is absent from the other two Synoptic Gospels. Though it is true that Jesus is also for Mark and Matthew "the Lord" (see Mark 1:3; Matt 3:3), Luke makes this characterization of Jesus explicit through his recurring narrative use of "the Lord" in reference to Jesus (7:13, 19; 10:1, 39, 41; 11:39; 12:42; 13:15; 17:5, 6; 18:6; 19:8; 22:61; 24:3; see the numerous occurrences of the same feature in Luke's Acts), no doubt reflecting the post-resurrection terminology of the early church and revealing thereby its lofty Christology.[31] As for the significance of Luke's narrative use of "Lord" for Jesus, after noting that "what was in the OT [LXX] the name of God has been applied to Jesus," and that ὁ κύριος (*ho kurios*, "the Lord") "is used of both God and Jesus quite indiscriminately [in Acts], so that it is often hard to determine which Person is meant," I. Howard Marshall declares that in his Gospel Luke employs it particularly to introduce authoritative statements by Jesus, and concludes from all this that "Jesus...is for Luke the Lord [in the Yahwistic sense] during his earthly ministry,"[32] although Luke, of course, is careful not to place the title with that significance on the lips of the disciples in an indiscriminate, anachronistic way.

The only legitimate judgment that can be passed in view of their

---

[31]Geerhardus Vos, *The Self-Disclosure of Jesus*, p. 119, writes on this Lucan feature:

> In [the case of the Evangelist using the title "the Lord" of Jesus] we have, of course, nothing but an instance of the custom which generally prevailed at the time the Gospels were written, of referring to Jesus as "the Lord." The Evangelist must have followed this custom in his daily speech, and no reason can be discovered why he should have refrained from following it in writing, even though it should have been, strictly speaking, an anachronism. For not only the Evangelist, but also the readers for whom he proximately wrote, daily so expressed themselves. Grammatically analyzed...the language used means simply this: "He, whom we now call the Lord...."

[32]I. Howard Marshall, *Luke, Historian and Theologian*, 166-67.

united testimony is that for the Synoptic Evangelists Jesus is God incarnate.

THE AUTHOR OF HEBREWS' WITNESS TO JESUS

Most likely in the late sixth or seventh decade of the first century, but almost certainly before the destruction of Jerusalem in A.D. 70, the Author of Hebrews penned his exhortation to Jewish Christians.[33] If Paul wrote it,[34] then it would have had to be written, of course, before his martyrdom in Rome around A.D. 64-67.

---

[33]The letter had to be written before A.D. 96 since Clement of Rome in A.D. 96 made use of it in his letter to the Corinthians. Most likely it was written in the late sixth or early seventh decade of the first century and almost certainly before the destruction of Jerusalem in A.D. 70 since no reference is made to that event which would have been a telling historical confirmation of his argument and since the temple service appears to be represented as still continuing in Jerusalem (see the present tenses in Hebrews 8:4, 13; 10:1, 8, 11; 13:10, 11). Moreover, no reference is made to such important events as the outbreak of the Jewish War (A.D. 66) or the Neronian persecution (A.D. 64). If Paul wrote it, Hebrews would have had to be written, of course, before his martyrdom in Rome around A.D. 65, but possibly as late as A.D. 67, most likely during his second imprisonment.

For representative synchronous discussions of the issue of dating, see Guthrie, *New Testament Introduction*, 716-18; F. F. Bruce, *Commentary on the Epistle to the Hebrews*, xlii-xliv; P. E. Hughes, *A Commentary on the Epistle to the Hebrews*, 30-32.

[34]Who is the author of this magnificent homily on the high priestly work of Jesus Christ? This is an *extremely* difficult question to answer, with Paul, Barnabas, Luke, Sylvanus, Apollos, Aquila and Priscilla, Priscilla alone, Philip, and even Clement of Rome all having been advanced as the author by some authority at one time or another. Donald Guthrie's conclusion—"an open verdict is clearly the safest course and in this the opinion of Origen can hardly be improved upon"—reflects the most common course followed today. But it is regrettable that about the only thing one hears popularly expressed about this question today is this referred-to opinion of Origen (c. 185-c. 254) to the effect that "in truth God [alone] knows [τὸ μὲν ἀληθὲς θεὸς οἶδεν, *to men alēthes theos oiden*]" the real truth of the matter. It is not so commonly recognized that the immediately preceding context of this remark suggests that in Origen's opinion the letter was Pauline—certainly in content if not by the actual pen of Paul. He writes:

The Christ of Hebrews is arguably as fully and truly human as everywhere else in Scripture—he shared our humanity (2:14), was made like his brothers in every way (2:17), was a descendant of Judah

---

...that the thoughts of the epistle are admirable, and not inferior to the acknowledged writings of the apostle, to this...everyone will consent as true who has given attention to reading the apostle.... But as for myself, if I were to state my own opinion, I should say that *the thoughts are the apostle's*, but that the style and composition belong to one who called to mind the apostle's teachings and, as it were, made short notes of what his master said. If any church, therefore, holds this epistle as Paul's, *let it be commended* [εὐδοκιμείτο, ***eudokimeito***]. For *not without reason* have the ancients [from only about a century and half earlier] handed it down as Paul's. (cited by Eusebius, *Ecclesiastical History*, 6.25.12-13; emphasis supplied).

The letter, admittedly, is anonymous. But whoever the author was, it is clear that the letter's original recipients knew who it was who was speaking to them, for he calls upon them to pray that he would be restored to them shortly (13:18-24). Could Paul be the author, as I think? In Egypt and North Africa Paul's authorship seems never to have been a matter of serious dispute. Primarily in Italy and particularly in Rome it was later disputed for a time.

As evidence of this Eastern tradition, while it is true that Paul in every other instance that we know of indicated authorship by name, Eusebius informs us that Clement of Alexandria (A.D. 155-215) declared (1) that Paul wrote the letter to Hebrew Christians in Hebrew and that Luke had carefully translated it into Greek and had published it for Greek-speaking Christians, and (2) that Paul had omitted his name in the letter both out of deference to his Lord whom he looked upon as the real Apostle to the Hebrews (3:1; see Rom 15:8) and to avoid Jewish prejudice against the letter which would have surely come were they to know that he had authored it. Eusebius's exact words (*Ecclesiastical History*, 6.14.2f.), summarizing a passage in Clement of Alexandria's *Hypotyposeis*, are as follows:

...as for the Epistle to the Hebrews, [Clement] says indeed that it is Paul's, but that it was written for Hebrews in the Hebrew tongue, and that Luke, having carefully translated it, published it for the Greeks; hence, as a result of this translation, the same complexion of style is found in this Epistle and in the Acts: but that the [words] "Paul an apostle" were naturally not affixed. For, says he, "in writing to Hebrews who had conceived a prejudice against him, he very wisely did not repel them at the beginning by putting his name."

(7:14), who could sympathize with human weakness, having been tempted in every way like we are (4:15), and who "in the days of his flesh" offered up prayers and petitions with loud crying and tears (5:7), as he "learned obedience from the things which he suffered" (5:8).

If Clement is right (admittedly, he may not be)—that what we have in Hebrews is a Lukan rendering in Greek of Paul's letter composed originally in Hebrew—this could account for all the much discussed differences in style and vocabulary with the known letters of Paul. Eusebius (*Ecclesiastical History*, 6.14.4) then quotes Clement as having written:

> But now, as the blessed elder [Pantaenus (died c. A.D. 200), first catechist of the catechetical school at Alexandria] used to say, since the Lord, being the apostle of the Almighty, was sent to the Hebrews, Paul, through modesty, since he had been sent to the Gentiles, does not inscribe himself as an apostle to the Hebrews, both to give due deference to the Lord and because he wrote to the Hebrews also out of his abundance, being a preacher and apostle of the Gentiles.

Moreover, Hebrews was accepted from the very first both in the Eastern and the Western church, being both known and quoted. Paul's authorship of Hebrews, as we have noted, was apparently never a matter of serious dispute in Egypt and North Africa. In the West the letter to the Hebrews asserted its intrinsic authority in *1 Clement* , written in Rome c. A.D. 95-97, and the *Shepherd of Hermas*, written in Rome between A.D. 120 and 140. Only later in the Western church—primarily in Italy, particularly in Rome, and *on dogmatic grounds*—did the dispute arise over the acceptance of the letter. The Western church's dispute over Hebrews, while it placed the question of its authorship in the foreground, was certainly connected with the particular way the Montanists attached themselves to Hebrews 6:4-8 which treats the problem of the lapsed or those who had denied the faith under persecution. But the recently discovered *The Gospel of Truth* (Codex I, known as the Jung Codex), possibly authored by the gnostic teacher Valentinus himself, near Nag Hammadi shows that around A.D. 150 the letter to the Hebrews did not have lesser authority in Rome than Paul's other letters. And although the letter is omitted from the Muratorian Canon (due perhaps to the corrupt state of the text of that Canon), Eusebius himself grouped it with the "fourteen" epistles of Paul (*Ecclesiastical History*, 3.3.5), this striking notice no doubt reflecting an earlier opinion such as is found (1) in the Chester Beatty papyrus P^{46} (c. A.D. 200) which places Hebrews between

But the Christ of Hebrews is indisputably divine as well. While the usual New Testament designations of Christ may be found scattered throughout the letter—the simple "Jesus" (2:9; 3:1; 6:20; 7:22; 10:19; 12:2, 24; 13:12), "[the] Christ" (3:6, 14; 5:5; 6:1; 9:11, 14, 24, 28; 11:26), "Jesus Christ" (10:10; 13:8, 21), "[the] Lord" (1:10; 2:3; 7:14; perhaps

---

Romans and 1 Corinthians, (2) in the ancestor of Vaticanus which places it between Galatians and Ephesians, and (3) in the majority of ancient Greek copies which place it after 2 Thessalonians, all three positions implying Pauline authorship. Both Jerome in Jerusalem (*Vir*. 5; *Ep*. 53.8; 129.3) and Augustine in North Africa (*Doctr. Christi*. 2.8; *Civ. D*. 16.22) cite it as Paul's, and Theodore of Mopsuestia (c. A.D. 350-428) tells us that believers "accept the epistle as having been written by Paul, like the others. If this were not so, what is written [in it] would not be profitable to them."

Internal evidence also supports the legitimacy of holding that Paul could have been the author. It is consistently Pauline to call upon his readers to pray for him (1 Thes 5:25; Rom 15:30-31; Eph 6:19-20). Moreover, the author's reference to "our brother Timothy" (13:23) surely has a Pauline ring about it (see 1 Thes 3:2; 2 Cor 1:1; Col 1:1; Philemon 1). Furthermore, there is a definite affinity of language and thought between the letter and the recognized Pauline letters (compare Heb 1:4 and Phil 2:9; Heb 2:2 and Gal 3:19; Heb 2:10 and Rom 11:36; Heb 7:18 and Rom 8:3; Heb 7:27 and Eph 5:2; Heb 8:13 and 2 Cor 3:11; Heb 10:1 and Col 2:17; Heb 10:33 and 1 Cor 4:9; Heb 11:13 and Eph 2:19; Heb 12:22 and Gal 4:25, 26). As a sampling of these, first, the statement in Hebrews that the Son obtained his "more excellent name" (1:4) has an affinity with Paul's statement that the Father gave Jesus "the name which is above every name" (Phil 2:9); second, the author's treatment of the new covenant has some parallels in 2 Corinthians 3; third, his assessment of the law as "a shadow of good things to come" (10:1) is paralleled by Paul's statement that the ritual law was "a shadow of things to come" (Col 2:17); fourth, although the author's treatment of Christ's high-priesthood is undeveloped in the acknowledged letters of Paul, the person and work of Christ in general are undeniably central in Hebrews as in Paul's acknowledged epistles and Christ's high-priesthood in particular has at least a foothold in Paul at Romans 8:34; fifth, the Old Testament quotation in Hebrews 10:30 departs from the Septuagint text in the same way that the same quotation does in Romans 12:19.

In my opinion, far too much weight has been given to the statement in 2:3 ("...so great salvation, which having first been spoken by the Lord, was confirmed to us by the ones who heard") as being "the most significant point" (so Simon J. Kistemaker, *Exposition of the Epistle to the Hebrews*, 7) *against* Pauline authorship. The statement, by this construction, supposedly

12:14; the first two occurrences of which clearly intended in the Yahwistic sense), "Lord Jesus" (13:20), "Jesus, the Son of God" (4:14)—the Author's favorite title for Jesus, above all others, is "[the] Son" (1:2, 5 [twice], 8; 3:6; 5:5, 8; 7:28) or its fuller form "[the] Son of God" (4:14; 6:6; 7:3; 10:29). Indeed, it is as God's Son in the preeminent (divine) sense of that title that the Author first introduces Jesus to his readers (1:2).

As God's "Son" he is the highest and final form of revelation to men, and as God's "Son" he is higher than the greatest representatives of God on earth, that is, the prophets of the Old Testament (1:1-2), higher even than Moses who in comparison was only a servant in God's house (3:5-6). Finally, his name as "Son"—whose Bearer is (1) the heir of all things, (2) God's cooperating agent in the creation of the world, (3) the radiance of God's glory, (4) the very image of his nature, (5) the sustainer of all things, (6) the purifier from sin, and (7) the Lord (of Ps 110:1) sitting at the right hand of the Majesty on high

---

teaches that the author was a "second-generation" Christian who had heard the gospel from the Apostles and who was converted as a result of their preaching, thus precluding Paul as the author because he claims in Galatians 1:12 that he received the gospel directly from Christ (see Acts 9:1-9). But Hebrews 2:3 does not say what this construction would imply that it says. It does not say that the author had first heard the gospel from the Apostles and was converted thereby. Rather, it says that the Apostles *confirmed* the message of salvation to him, implying thereby that the author was already in possession of it at the time of the act of confirmation, an activity which the Apostles could have done for Paul on the occasion of his second visit to Jerusalem about which he speaks in Galatians 2:1-10. The actions of the Apostles, as described by Paul in Galatians 2, have the appearance of being a "confirming activity."

As for its style and grammar and its doctrinal content, I grant that these matters are different in some ways from Paul's other letters to specific churches and individuals, but its recipients, its subject matter and its purpose undoubtedly had much to do with regard to the style and vocabulary of the letter. There is nothing in the content of the letter that Paul could not have written. I would recommend that the reader consult R. Laird Harris, *Inspiration and Canonicity of the Bible* (Grand Rapids: Zondervan, 1957), 263-70, who carefully surveys the patristic evidence and concludes that Hebrews is "a genuine Epistle of Paul using Barnabus as his secretary" (269) though he concedes that another person may well have served Paul as an amanuensis. In my opinion Luke is the best candidate here.

(1:2-3)—is "more excellent" even than that of the highest of creatures, that of "angel" (1:4), whose bearers are only "ministering spirits" (1:14) and whose duty it is to worship him (1:6).

As explications of the content of that super-angelic "more excellent name" of "Son," and *not simply new names* adduced in addition to that of "Son," he is the "God" (θεός, *theos*) of Psalm 45:6-7 and the "Lord" (κύριος, *kurios*), that is, the Yahweh, of Psalm 102:25-27.[35]

When he wrote, "To the Son, on the other hand, [God says], 'Your throne, O God, will last for ever and ever'" (1:8), the Author of Hebrews became the fourth person in the New Testament to use θεός, *theos*, as a Christological title. The controversy surrounding this verse is over whether ὁ θεός, *ho theos*, is to be construed as a nominative (if so, it may be a subject nominative: "God is your throne for ever and ever," or a predicate nominative: "Your throne is God for ever and ever") or a vocative, which would yield the translation given above. With the "overwhelming majority of grammarians, commentators, authors of general studies, and English translations,"[36] I believe that the Author applies Psalm 45:6 to Jesus in such a way that he is addressed directly as God in the ontological sense of the word. This position requires (1) that ὁ θεός, *ho theos*, be interpreted as a vocative, and (2) that the theotic character ascribed to Jesus be understood in ontological and not functional terms.

That ὁ θεός, *ho theos*, is vocatival is apparent for the following reasons: first, the fact that the noun appears to be nominative in its inflected form means nothing. The so-called articular nominative with vocative force, as we had occasion to note in connection with our exposition of John 20:28, is a well-established idiom in classical Greek, the Septuagint, and New Testament Greek. The case of the noun in Hebrews 1:8 must be established then on other grounds than its case form. Second, the word order in Hebrews 1:8 most naturally suggests

---

[35]Warfield, "The Divine Messiah in the Old Testament" in *Biblical and Theological Studies* (Philadelphia: Presbyterian and Reformed, 1952), 81.

[36]See Murray J. Harris, "The Translation and Significance of ὁ θεός [*ho theos*] in Hebrews 1:8-9" in *Tyndale Bulletin* 36 (1985): 146-48; see fns. 56, 57, 58, 59. To the sources which Harris cites should be added his own definitive article and the one which appeared subsequent to it: "The Translation of אֱלֹהִים [*'elōhîm*] in Psalm 45:7-8" in *Tyndale Bulletin* 35 (1984): 65-89.

that ὁ θεός, *ho theos*, is vocatival. A vocative immediately after "Your throne" would be perfectly natural. But if ὁ θεός, *ho theos*, were intended as the subject nominative ("God is your throne"), which Turner regards as a "grotesque interpretation,"[37] it is more likely that ὁ θεός, *ho theos*, would have appeared before "your throne." If it were intended as a predicate nominative ("Your throne is God"), which Turner regards as "only just conceivable,"[38] it is more likely that ὁ θεός, *ho theos*, would have been written anarthrously, appearing either before "your throne" or after "for ever and ever." Third, in the LXX of Psalm 45, which the Author is citing, the king is addressed by the vocative δύνατε (*dunate*, "O Mighty One") in 45:4 and 45:6. This dual vocative heightens the probability, given the word-order, that in the next verse ὁ θεός, *ho theos*, should be rendered "O God."[39] Fourth, although "about" or "concerning" is probably the more accurate translation of the preposition πρὸς, *pros*, in Hebrews 1:7 (given the cast of the following quotation), it is more likely that προς, *pros*, introducing the quotation in verse 8 should be translated "to" in light of the second-person character of the quotation itself and on the analogy of the formula (a verb of speaking followed by πρός, *pros*) in Hebrews 1:13, 5:5, and 7:21. This would suggest that ὁ θεός, *ho theos*, is vocatival. Fifth, the following quotation in Hebrews 1:10-12 (from Ps 102:25-27) is connected by the simple καί, *kai*, to the quotation under discussion in verses 8-9, indicating that it too stands under the regimen of the words introducing verses 8-9. In the latter verses the Son is clearly addressed by the vocatival κύριε (*kurie*, "O Lord"). These five textual and syntactical features clearly indicates that ὁ θεός, *ho theos*, should be construed vocatively, meaning that the Son is addressed as "God."

But what did he means by this address? Opinions run the gamut from Vincent Taylor's question-begging comment that "nothing can be built upon this reference, for the author shares the same reluctance

---

[37]Nigel Turner, *Grammatical Insights into the New Testament* (Edinburgh: T. & T. Clark, 1965), 461.

[38]Nigel Turner, *A Grammar of New Testament Greek* (Edinburgh: T. & T. Clark, 1963) III, 34.

[39]Harris, "The Translation and Significance of ὁ θεός [*ho theos*] in Hebrews 1:8-9," 142.

of the New Testament writers to speak explicitly of Christ as 'God,'"[40] to Oscar Cullmann's comment that "the psalm is quoted here precisely for the sake of this address,"[41] the chapter in which it occurs leading him to declare that "Jesus' deity is more powerfully asserted in Hebrews than in any other New Testament writing, with the exception of the Gospel of John."[42] What should we conclude? I would urge from the context of Hebrews 1 itself that the Son is addressed as God in the ontological sense. This may be seen from the fact that, as a "Son-revelation," as the final and supreme speech of God to man (vs 2), he is the heir of all things and the Father's agent in creating the universe. He abides (see the present participle ὤν, *ōn*, in vs 3) as the "perfect radiance of God's glory" and the "very image of his nature" (vs 3). As God's Son, he is superior to the angels, such that it is appropriate that they be commanded to worship him (vs 6). He is the

---

[40]Vincent Taylor, *The Person of Christ in New Testament Teaching* (London: Macmillan, 1959), 96. Raymond E. Brown's comment in "Does the New Testament Call Jesus God?" in *Theological Studies* 26 [1965], 4, 563 is also quite to the point: "...we cannot suppose that the author did not notice that his citation had this effect" of addressing the Son as God.

[41]Oscar Cullmann, *The Christology of the New Testament* (London: SCM, 1980), 310.

[42]Cullmann, *The Christology of the New Testament*, 305. I must register a caveat here. Cullmann, of course, must say these things if he is simply to be exegetically honest. But one must not forget that Cullmann is a "functional Christologist." In his *Christ and Time* (1946), he writes, "...we must agree with Melanchthon when he insists that the knowledge of Christ is to be understood only as a knowledge of his work in redemptive history.... All speculation concerning his natures is...un-Biblical as soon as it ceases to take place in the light of the great historical deeds of redemption" (128). He says again in his *The Christology of the New Testament:* "We come to the conclusion that in the few New Testament passages in which Jesus receives the title 'God,' this occurs on the one hand in connection with his exaltation to lordship..., and on the other hand in connection with the idea that he is himself the divine revelation" (325), and again: "Therefore, in the light of the New Testament, all mere speculation about his natures is an absurdity. Functional Christology is the only kind that exists" (326). In other words, after all is said and done, in spite of his splendid exegetical work in Chapter 11 on "the designation of Jesus as 'God,'" Jesus for Cullmann is not God in himself but only God in self-revelation or *Heilgeschichte* ("holy- or salvation-history").

Yahweh and the Elohim of Psalm 102 who eternally existed before he created the heavens and earth (vs 10) and who remains eternally the same though the creation itself should perish (vss 11-12; see Heb 13:8). Because he is all these things, it is really adding nothing to what the Author has said to understand him as describing the Son as God in the ontological sense in 1:8.

E. C. Wickham and others have suggested that if ὁ θεός, *ho theos*, is really ascribing ontological deity to the Son, the climax of the Author's argument would come at verse 8 since nothing higher could be said about him. But, it is urged, since in fact the Author goes on in verse 10 to describe the Son as κύριος, *kurios*, this further development of the Son's character becomes the climax, indicating that the former description cannot be construed ontologically. But this objection fails to apprehend the significance of the two terms. While θεός, *theos*, is indeed a term of exalted significance when used ascriptively of the true God, it speaks only of his divine essence. It is κύριος, *kurios*, coming to us out of the Old Testament citation here, that is God's personal name. In the covenantal sense, it is the more sacred of the two! So actually, the Author's argument, even though it ascribes ontological deity to the Son in 1:8, does not reach its climax until it ascribes the character of Yahweh himself to the Son, indicating by this ascriptive title that the Son is not only the Creator but the covenant God as well. The Author truly can say nothing higher than this.

Two of the descriptive phrases above deserve further comment. In addition to ascribing to him the divine work in eternity of creating the world, and the divine work in time of sustaining the universe, the Author describes the Son as "the Radiance [ἀπαύγασμα, *apaugasma*] of God's glory [δόξα, *doxa*]" and "the very Image [χαρακτήρ, *charaktēr*] of his nature [ὑπόστασις, *hupostasis*]." In the former expression, with God's δόξα, *doxa*, denoting his nature under the imagery of its splendor, as his ἀπαύγασμα, *apaugasma* (from ἀπαυγάσειν, *apaugasein*, "to emit brightness"), one has to do in Jesus with the personal "outshining" of God's divine glory as "the radiance shining forth from the source of light."[43] In the latter

[43]Bruce, *Commentary on the Epistle to the Hebrews*, 5.

expression, with God's ὑπόστασις, *hupostasis*, denoting his "whole nature, with all its attributes" (Warfield), his "real essence" (F. F. Bruce), or his "very essence" (P. E. Hughes), as his χαρακτήρ, *charaktēr* (from χαράσσειν, *charassein*, "to engrave, to inscribe, to stamp"), one has to do in Jesus with God's "very image" by which is meant "a correspondence as close as that which an impression gives back to a seal" (Warfield), his "exact representation and embodiment" (Bruce), or the "very stamp" (Hughes) of God. Clearly, such exalted descriptions intend the ascription of divine status to the Son. Accordingly, it is altogether likely, inasmuch as the Son is the Yahweh of Psalm 102:25-27 who remains forever the same (1:11-12) and who in the person of Jesus Christ is "the same yesterday, today, and forever" (13:8), that he is the subject of the doxology in 13:21, to whom eternal glory is ascribed. Certainly, the collocation of the relative pronoun and the title "Jesus Christ" in 13:21 favors such an interpretation.

But whatever the case may be with regard to the rather minor matter of the subject of the concluding doxology of the letter, there can be no doubt in view of the content of his first chapter that for the Author of Hebrews all that God is as God, that Jesus is as the Son, from, to, and throughout eternity.

This conclusion has not gone unchallenged. J. A. T. Robinson, for example, has urged that all of these exalted descriptions are true of Jesus as "God's Man," with only his functional relationship to God as God's "son" being "decisively different" from the relationship that obtains between God and other men.[44] He adduces in support of his view (1) the supposed derivation of the descriptions of 1:3 from Philo and Wisdom 7:26 and (2) what he terms "adoptionist" terminology in 1:2, 4, 9, 13; 2:9, 10, 12f., 16; 3:2f.; 5:1-6, 8, 10; 7:28.[45] James D. G. Dunn also insists (1) that "there is more 'adoptionist' language in Hebrews than in any other NT document,"[46] and (2) that "the element of Hebrews' christology which we think of as ascribing pre-existence to the Son of God has to be set within the context of his indebtedness

---

[44]John A. T. Robinson, *The Human Face of God* (London: SCM, 1973), 156.

[45]Robinson, *The Human Face of God*, 156-61.

[46]James D. G. Dunn, *Christology in the Making*, 52.

to Platonic idealism and interpreted with cross-reference to the way in which Philo treats the Logos," that is to say, "what we may have to accept is that the author of Hebrews ultimately has in mind an *ideal* pre-existence [of the Son], the existence of an idea [of the Son] in the mind of God,"[47] and this within a strict monotheism in which the concept of pre-existent Sonship is "perhaps more of an idea and purpose in the mind of God than of a personal divine being."[48] In sum, for Dunn, the Christology of Hebrews views Jesus in terms of Wisdom language, so that "the thought of pre-existence is present, but in terms of Wisdom Christology it is the act and power of God which properly speaking is what pre-exists; Christ is not so much the pre-existent act and power of God as its eschatological embodiment."[49]

I concur with I. Howard Marshall's assessment that this impersonal construction of the Author's doctrine of divine Sonship is "very alien to the biblical understanding of God as personal, quite apart from imposing a very artificial interpretation upon the biblical text."[50] For while it is true that the Son "was *appointed*" heir of all things (1:2), and "sat down on the right hand of the Majesty on high, *having become* by so much better than the angels, as he has *inherited* a more excellent name than they" (1:4), this need not be "adoptionist" language, but rather, language that envisions the glory which became his following upon the conclusion of his humiliation in his role as Messiah and Mediator (see Heb 2:9; Ps 2:8). Hughes concurs that this is how the so-called "adoptionist" language should be construed, writing on 1:4:

> It is true, of course, that by virtue of his eternal Sonship he has an eternal inheritance and possesses a name which is eternally supreme—*the name* signifying, particularly for the Hebrew mind, the essential character of a person in himself and in his work. But our author at this point is speaking of something other than this: the Son who for our redemption humbled himself for a little while to a position lower than the angels has by his ensuing exaltation *become* superior to the

---

[47]Dunn, *Christology in the Making*, 54.

[48]Dunn, *Christology in the Making*, 56.

[49]Dunn, *Christology in the Making*, 209.

[50]I. Howard Marshall, "Incarnational Christology in the New Testament" in *Christ the Lord*, 11, fn. 25.

> angels (2:9 below), and in doing so has achieved and retains the inheritance of a name which is *more excellent than theirs.*[51]

And if he is said to have "inherited" the name of "Son," as Bruce declares,

> this does not mean that the name was not His before His exaltation. It was clearly His in the days of His humiliation: "Son though He was, He learned obedience by the things which He suffered" (Ch. 5:8). It was His, indeed, ages before His incarnation: this is the plain indication of the statement in Ch. 1:2 that God has spoken to us "in his Son,...through whom also he made the worlds."[52]

All of the so-called "adoptionist" language of Robinson and Dunn can be similarly explained; none of it requires that the Son's personal pre-existence has to be forfeited in deference to an ideal, impersonal pre-existence in the mind of God. And even if the Author's language is that of Philo and the Book of Wisdom, again as Bruce affirms,

> his meaning goes beyond theirs. For them the Logos or Wisdom is the personification of a divine attribute; for him the language is descriptive of a man who had lived and died in Palestine a few decades previously, but who nonetheless was the eternal Son and supreme revelation of God.[53]

Viewed, then, from the Scriptural perspective of the *humiliatio-exaltatio* paradigm, as they rightly should be, the supposed "adoptionist" passages in Hebrews are not "adoptionist" at all. The full unabridged deity of the Son is secure and intact throughout the letter to the Hebrews.

---

[51]Hughes, *A Commentary on the Epistle to the Hebrews*, 50.

[52]Bruce, *Commentary on the Epistle to the Hebrews*, 8.

[53]Bruce, *Commentary on the Epistle to the Hebrews*, 5. Citing the opinion of E. Lohmeyer as a correct one, M. Hengel (*The Son of God* [Philadelphia: Fortress, 1976), declares that "the divine nature of the 'Son' in Hebrews is...established from the beginning. The approach...is the same as in the hymn [Phil 2:6-11] which Paul quotes; the difference is that [in Hebrews] it is made more precise in terms of the metaphysical substantiality of Christ." (87)

JOHN'S WITNESS TO JESUS

Sometime during the last four decades of the first century (it is impossible to be more specific), John the Apostle[54] wrote his Gospel, the three letters which bear his name, and finally the Revelation.[55] The Christology found in the Johannine corpus is as explicitly incarnational as is humanly conceivable, a fact which even the most radical critics recognize.

John's Gospel Witness

We considered in Chapter Four the John 20:28 occurrence of θεός, *theos*, as a Christological title in Thomas' great confession. But precisely because this title occurred in John's reported confession of someone else and was not an affirmation on John's own part, though it would be sheer wrong-headedness to argue so, someone might still insist that Thomas' confession of Christ as θεός, *theos*, does not necessarily reflect the Christological thinking of John. We are not shut up, however, to this single occurrence of θεός, *theos*, as a Christological title in John's Gospel. The title occurs as such also in John 1:1 and 1:18. These two verses now warrant our closest attention.

---

[54]I am assuming that the Apostle John rather than Papias' "John the Elder" or someone else was, both in substance and (in the main) literary composition, the author of the Gospel and the Johannine letters. For a full discussion of the question of authorship, see Donald Guthrie, *New Testament Introduction* (Third edition; London: Tyndale, 1970), 241-71, 864-69. See also B. F. Westcott, *The Gospel According to St. John* (London: John Murray, 1908), I, ix-lxvii, and Leon Morris, *The Gospel According to John* (Grand Rapids: Eerdmans, 1971), 8-30.

[55]See Guthrie, *New Testament Introduction*, 282-87, 883-84, 894, 898, and 949-61, for discussions of the respective dates of each. Leon Morris, *The Gospel According to John*, 30-35, suggests a date before A.D. 70 for John's Gospel, a view shared by J. A. T. Robinson, *Redating the New Testament* (London: SCM, 1976), 254-84, who places the Johannine letters (as well as the Revelation) also in the general time frame of the seventh decade of the first century. Precise dating of the Johannine corpus is extremely difficult if not impossible with the knowledge presently available to us. Suffice it to say, however, that nothing requires that any of the Johannine literature be dated after A.D. 100. All of it can be placed well within the first century A.D.

John 1:1

The Apostle John begins his Gospel with a powerful statement concerning the Logos (ὁ λόγος, *ho logos*—a term, according to his usage, meaning "[the independent, personified] Word [or Wisdom] [of God])."[56] He deliberately repeats the term three times in verse 1 to refer to the Son of God—against the background of the first-century forms of pre-Gnostic and Stoic theology—in order to warn his readers against all of the then-current false forms of the Logos doctrine. Translated literally, verse 1 reads:

> In the beginning was the Word,
> and the Word was with God,
> and God was the Word.

The term occurs in each clause, each time in the nominative case (subjective nominative), and three times ἦν, *ēn*, the imperfect of εἰμί, *eimi*, occurs, "expressive in each case of continuous existence."[57]

In the first clause, the phrase "In the beginning," as all commentators observe, is reminiscent of the same phrase in Genesis 1:1. What John is saying is that "in the beginning," at the time of the creating of the universe, the Word "[continuously] was" already, not "came to be." This is clear not only from the imperfect tense of the verb but also from the fact that John declares that the Word was in the beginning with God and that "all things were made by him, and without him nothing was made which has been made" (vs 3). In short, the Word's pre-existent *being* is antecedently set off over against the *becoming* of all created things.

In the second clause, the Word is both coordinated *with* God and distinguished in some sense from God as possessing an identity of its own. The sense in which the Word is distinguishable from God may be discerned by comparing the phrase in 1:1, ἦν πρὸς τὸν θεόν, *ēn pros ton theon*, with its counterpart in 1 John 1:2 where we read that "the Word," which was "from the beginning" (vs 1), "was with

---

[56]BAGD, *A Greek-English Lexicon of the New Testament*, 480.

[57]J. H. Bernard, *A Critical and Exegetical Commentary on the Gospel According to St. John* (ICC) (Edinburgh: T. & T. Clark, 1928), I, 2.

the Father" (ἦν πρὸς τὸν πατέρα, *ēn pros ton patera*). This shows that the "God" of John 1:1b is God the Father. The Word which stands coordinate with and yet distinguishable from God as *Father* is by implication then the pre-existent Son, which means that John is thinking of the Word in personal terms. This thought is reminiscent of Hebrews 1:8-9 where, as we have seen, the Son is both identified as himself God but distinguished from God the Father.

In the third clause, John now asserts the obvious: "The Word was God" (KJV, RV, ASV, RSV, NASV, NIV, NKJV). That ὁ λόγος, *ho logos*, is the subject with θεός, *theos*, the predicate nominative is evident from the fact that θεός, *theos*, lacks the article while λόγος, *logos*, has the article. But the fact that θεός, *theos*, is anarthrous does not mean that it is to be construed qualitatively, that is, adjectively ("divine," as Moffatt's translation suggests) or indefinitely ("a god," as the silly schoolboy translation of the Jehovah's Witnesses *New World Translation* suggests). No standard Greek lexicon offers "divine" as one of the meanings of θεός, *theos*, nor does the noun become an adjective when it "sheds" its article. If John had intended an adjectival sense, he had an adjective (θεῖος, *theios*) ready at hand. That the anarthrous noun does not connote indefiniteness as the Jehovah's Witnesses contend is evident from the recurring instances of the anarthrous θεός, *theos*, throughout the Johannine Prologue itself (vss 6, 12, 13, 18) where in each case it is definite and its referent is God the Father.

That θεός, *theos*, is definite in meaning is suggested by its position in the clause before the copula ἦν, *ēn*, in accordance with E. C. Colwell's observation.[58] But that John wrote θεός, *theos*, anarthrously is due most likely to his desire to keep the Word hypostatically distinct from the Father to whom he had just referred by τὸν θεόν, *ton theon*. If John had followed 1:1b by saying: "and ὁ θεός [*ho theos*] was the Word" or "and the Word was ὁ θεός [*ho theos*]," he would have implied a retreat from, if not a contradiction of, the clear distinction which he had just drawn in 1:2b, and thus he would have fallen into the error later to be known as Sabellianism.

Here then John identifies the Word as God (*totus deus*) and by so

---

[58]See E. C. Colwell, "A Definite Rule for the Use of the Article in the Greek New Testament" in *Journal of Biblical Literature* LII (1933): 12-21.

doing ascribes to him the nature or essence of deity. When John further says in 1:2 that "This one [οὗτος, *houtos*; the one whom he had just designated "God"] was in the beginning with God," and in 1:3 that "through him all things were created," the only legitimate conclusion that one can draw is that as God his deity is as ultimate as his distinctiveness as Son while his distinctiveness as Son is as ultimate as his deity as God.

When John then declares that the Word, whom he had just described as eternally pre-existent, uncreated, personal Son and God, "became flesh," he not only goes beyond anything in the first-century pre-Gnostic theology but also ascends to the high ground of incarnational Christology. I. Howard Marshall has observed:

> ...the prologue of the Gospel comes to a climax in the statement that the Word who had been from the beginning with God and was active in the work of creation and was the light and life of men became flesh and dwelt among us. It is noteworthy that the subject of the passage is the Word or Logos. It is the career of the Logos which is being described, and not until verse 17 is the name Jesus Christ used for the first time, thereby identifying the Word who became flesh with the historical figure of that name. From that time onwards John ceases to use the term Logos and writes about Jesus, using his name and a variety of Jewish messianic titles to refer to him.
>
> . . . For John, then, Jesus is undoubtedly the personal Word of God now adopting a fleshly form of existence. When we talk of incarnation, this is what is meant by it, for it is here that the New Testament offers the closest linguistic equivalent to the term "incarnation": *ho logos sarx egeneto.*[59]

John 1:18

In this verse we face a problem which we have not faced before in our appraisal of those verses in which Jesus is either described or addressed as θεός, *theos*. Here any conclusions we reach must be made on the basis of determining the original reading in the Greek text. Did the original text of John 1:18 read (1) ὁ μονογενής, *ho*

---

[59] I. Howard Marshall, "Incarnational Christology In the New Testament" in *Christ the Lord*, 2-3.

monogenēs,[60] (2) ὁ μονογενής υἱός, *ho monogenēs huios*, (3) μονογενὴς θεός, *monogenēs theos*, or (4) ὁ μονογενὴς θεός, *ho monogenēs theos*?

The first reading, although it has in its favor the fact that it is the shortest reading, may be dismissed because it has no Greek manuscript support whatsoever. The second reading has in its favor the support of the Greek uncials A, the third corrector of C, K, a later supplement to W, X, *D*, *Th*, 063, and many late minuscule manuscripts from the "Byzantine" tradition. It is also found in the Old Latin, the Latin Vulgate, the Curetonian Syriac, the text of the Harclean Syriac, and the Armenian version. It is also found in about twenty church fathers. In addition, it has in its favor the fact that, apart from John 1:14 where it stands alone, in the other three places where μονογενής, *monogenēs*, occurs in the Johannine literature, it appears in a construction with υἱός, *huios* (John 3:16, 18; 1 John 4:9). But this reading has three strikes against it. First, on the basis of the text-critical canon that "manuscripts are to be weighed, not counted," the textual support for this reading, in comparison with the two remaining readings, is not impressive, being found mainly in inferior and late manuscripts. Second, the fact that it is found in some significant church fathers is not a substantive argument in its favor inasmuch as the Ante-Nicene Fathers tended to "follow the analogy of the versions,"

[60]That μονογενής, *monogenēs*, does not mean "only begotten," alluding to some form of generation or to the virginal conception of Jesus, but rather "one and only," "only one of [his] kind," or "unique," enjoys wide consensus today. Warfield writes: "The adjective 'only begotten' conveys the idea, not of derivation and subordination, but of uniqueness and consubstantiality: Jesus is all that God is...." (*Biblical Doctrines* [New York: Oxford University], 194). See also Dale Moody, "God's Only Son: The Translation of John 3:16 in the Revised Standard Version" in *Journal of Biblical Literature* LXXII (1953): 213-219); Richard N. Longenecker, "The One and Only Son" in *The Making of the NIV* (Grand Rapids: Baker, 1991), 117-24; Karl-Heinz Bartel, "μονογενής [*monogenēs*]" in *The New International Dictionary of New Testament Theology*, edited by Colin Brown (English edition; Grand Rapids: Zondervan, 1976), 2.725; D. R. Bauer, "Son of God" in *Dictionary of Jesus and the Gospels*, edited by Joel B Green, Scott McKnight, and I. Howard Marshall (Grand Rapids: InterVarsity, 1992), 775a; and finally, BAGD, *A Greek-English Lexicon of the New Testament*, 529.

υἱός, *huios*, being "one of the numerous Ante-Nicene readings of the 'Western type'...[which fail to] approve themselves as original in comparison with the alternative readings."[61] Third, while it can be readily understood, if θεός, *theos*, were the original reading how υἱός, *huios*, could have arisen, namely, through the scribal tendency to conform a strange reading to a more common one (in this case, to the formula in John 3:16, 18, and 1 John 4:9), it is difficult to explain, if υἱός, *huios*, were the original reading, why a scribe would have changed it to θεός, *theos*.

The two remaining readings, both supporting an original θεός, *theos*, differ only in that the former omits the article while the latter retains it before μονογενής, *monogenēs*. The manuscript support for the former is Bodmer Papyrus 66, the original hand of א, B, the original hand of C, and L, plus the Syriac Peshitta, the marginal reading of the Harclean Syriac, the Roman Ethiopic, the Diatesseron, and about seventeen church fathers, including the heretical Valentinians and Arius. The manuscript evidence for the latter is Bodmer Papyrus 75, the third hand of א, the Greek minuscule 33 (the best of the cursives), and the Coptic Bohairic. Of these two, the former has the better manuscript support. But the *combined* weight of both, speaking purely from the perspective of manuscript support, lends exceedingly strong support for the originality of θεός, *theos*, in John 1:18. It has also in its favor the fact that it is the harder reading (the *lectio difficilior)*. The reputable textual critic must admit that the evidence points rather decisively in favor of an original θεός, *theos*. Of course, because the nature of the problem calls for a judgment of evidence,

---

[61]F. J. A. Hort, *Two Dissertations* (Cambridge: Macmillan, 1876), 7-8. Hort's dissertation laid the ground work for virtually all subsequent text-critical work on John 1:18 and provided the single greatest impulse toward the conclusion that θεός, *theos*, is the original reading. What is most telling as an indication of his careful scholarship is the fact that Hort did his work without the advantage of having the two great Bodmer Papyri 66 and 75, the later discovery of which vindicated his conclusion. Metzger writes: "With the acquisition of P^{66} and $P^{75,}$ both of which read θεός [*theos*], the external support of this reading has been notably strengthened" (*A Textual Commentary on the Greek New Testament*, 198.) See J. Finnegan, *Encountering New Testament Manuscripts* (London: SPCK, 1975), 111-77 (summarized on 174-77) for a textual history of John 1:18.

the final decision will always have an element of uncertainty about it, but the evidence is so weighty in one direction that it puts θεός, *theos*, as the original reading beyond reasonable doubt. Indeed, if it were not for the Christological implications in the reading itself ("[the] only [Son], [himself] God") one suspects that such combined manuscript support and the fact that it is the harder reading would be sufficient under less doctrinally-pregnant circumstances to carry the field of scholarly opinion. Even so, there is a trend in modern translations to adopt θεός, *theos*, as the original reading (NASV, NIV). Therefore, I would suggest that John 1:18 be translated as follows:

> God no man has seen at any time;
> the only [Son], [himself] God, who is [continually][62] in the bosom
> of the Father—
> that One revealed him.

Here then in John 1:1 and (quite probably) in 1:18 we have two more uses of θεός, *theos*, as a Christology title, the contexts of which place beyond question that John regards Jesus as the God the Son incarnate.

Continuing Johannine Witness to Jesus' Deity

Continuing now our investigative analysis of John's Gospel for its Christology, we should note that we consulted John's Gospel earlier when we were considering Jesus' self-understanding as that understanding was borne to us particularly in his "Son of God" sayings (see, for example, 5:17-26; 10:30, 36), his "Son of Man" sayings (see, for example, 3:13; 6:62), and his "I am" sayings (see, for example, 8:24, 58).

We sought its counsel yet again when we were amassing the pre-resurrection corroborative evidence in support of his deity in, for

---

[62]Warfield, "The Person of Christ According to the New Testament" in *The Person and Work of Christ*, 55-56, underscores the truth, on the basis of ὤν, *ōn*, the present participle in 1:18, that the divine state of the Logos "is not one which has been left behind at the incarnation, but one which continues uninterrupted and unmodified."

example, his recorded "works" and his disciples' testimonies respecting him (see, for example, 1:34, 49; 6:69; 11:27; 16:30).

Now in that John incorporated these data in his Gospel, we may assume that they reflect his Christology as well, for he expressly declares that he wrote what he did in order to bring his readers to faith in Jesus as "the Christ, the Son of God" (20:31). Surely, for example, the high incarnational Christology in his Prologue reflects his personal Christology as well. But there are three other features in John's Gospel which we have not yet treated in any direct way which afford still further insight into his personal Christology.

I refer, first, to the two paragraphs in 3:16-21 and 3:31-36, which may be in their contexts continuing remarks by Jesus and by John the Baptist respectively (the NIV seems to construe them as such), but which may also, in fact, be reflections by John the Evangelist himself on the themes touched upon by Jesus and the Baptist.[63] If the latter case is the correct reading of the matter, we have in both instances discourses by John upon the transcendent nature and origin of Jesus. In 3:16-21, he speaks of Jesus as God's "unique Son" (ὁ υἱὸς ὁ μονογενής, *ho huios ho monogenēs* (3:16, 18), whom God "sent into the world" (3:17), who himself, as the Light, "has come into the world" (3:19), and through faith in whom eternal life is mediated (3:16, 18). In 3:31-36, the same themes are advanced: Jesus is God's Son, whom God "sent" (3:34), and who may be thus characterized as himself "the one who comes from above" (3:31a) and "the one who comes from heaven" (3:31b). What Jesus declares is what he himself has seen and heard in heaven (3:32). He is "over all" (3:31) in that his Father "has given all things into his hand" (3:35), including the Spirit without limit (3:34). And, as in the former paragraph, the destiny of men turns upon their relation to him (3:36). These features—"the descent of Christ from the supernal world, the experiential character of his knowledge of the things of heaven, his identification with God, so that to hear him is to seal the veracity of God, his all-comprehensive

---

[63]Morris, *The Gospel According to John*, 228, 242, regards both pericopes as Johannine reflections. While Vos comments only on the latter passage, he too suggests that the evidence, when all of it is taken into account, "slightly favors attribution of the words to the Evangelist" (*Biblical Theology*, 352). So also Westcott, Lagrange, and Lightfoot.

authority in the sphere of revelation, the function of faith [in him] as mediating eternal life...whilst unbelief with reference to him results in exclusion from life and permanent abiding under the wrath of God"[64]—these features, I say, as a piece of John's Christology all serve to underscore both the pre-existence and the absolutely transcendent character of the one who occupies center stage throughout his Gospel.

When this perception of Jesus is coupled—and this is the second new feature I wish to highlight—with John's citation of Isaiah 6:10 in 12:40, which citation itself brings out the divine sovereignty in salvation and reprobation and concerning which citation John declares: "These things Isaiah said because he saw his [the preincarnate Son's] glory, and spoke concerning him," one must conclude that the transcendent character of Jesus Christ is just the transcendence of Yahweh himself, for it was "Yahweh, seated on a throne, high and exalted" (Isa 6:1; see 57:15) whom Isaiah reports that he saw in vision when he spoke the words of the citation. Leon Morris quite properly remarks:

> John sees in the words of the prophet primarily a reference to the glory of Christ. Isaiah spoke these things "because he saw his glory". The words of Isaiah 6:3 refer to the glory of Yahweh, but John puts no hard and fast distinction between the two. To him it is plain that Isaiah had in mind the glory revealed in Christ.[65]

This being so, it should not go unnoticed that it was the preincarnate Christ who commissioned and sent Isaiah on his prophetic mission, a fact which Jesus himself noted in Matthew 23:34 (see Luke 11:49) and which Peter alludes to in 1 Peter 1:11.

Since for John the glory of Christ is equivalent to the glory of Yahweh himself, it is not unlikely, indeed, it is highly probable—and this is the third new feature I desire to bring out—that when John refers to Christ as "the Lord" (ὁ κύριος, *ho kurios*) in the narrative of his Gospel (see 4:1; 6:23; 11:2; 20:20; 21:12), he intends the title, used as it is in the Septuagint to translate the divine name Yahweh, in its most eminent, that is to say, in its divine, Yahwistic sense.[66]

---

[64]Vos, *Biblical Theology*, 352-53.

[65]Morris, *The Gospel According to John*, 605.

[66]I would remind the reader once again of Cullmann's trenchant insight: "If...the whole Gospel culminates in [Thomas'] confession, and, on the other

There can be no doubt that John's Christology is incarnational in the highest conceivable sense, Jesus Christ being true God and true man. No view of John's Christology which would claim otherwise can claim to be exegetically sound.

John's Epistolary Witness

The *Sitz im Leben* behind First and Second John seems to be a situation in which certain heretical teachers (precursors or followers of Cerinthus?) were denying the possibility of a real incarnation, quite possibly insisting rather that Jesus began his earthly life as a mere man and that "the Christ" or "the Son of God," a higher divine power or emanation, came upon him at his baptism and departed from him just prior to his crucifixion. It is likely that this is the view which John was combating in 1 John 5:6 when he tells us that Jesus Christ, the Son of God, is "the One who came through water [that is, the event of baptism] and blood [that is, the event of crucifixion]." Alexander, with admirable clarity, explains:

> The Greek [aorist participle, ἐλθών, *elthōn*, meaning "came"] makes the 'coming' refer to a definite historical event, [showing that] *came by water and blood* must refer to specific events in Christ's Incarnate experience.... This is not quite all. John adds: *not by water only, but by water and blood.* Great weight is thus thrown on the words *and blood.* Some must have been saying that Jesus Christ *did* come by water but not by *blood.* What heresy is this? Probably Cerinthianism. Cerinthus taught as follows. At the baptism the Divine Christ came into the man Jesus. Jesus, allied now to the Divine Christ, brought news of the hitherto unknown God and lived and ministered in perfect virtue. Just before the Crucifixion the Christ left Jesus and returned to glory. The man Jesus was crucified and resurrected.
>
> This view accepted Christ's coming 'by water'; it denied (since for no Gnostic could the Divine suffer) Christ's coming 'by blood,'

---

hand, the author writes in the first verse of the first chapter, 'And the Logos *was God*,' then there can be no doubt [presuming the legitimacy of *inclusio*] that for him all the other titles for Jesus which are prominent in his work ('Son of Man,' 'Son of God,' 'Lord,' and in the prologue, 'Logos') ultimately point toward this final expression of his Christological faith." See his *The Christology of the New Testament*, 308.

> the blood of the Cross. John's seceding teachers seem to have been tarred with this Cerinthian brush.[67]

Accordingly, to combat this specific form of docetic or adoptionist Christology John wrote his letters.

It will be immediately evident from even a cursory reading of these letters that "the same concept of incarnation as in the Gospel is present in 1 and 2 John, and indeed it is the principal Christological idea in these Epistles."[68] This is plain from the fact that John defends (1) the dual confession that Jesus is both the Christ (1 John 2:22; 5:1) and the Son of God (1 John 2:22-23; 4:15; 5:5; see 1:3, 7; 2:24; 3:8, 23; 4:9, 14; 5:9, 11, 12, 13, 20), and (2) the incarnational prerequisite that God the Father "sent" his Son into the world (1 John 4:9, 10, 14), and that, having been "sent," the Son was "sent" in such a way that he "came in the flesh" (1 John 4:2; 2 John 7; see 1 John 5:6, 20) and thus was "manifested" to men (1 John 1:2 [twice]; 3:8) in such a way that, while still "the Eternal Life, which was with the Father" from the beginning (1 John 1:1-2), he could be heard, seen with the human eye, gazed upon, and touched by human hands. So intense is John's conviction as to the necessity of a real Incarnation that he makes the confession, "Jesus Christ has come in the flesh," a test of orthodoxy—to confess the same is to be "of God"; to deny it is to be "not of God" but "of Antichrist" (1 John 4:2-3). And quite likely does John speak in 1 John 5:20 of Christ's deity by using θεός, *theos* once again as a Christological title.

1 John 5:20

In this verse John quite likely intends to employ θεός, *theos*, once again as a Christological title.[69] Translated literally, the verse reads:

---

[67]Neil Alexander, *The Epistles of John: Introduction and Commentary* (London: SCM, 1962), 118-19; see F. F. Bruce, *The Epistles of John: Introduction, Exposition and Notes* (London: Pickering & Inglis, 1970), 118-19; see also I. Howard Marshall, "Incarnational Christology in the New Testament" in *Christ the Lord*, 4-5.

[68]Marshall, "Incarnational Christology in the New Testament" in *Christ the Lord*, 5.

[69]I have examined the remaining passages which are often cited as

> And we know that the Son of God has come, and he has given us understanding in order that we may know the True One. And we are in the True One in his Son Jesus Christ. This is the true God and life eternal.

The issue facing the interpreter is to determine who it is that John had in mind when he wrote: "This is the true God...." We must choose between the Father and the Son. Since a case can be made for either, our conclusion will be of the nature of a choice between two possibilities. I am personally persuaded that a better case can be made for understanding θεός, *theos*, as referring to the Son.

The case for the Father being the referent of "the true God" highlights the following features in the verse. First, reference to the Father is indirectly but clearly present in the verse in the genitives τοῦ θεοῦ, *tou theou*, and αὐτοῦ, *autou*, following the two occurrences of "the Son." This fact makes it evident that the Father is a bonafide possibility as the referent. Second, it is likely that the two occurrences of "true One" (τὸν ἀληθινόν, *ton alēthinon*, τῷ ἀληθινῷ, *tō alēthinō*) both refer to the Father rather than to the Son for the following reasons: (a) it would be a harsh rendering to interpret John as saying that "he [the Son] has given us understanding that we may know the true one [that is, himself]"; if this is what he had intended John would more likely have written "the Son" than the "true one." (b) The Father clearly seems to be the referent of the second occurrence of "true one" (and by forward extension to the first occurrence as well) because of the αὐτοῦ, *autou*, in the phrase immediately following it: "in *his* Son" (the NIV rendering, "even in his Son," implies the presence of a καί, *kai*, before the prepositional phrase, but there is no καί, *kai*, in the Greek text). (c) It is more true to Johannine thought to represent the Son's messianic mission as a revelation of the Father than as a revelation of himself (see John

---

ascribing deity to Jesus by the application of θεός, *theos,* as a title to him and have concluded that Acts 20:28 is *quite possibly* doing so (see Nigel Turner, *Grammatical Insights into the New Testament*, 14-5), that 2 Thessalonians 1:12 is *only possible* doing so, that Ephesians 5:5 is *probably not* doing so, and that Galatians 2:20, 1 Thessalonians 4:9, Colossians 2:2, 1 Timothy 1:17, 3:16, 5:21, James 1:1, and John 17:3 are *positively not* doing so.

1:18; 17:3-4). These features, it is urged, since it is highly unlikely that John would have referred to two different persons so closely in the same verse by the one adjective "true," point to the Father as the referent of John's phrase "the true God." Furthermore, this would accord with John's clear reference to the Father as "the only true God" in John 17:3. Both exegetically and theologically, this interpretation is possible, and it has been espoused by such notable expositors as Brooke (ICC), Westcott, Dodd, and M. Harris.[70]

But, in my opinion, there are four grammatical or exegetical considerations which tell against it, favoring as a result the greater likelihood that the last clause refers to Jesus Christ. First, the nearest possible antecedent to οὗτός (*houtos*, "This One") is the immediately preceding phrase "Jesus Christ," and it is an exegetically sound principle to find the antecedent of demonstrative pronouns in the nearest possible noun unless there are compelling reasons for not doing so. There are no such reasons here, as there are in the oft-cited counter examples of 1 John 2:22 or 2 John 7, which require that one go forward still further in the sentence to "his" or to "true one" or to "God." (The suggestion of some critics that "in his Son, Jesus Christ" is a gloss and should therefore be omitted, this being suggested in order to make "the true one" the nearest antecedent, has no manuscript support and must be judged for what it is—a mere expedient.) Second, to choose the more distant antecedent—that is, the Father—injects a tautology, if not an inanity, into the verse, for one does not need to be informed that the Father, who has just been twice identified already as the "true one," is "the true God," whereas John advances the thought and avoids the tautology if he is saying that Jesus Christ is "the true God." It is true that Jesus describes the Father as "the only true God" in John 17:3, but there the Father has not been previously identified as the "true One." Third, the singular οὗτός, *houtos*, and the fact that "true God" and "eternal life" both stand under the regimen of the single article before "God," thereby binding the two predicates closely together on the pattern, for example, of "the true God who is (for us) eternal life" (unless both are *titles* of a person, which seems preferable for this avoids placing a person and an abstract concept

[70]See Murray J. Harris, *Jesus as God: the New Testament Use of Theos in Reference to Jesus* (Grand Rapids: Baker, 1992), 239-53.

under the regimen of a single article) indicate that *one* person is before the mind of the Apostle. This eliminates the suggestion of some that the first title refers to the Father and the second refers to the Son. And while it is true that the Father has life in himself (John 5:26; 6:57) and gives to men eternal life (1 John 5:11), he is nowhere designated "the Eternal Life" as is Jesus in 1 John 1:2 (see also John 1:4; 6:57; 11:25; 14:6). "This predicate fits Jesus better than it fits God," writes Brown.[71] But then if Jesus Christ is the referent of "Eternal Life," and if both titles refer to one person, it would follow that he is also the referent of "the true God." Fourth, while John reports that Jesus describes the Father as "the only true God" (John 17:3), he himself either describes or records that Jesus describes himself as "the true Light" (John 1:9; 1 John 2:8; see John 1:14, 17), "the true Bread" (John 6:32), "the true Vine" (John 15:1), "the true one" (Rev 3:7; 19:11), "the true Witness" (Rev 3:14), and "the true Sovereign" (Rev 6:10). We have already established that John is not at all reticent about designating Christ as "God" (see John 1:1, 1:18, 20:28). So just as "the true one" can refer as a title both to the Father (1 John 5:20) and to the Son (Rev 3:7), there is nothing that would preclude John from bringing the adjective "true," which is used of Jesus elsewhere, and the noun "God," which he himself has used of Jesus, together here and applying both in their combined form as "the true God" to Jesus Christ. I am persuaded that these considerations make it highly probable that 1 John 5:20 is another occurrence of θεός, *theos*, as a Christological title. Athanasius, Cyril of Alexandria, Jerome, Bede, Luther, and Calvin in earlier times, and Bengel, Warfield, Brown, Bruce, (even) Bultmann, Marshall, Murray, Olshausen, Schnackenburg, and the recent translators of the NIV, to name only a few in more modern times, have so interpreted John here.

Portraying Jesus Christ, the Son of the Father, then, as "the true God and Eternal Life" (1 John 5:20) and the co-source with the Father of the blessings of grace, mercy, and peace (2 John 3), who "came in the flesh" and who also came "through water and blood, not with the water only but with the water and with the blood," John asserts a "real and lasting union between the Son of God and the flesh of

---

[71]Raymond E. Brown, *The Epistles of John* (AB) (Garden City, New York: Doubleday, 1982), 626.

Jesus"[72] from the very beginning of Jesus' life and throughout his ministry, including even the event of his death. Presupposing the same concept of Incarnation as is found in John 1:1-3, 14, John leaves no room for a docetic or an adoptionist Christology. Only the real Incarnation of the Son of God satisfies all the doctrinal affirmations of these letters.[73]

The Christology of the Revelation

When one analyzes the "Revelation of Jesus Christ" (1:1) for its Christology—its nature as "apocalyptic" being unique within the New Testament corpus itself, one should not be surprised if he finds the Christology contained therein to be more "marvelous," if not more "other worldly," than elsewhere in the New Testament. Indeed, this is what one does find. But this is not to suggest that its representation of Christ differs in any essential way from the Christology of Paul, of the Synoptic Evangelists, of the writers of the general epistles, of Hebrews, or that of the rest of the Johannine corpus. But it must be acknowledged that its Christology is more consistently "advanced," to use Beasley-Murray's term,[74] in that it portrays Christ almost singularly from the perspective of his state of exaltation. The customary names and titles for Jesus are still present—"Jesus" (1:9 [twice]; 12:17; 14:12; 17:6; 19:10 [twice]; 20:4; 22:16), "Christ" (20:4, 6; see also "his [the Lord's] Christ," 11:15; "his [God's] Christ," 12:10), Jesus Christ" (1:1, 2, 5), "Lord" (11:8; probably 14:13; see also "the Lord of lords," 17:14; 19:16; and "the Lord's Day," 1:10), "Lord Jesus" (22:20,

---

[72]Marshall, "Incarnational Christology in the New Testament" in *Christ the Lord*, 5.

[73]There is no explicit Christology in 3 John, the only allusion to Christ being the reference to "the Name" in verse 7. But about this term Westcott writes: "From the contexts it is evident that 'the Name' is 'Jesus Christ'..., or, as it is written at length, 'Jesus Christ, the Son of God' (John xx.31; I John iv.15). This 'Name' is in essence the sum of the Christian Creed.... When analyzed it reveals the triune 'Name' into which the Christian is baptized, Matt. xxviii.19." See his *The Epistles of St. John* (Third edition; London: Macmillan, 1892), 238-39; see also Warfield, *The Lord of Glory*, 274.

[74]G. R. Beasley-Murray, *The Book of Revelation* (London: Oliphants, 1974), 24.

21), "a son of man," meaning "a man" (1:13; 14:14; see Dan 7:13-14), "the Son of God" (once, in 2:18; but see "my Father," 2:27; 3:5, 21; and "his God and Father," 1:6), and "the Word of God" (19:13). But by far, the most common (twenty-eight times), almost personal, "new" name which John (1:1, 9; 22:8), as the Apocalyptist, uses for the glorified Christ is "the Lamb" (ἀρνίον, *arnion*, 5:6, 8, 12, 13; 6:1, 16; 7:9, 10, 14, 17; 12:11; 13:8; 14:1, 4 [twice], 10; 15:3; 17:14 [twice]; 19:7, 9; 21:9, 14, 22, 23, 27; 22:1, 3), a representation found elsewhere in the New Testament only at John 1:29, 36, and 1 Pet 1:19 (see Acts 8:32) where the word is ἀμνός, *amnos*. What is truly remarkable about this title in the Revelation is the fact that, while "the Lamb" is identified as "the Lamb that was slain" (5:6, 9, 12; 13:8), with allusions to his death in such an expression as "the blood of the Lamb" (7:14; 12:11), and while the term itself, as Warfield notes, always carries the "implied reference to the actual sacrifice,"[75] never is the one so designated now a figure of meekness in a state or condition of humility. Beckwith observes:

> [Lamb] is the name given to him in the most august scenes. As the object of the worship offered by the hosts of heaven and earth, chapts. 4-5; as the unveiler of the destinies of the ages, chapts. 5-6; as one enthroned, before whom and to whom the redeemed render the praise of their salvation, 7:9ff.; as the controller of the book of life, 13:8; as the Lord of the hosts on mount Zion, 14:1; as the victor over the hosts of Antichrist, 17:14; as the spouse of the glorified Church, 19:7; as the temple and light of the new Jerusalem, 21:22f.; as the sharer in the throne of God, 22:1,—Christ is called the Lamb. Nowhere in the occurrence of the name is there evident allusion to the figure of *meekness and gentleness* in suffering.[76]

In other words, if Jesus is "the Lamb" in the Revelation, it is as the "Lamb glorified" that he is depicted. And it is this depiction of Christ as the glorified Lamb which is dominant throughout the Apocalypse.

Of course, he is certainly a *human* Messiah still, as the "male child" (12:5, 13), the "Lion of the tribe of Judah" (5:5), and the "Root

---

[75] Warfield, *The Lord of Glory*, 290.

[76] Isbon T. Beckwith, *The Apocalypse of John* (Reprint; Grand Rapids: Baker, 1967), 315.

and Offspring of David" (5:5; 22:16) who is capable of dying and who did die, but who by his exaltation is the "Firstborn from the dead" (1:5), and thus the "Ruler of the kings of the earth" (1:5), indeed, the "King of kings and Lord of lords" (19:16; see 17:14). And while he is set off over against God in that he is the Son of God (2:18) and the Word of God (19:13), and in the sense that God is his Father (1:6; 2:27; 3:5, 21; 14:1), indeed, even in the sense that God is his God (1:6; 3:2, 12; see 11:15; 12:10) who gives to him both the authority to rule (2:27) and the Revelation itself to show to his servants (1:1), he is represented as being himself divine. Beckwith observes again in this connection:

> ...nowhere else are found these wonderful scenes revealing to the eye and ear the majesty of Christ's ascended state, and these numerous utterances expressing in terms applicable to God alone the truth of his divine nature and power. He is seen in the first vision in a form having the semblance of a man, yet glorified with attributes by which the Old Testament writers have sought to portray the glory of God; his hair is white as snow, his face shines with the dazzling light of the sun, his eyes are a flame of fire, his voice as the thunder of many waters; he announces himself as eternal, as one who though he died is the essentially living One, having all power over death, 1:13-18. He appears in the court of heaven as coequal with God in the adoration offered by the highest hosts of heaven and by all the world, 5:6-14. He is seen coming forth on the clouds as the judge and arbiter of the world, 14:14-16. Wearing crowns and insignia which mark him as King of kings and Lord of lords, he leads out the armies of heaven to the great battle with Antichrist, 19:11-21. In keeping with these scenes, attributes and prerogatives understood to belong to God only are assigned to him either alone or as joined with God; he is the Alpha and Omega, the first and the last, the beginning and the end, 22:13, 1:17, 2:8—a designation which God also utters of himself, 1:8, see Is. 44:6, 48:12; worship is offered to him in common with God, 7:10, 5:13—a worship which angelic beings are forbidden to receive, 19:10; doxologies are raised to him as to God, 1:6; the throne of God is his throne, the priests of God are his priests, 3:21, 22:1, 20:6; life belongs essentially to him as to God, compare 1:18 with 4:9, 10.[77]

---

[77]Beckwith, *The Apocalypse of John*, 312-13. In this same regard, H. B. Swete, *The Apocalypse of St John* (Third edition; London: Macmillan, 1911), clxii, writes:

Beasley-Murray likewise affirms:

> Constantly the attributes of God are ascribed to Christ, as in the opening vision of the first chapter, which is significantly a vision of Christ and not of God. The lineaments of the risen Lord are those of the Ancient of Days and of his angel in the book of Daniel (chs. 7 and 10). Christ is confessed as Alpha and Omega (22:13), as God is also (1:8). The implications of the claim are drawn out in the book as a whole.... In the closing vision of the city of God...God and the Lamb are united as Lord of the kingdom and source of its blessedness. It is especially noteworthy that John depicts the throne of God and the Lamb as the source of the river of water of life in the city, thereby conveying the notion of a single throne, a single rule, and a single source of life. He adds, 'his servants shall worship him; they shall see his face, and his name shall be on their foreheads' (22:3f.). In the context it is difficult to interpret the pronoun 'his' as meaning anything other than 'God and the Lamb' as a unity. The Lamb remains the mediator..., yet he is inseparable from the God who enacts his works...through him.[78]

In light of these facts, we may bring this overview of the Revelation to a close by concluding that any reader who will take the time to check for himself will discover that the Revelation sets before its

---

> What is the relation of Christ, in His glorified state, to God? (i) He has the prerogatives of God. He searches men's hearts (2:23); He can kill and restore to life (1:18; 2:23); He receives a worship which is rendered without distinction to God (5:13); His priests are also priests of God (20:6); He occupies one throne with God (22:1, 3), and shares one sovereignty (11:15). (ii) Christ receives the titles of God. He is the Living One (1:18), the Holy and the True (3:7), the Alpha and the Omega, the First and the Last, the Beginning and the End (22:13). (iii) Passages which in the Old Testament relate to God are without hesitation applied to Christ, e.g., Deut. 10:17 (Apoc. 17:14), Prov. 3:12 (Apoc. 3:19), Dan. 7:9 (Apoc. 1:14), Zech. 4:10 (Apoc. 5:6). Thus the writer seems either to coordinate or to identify Christ with God. Yet he is certainly not conscious of any tendency to ditheism, for his book...is rigidly monotheistic; nor, on the other hand, is he guilty of confusing the two Persons.

[78]Beasley-Murray, *The Book of Revelation*, 24-25. See also Warfield, *The Lord of Glory*, 294-97.

reader an awe-inspiring divine Christ and thus unites its witness, and that in a singularly marvelous way, to the consentient testimony of the New Testament as a whole in support of the full and unabridged deity of the Son of God.

* * * * *

In this chapter we reviewed the remaining New Testament witness to Jesus as that witness is set forth in the Christologies of James, Jude, Peter, the Synoptic Evangelists, and particularly the Author of Hebrews and John. It was our intention throughout to discern as clearly and as accurately as possible the nature of the Jesus about whom they spoke, the Jesus in whom they themselves believed, and the Jesus whom they proclaimed to others. I think it a fair deduction that Jesus was for all of them,[79] as well as for the entire early Christian community which followed the teaching of the Apostles, the promised Messiah of Old Testament hope and expectation who, while being certainly human in every sense of the word, exhibited by his life, his words, and his works that he was also the divine Son of God and thus God incarnate. *Theirs, in a phrase, was an incarnational Christology.* This is not to suggest that there were no differences in emphasis between them for such differences in emphasis there certainly were. Nor is this to suggest that one can find in their writings Christological formulas that set forth their views with the later formulaic precision of the Fathers at Nicaea or at Chalcedon. Such later formulas would have to come as the hard-won systematized responses to specific, sometimes bizarre, doctrinal errors which would circulate in later times about Christ. But I would urge that these New Testament writers provide such an all-pervasive and singularly united witness to a Christ who is both true God and true man that only Christological formulas such as those that came forth from Nicaea in A.D. 325 and from Chalcedon in A.D. 451 do full justice to all of the biblical data.

Furthermore, having now surveyed the whole of the New

---

[79]The reader is urged to read Gerald Bray's excellent defense of the doctrinal unity of the Apostles and the New Testament writings found in his *Creeds, Councils and Christ* (Reprint, Ross-shire, Scotland: Mentor, 1997), 54-59.

Testament for its Christology, with the necessary data now at hand to draw certain basic conclusions, I want to deal with one final, very significant issue. One finds it often said in critical circles today that if Jesus had really believed that he was God, one would think that such an explicit claim would be found on his own lips and not just on the lips of others. Moreover, it is said, if Jesus had really been regarded by the New Testament witness as God manifest in the flesh, one would expect to find the New Testament filled with explicit statements to that effect and not just the (at least) eight occurrences of θεός, *theos*, which we have culled from the New Testament record (in their historical order of occurrence, John 20:28, Romans 9:5; Titus 2:13; 2 Peter 1:1; Hebrews 1:8; John 1:1; John 1:18; and 1 John 5:20). What shall we say to these observations.

I would begin by saying that even if we had needed to conclude from our investigation that Jesus was never called "God" in the New Testament, his deity is still solidly evidenced to us, as we have seen, on the New Testament grounds that he portrays himself and is portrayed therein as possessing divine attributes, as exercising divine functions, as the recipient of both angelic and human worship, as the respondent to the petitionary prayers of the saints, and as the object of saving trust. I would also say that while it true that one never finds Jesus in any Gospel making the explicit claim in so many words,' Εγώ εἰμι θεός, *Egō eimi theos*, or אֲנִי אֱלֹהִים, *'ănî 'elōhîm* ("I am God.") just as he did not regularly go around claiming in so many words to be the "Christ," one may understand, given his *Sitz im Leben*, why Jesus deemed it wise, before his hearers' minds and hearts had been prepared for such and before his own ministry had been completed, that he not travel around in the intensely monotheistic setting of pre-Christian Palestine claiming in so many words to be God. As for the relatively few occurrences of θεός, *theos*, as a Christological title throughout the New Testament, Murray Harris has quite properly noted that

> in all strands of the NT θεός [*theos*] generally signifies the Father. Short of coining a new theological term to denote deity, writers who believed in the divinity of Jesus were forced to employ current terminology and run the risk of being branded ditheistic. One reason for the relative infrequency of the NT use of θεός [*theos*] in reference

> to Jesus may in fact have been the danger recognized by the early church that if θεος [*theos*] were applied to Jesus as regularly as to the Father, Jews would have tended to regard Christianity as incurably deuterotheological, and Gentiles would probably have viewed it as polytheistic.[80]

So faced with the fact that "the Old Testament heritage dominated the use of the title God [for the Father],"[81] and yet having the need to address not only the Father but also the Son as God and needing at the same time to distinguish between them, the church, under the wise guidance of the Apostles, adopted the practice which is observed to this very day of addressing primarily the Father as θεός, *theos*, and addressing primarily the Son as κύριος, *kurios*, the latter however certainly intending deity as fully as the former, but also containing the suggestion of the exalted status which became his as God incarnate by virtue of his incarnational work as Messiah and Savior (see Acts 2:36; Phil 2:6-11). The fact that the references to Jesus as θεός, *theos*, are few in number is no argument, therefore, against his being deity. The sparse number simply reflects the exigencies which obtained under the given circumstances and needs of the time.

With respect to the eight occurrences of θεός, *theos*, as a Christological title themselves, while it is still in vogue in some quarters to argue that none are undisputably clear references to Jesus, justifying Nigel Turner's comment that "the simple grammarian may be forgiven for suspecting that special pleading has contributed to the debilitation of tremendous affirmations in the New Testament" respecting the deity of Jesus Christ,[82] it is increasingly being urged that the New Testament employment of θεος, *theos*, as a Christological title had its origin, not in apostolic teaching, but in the liturgy and prayers of the worshiping community. As evidence of this theory, Brown points out

---

[80]Murray J. Harris, "Titus 2:13 and the Deity of Christ" in *Pauline Studies: Essays Presented to Professor F. F. Bruce on His 70th Birthday*, edited by Donald A Hagner and Murray J. Harris (Grand Rapids: Eerdmans, 1980), 265-66.

[81]Raymond E. Brown, "Does the New Testament Call Jesus God" in *Theological Studies* 26 (1965): 4, 569.

[82]Nigel Turner, *Grammatical Insights into the New Testament*, 16.

that the occurrences in Romans, Titus, 2 Peter, and 1 John are doxological in character, that the occurrences in Hebrews and John's Prologue appear respectively in the citation of a Psalm and in a hymn, and that Thomas' confession occurred on Sunday (!), suggesting that "my Lord and my God" was a "confessional formula used in liturgy."[83] He also asserts that "...the usage of calling Jesus God was a liturgical usage and had its origin in the worship and prayers of the Christian community."[84] A. W. Wainwright, agreeing that some if not all of these uses have a "liturgical background," explains that the Apostles and the early church could only express in worship what they, in their inmost feelings, surmised but were unable to adjust to their monotheism:

> The writers of the New Testament seem to have been reluctant to commit to writing the confession that Jesus is God. The reluctance of St. Paul and the author of the Epistle to the Hebrews may have been caused by their inability to give an account of the relationship of this belief to the Jewish monotheism to which they continued to subscribe. Their faith outstripped their reason, and they were able to give joyful utterance to a belief which they felt incapable of expounding. But each of these writers, on one occasion [*sic*], allowed himself to give expression to this deep-seated belief, and to include in the text of an epistle language which he used more frequently in private and public worship. [How does Wainwright know that these writers used this language more frequently in their private worship?]
>
> The author of the Fourth Gospel interwove this belief into his thought... St. John too was in contact with a liturgical tradition in which Jesus was hailed as Lord and God. Perhaps, by placing the confession of Thomas at the very end of the Gospel, he was suggesting that it was only in the moment of worship that men were able to comprehend that Jesus was God.[85]

---

[83]Brown, "Does the New Testament Call Jesus God" in *Theological Studies*, 570-71.

[84]Brown, "Does the New Testament Call Jesus God" in *Theological Studies*, 570-71. In his *The Gospel According to John I-XII* (Garden City, New Jersey: Doubleday, 1966), I, 24, Brown declares that "the title 'God' was applied to Jesus more quickly in liturgical formulae than in narrative and epistolary literature."

[85]A. W. Wainwright, "The Confession Jesus is 'God' in the New Testament" in *Scottish Journal of Theology* X (1957): 295.

This theory must be roundly rejected. It is the offspring of a form-critical approach that will not permit a teaching or an event in the New Testament documents to be untouched history but views them rather as the result of theological reshaping of an early Christian community. It is mere expediency to declare that the occurrences of θεός, *theos*, in Titus, 2 Peter, and 1 John are doxological in character, as Brown does. And it is surely a case of special pleading to say, because the Author of Hebrews is quoting a Psalm, that Hebrews 1:8 is liturgical. But even if it were, is not Psalm 45 part of Scripture and "profitable for doctrine"? To make John 1:1 fit the theory, Brown must argue that the prologue of John is "an early Christian hymn, probably stemming from Johannine circles, which has been adapted to serve as an overture to the Gospel narrative."[86] But this view of John's prologue is not shared by all by any means. Morris, for example, describes the language of the prologue as being, at most, "elevated prose" and not hymnic.[87] And to suggest, as Wainwright does, that the early church could confess in worship what it neither could conceptualize nor dare to express in non-liturgical prose or narrative is to impute an uncommonly low level of reflective capability to the first-century Christians and their leaders and is to suggest that it was not their primary concern that their worship be in accordance with truth and fact. Worship must be grounded in sound doctrine. Any confession of faith must be sound likewise. Are we to suppose that the early church did not understand this? The biblical evidence would indicate that they understood this better than Wainwright gives them credit for doing. The Apostles and the early church were deeply concerned with sound doctrine and aberrations were not tolerated (see 1 Cor 1:10-13; 3:4-9; Rom 16:17; Gal 1:6-9; Eph 4:3-6; 2 Tim 1:13-14; 2:2; 4:1-4; Tit 1:9-11; 2:1; 1 John 4:1-3; 2 John 7-11; Jude 3-4). They would not have expressed in their liturgy what they could not express in their prose.

These scholars have misread the facts governing the situation. It is true that the early church did worship Jesus as God, and it is true

---

[86]Brown, *The Gospel According to John I-XII*, 1.

[87]Morris, *The Gospel According to John*, 72. Morris further comments: "[The prologue] is written in a meditative strain.... This lends a musing air to the passage. But it does not make it poetry." (72)

that the Apostles upon occasion, as we have seen, actually gave expression to the fact of Jesus' *theotic* character in their writings by the explicit use of θεός, *theos*, as a Christological title. But it was not the church's worship which induced the Apostles to include such expressions in their writings. Rather, it was the teaching of Jesus himself and that of his Apostles which grounded for Christians the appropriateness of the worship of Christ as God.

It is also incorrect to insist, with Raymond E. Brown and many others, that "although the Johannine description and acceptance of the divinity of Jesus has ontological implications...in itself this description remains primarily functional" because "the Johannine acceptance of Jesus as divine or equal to God...is not divorced from the fact that Jesus was sent by God and acted in God's name and in God's stead."[88] Brown goes even farther in another place and states categorically that "...no one of the instances [where Jesus is called God] attempts to define Jesus essentially."[89] Even apart from the fact that John the Baptist also claimed to have been sent from God and in fact acted in God's name and in his stead (John 1:6) with no charge of blasphemy ever being levelled at him for claiming such, in both John 1:1 and 1:18 θεός, *theos*, is used of the Father, unquestionably designating what he essentially is. It is difficult to believe that θεός, *theos*, means something entirely different in these same two verses when applied to Jesus. A tough-minded reading of the three occurrences of the title in the Fourth Gospel will reveal that its first usage in 1:1 as a description of the pre-existent Logos provides the governing control over the meaning of its description of him in 1:18 as the incarnate Logos and the later description of him in John 20:28 as the risen Christ. In each case the term "does not describe [Jesus'] function, but indicates who he is."[90]

These unmistakably clear New Testament attributions of deity to Christ also explain a phenomenon in early patristic literature. Ignatius, third bishop of Antioch (Syria) who was martyred in Rome in A.D.

---

[88]Brown, *The Gospel According to John I-XII*, 408.

[89]Brown, "Does the New Testament Call Jesus God?" in *Theological Studies*, 572.

[90]See B. A. Mastin, "A Neglected Feature of the Christology of the Fourth Gospel" in *New Testament Studies* 22, (1976): 43-6.

108 is, along with Clement of Rome, the earliest of the extra-biblical Christian writers. In his letter to the Ephesians Ignatius speaks of the "blood of God" (αἵματι θεοῦ, *haimati theou*) 1:1; see Acts 20:28) and says that "our God, Jesus the Christ [ὁ θεὸς ἡμῶν' Ιησοῦς ὁ Χριστός, *ho theos hēmōn Iēsous ho Christos*]" was conceived by Mary (18:2), and that "God was manifest as man [θεοῦ ἀνθρωπίνως φανερουμένου, *theou anthrōpinōs phaneroumenou*]" (19:3). In his letter to the Smyrnaeans he glorifies "Jesus Christ, the God [Ἰησοῦν Χριστὸν τὸν θεόν, *Iēsoun Christon ton theon*]" who had given them wisdom (1:1). In his letter to the Romans, twice in the salutation he refers to "Jesus Christ, our God" ['Ιησοῦ Χριστοῦ τοῦ θεοῦ ἡμῶν, *Iēsou Christou tou theou hēmōn*; Ἰησοῦ Χριστῷ τῷ θεῷ ἡμῶν, *Iēsou Christō tō theō hēmōn*], and later to "the passion of my God [τοῦ πάθους τοῦ θεοῦ μου, *tou pathous tou theou mou*]" (6:3). In his letter to Polycarp he bids Polycarp farewell "in our God, Jesus Christ [ἐν θεῷ ἡμῶν 'Ιησοῦ Χριστῷ, *en theō hēmōn Iēsou Christō*]" (8:3). In the mid-second century, in so-called 2 Clement 1:1, Clement informs his Christian brothers that it is necessary to think "of Jesus Christ as of God [περὶ 'Ιησοῦ Χριστοῦ ὡς περὶ θεοῦ, *peri Iēsou Christou ōs peri theou*]." The pagan Pliny the Younger (A.D. 61-112), governor of Bithynia in Asia Minor, in *Letter* 10. 96. 7 reports that Christians of his day were chanting verses "to Christ as if to a god" (*Christo quasi deo*). Without the clear New Testament titular descriptions of Jesus as θεός, *theos*, we could still always argue that the early Fathers had deduced, and rightly so, the propriety of their use of the title from all the other New Testament data which treat him as divine. But it could also be argued that the church had deduced too much. As it is, with these references to Jesus as "God" embedded in the New Testament literature, we stand on the "concrete" which bridges the Apostolic Age and the age of the earliest church fathers and the later church beyond. Here—in what the New Testament reports that he taught about himself and in what he led the Apostles to affirm about him—is the exegetical grounding for the church's freedom today to speak of Jesus as the two-nature divine-human Son of God incarnate, to worship him as the Son of God, and to serve him as its Lord.

EPILOGUE

MY PERSONAL WITNESS

Throughout the foregoing chapters we have been seeking from both the Old and New Testament literature the basic answer to the perennial question: Who is Jesus Christ? Jesus himself in his own day forced this question on every man with his penetrating interrogations: "Who do people say the Son of Man is?...Who do you say I am?" (Matt 16:13, 15), and "What do you think of the Christ? Whose son is he?" (Matt 22:42) Jesus' questions here focus our attention not directly upon his teachings or his deeds but upon *him*. Both the Old Testament, the New Testament, and the historic Christian church have declared in response to his questions that Jesus is the eternal Son of God who, as God's ordained Messiah, became incarnate for us men and for our salvation and who then went to the cross to pay the penalty for the sin of his people. My own assessment, it should be apparent to the reader by now, accords with that finding.

Jesus' questions, interestingly, have to do not only with *him* but also with *thoughts* about him: "What do you *think* of the Christ?" Thoughts are all-important in this world. They determine every human action, either directly or indirectly. And thoughts about Christ, I would suggest, are of paramount significance. Whatever else one may think of Karl Barth's total theological edifice (and for myself I find much in it with which I must disagree), he was absolutely right when he declared that what a man thinks about Christ will determine what he ultimately thinks about everything else. Jesus even declared that a man's eternal destiny would be determined by his thoughts about him (John 8:24).

Jesus' questions are also eminently *personal*: "Who do *you* say I am?...What do *you* think of the Christ?" It is very easy for one to immerse himself so deeply in the communities of mankind that he lets those communities think for him without realizing it. For instance, one can say, "I believe whatever my church believes about him although I am not sure I know what that is. Nevertheless, I am certain my church is right." Perhaps one will say, "I believe what my university professor told me about him." But when it comes to thoughts about Christ, these are perilous paths to follow. It is very tempting today for one to feel out which way the theological wind is blowing in the church or in the academic world and to conclude that, enlightened as these sources of information must be, surely the numerous voices within their venues must be right if now they urge upon men a "modern Christ" different in kind from the two-natured Christ which the Bible and the Christian church have always confessed and urged upon people. Here I would urge unusual caution, but since I have given many reasons already for such counsel, I will let someone else explain why this is not wise. While I was writing this book at Tyndale House in Cambridge, England in 1986 the editor of the London daily, *The Daily Telegraph,* in his lead editorial for the Christmas Eve edition, entitled "God Bless Us, Everyone," wrote:

> The aspect of the [Christmas] festival which most continues to fascinate modern industrialised man (...flying in the face of the conventional wisdom) has to do with its miraculous character. Those who crowd the churches tonight...will not be celebrating the birth of a good man, simply. The wonder of Christmas is precisely that God himself, by whom the heavens and earth were made, was born as a tiny child, humbling himself to share in our humanity.... The Bishop of Durham describes the biblical narrative of Christ's birth as "unlikely." But the entire point of the story is that it is not only unlikely but wholly unique; quite impossible to accept without the belief that God can and does intervene in the affairs of men. It may be that our culture has a deeper instinct than many within the Church have realised that this belief is actually true. And it needs to be said that until this realisation sinks home, the crisis within the Church...will grow increasingly grave.
>
> That the Church is in deep crisis becomes increasingly clear.... At a time when industrialised man [is] weary of being the plaything of large-scale processes, and hungry for a resacralised understanding of human existence, the Church is becoming more and more committed to...a non-supernatural version of traditional Christian doctrine....
>
> The only way the Church can become again a vehicle for divine truth is to understand once more how ephemeral and how worthless

> is all the wisdom of the rulers of this world.... A first step would be to understand that the Church has put its money on a liberal secularist biblical criticism to the point of intellectual collapse.

The editor concluded his editorial with this observation:

> When [this] reality [of the supernatural Christ] has thus been faced [by the Church] the Church may be in a position to kneel before the Christ child, and to say in all humility, in the words of THOMAS the Doubter, 'My Lord and my God.'"

The editor revealed uncommon insight into the intellectual currents of the church today. With exceptionally clear vision he understands where the modern church is intellectually and spiritually. It is in deep crisis as he says, having lost its way precisely for the reason that he indicates: Insensitive to the worthlessness of the wisdom of this world, a large segment of the church's educators and ministers at the level of their intellectual life has "put its money" on a liberal secularist biblical criticism to the point that the church faces not only intellectual collapse but also wholesale loss of respect on the part of the man both in the pew and on the street who still believes or would like to believe that the biblical message is true or who at least believes that there is a supernatural dimension with which we have to do. I would urge my readers not to listen to the modern doctors of the church who would deliver the church from what they say is its bondage to the Bible's "arcane model of vertical transcendence" but to "search the Scriptures" for themselves as the Bereans did (Acts 17:11) to see if what the church has historically maintained is true with respect to the all-important question concerning who Jesus was and is. Occasionally, the Christian even hears the admonition to "face reality," to "wake up and to begin to live religiously in the real world." In response, I would urge that to enter believingly into the world of the Bible's witness concerning Jesus Christ *is* to enter into the real world and to begin to understand things as they really are.

At the end of the first chapter I invited my reader to continue with me on my investigative pilgrimage through the evidence from Scripture for Jesus Christ as both God the Son incarnate and the promised Old Testament Messiah. I suggested then that there was more at stake than just an *intellectually* satisfying faith. That journey has now reached its end. Now I invite my reader, if he has not already done so, to face squarely the fact that Jesus Christ is both God the Son incarnate and the promised Old Testament Messiah and that as God's Son he came into the world to save sinners because his Father in heaven "so loved the world that he gave his one and only Son that whoever believes in him shall not perish but have eternal life" (John 3:16). In sum, the real issue that the reader must face is that, according to the Bible, one's eternal destiny hangs upon what he thinks about Jesus' person and work. If the reader has been convinced from the biblical data that what we have argued is true, I urge him to bow in faith before Christ's saving scepter and to join Christ's witnesses in their effort to make the salvation that he accomplished at his cross known to the rest of mankind. But it should be apparent to him by now that the one thing he cannot and must not do is simply say, "What a nice argument," and then yawn and turn away, because biblical Christianity, if false, is of *no* value, but, if true, it is of *infinite* value. The one thing it is not is simply a "nice" argument. The Holy Scriptures will not allow one to stop at that conclusion with impunity. It should be obvious by now to the reader why I say this, but I will explain what I mean.

The "good news" of the gospel is not the mere "offering" of Christ's saving benefits to those who apathetically may or may not want them, that is, to those who have no sense of their spiritual poverty. It has never been this. Paul would no more have said to his auditors, "If you would like to have the experience of living under an emperor, you might try the Jewish Messiah," than would Caesar's herald have said: "If you would like the experience of living under an emperor, you might try Nero." Just as Caesar's herald would have announced: "Nero has ascended the throne of Rome and has been crowned as your emperor; submit to his imperial authority or refuse him such submission upon pain of death," so also by his gospel Paul proclaimed: "Christ by his obedient life and sacrificial death has become the Lord of the universe and your sovereign King! Submit to him if you would be delivered from the bonds of sin that enslave you or refuse him such submission upon pain of eternal death!" In short, the gospel, that is, the "good news" concerning God's Son, is the proclamation that through the death and resurrection of a very human—even a Jewish—life the living God in the person of Jesus Christ has become the sovereign King and Savior of the world and demands the repentance and the obedience that flows from faith in him. And only to those who *from the heart* submit to his authority and trust in his saving work will he grant the gift of eternal life. All others, in his wrath, he will destroy.[1]

By the "folly" of the cross—regarded by the world as folly because a Roman cross admittedly is the last place in the whole wide world where one would think to find God—God has reversed the world's values, turning its shame into glory and all human glory into shame. By the folly of the cross he has outsmarted the wise, by the weakness of the cross he has overpowered the strong. But how? Hundreds of Jews had been crucified by the Romans in that first century. Why was his crucifixion so special? As we have seen, because of who he was and because of what happened on the third day after his crucifixion.

Who was he? Not just the son of David and thus mere earthly royalty but also the Messianic Son of Man and the divine Son of God, the majesty of whose person outrivals all the combined pomp of all the earthly kings who have ever lived, the might of whose power is infinite, upholding all things even as he hung upon the cross making purification for our sins, and who was declared to be the Son of God by what happened next, namely, by his physical resurrection from the dead.

By his physical resurrection from the dead, which we have argued was a historical reality, Christ's crucifixion for our sins was turned into a great victory. By his resurrection Jesus went through death for sinners and emerged victoriously on the other side. His resurrection means that Christ really is God's anointed King and Lord. He has brought to light life and immortality. The Age to Come has already come in its saving power. And the gospel is the announcement of that great victory. But it is the announcement of even more than that! It goes beyond the simple glad tidings that Jesus Christ reigns today as Lord and King. It also announces that the sinner who trusts Christ's

---

[1]I am indebted to N. T. Wright, *What Saint Paul Really Said* (Grand Rapids: Eerdmans, 1997), 41-45, for some of the insights of this section.

active and passive obedience will receive the forgiveness of sins and right standing before God and will live forever. This is just to say that the gospel is to be enunciated precisely in terms of the doctrine of justification by faith alone in Jesus Christ, the King and only Savior of men. And because he lives and reigns, we too shall someday live and reign, and the cosmos itself will someday be restored to its paradisiacal state at his return and the resurrection of our bodies. By his cross and resurrection Jesus Christ has inherited that title above all titles—the title of lord.

The gospel then is indeed a royal announcement—the King's proclamation of the appearing of a great victor and of an equally great victory over sin and death. And to make light to any degree of God's forgiveness by the cross is to make light of the great price God paid in order to do away with sin. Trivializing the gospel by treating it as something about which one may simply say, "How nice," then yawn and turn away, that is, to treat it as something that one may choose or reject with impunity *if* one pleases, *as* one pleases, *when* one pleases, *how* one pleases, is to fail to recognize its true worth. The reader must clearly understand that he refuses to bow before this heavenly Emperor at the peril of his eternal soul, that he will know only eternal misery and woe if he continues in his rebellion against Jesus' lordship, and that he will know this misery and woe someday at Jesus' hands!

Subject Index

Introduction

Part One: the Old Testament Witness

Part Two: the New Testament Witness

Epilogue

Persons' Index

Select Scripture Index

Other books in the MENTOR imprint from

Christian Focus Publications

Paul – Missionary Theologian

A Survey of his Missionary Labours and Theology

Robert L Reymond

This is quite a book! It tackles a big subject and grapples with it in a big way. Scholars, ministers, theological students and many general Christian readers will find much to stimulate and instruct them here.

Dr Geoffrey Grogan
Glasgow Bible College

This excellent volume examines Paul's theology and practice of mission. Its scope is wide and touches upon many areas of Pauline studies that have caused and continue to cause controversy. It is undoubtedly an inspiring and thought-provoking work. **Paul Gardner**, Vicar, Hartford, Cheshire

Robert Reymond has written a useful survey of Paul's missionary life and theology. The approach to the New Testament materials reflects a high view of their divine origin and authority. Of particular note is a serious defense of the now generally abandoned view that Paul was the author of Hebrews.

Dr. Douglas Moo
Trinity Evangelical Divinity School

Dr. Reymond has applied his considerable skill in systematic theology to the study of the writings of the Apostle Paul. The approach that my former colleague takes is the fascinating aspect of this study. He is not writing about Paul as the great theologian, albeit he does do that, but about him as the great missionary/theologian.

Dr. George W. Knight III
Greenville Presbyterian Theological Seminary

Those who have read and appreciated Robert Reymond's *A New Systematic Theology of the Christian Faith*, will be delighted with this new volume on the apostle Paul. Reymond's biblical and theological exposition of particular themes, for example, on canonicity, imputation, justification and the Holy Spirit, is superb and stimulating.

Dr A.T.B. McGowan
Highland Theological College

The writings of Paul are a major contribution to our understanding of the doctrines of Christianity. This new study, by a world class theologian, is set to become the staple book in colleges, seminaries and mission agencies.

ISBN 1 85792 497 5

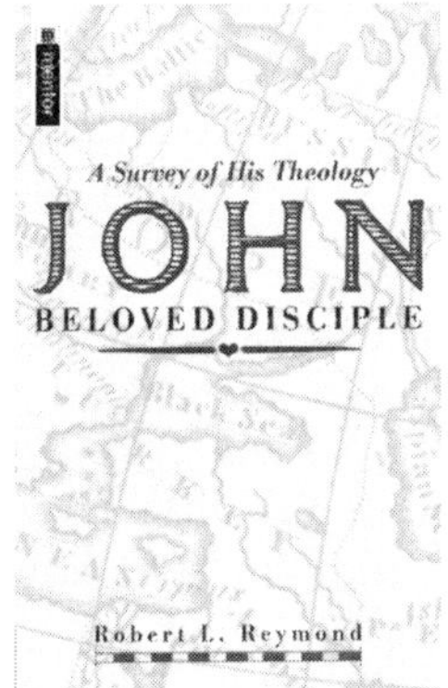

John: Beloved Disciple
A Survey of His Theology
Robert Reymond

Writing on a Biblical subject can be a major test for a Systematic theologian for it will reveal the quality of his Biblical exegesis and so whether his theology is likely to be faithful to Scripture. Robert Reymond passes this test with flying colours. This is a most valuable study of the doctrinal content of five New Testament books. He has a direct, unfussy style, quickly gets to the heart of each issue, marshals his arguments with admirable clarity, and shows deep concern that the witness of John to Christ should be taken with real seriousness. **Geoffrey Grogan**, Glasgow Bible College

Having whetted our appetite with his excellent book Paul, Missionary Theologian, we are now further in the debt of the publisher through the publication of this work on John. Reymond is a significant scholar in the Reformed tradition but above all he is a biblical theologian. Indeed, he is quite prepared to be critical of the tradition if he believes that the biblical evidence justifies it. This book is the result of detailed and painstaking study and yet it remains accessible and useful to all who have a serious interest in Scripture. **A.T.B. McGowan**, Highland Theological College

In this book Dr. Reymond again demonstrates his love for God, commitment to Scripture, and his theological expertise and learning. This very readable work examines John's theology in considerable depth. Dr. Reymond takes the view that the Gospel, the Johannine epistles, and the book of Revelation come from the aposlte John's pen. Building on this he writes, he counters much modern work on John and leaves us in no doubt that the apostle has presented to us the true Jesus, the incarnate God. Certainly this is a worthy introduction to John's theology. **Paul Gardner**

> "As the reader studies these five literary pieces with me, he should understand that in my opinion he is studying the inspired Word of God. Hopefully the reader will be persuaded concerning these matters by the time he has completed reading this book." *Robert Reymond*

ISBN 1 85792 6285

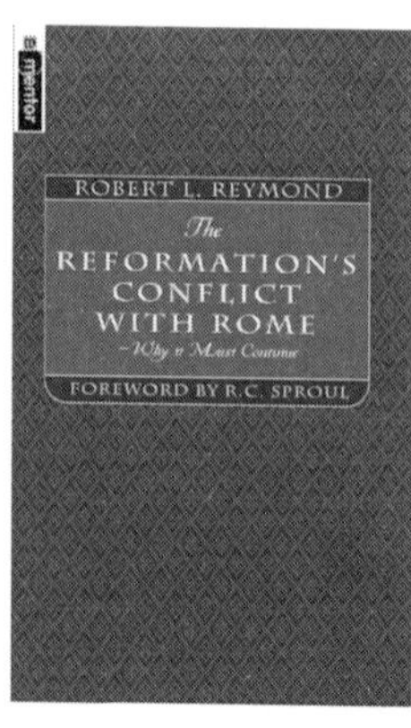

The Reformation's Conflict with Rome – Why it Must Continue
Robert L Reymond
Foreword by R.C. Sproul

Dr. Reymond clearly demonstrates in this monograph that there are several serious doctrinal differences between Roman Catholic teaching and Biblical Christianity... I am confident the reader will find this work clear, fair and accurate. I highly commend its close reading. **R.C. Sproul**

The Christian public is indebted to Dr. Reymond for producing such a lucid and incisive volume evaluating modern attempts to rejoin Protestant churches with the Roman Catholic Church... The reader will be well-informed by this decisive, but irenic, rejection of the notion that the Roman church has always embraced the biblical concept of justification by faith.

Dr. Richard L. Mayhue, The Master's Seminary

Robert Reymond is to be warmly commended for producing such a lucid book on the Reformation controversy with Rome, and why that controversy must continue even today.

Dr Nick Needham, Highland Theological College

Written in an inoffensive yet honest way, Robert Reymond has studied the essential divisions between Roman Catholics and the Reformed church to find out the real issues and points of conflict.

Reymond looks at historical watersheds of doctrine, the development of Roman Catholic authority and contemporary attempts at rapprochement (including *'Evangelicals and Catholics Together'* and Robert Sungenis' *'Not by Faith Alone'*). In doing so he helps us understand the great truths of salvation worked out through the sacrifice of Jesus, the Messiah.

ISBN 1 85792 6269

Standing Forth

Collected writing of Roger Nicole

Roger Nicole

Long regarded as one of the pre-eminent theologians in America, Roger Nicole has devoted a lifetime to defending the orthodox belief on issues under attack including the inspiration of scripture, the nature of the atonement, the existence of hell, and more recently the openness of God issue. Presently he is a Professor of Theology at Reformed Theological Seminary in Orlando, Florida

As well as his major theological works, Roger Nicole has had a productive ministry writing essays for publication. For the first time a selection has been compiled into a book.

Wherever your eye alights in this book you will always find something fresh, something deep, something relevant or something arresting to take away with you.

'Dr. Roger Nicole is one of God's great gifts to the church. His careful study and thoughtful analysis serve as models of evangelical scholarship.'
R. Albert Mohler Jr.,
President, Southern Baptist Theological Seminary, Louisville.

'Roger Nicole's insight, clarity, patience, thoroughness, geniality and good sense have given him anchor-man status for over a generation in the ongoing task of declaring and vindicating classical Reformed theology.' **J. I. Packer,**
Regent College, Vancouver

'This is a marvelous book, a treasure trove of godly wisdom from one of the master theologians of our times. Dr. Roger Nicole has had a shaping influence on several generations of students..' **Timothy George, Executive Editor, *Christianity Today* and Dean of Beeson Divinity School**

'Every pastor will want to have this valuable resource close at hand.'
Thomas Ascol, Editor, The Founders Journal

'...one of the premier Reformed theologians of our time. Dr. Roger Nicole, whose encyclopedic knowledge of the entire theological discipline most of us can only dream of acquiring, has for many years been a winsome apologist for biblical inerrancy and the Reformed faith. This volume contains the 'cream of the crop' of his literary output...the reader has several rich hours of reading in store for him.' **Robert L. Reymond, Knox Theological Seminary**

ISBN 1 85792 6463

Creation in Change
Genesis 1:1 – 2:4 in the Light of Changing Scientific Paradigms
Douglas F. Kelly

In this book Professor Douglas Kelly persuasively argues for a literal interpretation of the seven day account of creation found in Genesis chapters 1 and 2. He assesses both the biblical details and the scientific data to show that there is a convincing case for this understanding and how it is scientifically viable.

A Highly intelligent engagement with these crucial verses with which God declares himself to be a speaking God who is our maker. The discussion is scholarly but accessible, a model of the kind of exegetical thinking which the church of our day needs.

Nigel M. de S. Cameron, Executive Chairman, The Centre for Bioethics and Public Policy, London

Douglas Kelly is a theologian who also displays a deep understanding of science and philosophy. The result is this thoughtful, thorough and well researched book that will be valuable to anyone wishing to dig deeper. I highly recommend Creation and Change.

Walter E Brown – Center for Scientific Creation, Phoenix

It is an excellent work... I believe it will be an important contribution to the field. **John Currid – Reformed Theological Seminary, Jackson.**

I greatly appreciate the content as well as the style of this book. It is the best work that I have read on this subject. The author's statements concerning the role of faith in science are very important; the subject is frequently misunderstood. With regard to the exegesis of the biblical text I hope that Douglas Kelly's courageous voice will be listened to.

Frederick N. Skiff – Associate Professor of Physics, University of Maryland.

Douglas F. Kelly is Professor of Systematic Theology at Reformed Theological Seminary, Charlotte, North Carolina. Having studied in France, Scotland and America, he is a scholar in international demand for conference speaking engagements as well as being an established author. His other books include If God already Knows - Why Pray? *ISBN 1 85792 1461.*

ISBN 185792 283 2

Towards a Sure Faith

J. Gresham Machen and the Dilemma of Biblical Criticism, 1881 – 1915

Terry A. Chrisope

Church historisna and other scholars are aware of the significance of J. Gresham Machen. He was the New Testament professor at Princeton Theological Seminary from 1906 to 1929, when he resigned to found Wesminster Theological Seminary in Philadelphia.

MACHEN is best known as a capable apologist for Christian orthodoxy, especially through the publication of his masterful Christianity and Liberalism. That he is recongnised as a significant figure is shown by one of his sermons being included in the publication *American Sermons: The Pilgrims to Martin Luther King jr.*

A major question facing Machen, nad which still faces Christians today, is whether or not Biblical authority can be maintained in the face of moder historical scholarship. Machen knew the critical views firsthand, and often felt the appeal of liberal positions, so his answers are the product of hard fought battles. Machen arrived at his conclusions using a rigorous methodology and complete honesty.

That is what makes his work, present here, so usedful today.

In the last decade J. Gresham Machen has attracted the attention, adn gained the appreciation, of even some Roman Catholic and main-line Protestant writers. Terry Chrisope's excellent study of Machen as a New Testament scholar adds another dimension to the understanding of this conservative theologian of the early 20th century who yet speaks into the post-modern culture of the 21st century. Machen upheld principles that still serve well the Christian faith more than two generations after his death in 1937.

William S. Barker
Professor of Church History
Westminster Theological Seminary

Although historical biblical criticism is the focus of this book, Dr. Chrisope skilfully weaves in much valuable information about Machen and his times. Especially important is his description of the conservative Christian movement in the 1920s and his reflections on the direction of American intellectual and religious culture. **David B. Calhoun, Covenant Theological Seminary, St. Louis**

ISBN 185792 439 8

Christian Focus Publications

publishes books for all ages

Our mission statement –

STAYING FAITHFUL

In dependence upon God we seek to help make His infallible word, the Bible, relevant. Our aim is to ensure that the Lord Jesus Christ is presented as the only hope to obtain forgiveness of sin, live a useful life and look forward to heaven with Him.

REACHING OUT

Christ's last command requires us to reach out to our world with His gospel. We seek to help fulfill that by publishing books that point people towards Jesus and help them to develop a Christ-like maturity. We aim to equip all levels of readers for life, work, ministry and mission.

Books in our adult range are published in three imprints.

Christian Focus contains popular works including biographies, commentaries, basic doctrine, and Christian living. Our children's books are also published in this imprint.

Mentor focuses on books written at a level suitable for Bible College and seminary students, pastors, and other serious readers. The imprint includes commentaries, doctrinal studies, examination of current issues, and church history.

Christian Heritage contains classic writings from the past.

For a free catalogue of all our titles, please write to

Christian Focus Publications, Ltd
Geanies House, Fearn,
Ross-shire, IV20 1TW, Scotland, United Kingdom
info@christianfocus.com

www.christianfocus.com